Year One of the Russian Revolution

Year One of the Russian Revolution
Victor Serge

TRANSLATED AND EDITED BY

PETER SEDGWICK

PHOTOGRAPHIC RESEARCH BY

CELESTINE DARS

HOLT, RINEHART AND WINSTON

CHICAGO   NEW YORK   SAN FRANCISCO

First published as *L'An 1 de la revolution russe* in 1930
Translation, Editor's Introduction, and Notes
copyright (c) 1972 by Peter Sedgwick

Library of Congress Catalog Card Number: 77-117275
First published in the U.S. in 1972
ISBN: 0 7139 0135 7

Printed in the United States of America

Contents

I dedicate this work to two proletarian revolutionaries:
to one now dead,
dear Vassili Nikiforovich Chadayev,
militant in the Leningrad communist organization, 1917–28, whose
principled intelligence, firmness of character and absolute devotion
– a unique flame burning within him – never wavered even in the
bitterest torment and who perished before he could show the fullness
of his powers in the service of the revolution, murdered while
accomplishing a mission on 26 August 1928, not far from Armavir
(Kuban); and

TO A GREAT LIVING REVOLUTIONARY.

V.S.

Year One of the Russian Revolution

Editor's Introduction

The present book is one of the first works produced by Victor Serge following the decision he took in 1928, when he was confined in a Leningrad hospital with a near-mortal illness, to turn his literary talents from the fields of immediate agitation and propaganda (now denied to him as a result of the victory of Stalinism) into more permanent forms of political and artistic testimony. Like the other works produced by Serge for publication abroad during his disgrace as a former Left Oppositionist in the Soviet Union, it was composed according to a peculiar format: 'in detached fragments which could each be separately completed and sent abroad post-haste and ... could, if absolutely necessary, be published as they were, incomplete'.[1]*

In these early years of Stalin's hegemony, the mere act of dispatching a manuscript to a Western publisher was not regarded by Soviet officialdom, as it is today, as in itself tantamount to an act of treason. During the 1920s it had been relatively common for Soviet writers to bring out their work abroad, in order to establish copyright, before it appeared in Russia. This relative freedom was not to last very long: in 1929, for example, Boris Pilnyak was savagely attacked in the Russian press for his publication of the novel *Mahogany* in Berlin, and was removed from his post in the All-Russian Writers' Union for this supposedly 'anti-Soviet' action. Thus by 1930 when *Year One of the Russian Revolution* appeared from the presses of a Paris publishing house, Serge must have had grounds for fearing that an historical work which challenged, implicitly but still definitely, the Stalinist re-writing of party history might bring unpleasant consequences upon its author. Only a year later, in a novel devoted to the civil war period, he felt it necessary to omit the names of Lenin and Trotsky in a scene which clearly described the two leaders together in close conversation;[2] and in 1936, when Victor Serge was allowed to leave the Soviet Union after three years of deportation in central Asia, the GPU censorship took care to seize all his manuscripts, including *Year Two of the Russian Revolution*, the sequel to the present work. This book then, like Victor Serge himself, is a specimen of uncompromising heresy which survived the risks of Stalinist repression through a combination of skilful timing and historical good luck.

In contrast with Serge's other works of political history, *Year One of the Russian Revolution* contains no autobiographical element: it is in no sense an eye-witness account, since its narra-

*References are noted at the end of the book, pp. 373 ff.

tive breaks off precisely at the point in January 1919 when Serge
was beginning his own personal experience of the Bolshevik
Revolution, setting foot on Russian soil for the first time in his
life as the returned son of exiled Narodnik parents. Serge's initia-
tion into the stern realities of Red Petrograd at the end of Bolshevism's Year One dealt him (as he tells us in his memoirs)[3] a
considerable shock: despite the recent promise of a Soviet democracy based on mass participation, here was a revolution at death's
door, its freedom checked and controlled by a rigorous party
monopoly which maintained the 'Proletarian Dictatorship' in the
face of a starving, embittered and depopulated proletariat. Even
with this restricted basis of legitimacy, the Soviet regime could
still exert a powerful claim of fealty upon socialists and internationalists; Serge was not at this point prepared to declare (as he
did, in confidence, in 1921 to an anarchist visitor to Moscow)
that 'the Communist party no longer exercises a dictatorship *of*
the proletariat but *over* the proletariat'.[4] The bond between the
ruling party and the class it represented could still be renewed
from time to time, in periodic feats of mass heroism in the war
against White restoration or in the pioneering work of construction within new institutions and a new culture. Serge is too honest
not to see that the ideals of 'Soviet Democracy', which had fired
the hearts of millions in Russia and throughout the world in 1917,
have given way to the authoritarian monopoly ('the dictatorship
of the centre', as he puts it) of the Bolshevik leadership. The purpose of *Year One of the Russian Revolution* is essentially one
of reconstructing the chain of events, in the Russia of revolution
and counter-revolution, which has led from the 'Commune-State'
of 1917 to the party dictatorship of late 1918. The terms of the
narrative are fixed by Serge's basic convictions, firstly, that the
October Revolution of 1917 was a genuine expression of mass
feeling by workers and peasants in their overwhelming majority,
and secondly that the revolutionary wave had very quickly exhausted itself, or rather bled itself dry, through the military
depredation and economic ruin which wrought havoc in an already
enfeebled Russia during the early months following the Bolshevik
seizure of power.

Serge's outline of the early development of Bolshevism is therefore likely to dissatisfy at least three classes of historians and commentators upon Communism. There are those who reject the first
cornerstone of Serge's narrative, arguing that the Bolshevik revolution of 1917, far from being an expression or representation of
popular desires, was a mere *coup d'état* or conspiracy: on this
argument a detailed account of the revolution's fortunes over the
year 1917–18 would possess little historical relevance in explaining
the frustration of the Communist ideal, since the regime from the
outset would be a minority dictatorship masquerading behind the
banner of the Soviets. There are many, too, on the Left who

would gladly endorse Serge's characterization of Bolshevism's initial victory, as the advent to power of authentically revolutionary mass institutions, and yet would reject his chronology of the movement's speedy decline. 1918 has indeed been offered but rarely as a significant date by Left-wing interpreters of Russian Communist history; most accounts of the trajectory of Stalinism are sprinkled with references to such salient years as 1937–8 (the great purge), 1929–30 (collectivization and famine), 1927 (defeat of Left Opposition, expulsion of Trotsky), or – if a critic is sufficiently bold – 1921, the year of the suppression of the Kronstadt rebellion and the banning of factions inside the Bolshevik party. There are very few interpretations which both proclaim the 1917 October Revolution as a valid and genuine proletarian insurrection and go on (as Serge does) to date the erosion of mass involvement in the revolution within a matter of months. Quite recently, however, a third group of critics of Bolshevik history has attracted public attention. These would share Serge's chronological focus, in concentrating on developments in Soviet Russia during the immediate aftermath of the Bolshevik assumption of authority, but would offer a radically distinct explanation for the tendencies towards political repression, centralization and monopoly that are evident in the practice of Lenin's party as early as 1918. Such writers as Noam Chomsky, the Cohn-Bendit brothers and Paul Cardan are inclined to ascribe the Bolshevik expropriation of the Soviets not to the sheer pressure of historical events (though it is conceded that these may have played their part) but to specific ideological drives towards the centralization of authority at the expense of the workers; these conceptual deformities within Bolshevism are seen as pre-dating the October Revolution and are variously traced back to Lenin's centralizing politics in the 1902–3 split with the Mensheviks, or to a residue of orthodox social democracy still latent within Russian Bolshevism, or to elements in the philosophy of the Proletarian State as developed by Marx himself in the old controversy with anarchism.[5]

It might be thought that a work such as the present one, composed under conditions by no means propitious for mature historical research, and expressing the political outlook of a revolutionary tendency defeated by history, would have very little chance of withstanding the criticism that might be directed upon it from any of these rival currents of explanation, based as these are on several more decades both of detailed scholarship and of international revolutionary experience. However, when due exception is made of a number of biases and inadequacies which are evident in certain points of Serge's narrative (none of them crucial to his case), the book's general schema of the Russian revolution's 'Year One' makes extremely good sense when contrasted with alternative explanations of what happened. It is unlikely, perhaps, that any one interpretation of so complex and significant an event as the Bolshevik revolution will ever be accepted as definitive, expecially in a world still rent by political divisions stemming in large part from that very revolution; still, it is possible to point to particular features in the march of events during 1917–18 which raise certain theoretical or empirical difficulties for the alternative standard views of the Bolshevik triumph.

BOLSHEVISM: COUP OR MASS RISING?

Let us consider first the position, made out by successive waves of opponents of the October Revolution ever since the Bolshevik uprising itself, which sees the transition simply as the outcome of a *putsch* or military conspiracy, resting on no political mobilization of the Russian masses. History, unfortunately, affords the commentator no ready-made index with which one can compute unambiguously the depth and the quality of a social upheaval. Every modern revolution, from 1789 onwards if not further back, has had a question-mark placed by some of its critics over its popular character as well as upon its social content. (To take one dramatic example: not merely the depth and the range, but even the very existence of the Spanish workers' and peasants' revolution of 1936 went unrecognized for many years after the event by thousands of liberal observers – including even, as he has candidly admitted, so trained an analyst as the present Regius Professor of Modern History at Oxford.)[6] The recognition or the denial of the majority character of an insurrection must inevitably, by comparison (say) with the registering of a majority in a parliamentary election, proceed from the exercise of a fairly complex political and historical judgement. The position is further complicated, in the case of the Russian revolution, by at least two other factors. In the first place, there is an evident tendency among writers on Russian affairs to characterize the October rising of the Bolsheviks as the decisive founding act of one of the world's modern industrial super-States – a judgement which concedes the world significance and even the historical necessity of October without evaluating it within the mass revolutionary politics of its own day. And secondly, there is so much in the actual conduct of the insurrection in Petrograd during the closing days of October 1917 which lends colour to a purely conspiratorial view of the events. Trotsky himself admits almost as much in the final pages of his great history:

Where is the insurrection? There is no picture of the insurrection . . . a series of small operations, calculated and prepared in advance, remain separated one from another both in space and time . . . there is no action of great masses. There are no dramatic encounters with the troops, there is nothing of all that which imaginations brought up on the facts of history associate with the idea of insurrection.[7]

Trotsky, it is true, goes on to present the absence of the masses from the rising as a positive proof of the movement's coherence and popular support:

The workers had no need to come out into the public square in order to fuse together: they were already politically and morally one single whole without that. . . . These invisible masses were marching more than ever before in step with the events.[8]

The pro-Bolshevik temper of the masses in the cities during late 1917 is, however, attested by evidence of a far less 'invisible' nature. 'In August, September and October' – i.e., when the Bolsheviks were once again issuing the call for the replacement of the Provisional Government by Soviet power – 'manifold indications,' as a recent historian puts it, 'disclosed the growing popularity of Bolshevism.'[9] The congress of Soviets of the northern region, whose delegates were drawn from Petrograd, Kronstadt, Moscow, Helsinki and Reval, unanimously passed Trotsky's resolution for the transfer of the central government to the Soviets. A similar swing towards the Bolshevik line – often, it is true, in terms which left open the possibility of a peaceful transfer of power – was seen in the resolutions passed by many regional and local Soviet assemblies in this period, for example, at Kiev and Minsk, in Siberia and the Urals. On 19 October the All-Russian Conference of factory and shop committees, with a Bolshevik majority among its 167 voting delegates lining up with the twenty-four SR delegates against an opposition consisting of seven Mensheviks and thirteen anarcho-syndicalists, came out for the immediate passing of power to the Soviets: this, as Trotsky put it, was indeed 'the most direct and indubitable representation of the proletariat in the whole country'.[10] For the situation following the successful Petrograd rising, the results of the All-Russian Constituent Assembly elections, often cited as an indication of the relative unpopularity of the Bolsheviks, in fact show a continuance of the Bolshevik landslide in the key industrial centres and the nearby garrisons.[11] By the time the elections were held, eighteen days after the ousting of the Provisional Government and the installation of the Bolshevik government by the Second Congress of Soviets, none could have doubted the definitely insurrectionary character of the slogan 'all power to the Soviets' as proclaimed by Lenin and Trotsky. Yet the Bolsheviks' main rivals for the allegiance of popular masses, the Menshevik and SR opponents of the insurrection, were decisively beaten in the main cities of Russia: the wave of pro-Bolshevik extremism which had already ousted the Mensheviks from their leading positions in the urban Soviets rolled forward still to reduce the total Menshevik vote for the empire to 1,700,000 (nearly half of this drawn from Jordania's nationalist, non-proletarian stronghold of Georgia); while in the sole industrial centre which had been under SR control during 1917, Moscow itself, the sensational swing towards the Bolsheviks manifested in the city's two municipal elections earlier in the year was sealed by the SR party's crushing defeat in the ballot for the Assembly, by an electorate now polarized between a Red plurality and a Kadet counter-revolution.[12]

The sweep of popular Bolshevism in late 1917 extended far into the countryside of Russia, as the radicalized soldiers returned to the villages, drawing masses of rural toilers into their mood. The formal constitutional majority (both of votes and of actual seats) enjoyed by the SR party in the Constituent Assembly elections provides no indication of the real scope and power of the radical movement among the peasantry. Not only had the selection of candidates for the election by the SR party machine been consciously operated so as to under-represent the party's Left fraction (forty Left deputies out of the total SR delegation of 339 were elected) and even the 'centre' fraction of Victor Chernov (whose delegation of fifty was grossly under-sized in proportion to the influence of the Chernov group in the Central Committee elections during November).[13] For outside the fractions and committees, in the grassroots base of Social Revolutionism, the peasantry of Russia, the SR party was losing ground rapidly, not only to its Left breakaway but even to the Bolsheviks; Radkey's careful analysis of a number of widely varying peasant regions during late 1917 confirms this trend in detail.[14] The self-proclaimed party of the Russian peasantry proved, as Radkey puts it, to be 'the chief roadblock in the path of the agrarian revolution'[15] that rolled across the empire. The apparently overwhelming SR electoral 'majority' in the Constituent Assembly returns was based on a feeble minority among the actual social forces of the Russian nation; it would be futile and sophistical to try to prove, conversely, that the Bolshevik and Left SR vote reflected a conscious majority of the total population of the toilers, except in the key industrial centres, but it was certainly the expression of a half-conscious mood of 'popular Bolshevism' at work in the hearts of millions.

To say this much is to leave open very wide areas for serious argument over the strength, the sources and the conscious quality of the revolutionary mass-mobilization that was seized and shaped at the pinnacles of society by the organizational and political actions of Lenin and Trotsky. A final word in the dispute over the 'minority' or 'mass' character of the October Revolution may perhaps be left with the spokesmen for the defeated and discredited party of Mensheviks. This party, whose leadership had assailed the Bolshevik rising on its morrow as a pure 'military conspiracy', an 'adventure' conducted in isolation from the masses, reversed its judgement at its Central Committee meeting of 17–21 October 1918, in a resolution which declared:

The Bolshevik revolution of October 1917 has been historically necessary [and] expressed the endeavour of the toiling masses to steer the course of the revolution wholly in their interest, without which the liberation of Russia from the vice of Allied imperialism, the pursuit of a consistent peace policy, the radical implementation of the agrarian reform and the regulation by the state of the whole economic life in the interests of the masses of the people would have been inconceivable.[16]

This endorsement of the authentically revolutionary character, in terms both of popular base and of historical significance, of the Bolshevik insurrection was, of course, not undertaken without serious criticism of the post-revolutionary conduct of the Communist regime. But these criticisms do not diminish the *de jure* and *de facto* recognition of October accorded by the revolution's old opponents.

THE DECAY OF THE REVOLUTION

In tracing the decline in the active mass support enjoyed by the Bolshevik party, we are at once faced by the loss, over 1918, of such indispensable indicators as the distribution of the vote, between Bolshevik candidates and their rivals, in Soviet and other elections. It should not now be necessary to attribute the early Bolshevik dominance of the Soviets and trade unions exclusively to the effects of dictatorial repression: the pitiful showing made by the non-Bolshevik but 'Sovietist' organizations such as the sections of anarchists and SRs loyal to the regime is probably due not simply to police action, but to the phenomenon (very common nowadays in the underdeveloped world) of the 'funnelling' of prestige and enthusiasm into the party machine which bears the credit for the foundation of the new regime. The excessive 'homogeneity' noted by Serge in the All-Russian Soviet Congress of November 1918 has its parallel in the legislative assemblies of many contemporary states of recent inauguration. Nevertheless, Serge is evidently right to signal 'the end of the Soviet bloc' of fraternal but contending parties, soon after mid-1918, as a crucial stage in the replacement of popular Bolshevism by *élite* party control. In this respect, his analysis (even though formulated during a phase when he was a convinced member of the Trotskyist opposition) differs sharply from that made by Trotsky himself. For Trotsky, writing in late 1937 to refute the theory that Stalinism sprang from Leninism as a direct progression, the monopoly of the party in the Soviets appears to be completely unproblematic. He concedes to the Left-wing critics of Bolshevism the bare facts of their case:

the Bolsheviks ... replaced the dictatorship of the proletariat with the dictatorship of the party; Stalin replaced the dictatorship of the party with the dictatorship of the bureaucracy. The Bolsheviks destroyed all parties but their own; Stalin strangled the Bolshevik party in the interests of a Bonapartist clique.

Trotsky adds, however, that 'one can make such comparisons at will. For all their apparent effectiveness they are entirely empty.' The party monopoly, indeed, is the natural form by which the dictatorship of the proletariat is exercised: 'The proletariat can take power only through its vanguard. ... The Soviets are only the organized form of the tie between the vanguard and the class. A revolutionary content can be given to this form only by the party.' Trotsky concludes: 'The fact that this party subordinates the Soviets politically to its leaders has in itself abolished the Soviet system no more than the domination of the Conservative majority has abolished the British parliamentary system.'[17] (To which it might be replied that a Conservative 'domination' using the same methods of repression as the Bolsheviks employed against the other parties would certainly abolish the parliamentary system as it has been known in Britain.)

Without statistics for the elections to Soviet institutions (and doubtless some useful findings could be gleaned for the period when balloting still went on) it is impossible for us to monitor the process of working-class disillusionment with the Soviet regime. The centralization of Soviet economic institutions, through the creation of 'the Supreme Council of the National Economy' with its branches in the different industries in place of the localized, uncoordinated organs of 'workers' control', did not involve the Soviet government in any collision with the mass of workers.[18] Despite the vested interest in local separatism that was characteristic of many factory Soviets, the factory-committee movement collaborated with the transition towards centralism, doubtless for the greater economic security it conferred as well as for the regime's defence requirements. Pankratova even states that the idea of establishing the Supreme Council of the National Economy

was actually initiated and given shape within the movement of factory-committees itself. The Central Soviet of Factory Committees took a very active part in its formation, gave it its own best workers and offered its apparatus to it. The factory committees of Petrograd, who at their First Conference of May 1917 had proclaimed workers' control, buried it unanimously at their Sixth Conference.[19]

It was not, it would seem, any confrontation between the Bolsheviks and the working class over this or, probably, any other single issue that drove a wedge between the regime and its proletariat, so much as the cumulative pressures that bore down relentlessly upon the people throughout Bolshevism's Year One.

That there was, by the end of 1918, a yawning void filled by apathy at best, and hostile bitterness at worst, between the Soviet regime and the working class appears to be an irresistible conclusion. The portrait sketched by Serge at the end of the present book accords very closely with the summary given in his own reminiscences: 'it was the metropolis of Cold, of Hunger, of

Hatred, and of Endurance. From about a million inhabitants its population had now fallen, in one year, to scarcely 700,000 souls.' Here was 'a revolution dying, strangled by blockade, ready to collapse from inside into the chaos of counter-revolution'.[20] Within weeks of Serge's arrival, the huge factories of Petrograd, once the pride and the powerhouse of working-class Bolshevism, would explode in spectacular disturbances involving thousands of workers in action against the regime. These strikes and demonstrations were eagerly observed and, wherever possible, encouraged by the domestic and foreign forces that were working for the overthrow of the Soviet government. Paul Dukes, the head of the British intelligence network then operating clandestinely in Petrograd, recalls the 'bloody encounters between large bands of workers and the forces of the Cheka', and records one workers' demonstration which paraded a banner with the ironic couplet:

> *Doloi Lenina s koninoi,*
> *Daitye tsarya s svininoi!*
> (Down with Lenin and horseflesh,
> Give us the Tsar and pork!)

In an intelligence report smuggled back from Russia at the time, Dukes reported on the mass anti-Bolshevik agitation in a factory that a short while ago had been a stronghold of the revolution:

On 10 March a mass meeting was held at the Putilov Works. Ten thousand men were present and the following resolution was passed with only twenty-two dissentients . . .

We, the workers of the Putilov Works, declare before the labouring classes of Russia and the world that the Bolshevist government has betrayed the ideals of the revolution, and thus betrayed and deceived the workers and peasants in Russia; that the Bolshevist government, acting in our names, is not the authority of the proletariat and peasants, but a dictatorship of the Bolshevik party, self-governing with the aid of Cheka and the police. . . . We demand the release of workers and their wives who have been arrested; the restoration of a free press, free speech, right of meeting and inviolability of person; transfer of food administration to cooperative societies: and transfer of power to freely elected workers' and peasants' Soviets.[21]

Dukes's report was promptly published by the British government in the official *Collection of Reports on Russia* put out in 1919 in the attempt to convince a wavering parliament and public of the horrors of Bolshevism and the necessity for continued support to the White forces.[22]

Victor Serge is candid in his own account of this erosion of the regime's proletarian base. Despite the Soviet government's unpopularity among the working class, he remained committed to its survival and continued to defend its authenticity as a 'dictatorship of the proletariat', defined as such now not sociologically (through the active adhesion of the Russian working class in its majority) but ideologically (through the Marxist perspectives and the revolutionary determination displayed in the thousands of Bolshevik cadres that constituted the new State). It was relatively easy for Serge to make this leap from a mass identification to the hero-worship of a glorious minority, from (one might almost say) the criteria of Marxist politics to those of an aesthetically and psychologically grounded romanticism. For his own adoption of the Marxist class vision was, in 1919, of relatively recent formation; as Jean Maitron has convincingly shown,[23] the first political position of the young Victor Lvovich Kibalchich, before he took the name of 'Victor Serge', was one of rampant anarchist individualism, glorifying the desperate violence of his close friends in the 'Bonnot gang' of bank-robbers and despising the stultified beasts of burden who were the modern proletariat. '*Je suis avec les bandits!*' Serge had proclaimed in his organ *L'Anarchie* in 1911, as his friends were shooting out their last battles with the French gendarmerie. The bandits were at least men, bravely defying the corrupt bourgeois society they could not hope to defeat. This élitist revolutionary loyalty was available for Serge to fall back on if the masses failed him, as they did in Petrograd almost as soon as he arrived there. The Bolsheviks, that beleaguered commando of revolutionary fighters, daring to the death, could be accepted on the same grounds as his old bandit comrades. However logically or morally vulnerable this position was, it at least enabled Serge to face reality squarely and admit that the working class was not, in this situation, fulfilling the revolutionary expectations held out for it by the official creed of Marxism. Other Communist publicists, less inclined towards romantic heroics than he was, would through that very fact also tend to cling to the mass criterion for supporting the regime long after the actual behaviour of the masses had made nonsense of their theory. For such as these, 'Soviet power' as the exercise of the majority will of the real Russian proletariat would necessarily continue to function, until the strain on theory imposed by the reality grew to breaking-point.

It was not, of course, necessary to be either an Ibsenesque hero-worshipper or a naive pro-Bolshevik in order to rally to the support and defence of the Soviet regime in the Civil War period. The sheer peril of counter-revolution, seconded by the active intervention of the Allies, caused most Socialists and internationalists at this time to solidarize with the Soviet government against even its Left-wing dissidents when the survival of the regime was in question. In a later work (*Destiny of a Revolution*, published in 1937) Serge explained why, in his view, no revolutionary could support the working-class demonstrations against the government in the Petrograd of early 1919. The very success of the Menshevik and Left SR agitators in rallying the city's workers testified to the absence of the proletariat's conscious and revolutionary elements

from the factories: for the most dedicated and idealist workers
had volunteered in thousands for the civil war front. Those that
remained, although a majority, were the proletariat's 'backward
elements, the least conscious and most selfish, those least inclined
to sacrifices demanded by the general interest ... discouraged
rearguards who are ready unconsciously to second a counter-
revolution'. To attempt 'a general strike in famished Petrograd,
threatened from two sides by the Whites, in the factories which all
the revolutionists have left' was simply 'suicide for the revolution'.[24] It should be remembered that in the spring of 1919
General Yudenich was grouping the forces of his White army in
Estonia for the offensive which in May would win substantial
territory from the Baltic coast down to Pskov and which, when
renewed more vigorously later in the year, would take his troops
into the very suburbs of Petrograd. In March 1919 also, an intervention by Finland to capture the city for the counter-revolution
was already being lobbied in Allied circles. This was an epoch
when 'counter-revolutionary peril' was far more than a bureaucratic excuse to justify the repression of dissidence: even though it
might be expressed formally in the same terms used during later
repressions, the logic of Communist violence in 1918 proceeds
from real and distinctive pressures which are not those of 1968,
or 1956, or 1937 or (even, be it said) 1921.

THE IDEOLOGICAL ALTERNATIVE

The whole blame for the evolution of the Commune-State into the
Party-State is therefore laid by Victor Serge to the account of the
counter-revolutionary peril. It was the opening of the civil war by
the Whites, regularly and lavishly funded by the Allies, that dissipated and destroyed the active forces of the Russian working
class in a literal haemorrhage of the revolution's social basis. It is
to the activity of the counter-revolution, in the repeated plots,
assassinations and uprisings conducted by the anti-Bolshevik
parties of both Right and Left, that we must look for the explanation of the Communist party's monopoly of power and terror.
Here Serge parts company with all those critics of Bolshevism who
have predominantly emphasized the ideological factor of 'Jacobinism' or 'Leninism' (detected as residing within the intellectual
marrow of the Bolshevik party since 1903) as the germ of the later
State autocracy under Lenin or even as a prime cause of Stalin's
totalitarian rule.[25] The ideological case may be illustrated very
simply by quoting one or two predictions made by Leon Trotsky
in his pre-revolutionary polemics against Lenin's centralism. 'In
the internal politics of the party these [Lenin's] methods lead the
party organization to "substitute" itself for the party, the Central
Committee to substitute itself for the party organization, and
finally a "dictator" substitutes himself for the Central Committee.'
And: 'If the anti-revolutionary characteristics of Menshevism are

already in full view, the anti-revolutionary features of Bolshevism run the grave risk of only revealing themselves after a revolutionary victory.'[26] These are only the most sensational extracts from an indictment of bureaucratic 'Leninism' developed by Trotsky, Rosa Luxemburg[27] and the Menshevik wing almost a decade and a half before Lenin's politics found a manifest application in the exercise of State power. To refuse any validity to the ideological explanation of Bolshevism's degeneracy is tantamount to saying that any similarities that arose between Communist practice and these startling early prophecies were the result of pure coincidence: an implausible judgement, one might suppose.

And yet, why should the parallelism not be one of coincidence, given that the historical context in which the October Revolution was embedded was so unpropitious to the free flowering of democratic Socialist institutions? The 'objective' social circumstances of Russia's revolution and civil war already contain the sufficient conditions for the collapse of the mass-revolutionary wave, without any recourse to causal factors stemming from the 'subjective' deficiencies of Lenin's early formulations. The impact of historical causes pressing on actors from the urgent dilemmas of 1917 must have had a far greater importance in determining what happened in 1917 (and 1918) than did the ideational influence of exile controversies in 1902. There is enough 'Jacobinism' and 'substitutionism' present in the basic political premises of the October insurrection, that uncertain alliance between a tiny proletariat and a vast and land-hungry peasantry; in what scale can any verbal Jacobinism, the substitutionism of paper (and faded paper at that), be made to balance against the insistent, leaden weight of historical impossibility?

In any case, the account of pre-revolutionary 'Leninism' presented by the ideological critics of Lenin is seriously misleading. Ideological explanation requires, in the first place, an accurate description of the ideas which are alleged to have been causally operative: and the description of Lenin as a 'centralist' or 'Jacobin' is only a half-truth at best. The Lenin of 1905–6, for example, is not the 'centralizer' of 1902–4; the Leninist model of party organization developed for the unification of Russia's warring factions (following the joint Bolshevik-Menshevik congress of 1906) was fully democratic in content, involving not only normal election procedures for leading committees but also the use of referenda among the membership on controversial issues and the strict mandating of delegates by their local branches.[28] (It is this model of organization, incidentally, that was first termed 'democratic centralism' – a formula acceptable to Mensheviks no less than to Leninists – in distinction from the unqualified and explicit 'centralism' of Lenin's position in 1902–4.) For the first year or so after the Bolshevik seizure of power, the democratic and even semi-anarchist strains in Lenin's organizational theory become even more pronounced: Serge is eager to emphasize these elements (visible not only in the classic *State and Revolution* but in many speeches and writings of the period) in his own narrative of the Year One, and the excessive significance attached to these libertarian statements by Serge (understandable in a former anarchist trying to reconcile himself to Soviet authority) should not blind us to the persisting reality of a Lenin who found both 'democracy' and 'centralism' to constitute key values in the construction of a Socialist order.[29]

Another very common ideological explanation of Bolshevik policy during the Year One may also be answered here: it is often asserted that, in the vital field of economic decision-making, the bureaucratic imperatives of Leninist orthodoxy ensured the replacement of localized, libertarian structures of 'workers' control' by a centralized planning machinery in the hands of a party *élite*.[30] The eclipse of the factory-committee movement in early 1918 is thought to be symptomatic of this bureaucratic trend, whose causes can once again be traced to the ideological presuppositions of Leninist (or even Marxist) 'State Socialism'. But there is no evidence that Bolshevik industrial policy in the pre-revolutionary period had any disposition towards centralization and State planning at the expense of local initiatives. Economic gradualism, indeed, entailing a long epoch of co-existence between capitalists (politically dispossessed, it is true) and workers on the shop-floor, was the most obvious theme of Marxist industrial policy as envisaged by Marx, Engels and later by Lenin.[31] The 'State capitalism' advocated by Lenin in the first year of Soviet rule referred precisely to such an extended period of joint management within a privately owned industry, and not to any system of State ownership and centralized management. And the forces within the Bolshevik party that were responsible for the shift away from 'workers' control' by factory committees were neither 'Leninist' in inspiration nor 'bureaucratic' in general tendency. Lenin's gradualist line for industry came under fire, from late 1917 onwards, from two sorts of Communist, at opposite ends of the many-hued ideological spectrum of Bolshevism.[32] On the Right, the improvisations of the factory-committee structure were resisted by spokesmen for the official trade-union machine, Communists like Larin, Lozovsky and Ryazanov who were politically the most liberal of all Bolsheviks in their insistence on a broad all-party Socialist coalition and their opposition to the suppression of hostile newspapers.[33] Within this small but (on industrial matters) influential current of Bolshevism a concern for economic centralization was actually correlated with a pluralistic and constitutional perspective for the political structure of the Soviets. At the other extreme, the incipient tendency of 'Left Communism' opposed the half-measures of 'workers' control' with the demand for the outright expropriation of all employers by the State and for the introduction of a system of 'workers' management' which would embody both a centralized regulation of the whole nationalized economy and the running of factories by collegiate bodies with a sizeable (ideally a majority) representation of directly elected factory workers.[34] The polarity between 'centralism' and 'democracy', 'Leninism' and 'libertarianism', is wholly inadequate to encompass the diverse tendencies of this crucial economic debate. The Bolsheviks are to be reproached in this field not, it would seem, for adhering to a doctrinaire imperative of State centralism but rather for having entered on the course of Socialist revolution without any worked-out programme for the control of industry. An excess of improvisation rather than of ideological rigidity was the real weakness of Russian Communism in the critical Year One.

The general case for regarding the development of Russia's one-party Communist regime as the outcome of improvised emergency measures in response to a crisis situation, rather than as the result of a central ideological drive towards repression, is given in ample detail within Serge's history. In going through this record, the reader should perhaps try to ask himself whether the coercive and élitist features of Russian Bolshevism were really any more significant than the similar political traits that were manifested in the ideas and the behaviour of their opponents in the revolution. The Bolsheviks outlawed those newspapers that were hostile (or unsympathetically neutral) towards them in the civil war; Kerensky had outlawed the monarchist press on roughly the same grounds. The Bolsheviks engaged in an armed insurrectionary conspiracy at the head of a vast mass movement of workers and peasants; the Left and Right SRs and the anarchists (not to speak of the monarchists and liberal-capitalists) conducted futile *putsches*, or preparations for *putsches*, without the slightest popular backing.[35] The Bolsheviks set up a powerful and hideous secret police; the anarchist Makhno established two such forces with a horrific reputation in their territory, repressing all political parties as mercilessly as the Reds suppressed all parties save their own. Only the Left-wing Mensheviks around Martov can be excused from the general charge of indiscriminate terror and violence: and these avoided the dangers of revolutionary excess only at the cost of avoiding any positive perspective for the revolution itself.

BALANCE-SHEET OF 'THE YEAR ONE'

Victor Serge's narrative is itself not exempt from the sectarian intolerance characteristic of a period of mortal combat between rival doctrinal currents. Despite his real effort to retain historical detachment amid the pressures of his confessed partisanship, his judgement on several important points was warped by fervour. He is unfair and inaccurate on the pre-revolutionary politics of the Menshevik party, and evasive in recounting the story of the

Cheka's suppression of the anarchists. (Himself an ex-anarchist of very recent conversion to Bolshevism, he must have found it impossible to be objective towards those who still adhered to the ideology he had spurned.) There is also, from time to time, an excessive readiness to offer simple, conspiratorial explanations for complex events – a tendency doubtless deriving from Serge's long immersion in the archives of the Tsarist secret police, that fund of startling secrets on the infiltration of the revolutionary movement by spies and agents. More generally, Serge's command of Marxist sociology is sometimes surprisingly crude in relating ideological divergencies to variations of social class. What he calls Lenin's 'proletarian realism' was not by any means a characteristic of Russian working-class militants in the issue concerned (the Brest-Litovsk treaty); many Communists in industrial centres favoured the continuation of the war with Germany. Equally, while Serge is correct in naming the middle peasants as the sociological base of the SR party, he is unconvincing in his suggestion that the SRs' vacillation and Utopianism expressed the mentality of a rural 'petty-bourgeois' stratum: this mindless enthusiasm, alternating between patriotic euphoria and ultimatist violence, was surely typical of a floating urban intelligentsia rather than of a stolid peasantry.

Despite these shortcomings (remarkably few considering the circumstances of its composition), *Year One of the Russian Revolution* seizes the thread of reason, of causality, from out of the chaos of miseries and exaltations, ideals and their disappointments, bloody precedents and bloodier consequences, that constituted the early fortunes of Russian Bolshevism. In our own era, when the forces of Marxist and libertarian radicalism are asserting and assembling a fresh identity, it may not be too much to hope that this work will fulfil the main purpose intended by its author: that of drawing the lessons of the last victorious workers' revolution, as a necessary preparation for the successful advent of the next.

Peter Sedgwick

Acknowledgements

The editorial apparatus to this version is extensive, for a variety of reasons. It has been necessary to update some of Serge's biographical and political addenda; to correct or amplify some of his conclusions in the light of later research; and to fill out the short bibliographical references of the original edition.

Both the inaccessibility of many of the texts cited and my own linguistic incapacity have made it impossible to provide page-references for most of the sources. An exception has been made for the frequent quotations from Lenin, where reference is given to the corresponding passages in the English edition of the *Collected Works* published by Lawrence & Wishart in London in 1969; these citations (like many from other authors) are given by Serge in his own French translation, often with slight paraphrases or personal renderings. Serge's version has been translated throughout the text; i.e. there has been no recourse to the original source even when this is in English or has an alternative English version.

A few of the notes are the result of my own research in the archives of the British government for 1917–18. 'Allied policy towards Russia,' as Professor Richard Ullman has remarked, '... in these years largely originated in London'; when intervention got under way, 'Of all foreign governments, that of the United Kingdom was the most heavily involved ... both directly, through the use of its own military, naval and air forces, and indirectly, through the provision of material assistance and advice in the campaign to unseat the Bolsheviks' (R. H. Ullman, *Intervention and the War* (Princeton, 1961), p. vii; *Britain and the Russian Civil War* (Princeton, 1968), p. vii). Since, to quote Ullman once again (1961, p. 334), 'there is considerable truth in the often repeated Soviet assertion that the terror was a direct result of intervention', it has seemed worthwhile to explore the responsibilities of British policy in some of the earlier episodes of the civil war recorded by Serge. The Milner papers kept in the Bodleian Library, Oxford, and the State papers in the Public Record Office (these last having been still unavailable to scholars at the time of Professor Ullman's first volume) have been used in addition to published accounts by scholars and biographers.

My acknowledgements for the production of the editorial material must extend firstly to several invaluable books: Ullman's two rich and detailed volumes mentioned above; Robert Conquest's *The Great Terror* (London, 1968); and W. H. Chamberlin's classic, *The Russian Revolution, 1917–1921* (London, 1935). I am indebted to Paul Avrich both in respect of his fine book *The*

Russian Anarchists (Princeton, 1967) and for an illuminating correspondence; to Oliver Caldecott of Penguin Books for patient advice during the writing and for the enthusiasm of a Serge devotee; and to Edie Sedgwick for her encouragement and much lively discussion on Russian anarchism.

All citations from British government papers appear by permission of the Controller of Her Majesty's Stationery Office, in whom the Crown copyright is vested for the material quoted both from the Public Record Office archives and the Milner papers. I am grateful to Dr G. V. Bennett, the Librarian of New College, Oxford, for according me, on behalf of the Warden and Fellows of that college, permission to work in the Milner papers deposited in the Bodleian. My thanks are finally due to the staff of the following libraries for their promptness and care: the Bodleian Library, Oxford; the British Museum Reading Room; Liverpool Public Libraries; the London School of Economics Library; the Library of the London School of Slavonic Studies; New York Public Library; the Public Record Office; York City Library; and York University's Morrell Library. It remains to thank Deborah Thompson for the thoroughness of the index.

The publishers wish to acknowledge the following permissions for illustrations reproduced in this volume:

Novosti: 1, 3, 12, 17, 20, 21, 25, 27, 33, 35, 38, 40, 46, 50, 52, 54, 55, 56, 57, 62, 64, 69

Ringart: 2, 4, 6, 9, 19, 26, 28, 30, 31, 41, 44, 63

Ullstein Bilderdienst: 5, 13, 15, 16, 22, 23, 29, 34, 42, 43, 48, 51, 58, 61, 65, 66, 67, 68, 70

H. Roger-Viollet: 7, 10

Mansell Collection: 8, 36, 47

Snark International: 11, 24, 32, 59, 60

U.P.I.: 14

Imperial War Museum: 18, 45

Punch: 36

Établissement Cinématographique et Photographique des Armées: 37

Lehtikuva Oy: 39

Thomson Newspapers: 49, 53

Foreword

In this book I have tried to provide a truthful, reasonable and living portrayal of the first struggles of Russia's Socialist revolution. My chief aim has been to display, for the benefit of the proletarian classes, those lessons which can be drawn from one of the greatest and decisive epochs of class struggle in modern history: with this in mind, I could express no other point of view but that held by the proletarian revolutionaries. This has an advantage for the reader who does not accept Communist doctrines: it enables him to acquire an idea of how the revolution was understood, and is still understood, by those who actually made it.

The impartiality of the historian is no more than a myth, designed to prop up certain convenient opinions. It has been destroyed (if it needed destroying) by the character of the historical works which emerged from the Great War. The historian is always 'a man of his time': of his social class, of his nation, of his political habitat. Today, however, the only open partiality which is compatible with complete devotion to the truth is that of the proletarian historian. The working class is the only class which has everything to gain, whatever the circumstances, by knowing the truth. It has nothing to keep hidden, at any rate not in history. Social lies have the same function as they ever had: that of deceiving the working class. This class refutes deception in order that it can conquer; its refutation of deceit is the measure of its conquest. There are, doubtless, certain cases of proletarian historians who have bent history to suit the biases of contemporary politics. In doing so, they have surrendered to traditions which are totally alien to their calling and have subordinated, to sectional and temporary interests, the prior and permanent interests of their class. It is an example from which I have shrunk. If, as is probable, my account turns out, at various points, to be a misrepresentation of the truth, it will have been unintentionally so, either through lack of information or through my own error.

As it is, the book is bound to be very defective. I have been absorbed by other tasks, leading the life of a militant in an age filled with commotion; I have always lacked the repose and leisure which are so necessary for historical research. It is for these reasons that those who make history rarely have the opportunity to write it. Besides, the material that forms the basis for the present study is not in a fit state to be worked with. The facts are too recent and too alive; the ash in the crucible is too warm, it burns you when you touch it. The literature existing in Russia on the subject of the October Revolution bears the character of abundance rather than of richness. Memoirs, reports, notes, documents, fragmentary studies have been appearing in profusion. It must, however, be remarked that it is extraordinarily difficult to know what use to make of this immense documentation, excessively subordinated as it is to agitational aims: systematic studies, aiming to cover the whole field, are almost completely absent. The history of the parties, of the civil war, of the Red Army, of the terror, and of the various workers' organizations has not been begun, even in outline. Apart from a few writings of a very summary description, not one serious history of the revolution has yet been published in the USSR (not that anybody should be surprised at this). The writers on military topics are the only ones who have undertaken any fundamental appraisal of at least some of the problems that interest them. In these circumstances, one has no alternative but to refer to the autobiographies of participants, which have serious faults. Even in the best cases, revolutionaries make only tolerable chroniclers; what makes matters worse is that they have usually set pen to paper for certain very restricted ends – commemoration at anniversaries, homage, polemic and even the deformation of history at the whim of certain momentary interests. The more specialized works, e.g. monographs on local episodes, offer few indications of scientific worth. In turning to some use the bulk of this documentation, I have been mainly concerned to search in it for the significant particular. In order that the reader can be provided with concrete data for his own evaluation, I have provided details and quotations quite extensively. My sources have been indicated only when I was dependent on previous writings of genuine value, or when I felt that I should emphasize the authority of a particular witness, or, finally, with the aim of easing the reader's own investigations into the period.

I intend to continue this work if I have any chance of doing so. I shall be particularly grateful to any readers who may like to write to draw my attention to this book's deficiencies, or to any questions on which they would like some further enlightenment.

I shall now try to situate 'The Year One' in its context within the history of the revolution.

The Year One of the proletarian revolution, or of the Soviet Republic, begins on 7 November 1917 (25 October, Old Style) and ends, of course, on 7 November 1918, at the moment when the German revolution erupts. There is an almost perfect coincidence between the dates of the calendar and that first phase of the historic drama which starts with the victorious insurrection and ends with the spreading of the revolution to central Europe. In this period, we see the appearance, for the first time, of all the problems which the dictatorship of the proletariat is called upon to resolve: organization of distribution and production, internal and external defence, policy towards the middle classes, intellectuals and peasantry, the life of the party and the Soviets.

We shall call this first period *the phase of proletarian conquest*: it comprises the seizure of power, the conquest of territory, the mastery of production, the creation of State and army, the acquisition of the right to survive.

The German revolution marks the opening of the next phase, that of *the international struggle* (or more exactly, the armed defence, sometimes an aggressive defence, of the base of the international revolution). In 1919, a 'First Coalition' is formed against the Soviet Republic. The Allies, finding the blockade insufficient to achieve their purposes, encourage the establishment of counter-revolutionary states in Siberia, Archangel, the south and the Caucasus. In October 1919, at the end of the Year Two, the Republic seems to be at death's door, besieged by three White armies. Kolchak is marching on the Volga; Denikin has invaded the Ukraine and marches upon Moscow; Yudenich, with support from a British naval squadron, marches on Petrograd. By a miracle of energy, the Republic gains the victory. The famine, the invasions, the terror, the heroic, implacable, ascetic regime of 'War Communism' continue. In the following year the European coalition drives on Poland to attack the Soviets at the very moment when the end of the terror has been decreed. While the Second Congress of the Communist International is sitting in Moscow, the Red Army arrives at the gates of Warsaw and causes the threat of a new revolutionary crisis to cross Europe. This period ends in November–December 1920 with Wrangel's defeat in the Crimea and the conclusion of peace with Poland. The civil war appears to be at an end; however, peasant insurrections and the Kronstadt rising give a brutal revelation of the gravity of the conflict between the Socialist regime and the peasant masses.

A third phase, which could be called that of *economic reconstruction*, opens in 1921 with the New Economic Policy (*Nep* for short), and ends in 1925–6 with the recovery of production to its pre-war level (admittedly with an increased population). We must briefly recall what *Nep* amounted to. The proletarian dictatorship found itself compelled, after the defeats of the European working class, to make economic concessions to the rural petty-bourgeoisie: the abolition of the State grain monopoly, freedom of trade, the toleration of private capitalism within certain limits. The Socialist State maintains all its commanding positions in the economic field, and makes no concessions in politics. This serious 'retreat' (the word is Lenin's), undertaken to prepare a later progress towards Socialism, restores peace to the country and facilitates recovery. From 1925–6 onwards, the history of the proletarian revolution in Russia enters its fourth phase. Economic reconstruction is completed in five years after the end of the civil war, a remarkable accomplishment for a nation so severely depleted and then thrown back on its own resources. From this point on, the task is to enlarge production and match the productive level of the great capitalist powers. All the old problems present themselves again in a fresh light. This is the phase of industrialization: resumption of struggle between the classes, growing more and more bitter; intensification of the evils of a proletarian revolution which is confined within national boundaries and surrounded by capitalist states. But now we are in the present, in life, in struggle. Nothing can form a better grounding for an appreciation of these recent issues than the knowledge of the revolution's heroic beginnings, in which men were steeled, ideas were developed, institutions were moulded.

Since the events studied in this book, twelve years have passed. The proletarian Republic, founded by the insurrection of 7 November 1917, is still alive. In Russia the working class has shown itself capable of exercising power, of organizing the economy, of vanquishing its enemies within and without, and of persevering in its historic mission: all this in the most unpromising of conditions. All the uncertainties and errors of men, all the dissensions and political battles must not be allowed to blur this great fact, but rather emphasize it further in our eyes. The proletarian revolution is continuing. Upon all those whose class interests do not range them against the revolution, a double duty now falls: internally – that is, within the USSR and in the international revolutionary movement of workers – to serve the revolution by fighting the evils which afflict it, by learning to defend it against its own defects, by making every effort towards the ceaseless elaboration and practice of a politics inspired by the higher interests of the world proletariat; externally, to defend the first Workers' Republic, to be vigilant for its security; and to note its deeds and its struggles with the aim of drawing those lessons which tomorrow, for other peoples, will throw light on the future paths of the world's transformation.

Since the greater part of this book was written in the USSR, I must apologize for having been unable to use a number of important texts which have recently been published abroad. It has been impossible for me to obtain them.

Victor Serge
January 1930

1. The 1861 proclamation on land distribution is read out on an estate near Moscow

1 · From Serfdom to Proletarian Revolution

1861: THE EMANCIPATION OF THE SERFS

Sequences in world history are so tightly interconnected that it is often necessary to go back a long while in order to get some more than arbitrary idea of the causes of an event – especially when the event concerned is as grandiose as the Russian revolution.

The close of the eighteenth and the first half of the nineteenth century are marked in the history of western Europe by a social transformation which is painful, radical and pregnant with immense possibilities: the *bourgeois revolution*.

The *ancien-régime* monarchies were the heirs of the feudal system over which they had triumphed in the bloody struggles of an earlier age, aided by the people of the communes, a revolutionary force of their time. These kingdoms rested on large-scale landed property (noble or feudal), on the bureaucratic absolutism of the royal dynasty, and on the hierarchy of orders in the realm, with the nobility and clergy taking precedence over the bourgeoisie. Of these social classes, the older dominant orders were in a state of decline and the other, the bourgeoisie of commerce, manufacturing, finance and parliament, was sinking powerful roots among the lower artisan classes, and developing traditions of work, thrift, business honesty, dignity and political liberty – the latter, as always, being greatly valued among the subject classes of society. Growing in strength and in the consciousness of its own needs – and principally of the necessity to sweep away all obstacles in the way of its own advancement – the bourgeoisie was making its way towards power. The French Revolution of 1789–93 opened the series of bourgeois revolutions. 'What is the Third Estate [meaning the bourgeoisie]?' the Abbé Sieyès, one of the future men of Thermidor and Brumaire, speculated in 1789. 'Nothing. What must it become? Everything.'

It took until about 1850 to complete the bourgeois revolution in Europe. Napoleon's armies carried it from Madrid and Lisbon as far as Vienna and Berlin. The revolutions of 1830 and 1848 are its final political convulsions. In the meantime, the industrial revolution had begun, a revolution perhaps even more radical (the first steam-engine, that produced by Watt, dates from 1769; Fulton invents the steam-boat in 1807 and Stephenson the locomotive in 1830; Jacquard's loom is from 1802). Large-scale mechanized industry, with assistance from the railways, fills the cities of work and misery with a new transforming force: the proletariat. Hot in the steps of the bourgeois revolution – characterized by the abolition of feudal privileges and the system of monarch, nobles and castes, the conquest of the freedoms necessary for industrial growth, the social hegemony of the bourgeoisie and the omnipotence of money – fresh battles break out in the newly won terrain: the proletariat, even before it recognizes its mission as the liberator of humanity, demands its right to a human existence.

Throughout the first half of the nineteenth century, Russia remains outside the influence of the revolutionary convulsions in the West. The *ancien régime* (serfdom, privileges of nobility and Church, Tsarist autocracy) is here impregnable: the 'Decembrist' military conspiracy of 1825 scarcely ruffles it. From 1840 onwards, the need for serious reform does begin to be apparent: agricultural production is poor, grain exports low, the growth of manufacturing industry slowed down through the shortage of labour; capitalist development is being impeded through aristocracy and serfdom. It is a perilous situation, which is given a fairly astute solution in the act of 'liberation' of 19 February 1861, abolishing serfdom. The 'emancipated' peasant now has to buy up tiny, neatly truncated plots of land, and passes from a feudal subjection to an economic one. He must now work harder, and manufacturing industry will find in the countryside the 'free' manpower it needs so badly. With a population of sixty-seven million in this epoch, Russia had twenty-three million serfs belonging to 103,000 landlords. The arable land which the 'freed' peasantry had to rent or buy was valued at about double its real value (342 million roubles instead of 180 million); yesterday's serfs discovered that, in becoming free, they were now hopelessly in debt. Between this great reform of Alexander II, the 'Tsar Liberator', and the revolution of 1905, the lot of Russia's peasants will worsen uninterruptedly. The reform of 1861 gave them about five hectares[1] of land per male inhabitant; by 1900 the rapid population increase will leave the muzhiks with less than three hectares per head – seventy per cent of the farmers possessed an area of cultivation below the minimum needed to support their families. On the other hand, in 1876, fifteen years after the reform, the export sales of Russian grain on the European market had risen by 140 per cent, causing a fall in the world price of cereals. In 1857–9 Russia exports only 8,750,000 quarters (English measure) of cereal crops; in 1871–2 it exports 21,080,000. For commerce, for industry, for landed property and for the governing bureaucracy, the emancipation of the serfs was good business. The peasants simply exchanged one form of slavery for another and became subject to periodic famines.

The abolition of serfdom in Russia coincides with the War of Secession and the abolition of slavery in the United States of America (1861–3). Both in the Old World and the New, the growth of capitalism demands the replacement of the slave or serf by the free worker – free, that is, to sell his toil. The free worker works better, more intensively and more conscientiously. Large mechanized industry is incompatible with primitive methods of compulsion; in their place it substitutes economic constraint, the concealed compulsion of hunger whose efficacy is different in nature from that of naked violence.

1881: THE 'PEOPLE'S WILL'

At the very time when his great reform was being implemented, in the year 1863, the Tsar Liberator crushed the Polish rising in the blood of its patriots: there were 1,468 executions.

The initial path of capitalist development in Russia may have been cleared by the reform of 1861, but the way ahead for it was not without obstacles. There was no equality of civil rights. Initiative was clogged by a rigid bureaucratic and police apparatus. Privileged castes maintained their position in the State; the bourgeoisie was kept at a distance from the levers of power, and saw its interests (which it sincerely identified with the general interests of progress) constantly misrepresented by reactionary values, or else sacrificed to the demands of the Tsarist court, the nobility or the big landlords.

Disturbances among the peasantry became a constant problem. Within the petty-bourgeoisie, deprived of any rights or assured future, and mauled both by the old regime and by ascendant capitalism, the young intelligentsia had become captivated by the advanced ideas of the West, and promised to be a favourable ground for the seeds of revolution. New reforms, such as the reorganization of the judiciary, the statute on local governments and the abolition of corporal punishment, co-existed with pitiless acts of repression such as the deportation of the thinker Chernyshevsky to Siberia, where he spent twenty years. The first important revolutionary movement in Russia, that of the Narodniki or Populists (from the word *narod*, meaning 'people'), was impelled by a number of factors: the weakness of the Russian bourgeoisie proper, which constantly tended towards compromise with reaction; the non-existence of any liberal movement; the desperate plight of the peasantry, the common people and the propertyless intellectuals; the rigours of repression and the influence of Western Socialism, with its heritage from the revolutionary tradition of 1848. The Narodniki hoped for a popular revolution and saw the old Russian rural commune, or *mir*, as the foundation on which a peasant Socialism could be built. They believed that enlightened minorities owed imperious duties towards the people; they had faith in an intellectual *élite*, in human personality, in 'critical thought' and in idealism. Pyotr Lavrov and Mikhailovsky[2] equipped the movement with a philosophy, and the indomitable Bakunin gave it the lesson of struggle.

This is the period of 'going to the people'. In their thousands, young men and women from the aristocracy, the bourgeoisie and the petty-bourgeoisie go to the people, forsaking career and comfort to work in manual labour, to experience hardship, hunger, toil and prison, Siberia and Geneva. Circles of 'rebels' are formed,

attracting the sympathy of enlightened elements. They are persecuted and repressed. Out of their wreckage, in 1878, comes the
secret society 'Land and Liberty', which soon splits into two
parties, the 'Black Partition', which advocates propaganda in the
countryside, and the Narodnaya Volya ('People's Will'), which
promotes terrorism. 'History is too slow,' says one of its leaders,
Zhelyabov. 'We must hurry it on, or the nation will have degene-
rated before the liberals wake up and start work again.' The
party's programme is somewhat confused: the land to the people,
the factories to the workers; a Constituent Assembly and a
republic; a constitution. Some of the Narodniki would have been
content with a constitutional monarchy. They had a very clear
idea of what had to be destroyed: they were far less preoccupied
with what had to be built afterwards. In the absence of any other
method of action, the men of the 'People's Will' resorted to the
assassination of individuals: 'Our party has no other method it
can use,' one of them wrote a few days before mounting the
scaffold. 'Political assassination is one of our most efficient
weapons in the struggle against Russian despotism,' wrote the
party's organ *Land and Liberty*. The party numbered fewer than
fifty members, but these were heroic and dedicated men, energetic,
fearless, intelligent, willing to face death.

The first important attempt was that made by the student Vera
Zasulich,[3] who shot at General Trepov in 1878. A monster trial
had just taken place, in which 193 defendants accused of revolutionary activities had appeared before the judges of St Petersburg.
Out of 770 arrested, seventy had died in prison during the preliminary investigation, which had taken several years. The trial,
which was a complete farce, ended with ninety-four acquittals,
thirty-six deportations and one sentence of ten years' hard labour.
Meanwhile, Trepov, the St Petersburg Chief of Police, had a
student who was in prison beaten with sticks. 'The punishment
was quite legal,' he explained afterwards. 'After all, B—, the
condemned student, was not of noble blood.' Vera Zasulich was
acquitted in her trial. Russian terrorism, as can be seen, came to
its fruition in a supercharged atmosphere.

Assassinations soon followed. The dreaded 'Executive Committee of the People's Will Party' met in secret to pass sentences
of death, complete with a statement of charges, and these were
communicated to the persons concerned: the Tsar duly received
his. Then the tribunal carried out sentence. The police chief
Mezentsev was stabbed by unknown assailants[4] in a St Petersburg
street; the governor of Kharkov, a prince of the Kropotkin
family, was executed. The Tsar replied to the murder of his servants by referring all political cases before courts-martial and by
having gallows erected for any who fell foul of police revenge. The
nation was a mute bystander in this duel between the autocracy
and a handful of revolutionaries. Between 1872 and 1882 there

were six attempted assassinations (three of these successful) against high officials, four against police chiefs, four against Alexander II, nine executions of informers and twenty-four cases of armed resistance to the police. Thirty-one revolutionaries were hanged or shot.

The prime target for the 'People's Will' was the head of the whole system, the 'king stag' of the herd. On 14 April 1879, the student Soloviev fired five pistol-shots at Alexander II. On 1 December the same year an explosion derailed the Imperial train not far from Moscow. On 17 February 1880, the dining-room in the Winter Palace exploded seconds before the Imperial family was due to enter it. On 1 March 1881, Alexander II at last met his death in St Petersburg, mangled by bombs. His five executioners, Sophia Perovskaya, Zhelyabov, Kibalchich, Mikhailov and Russakov, were hanged. With these casualties the party lost its finest leaders, some of them the finest revolutionary personalities known to history. The party was decapitated.

Other social forces, as yet unperceived, were now entering the battle.

1885: THE BIRTH OF THE LABOUR MOVEMENT

Over the next ten years, from 1881 to 1890, reaction makes a determined counter-attack; serfdom is more than half reinstated. At his accession, the new Tsar, Alexander III, proclaims the autocracy to be 'unshakable': the establishment of the Okhrana ('The Defensive') follows, a political police armed with extensive powers and funds. A press law lays down preventive censorship for journals suspected by the authorities (1882); they can even be suppressed. In 1889 the legalized servitude of the peasant is sanctified with the creation of headships of rural communes (*zemskye nachalniki*), chosen from among the nobility on the nomination of the big landlords and endowed with wide authority. The rights of the aristocracy are extended; higher education is reserved by law for the governing classes; students have to wear compulsory uniform and are placed under strict police surveillance. A Nobles' Rural Credit Bank and a Peasants' Rural Credit Bank are founded, the first to assist the squirearchy and landed gentry, the second to further the progress of the rich peasants. The Russification of Poland, Finland, the Baltic provinces and the Caucasus is pursued relentlessly. The Jews, who have been harried by the recent pogroms of 1881–2, are now compelled to reside in the gubernias of the south-east and in Poland; residence in the provincial capitals is forbidden to them, and nearly a million and a half Jews, hounded from the cities where they were settled, return to their places of origin (1888). Overcrowding and indescribable misery in the Jewish centres are the results of this legislation; it will not be repealed until 1917. The quota of places permitted to Jews in the universities is limited to ten per cent in so-called 'Jewish territory' and to two per cent in the capitals. M. Rambaud has remarked that under Alexander III 'the fate of the Jews was rather like that inflicted on the Huguenots in France through the revocation of the Edict of Nantes'.[5]

The causes of this phase of reaction were entirely economic, as M. N. Pokrovsky has demonstrated.[6] We have noted the added impetus in corn exports from Russia (i.e. in the development of commercial capital) as the result of the emancipation of the serfs. At that period world corn prices were high: from 1870 onwards they declined. The price of Russian wheat abroad fell from 1 rouble 54 kopeks per pood (a pood being about thirty-seven pounds in weight) to 74 kopeks, or less than half. The export of grain now played a leading role in the Russian economy. The autocracy entered on a protectionist policy and insisted that customs dues had to be paid in gold. The cost of manufactured goods to the peasantry rose sharply; and since the best land had been taken off him after the 'emancipation' of 1861, he had to work still harder to make a living, and had to rent land – often the same land that had been wrested from him – at a high charge. (The amount of rented land increased *tenfold* in the Saratov gubernia between 1860 and 1880.) The pauperization of the peasantry was quick to follow: in eleven years in the province of Orel the number of cattle owned by the peasants fell by one fifth. In 1884 two and a half million peasant families out of a total of nine million did not own a horse (see Pokrovsky). The legal measures taken to prevent the proletarianization of the peasantry, according to the official dream, by attaching him to his plot, were powerless in the face of these economic factors.

It is at this moment that Russian industry begins to expand. Through the impoverishment of the countryside, ten million starving proletarians are placed at its disposal. A vast internal market is assured to it thanks to the more intensive labour of the peasants who are, increasingly, devoting all their time to the farming of grain crops and abandoning the local production of the fabrics, tools, etc. that they consume. Foreign capital gushes in. The total industrial production of Russia, valued in 1877 at 541 million roubles, rises to 1,816 million in 1897; and the stake of foreign capital in it rises to 1,500 million roubles. In ten years, from 1887 to 1897, the number of proletarians in the engineering industry goes up from 103,000 to 153,000 and in the textile industry from 309,000 to 642,000.

The condition of this proletariat was pitiful. The textile workers in the Moscow region usually lived inside the mill itself, sleeping in the workshops. Even in the case of the best-paid workers it was rare for a family to have the use of one whole room; several families would generally be crowded together in a single room. There was an entire population of wretched cellar-dwellers in the cities. Infant mortality was frightful, and the working day was often as long as

2. A peasant dwelling in Russia before the First World War

fourteen hours. In 1899 the weavers of Petrograd, who till then had worked fourteen hours a day, waged a strike which won them a legal day of $11\frac{1}{2}$ hours. Wages were very irregularly paid. In 1883, in 110 Moscow factories out of a total of 181 the payment of wages was entirely dependent on the employer's goodwill! Fines, inflicted on the slightest pretext, rained down on the worker's wage-packet. Industry was a gold-mine for its owners.

From 1850 onward, strikes began to multiply. Towards 1875 Chaikovsky's[7] little group, which includes Pyotr Kropotkin, is active among the workers of St Petersburg. In 1877, during a trial of working men, the weaver Pyotr Alexeyev utters memorable words: 'The brawny hand of the worker will one day crush the autocracy into dust.' The first Socialist demonstration by workers takes place in St Petersburg, in the open square before the Kazan Cathedral, on 6 December 1876: at it the student G. V. Plekhanov, the future leader of Russian Social-Democracy, unfurls the Red Flag for the first time on Russian soil.

The 'Association of Workers of the North' is founded in 1878–9 by the joiner Stepan Khalturin, a friend and comrade of Zhelyabov. Khalturin fails in his aim of forming a workers' organization, turns to terrorism and dies on the gallows in 1882. The first victorious strike by Russian workers – victorious, in fact, despite the intervention of troops and the 600 arrests that initially gave formal victory to the employers – took place at the Morozov spinning-mills at Orekhovo-Zuev in 1885. In the following year a law was passed which satisfied the strikers' demands.

The first Russian revolutionary grouping with a Marxist tendency is founded in Switzerland by G. V. Plekhanov in 1883, a year before the dissolution of the Executive Committee of the 'People's Will'. It is called the 'Emancipation of Labour' group, and numbers no more than five *émigrés*. The first Social-Democratic organization in Russia itself will not be founded till ten years later.

It is in 1892 that we see the beginnings, in St Petersburg and Moscow, of the 'Unions of Struggle for the Emancipation of the Working Class'. These are formed definitively only in 1895. The branch in St Petersburg has two founders: V. I. Lenin and Y. O. Martov.[8] The school-teacher, N. K. Krupskaya, is also involved. Vladimir Ilyich Ulyanov, who will later sign his writings N. Ilyin and then N. Lenin, is twenty-five. The son of a head teacher at Simbirsk, he is of petty-bourgeois stock, like most of the revolutionary intellectuals who founded the Russian Socialist movement. His brother Alexander, implicated in one of the last conspiracies of the 'People's' Will, was hanged in 1887. The adolescent Lenin has matured in the shadow of the gibbet erected for his elder brother. His subversive opinions have caused him to be expelled from the University of Kazan, where he was reading law.

1895–1903: THE PARTY OF THE PROLETARIAT

From now on, the history of Russia will follow two paths, distinct though converging. The attention of scholars has been focused only on one of these, the one that appears in broad daylight. Historians study the deeds and the laws of emperors, diplomatic activities, military conquests, changes of government and the various reforms; they perceive the famines (especially the great one of 1891) and sometimes the civil commotions. These events have their importance, which we would be the last to decry: but any observer today who wants to understand the history of Russia – and, indeed, of the world – must pay the greatest possible attention to other happenings: the troubles in the countryside, the strikes, the formation of the revolutionary parties, and the economic necessities which are linked with these events by bonds of direct causation.

The period we are now viewing, 1890 to 1903, is that of the rise of the proletarian party. It is marked by the Franco–Russian understanding, soon to become an actual alliance (1891–4), by the advance of the Russians into central Asia (Turkestan and Pamir), where they collide with British interests, and into the Far East, where they help to rob Japan of the full fruits of her victory of 1895 over China; by the massacre of the Armenians in Turkey and the Balkan intrigues of Russian diplomacy, which succeed in getting the Bulgarian statesman Stambulov assassinated (1894); by the first Peace Conference at The Hague, summoned on the initiative of Nicholas II; by the war in the Transvaal, the Spanish–American war, the war against China, the Anglo–Japanese alliance, the beginnings of the encirclement of Germany. The colonial expansion of the European powers (in other words, the division of the globe among capitalist national blocs) is completed. This summary cataloguing of dates should be enough to display the profound forces which were already propelling capitalist society towards that final parting of the ways: the imperialist Great War. Equally in preparation were the forces of revolution, engendered by the same forces of capitalist development, but growing outside the public view, in the shadows.

The Second International of world Labour is resurrected in 1889, at its Paris Congress, where Plekhanov, as the representative of Russia's first Social-Democratic group, affirms that 'the Russian revolution will triumph as the revolution of the working class – else not at all'.

Lively polemics are being conducted in Russia within Socialist circles, between Populists (Narodniki) and Marxists. The former contend that the evolution of capitalism in agrarian Russia is neither necessary nor probable: in the ancient rural communities they discern the embryonic forms of a specifically Russian agrarian Socialism. The proletariat appears to them as an important but secondary element in the revolution, and the revolution itself is conceived by them as one which must replace the autocracy by a democratic regime founded on the people's rights. Plekhanov and Lenin reply to them by establishing the inevitable nature of capitalist development in Russia, and by formulating the theory of the dominance of the proletariat, which is destined not to serve a revolution made by other classes but to make its own revolution, that is, to play the decisive role in the country's destinies.

'Unions of Struggle for the Emancipation of the Working Class' now exist in a number of places: in the St Petersburg branch the student Krassin is working, in Odessa Ryazanov, Steklov and Tsyperovich are active; in Tula there is Khinchuk. A little later, in 1896, at Nikolayev the student Bronstein, later to be known as Trotsky, assists in the foundation of the 'Workers' Association of South Russia'.

The first congress of Russian Social-Democracy is held at Minsk (White Russia) in 1894. It is attended by nine delegates. Pyotr Struve[9] is there, and draws up the manifesto of the party. In it we find the following pregnant statement: 'The farther east one goes in Europe, the more base, weak and cowardly does the bourgeoisie appear, and the more gigantic are the cultural and political tasks that fall to the lot of the proletariat.'

As Socialist propaganda penetrates the consciousness of the

Russian labour movement, it falls also under the influence of the more advanced elements in the liberal bourgeoisie, who have joined Social-Democratic organizations: people like Prokopovich and Kuskova.[10] Russia's brand of opportunism in this period receives the description of 'Economism'; it declares that the workers' only interest is in economic matters, that politics is of little or no account. It tries to direct the proletarian movement into a simple non-political trade-unionism. It condemns the idea of violent revolution (coinciding on this point with Bernstein, who is working away within German Social-Democracy on the 'revision' of Marx), and places its faith in the evolution of capitalism. This is the time when 'Legal Marxism' takes root in Russia: the liberal bourgeoisie finds it an excellent weapon. Plekhanov and Lenin devote themselves to fighting these ideologies, whose triumph would confuse and mislead the workers' movement. The keen judgement, sharpness of view and proletarian intransigence evident in their polemic earn them much admiration. Later, Plekhanov will change: he will fail and then betray. Lenin will remain the same throughout his life, unshakably loyal to the class he has elected to serve, with the clear vision of genius.

It is in prison, in 1896, that Lenin writes his pamphlet *On the Strikes*. It is in exile in Siberia, in 1897, that he formulates the 'Tasks of Russian Social-Democracy' in a short programmatic text. Out of deportation, as an exile in Munich, he publishes in 1900 the first numbers of the first journal *Iskra* (*The Spark*),[11] which devotes itself to two tasks: to safeguard proletarian ideology against deviations, mutilations and degeneracies; and to direct the sympathies of all revolutionary oppositional elements towards the proletariat. *Iskra* fights against all the varieties of Russian opportunism, the equivalent of Bernsteinism and French Millerandism;[12] it crosses swords with the first 'Socialist-Revolutionary' organizations of Russia; it struggles to rally the students and intelligentsia to the side of the proletariat. In the period 1894–1903 the students are in the vanguard of the revolutionary movement; with increasing sharpness, the middle classes are taking up a stand against Tsardom. 'Lenin,' V. Nevsky has written,[13] 'and the other editors of *Iskra* repeatedly undertook the defence of the revolutionary intellectuals against the demagogic speeches of those who cried "Down with the intellectuals!"' *Iskra*, finally, condemns the individual terrorism practised by the Socialist-Revolutionaries, preaching instead the cause of action by the masses.

In 1902 there appears *What Is To Be Done?*, one of Lenin's key works. In it he insists on the necessity for forming, at long last, a revolutionary organization capable of decisive and consistent activity; its mainspring must be a body of 'professional revolutionaries' who are totally dedicated to the movement; only at this price will resistance to the autocracy's formidable machine, and the final overthrow of the latter, be possible. Henceforth the building of this organization will guide all Lenin's indefatigable efforts.

The Second Congress of Russian Social-Democracy meets in 1903 at Brussels; police interference compels the delegates to move from there to London. Sixty militants are present. They include Trotsky, now back from Siberia, Noah Jordania[14] and N. Bauman (who will be killed in 1905). The Congress splits into 'majoritarians' (Bolsheviki) and 'minoritarians' (Mensheviki), on a number of points defined by Plekhanov and Lenin, both of them Bolsheviki. Plekhanov demands a policy of no compromise with the liberals, defends the use of the death penalty against landlords and members of the Tsarist dynasty, and denounces parliamentary fetishism. Lenin, in a memorable debate on Article One of the Party Rules, insists that a condition of membership must be active participation in active work in an illegal organization – a condition which the Menshevik draft version tries to evade in order to keep the party open to sympathizing intellectuals. The Congress marks the definite split between Bolsheviks and Mensheviks.

THE 'SOCIALIST-REVOLUTIONARY' PARTY

The Socialist-Revolutionary party[15] grows up concurrently with a host of other groups which continue the Narodnik traditions opposed by Plekhanov and Lenin. In distinction from the Social-Democrats, who form the party of the proletariat, the Socialist-Revolutionary party tries to be the party of the proletariat, the peasantry and the advanced intelligentsia, all at once. As with the first Marxist organizations, the intellectuals are the most numerous element in it, but whereas Social-Democracy demands that these enter the service of the proletariat, and only gives them a hearing to the extent that they speak for the proletarian cause, in the Socialist-Revolutionary party it is the intellectuals *as such* who are given a decisive role. Narodnik theory teaches, in effect, that conscious individual personalities, 'endowed with critical thinking' and constituting a minority *élite*, have a crucial influence over the destinies of society. This conception, typical for an advanced intelligentsia in that it assigns a grossly exaggerated weight to 'critical thinking' and individual moral worth, is evidence of a serious failure to grasp economic factors, the role of the masses, the activity of the masses and the class struggle. The very idea of struggling against Tsardom by means of a single-party bloc of workers, peasants and intellectuals (i.e. the educated petty-bourgeoisie of the cities) represents, moreover, a misunderstanding of the class struggle. In such a party the workers will of necessity be kept in a subordinate role, cannot aspire to the working-out of their own politics, and in the end are bound to be used for the politics of the middle classes. Reviving the theories of the old

Narodniki, the SRs saw the peasant communes as the basis for a future Russian Socialism. Their activity leant principally towards the young intelligentsia and the peasantry. As against the Social-Democrats, who condemned the tactic in the name of mass action (without, however, denying that some acts of reprisal or legitimate defence against the rulers were perfectly natural), they elevated individual terrorism into a strategy. Their resolutions demanded that such terrorism be exercised in step with the action of the masses, or else in order to stimulate mass action, and in any case under the strict control of the party. A party of intellectuals leaning on the peasantry for support is incapable of utilizing the activity of the worker-masses, of which the strike and the street demonstration are the simplest forms: it has no alternative but to resort to terrorist acts. The immensity of the abyss separating the SRs from the revolutionary Marxists is evident. In fact – as Lenin wrote long ago and as history has abundantly demonstrated – the SR leaders were often no more than liberals armed with bombs and revolvers. Even so, up to 1917 (when it collapsed politically following the March revolution), the SR party gave proof of excellent revolutionary qualities. Its petty-bourgeoisie fought hard and well. The mass membership of the party can only be admired. Along with the Social-Democrats (and that energetic minority, the anarchists) it was the SRs that populated the prisons, the convict settlements and the remotest corners of Siberia; they included many fine professional revolutionaries; they gave heroes and martyrs in hundreds to the cause of revolution. Their downfall following March and October 1917 is all the more disillusioning: it reveals the incapacity of the middle classes to lead any revolution in our epoch, and the terrible danger of confused ideologies.

The various SR organizations fused into one party in 1901. The main leaders of the party were: Catherine Breshko-Breskhovskaya, an old militant of great courage who, since her first arrest in 1874, had undergone two sentences of penal servitude, experiences of exile, and a life of permanent illegality; Grigori Gershuni, the founder of the party's Battle Organization and a militant of sparkling intelligence and limitless devotion; Mikhail Gotz, an experienced veteran of the 'People's Will'; the politician Victor Chernov;[16] the engineer Evno Azef, a secret Okhrana agent who was later appointed to direct the party's Battle Organization.

This organization was founded by Gershuni in 1902; its first act, in the same year, was the execution of the Minister of Education Sipyagin by the student Balmashev (who was later hanged). On the day after the murder, the SR party published an official justification of the act. The following year Bogdanovich, Governor of Ufa, perished under a similar verdict. The arrest of Gershuni, who was delivered to the police by Azef, caused the latter's promotion to the top leadership of the terrorist detachment. A man

3. I. P. Kalyaev

named Boris Savinkov, for whom terrorism was a vocation and whose courage was indomitable, now found himself under the orders of the agent-provocateur. In 1904 the Prime Minister, von Plehve, fell mutilated by Yegor Sazonov's bomb. Sazonov had organized the assassination on instructions from Azef. Next came the turn of the Regent of Moscow, Grand Duke Sergei Alexandrovich, who was executed by Ivan Kalyaev. The terrorists Sazonov and Kalyaev should be numbered among the most impressive figures of Russian revolutionary history. Assassinations followed at a quickening pace. During the 1905 revolution, after the Imperial Edict of 17 October, the SR party became totally demoralized and ordered an end to the terror; in the new era of reaction which followed, it ordered its Battle Organization into fresh activity. The number of terrorist acts committed by the party was fifty-eight in 1905, ninety-three in 1906 and seventy-four in 1907.[17]

As it was composed of very disparate trends the SR party frequently experienced the departure from it of various elements of the Left or the Right. Around 1906 a Left wing with anarchistic tendencies broke off to form 'The Union of Maximalists', whose small groups distinguished themselves by terrorist acts of extraordinary daring.

1905: THE FIRST RUSSIAN REVOLUTION AND ITS CAUSES

It has often been remarked that the revolution of 1905 was the 'dress rehearsal' for the one of 1917.[18] It was a rehearsal for which the whole of previous Russian history had been preparing.

On the eve of 1905, ten million peasant families own seventy-three million *desyatins*[19] of land; there are 27,000 landed proprietors of whom 18,000 own sixty-two million *desyatins*; and of this huge area about one third belongs to 699 extremely rich landlords, the autocracy's firmest backers. Naturally, the best of the land is kept out of the hands of the peasants. Ever since 1861 the plots of land have been parcelled out in such a way as to leave the former serf as dependent as possible on the old landlord, from whom he had to rent, usually on ruinous terms, more land in order to keep a livelihood. The peasant pays dues or 'rights' for farming on untilled land along the roads into his village, for grazing his cattle, for a thousand other pretexts. From 1900 world prices of cereals begin to recover; eager for their profit, the landed gentry raise land prices and rents, sometimes doubling them. The population on the land has now increased: in 1861 the peasantry owned an average of five *desyatins* of land per male inhabitant, in 1900 a holding of less than half this size is common. Statistical estimates of rural unemployment now run to ten million. 1895-6, 1897 and 1901 are famine years (and during them the export of grain continues ...).

The misery of peasant and worker is a source of wealth for the propertied classes. From 1893 to 1896 the average annual value of Russian exports is 661 million roubles; from 1905 to 1908, in spite of an industrial crisis, the Russo–Japanese war and the revolution, the export average rises annually to 1,055,000,000 roubles. The annual accumulation of profits grows over the same period from 104 million to 339 million. Foreign capital flows into this land where labour is so cheap and fortunes are so quickly amassed. Between 1894 and 1900, nearly 500 million gold roubles' worth of foreign investments enters Russian industry.

Despite its recent origins, Russian industry develops vigorously within its own peculiar terms. Its reserves of manpower are limitless but skilled workers are very scarce: no labour aristocracy is formed. The technical level of industry in this backward country is usually primitive: it is just too easy to do good business. On the other hand, concentration of capital, under the influence of foreign investors, is more intense even than in German industry. Here is a capitalism with a modern structure, impeded by institutions which, compared with it, are more than a century behind the times.

There is little or no labour legislation; no trade unions; no rights of combination, assembly, strike or speech. The working class, quite simply, *have no rights*. The working day varies between ten and fourteen hours. In the engineering factories at Bryansk in the south, wages in 1898 are 70 kopeks for a twelve-hour day. Textile workers get 14 to 18 roubles a month, with swingeing deductions from the wage-packet. The working day is longer and the level of wages lower than anywhere else in Europe. This proletariat of mill and factory, concentrated in a few large centres, forms a compact mass of 1,691,000 workers (as of 1904).

This state of affairs had its repercussions even among the industrialists. The textile employers, who had only a wretched domestic market in the pauperized countryside, sympathized with the 1905 revolution, at least at first. The engineering employers, working on State orders, yielded, numbed, after the military disasters in Manchuria.

Discontent among the petty-bourgeoisie was mounting. The wealthy peasants could see the big land-owners blocking any further progress for them. Merchants, artisans, poor folk and, still more, the intellectuals felt their interests profoundly thwarted and their dignity affronted by the caste-system and its bureaucratic despotism. With the exception of the big landlords, the rich nobility, the Court and the fraction of the top bourgeoisie that was linked with Tsardom, all classes in society felt the need for serious changes.

1902 was marked by troubles in the rural districts. Whole villages were shot down or flogged. The great mass strike at Rostov-on-Don revealed the power of the working classes. In the next year, what amounted to a general strike swept the south. The anti-semitic progroms at Kishinev, organized by von Plehve's police, were a response to these stirrings among the people: several hundred Jews were butchered. In this period, it occurred to the Tsar's police officials that the labour movement might just as well be staffed and run by themselves. The police chief Zubatov encouraged the establishment, first at Moscow and then at St Petersburg, of working men's associations enjoying the threefold protection of police, employers and clergy. However, the pressure of circumstances compelled even this 'police Socialism' to lend support to strikes: in 1905 a struggle broke out at the Putilov Works between the workers and the management, who had just sacked four members of the workers' association patronized by the authorities and directed by the priest Gapon. This 'black trade-unionism' was thus catapulted into the leadership of an entire proletariat that had reached the limit of its patience.

Gapon is a remarkable character. He seems to have believed sincerely in the possibility of reconciling the true interests of the workers with the authorities' good intentions. At any rate it was he who organized the movement to petition the Tsar which ended with the massacre of 22 January (9, Old Style) 1905. The petition of the workers of St Petersburg to Nicholas II, drafted by Gapon

4. Gapon leading a workers' deputation in audience before the Tsar

and endorsed by tens of thousands of proletarians, was both a lugubrious entreaty and a daring set of demands. It asked for an eight-hour day, recognition of workers' rights and a Constitution (including the responsibility of ministers to the people, separation of Church and State, and democratic liberties). From all quarters of the capital the petitioners, carrying icons and singing hymns, set off marching through the snow, late on a January morning, to see their 'little father, the Tsar'. At every cross-road armed ambushes were waiting for them. The soldiers machine-gunned them down and the Cossacks charged them. 'Treat them like rebels' had been the Emperor's command. The outcome of the day was several hundred dead and as many wounded.[20] This stupid and criminal repression detonated the first Russian revolution. It also ensured the suicide – for a date twelve years hence – of the Russian autocracy.

1905: THE BATTLE

Over the length and breadth of the nation, whose discontents were already magnified through the Russo–Japanese war, this massacre of workers sent a gust of revolution. A general strike, virtually total, swept through 122 towns and industrial centres and along ten main railway-lines. At Warsaw the strike took on the character of an insurrection, attested by ninety dead, 176 wounded and 733 arrests. For a whole year the Russo–Japanese war had been simply a succession of defeats. The war's causes were various. Tsardom, in furtherance of its policy of territorial aggrandisement, had cast its net into Manchuria, an excellent zone for colonization: possession of Port Arthur would open up China for Russian commerce; French capital, now engaged in the construction of the Trans-Siberian Railway, had Far Eastern ambitions; the Tsar, now heading an Imperial family whose increasing numbers made it more difficult to provide them with endowments, dreamed of Korea as a base for extending the Romanov fortunes; finally, the statesmen of Russia were by no means averse to the prospect of strengthening the autocracy at home by means of a military victory. Japan, for its part, had been deprived by Russia in 1894 of its spoils of victory over China; it was resolved to conquer Korea; and its designs for a forcible settlement of accounts with Russia were now being encouraged by British imperialism, which wanted a weakening of Russian influence in Asia. The war broke out in February 1904 and was ended by the treaty of Portsmouth on 5 September 1905. The Russians were defeated in every single engagement (on the Yalu, at Lyao-Yang, at Mukden, at Port Arthur where they had to capitulate) and lost their entire fleet at the naval battle of Tsushima (May 1905). Each defeat, in displaying the military feebleness of the autocracy (which had never doubted its prospects of a hands-down victory), had even more serious repercussions on the domestic front than on the battle-field. These shameful defeats were the result of administrative incompetence, the incapacity of the men in charge, and the troubled situation at home, where most of the best troops had to be left. The war cost 1,300 million roubles. Nicholas raised practically the whole sum (around 1,200 million) from abroad, principally on the Paris Stock Exchange.

We can make no attempt to trace through, in a few pages, the complex fortunes of the 1905 revolution; we shall sketch only the most important dates and details. The rural troubles began in February. On the 4th of the month the Grand Duke Sergei was executed by the SR party; on 17 April an Imperial edict (*ukaz*) proclaimed freedom of conscience for all – without touching the powers of the State Orthodox Church. In May there is the London Bolshevik Congress, the third congress of Russian Social-Democracy.

The Bolshevik faction of the movement has been going through a difficult phase since 1903. Plekhanov, the party's leader, had shortly after the Second Congress gone over to the Mensheviks, as had Trotsky (the latter only for a short time: throughout the whole revolution he was to work with the Bolsheviks and was even somewhat to the Left of them). 'It was a period of collapse, hesitation and disarray,' Lenin observed. But in reality the Bolshevik party was forged in these terrible internal struggles. On the eve of the revolution it found itself the only organization that was in a state of readiness, the only one armed with clear ideas. The Mensheviks held power in the leading bodies of the party: despite the seriousness of the situation, they refused to call a Party Congress where they would have been put into a minority. The Bolsheviks held their own conference in London and the Mensheviks called one in Geneva.

Nothing can explain the Bolshevik victory of 1917 better than their attitude in 1905. The Mensheviks maintained that the coming revolution would be a bourgeois one, carrying the bourgeoisie into power and consolidating their rule, opening an era of expanding capitalist development in Russia. A workers' insurrection would be madness. The Bolsheviks accused their adversaries of trailing behind the possessing classes. The proletariat, they insisted, must place itself at the head of the popular upheaval; a bourgeois revolution could only be truly realized within 'the democratic dictatorship of the workers and peasantry', whose victories would enable the proletariat to advance towards Socialism in the next stage. Lenin's guiding idea was that, in the presence of a numerous, powerful and politically conscious proletariat, there could be no question of a purely bourgeois revolution. At this time Trotsky and Parvus formed a third tendency within Russian Social-Democracy: while steering clear of the opportunism of the Menshevik members, they linked the destinies of the Russian revolution to the fate of the European workers' movement (in their theory of 'permanent revolution').

Lenin and Krassin persuaded the London Congress to agree to the party's participation in the revolutionary government which would not recoil either from the accusation of 'Jacobinism' nor from the use of terror. 'In a revolutionary period it is stupid and criminal to be afraid of participation in power.' Following the report presented by Lunacharsky and Bogdanov, the Congress mandated the party with the task of preparing insurrection.

The first phase of the revolution was one of mobilization. Parties and groupings formed themselves: reactionaries, liberals, Zemstvos,[21] various petty-bourgeois societies, the peasants' congress, the workers' trade union.

Immediately after Bloody Sunday, trade unions began to spring up everywhere, illegal or semi-legal, often holding their meetings in the woods. Then events accelerated. On 15 June the battleship *Knaz-Potemkin* mutinied.[22] At the camp of Novaya Alexandria a soldiers' mutiny erupted, organized by the officer Antonov-Ovseyenko.[23] There was street-fighting at Lodz, in Poland: 500 dead. The autocracy saw that it had to manoeuvre. On 6 August, an Imperial edict established the Duma of the Empire, in accordance with the project of the Bulygin commission. This assembly, purely consultative in character, was to be elected on a restricted franchise, by electoral colleges, through an extremely complicated system. Every big land-owner was an elector, but every ten small land-owners elected only one elector in their own college. In the towns only bourgeoisie could vote, the working classes being excluded. Of the intellectuals only the rich could vote (those with a salary of 1,300 roubles per annum). St Petersburg had an electorate of 9,500 out of its population of one and a half million. The bourgeoisie tried to console itself with this shadow of a parliament.

At the beginning of October, a general strike broke out, from a dispute which appeared to be very trivial. The compositors in Moscow came out to demand payment for punctuation marks at the same rate as for letters. Gradually, through solidarity action, the strike spread to the whole of Moscow: then the railway workers joined in throughout the country. It was a formidable stoppage, and a complete one: even the shops closed down. On the 13th the Soviet (or Council) of the St Petersburg workers was founded, on the basis of one deputy for every 500 workers. At this moment the revolt of the peasants engulfed almost the whole of Russia. The 'lords' nests' were burnt down in hundreds. Two thousand land-owners' homes were reduced to cinders. The autocracy hesitated between the path of military dictatorship and that of surrender. The rail strike and the poor state of the troops' loyalties caused it to choose Count Witte's plan, a relative surrender: the Imperial edict of 17 October elevated the Duma into a legislative assembly and gave the suffrage (at the second and third stages of election) to the urban petty-bourgeoisie and the workers. But this only became a further stimulus; all the democratic freedoms were seized as an accomplished fact; a revolutionary press sprang up and the authorities, powerless, had to tolerate it.

The following days saw more anti-semitic pogroms,[24] an amnesty for political offences and the granting of autonomy to Finland. The end of October was marked by the military rising of Kronstadt; then came the revolt of the Black Sea fleet, whose inspirer, Lieutenant Schmidt, a brave but irresolute man, knew only how to die courageously. A single decisive fact dominates these events: the army, in spite of these explosive defections, remains *generally* in a state of obedience.

The St Petersburg Soviet had been led at first by a popular lawyer, Khrustalev-Nosar: he was arrested after a short while and replaced by Trotsky. The Soviet, led by Trotsky and inspired by the Bolsheviks, waged a struggle that was all the more difficult since the weariness of the St Petersburg proletariat was becoming increasingly acute. It tried in vain to win the eight-hour day by strike action, but failed. A year of struggle had exhausted the workers of the capital: the arrest of the Soviet precipitated only a short strike by a section of workers.

In Moscow, on the other hand, where the proletariat had been less active over the preceding months, the fever of rebellion now reached its peak. In vain did the more far-sighted revolutionaries point to the probability of a defeat. The general strike began on 7 December, with the backing of the SRs and the Bolsheviks. It immediately took on an insurrectional character: the small combat-groups of the workers' organizations covered the city with barricades, ready to resist the use of troops. They were too few, and too poorly armed; the movement had appeared too late, for a regiment in sympathy with the revolutionaries had been disarmed a short while before. The insurrection was decapitated by the chance arrest of most of the members of its leading committee. The working-class quarter of Krasnaya Presnya came late into the battle but defended itself magnificently. The artillery had to be brought in to crush it. Most of the insurgents managed to make good their escape. Nevertheless Admiral Dubasov, acting on the caprice of informers, had over 250 people shot.

The revolution had substantial successes in the south, and real victories in the Caucasus. January 1906 was a month of firing-squads. Punitive expeditions restored order everywhere with a cold ferocity. In the Baltic provinces, Siberia and the Caucasus they sowed the seeds of terrible hatreds.

Russia's first revolution cost her people almost 15,000 dead, over 18,000 wounded and 79,000 imprisoned.

In 1905 the autocracy was saved through the hesitations and reactionary sympathies of the liberal bourgeoisie, the hesitations of the revolutionary middle classes, the inexperience and poor

5. Matsushenko (sailor in white jerkin), leader of the *Potemkin* mutiny, shortly after its surrender

organization of the proletariat (for which its enthusiasm and solidarity were no substitute), the weakness of the proletarian party,[25] the primitive character of the movement in the country-side, the relative loyalty of the troops and the availability of French money.

1905: THE RESULTS

The defeat of the first Russian revolution was by no means total. The workers and peasant masses had lost their respect for the autocracy and learnt to engage in combat against their oppressors. It was a psychological change of incalculable importance. Now, the workers could see a clearer pattern in the mosaic of parties: from now on, in increasing numbers, they turned to the party of their class. The hard core of the Bolshevik party steeled itself for the struggles to come, and drew the lessons of an experience already formidable, during the moral crisis which followed. The years of reaction were painful to endure, like every aftermath of defeat: individualism, scepticism, discouragement, the spurning of the weak, all manifested themselves in a variety of forms. But the proletariat has no other school but struggle. The exploited class, the oppressed class, the class of the vanquished by definition, it learns, in its periods of reverse, how to conquer; the very fact that it rises from its feet and acts is already, in a certain sense, a victory; and its most telling defeats sometimes count, in the scale of history, as the equal of fruitful victories. So it was in 1905.

For the Russian bourgeoisie, by contrast, 'its' democratic revolution of 1905 was an unmitigated failure. The role played in it by the proletariat struck them as singularly disturbing. The bourgeoisie had lacked all unity. The middle classes, in moments of ardour during the struggle, had supported the workers. But the big bourgeoisie, the financiers, the engineering bosses, terrified by the advance of Socialism, had shown themselves as only too inclined to make a deal with the large landlords and the autocracy. The caste-divisions of Russian society, the privileges of nobility, landlords, Church and Crown, the civil inequality, the autocracy, all survived the crisis of 1905; Russian capitalism remained tied down at every move, even with the wide possibilities of development that were offered it through the influx of foreign capital. The corruption, incompetence and bureaucracy of Tsardom continued their work of obstruction. None of the causes of the revolution had been removed, or suppressed.

The Witte Cabinet had rendered a signal service to Tsarism through its constitutional juggling; liberalism and conservatism had met in the service of counter-revolution. It was succeeded by Stolypin's reactionary government, which was only too well aware that a final settling of accounts had only been postponed. In the face of this threat it undertook an intelligent manoeuvre in the agrarian reform of 1906–10, which encouraged the development of private property among the peasantry and the further enrichment of the better-off farmers. A 'Peasant Bank' allotted an extension of land, though not nearly enough, among the peasantry. The poor peasants were urged to colonize Siberia, central Asia and the Far East. Stolypin's policies were aimed at creating a stratum in the countryside that was rich, numerous, loyal to the regime and privileged; its property instincts would turn it into the ally of the reactionary nobility and the big bourgeoisie. Stolypin believed that the formation of this class of rich peasants would exorcise the peril of revolution forever within a space of twenty years. However, after 1912 came the revival of the working-class movement: then, the imperialist war.

While the Mensheviks were digesting 'the historic error of the Moscow uprising' ('They should not have taken up arms!' declared Plekhanov), Lenin and the Bolsheviks were drawing out the lessons of 1905. Lenin's writings of 1905–6 should be required reading. They are a model of revolutionary dialectic, and more: an

6. Aftermath of a pogrom in Odessa

introduction to the history of the October Revolution. Lenin
emphasized the significance of the Soviets as 'organs of direct
struggle by the masses', 'organs of insurrection', and hence their
fundamental incompatibility with the Tsarist regime. He used the
Moscow events to demonstrate the necessity for revolutionary
organization in an insurrection. He advocated guerrilla warfare,
which the Bolsheviks took up in many areas (notably in Latvia) in
order to resist reaction and prepare for later action. He developed
his theory of the united front, 'an agreement for purposes of
struggle concluded by the proletarian party with the parties of
revolutionary democracy'; he studied the technique of insurrection. Recent history had confirmed his evaluations of the liberal
bourgeoisie and of Socialist opportunism. His active thought, the
thinking of a revolutionary Marxist, was in constant opposition
to the tired, rigid, bookish doctrines of the Mensheviks. On 30
September 1906 he wrote, in reply to those who accused him of
being a 'Blanquist', 'anarchist' or 'Bakuninist':

Marxism distinguishes itself from all primitive forms of Socialism in the fact that it does not attach the revolutionary movement to any one form of struggle. It admits of the most different methods of action, without, however, 'inventing' them. It confines itself to generalizing, organizing and giving conscious purpose to those modes of action by the revolutionary classes which arise spontaneously in the course of the movement. A resolute enemy of all abstract formulas, all recipes invented by doctrinaires, Marxism demands an attitude of attention towards the struggle of the masses, a struggle which, in parallel with the development and the consciousness of the masses, and with the severity of economic and political crises, constantly calls forth new methods of attack and defence. Marxism does not reject any form of struggle. . . . Marxism never contents itself with forms of struggle which are actual or possible at a given moment: it recognizes the inevitability, as the situation changes, of modes of action which are still unknown to the militants of the present day. On this point it can be said that, far from having any pretensions to educate the masses in modes of action imagined by armchair inventors of systems, Marxism is always and only the school of the masses' own practice.

. . . Marxism demands, unconditionally, the historical examination of the problem of forms of struggle. To pose this question outside the concrete historical situation is to fail to understand the ABC of dialectical materialism. To different moments of economic evolution, there correspond different forms of struggle, conditioned by political, national and cultural situations, as well as by customs which in their turn modify the auxiliary and secondary forms of action.[26]

His theory of civil war, whose application we shall see in October 1917, was already developed. One might well believe that these lines, extracted from an article of 29 August 1906, date from 1917:

Let us bear in mind that the great struggle of the masses is approaching. It will be the armed insurrection. It must be, as far as possible, simultaneous over the whole country. The masses must know that they are coming to an armed, bloody and desperate struggle. Contempt for death must imbue them and assure them of victory. The offensive must be pursued with all possible energy: attack and not defence must be the masses' common slogan, the pitiless extermination of the enemy their objective; the organization of the struggle will be flexible and mobile; the vacillating elements among the fighters will be led on to enter battle. The party of the conscious proletariat must carry out its duty in this great struggle.

1907–14: REACTION AND FRANCO–RUSSIAN IMPERIALISM

The first fourteen years of the twentieth century are occupied by the preparation of the imperialist war. The division of the world, among great powers governed economically and politically by high finance, is now complete. Germany, deprived of satisfactory colonies, threatens Britain's control of the seas and, over the whole world, confronts British commerce with a competition for which there is no remedy except cannon-fire. On the two sides of the Rhine, the German and French engineering industries square up to one another. The German Empire covets France's colonies and dreams of consolidating her own influence over Turkey. Her interests, along with those of the Austrian Empire, clash with the interests of Russia: for more than thirty years, Tsarist intrigues have dominated the politics of the small Balkan states, and Russia now casts longing eyes at Constantinople, essential to her grain exports. 'From the end of the nineteenth century,' writes M. N. Pokrovsky, 'there exists a Franco–Russian imperialism.'[27] In 1900 the capital invested in Russian industry (in millions of gold roubles) had reached the following levels: Russian capital, 447·2 (or twenty-one per cent); foreign capital, 762·4 (or 35·9 per cent); capital raised by selling Russian stocks abroad, 915·6 (or 43·1 per cent). In all, seventy-nine per cent of the capital invested is of foreign origin! When one adds the 9,349,000,000 gold francs lent by the French Republic to Nicholas II, some idea will be conveyed of the hold exerted by French finance on the destinies of the Russian Empire. In 1914 the French capitalists had control of 60·7 per cent of Russia's output of pig-iron and of 50·9 per cent of its coal. On the eve of the revolution the banks of Petrograd disposed of a capital of 8,500 million roubles, fifty-five per cent of which belonged to the French banks.

We shall not relate here the military preparation for the war, undertaken ever since 1907, if not before, by the French and Russian General Staffs in collaboration with the British Admiralty. At Irkutsk in 1920, shortly before he was shot, Admiral Kolchak testified that ever since 1907 the Russian General Staff and Admiralty had determined 1915 as the date for the outbreak of the European conflagration. It is known that the Russian General Staff speeded up the march to war (so ably directed by M. Poincaré) through the provocation at Sarajevo.[28]

At the time when war broke out, large strikes in St Petersburg had just taken place, a symptom of working-class strength. The Bolshevik party had succeeded in publishing newspapers and magazines inside Russia (ceaselessly suppressed, and as ceaselessly springing up again), and in penetrating all working-class concentrations: it now participated in all movements by the proletarian masses. From 1910 on, the Russian proletariat had entered a phase of upsurge and activity: it was managing to increase its wages and reduce its working hours. The protests that followed the massacre at Lena were a witness to its awakening. The workers in the goldfields at Lena, in the gubernia of Irkutsk in Siberia, were hideously exploited. Lodged in insanitary barracks, paid in truck by their company (which had British capital), they began a strike at the end of May 1912, demanding an eight-hour day (instead of ten hours), a thirty-per-cent wage increase and the dismissal of various members of the staff. At the company's instigation, the crowd of strikers, unarmed, are fired on: there are 270 dead. Both in Moscow and in Petrograd huge strikes take place in protest against this employers' crime.

In Russian Social-Democracy the split between Bolsheviks and Mensheviks (who had been briefly reunited at the Unity Congress at Stockholm in 1906) widens between 1906 and 1914. The Bolsheviks had been attacking the 'liquidationist' tendencies that have arisen from the defeat of the revolution. (The liquidation in question is that of illegal work and revolutionary action.)

The war widens the gulf still further. The SRs have become converted to patriotism, and the Menshevik liquidators, in reply to a telegram from Vandervelde,[29] declare that 'they are not opposing the war'; whereas the Bolshevik Central Committee, looking back to the Paris Commune and the decisions of international Socialist Congresses, adopts the slogan formulated by Lenin: 'turn the imperialist war into civil war'. The five Bolshevik deputies in the Duma are arrested in November 1914, along with Kamenev, and deported to Siberia. In Petrograd the Bolsheviks now number no more than a dozen groups of some 120 members altogether.

They set to work at once for the re-foundation of the International, which has expired on 2 and 4 August 1914.[30] They travel to Zimmerwald and Kienthal. The line taken by Trotsky, now outside both the main factions of Russian Social-Democracy, differs very little from that of the Bolsheviks.[31]

1917

The Russian bourgeoisie, in contrast with the ruling clique of landlords, nobles and bureaucrats, welcome the war with enthusiasm. Surely the war was going to fulfil its dearest wishes, by compelling the autocracy to abdicate constitutionally, or at the very least to introduce far-reaching reforms? Besides, this bourgeoisie, with all its links with the capitalist classes of western Europe, was imperialist-minded.

The next years were to bring a number of fantastic spectacles: whole armies entering the field without munitions, fighting it out with sword and bayonet in mid-battle; treason at work in the General Staff and perhaps in the Court; sudden fortunes in the hands of manufacturers of war supplies; incompetent drunkards in responsible posts; a rakish *staretz* (or 'holy old man'), Rasputin, as close adviser to the Tsar, appointing and dismissing ministers between one drunken orgy and the next; Russia sliding towards the abyss while the world watched. The war revealed the gangrene of the whole system.

In January 1917 higher prices were obviously outstripping wage increases, in the proportion 163 to 130. Production was declining. The Allies had urged Russia into its immense effort, which reached a climax in 1916 and then left the nation exhausted.

Inflation. The railways worn down. Crisis of food supplies. The capital faced a bread and a fuel shortage. Assailed by speculation, the government vainly tried to tax foodstuffs and regulate the economy. The bourgeoisie under Allied influence would have liked a *rapprochement* with the autocracy, but the Court and the land-owning caste around the Tsar were inclined to see a separate peace with Germany as their only hope. This disquieting vacillation, and the terrible defeats sustained by the Russian armies, encouraged the Allies to nurture dreams of a *coup d'état* in the breasts of the Russian bourgeoisie. In 1917 most Russian politicians and generals, not to mention several Grand Dukes, were thinking of how they might avert a revolution in the streets by conducting one in the palace. Nobody dared to do anything. These conspiracies of the drawing-room resulted in nothing except the murder of Rasputin by Purishkevich, the leader of the extreme Right, acting with Prince Yusupov.

The revolution did come into the streets: it came down from the factories with thousands of workers out on strike, to cries of 'Bread! Bread!' The authorities saw it coming but could do nothing: it was not in their power to remedy the crisis. In the streets of Petrograd the troops fraternized with the workers' demonstrations, sealing the fate of the autocracy (25–7 February 1917). The speed of events took the revolutionary organizations by surprise even though they had been working towards this goal.

Two governments soon come on the scene. The Duma's Provisional Committee was a makeshift government of the bourgeoisie, headed by landed reactionaries whose sole idea after the abdication of the Tsar was the drafting of a constitution to preserve the royal dynasty and get the lower orders back into obedience; the Soviet of Workers and Soldiers was the government formed by the proletariat. The two rival powers at first hold their sessions side by side in the Tauride Palace, observing one another and avoiding collisions. The Mensheviks and SRs constituted the leadership of the Soviet: but the masses below pushed them, watched them and goaded them. The first Provisional Government headed by Prince Lvov, was actually steered by Milyukov, the leader of the Kadet (Constitutional Democrat) party of the liberal big bourgeoisie; its perspective was a constitutional monarchy under the Regency of Mikhail Romanov until the Tsarevich Alexei should attain his majority.

But the Soviet was acting. Its Decree (*prikaz*) No. 1, of 1 March,

8. Meeting of soldiers' delegates sent from the front to the Duma

abolished all titles of rank in the army, ordered the election of committees in all military units, and thus placed the soldiers at the effective disposition of the Soviet. It was at the Soviet's insistence that the Emperor and Imperial family were arrested, it was the Soviet that stopped the Tsar from escaping to England. The Soviet proclaimed its desire for peace; the Provisional Government, its loyalty to the Allies. The duality of power meant a conflict of power.

A coalition ministry, consisting of bourgeois-liberals, Kadets, Mensheviks and SRs with Kerensky as Prime Minister, is formed in the first days of May. Its programme consists of a couple of words: democracy, Constituent Assembly. It proves powerless to meet the economic crisis: for that, energetic measures, which would have hurt the bourgeoisie, would have been necessary. It yields to Allied pressure and launches the offensive of 18 June, a futile slaughter, as was obvious beforehand. It refuses national independence to Finland and disintegrates, with the resignation of the bourgeois ministers, on the question of the Ukraine's independence. A new Kerensky Cabinet follows, and in this the influence of the Kadets, who are determined to sabotage the revolution, is even stronger. This ministerial shuffle takes place amid the July rising, which foreshadows the October Revolution. The proletariat and the garrison have had enough of these ministerial games: 'All power to the Soviets.' The Bolshevik party judges the offensive to be premature: the provinces will not follow. Nevertheless, it supports the action of the masses, and is promptly outlawed. Trotsky is arrested, Lenin and Zinoviev are wanted men. The press denounces the Bolsheviks as paid agents of Germany.

Russia has the choice of two dictatorships: either that of the proletariat or that of the bourgeoisie. The 'State Conference' in Moscow acclaims General Kornilov, the prospective dictator, who wants discipline in the army – through the death penalty – order on the home front and a strong government. He attempts a *coup* on 9 September, in concert with Kerensky and the veteran SR terrorist Savinkov. Kerensky lets him down and the *coup* collapses. But this exercise in adventurism has mobilized the masses and restored the streets to the proletariat. We will give some little-known quotations which reveal the bourgeoisie's intentions in the period before Kornilov's *coup*. At the 'State Conference' in Moscow on 13 August, Prokopovich puts the programme of the bourgeoisie: 'Guaranteeing of proprietors' rights, State control over production, maximum prices to regulate profits, compulsory labour (with specified work-standards) for the proletariat.' A few days later Ryabushinsky, one of the big Russian capitalists, declares at the Conference of Industry and Trade that 'the Government must begin to think and act from the bourgeois viewpoint. ... Perhaps it may need the bony hand of famine to take the false friends of the people by the throat. ...' 'Let the capitalist give up his excessive profits,' says Prokopovich, 'and the worker his surplus leisure.'

The S R party, which is now the real governing party, postpones the implementation of its agrarian programme, puts off the election of the Constituent Assembly, yields to the pressures of the bourgeoisie and does what the Allies demand. Famine is swiftly approaching. The Germans capture Riga and menace Petrograd, which seems abandoned to their invasion plans. After all, would not Ludendorff take over the pressing problem of controlling the proletariat of the capital? In the countryside, peasant rebellion is flaring up.

Three great problems cry out for urgent solution, expressed in the three words: *peace, land, bread!* Peace is wanted by millions of peasants and proletarians in the army, and the bourgeoisie cannot give it them because it is too busy waging its own war. Land is desired by millions of peasants: the bourgeoisie will not give it, because it is allied with the big land-owners and because it rejects any attack on private property, the principle of its own domination. Bread is demanded by the proletariat of the cities: the bourgeoisie cannot give it, for the famine is the offshoot of *its* war and *its* policies. ... The overthrow of Tsardom has solved nothing. Another revolution has to be made.

This is what the masses feel and want. This is what the party of the proletariat knows and arms for.

2 · The Insurrection of 25 October 1917

From the rostrum Trotsky had just announced the withdrawal of the Bolsheviks from the Pre-Parliament (Democratic Conference). His voice, grating metallically, hurled the defiance of proletariat and peasantry before the highest authority of the Republic. Then he went out, passing in front of the sailors who were guarding the hall. As he passed them their bayonets wavered, and hard faces with burning eyes turned to the man who had just spoken. Gesturing with their bayonets, they asked him:

'When do we use these?'

It was 6 October. The Democratic Conference, a mock parliament for the revolution summoned by the SRs and Mensheviks, had opened in Moscow in the middle of the previous month. Strikes had forced it out of the city; the staff in hotels and restaurants had refused to wait upon its members. It had now been transferred to Petrograd, and was deliberating under the protection of a picked unit of the most reliable sailors. But the bayonets of these men shuddered at the passage of a Bolshevik spokesman:

'When do we use these?'[1]

This state of feeling was general in the fleet. Two weeks before 25 October, the sailors of the Baltic squadron, anchored at Helsinki, demanded that no more time be lost, and that 'the destruction of the fleet by the Germans, which now appears to us to be inevitable, should be made holy' by insurrection.[2] They were willing to die: but only for the revolution. Since 15 May the Kronstadt Soviet had refused to recognize the Provisional Government. After the July riots, the commissars sent by Kerensky to board ships and arrest 'Bolshevik agitators' received only this curt response: 'Agitators? We are all agitators.' It was true. The masses had innumerable agitators.

Delegates from the trenches came to the Petrograd Soviet with speeches of denunciation:

How much longer is this unbearable situation going to last? The soldiers have mandated us to tell you that if peace proposals are not presented immediately and seriously, the trenches will empty and the whole army will come home. You are forgetting all about us! If you cannot find the answer to the situation we shall chase out our enemies ourselves, at bayonet-point – but you will go with them!

Such, Trotsky relates, was the language of the front.[3]

At the beginning of October the insurrection broke out everywhere, spontaneously; peasant risings spread all over the country.

The provinces of Tula, Tambov, Ryazan and Kaluga are in revolt.

9. A revolutionary demonstration in the countryside some time in 1917. A Social Democratic (either Menshevik or Bolshevik) party banner is followed by that of the SR party

The peasants have been expecting peace and land from the revolution. They have been disappointed; and so they rise, seize the granaries of the landlords, and burn down their houses. The Kerensky government represses the risings wherever it has the force to do so. Fortunately its resources are limited. Lenin warns that 'to crush the peasant upsurge means the murder of the revolution'.[4]

Within the Soviets of the cities and the armies, the Bolsheviks, until recently a minority, become the majority. In the Moscow Municipal Duma elections, they win 199,337 votes out of 387,262. Of the 710 members elected, 350 were Bolsheviks, 184 Kadets, 104 Socialist-Revolutionaries, thirty-one Mensheviks and forty-one other groups. On the eve of civil war, the moderate, middle-ground parties now fall back, and the extreme parties gain. At a time when the Mensheviks are losing all real influence, and the governing SR party, which only a short while before appeared to carry immense weight, is reduced to the third place, the Kadets – the bourgeoisie's own party – acquire new strength as they line up to face the revolutionaries. At the last elections in June the SRs and the Mensheviks had obtained seventy per cent of the vote:

their share now is eighteen per cent. Of the 17,000 soldiers who vote, 14,000 are for the Bolsheviks.

The Soviets are becoming transformed. Once the strongholds of the Mensheviks and the SRs, they are becoming Bolshevized. There are new majorities forming in them. On 31 August in Petrograd and on 6 September in Moscow, the Bolshevik resolutions put before the Soviet obtain a majority for the first time. On 8 September, the Menshevik–SR executives of the two Soviets resign. On 25 September, Trotsky is elected President of the Petrograd Soviet. Nogin[5] is elected to the same position in Moscow. On 20 September, the Soviet in Tashkent takes power. It is suppressed by the troops of the Provisional Government.[6] On 27 September, the Soviet in Reval decides in principle for 'all power to the Soviets'. A few days before the October Revolution, Kerensky's 'democratic' artillery fires upon the revolutionary Soviet at Kaluga.

A little-known fact is worth recording here. At Kazan, the October insurrection triumphed before it had even begun in Petrograd. One of those who took part relates this dialogue between two militants at Kazan:

'What would you have done if the Soviets had not taken power in Petrograd?'

10. May Day 1917: a Bolshevik agitator addresses the crowd

'It was impossible for us to refuse power, the garrison wouldn't let us.'

'Moscow would have rubbed you out.'

'No, you are wrong. Moscow could never have got past the forty thousand soldiers we had at Kazan.'[7]

All over this immense country, the whole labouring masses are moving towards revolution: peasants, workers, soldiers. It is an elemental, irresistible surge, with the force of an ocean.

THE PARTY OF THE PROLETARIAT

The masses have a million faces: far from being homogeneous, they are dominated by various and contradictory class interests; the sole means by which they can attain a clear-sighted consciousness – without which no successful action is possible – lies in organization. The rebel masses of Russia in 1917 rose to a clear consciousness of their necessary tasks, of their means and the objectives, through the organ of the Bolshevik party. This is not a theory, it is a statement of the facts. In this situation we can see, in superb relief, the relations that obtain between the party, the working class and the toiling masses in general. It is what they actually want, however confusedly, the sailors at Kronstadt, the

soldiers in Kazan, the workers of Petrograd, Ivanovo-Voznesensk, Moscow and everywhere, the peasants ransacking the landlords' mansions; it is what they all want without having the power to express their hopes firmly, to match them against the economic and the political realities, to formulate the most practical aims and choose the best means of attaining them, to select the most favourable moment for action, to extend the action from one end of the country to the other, to provide the exchanges of information and the necessary discipline, to co-ordinate the innumerable separate efforts that are going on – it is what they really want, without being able to constitute themselves into (in a word) a force of the requisite intelligence, training, will and myriad energy. What they want, then, the party expresses at a conscious level, and then carries out. The party reveals to them what they have been thinking. It is the bond which unites them from one end of the country to the other. The party is their consciousness, their organization.

When the gunners of the Baltic fleet grew anxious for the perils hanging over the revolution, and sought a way forward, it was the Bolshevik agitator who pointed a way. And there was no other way, that much was clear. When the soldiers in the trenches wanted to voice their determination to finish with the butchery, they elected, to the committee of their battalion, the candidates of the Bolshevik party. When the peasants became tired of the procrastinations of 'their' Socialist-Revolutionary party, and began to ask whether it was not time to act for themselves, it was Lenin's voice that reached them: 'Peasant, seize the land!' When the workers sensed counter-revolutionary intrigue all about them, it was *Pravda* that brought them the slogans of action that they already half-knew, the words of revolutionary necessity. In front of the Bolshevik poster the wretched folk passing by in the street stop and exclaim, 'That's just it!' That is just it. This voice is their own.

That is why the progress of the masses towards revolution is reflected in one great political fact: the Bolsheviks, a small revolutionary minority in March, become in September and October the party of the majority. Any distinction between the party and the masses becomes impossible, it is all one multitude. Doubtless, scattered among the crowds, there were many other revolutionaries: Left SRs (the most numerous), anarchists and Maximalists,[8] who also aim towards the revolution. These are a handful of men swept along by events, leaders who are being led. How clouded their perception of realities is, we shall see by many instances. It is the Bolsheviks who, owing to their accurate theoretical appraisal of the dynamism of events, become identified both with the labouring masses and with the necessity of history. 'The Communists have no other interests distinct from those of the working class as a whole': thus the *Manifesto* of Marx and Engels. This sentence,

11. Petrograd, 1917: a crowd is dispersed under fire during the 'July Days'

written in 1847, now appears to us as one of fantastic foresight.

Since the July days, the party has passed through a period of illegality and persecution, and is now barely tolerated. It forms itself into an assault column. From its members, it demands self-denial, passion and discipline; in return, it offers only the satisfaction of serving the proletariat. Yet we see its forces grow. In April it had numbered seventy-two organizations with a membership of 80,000. By the end of July its forces numbered 200,000 members, in 162 organizations.

ON THE ROAD TO INSURRECTION

The Bolshevik party had been marching towards the seizure of power, with its astonishing steadfastness, lucidity and skill, ever since the fall of the autocracy. To be convinced of this it is necessary simply to read *Letters from Afar*, written by Lenin before his departure from Zurich in March 1917. But perhaps, like any historical definition that tries to be precise, that is too narrow a statement. The party had been marching towards power ever since the day when its obscure Central Committee of *émigrés* (like Lenin and Zinoviev) declared, in 1914, that 'imperialist war must be transformed into civil war', or since the even earlier day when it was born as a party of civil war at the London Congress of 1903.

When Lenin arrived in Petrograd, on 3 April 1917, he proceeded to amend the political line of the party's central newspaper; this done, he set about defining the objectives of the working class. Tirelessly he urged the Bolshevik militants to use persuasion to win the working masses. In the first days of July, when an infuriated popular upsurge broke for the first time against the Kerensky administration, the Bolsheviks refused to follow this movement. These are leaders, in the real sense of the word, who are refusing to be led. They want to avoid a premature insurrection: the provinces are not ready, the situation is not ripe. They pull back the movement, resist the stream, risk unpopularity. The proletariat's consciousness embodied in the party is entering into a momentary conflict with the revolutionary impatience of the masses. It is a dangerous conflict. If the enemy had been bolder and more intelligent, the masses' impatience would have given it an easy victory. 'Now,' said Lenin to his friends, just after the July riots, 'they're going to shoot the lot of us.' In theory Lenin might have been right; it was perhaps the bourgeoisie's sole chance to reduce the proletariat with a preventive slaughter that would have been effective for months, if not years. Fortunately, the bourgeoisie was less skilful at its own game than Lenin was. It lacked daring (it certainly did not lack the intention).

After July, the more energetic bourgeois leaders thought of remedying this deficiency. They had ideas of a 'strong' authority. Russia was between two dictatorships – Kerensky's administration could now be no more than an interregnum. Kornilov's abortive *coup* (secretly aided by Savinkov and Kerensky) unleashed a fresh mobilization of the proletariat. The situation worsened, threatening to become quite desperate for the proletariat, whose privations grew daily. The workers felt, correctly, that if they could not win they would be beaten into the ground. Likewise for the peasantry: the situation worsened as they saw the agrarian revolution, promised to them by the SRs who were now in power, constantly deferred and in danger of summary suppression by some Napoleon of counter-revolutionary reaction. For the army and the fleet it worsened as they were still compelled to wage a hopeless war in the service of enemy classes. It worsened for the bourgeoisie, whose position was getting more precarious each day through the collapse of the transport system, depreciation of industrial equipment, defeats at the front, the crisis of production, the famine, the unruliness of the masses, the lack of authority of the new government, and the feebleness of its coercive machine.

After the July days, Lenin had remarked to V. Bonch-Bruyevich: 'The insurrection is absolutely unavoidable. In a short while it will become imperative. It cannot fail to take place.' From mid-September on, the party begins to prepare itself decisively for the battle. The Democratic Conference, which is supposed to act as a preparatory Parliament, is in session from 14–22 September.

Lenin, in hiding at the time, insistently demands the recall of the Bolshevik faction from the Conference, where some of the comrades would be tempted to take the role of a parliamentary opposition (though a vocal one). Supported by the majority of the party, Lenin's line carries the day, and the Bolsheviks march out, slamming the door behind them. Trotsky reads their declaration to the remaining delegates.

The impassioned speech of L. D. Trotsky, who had just tasted the joys of prison life under the government of the bourgeoisie and the Mensheviks, cut like a sword through all the plots concocted by the various orators of the Centre. He told them, clearly and unmistakeably, that there was no road back for us; that the workers had no retreat in mind, and saw no other way forward except that of a new revolution. He was heard in complete silence; a tremor passed over the comfortable seats and the boxes occupied by the leaders of the bourgeoisie. ... From the gallery and balcony, applause thundered down. ... With this the will to insurrection was clearly affirmed, and all the tact and authority of the Central Committee was needed to stop it from proceeding to immediate action, for it was still too soon – the July days could have had an even bloodier repetition.[9]

In the last days of September (alternatively the first days of October) the Central Committee of the Bolsheviks (Lenin, Trotsky, Stalin, Sverdlov, Yakovleva, Oppokov, Zinoviev, Kamenev) met in Petrograd, in the apartment of the Menshevik Sukhanov. Even the principle of the insurrection was in dispute. Kamenev and Zinoviev (Nogin and Rykov, who were of the same opinion, being absent from this meeting) stated their view that the insurrection might perhaps itself be successful, but that it would be almost impossible to maintain power afterwards owing to the economic pressures and the crisis in the food supply. The majority voted for the insurrection, and actually fixed the date for 15 October.[10] Let us insist on one point in this connection. This difference of judgement must emphatically not be taken as a sign of any tendency towards opportunism or Menshevik feebleness in men who had proved themselves in years of struggle and who later, throughout the whole of the civil war, were exempt from any charge of faintheartedness. It may be taken as indicating that certain tried revolutionists were inclined to overestimate the strength of the enemy and to lack confidence, to a certain extent, in the forces of the proletariat. One does not play at insurrection. It is the duty of all revolutionaries to weigh in advance every eventuality and possibility. If they are concerned at the possible defeat of the revolution their apprehension has nothing in common with the counter-revolutionary fears of opportunists, who dread nothing more than the victory of the proletariat. Still, since these legitimate fears rested on a faulty interpretation of reality, they were immensely dangerous for the party's whole activity, which they could have warped irreparably. Time works in favour of revolution at certain hours; works against it once the hour has passed; and an action postponed may well become an action lost to history. For its hesitation in 1920, the Italian proletariat has paid very dearly; the opportunity which was offered the German proletariat in 1923[11] will, no doubt of it, recur: but when? The error of the Bolshevik opponents of the insurrection was therefore a most serious one, as they have since admitted.[12]

On 10 October, the Central Committee of the Bolshevik party (present: Lenin, Zinoviev, Kamenev, Stalin, Trotsky, Sverdlov, Uritsky, Dzerzhinsky, Kollontai, Bubnov, Sokolnikov and Lomov) voted ten to two in favour of immediate preparation for the insurrection. The work of preparation was assigned to a Political Bureau consisting of Lenin, Trotsky, Zinoviev, Stalin, Kamenev, Sokolnikov and Bubnov.

THE PROLETARIAN LEADERS

Within the party, the relationship which holds between the mass of militants and the leadership may be compared to that obtaining between the working masses and the party itself.

The party is the nervous system of the working class, its brain. The leaders and the key members perform the role of brain and nervous system within the organism of the party also. This comparison must not be taken in a literal sense: functions in a biological organism are differentiated in a manner very different from the allocation of functions in a social group. But, however politically conscious they may be, the rank and file of the party is unable to get to know the situation as a whole. Whatever the personal worth of these comrades, they must inevitably lack information, liaison, training and the revolutionary's theoretical and professional preparation, if they are not within that core of party members who have been selected and tried by long years of struggle and work, enjoy the goodwill of the movement as a whole, have access to the apparatus of the party, and are accustomed to thinking and working collectively. Just as the soldier in the trenches sees only a tiny portion of the battlefield and cannot, whatever his personal talents may be, acquire a clear picture of the action under way, just as the engineering worker at his machine cannot take in the functioning of the whole factory at a glance, so the rank-and-file party member, on the basis of his own resources, can only make his mind up through general ideas and judgements, and through acquaintance with a partial area of reality. True proletarian leaders are, all at the same time, guides, pilots, captains and directors of enterprises: I mean the formidable enterprise of demolishing a social system and constructing another. They have to uncover, by the scientific analysis of historic processes, the tendency of events and the possibilities that are open in them. They have to grasp the action that is possible and necessary for the proletariat, according with historical necessity and not with its wish or hope of the moment.[13] In a word, they must see reality, grasp possibility, and conceive the action which will be the link between the real and the possible. In doing so, the only vantage-point they can ever adopt is that of the proletariat's own higher interests. Their whole thinking has to be that of the proletariat, with the advantage of scientific discipline. Proletarian class-consciousness attains its highest expression in the leaders of the organized vanguard of the working class. As personalities, they are great only in the measure that they incarnate the masses. In this sense only they are giants – anonymous giants. In voicing the consciousness of the mass they display a virtue which, for the proletariat, is sheer necessity: a terrible impersonality.

So much is true. But the value of such leaders – the genius of a Lenin – lies in the fact that the development of class-consciousness is not foreordained from all time; mass consciousness can remain latent and unexpressed at a particular moment; the possibilities contained in the situation need never be perceived; the action necessary for the victory or the safety of the proletariat may never be devised. The recent history of the proletariat in western Europe offers only too many examples of opportunities missed through the failure of class consciousness to crystallize.

We can define the proletarian leader, finally, this man of a new epoch, by contrasting him with the leaders of the possessing classes both of today and of previous eras. The latter are the blind instruments of history; the revolutionary is its conscious instrument.[14]

The October Revolution offers us an almost perfect model of the proletarian party. Relatively few as they may be, its militants live with the masses and among them. Long and testing years – a revolution, then illegality, exile, prison, endless ideological battles – have given it excellent activists and real leaders, whose parallel thinking was strengthened in collective action. Personal initiative and the panache of strong personalities were balanced by intelligent centralization, voluntary discipline and respect for recognized mentors. Despite the efficiency of its organizational apparatus, the party suffered not the slightest bureaucratic deformation. No fetishism of organizational forms can be observed in it; it is free of decadent and even of dubious traditions; its dominant tradition is that of the war against opportunism – it is revolutionary down to the marrow of its bones. This makes it all the more remarkable that profound and persistent hesitations arose in its leading circles on the eve of action, and that several of its most important members declared themselves strongly opposed to the seizure of power.

LENIN

We have already remarked the powerful unity of character possessed by Lenin. He was a man hewn of a single block, totally devoted, at every moment of his life, to one sole work. He was one with his party, and through the party, with the proletariat. In the decisive hours he was one with the whole working people of Russia, and with the proletarians and oppressed peoples of all the countries in the world that lay beyond the bloody frontiers. That is the reason for his emergence in October 1917 as the unchallenged, unrivalled leader of the proletarian revolution.

The spirit of the masses during September and October has been described. In the middle of September Lenin sends an urgent letter to the Central Committee calling on them to seize power without delay. Another letter follows almost immediately, dealing with *Marxism and Insurrection*. Even before the seizure of power, Lenin (who knows that power is sometimes harder to hold than to acquire, and that it is essential to disclose to revolutionaries what strength they have) writes his pamphlet entitled *Will the Bolsheviks Retain State Power?* This is at the end of September. On 7 October, a new article, a new call: 'The Revolutionary Crisis has Matured'. From this moment on, he is possessed by a raging impatience. His letters follow, persuasive, authoritative, urging, hectoring, to the Central Committee, to the party, to the membership. Over the head of the Central Committee he addresses the Moscow and the Petrograd committees at the beginning of October: 'To Temporise Now is a Crime'. On 8 October, his 'Advice from an Outsider' on the insurrection appears. On 16–17 October comes a long and memorable letter, 'To the Comrades', energetically refuting the arguments of those opposed to the rising. The last hesitations are now overcome. Lenin the leader, moulded over twenty-three years of struggle since 1895, acting in unison with the peasants, workers, soldiers, sailors and the whole labouring people, has marked the hour and given the signal for the crucial act. It still needed all his energy, allied with the efforts of other comrades, to surmount the hesitations that might have proved fatal.

His writings of this period have been collected in a book with the apt title *On the Road to Insurrection*. It is a vital work, whose significance has yet to be fully valued. A model of revolutionary dialectics, a treatise on the theory and practice of insurrection, a textbook on the art of winning the class war: we believe that it ranks with the *Communist Manifesto*, to which it forms, on the eve of the proletarian epoch, a necessary complement.[15]

Lenin's doctrine of insurrection may be summed up in these lines:

In order for an insurrection to be crowned with success it should have the support, not of a conspiracy, not of a party, but of the advanced class: that first of all. The insurrection must rest on a popular revolutionary upsurge: that is second. The insurrection must come at the historic turning-point of the expanding revolution, at the moment when the activity of the masses reaches its peak, and when the hesitation in the ranks of the enemy, and among the false friends of the revolution, the double-dealers and the fainthearts, reaches its peak. That is third. By thus posing the three conditions of insurrection, Marxism distinguishes itself from Blanquism [*Marxism and Insurrection*][16].

It is also summarized in this dictum of Marx: 'Never play with insurrection, but once it is begun remember that it must be carried through to the end.'[17]

Why is it that Lenin, among so many good revolutionists who like him aimed for the proletarian revolution, many of whom saw the way forward as clearly as he, still stands out at this time as the chief? Many responsible members in Moscow and Petrograd – and it would be wrong simply to restrict ourselves to the two capitals and the principal leaders – are going consciously on the same road to insurrection. Trotsky, the President of the Soviet, never had the slightest hesitation, from the moment of his arrival in Russia, on the road that must be followed; he was in complete agreement with Lenin, except over details of execution.[18] In the party's Central Committee, the great majority of the militants vote for action. But none among these revolutionaries enjoys an ascendancy comparable to Lenin's. Most of them are his pupils and recognize him as their master. Trotsky, whose talents as an organizer of victory now become strikingly revealed, has for many years been an isolated figure in the Russian Social-Democracy, equally distant both from the Bolsheviks and the Mensheviks; to tell the truth, he has never presented the impression of being a

12. A Red Guard
rkers' detachment

party leader. Many Bolsheviks still remember him as an adversary. He is a great newcomer, who has come on to the Central Committee at the end of July (at the Sixth Bolshevik Congress) a few days after joining the party. The simple, basic truth is that it is the party that makes the leader, for without the party there can be no leader. It is because he has been the creator of the proletarian party that Lenin becomes the leader of the revolution.

THE RED GUARD

The events which now unfold in the two capitals are very different, but display a remarkable basic parallelism.

The initiative in forming the Red Guards in Petrograd came from the factory workers, who began it instinctively after the fall of Tsardom. In disarming the old order they had to begin to arm themselves. In April, two of the Bolshevik militants, Shlyapnikov[19] and Yeremeyev, began to put the spontaneous organization of the Red Guards into a systematic shape. The first regular units, if they can be called such, of this workers' militia were formed in the outlying proletarian districts, principally in Vyborg. The Mensheviks and SRs tried, at first, to oppose the movement. At a closed session of the Soviet held in June, when they still had a majority, the Social-Democrat Tseretelli demanded the disarmament of the workers. He was too late. Proletarian command units had now been set up in every ward, and these were co-ordinated by a General Staff Headquarters for the city. Formed on a factory basis as a volunteer army – it was not individual workers but the factory as a whole that took the decision to enlist together or form its own unit–the first Red Guard detachments undertook the duty of protecting the great working-class demonstrations. During the July riots the Vyborg section kept the troops sent by Kerensky at a respectful distance. At this time Petrograd had about ten thousand Red Guards.

With Kornilov's *coup d'état* (25–30 September) and the march of a Cossack division on the capital, the imminence of counter-revolution forced the Menshevik–SR Soviet to arm the workers at speed. Not without friction: the munitions workers at Schüsselburg sent a bargeload of grenades, but the Soviet refused to take delivery of them – whereupon the Red Guard took delivery without further ado. The initiative of the workers made up for everything, sweeping past the insincerity and feeble will of the Socialists of 'social peace'. The mobilization of the proletariat against Kornilov showed that an abortive counter-revolution can be as disastrous for the bourgeoisie as the failure of an insurrection is for the workers.

In September, the use of weapons was being taught in seventy-nine Petrograd factories. In a good many factories all the workers carried arms. The military organization of the Bolshevik party could not find enough instructors for these masses. On the eve of the October rising, the Red Guard numbered 20,000 men, organized in battalions of 400 to 600 each divided into three companies, a machine-gun section, a liaison section and an ambulance section. Some of the battalions had an armoured car. Non-commissioned officers (workers) headed the battalions and the companies. Duties were performed on a rota system, with two thirds of the workers at their jobs in the factory at any time, and the other third 'on guard', with wages at their job rate paid for time on duty. The rules of the Red Guard required, for admittance, sponsorship from a Socialist party, a factory committee or a trade union. Three absences without excuse were grounds for expulsion. Infractions of discipline were tried by a jury of comrades. Unauthorized use of arms was an offence, and orders had to be obeyed without discussion. Each Red Guard carried a numbered identity card. The officers were elected; in practice, though, they were often selected by factory committees and other working-class bodies, with nominations for senior posts always submitted to the ward Soviets for approval. If the officers had not already received military training they were obliged to take special courses.[20]

It is worth remarking that this impressive initiative on the part of Petrograd's proletariat was the fulfilment of Lenin's own wishes in the urgent advice he gave in one of his *Letters From Afar*, written from Zürich on 11 March 1917 (24, Old Style). This advice was ignored at the time and the letter was only published later on as a historical document. In it Lenin discusses the 'proletarian militias' and appeals to the workers: 'Do not allow the police force to be re-established! Do not give up your own local organizations!' And form a militia without delay, including the women and the young people. ' Miracles of organization must be achieved', he concluded.

In Moscow, it proved to be much harder to establish the Red Guard. The authorities, who were headed by S Rs and Mensheviks, succeeded in virtually disarming the workers and part of the garrison. Grenades had to be manufactured in secret and explosives obtained from the provinces. The organization of the command and of communications was deplorably late. These weaknesses and delays were to cost the proletariat of Moscow a bloody street battle lasting six days.

The military organization of the party now numbered more than 100,000 soldiers and a certain number of officers. Out of this, Military Revolutionary Committees were to be formed everywhere, the organs that directed the insurrection.

THE ARMED WATCH

The conflict between the two powers (Kerensky's Provisional Government and the Soviet) entered a new, sharp phase from

16 October, when the Military Revolutionary Committee, headed by Antonov-Ovseyenko, Podvoisky and Chudnovsky, was formed by the Soviet. The garrison in Petrograd had now been won over to the Bolsheviks. The government tried to send the most revolutionary regiments off to the front, arguing that a German offensive was imminent. The MRC, now with its own communications, intelligence and munitions departments, began by appointing commissars in every unit of the troops. The bourgeoisie was arming – but the appointment of commissars at the arms depots put a stop to that. The delegates of the MRC were welcomed warmly by the soldiers, who knew that the Committee was determined to prevent them being sent off to the front. The MRC in effect refused to countersign the order for the departure of the Red regiments, pleading that it needed further information on the defence forces now available. The MRC now assumed the functions of a General Staff for the Red Guards, and issued definite instructions to the troops not to pay any attention to orders proceeding from their regular commanders. From then on, the insurrection was, as it were, latent. Two powers took the measure of one another, and two military authorities, one of them insurrectionary, deliberately countermanded each other's orders.

The Second All-Russian Congress of Soviets was due to meet in Petrograd on 15 October. The Mensheviks succeeded in having it postponed until the 25th (7 November, New Style), thus gaining a respite of ten days for the bourgeoisie's Provisional Government. Nobody could doubt that the Congress, where the Bolsheviks were certain of a majority, would vote for the seizure of power. 'You are fixing the date of the revolution!' said the Mensheviks to their Bolshevik opponents. In order that the predetermined conclusion of the Congress should not be a simple pipe-dream, it was necessary to support that decision by force of arms. Concerning the date of the uprising, two points of view were manifested: Trotsky wanted to link the action to the Congress itself, believing that an insurrection conducted on the party's own initiative would have less chance of winning mass support; Lenin believed it 'criminal' to temporize until the Congress, since he feared that the Provisional Government would forestall the insurrection by a vigorous offensive. This fear, though legitimate, was not justified by the actual march of events: the enemy was caught napping.

In our opinion, the conflict here arose from two perfectly correct conceptions arising from different vantage-points. One stemmed from the *strategic* consideration of linking the party's action with a demand immediately intelligible to the broadest mass of people ('All power to the Soviets!'); this is, naturally, a condition of success. The other was based on the general policy of shattering any illusion that genuine proletarian power could be instituted *before* the insurrection. Once this possibility was admitted in theory, why not allow of power *without* an insurrection? There lay the slippery slope. Ever since 1906, Lenin had attacked the tendency to 'gloss over or discard the question of insurrection, in favour of the question of the organization of revolutionary power ...'. His position of realism could be summarized as: Conquer first! And so Lenin wanted the insurrection to precede the Congress, which would have no alternative but to sanction the accomplished deed. He urged this policy in a personal meeting with the organizers of the insurrection.[21] The details of the preparation interested him passionately: he would not have the attack put off at any price. Nevsky and Podvoisky tried vainly to persuade him that a few days' extra preparation would only increase the chances of success. 'The enemy will profit by it too,' he replied obstinately.

Antonov-Ovseyenko has left a vivid account of his meeting with Vladimir Ilyich a few days before the rising, in a house in the working-class district of Vyborg. Lenin arrived in disguise; he was wanted by Kerensky's police and in the event of capture would doubtless have ended his days through an 'accidental' bullet.

We found ourselves in the presence of a little, grey-haired old man wearing pince-nez, wearing them with a proper, almost debonair style. One would have taken him for a musician, a schoolmaster or a secondhand book-dealer. He took off his wig, and we recognized his eyes, sparkling as usual with a glint of humour. 'Any news?' he asked. He was full of confidence. He wondered about our chances of calling the fleet up into Petrograd. Somebody objected that this would leave the front at sea undefended, and his reply was brusque: 'Come now, the sailors must know that there is more danger to the revolution in Petrograd than on the Baltic.'

The Peter-Paul Fortress was a source of considerable disquiet to the Military Revolutionary Committee; it was situated in the centre of the city on an island in the Neva, and bristled with guns. Its artillery overlooked the Winter Palace and its armoury held 100,000 rifles. Its garrison appeared to be loyal to the Provisional Government. Trotsky proposed that the fortress should be taken from the inside – by holding a meeting there. He went there with Lashevich, and succeeded.

22 October was the Day of the Petrograd Soviet, the occasion of the great plebiscite of the insurrection, as it were. The immediate cause of its meeting was fairly trivial, as often happens when events of immense importance are in the course of accomplishment and the last link, often a slender one, appears in the long chain of causes. The Central Executive Committee of the Soviets, still under the sway of the social-peace Socialists, had charge of the funds of the Petrograd Soviet. The latter body needed a newspaper. It was decided to hold a series of large mass meetings on

the 22nd with the aim of raising money for the foundation of the journal. The bourgeois press, terrified by this mobilization of masses, proclaimed that it was a riot, Kerensky gave out apparent-ly forceful utterances which were nothing but wind: 'All Russia is with us! We have nothing to fear!' He issued a threat against 'all those elements, groups and parties who are menacing the liberty of the Russian people, running the risk of opening the front to Germany, of a final and complete catastrophe'. A regular Galliffet or Cavaignac,[22] to all appearances. But his threats were empty. The 22nd saw a tremendous mobilization of the masses.

Every hall was filled to capacity. At the House of the People (*Narodny Dom*) thousands crammed the halls, the galleries, the corridors; in the great auditorium, human clusters were hanging, palpitating, like grapes from the metal structure of the building. John Reed was present. His notes on the gathering, where it was Trotsky's voice that thrilled the crowd, deserve to be quoted:[23]

The people around me appeared to be in ecstasy. They seemed about to burst forth spontaneously in a religious hymn. Trotsky read a resolu-tion to the general effect that they were ready to fight for the workers and peasants to the last drop of their blood. . . . Who was in favour of the resolution? The innumerable crowd raised their hands as a single man. I saw the burning eyes of men, women, adolescents, workers, soldiers, muzhiks. Trotsky went on. The hands remained raised. Trotsky said, 'Let this vote be your oath. You swear to give all your strength, not to hesitate before any sacrifice, to support the Soviet, which undertakes to win the revolution and give you land, bread and peace.' The hands remained raised. The crowd approved; they took the oath. . . . And the same scene was repeated all over Petrograd. The last preparations were made everywhere; everywhere they swore the last oath; thousands, tens of thousands, hundreds of thousands of men. It was the insurrection.

KRONSTADT AND THE FLEET

On the morning of the 25th, the revolutionary forces at Kronstadt received orders to prepare to undertake the defence of the Soviet Congress (for the whole offensive was conducted under the formal pretext of defence). We may pause for a moment at the prepara-tions in Kronstadt, one of whose participants (I. Flerovsky) has left an excellent account.[24] The rational element of co-ordination, the superb organization of the rising as a military operation con-ducted along the rules of the war-making art, is clearly demon-strated here, and forms a striking contrast with the spontaneous or ill-organized movements which have been so numerous in the history of the proletariat.

The work of preparation for our intervention at Petrograd was car-ried on entirely at night. . . . The Navy Club was crammed with soldiers, sailors and workers, all of them obviously ready for battle. . . . The revolutionary General Staff worked out the plan of action precisely,

designated the different units and sections for each task, checked off the
inventory of supplies and ammunition, and picked the leading personnel. The night was one of strenuous work. The following ships were
selected to take part in the operation: the torpedo-boat and minelayer
Love, the old cruiser *Dawn of Liberty* (formerly *Alexander III*), the
monitor *Vulture*. *Love* and *Vulture* were to land troops in Petrograd.
The cruiser was to take up a position at the entrance to the maritime
canal, commanding the coastal railway with its guns. In the streets an
intense but noiseless activity went on. Army detachments and squads of
sailors marched towards the harbour. Only the serious, resolute faces of
the leading ranks could be seen by the light of the torches. There was no
laughter, and no talk. The silence was broken only by the military tread
of marching men, by brief commands, and by the grinding of the lorries
as they went past. At the harbour, the ships were speedily loaded.
Detachments of men waited in line on the quay patiently awaiting their
turn to embark. Is it possible, I could not help thinking, that these are
the last few moments before the great revolution? Everything is going
off with such simplicity and neatness that one would imagine some perfectly ordinary military manoeuvre was involved. It all has so little
resemblance to the vistas of revolution that we remember from history.
... 'This revolution,' my companion said to me, 'will go off in style.'

The revolution did, indeed, go off in proletarian style – with
organization. That is why, in Petrograd, it won so easily and completely.

Another significant scene may be borrowed from Flerovsky's
memoirs. It is on board a ship steaming towards the insurrection.
The delegate from the revolutionary headquarters enters the
officers' mess.

Here, the atmosphere is different. They are worried, anxious, dis-
oriented. As I enter and salute, the officers rise. They keep standing
while they listen to my brief explanation, and the orders I give. 'We are
going to overthrow the Provisional Government by force. Power is
being transferred to the Soviets. We are not relying on your sympathy:
we have no need of it. But we do insist that you remain at your posts,
going about your duties punctually and obeying our orders. We shall
not give you any unnecessary trouble. That is all.' 'We understand,' the
captain answered. The officers went off immediately to their posts, and
the captain mounted the bridge.

13. M. Lashevich

A numerous flotilla came to the assistance of the workers and
the garrison. Up the Neva sailed the cruisers *Aurora, Oleg, Novik,
Zabyika* and *Samson*, two torpedo-boats, and various other ships.

THE TAKING OF THE WINTER PALACE

Three comrades had been deputed to organize the seizure of the
Winter Palace: Podvoisky, Antonov-Ovseyenko and Lashevich.[25]
With them Chudnovsky was working, a splendid militant from
the earliest days of the party, who was soon to meet his death in
the Ukraine. The former Imperial residence is situated in the centre of the city on the banks of the Neva; the Peter-Paul Fortress

faces it 600 yards away on the other bank. To the south, the palace's façade looks out over a vast paved square which contains the Alexander I Column. A historic spot. At the back of the square, in a semi-circle, lie the huge, respectable offices of the former War Department and Ministry of Foreign Affairs. Over this square, in 1879, the revolver shots fired by the student Soloviev cracked out, and the autocrat Alexander II could be seen running zigzag across the stones, with his head down, and pale with fright. In 1881 these dismal buildings were rocked by the dynamite charge set off under the Imperial apartments by the carpenter Stepan Khalturin. Under these windows, on 22 January 1905, soldiers opened fire on a crowd of workers who had come, carrying ikons and singing hymns, to petition the Tsar, the 'little father' of his people. Here lay about fifty dead and more than a thousand wounded; and the autocracy was wounded, too, to the death, by its own bullets.

Now, on 25 October, from the morning onwards, the Bolshevik regiments and the Red Guards began to encircle the Winter Palace, where Kerensky's government had its offices. The assault was planned for 9 P.M., although Lenin was impatient and wanted it all over before then. While the iron ring closed slowly around the Palace, the Congress of the Soviets was assembling at Smolny, in a former high school for young ladies of the nobility. In a small room in the same building, Lenin was pacing up and down nervously, still an outlaw, still in his old man's disguise. Of every new arrival, he asked, 'The Palace – has it not been taken yet?' His fury mounted against the ditherers, the procrastinators, the indecisive ones. He threatened Podvoisky – 'We shall have to shoot him, yes, shoot him!' The soldiers, huddled around fires in the streets near the Palace, showed the same impatience. People heard them murmur about how 'the Bolsheviks are starting to play at diplomacy too'. Once more, Lenin's feelings even on a point of detail were those of the mass. Podvoisky, certain of victory, kept back the assault. The doomed enemy was demoralized with all the anxiety. Revolutionary blood was now easily spared, and each drop was precious.

The first summons to surrender was conveyed to the ministers at six o'clock. At eight, there was a second ultimatum. Under a flag of truce, a Bolshevik orator addressed the defenders of the palace, and the soldiers of a crack battalion crossed over to the revolutionaries. They were welcomed by loud hurrahs over the square which was now the field of battle. A few minutes later, the Women's Battalion surrendered. The terrified ministers, guarded in a vast room without lighting by a few young officer-cadets, still hesitated to give in. Kerensky had run off, promising them that he would return shortly at the head of a troop of loyal soldiers. They expected to be torn to pieces by a howling mob. The guns of the *Aurora* – firing only blank cartridges! – finally demoralized the

14. The storming of the Winter Palace (from a commemorative re-enactment
staged in 1920)

defending side. The Reds' attack met only very slight resistance.
Grenades exploded on the great marble staircases, there were
hand-to-hand tussles in the corridors. In the twilight of a great
ante-chamber, a thin line of pale cadets stood with bayonets
crossed before a panelled door.

It is the last rampart of the last bourgeois government of
Russia. Antonov-Ovseyenko, Chudnovsky and Podvoisky push
past these powerless bayonets. One youngster whispers to them,
'I'm on your side!' Behind the door is the Provisional Government: thirteen wretched, trembling gentlemen, thirteen crestfallen
faces hidden by shadow. As they are escorted out of the Palace by
Red Guards, a cry for their blood goes up. Some soldiers and
sailors have a fancy for a massacre. The worker-guards restrain
them: 'Don't spoil the proletarian victory by excesses!'

The ministers of Kerensky go off to the Peter-Paul Fortress, that old Bastille which has held all the old martyrs of Russian freedom. There they meet the ministers of the last Tsar. It is all over.

In the adjoining areas of the city, normal traffic had not been interrupted. On the quays, the idlers were staring peaceably.

One detail more on the organization of the attack. In order to ensure that any temporary successes won by the enemy should not interrupt their work, the military leaders of the uprising had prepared two reserve headquarters.

THE CONGRESS OF THE SOVIETS

Just as the Reds are surrounding the Winter Palace, the Petrograd Soviet meets. Lenin comes out of hiding, and he and Trotsky announce the seizure of power. The Soviets will offer a just peace to all the belligerent powers; the secret treaties are going to be published. Lenin's first words underline the importance of the bond between workers and peasants, which is yet to be consolidated:

All over Russia, the vast majority of peasants have said: Enough of playing with the capitalists, we are marching now with the workers! One single decree, abolishing the landlords' property, will win us the trust of the peasantry. They will realize that their only safety lies in their

15. Martov (centre), with Axelrod and Martynov, in Stockholm at the time of the 1917 international socialist conference

association with the workers. We shall inaugurate workers' control of industry ...

The All-Russian Congress of Soviets opens in the evening in the great white ballroom at Smolny, flooded with light from enormous chandeliers. 562 delegates are present: 382 Bolsheviks, thirty-one non-party Bolshevik sympathizers, seventy Left Socialist-Revolutionaries, thirty-six Centre Socialist-Revolutionaries, sixteen Right Socialist-Revolutionaries, three National Socialist-Revolutionaries, fifteen United Internationalist Social-Democrats, twenty-one Menshevik supporters of national defence, seven Social-Democratic delegates from various nationalist groups and five anarchists. The hall is packed tight, the atmosphere is feverish. The Menshevik Dan opens the Congress on behalf of the outgoing All-Russian Executive; as the new officers are elected, guns thunder on the Neva. The resistance at the Winter Palace is still dragging on. Kamenev, 'dressed in his Sunday best, and beaming',[26] becomes Chairman in place of Dan. He proposes an agenda with three headings: organization of authority; war and peace; the Constituent Assembly. The oppositional Menshevik and SR parties take the floor first. For the Mensheviks there is Martov, their most honest and talented leader, whose extreme physical weakness seemed to symbolize the bankruptcy, despite his great personal courage, of the ideology he served. 'Martov, planted on the rostrum as usual, with a trembling, bloodless hand over his hip, an undulating, half-comical figure, shaking his head of unruly hair, urges a peaceful solution to the conflict. ...' A fine time to say it! Mstislavsky speaks for the Left SRs. His party mistrusted the Provisional Government and was sympathetic to the seizure of power by the Soviets, but had refused to join in the rising. His speech is one qualification after another. Yes, all power to the Soviets – particularly since they have already seized power. But military operations must be stopped immediately. How could we deliberate in the middle of gunfire? To this, Trotsky replies with alacrity: 'Who, now, is going to be upset by the sound of the guns? On the contrary, it can only improve our work!'

The roar of the guns makes the glass in the windows rattle. The Mensheviks and Right SRs denounce the 'crime which is taking place against Fatherland and Revolution', and a sailor from the cruiser *Aurora* comes to the rostrum to answer them.

A bronzed figure he was [Mstislavsky relates], with brusque, confident gestures, and a voice that came straight out, cutting the air like a knife. As soon as he mounted the rostrum, stocky and sinuous, his shaggy chest showing below the high collar that curved back gracefully around his tousled head, the hall rang with cheers. ... 'The Winter Palace is finished,' he said. 'The *Aurora* is firing at point-blank range.'

'Oh!' groaned the Menshevik Abramovich, standing up distraught and twisting his hands. 'Oh!' The man from the *Aurora* responded to this outcry with a large-hearted, graceful gesture, and made haste to calm Abramovich down with a loud whisper that trembled with quiet laughter: 'They're firing with blanks. That's all that will be needed for the ministers and the ladies of the Women's Battalion.' Tumult in the hall. The Mensheviks of national defence and the right SRs, about sixty delegates, leave, determined 'to die with the Provincial Government'. They do not get very far: their diminutive procession finds the streets barred to them by the Red Guards, and disperses one by one . . .

Late in the night, the Left Socialist-Revolutionaries resolved in the end to *follow* the Bolsheviks and remain in the Congress.

Lenin did not come to the rostrum until the session of the following morning, when the great decrees on land, peace and workers' control of production were voted. His appearance set off an immense acclamation from the whole hall. He waited for it to end, looking out calmly over the triumphant crowd. Then, quite simply, without any gesture, his two hands resting on the stand, his broad shoulders leaning forward slightly, he said:

16. R. Abramovich

'We will proceed to construct the Socialist order.'

MOSCOW: ECONOMIC CRISIS AND INSURRECTION

The economic necessities behind the revolution were expressed much more directly in Moscow. The city was governed by a Municipal Duma composed of bourgeois, petty-bourgeois and intellectual elements, where the SRs and the Kadets enjoyed a fairly stable majority which was often reinforced by the Mensheviks. It was an unpopular assembly, and the audience in the galleries used to demonstrate noisily – as in the Convention of the French Revolution – by applauding the Bolshevik opposition. An election for the Ward Dumas on 24 September gave the Bolsheviks their opportunity to sound out the masses. The election gave a majority to the Bolsheviks in fourteen wards out of seventeen. The Kadets also made gains. The parties of social peace were crushed.

The Bolsheviks' victory was a tribute to their understanding of the workers' needs. The famine was acute; the last of the grain reserves were being exhausted; the day was approaching when the city would have no more bread. The bread ration was cut to 100 grams per person per day.[27] The collapse of the transport system blocked any possible improvement. Extremely energetic measures were needed if the population was to be saved: centralization of the food supply system, municipal control over bread production – i.e. the expropriation of the bakeries – requisition of buildings, compulsory registration of all inhabitants on a single ration list. These measures formed the programme of the Bolsheviks. They had serious implications. The food crisis fitted in with the class war now being conducted by the propertied classes. It complemented the effects of the employers' sabotage of production. In order to produce a real answer to the famine it would be necessary to take control of the whole of production.

The Bolshevik demands were:

1. The immediate switching from war production of all enterprises which were manufacturing basic necessities before the war. 'The continuation of the war was causing a failure of the capacity for revolutionary action among the proletariat and the army, in the end the failure of the revolution' (A. Schlichter).

2. Requisition of factories so as to put an end to the sabotage of production by the management and bring about the rapid return of peacetime production. The aim here would be to exchange industrial products for the peasants' grain.

3. Compulsory labour for all industrial employees, who might be tempted to go on strike against socialization.

4. Requisition of stores in order to put an end to speculation.

By the end of the first week of October, the leather-workers of Moscow had entered the tenth week of a strike: no mean achievement on a bread ration of ten grams per day. The woodworkers', engineering, textile and municipal workers' unions were preparing to strike. On their side, the employers organized a kind of strike of capital: partial lock-outs, shut-down of factories on a variety of pretexts, covert or blatant restrictions in production, sales of equipment, liquidation – all justified by 'general economic difficulties'. The condition of the Moscow worker now became desperate. Since the beginning of the war the cost of living had increased six and a half times; the cost of manufactured necessities (cloth, shoes, firewood, soap, etc.) had gone up twelvefold. Wages, on the other hand, had only quadrupled. The workers' demands for the recognition of their factory committees were rejected. The Provisional Government, which sympathized with the employers, made no secret of its ill-will towards the working class. Fierce strikes were ready to break out at any moment. The crisis had matured. On 19 October, the Bolshevik majority in the Moscow Soviet, on the motion of Bukharin and Smirnov, adopted a series of resolutions of a quasi-insurrectional character.

The Soviet decreed that the demands of the strikers must be satisfied, by agreement with the trade unions; capitalists guilty of industrial sabotage to be arrested; suspension of rent collections; the mobilization of the masses for the seizure of power by the revolutionary people. The trade unions were asked to implement the eight-hour day under their own responsibility, and the leather-workers who were on strike were told to get the factories running themselves.

A few days later a city conference of the party was held. Semashko, Ossinsky and Smirnov dealt with the insurrection. As one witness recounts,

Figures and statistics at their fingertips, they demonstrate that if the proletariat, which alone is capable of ending the war, does not take power, Russia will be ruined, there will be no bread or fuel, the railways

17. Red soldiers in a Moscow demonstration, 1917: their banner says
'Communism'

and the factories will cease to function. ... Their speeches have a scientific, almost academic tone. It did not seem so much like an assembly of
revolutionists planning a social upheaval, as the meeting of some
learned society. The audience, made up for the most part of delegates
from the military branches, seemed apathetic. Nobody took the floor to
make any objection. When the vote was put, all hands were raised for
the motion; the meeting voted unanimously for the insurrection.

The topic under discussion was regarded as only too obvious.[28]

On 23 October, the Moscow Soviet issued its Decree No. 1,
making the hiring and firing of all workers the responsibility of
the factory committees. On 24 October, the Soviet voted for the
organization of a Red Guard. Each of these votes occasioned
stormy battles with the Mensheviks and SRs, both of whom
defended what they called democracy and legality, every inch of
the way.

On 25 October, while the insurrection was under way at Petrograd, the Moscow Soviet instituted, somewhat late in the circumstances, its own Military Revolutionary Committee. The SRs and the Mensheviks exhorted the workers to control themselves, and avoid the dreadful example of the usurpers in Petrograd: only the Constituent Assembly would have the right to adjudicate on the destinies of Russia. Defeated in the vote, the Mensheviks still entered the MRC 'in order to mitigate as far as possible the effects of the Bolsheviks' projected *coup d'état*' – in other words, to sabotage the insurrection. They were allowed to go on the Committee.

The City Duma had met the same night in secret session, without the Bolshevik representatives, and there had set up its own Committee of Public Safety. The Mayor, Rudnev, a Socialist-Revolutionary, presided over its preparation for battle. Colonel Ryabtsev, another SR, made haste to arm the cadets in the military schools – the Junkers – as well as the students and high-school youth: in short, the youth of the bourgeoisie and middle classes.

THE START OF THE WHITE TERROR

The battle in the streets lasted six days and was very hard going. The initiative in the operations was taken by the Committee of Public Safety which, on the 27th, during the joint session of the Dumas, ordered the MRC to dissolve itself within fifteen minutes. It was a ragged, bitter and bloody struggle, whose manoeuvres we shall not recount in detail. The urban physiognomy of Moscow is that of a city that has grown up in concentric rings over several centuries around the palaces and churches of the Kremlin, which is itself a sort of city, fortified and surrounded with high crenellated walls and pointed towers. A bird's-eye view of the Kremlin would reveal it to be a triangle, whose base is the left bank of the River Moskva. The city, built on a number of hills, all in narrow streets whose irregular circuits run in and out of each other, with innumerable churches set in gardens, and long, tree-lined boulevards throughout, offers numberless possibilities both for attack and for defence. However, the strategic options of the opposing sides were delimited from the beginning. The MRC shared offices with the Soviet in the centre of the city at the top of Tverskaya Street, in the former residence of the governor. The liquidation of this headquarters became the objective of the government troops. The MRC's problem was to hold on to its premises long enough for the Red Guard to come to its help from the suburban districts, taking the Whites from the rear. Under these terms, the Whites' capture of the Kremlin was no more than an episode, though doubtless a significant one.

The Reds had the advantage in numbers:

Our enemies [writes Muralov] must have had about ten thousand
men: two military schools, six NCO training-schools, the military sections of the SRs and the Mensheviks, the youth from the schools. We
had at least fifty thousand reliable fighters: about fifteen thousand
active troops, twenty-five thousand reserve troops, three thousand
armed workers, six light-artillery units and several heavy guns.

On one side, the bourgeoisie and petty-bourgeoisie and their intel-
ligentsia; on the other, the grey mass of soldiers and workers.
Nevertheless, the faulty organization and the hesitations of the
Red side kept the outcome of the struggle uncertain.

On the 28th, at midnight, the Junkers (cadets from the military
colleges) surround the Kremlin. Already the Committee of Public
Safety is taking over the railway stations, the power station, the
central telephone exchange. Cut off from the MRC, Berzin, the
commander of the Kremlin, surrenders it after being told that
'order has been restored' and given a solemn promise that the
lives of his men will be spared. He goes personally to open the
doors, and is at once struck down, stabbed and savaged by the
Junkers. One of their colonels says, 'What, you're still alive, are
you? You have got to be killed.' The workers in the Kremlin
Arsenal do not hear of the surrender until the cadets come to
arrest their Works Committee. In the morning, they are ordered
to line up in one of the vast courtyards of the Kremlin wearing
their identity discs, not far from Tsar Fyodor Ivanovich's massive
cannon. There, the covers are suddenly taken off three machine-
guns in front of them. I quote the account of one of them who
managed to get away.[29]

The men still cannot believe that they are going to be shot like this,
without trial, without sense – they have taken no part in the fighting. A
command bellows out: 'In line now! Eyes front!' The men stand rigid,
fingers along the seams of their trousers. At a signal, the din of the three
machine-guns blends with cries of terror, sobs and death-rattles. All
those who are not mown down by the first shots dash towards the only
exit, a little door behind them which has been left open. The machine-
guns carry on firing; in a few minutes the doorway is blocked by a heap
of men, lying there screaming and bleeding, into which the bullets still
rain. ... The walls of the surrounding buildings are spattered with blood
and bits of flesh.

This massacre is not an isolated act. Practically everywhere the
Whites conducted arrests followed by executions. At the Alexan-
drovskoye Military College, a court-martial took thirty seconds to
pass sentences of death which were carried out forthwith in the
courtyard. Let us remember these facts. They show the firm intention of the defenders of the Provisional Government to drown the
workers' revolution in blood. The White terror had begun.

The news of the massacre at the Kremlin came in the middle of
the negotiations that were being conducted for an armistice between the MRC and Colonel Ryabtsev. The Whites were only

trying to gain time until reinforcements could arrive. The MRC now understood that it was victory or death. Its headquarters were almost surrounded; but, from every working-class quarter, Red Guards and revolutionary regiments sprang up in masses to their help, so that the besiegers were themselves encircled in a ring of steel. On the 29th, in the evening, after a terrible day in which the headquarters of the insurrection nearly fell, a twenty-four hours' truce was signed: it was quickly broken by the arrival of a shock battalion to join the Whites. The Reds on their side were reinforced by artillery. Gun batteries went into action on the squares, and the Whites retreated to the Kremlin. After long vacillations, due to their desire to avoid damage to historic monuments, the MRC decided to order the bombardment of the Kremlin. The Whites surrendered at 4 P.M. on 2 November. 'The Committee of Public Safety is dissolved. The White Guard surrenders its arms and is disbanded. The officers may keep the sidearms that distinguish their rank. Only such weapons as are necessary for practice may be kept in the military academies. . . . The MRC guarantees the liberty and inviolability of all.' Such were the principal clauses of the armistice signed between Reds and Whites. The fighters of the counter-revolution, butchers of the Kremlin, who in victory would have shown no quarter whatever to the Reds – we have seen proof – *went free*.

Foolish clemency! These very Junkers, these officers, these students, these socialists of counter-revolution, dispersed themselves throughout the length and breadth of Russia, and there organized the civil war. The revolution was to meet them again, at Yaroslavl, on the Don, at Kazan, in the Crimea, in Siberia and in every conspiracy nearer home.

ORGANIZATION AND SPONTANEITY

The differences between the Petrograd and the Moscow insurrections are striking.

At Petrograd the movement, prepared minutely over many weeks, is essentially political, a conscious seizure of power. The revolution took place sharp on the hour, as Trotsky put it. Two factors dominated events: the party and the garrison. The action was energetically planned and implemented without hesitation. Its success was rapid, with scarcely any bloodshed. The Petrograd insurrection offers us the model of a mass movement with perfect organization.

At Moscow the spontaneity of the masses outran their organization. The movement responded directly to economic pressures, with a less developed consciousness of political ends and means. Waverings, hesitations and delays formed considerable obstacles. The enemy, though numerically inferior, was well-organized, resolute and equipped with a clear political understanding of the end – the restoration of order – and the means – terror. It therefore was able to hold the proletariat in check for a long while and inflicted cruel losses on its ranks. In their districts the workers armed themselves as best they could. They came often to battle, on their own initiative. They were short of arms, short of ammunition. When they had cannon, there were no shells. When there were shells, the sights on the guns were all wrong. Communications were appalling. Reconnaissance hardly existed. 'We fought very badly,' said Muralov (who led the Red forces), 'we were carried along by the elements.' There was no united command, and the Whites had the initiative; at times their occupation of strategic points compensated for their numerical weakness.

The enthusiasm of the militants was undoubtedly admirable: equipped with good organization it would have been miraculous. Enthusiasm on its own could not prevent a long, perilous and costly battle. The MRC was set up on the 25th, much too late, and then was prone to vacillation. It conducted quite unnecessary parleys with the SRs and Mensheviks, made the mistake of signing an armistice on the 29th just as the Reds were about to capture the telephone exchange, and once the counter-revolutionaries were vanquished displayed a deplorable magnanimity towards them.

In our opinion, the insurrections at Petrograd and Moscow were *different types* of movement. The Moscow insurrection is related – *very distantly*, we must add – to the more backward type of proletarian rising whose model instance is the revolt of the workers in Paris in June 1848, consciously provoked by the bourgeoisie's economic policies. Provocation played a considerable part in the events at Moscow: the revolt was a response to it, and often became outmanoeuvred. The enemy, on the other hand, was all out for a massacre. The Petrograd insurrection, by contrast, is the first practical example of a *new type* of armed uprising which was later followed in the Hamburg insurrection of 1923.[30] Here, the conspiracy of a large party is co-ordinated with the action of the masses; both are launched at a selected moment after a detailed preparation; the element of the unforeseen is reduced to a minimum; the forces in battle are deployed with maximum economy. At Hamburg, the defeat – which was actually much more of a retreat[31] – entailed only slight losses. As a rule, of course, defeats are very costly.

The contrast between the Petrograd and the Moscow events demonstrates the enormous superiority, under equivalent conditions, of efficiently organized actions over movements in which spontaneity predominates. In the light of these experiences, the preconditions for a proletarian victory can be reduced to the following elementary rules of the military art: maximum of organization and energy in action; and the placing of superior forces at the decisive moment at the decisive points.

18. Soldiers and car, red flag and bayonet: Petrograd in the revolution

3 · The Urban Middle Classes against the Proletariat

After the departure of the Mensheviks and the Right SRs, the Second All-Russian Congress of the Soviets noted, in a brief motion, that 'the exit of the conciliators, far from weakening the Soviets, strengthens them by purging the workers' and peasants' power of counter-revolutionary elements'. It is the all-clear, a complete victory. Behind the scenes, negotiations begin with the defeated parties, and with the powerful railwaymen's union, under Menshevik influence. The ground is cleared for further progress, but there are immense dangers, how immense we shall shortly witness. Speedy action is now needed. The Congress has the initiative. If it hesitates or fools itself, if what it proclaims does not chime in with the masses' longings, all will be lost tomorrow. The delegates must find the words that can conquer, vote the decrees which will win for the revolution the embittered people of the trenches, the impatient people of the countryside, the people of the cities.

The decree on peace is the first to be passed.

The Workers' and Peasants' Government, established by the revolution of 24–5 October, and based on the Soviets, invites all the belligerent nations and their governments to open negotiations without delay for a just and democratic peace ...

The Italians have just been routed at Caporetto; Rumania is being invaded: with the advent of submarine warfare, every ship on the seas is now a hunted prey; German ballistics experts are preparing the long-distance bombardment of Paris; France, Germany, Italy and Austria, bleeding, depopulated, rationed to the bone, are beginning to falter.

The decree defines as just and democratic 'an immediate peace without annexations (that is, without conquest of foreign territories or forcible adherence of foreign nationalities) and without indemnities'.

The Government declares that it considers none of these conditions of peace as an ultimatum; it is willing to examine any other conditions that may be proposed, insisting only on their prompt discussion by any other belligerent power involved, on the utmost frankness and on the exclusion of all equivocation and secrecy.

The decree pronounces the abolition of all secret diplomacy, and the 'immediate, unconditional' cancellation of the secret treaties 'which have usually served to secure advantages and privileges for the capitalists and landlords of Russia' or for the

Great-Russian nationality. All the belligerent nations are invited to sign an immediate armistice of at least three months. The document ends with an appeal 'to the workers of the three most advanced countries of mankind, France, Britain and Germany'. It recalls these workers' services to the cause of progress and Socialism, and exhorts them to dedicate themselves to the cause of peace and the emancipation of all toilers.

When the vote is taken, the Left S Rs announce that their party will support the decree even though they do not agree with its terms. Lenin replies to the critics of the decree, some of whom find its language too moderate.

We are being told [he says] that failure to use the terms of an ultimatum means a display of our feebleness. But it is time for us to finish with the old bourgeois sham of phrases about 'the power of the people'...

In the eyes of the bougeoisie, strength is manifested when the masses go blindly to the slaughter. The only government which the bourgeoisie recognize as strong is one which can use all the power of the state machine to push the masses anywhere it pleases. Our conception of strength is different. In our eyes, a government is strong in proportion to the consciousness of the masses. It is strong when these masses know everything, judge everything, accept everything consciously.[1]

We desire general peace, but do not shrink from revolutionary war. If the German people sees that we are ready to discuss every kind of peace proposal, that will be the spark, the beginning of the German revolution. We are ready to discuss all proposals; that does not mean that we will accept them. That was how Lenin argued. The decree was passed unanimously. 'The war is over! Faces lit up.'[2] The *Internationale* rose from the hall, and then the *Farewell to the Dead*, plaintive as a crowd's deep sigh.

We shall analyse the peace policy of the Soviets when we come to our chapter on the treaty of Brest-Litovsk. This first, symbolic act of the revolution meant that from its very first day it possessed an international character. It was a gesture of defiance to the old order; an appeal directed daringly towards the peoples, over the heads of the old society; an appeal that was bound to reach the ears of men in very distant places. Immediate peace, without annexations or indemnities! Compare this with the war aims of the two imperialist coalitions.[3]

THE LAND

Lenin had spent part of the night in drafting the decree on land. This decree alone would make the new authority invincible, by assuring it of the support of millions of peasants. Lenin knew this. On the morning of the 26th, he exclaimed, 'Let us just have enough time to promulgate this law – after that, just see them try to take it off us!' In drawing up this crucial draft, Lenin took the wording from the 242 decrees which local peasant Soviets had passed in conformity with the agrarian programme of the Socialist-Revolutionary party. This measure, which the SRs had incessantly talked of, the Bolsheviks actually carried out, thereby depriving yesterday's governing party of the programme which had been the basis of its influence in the countryside. The first clause of the decree is short: '1. The land-owners' right of ownership over the soil is abolished forthwith, without compensation.'

The estates of the landlords, the land of the monasteries, churches, etc., along with their livestock and other material, become the property of the Peasant Soviets. Revolutionary tribunals are to punish any damage to these goods, which now belong to the nation (this clause was anticipating the possible destruction of equipment or buildings by the dispossessed land-owners). In the implementation of these measures, the lists of peasants' demands (or decrees) are to serve as a guide, pending 'the definitive decisions to be made by the Constituent Assembly'.

In expropriating the land-owners, possessors of estates, the decree did not abolish private property in land: the possessions even of the rich peasants were not disputed. The landed proprietor, the descendant of ancient feudal families or a newly enriched bourgeois, was hated equally by the rich, poor and middle peasants, who were all the descendants of serfs. Thus the decree created a united front of the whole of the peasantry around the Soviets. The doctrinaires – for some existed – judged Lenin to be timid, precisely when he was proving that he – and his party – were serious revolutionaries, realists free of routine thinking. This revolution, they said, was surely that of the proletariat. But the abolition of *feudal* property was the outcome, over virtually the whole of Europe, of the bourgeoisie's own revolutions. Here was the triumphant proletariat limiting itself to achieving the *bourgeois* revolution in the countryside. It was doing for the Russian peasants what the Third Estate (French bourgeoisie), soon to be represented by the Jacobins, had achieved in 1789–93 for the French peasant, by giving him property rights and freeing him from subjection. The bourgeois revolution was being achieved, and indeed surpassed by the vigour of the attack against private property. But was not this a breach of the Bolshevik party's programme, which advocated the nationalization of the soil? Lenin was blamed for applying the agrarian programme of the SRs, not his own.

That is unimportant [he replied]. As a democratic government, we cannot simply ignore the wishes of the popular masses, even if we are in disagreement with them.

Life will show who is in the right. In the development of new forms of government, we must follow the demands of life, and leave complete freedom to the creative activity of the popular masses. The last government tried to solve the agrarian question by agreement with the ancient, immovable bureaucracy of the Tsar. Far from settling the problem, the bureaucracy simply attacked the peasants. ... So the peasants want to solve the agrarian question themselves. Let there be no amendments to their plan! Will the peasantry act in the spirit of our programme or in that of the SRs? It is of little importance: the main thing is for them to have the firm assurance that there will be no more landlords and that they can set about organizing their own lives.[4]

Unfortunately the only reports of these debates are summaries by the secretaries in charge of the sessions. The stenographers had left the Congress at the same time as the opponents of the Bolsheviks. The decree on land was voted unanimously except for one vote against and eight abstentions.

What advantages did this law bring to the peasantry? In the Ukraine and the regions bordering the Black Sea, the big landowners possessed about a fifth of all cultivated land. In central Russia the proportion was only about 7·5 per cent (2,916 *desyatins*, out of the 39,222 *desyatins* in thirty-six gubernias: a *desyatin* is about 2,500 acres). But over the whole of Russia, the peasants were burdened with taxes, compulsory duties and debts, which made their income inferior to that of the workers. They now found themselves free of these exactions.

THE FIRST COUNCIL OF PEOPLE'S COMMISSARS

The first Government of the Soviets was established at this same session, after heated debates. The Congress elected a new All-Russian Executive of the Soviets, consisting of 102 members: sixty-two Bolsheviks, twenty Left Socialist-Revolutionaries, some Internationalist Social-Democrats and other groups of less importance. The first Council of People's Commissars – the term had been suggested by Trotsky to avoid the discredited title of 'Ministers' – was composed solely of Bolsheviks, as follows: Chairman, N. Lenin; Interior, A. I. Rykov; Agriculture, V. P. Milyutin; Labour, A. G. Shlyapnikov; War and Navy, a committee of three (V. A. Antonov-Ovseyenko, N. V. Krylenko, P. E. Dybenko); Commerce and Industry, V. P. Nogin; Education, A. V. Lunacharsky; Finance, I. I. Stepanov-Skvortsev; Foreign Affairs, L. D. Trotsky; Justice, G. I. Oppokov (Lomov); Food, I. A. Teodorovich; Posts and Telegraphs, N. P. Glebov-Avilov; Nationalities, J. V. Dzugashvili (Stalin). No People's Commissar for Transport and Communications was appointed, doubtless because of the strained relations that existed with the All-Russian Railway Workers' Committee.

The Left SRs, always prone to incessant hesitations, had refused to participate in the government, although invited by the Bolsheviks, who had no wish to govern alone. To govern alone was, in effect, to assume, undivided, all the overwhelming responsibilities of the moment, and to leave open to rivals, to hidden opponents and to waverers, the advantageous role of the opposition. It was a difficult situation for a party which had been denounced for months unanimously by the bourgeois press as a nest of enemy agents, and whose leaders, with high treason charges hanging over their heads, had arrived via Germany in a sealed train.... But the Left S Rs, who actually would have been precious allies, on account of their representation of the peasantry, wanted a coalition government which would have included every party in the Soviet, in which the Girondin followers of counter-revolution would be given ministerial posts. 'We had no alternative,' writes Trotsky, 'but to leave the Left S Rs to their efforts of persuading their more Right-wing neighbours to rally to the revolution. While they devoted themselves to that hopeless enterprise, we deemed it our duty to assume all responsibility in the name of our party.'[5]

The Second All-Russian Congress of Soviets broke up on the morning of 27 October, after an all-night session. On the same day, while it was dispatching its peace proposals to all the belligerent powers, the Council of People's Commissars passed a decree abolishing the death penalty.

THE JUNKERS' MUTINY

The insurrection was victorious. The situation still appeared desperate.

Petrograd had food supplies for no more than ten days. None of the government offices was functioning. The new administration had neither premises nor staff. Doubtless, from one hour to the next, the sympathy of the masses would be conveyed to it by delegates from the armies, from regiments, from provincial Soviets and trade unions; but telegrams of condemnation also rained in on Smolny: committees of the army, military headquarters, Municipal Dumas, provincial administrations, in short, every established body and command post in the land, declared to the 'usurpers', the 'traitors', the 'bandits who are launching civil war', that the restoration of order and speedy chastisement was on its way. The newspapers of the bourgeoisie continued to appear, full of sensational revelations on the dark goings-on behind the *coup*, announcing that regiments were on their way from the front, that Kerensky was now a few kilometres from the capital, at the head of two armoured corps. A new clandestine Provisional Government had been set up, and the socialists of counter-revolution, the Mensheviks and S Rs, were preparing to take up arms. The Central Telegraph Agency refused to transmit the People's Commissars' dispatches and the railwaymen's executive, which was bitterly opposed to the new government, was sabotaging communications. The news from Moscow was confused: battles in the streets, negotiations, the Whites' capture of the

Kremlin. The 'public opinion'of the bourgeoisie, middle classes, press and foreign observers declared that the Bolshevik escapade would not last for long. First it was given a few days to hang on, then a few weeks (and eventually a few months). The very idea that the proletariat could stay in power was preposterous.

On the Nevsky Prospect, the central thoroughfare of Petrograd, a well-dressed throng used to crowd around, discussing the latest news, uttering loud predictions of the restoration of order, sometimes jeering at the Red Guards.[6] Isolated murders of workers and soldiers took place. The Junkers (military cadets) succeeded in taking over the central telephone exchange. On 29 October, the Engineers' Castle and the Military College, where these Junkers were housed, were surrounded by Red Guards, and armoured cars took up their stations in the approaches. The slender shadows of artillery gun-barrels drooped along the pavements. Summoned to surrender within ten minutes, the Junkers replied with rifle-shots. Their resistance was broken by the first shell, which tore a large gap in the façade of the Military College. Some of the Junkers tried to flee, still resisting; they were massacred.

Why did these sons of the petty-bourgeoisie take up arms? One of the military leaders of the SRs wrote at this time to General Krasnov, then marching towards Petrograd: 'Our forces consist of two to three hundred Junkers, and fifty militants armed with grenades.'[7] The SR party, which had at its disposal only these forces, with no proletariat to speak of, had banked on offering support, from inside the city, to the military offensive conducted by Kerensky, Krasnov and the Stavka (General Headquarters) at Mogilev.

THE COSSACK MARCH ON PETROGRAD

We must now consider the forces at the disposal of the 'head of the Provisional Government' at his outpost of Gachina, and the forces ranged against him. The troops of the Petrograd garrison, so confident when in the grip of agitation, were now very reluctant to start fighting. Many of their officers had gone into hiding. The rest, with few exceptions, were hostile. When the revolutionary government convoked a meeting of officers, attended by Lenin and Trotsky, not one at first could be found who was willing to accept the supreme command over the Red forces. In the end, Colonel Muraviev volunteered enthusiastically: a talented man, vigorous and ambitious. A member of the Socialist-Revolutionary party, he had taken part here and there in repressions of 'Bolshevik conspiracies' in the army, and then had rallied to the Left SRs. He was entrusted with the command, with a Committee of Five at his elbow whose duty was to keep an eye on him, relieve him of his functions if necessary, and shoot him at the first sign of treason. He proved to be loyal, passionately energetic, and a good organizer and soldier. With Trotsky he shared the honours for the victory of Pulkovo. (A few months later, the adventurer came out in him: while commander-in-chief on the Czechoslovak front he tried to cross over to the enemy, and when caught blew out his brains.) Other officers joined him, often motivated by their dislike of the Kerensky regime; in their hatred of democracy they chose what was for them the lesser evil. They were useful. Thus an old colonel, Walden by name, was in command of the Red artillery on the heights of Pulkovo which saved Petrograd.

Everything had to be improvised. Sabotage was at work in all the army departments. Cartridges, shells, spare parts for the weapons were hidden; telephone and engineering apparatus had disappeared. The Red Guards and the factories made up all the deficiencies, did all the jobs themselves, from keeping the artillery supplied with ammunition to digging the trenches.

At Petrograd, Podvoisky had just taken over the command from Antonov-Ovseyenko, who was exhausted. He has told the story of how Lenin burst into his office, announcing, 'The Council of People's Commissars has appointed me, along with Stalin and Trotsky, to come and help you.' Actually Lenin had come along to follow operations himself, without telling anyone else. He at once gathered assistants round him and began, apparently without realizing it, to give orders. Eventually Podvoisky, unnerved at this, protested at this interference in his duties and asked to be allowed to resign. Lenin then turned threatening: 'What? What? I'll have you brought before a party tribunal! We'll have you shot! I order you to continue your work and let me get on with mine!'

It was only the next day [writes Podvoisky] that I realized, by looking at its results, the effectiveness of Lenin's work ... and the source of its strength: at the most serious crises, when we were wasting ourselves in dispersed efforts, in him concentration of reasoning, of inner powers and resources, reached its highest peak.[8]

Kerensky had taken refuge among General Krasnov's Cossacks. In the old army, the Cossacks were the embodiment of reactionary ideas: caste-consciousness had been sedulously fostered among these privileged peasants from their distant regions of the south-east. Krasnov, an ambitious monarchist, who was to become during the civil war one of the leading lights of the counter-revolution, assured them that they would have no difficulty in vanquishing the anarchy that was now instituted at Petrograd. Was not the military rising prepared by the SRs about to smooth their path within the capital itself?

The White forces occupied Gachina and Tsarskoye-Seloe, less than twenty kilometres from the capital. Between them and Petrograd rose the heights of Pulkovo. From the top of these hills, the Red artillery inflicted severe losses on them (between 300 and 500 dead). This was on 30 October. The Cossacks, taken aback by this

19. General Alexeyev and Kerensky

resistance, demoralized by agitation and surrounded by hostile populations of workers, drew back in disorder. The railway workers got a train going for them, but with such poor enthusiasm that the job took an hour instead of fifteen minutes. The telephone operators refused to transmit Krasnov's telegrams.[9] This last adventure of the 'people's tribune' Kerensky, 'head of the Provisional Government, Supreme Commander of the Armies of the Republic', an impressive orator and mediocre character, had a pitiful finale. Once again, democracy's tribune managed to escape just in the nick of time as Krasnov, his subordinate who despised him, was about to hand him over to the Bolsheviks 'to see if he was a coward or not'.[10] Krasnov himself was finally handed over by his own Cossacks, who offered no resistance to the Reds' occupation of the palace at Gachina.

The revolution made the mistake of showing magnanimity to the leader of the Cossack attack. He should have been shot on the spot.[11] At the end of a few days he recovered his liberty, after giving his word of honour never to take up arms again against the revolution. But what value can promises of honour have towards enemies of fatherland and property? He was to go off to put the Don region to fire and the sword.

SOCIALISM OF THE COUNTER-REVOLUTION

Nothing is more tragic at this juncture than the moral collapse of the two great parties of democratic socialism. The Socialist-Revolutionaries had carried considerable weight, through their distinguished record and their influence in the countryside, on the intellectuals and middle classes and, not so long ago, among powerful minorities of workers: they had enjoyed every opportunity of taking power without any transgression of the established legality and of governing as Socialists. The country would have followed them. At its Fourth Congress the majority of the party castigated the Central Committee for not having done so. But the SR leaders, ridden by a fetishism for formal democracy, fearing more than anything else the anarchy of the masses and peasant *jacquerie*, and dreaming of a parliamentary democracy where their eloquence would have held sway, rejected the arduous Socialist road in favour of collaboration with the liberal bourgeoisie. The SRs had exercised a paramount influence within the Kerensky government. Kerensky himself was a member of their party, as was his Minister of Agriculture, Victor Chernov, a verbose theoretician of populist Socialism and the author of a programme of agrarian reform whose implementation he constantly deferred. In the Soviets, the SRs, with Menshevik support, had enjoyed the majority. They had a majority in the Municipal Duma of Moscow and had controlled about half the votes in the Petrograd Duma. Their leader Avksentiev was Chairman of the Provisional Legislative Council of the new Republic. They appeared to possess powerful teams of men accustomed to action. Their Central Committee, initiating waves of terrorist activity at the word of command, sending hundreds of militants to become heroes and martyrs of the revolution, had in its best days made Tsardom tremble.

The Mensheviks, a minority of the Russian Social-Democratic Workers' party who had tussled over twenty years with the Bolsheviks (in factional struggles which were actually contests between revolutionary intransigence and Socialist opportunism), were influential in the industrial centres, among the intelligentsia, in the cooperatives, in the trade union leadership, and in the circles around the late government. They had contributed statesmen as remarkable, for their personal qualities and their revolutionary past, as Chkeidze and Tseretelli, and theoreticians and agitators as gifted as G. V. Plekhanov, the great founder of Russian Social-Democracy, Y. Martov, Dan and Abramovich. But the Mensheviks, with similar hesitations to those of the SRs, declared themselves on the side of class collaboration, democracy and the

Constituent Assembly, and against 'anarchy', 'premature social-ism', 'Bolshevik hysteria' and (even) 'civil war'.

On 26 October, both these Socialist parties took the initiative within the Petrograd Municipal Duma in forming a Committee of Safety for Fatherland and Revolution, to whose membership they admitted three Kadets, representatives of the big bourgeoisie (Nabokov, Countess Panina and one more obscure). The SRs' military branch undertook to arrange the Junkers' mutiny. Gotz picked a colonel to lead the rising, and Avksentiev signed the order to the military colleges to seize arms and start the fighting.[12] *Dyelo Naroda* (*People's Cause*), the party's official organ, an-nounced that 'The President of the Party's Central Committee and Honorary President of the All-Russian Soviet of Peasants, V. M. Chernov, is now at the head of General Krasnov's troops.'

Once the Junkers were disarmed, the Committee of Public Safety, the SR Central Committee, and the two signatories of the order to fight (Avksentiev and a Menshevik) united in *repudiating* – simply through fear of the consequences and the wish to fight another day – the attempted *coup* which they themselves had instigated and for which several hundred young men had paid with their lives.[13] The appeal from the Committee of Public Safety, sent out on 27 October, had openly said: 'Arm to resist the mad adventure of the Bolshevik MRC! We call on all troops loyal to the revolution to assemble at the Nikolai Military College and unite around the Committee of Public Safety!' Not a single army unit responded to this appeal.

After this dishonest escapade, the Girondin conspiracy against the revolution took on a permanent shape. Here the SRs, who were more actively inclined than the Mensheviks and more used to illegal work, took the dominant role.

Not that the counter-revolutionary attitude of the Social-Democrats was any less incriminating. In the middle of the fight-ing they wrote: 'In the serious crisis which has stricken Petrograd and the nation, the revolution has received a terrible blow: and not a blow in the back from General Kornilov but a blow to the heart from Lenin and Trotsky.' The conclusion of the document was that 'in order to avoid civil war' (!) workers should align themselves with the Committee of Public Safety, i.e. with reaction. On 3 November, nine days after the revolution, a Menshevik, conference was held at Petrograd. The two opposed viewpoints that emerged there were summarized by Abramovich:

The minority says that Bolshevik force must be opposed with the force of bayonets. The majority says that the Bolsheviks have the sym-pathy of the proletariat and the army, it is an insurrection of *sans-culottes*, whose suppression would drive the soldiers into the arms of black reaction and anti-semitism and unleash the forces of the Right. ... And so, civil war has to be avoided by conciliation.

Dan stated there: 'In the first few days, we had hoped that the Bolshevik conspiracy could be liquidated by force of arms. The attempt failed. ...' (These are Dan's actual words.) '*That is why,*' he went on, 'we have now taken up the position of conciliation.' These unsuccessful executioners of the Russian proletariat were now against the civil war since they had not been able to win it! Dan advocated a policy aimed at splitting the Bolsheviks, which would win over 'the reasonable Bolsheviks' for a broad democratic front, isolate the others, and finally crush 'the military-minded faction around Lenin and Trotsky'. The argument of a certain Weinstein deserves to be cited as a model of Socialist jesuitry in the service of reaction: 'If democracy does not suppress Bolshevism, even with force of arms, others will do it instead.'[14] On the vote, the irreconcilable tendency, of all-out struggle against Bolshevism, had the majority.

20. G. V. Plekhan[

The men who used this sort of language were not on the party's Right wing. The Right of Social-Democracy is represented in the 'national defence' tendency, whose organ is *Edinstvo* (*Unity*) and whose leader is the grand old man George Valentinovich Plekhanov, the Russian equivalent to Guesde.[15] Sick and confined to bed, old Plekhanov receives Jacques Sadoul on 17 October and says to him of the Bolsheviks, 'We must not only master but crush this vermin, drown it in blood. That is the price of Russia's safety.'

Plekhanov [Sadoul wrote later to Albert Thomas] is convinced that the final struggle is coming soon, in fact passionately desires it, even to the point of hinting – and you know Plekhanov's democratic scruples – that if the rising does not come spontaneously then it must be provoked.

In Plekhanov's eyes the 'Bolshevik bandits' are a 'revolting mixture of Utopian idealists, imbeciles, traitors and anarchist provocateurs'.[16] The depth to which old Plekhanov had fallen was low, indeed abysmal. At least, however, there was a ruthless logic in his pursuit of all the implications of his position as a 'Socialist of national defence'.

Maxim Gorky's journal *Novaya Zhizn* (*New Life*), which at this point took an attitude of neutrality, described the politics of 'moderate democracy' (meaning the Socialists principally) in th: following terms: its organizations 'call upon all citizens to refuse to obey the Bolsheviks, to resist the rising actively, to undertake sabotage and the disorganization of food supplies. Their motto is: against the Bolsheviks, all methods are good.'[17]

SABOTAGE

'All methods are good!' These were not mere words. The counter-revolutionary democrats made wide use of a ruthless weapon, outside the normally understood customs of war: the systematic sabotage of all enterprises serving the general population (food supplies, public services, etc.). From its outset the war of classes broke the conventional mould of what is permissible in war.

When the victorious Reds entered the offices of the Municipal Duma in Moscow, they found nothing but debris. The records had been used to stop up the windows. The cupboards and desks were empty, the typewriters unusable. The municipal employees, 16,000 of them, were out on strike. Their strike against the workers' revolution was to last *four months* in a city already, immediately after the insurrection, threatened by famine and epidemics.

In these conditions it was indescribably difficult to get the various departments of the city administration running again. A strike of all the staff without exception, doctors, teachers and engineers; the boycotting of their jobs; the sabotage practised by the new officials, along with the need to pay the manual workers their normal wages (the civilian and military administrations in Moscow employed over two hundred thousand of these workers); the need to feed tens of thousands of refugees and maintain the services for water, sewage, tramways, abattoirs, gas, and electricity, at all costs: such was the problem which our workers and militants, very inexperienced in these matters, had to face immediately, with nothing to meet the situation except their own wits.[18]

A number of sections of skilled workers joined the sabotage and the strike, another indication of the role played by the influence of the Socialists of counter-revolution.

The situation at Petrograd was very similar. Here the effects of sabotage can be seen at work in the great departments of State. In the agricultural section of the Ministry of Food, all the officials and staff without exception went on strike, and took the files on current business away with them. The Soviet's Food Department, a mere handful of militants, occupied the vast, deserted premises. Everything was gone. 'Kalinin and I,' writes one comrade, 'found a few lumps of sugar tucked away in a safe. ... We made some tea. ... The Ministry of Food had been captured by Schlichter at the head of a Red Guard unit. There was hardly anybody inside it. ...'

The strike at the State Bank did not begin until 14 November. One militant reports on it:

I found the premises deserted. Obolensky, Pyatakov and Smirnov were meeting in one of the offices, discussing how they could get some money out for the Council of People's Commissars, who possessed neither paper nor ink. Negotiations went on with some junior staff. There was one lone official who was still at his post...

After a good many formalities the Bolsheviks eventually got five million roubles turned over to them. V. Bonch-Bruyevich administered this treasure thriftily.[19] In some banks the employees were willing to work but, being afraid of having to answer later for their compliance, begged to be compelled, with Red Guards installed in their offices. The officials at the Treasury were still on duty, keeping watch over the money they had charge of.

At the Ministry of Foreign Affairs, Trotsky found nobody in. A certain Prince Tatishchev, who had been put under arrest, eventually agreed to open the office desks for him. The Commissariat for Foreign Affairs operated from Smolny, without equipment or staff. Trotsky, who was in any case absorbed with military duties, formulated at this point a rather abbreviated definition of foreign policy. 'I have only undertaken this work,' he said, 'so that I shall be able to give more time to the party. My mandate is simple: publish the secret treaties and then shut up shop.'[20] A number of the documents had disappeared.

At the Ministry of Justice twelve office boys and one functionary were to be found.

Let us close this catalogue. In all the ministries, all the public offices, all the banks, the picture presented was similar, and the funds and the most important files had disappeared.

A shadow government was functioning, presided over by Prokopovich, who had officially taken over the succession from Kerensky, who was said to have 'resigned'. This clandestine Cabinet directed the strike of officials in concert with a strike committee. The large firms of industry, commerce and banking, such as the Rural Bank of Tula, the Moscow Popular Bank and the Bank of the Caucasus, continued to pay their officials who were out on strike. The former All-Russian Soviet Executive (Menshevik and SR) used its funds, stolen from the working class, for the same purpose.

THE INITIATIVE OF THE MASSES

'Miracles of proletarian organization must be achieved.'[21] This idea of Lenin's provided the key to the people's salvation. This many-headed resistance of entire classes could be combated only by the initiative of masses more numerous and more energetic. In this period the policy of the Soviet authority consisted principally in awakening, stimulating, sometimes guiding, but more usually simply of endorsing the initiative of the masses. The People's Commissariats were ordered, by decree, to work 'in close contact with the mass organizations of the working men and women, the sailors, the soldiers and the employees'. The decree of 28 October (10 November) allotted the work of local supplies to the municipalities. Another decree the same day urged them to solve the housing crisis by taking their own measures, and gave them the right to requisition, sequestrate and confiscate premises. This decree is characteristic: it both orders and takes initiative, in an area of grave importance, with a serious incursion made against the rights of private property. The decree of 14 November invites the workers to use their own committees to control the production, accounting and financing of the firms they work in. We have already pointed out that in the decree on land the greatest initiative was left in the hands of the rural Soviets.

As there was no central government, the initiative of the masses counted for everything. The Council of People's Commissars was a very high authority, but one of a moral description. 'Its first meetings,' writes Shlyapnikov,[22] 'took place in Lenin's little office on the second floor of Smolny. At the beginning its staff was very small: V. Bonch-Bruyevich as head of department, and two assistants. I believe that they did not even keep proper minutes of the first few meetings.'

The sessions of the Council were long. There were a large number of practical questions demanding immediate solution. They were discussed with delegations of workers. The council decided that its People's Commissars would receive a salary equal to the average wage of a skilled worker (500 roubles a month), with an extra 100 a month for each dependent. As the head of this government of revolution, Lenin was concerned to establish its authority. He insisted on the precise observance of formalities, and observed them himself, thus inspiring among his colleagues and, by diffusion, throughout the administration, a feeling of power, trust and respect for the authority he had created.[23]

Some examples of mass initiative may be relevant. The Metalworkers' Union, whose secretary, Shlyapnikov, had just become People's Commissar of Labour, provided this department with its first new members of staff. The Central Committee of the Seafarers' and Bargemen's Union undertook to organize the new administration of the ports. In many offices and enterprises, the junior staff found itself left in a position of management (which it promptly exercised) through the defection of its superiors. The courts had disappeared, except for a few which the Red Guard had to close down. One team of soldiers proceeded to dissolve the ancient 'Governmental Senate', which was composed of eminent members of the legal profession. The justices of the peace, a fairly popular system of justice, stayed in office. There was a constant procession to Smolny of arrested miscreants, functionaries, officers, looters and thieves. On the top floor there was a room crammed with old sheepskins and furnished with a table and two or three chairs, in which sat a 'Commission of Judicial Inquiry' which was actually no more than one very overworked party member. It conducted summary investigations and passed sentences of imprisonment in the cellars of this former school for daughters of the nobility. The workers themselves set up tribunals in their own districts. 'The first of these tribunals was established in the Vyborg area. The public prosecutor and the defence spoke before the public, who took part in the debates. The verdict was taken by vote among the audience. Composed for the most part of workers, the tribunal functioned quite well. ...'[24] At Smolny, a similar tribunal arose out of the 'Commission of Inquiry' just mentioned, and its main concern became that of combating banditry. The arrested malefactors were interrogated and tried without formalities by all persons present in Room 75.

> One day [relates Bonch-Bruyevich] they brought in a gang of coiners who refused to confess. Stared out by forty pairs of eyes, and harried by cross-examinations from the workers, they eventually broke down. One of them fell on his knees and shouted, 'I can't stand it any longer, I'll tell the whole truth. ...' We did not know what to do with these people any more, the Peter-Paul Fortress was jammed full.

Another defendant there was a madman who had stabbed twenty-two people in one of the main thoroughfares of the city.

The problem of criminality, inherited from the old regime, thus became immediately pressing. In the prisons the common-law criminals had a meeting and presented a petition asking that they be given the chance to start a new life. Most of them were released, many of them to return inside in no time. Formal tribunals were not organized until later: these were constituted from delegates to the Petrograd Soviet, each assisted by two workers drawn from the lists of the factory committees.

ALCOHOL

For a short period the counter-revolution might well have imagined that it had discovered its most murderous weapon, in the form of alcoholism. The frightful plan, conceived in clandestine circles, of drowning the revolution in liquor before going on to drown it in blood, of turning it into a tumult of drunken crowds, now began seriously to be executed. In Petrograd there were cellars richly stocked with wine, and precious stores of fine liqueurs. The idea of looting them would blossom – or more exactly, be implanted – in the breasts of the crowd. Frantic groups would then descend on the cellars of palaces, restaurants and hotels. It was a contagious madness. Picked detachments of Red Guards, sailors and revolutionaries had to be organized for protection against the danger at all costs. The cellars would get flooded by the hundreds of burst barrels, and people came to draw wine from the ventilating shafts. Machine-guns barred the way, but more than once the wine went to the heads of the gunners. Stocks of old wine were hastily smashed up, to let the poison run off quickly into the sewers.

Antonov-Ovseyenko reports:[25]

> The problem was particularly serious with the cellars at the Winter Palace. The Preobrazhensky Regiment, which had been put in charge of guarding them, got drunk and became quite useless. The Pavlovsky

Regiment, our sure revolutionary shield, went the same way. Teams of soldiers were sent, picked from various regiments: they too got drunk. The workers' committees attempted no further resistance. The crowd had to be dispersed by armoured cars, whose crews were soon reeling too. By nightfall it had become a wild orgy. 'Let's drink up the Romanovs' leftovers', they said gaily in the crowd. Order was restored in the end by sailors fresh from Helsinki, men of iron who had been more used to killing than to drinking. In the suburb of Vassili-Ostrov, the Finland Regiment, which was led by anarcho-syndicalist elements, decided to shoot the looters on the spot and blow up the wine-cellars.

These devotees of liberty took no half-measures, and a good job too.

These riots *were planned.* 'All methods are good.' Similar provocations took place all over Russia, and the hand of the enemy could frequently be detected. One of the October revolutionaries who was at the Rumanian front relates the following example:[26]

Alcohol suddenly made its appearance at the front in enormous quantities. Huge tanks full of it arrived, labelled *Paraffin* or *Benzine.* The troops, worn down by privation, quickly learned what was inside (and how? – that is a secret known to the corrupt originators of the cargo) and threw themselves, sometimes by whole battalions or regiments, upon this treasure; they would even get to the point of using bayonets or machine-guns to defend their tanks of liquor against others. We saw this happening at Minsk, and further in the rear at Orsha. At Orsha we received a first consignment of seventeen truckloads of alcohol which had been sent from Smolensk, we could not discover by whom, around 15 November. A few days later came a second train with twenty-two trucks labelled *Oats*, *Herrings* and *Wood*, with barrels of wine inside them. We had sent the first convoy back, but the soldiers still looted it on the way, addressing various threats in our direction. ... Even some of the members of the Revolutionary Committee yielded to the temptation to drink. ... We formed a detachment of seven men, absolutely reliable and well-armed, who worked non-stop from ten in the evening until eleven the following morning in an out-of-the-way spot, smashing up the oaken barrels of the second consignment ...

In Petrograd it became necessary, on 2 December, to institute a special Extraordinary Commission, armed with full powers, to combat this plague. Draconic measures were imposed: several looters of wine-cellars were shot on the spot. In his speech to the Soviet, Trotsky observed:

Vodka is as much a political force as the word. It is the revolutionary word which arouses men for the struggle against their oppressors. If you do not succeed in barring the path to drunken excess, all you will have left in the way of defences will be the armoured cars. Remember this: each day of drunkenness brings the other side closer to victory and us to the old slavery.

The evil was conquered within a week.

THE GOVERNMENT CRISIS

During the insurrection itself, at Petrograd, and throughout the street battles in Moscow, negotiations were going on between the Bolsheviks and the parties of 'Socialist democracy'. The Left SRs were insistent in their demand for the formation of a broad Socialist coalition government; as will be seen, this prospect was also favoured by a number of influential Bolsheviks. The negotiations opened under the auspices of the Vikzhel (All-Russian Executive of the Railwaymen's Union), where the Mensheviks and the Right SRs had the majority.

The Vikzhel was a sort of State within the State. On 26 October, when the Council of People's Commissars had no government machinery yet at its command, the writ of the Vikzhel ruled on all the railways. It was able to halt the transportation of troops and munitions at will, and was not slow to do so. 'Resolutely opposed to civil war', it blocked the transport both of Red troops and of White with a feigned impartiality. The negotiations went on at the Petrograd Municipal Duma, which was also the centre for the Committee of Public Safety's activities. Actually Lenin never took the negotiations seriously for a moment (though they were to preoccupy the enemy), and the majority of his party's Central Committee concurred with him.

At the beginning, as long as the outcome of the Moscow fighting was uncertain, the Vikzhel, and the democratic organizations grouped around it, proposed drastic conditions: (1) All troops to be placed under the authority of the Municipal Duma; (2) Disarmament of the workers and admission of Kerensky's forces into the city; (3) Release of all arrested persons; (4) Dissolution of the Military Revolutionary Committee. It was a demand for total capitulation. The victories at Pulkovo and Moscow made the Vikzhel considerably more amenable. Ryazonov,[27] who favoured conciliation, put before Vee-Tsik (the All-Russian Executive of Soviets) the new terms offered by the Social-Democrats. A Socialist government would be formed, in which the Bolsheviks would have half the portfolios, notably those of the Interior, Labour and Foreign Affairs; neither Lenin nor Trotsky would be included, in accordance with the previous plans of the Mensheviks. This government would be responsible to a Council of the Nation which would consist of 150 members from the All-Russian Soviet Executive, seventy-five delegates from the Peasant Soviets, eighty delegates from the army and the fleet, forty from the trade unions, and seventy Socialist members of the municipal Duma. A majority (sixty per cent of the seats) was promised to the Bolsheviks.

Acceptance of this proposal would have been a veiled capitulation on the part of the Bolsheviks. Their small majority in an assembly of a semi-parliamentary character would necessarily have been reflected in vacillations of policy; the strength of the minority Socialist opposition and its participation in the government would have led to the sabotage of all revolutionary measures; the consequent mass disillusionment would have weakened the Bolsheviks, while the bourgeoisie and upper middle classes would become alerted to danger. The majority of the Bolshevik Central Committee was astute enough to rely on the unreserved support it had from the mass of the party and the proletariat, and rejected the proposal.

Shortly afterwards a crisis arose in the party's Central Committee and in the Council of People's Commissars. We will quote here the Bulletin of the Central Committee of the Russian Social-Democratic Party (Bolshevik), No. 7, for 5 November 1917.

The Vee-Tsik, by 34 votes to 24, passed the resolution of Lenin and Trotsky on freedom of the press. The People's Commissars Nogin, Rykov, Milyutin, Teodorovich, Ryazanov and Derbyshev resigned. They addressed to the Vee-Tsik and the Council of People's Commissars the following declaration: 'We believe that it is necessary to form a Socialist government including all the parties in the Soviet. Only such a government can assure the fruits of the heroic struggles of the working class and the revolutionary army in the October and November days. We believe that a government which is exclusively Bolshevik can maintain power only by political methods of terror. The Council of People's Commissars is starting on this road: we cannot follow it.' Shlyapnikov was of the same opinion but did not believe that he should leave his post. Kamenev, Rykov, Milyutin, Zinoviev and Nogin have resigned from the Central Committee of the Bolshevik party.

(Actually Derbyshev and Ryazanov were not on the Council of People's Commissars; I have quoted the Russian text without amending this error.)

The majority attitude in the Central Committee was given in two documents, of which the first was the address of the majority to the minority, date 3 November:

The present political line of our party is contained in the motion put by Comrade Lenin and adopted yesterday, 2 November, by the Central Committee. This resolution considers as treason to the proletariat any attempt to induce our party to divest itself of the power which has been entrusted to us, on the basis of our programme, by the All-Russian Congress of Soviets, acting in the name of millions of workers, soldiers and peasants ...

The minority is told to submit or else get out of the party.

A split would be most unfortunate. But an open and honest split would be infinitely preferable to sabotage within the party, failure to implement our resolutions, disorganization and capitulation. ... We do not doubt for one moment that if our differences are placed before the masses, our policy will be supported unreservedly and with sacrifice by the revolutionary workers, soldiers and peasants, and that the vacillating opposition will speedily be condemned to isolation and impotence.

N. Lenin, L. Trotsky, J. Stalin, Y. Sverdlov, M. Uritsky, F. Dzerzhinsky, A. Yoffe, A. Bubnov, V. Sokolnikov, M. Muranov.

The crisis, serious though it was, remained confined to the top leadership of the party and was of short duration. At the All-Russian Soviet Executive Lenin made only a passing reference to it, in a disdainful remark on 'the departure of a few intellectuals'. He added: 'Only those who believe in the people, who throw themselves into the crucible of the living creativity of the masses, will maintain power . . .'

On 7 November, *Pravda* published an appeal to the masses, whose essential points were as follows:

May all the fainthearts, vacillators and sceptics, who have allowed themselves to be intimidated by the bourgeoisie or by the clamour of its direct or indirect agents, begin to blush. In the masses, there is not a shadow of hesitation . . .

Those who had resigned were roundly denounced as deserters. *Pravda*, on the same day or the next, published a 'Letter to the Comrades' signed 'G. Zinoviev'. Zinoviev reported that the Mensheviks and SRs had turned down the conditions put by the Soviets, and that in these circumstances he was withdrawing his resignation from the Central Committee; he called on his comrades in the opposition to do the same.

It is our right and our duty [he declared] to warn the party against mistakes. But we remain with the party. We prefer to make mistakes with millions of workers and soldiers and to die with them, rather than cut ourselves off from history at this decisive hour. . . . There is not and cannot be any split in our party.

In the whole history of the working-class movement we know of no example of a crisis as serious as this which was so simply and sanely resolved. Once more the great qualities of the Bolshevik party were displayed – its habits of collective thinking, its discipline, its strong morale, its searching exploration of differences, the unimportance of personal pride among its militants, their profound attachment to the working class and to organization. The patriotism of the British expresses itself eloquently in the powerful expression: *My country right or wrong*. The Bolshevik mentality implies a similar patriotism, one of inestimable value in the class war, a patriotism of class and party: better to be wrong with the party of the proletariat than right against it. There is no greater revolutionary wisdom than this.[28]

Those who had advocated a broad Socialist coalition were afraid that the Bolshevik party – which they were doubtless accustomed to conceive of as the most conscious minority of the working class – might find itself, once in authority, isolated from the worker and peasant masses. They did not have a clear picture of the immense influence that the party had acquired since the July days, or of its steadfast ability to develop policies which would conform to the vital interests of all toilers. They feared the prospect of civil war *within* the ranks of Socialism and democracy, and one cannot deny that this was a legitimate fear for them at that moment; the counter-revolutionary character of Socialist opportunism had not yet been revealed as abundantly as it later was, both in Russia and in Germany. It was perhaps permissible to hope – though in this hope there was a strong dose of dupery – that the Socialist parties would hesitate to side with the counter-revolution, to fire on the 'riots of the mob', i.e. the proletariat, and to take up arms against the true Socialists. Evidently this was an under-estimation of the democratic corruption of these parties, their subjection to influence from the bourgeoisie, the reactionary outlook of their leaders, and the special mentality and interests of the lower middle classes which they mainly represented. It was a patent error, particularly after the experience of 'the Socialism of national defence', which had been seen lined up on both sides of the battlefield in the service of the generals.

For its own part, the Socialism of counter-revolution, now-familiar with the corridors of power, was perfectly aware of its mission: it refused to compromise with the Bolshevik rising, which it dreamt of meeting, as we have seen, with a bloodbath. Its intransigence was of considerable use to the revolution: it speedily undeceived the few Bolsheviks who were still beset by illusions about the democratic party; it at once defined the situation sharply and accorded definite limits to the possibility of sabotaging the revolution. In Russia the revolution experienced no sabotage *from within*, had no enemies inside its inmost councils: among its leaders, treason had no ticket of entry. The reverse experience was the lot of the Hungarian proletariat in 1919. A few days before the seizure of power, the Communist party fused with the Social-Democratic party. During the entire period of the dictatorship of the proletariat in Hungary, Social-Democrats in brand-new Communist camouflage occupied the most important posts, with the result that no measure of revolution, or of defence against counter-revolution, was free from sabotage by the Social-Democracy: treason, whether conscious or unconscious, it matters little, was everywhere. Let us only recall that, after Bela Kun's retreat, a Social-Democratic Cabinet was formed which ensured the transition from the proletarian dictatorship to the Horthy regime. That is the mission of the Socialists of counter-revolution: to ensure the transition to the White terror. What Plekhanov dreamed of in Russia, the Social-Democrat Noske managed to achieve in Germany. In the light of these experiences, we can measure today the gravity of the mistake committed by those Bolsheviks who resigned on 4 November. Equally we can see the keen perceptiveness displayed in these days by Lenin, and the majority of the Central Committee who supported him. At this juncture the role of Lenin was similar in influence to the role he had played on the eve of the insurrection, and of equal importance for the success of the revolution.[29]

PROLETARIAN REALISM AND 'REVOLUTIONARY' RHETORIC

Other debates had taken place in the All-Russian Soviet Executive, in which the Left Socialist-Revolutionaries, who were inspired by a large-hearted, foggy idealism, took the attitude of a loyal opposition within the young Soviet regime. On 4 November, while the dissident Bolsheviks were resigning, the Left SRs, who also favoured a broad Socialist coalition, withdrew their representatives from the leading bodies of the Soviets. The debate on this day is worth noting: in it Lenin had to defend against the Left SRs the simplest, plainest revolutionary realism.

The topic under discussion was the freedom of the press, and in particular that of the journal *Rech* (*The Word*), the organ of Milyukov and the liberal big bourgeoisie. The bourgeois press was continuing to appear. Their role in the first exchanges of the civil war was one of considerable effect: in one direction they would breathe hatred, combativity, reactionary ideology; in the other, confusion, panic and slander. The problem before the Soviet Executive was that of silencing these journals, which turned out to be a lengthy process.[30] The Left SRs' orator Karelin paraded as a defender of fundamental principles, declaiming that the Bolsheviks were 'muzzling thought' and that the civil war was a 'disgrace'. Lenin retorted to this pitiful rhetoric:

Let us set up a commission to enquire into the dependence of the bourgeois newspapers upon the banks. We would like to know what sort of freedom it is, wouldn't we, that is allowing these journals to appear: isn't it the freedom to buy up tons of paper and hire hordes of scribblers? No more talk of this freedom of the press which is the slave of capital!

Lenin proposed a monopoly of advertising in order to deprive the bourgeois papers of their support from this quarter. And he had to reply to the objections of the print-workers, who supported capitalist advertising because it gave them a living.

The Left SRs also attacked the Council of People's Commissars for violating Soviet legality (yes, already) in issuing decrees without previous sanction from the All-Russian Soviet Executive. 'By what right? How arbitrary!' exclaimed these priceless revolutionaries. Lenin had to explain to them that the new government had not the leisure to spend on such formalities, that the crisis was too serious and no delay was possible. (This was inconceivable to the SRs.) Lenin concluded:

Nothing, not one article, not one pound of bread, will escape accounting: for Socialism is, above all, accounting. Socialism is not created by decrees coming from on high. It has nothing in common with official, bureaucratic routinism. Living Socialism is the work of the popular masses themselves.

A Left S R had said that 'The West is shamefully silent.' Lenin replied sharply:

Revolutions are not made at the word of command. Germany is at the same stage we were at, a while before the fall of Tsardom. Discrediting Socialism, are we?.[The S Rs had said this too, another of their gems.] Come now, really! ... Is not the present government appealing to the masses to create new forms of life? ... We are going to have a republic of labour: he who does not labour, neither shall he eat![31]

Lenin's proletarian realism was affirmed in the face of 'revolutionary' phraseology from the Left S Rs, who were excellent revolutionists in their sincere desire to serve Socialism, in their courage and honesty but who, like all the radical petty-bourgeois whose most advanced elements they were, were captivated by the fine phrases which form the whole content of the ideology of bourgeois democracy.

Lenin's invocation of the initiative of the masses is unceasing. Mass spontaneity is conceived by him as the necessary condition of the organized action of the party. On 5 November, he signs an appeal to the people, calling on them to fight against sabotage. The majority of the people is with us, so our victory is assured:

Comrades, workers! Remember that from now on *you yourselves* are administering the State. Nobody is going to help you if you do not yourselves unite, and take over *all* state affairs. Rally round your Soviets: make them strong. Get to work, there at the base, without waiting for orders. Institute the strictest revolutionary order, suppress without mercy the anarchic excesses of drunken hooligans, counter-revolutionary Junkers, followers of Kornilov, etc. Institute rigorous control over production and the accounting of products. Arrest and deliver to the tribunal of the revolutionary people whoever dares to raise his hand against the people's cause ...

The peasants are urged to 'take full power themselves, on the spot'.[32] *Initiative, once again initiative, and always initiative!* That is the slogan that Lenin flings to the masses on 5 November, ten days after the victory of the insurrection.

THE URBAN MIDDLE CLASSES AND THE REVOLUTION

The first days following the revolution are characterized by two outstanding facts:

(1) The middle classes in the towns (for the decree on land satisfies the corresponding classes in the countryside, who will only form a hostile force later) rally in their entirety to the counter-revolution. It is they who provide the counter-revolution's effectives and shock-brigades. In the street battles of Moscow and Petrograd, as at the heights of Pulkovo, the bourgeoisie is un-

doubtedly not defended by itself: its own forces consist only of organized mercenaries. Who, then, are its last defenders? The officers, the Cossacks (whom we shall discuss later), the students of the military colleges, the youth of the high schools, the officials, the senior staffs, the technicians, the intellectuals, the Socialists, all of them people of the middling sort, more or less exploited but highly privileged within the system of exploitation and participating in it. *The technical intelligence is simultaneously the organizer of production and of exploitation*:[33] it is thereby led to identify itself with the system, and to conceive of the capitalist mode of production as the only one possible. The petty-bourgeoisie, educated, comfortable and held in a position of subordinacy by the bourgeoisie, is often threatened with impoverishment, and consequently tends towards Socialism; it is, however, inclined towards fatal illusions. More cultured than the proletariat, more numerous and advanced in ideology than the bourgeoisie proper, it feels that its vocation is that of running society. Nineteenth-century democratic illusions were born out of this state of mind and have, in their turn, helped to nurture it. The Socialism of the petty-bourgeois is a Socialism of administrators: liberal, confused, individualist, sometimes Utopian, sometimes reactionary. Petty-bourgeois culture is capitalistic, fixated on the defence of the old order and on a mass education which will conform to the interests of the propertied classes. The petty-bourgeois mentality tends, above all in politics, to separate action from the word: the word is conceived as an antagonist to action or as a false substitute for it (compare the 'symbolic gestures' practised by French radicalism). The bravest souls of the Russian middle classes, who sympathized with the revolution long before it became a reality, thought it should be confined to the bourgeois revolution which would open an era of sound reforms. Proletarian revolution appears to them like an invasion of barbarians, a collapse into anarchy, a blasphemy against the idea of revolution itself. This point of view was forcibly expressed by Maxim Gorky in his *Untimely Thoughts* published by *Novaya Zhizn* (*New Life*). The middle classes wanted the bourgeois revolution to inaugurate a democratic republic in which they would have constituted the administrative classes and where capitalist development would have proceeded unchecked: this conception was particularly firm among the Mensheviks and the SRs who at this time were the most conscious ideologists of the petty-bourgeoisie.

The Utopianism of this class was also shocked by the reality of the revolution: the harsh, bloody reality that was so different from the romantic idyll they had often dreamed of. The workers and the soldiers had quite another approach here, accustomed as they were to living among harsh and bloody realities, enduring necessities in all their naked brutality, brought up in the school of repression and imperialist war.

To the enlightened middle classes, the October Revolution seemed like a *putsch* engineered by a handful of fanatical doctrinaires with the support of a frightful, anarchic movement of uncivilized commoners. Gorky employed these very words. The issue of war and peace wounds their patriotism (for patriotism is above all the emotion of this class, since the proletariat is internationalist and the bourgeoisie has no more than a businessman's patriotism diluted with the financier's cosmopolitanism), just as it wounds the petty-bourgeois revolutionaries' romanticism: it is the war issue that widens the abyss between the revolution and what was called – falsely – 'the democracy'. Before the actual events, it was impossible to foresee that the petty-bourgeois democracy would range itself so totally, with the energy of despair, on the side of the counter-revolution, even to the point of following the monarchist generals, looking for a new Galliffet, and proceeding to mass executions of insurgents. Hence the error made by some of the Bolsheviks. The Moscow Military Revolutionary Committee seems, right up to the massacre at the Kremlin, to have nursed the hope that the SRs and Mensheviks would not go fundamentally against the workers' rising. The minority in the Bolshevik Central Committee and the Council of People's Commissars believed, erroneously, in a concentration of the Socialist forces: in other words that the Socialist-minded petty-bourgeoisie could be won back to the proletariat.

As a matter of fact, the counter-revolutionary attitude of the middle classes was not rigidly predetermined by their class interests. With hindsight, one can see that submission to the Soviet regime would have held every advantage for them: through their small numerical importance, their failure to act unitedly and the formidable superiority of the proletariat in organization, morale and thought (with its party, its class consciousness and its Marxism), through, finally, the support given to the revolution by the rural petty-bourgeoisie, the urban middle classes were doomed to a cruel defeat, or rather to annihilation. Their resistance, moreover, created a pile of ruins, and devastated the country. Had they been only slightly more aware of the forces that were in motion, they would have saved themselves – and Russia – a host of calamities. Doubtless, the middle classes are not fated always to have this same hostility towards the proletarian revolution: it is more probable that, in the social struggles of the future, the power and the resolution of the working class will incline them towards an attitude of, first, neutrality, then support. In short, they follow, now and in the future, the strongest side, and when they see the working class is the strongest, they will follow that. In Russia in October 1917, the middle class fooled itself: it thought that the victory of the proletariat was impossible. For a long time they clung to this idea, anticipating the fall of Bolshevism in days or weeks. The only people who could believe in the victory of a class which had never triumphed previously in history, with no experience of power, no footing in society, no wealth, no institutions of its own, except for a few combat organizations – the only people who could believe this had to be as deeply imbued with the historic mission of the proletariat as the Bolsheviks were: had to be, in a word, revolutionary Marxists. The invalidation of this psychological motive that lay behind the counter-revolutionary attitude of the Russian petty-bourgeoisie is one of the great historical achievements of the October Revolution.

THE 'LAWS OF WAR' DO NOT APPLY TO CIVIL WAR

(2) These early days are also marked by the special features taken by the civil war. Here the Reds, still ignorant of the technique of repression, as well as of its actual necessity, and tending towards self-delusion on the nature of the Socialist democracy, are guilty of a deplorable leniency. It is enough to compare the conditions put by the MRC at Moscow, after its victory to the Committee of Public Safety, with those which the White Committee, at a time when it was far from winning, had tried to impose upon the MRC. The Whites massacre the workers in the Arsenal and the Kremlin: the Reds release their mortal enemy, General Krasnov, on parole. The Whites' conspiracy for the restoration of order is utterly ruthless: but the Reds hesitate over suppressing the reactionary press. Sheer inexperience was one of the main causes of this dangerous leniency on the Reds' side.

The counter-revolution, on the other hand, finds its commitment instinctively, immediately, and absolutely. The conflagration of the civil war, it is true, takes light only gradually, with assistance from foreign powers; but, already, from 26 October, the struggle was much more savage than that of wars between states. These are, generally speaking, limited by certain laws, and there are rules of war in them. But there are no rules, no Geneva conventions, no customs of chivalry, and no non-belligerents in the war between classes. From the outset, the bourgeoisie and the petty-bourgeoisie resort to strikes and sabotage in all the public utilities, in all administrations: a weapon quite outside the customs of war. When Belgium and France were invaded, nowhere did the technicians go on strike as the enemy entered their territory. The sabotage consisted of an attempt to engineer famine, that is, to strike at the whole working population, without any distinction between combatants and non-combatants. Equally significant is the use that was made of alcohol. And the entire counter-revolutionary conspiracy laid the groundwork for White terror.

For wars between states are customarily domestic wars within the possessing classes, who enjoy a common class ethic and a common conception of what is right and proper. In certain eras there was even a marked tendency to reduce the art of war to a rather conventional game. The modern art of war dates from the French Revolution, which pitched a nation-in-arms under bourgeois leadership against the professional armies of antiquated monarchies, armies based on forced conscription and the use of mercenaries and commanded by noblemen: the revolution thus immediately liquidated the old, outdated conventions of strategy and tactics. The Europeans depart from the current rules of war only when they are dealing with peoples they believe to be inferior:[34] so too with the wars waged by ruling classes convinced of their right to defend 'civilization' against working-class 'barbarism'; all means are considered permissible. The interests at stake are too great, all conventions are annulled, and ethics (for there is no human ethic, only the ethics of classes and social formations) no longer exert any moderating influence upon the contending forces: the counter-revolution views the rebellious exploited classes as 'banished from humanity'.

These truths can be seen in all their vividness at the end of the first week of the new Soviet authority. Later, we shall see the massacre of prisoners become a matter of routine in the civil war; and, for a whole period of years, the capitalist States will treat Communist Russia as an outlaw nation.

4 · The First Flames of the Civil War: The Constituent Assembly

THE RIGHTS OF NATIONALITIES

The great decrees of 26 October affirmed only one aspect of the Revolution. It was not enough to proclaim to millions of soldiers that a vigorous revolutionary initiative for peace had begun, not enough to announce to over a hundred million peasants that they were now the masters of their land. The decree on peace shook the yoke of imperialism whose bloody weight bore down upon millions of soldiers. The expropriation of the landlords shook the feudal yoke which had borne down for centuries upon the peasantry. The task remained of delivering a lethal blow against the imperialism which had inherited the domineering traditions of feudal and mercantile Great Russia. As Elisée Reclus had foreseen even in 1905,[1] any genuine Russian revolution, if it was not to undermine its own future irretrievably, had to give immediate freedom to the nationalities in bondage to the Empire that had now collapsed. In terms of nationalities, the population of the Empire was composed as follows:[2] Great Russians, 56,000,000; Ukrainians, 22,300,000; White-Russians, about 6,000,000; Poles, 8,000,000; Lithuanians, 3,100,000; Germans, 1,800,000; Moldavians, 1,100,000; Jews, 5,100,000; Finns, 2,600,000; peoples of the Caucasus, 1,100,000; peoples of Finnish origin (Estonians, Karelians, etc.), 3,500,000; peoples of Turco–Tartar descent, 13,600,000. The constitution of the Empire was characterized by the absolute hegemony of the conquering Great-Russian nation: its language was the sole official language, its religion (Greek Orthodoxy) the State religion. This though the Great Russians formed no more than a minority, fifty-six million out of 129 million. Between March and October 1917, the Provisional Government, in its concern to hold on to the territorial integrity of the old Empire, especially to the material advantages accruing to the Russian bourgeoisie from the subjection of conquered peoples, simply *continued* with the national policies of Tsardom, without even flinching before the dangerous conflicts that were now opened with Finland and the Ukraine. It was, for that matter, impossible for the old ruling classes to behave in any other way. And the fall of the autocracy had stimulated the appearance of national movements which became marked, notably in Finland and the Ukraine, by separatist tendencies. We must add, too, that the national question, among most of the non-Russian peoples, was closely related to the agrarian question, since the subject peoples in most of the territories were peasants.

On 2 November, while the fighting was still going on in Moscow (it was the very day when the Red artillery was firing on the Kremlin) and while the victorious fighters from Pulkovo were being hailed by the population of Petrograd, the government of the Soviets promulgated the 'Declaration of the Rights of the Peoples of Russia', which may be summarized by the three points: (1) Equality and sovereignty of all peoples; (2) Right of self-determination for the peoples, including that of separating to form independent States; (3) Abolition of all national and religious privileges; and free development of all national or ethnic minorities.

This essential text contained no more than the programme expounded by Lenin himself from April and May onwards.

It can be compared with an appeal to the Islamic workers of Russia and the East published twenty days later (22 November) under the signatures of Lenin and the Commissar for Nationalities, Dzugashvili-Stalin. Never before in history had Europeans spoken out in this manner to peoples who had been oppressed, enslaved, conquered and 'protected' for centuries. We have torn up the secret treaties giving Constantinople to Russia! Gone is the treaty for the partition of Persia! Gone is the treaty for the partition of Turkey! Cancelled, the annexation of Armenia! 'From now on, your beliefs and your customs, your national and cultural institutions, are declared free and inviolable. Go, organize your national life, freely and without fetters. ... You must become the masters in your own countries. ... Your destiny is in your hands.'

THE RESISTANCE OF THE GENERAL HEADQUARTERS: TROOPS AGAINST GENERALS

The General Headquarters – in Russian, the *stavka* – of a country at war is a sort of capital city no less important than the civilian metropolis. Immediately after the proletarian insurrection, the Stavka became the last hope of the counter-revolution. It held out tenaciously until 18 November.[3]

Fortunately for the Whites, it was situated a fair distance from both Petrograd and Moscow, at Mogilev, a small town in White Russia with 60,000 inhabitants, where the proletariat and the Bolshevik party were both equally weak. At the Stavka the supreme revolutionary authority was the Committee of the Armies, which had been elected at the beginning of the revolution and was controlled by the SR party. This committee hobnobbed amicably with the General Staff, denounced Bolshevik plots and affirmed the indefatigable loyalty of the army to fatherland and Allies, as well as 'the fervent desire of the soldiers to continue the war to the very end'. On 31 October it officially announced its intention to 'resist Bolshevik force by force'. Its troops were to 'march on Petrograd' to re-establish order. 'Not one drop of blood will be spilt unnecessarily,' the proclamation ran. 'If the

Right wing tries to make capital out of these events for the counter-revolution, we shall turn all our forces against them.'

On the same day, the commander-in-chief, General Dukhonin, summoned the Bolsheviks to surrender unconditionally to the Provisional Government. This forceful language was no more than verbiage. The mass of the troops welcomed the news of the new revolution with joy. The Committee of the Armies had to reduce its pretensions, and said it would be content with a broad Socialist coalition. It changed again on the arrival, at the Stavka, of the leaders of the SR party, Chernov and Gotz. The Rada, or National Parliament of the Ukraine, had just declared itself against the Bolsheviks. The idea of an alliance with the Rada now became current among the Socialists of counter-revolution.

21. N. V. Krylenko

The Committee of the Armies proposed the establishment of a 'government of order' whose Prime Minister was to be V. M. Chernov. These efforts were encouraged by the representatives of the Allies. In the middle of these negotiations, intrigues, faction-meetings and schemes, the soldiers and the masses acted. The armies of the North and the North-West went over to the Bolsheviks. The crack battalions of St George proved to be less than loyal: hostile to the generals and the SRs, they prevented the Stavka from moving to the south. Arrests of officers by their soldiers became more and more frequent.

On 9 November, Lenin, Stalin and Krylenko called General Dukhonin to the telephone and ordered him to begin immediate negotiations for an armistice with the Austrians and Germans. As the replies he gave were evasive, they ended the telephone conversation by dismissing Dukhonin from his command: 'Second Lieutenant Krylenko is appointed commander-in-chief.'

But how could the General Staff be disarmed? The Council of People's Commissars still had no governmental apparatus at their disposal. They were ignorant of the weakness of their adversary. Once again they relied on the masses. A radio appeal drafted by Lenin[4] called on the troops to intervene:

Soldiers, the cause of peace is in your hands. You cannot let the counter-revolutionary generals sabotage the great work of peace; you will place them under guard in order to prevent lynchings which are unworthy of the revolutionary army, and to ensure that they will not escape the tribunal which awaits them. You will observe the strictest revolutionary and military order.

The front-line regiments are immediately to elect delegates to begin formal negotiations with the enemy for an armistice. The Council of People's Commissars authorizes you to do this. Inform us by every means possible of the progress of negotiations. The Council of People's Commissars alone has the authority to sign the final armistice.

This document aroused a discussion in the All-Russian Executive of the Soviets (10 November), in the course of which Lenin explained his ideas.[5]

The only way we can defeat Dukhonin [he said] is by calling on the initiative and self-organization of the masses. Peace will not come about only from the top, it must be won from below. We have not the slightest confidence in the German generals, but we do have confidence in the German people. In the struggle we are waging against the Stavka, we must act thoroughly and without regard for formalities. I am against half-measures.

The Stavka's own troops turned against it; on 18 November, just as it was on the point of fleeing and transporting itself to the Ukraine, the General Staff was confronted by its soldiers. The *émigré* Stankevich, who was an eye-witness, writes, 'The Stavka had barely begun the preparations for its move when crowds of excited soldiers came on the scene, declaring that they would not let the GHQ go. . . . The Stavka had not a single soldier to defend it. Dukhonin remarked that he was being watched by his own batman.'[6] The Allied officers, a few generals, and some reactionary units were the only ones to escape. When Krylenko and the Red sailors arrived, Generalissimo Dukhonin was arrested, and summarily done to death in the railway station at Mogilev.

It should be noted that the Stavka's resistance marks the beginning of the intervention of the Allies against the revolution. General Lavergne, the head of the French Military Mission, and a senior American officer had given official encouragement to Dukhonin. This fact was pointed out in a menacing diplomatic Note from Trotsky.

On every front, the revolution similarly translated itself into a conflict between the masses on one side, and the command and leading officers on the other. And practically everywhere the outcome of the conflict was the same too.

KALEDIN: THE DEFEAT OF THE COSSACK
COUNTER-REVOLUTION

Broken in the two capitals, broken in the Stavka, the counter-revolution's resistance at once moved to the south. Asylum for the vanquished combatants of Petrograd, Moscow and Mogilev was found beyond the Ukraine (nationalistic and hostile to anything that savoured of the old Great-Russian yoke), in the provinces of the south-east and in the Don and Kuban Cossack territories. The Cossack population, a rural petty-bourgeoisie with strong military traditions enjoying special privileges under Tsardom, appeared to the generals as the ideal base for the recruitment of the counter-revolution's first troops. Autonomous governments had been set up in these areas. The Donski-Krai, or Don country, was a kind of Cossack Republic, whose president was an elected military leader, or Ataman, General Kaledin, a supporter of the counter-revolution. At Ekaterinodar, the capital of the Kuban, there was a Rada, or vague parliament, composed of Cossacks and Socialist intellectuals whose representation of the wealthy part of the population was so blatant that their 'constitution' excluded the workers and the poor, non-Cossack peasantry from the franchise.

Thereafter, over many bloody years, the history of the Don and the Kuban Cossacks, a typical rural petty-bourgeoisie, was one of interminable oscillation and internal feuding. Canvassed and attracted by revolution and by counter-revolution in turn, they showed themselves, in short, as absolutely incapable of taking up a definite position. As democrats, opposed to the restoration of Tsardom and hostile to the national patriotism of the Great-Russian bourgeoisie, they were constantly in conflict with the White generals in one way or another. The councils of the national armies were always being preoccupied by an embarrassing 'Cossack question'. As determined supporters of private property, they battled violently against the proletarian Communists. Following the October Revolution their ideal became one of regional independence: they wanted to maintain their territories intact from 'Bolshevik anarchy'. Here, as in everything else, the second-rate politicians of the Don and the Kuban displayed a very characteristic blindness.

While Krylenko was making his way into the Stavka at Mogilev, the man of September's unsuccessful *coup d'état*, the man who had re-introduced the death penalty in the army, the Russian and Allied bourgeoisie's recent candidate for the role of dictator, Kornilov himself, simply walked out of the monastery at Bykhov-skoye where the Provisional Government had interned him. Was it trickery or weak security? A mixture of both: Kerensky had entrusted the surveillance of his accomplice, who was a prisoner for the sake of public form, to a detachment of cavalry entirely devoted to the prisoner! Kornilov placed himself at the head of· his squadron and made his way towards the Don country; there he arrived at the beginning of December, alone and disguised as a peasant, having narrowly escaped being handed over to the Bolsheviks by his own loyal soldiery.[7]

In the Don, the old general Alexeyev[8] had been working away at the creation of an army of loyalist volunteers ever since the beginning of November. From all the corners of Russia, officers and Junkers flooded into Novo-Cherkassk and Rostov. The character of these counter-revolutionaries has been described with praiseworthy exactness by General Denikin:[9] the appeal for volunteers was responded to by

officers, Junkers, students, and very, very few others. ... The nation did not rise to the call. Under these conditions of recruitment the army from its inception suffered from a grave organic fault: it took on the character of a class army, inevitably. . . . It was evident that in these circumstances the Army of Volunteers could not fulfil its mission over the whole of Russia.

What, then, did the generals imagine they could do? Their objective, it is clear, was to contain Bolshevism while the latter was still unorganized – its phenomenal power of organization took them unawares – and to await the outcome of events.

The establishment of this army proved difficult. The majority of the officers hesitated, went into hiding, or adapted to the new regime. Once the basis for military authority had been shattered, these army professionals felt utterly lost. And, everywhere, the vigilant hatred of the masses barred their path. Those who managed to reach the Don did so after passing through innumerable perils: the fugitive officer *en route* for the south became an outlaw-figure for the soldiers, to be killed on sight. Alexeyev had to work with frenzied energy to get his first units going. Money was in short supply. The bourgeoisie in the towns gave too little; it was already hard-pushed. The day very soon came when they could give nothing. Denikin reports that 'The Embassies of the Allied Powers were in a state of terror.' Even the Cossacks looked with a jaundiced eye upon this ingathering of armed patriots on their soil. The reactionary generals, in their appeal of 27 December, had to include a reference to the sovereignty of the people, exercised by the Constituent Assembly. All the same, the Cossack Council at the Don decided to keep a strict watch on the Army of Volunteers and 'purge it of counter-revolutionary elements'. At its best, the army counted no more than three to four thousand men. By contrast, it teemed with senior officers. Two generalissimos, Alexeyev and Kornilov, who also were at loggerheads, held the supreme command. Together with Kaledin, they formed a ruling triumvirate.

The army began its career by putting down workers' risings at Rostov and at Taganrog (26 November, 2 January) after the Cossacks had refused to intervene. It very quickly found itself in an impossible situation, with the ground cut from beneath its feet. The workers in the nearby Donetz region were threatening; the Cossacks were mutinous, and kept clearing off, since their parochial patriotism moved them to defend no more than their own territory – i.e. the territory of their various villages – against Red incursions. The Red Guards and the Caucasian army, which was back from the front, were soon surrounding the Don and laying siege to the Kuban.

The Council of People's Commissars outlawed the leaders of the Cossack counter-revolution in an appeal on 28 November:

> The local garrisons are urged to act with all possible vigour against the enemies of the people, without waiting for orders. All negotiation with them is forbidden. Any local citizens or railway-workers who give

them assistance will be punished with all strictness of the revolutionary law.

The Soviet government did not rest with this: the workers' Red Guards from Petrograd, Moscow, Kharkhov and the Donetz mines, reinforced with sailors and some army units, began a huge pincer movement under the command of Antonov-Ovseyenko, designed to isolate the Don area from the Ukraine before going on to the capture of Rostov and Kiev.

Inevitably in this guerrilla warfare, fought mostly along the railways with assistance from armoured or simply armed trains, the Red military headquarters for the southern front could give only very general guidance. Under Antonov's command there were two remarkable leaders: Sablin, a Left SR who headed the workers' contingents from Petrograd and Moscow, and Sivers, a Bolshevik NCO who commanded the Don army and was shortly to be killed. At first the Reds suffered some defeats, notably at Matveyev-Kurgan near Taganrog: but a workers' rising in this city restored the situation by chasing out the Whites. The Cossacks were hesitant, and became subdivided into factions of young and old, rich and poor, front-liner and rearguard. Red Cossack units were formed, and the workers continued their actions: the doom of the counter-revolution, reduced solely to the officers and thrown on to its own resources (for no foreign support was forthcoming), was now assured. The war ended on 29 January with the suicide of the Ataman Kaledin, and Kornilov's hazardous retreat to the Kuban.

A short extract from Kaledin's last speech, made before the Don Cossack Council just as the Reds were entering Novo-Cherkassk, forms an admirable summary of the débâcle of this first phase of counter-revolution.

When Kornilov goes, we shall have only a handful of men, a hundred to a hundred and forty soldiers. ... How can one find words for this shameful disaster? We have been betrayed by the vilest kind of egotism. Instead of defending their native soil against the enemy, Russia's best sons, its officers, flee shamefully before a handful of usurpers. There is no more sense of duty or sense of honour or love of country, or even simple morality.

All that remained for the Ataman to do was to blow his brains out. His successor Nazarov was, in the collapse of the Cossack democracy, incapable either of organizing resistance or taking flight; the Reds surprised him in the middle of a session of the Cossack Council and shot him (12 February).

At around the same time the Kuban underwent confused fighting, similar to that in the Don area since they involved the same social elements. This ended on 1 March with a Red victory. Soviet power was installed in Ekaterinodar, only for a short time it is true. There was a rising of Cossacks in the Ural region between 25 November and 18 January which, under the command of General Dutov, succeeding in capturing Orenburg. This ended likewise in defeat.

The synchrony among these events is most striking.

2. General Dutov

THE UKRAINE

The vast region of the Dnieper, situated in the south of the Great Russian plain, is to Russia what Provence is to France. The people of the Ukraine are differentiated from their Great-Russian kin by a milder and sunnier climate, wonderfully fertile soil, a past of greater affluence, gaiety and freedom, and a southern language which is less modulated but more sonorous than Russian. The economic character of this differentiation can be seen clearly. Before the war of 1914–18 *three quarters* of all coal produced in the Empire came from the Ukraine, as did two thirds of the iron ore, three quarters of the manganese, two thirds of the salt, four fifths of the sugar and *nine tenths* of the wheat exported from Russia.[10] It was by far the richest land of the Empire. The Ukrainian national movement's theoreticians, bourgeois ideologists naturally, accused the Tsarist regime of systematically siphoning away the capital and natural wealth of the Ukraine for the benefit of Great Russia. Tsardom, they pointed out, had developed sea-traffic in the Baltic ports to the detriment of Black Sea shipping, and had restricted the growth of industry in the Ukraine. Finally, they waxed eloquent in their denunciations of the insupportable hardships of cultural Russification.

The Ukrainian national movement awoke immediately upon the fall of the autocracy. The Rada, a sort of Ukrainian National Assembly, was speedily constituted, and entered into conflict with the Provisional Government of Prince Lvov. The independence sought by the Ukraine was very far-reaching. The Bolsheviks alone supported the demand. Accordingly, the Rada hailed the October Revolution as an act of liberation, but, once it had shaken off the dominion of the Great-Russian bourgeoisie, the bourgeoisie and petty-bourgeoisie of the Ukraine had no intention of going with the proletariat along the path of social revolution. The Soviets of the Ukraine were now marching in step with those of Great Russia. The Kiev Soviet had organized a Revolutionary Committee on 22 October with the aim of seizing power. For a short while the Soviet and the Rada formed a united front against the Russian Kadets, Mensheviks and SRs in the Kiev municipal council who were siding with the Provisional Government in Petrograd. But as soon as Kerensky's cause was lost, another sort of united front was immediately set up: this time the Kadet party (the *Russian* Constitutional-Democrats, the party of the big Great-Russian bourgeoisie, be it recalled) joined forces with the Rada against Bolshevism. From now on, the conflict between the

'People's Republic of the Ukraine' and the Kiev Soviet could be resolved only by force of arms.

Our comrade G. Safarov has provided a most interesting analysis of the distribution of populations in the Ukraine. In the countryside, the Great Russians formed minorities often of tiny proportions (less than a thirtieth of the population in the Poltava gubernia, a tenth in the Kiev gubernia, etc.). In the towns on the other hand, i.e. in the industrial and commercial centres, the Great-Russian element was often more numerous than the Ukrainian; small towns were often dominated by the Jews.

More and more, the towns were falling under non-Ukrainian influence. The composition of Ukrainian society can be summarized schematically as follows: at the summit, the Russian bureaucracy, the landlords and the Russian capitalists; next down, the commercial, industrial and artisan petty-bourgeoisie of the towns, which was Russian and Jewish; next, the Ukrainian rural petty-bourgeoisie and its intellectuals; finally, at the bottom, the Russian and Ukrainian proletariat of the towns and the country.

The rural petty-bourgeoisie (rich and middle peasants), along with its intelligentsia, was the backbone of the nationalist movement. As among the Don and Kuban Cossacks, it was both democrat and counter-revolutionary. Independence, property, the republic: for these classic ideals of the young ascendant bourgeoisies of old it was ready to fight ferociously.

The Rada of Kiev was composed of 213 peasant representatives, 132 army representatives, and 100 workers, salaried employees, intellectuals, etc. It tried to manoeuvre with the social current. Its Manifesto of 7 November was a curious mixture drawn from the declarations of the Soviet government. It announced the confiscation of the land belonging to the big proprietors and the Crown, etc., which were henceforth the property of the nation, to be disposed of by a Ukrainian Constituent Assembly. It decreed the eight-hour day and instituted government control over industrial production (*government* control, be it noted, not workers' control, though the workers had to participate in it). It promised energetic measures to end the war; abolished the death penalty and decreed a far-reaching political amnesty; announced a reform of the law-courts in accordance with 'the spirit of the people'; proclaimed a large decree of autonomy for local institutions (without saying which); and fixed the date for elections to the Ukrainian Constituent Assembly as 27 December, and the date for its first session as 9 January.

At the same time as it issued this shrewd proclamation, the Rada gave free passage over its territory to the White officers and the troop-units who were on their way to the Don, refused the same right to the Red troops going south, and disarmed the Soviet formations. On 4 December, the Council of People's Commissars presented it with an ultimatum which began with the significant sentence: 'We recognize, without reservation or condition, the national rights and the national independence of the Ukrainian people ...'

The Rada had to drop its mask. Its reply attacked, in a blanket of confused reproof, the elements of the extreme Right and the Bolsheviks, the anarchy of the Red soldiery and the fratricidal struggle in the People's Commissars' own territory. The Rada demanded a broad Socialist coalition and a federal republic. This document, signed by Vinnichenko, Petlyura and Mirny, was a declaration of war.

Fighting had already begun. A general strike broke out in Kiev. The Rada collapsed under the combined blows of the Red Guards from Petrograd, Moscow and Kharkov, who were commanded by Muraviev, the victor of Pulkovo, and of detachments of Red troops from the Rumanian front. The Reds entered Kiev on 26 January. Their victory was not a total one: guerrilla warfare was to continue in the south of Russia until 1921. A government of the Soviets of the Ukraine was set up at Kharkov.

France's intervention on the side of the counter-revolution did not stop with its prompt recognition of the independence of the Ukraine, complete with the despatch of a Military Mission to Kiev. At the beginning of January, M. Stephen Pichon had agreed a loan of 180 million francs to the Rada. At the same time as it leant on the support of the French government and enjoyed the advice of French agents like General Berthelot, the Rada also sought the assistance of the Central Powers for the struggle against Bolshevism.

THE TRAGEDY OF THE RUMANIAN FRONT

For several months, the monarchy of Rumania, now under crushing pressure from the Central Powers, had been harassed by the behaviour of the Russian army of about a million men, under the command of General Shcherbachev, an incorrigible reactionary. The Court and the General Staff had taken refuge at Jassy after the capture of Bucharest by the Austrians and Germans; there, on 1 May, they saw to their horror the Russian regiments release Rakovsky from prison, hail him with ovations and applaud the idea of a Rumanian Republic. For a few hours, Jassy was within the pull of the Russian revolution: but this had yet to find its way forward, and the Rumanian monarchy was allowed to survive.

The Russian generals made haste to join with the Rumanian government, the Allied representatives and the reactionary officer-cliques, against the 'Bolshevist anarchy' they all dreaded. When the Ukrainian Rada announced its independence, Shcherbachev concluded an agreement with it. A confused and bloody struggle now opened out, destined to last for months, between revolutionary soldiers and a grand coalition against the second revolution formed by the generals, the officers, the Allies, the Rumanian government, the pro-government Socialists (Mensheviks and SRs) and Ukrainian nationalism.

For a short spell a handful of Bolsheviks led by Semyon Roshal, a young militant of great talent, managed to get the better of the General Staff and take command of the army. They were arrested after a few days (10 December). Roshal was murdered after capture by a group of Ukrainian officers, and his seventy-three fellow-prisoners were treated harshly and threatened each day with the same fate. (Later, in March, they were exchanged for representatives of the Rumanian bourgeoisie who had been arrested in Russia.) The Rumanian army, commanded by General Averescu, acquired enormous stocks of war material which were gladly left for it by the Russian high command. White fighting units were now formed by Russian officers: one of these, that led by General Drozdovsky, later took part in the establishment of Denikin's army. A number of Red units from the army in Rumania managed to fight their way through to the Ukraine.

With encouragement from the Allies, the Rumanian government had for some time been preparing the annexation of Bessarabia, which the Allies appear to have endorsed at the beginning of the revolution. The Central Powers had made the same offer previously. The 'Moldavian national movement' in Bessarabia[11] had a character similar to that of Ukrainian nationalism – except that its strongest base was in the funds it received from the Secret Service of the Rumanian General Staff. The Rumanian bourgeoisie's ancient appetites for expansion were fanned by the imperious fears of the present: in order to check the revolution, it had to be robbed of territory. Bessarabia was a dangerous focus of revolutionary contagion: the Wallachian and Moldavian boyars[12] were still haunted by the memories of the peasant rising of 1907, a repercussion from Russia's revolution. Their agents set up a so-called 'National Council', the Sfatul Țării: it was elected from non-existent organizations and Moldavians had the majority in it.[13] The Moldavian National Party began to recruit an army. However, the spirit of the soldiers was such that when, at the beginning of January, the Rumanians made a first attempt to enter Kishinev, the Moldavian soldiers acted in concert with the revolutionary Russian troops to halt the move. Around twenty revolutionary soldiers had to be sent to the firing-squad before obedience could be restored.

The Sfatul Țării, chaired by a former commissar of Kerensky's administration, who was also an SR, assembled on 21 November to talk in a language similar to that of the Ukrainian Rada. The opposition of some honest Socialists was not enough to prevent the establishment of a Directorate which was at the bidding of Rumanian interests. Every tactic of intrigue, intimidation, cor-

ruption and demagogy was used by this body, in which the Rumanian agents even went so far as to take the guise of Bolsheviks, like
a certain Buzdugan who, later, on 27 March, was to read the loyal
address of the Sfatul Ţării to the King of Rumania.

The Rumanians, assisted by General Shcherbachev, meanwhile
occupied strategic points and cut off the supplies of the revolutionary soldiers. Finally they occupied Kishinev, but only after a
fierce battle lasting several days in which they broke the resistance
of the Moldavian peasants and the Russian revolutionary
fighters.[14]

MASSACRES OF OFFICERS

It is against the background of this period and these events that
the spontaneous beginnings of the Red terror must be viewed. It
was the direct consequence of a whole series of factors. The General
Staffs had maintained discipline in the army only through the
death penalty, that is, by a systematic practice of legalized terror.
The memory of the merciless repressions of 1905–6 was still active
in the army and the fleet. Then too, the officers now appeared
everywhere to be the most active agents of the counter-revolution.
For months they had insistently demanded the reintroduction of
the death penalty in the armed forces, the only guarantee of
discipline. Accustomed in the course of war to treat mutiny as a
dangerous beast to be dispatched without any pretence of a trial,
they themselves were devotees of terror. Episodes like the massacre
of the Kremlin arsenal workers became current almost everywhere whenever the officers secured a temporary control. The
seeds of hate that they sowed so liberally became a rich harvest in
a few weeks. General Denisov gives some interesting statistics on
the massacre of officers by soldiers, in the Don region alone,
between 13 February and 14 April 1918: fourteen generals,
twenty-three colonels and 292 commissioned officers were killed
in this period.[15]

A few reports of episodes will prove revealing on the nature of
this wave of terror.

An officer was walking along a street in a small town of the
Crimea. Nobody paid any attention to him. A beggar, who was a
legless cripple, caught sight of him. This human trunk started off
on the heels of the officer shouting: 'Off with your epaulettes,
comrade, take them off!' The officer hurried on. At this, the beggar roused a mob with cries of 'Comrades, look! There goes the
counter-revolution!' This scene is recounted by an eye-witness.[16]

The same witness tells the story of the execution of some naval
officers at Sebastopol. The Red sailors took over the railway
station, and every officer who arrived there was summarily interrogated. If he had served in 1905–6, the period of the ruthless suppression by the tribunals of the fleet, he was at once stood up

against the wall and shot. Any other officers could pass unmolested through this bloody checkpoint, under the hard eyes of the sailors.

After the first engagements of the civil war, the betrayals on the Rumanian front, the conspiracies and risings of the Ukraine, the Don, the Kuban, the Ural and the Crimea, the fury of the sailors and soldiers ceased to make any distinctions among the officers.

The first messages from the south announcing mass executions of officers were published in Petrograd during the second half of January. They described events in the Crimea. The officers, at the head of Tartar detachments, had gained control over the peninsula for a short time, and proceeded to shoot their Bolshevik prisoners. The arrival of Red sailors restored the situation. A telegram dated 20 January told of the bombardment of Yalta by two Red torpedo-boats, and ended with these lines: 'Several dozen officers were executed. They were led to the edge of the sea with heavy stones tied round their necks, and thrown in to drown. The corpses are floating in the harbour.... Two big merchants have been shot.'

Similar episodes took place in most of the small towns of the Crimea. Here, in some of the gayest and most beautiful places in the whole of Russia, the Red terror was born.

So far it was confined to the massacre of officers by their own soldiers, in the areas where the civil war had begun. In the capitals and over the greater part of its territory, the revolution treated its enemies with a magnanimity which was still to last for some months.

THE ARMISTICE

The Council of People's Commissars was beginning its difficult struggle for peace.

The risks implicit in its initiatives were colossal. Could anything at all accurate be known about the internal situation of the other belligerent nations? Suppose that the Bolsheviks' calculations were correct, based as they were on their faith in the revolutionary proletariat and their sure knowledge of the devastation among the contending nations: then their tactic of audacity was the right one, for it could only assist in the maturation of events. But what if they were wrong? Supposing that they were wrong even on the degree to which events had matured? Would not the generals of the Central Powers reply to the armistice proposals by an overwhelming offensive against an army so obviously disintegrating, whose officers were no longer obeyed, whose soldiers were demobilizing themselves in entire units to return to their villages, without waiting for orders? The Bolsheviks seemed to be burning the revolution's boats. If Germany was still powerful enough to reject the peace proposals, would the Bolsheviks on their side be able to undertake the revolutionary war which they accepted in principle?

23. Some of the Soviet delegation to the Brest-Litovsk talks. Standing, left to right: W. Lipsky (Red Army General Staff); P. Stuchka; Trotsky; L. Karakhan, the secretary; sitting: L. B. Kamenev; A. A. Yoffe; A. A. Bitzenko

The success of Lenin's strategy in the struggle for peace should not cause us to forget the uncertainties amidst which action had to be framed.

On 18 November, just as the Stavka was collapsing, a special train went off to Brest-Litovsk with the Soviet delegation in charge of the armistice negotiations. It consisted of nine persons: A. A. Yoffe, a former political exile and Trotsky's old colleague on the Vienna *Pravda*; L. B. Kamenev; S. G. Mstislavsky, a Left SR officer and a talented journalist; G. Y. Sokolnikov; a woman, another Left SR, A. A. Bitsenko, who had lately been a terrorist; plus a sailor, a soldier, a peasant and a worker. Senior officers accompanied the delegation as advisers. Its secretary was a modest militant named Karakhan. When it reached the German lines, Prince Leopold of Bavaria came forward with a salute. The plenipotentiaries of the Central Powers were headed by General Hoffmann.[17]

These negotiations were a sort of duel. It was the first time in modern history that men so different, representing not hostile States, but warring social classes, faced each other calmly across a green tablecloth: polite, reserved, observant, dominated by a coldly calculating hatred. On the one side, embroidered uniforms, sparkling with decorations, the decorations of princes and generals: on the other, the insolence of a sailor's jerkin, a peasant's smock, a trooper's greatcoat, the blouse of the perpetual student-girl, sombre garments without a badge of rank, the plain dress of yesterday's exiles, who now had the sober bearing of victorious insurgents.

Each side's every word was carefully weighed. Over the heads of the generals, the Russians wanted to speak to the troops, to the masses; over the heads of the Central Powers, to all the belligerents. Their adversaries on the other hand were in pursuit of immediate and very practical objectives. The Bolsheviks' outrageous declarations of principle, read out impassively by Kamenev, were received in the same spirit. It was time to formulate concrete proposals; when the Russians were asked to present theirs, they were taken by surprise. Matters had been improvised so rapidly *nothing of the sort had been prepared*. They had to gain time. Hoffmann would not agree to speak first; he who makes the first proposal reveals his armament. After some reflection, the Russians proposed the following conditions; an armistice of six months; no switching of Austrian or German troops from the eastern to the western front; freedom of propaganda; fraternization among the troops; the Central Powers to evacuate the key strategic position of Moonsund.[18] This last clause was regarded by the Austro–Germans as an outrage, which, however, they submitted to without flinching. For their part they offered an armistice of fourteen days. They were taken aback when the Russians refused to accept this; the parties separated after agreeing on a simple suspension of hostilities.

When negotiations were resumed, the armistice was concluded on 2 December, for twenty-eight days, renewable for a further period. The Austrians and Germans were to desist from any movement of troops from one front to another, a pledge that was much more formal than real. The pact allowed the fraternization of troops in the form of 'organized contacts'. For a long time Hoffmann tried to keep this clause out, but Kamenev succeeded in having it included. 'Come now,' Hoffmann said to him, 'don't be so unreasonable: no prohibition will stop the troops from fraternizing.' General Hoffmann was a realist.

THE WORK OF THE SOVIETS

The period from the first days of November to the dissolution of the Constituent Assembly (7 January 1918) was marked, on the home front, by the economic resistance of the old ruling classes, by the political struggle around the Constituent Assembly, and by the struggle for peace. We shall have to analyse these three sets of events separately, although in reality they were aspects of a single process.

The general situation at this time has been outlined. A simple enumeration of the main decrees of the Soviet government will show the enormous amount of work accomplished.

10 November: Castes and the civil hierarchy[19] were abolished.

22 November: Warm clothes were requisitioned for the army.

26 November: The Commissar of Foreign Affairs, Trotsky, recalled twenty-eight Russian diplomats and consular agents in foreign countries (including all the Russian ambassadors to the Great Powers).

1 December: The Supreme Economic Council was set up.

7 December: The Extraordinary Commission for Struggle Against Sabotage and Counter-Revolution (known as the Vee-Cheka for short) was set up.

9 December: The Brest-Litovsk peace talks were opened.

11 December: The eight-hour day was enforced on the railways; the Commissariat of Public Education, which took education out of the hands of the Church, was established.

16 December: Ranks in the army were abolished; the Russo–Belgian Metal Company was confiscated.

17 December: The 1886 Electric Company was confiscated; the market in living accommodation was abolished in the cities.

18 December: Civil marriage was instituted.

19 December: Divorce was instituted.

21 December: Russian spelling was simplified; a code for the revolutionary courts was decreed.

24 December: The Putilov factories were confiscated.

29 December: The payment of interest and dividends on bonds was stopped.

31 December: The Institute for the Protection of Mothers and Children was formed.

3 January: The Russian Federation of Soviet Republics was proclaimed; a decree was issued for the organization of the Socialist Red Army.

It was a formidable agenda, a tremendous creative labour. Sabotage lay everywhere, and counter-revolution seeped through every crack. The actively counter-revolutionary elements were the big bourgeoisie round the Kadet party, some tens of thousands of officers, and the Socialist-Revolutionary party. On 6 November, Purishkevich, the old leader of the ultra-reactionary 'True Russians', was arrested. On his person was a letter addressed to Ataman Kaledin, part of which ran: 'The situation can only be saved by establishing regiments of officers and Junkers. . . . Authority is in the hands of a criminal mob who will only be brought to their senses by public shootings and hangings.'[20]

In a document drawn up by Trotsky and published by the Military Revolutionary Committee, dated 7 November, we can see the first intimations of the measures which will later form the system of 'War Communism'. The MRC notes that sabotage is driving the country into famine, and warns the wealthy classes that they are 'playing with fire'. 'They themselves will bear the first consequences of the situation they are creating. The rich and their abettors will be deprived of the right to purchase supplies. All their stocks will be requisitioned. The property of the principal offenders will be confiscated.' The working population is urged to boycott those responsible for sabotage.

At the beginning of December, the situation in Petrograd took a sharp turn for the worse, as a result of the ransacking of the wine-cellars. Drunken, angry, demoralized crowds menaced the capital with anarchy. In order to stop a riot from occurring, an Extraordinary Commission had to be selected, equipped with full powers.

In reply to the activities of the counter-revolution, Lenin proposed, in his speech of 1 December to the All-Russian Soviet Executive, to declare the Constitutional-Democrats (Kadets) enemies of the people. 'When a revolutionary class is at grips,' he said, 'with propertied classes who are resisting it, it must break that resistance. And we shall break the resistance of the property-owners by the same methods that they are using against the proletariat. No others have yet been invented.'[21]

Lenin was asked to confine the measures to particular individuals, but he refused; 'It is the general staff of an entire class that we have to strike at.' It was, in short, not a matter of picking on individuals, to weigh out degrees of justice. Milyukov's party found unexpected champions among the Left SRs and in Maxim Gorky. Once again, the great writer was misled by his love of culture. 'The Kadet party,' he wrote in *Novaya Zhizn* on 7 December, 'numbers the most cultivated men in the country.' As if the party of Thiers and Galliffet, in 1871, did not number the most cultivated men in France! Lenin's measures, in fact, were relatively mild. A few arrests followed.

A few days after this, after the majority of the Second All-Russian Congress of Rural Soviets had voted to support the October Revolution, the Left SRs decided to enter the government. Six of their leaders (Proshyan, Algasov, Trutovsky, Steinberg, Mikhailov and Ismailovich) became members of the Council of People's Commissars. Lenin believed that the bloc between Bolsheviks and Left SRs, who were influential in the countryside, 'could be an honest coalition, for there is no fundamental disagreement between the interests of the workers and the interests of the toiling and exploited peasants'.[22]

Lenin's general views at this point are best expounded in a speech he made on 22 November to the Congress of the Fleet.[23] Here are a few lines from it:

The oppressed masses are confronted with the most difficult task in the world: they have to build a state unaided. You see what powers of resistance the bourgeoisie has, now they are trying to block our activity by sabotage, the floods of lies and slanders that are poured upon us at every excuse and without excuse ...

We say: there must be a strong power, there must be constraint and violence. But we shall use it against a handful of capitalists, against the bourgeois class.

The labouring classes have nothing to rely on except themselves. We must have confidence in our own forces! ... Divided, the masses are powerless: when united, they are strong.

THE ELECTIONS TO THE CONSTITUENT ASSEMBLY

The elections to the Constituent Assembly, which had been postponed for so long by the Provisional Government under pressure from the bourgeoisie, took place in the middle of November.

Every class and every party participated in the elections, but with very varied expectations and attitudes. The bourgeoisie proper hoped for very little from the future Assembly. Numerous witnesses at this time recount its profound disarray: headless, leaderless, without a plan of action or a definite tactic. General Alexeyev's Army of Volunteers received no more than pitiful subventions from commercial and industrial circles: the military leaders were not understood, and individual egoism triumphed over bourgeois class solidarity.

Armed resistance to the revolution was in the hands of the reactionary generals and the military caste, a social stratum much swollen through the war. Among the career officers, the aristocracy and bourgeoisie were dominant; among the reserve officers, who were much more numerous, the intelligentsia and petty-bourgeoisie. It is the officers who are the virile elements of the counter-revolution. They laugh at the idea of the Assembly. For them, what has to be done is to organize loyal regiments around a new centre of authority and to restore order just as one makes war, without skimping the ammunition.

It was only the SR party that awaited the Constituent Assembly with an almost mystical faith. For long months this party had forgotten its revolutionary traditions and lived in a state of democratic befuddlement. Fortified by votes from millions of peasants, from the intellectuals and from the urban middle classes, and even from radical elements of the bourgeoisie, encouraged by the international Socialist movement and the Allied governments, certain of a large majority at the coming Constituent Assembly – which would assuredly be followed by a Legislative Assembly! – the SR party believed itself to be the great parliamentary and governmental party of tomorrow. How could it not be so?

The prospect of an SR electoral victory embarrassed the Bolsheviks. Lenin wanted to amend the electoral law so as to give the vote at eighteen years, legalize the recall of candidates and delegates, and refuse the Kadets and counter-revolutionaries the right

24. Canvassing in Moscow for the Constituent Assembly, October 1917

to vote. But the Bolsheviks had themselves urged the Assembly's convocation, which would indeed have marked a step of progress under the Provisional Government. And the provinces were looking expectantly towards its meeting.

'Will we be any better off,' asked Lenin, 'if the Constituent Assembly turns out to be composed of Kadets, Mensheviks and SRs?' Other Bolsheviks replied that 'We shall be stronger at the moment when it meets than we are today.' Lenin gave in to the majority, but vowed that 'this error shall not cost us the revolution'.[24]

He expounded his ideas on the Assembly in some theses he published in *Pravda* at the end of December. These ran as follows. The Constituent Assembly realized the highest form of democracy possible in a bourgeois republic, and therefore had its legitimate place in the programme of Social-Democracy. However, the Soviets were a form of higher democracy, the only form ensuring an uninterrupted transition to Socialism. The reckoning of the votes was false, because it was made on the basis of outdated electoral lists that had been drawn up before the great changes in the country. The party that was most popular among the peasantry, the SRs, went to the polls on the basis of single lists when it was in fact split.[25] The majority of the people had still not had time to take account of the implications of the Soviet revolution. Fresh elections in the Army Committees, Provisional Committees, etc., indicated that political regroupments were still taking place. Besides, the counter-revolutionaries had begun civil war in the south and in Finland, 'thereby removing any possibility of settling the most pressing questions by methods of formal democracy'.

These questions could be settled only by the complete victory of the workers and peasants, by the 'pitiless suppression of the slave-owners' rebellion'. To consider the Constituent Assembly outside the class struggle and the civil war was to take the viewpoint of the bourgeoisie. If the Constituent Assembly 'opposes Soviet power it is condemned to inevitable political death'. 'The interests of the revolution take precedence over the formal rights of the Constituent Assembly.' In order to resolve the crisis, the people must use their right to re-elect the members of the Assembly, and the Assembly itself must declare itself for the Soviets and against the counter-revolution. Otherwise 'the crisis can be resolved only by reactionary methods'.[26]

The elections were over by the end of November, and showed the following results on 30 December: 520 delegates were elected, of whom 161 were Bolsheviks, 267 SRs, forty-one Ukrainian SRs and Mensheviks, fifteen Kadets, three Mensheviks and thirty-three (most of these SR) from national minorities or small parties.[27] 36,262,560 voters took part in the ballot, with the following distribution of votes:

		per cent
Bourgeois parties (Kadets, etc.)	4,600,000	13
SRs	20,900,000	58
Mensheviks	1,700,000	4
Bolsheviks	9,023,963	25

Thus the Mensheviks and SRs together obtained 22,600,000 votes, or sixty-two per cent of the total. These figures, from a work of N. V. Svyatitsky,[28] an SR, were discussed by Lenin in 1919 in a remarkable study entitled *The Elections to the Constituent Assembly and the Dictatorship of the Proletariat*. The figures speak volumes if they are read aright. The rural areas had voted for SRs, the industrial cities for the Bolsheviks. The immense majority of the proletariat had gone over to the Bolsheviks. (The relatively imposing Menshevik vote was misleading, as they obtained 800,000 non-proletarian votes from their base in the Caucasus.) For the two capitals, Moscow and Petrograd, the combined results were:

Kadets	515,000
SRs	218,000
Bolsheviks	837,000
	1,570,000

The distribution of votes in the army and fleet was equally significant:

SRs	1,885,000
Kadets	51,000
National minorities	756,000
Bolsheviks	1,791,000

'More than half the army,' concluded Lenin, 'was with the Bolsheviks, or we could not have won.' Another decisive fact he noted was that on the fronts nearest the capital, which were the best informed and most decisive sections, i.e. on the western and the northern front, the Bolsheviks had an overwhelming majority: a million votes to 420,000 for the SRs.

Thus, although the Bolsheviks had only gathered a *quarter* of the votes, they were certain to win because of the distribution of their forces.

Have a crushing majority at the critical points at the decisive moment: this rule for military success also applies to political success, above all in the bitter class war which is called revolution.

In all the capitalist countries, the forces of the proletariat are infinitely greater than its numerical strength as a proportion of the population. The proletariat has economic domination over the centres and sinews of the entire capitalist economy.

The votes of the peasant masses, said Lenin, can only be won by the proletariat after it has seized power. 'Political power in the hands of the proletariat can and must become the means of drawing the non-proletarian toiling masses to its side, the means of wresting these masses from the bourgeoisie and the petty-bourgeois parties.'

Lenin was not to draw these lessons until the following year. In the days before the Constituent Assembly met, the Bolsheviks, while extremely sure of themselves, made every possible preparation to break the anticipated resistance of the SR 'democracy'.

Our mistake is obvious, said Lenin. We took power; and now we have put ourselves into a situation where we are forced to seize it all over again.[29] He doubted the reliability of the peasant regiments.

THE DEFENCE OF THE CONSTITUENT ASSEMBLY

It was impossible to foresee how powerless, in the event, the petty-bourgeois democracy would turn out to be. We owe to a militant of the SR party the detailed record of the preparation for the defence and consolidation of the Constituent Assembly. These are fascinating documents.[30]

The author remarks that the Constituent Assembly was above all the ideal of the SR party, the party of the democracy: it was an ideal rather remote from the people, who preferred the Soviets, which they understood better. 'The Soviets are ours!' was the current saying. The peasants were glad to vote for the SR party, 'their' party, and were quite definite that they wanted land: but they had only a vague idea of the Assembly, and even then as a means rather than an end.

Since the SR majority in the Assembly was bound inevitably to collide with the 'Bolshevik usurpers', they had to think of defence and armament. A 'Committee for the Defence of the Constituent Assembly' was set up, quite openly, in premises that were a hive of activity, in the centre of the city. As B. Sokolov admits, it was purely a committee of intellectuals, without contact with the workers or inside the garrison.

The SR party's Military Organization was much more a force to be reckoned with. It had a controlling influence on two regiments, the Semyonovsky and the Preobrazhensky, that were part of the garrison. Here it could count on as many as 600 of its members. It could also call on the armoured-car division, and published an anti-Bolshevik newspaper, *Seraya Shinel* (*The Grey Greatcoat*). Several dozen SR soldiers, who had been recalled from the front, were organized under the cover of a 'People's University for Soldiers'. There was also the Battle Organization of the party's terrorists, thirty or so hardened men led by one Onipko.

These forces were quite considerable. Had they been deployed properly, they would have been a power for the Bolsheviks to reckon with; since they were not deployed at all, they became demoralized and soon disintegrated.

The SR leaders, dominated by a parliamentary obsession hard to match in history, seemed to have lost all contact with reality. Sokolov's account of events is more comical than tragic. The SR fraction in the Constituent Assembly established an office not far from the Tauride Palace, in which it proceeded to a laborious work of preparation, under inspiration from Chernov and Avksentiev, the oracles of the party. Committees, sub-committees, working parties, all deliberated at length every day, detailing draft laws, studying the future democratic Constitution, preparing, in short, to legislate and govern, complete with an appropriate Western-style ceremonial.

Absorbed in their parliamentary antics, the deputies would not hear of any plans for resistance against possible Bolshevik violence. Their house was open to all. They had no idea of the invigilation being exercised over their telephone conversations. Dedicated to their labours, they never set foot in the barracks or in the factories, where their Bolshevik colleagues were busy recruiting.

The Federation of Employees and Public Officers offered to support them with a general strike; they turned down the offer. When the tasks of defence were mentioned, the reply was: 'Defend ourselves? Are we not the elected representatives of the sovereign people?' As Sokolov puts it: 'They thought that the Constituent Assembly was protected by some vague power: the great people of Russia would not permit any profanation of the noblest ideal which had sprung from the revolution. ...' Mouthing such words, they mistook them for ideas.

The SR leadership, and particularly Chernov, lived in this parliamentary hallucination, which was no doubt reinforced by the awareness of their fundamental impotence. 'The Bolsheviks will not dare ...', they kept declaring.

Gotz seems to have been a little less befuddled. He took an active part in preparing for the 'peaceful demonstration' of 5 January, which was intended to rally the streets for the Assembly on the day it had its opening. The SR Central Committee decided on this move only at the last moment. Everything was ready to transform the event into an insurrection. Thirty armoured cars were to advance against Smolny: the SR regiments would have supported the *coup*. But the Constituent Assembly fraction condemned the initiative just as it was ready.

Onipko's SR terrorist group made efficient preparations for the kidnapping, or assassination, of Lenin and Trotsky. Its members had managed to infiltrate the Smolny staff: one of them had become Lenin's chauffeur, and another was the porter at a house that Lenin often visited. An equally effective trap had been arranged around Trotsky. At the last minute the party's Central Committee refused to authorize these ventures. Their reasons? The two leaders of the revolution were too popular; their disappearance would have provoked terrible reprisals; besides, the era of terrorism was over. It was a strange mixture of political commonsense and sheer timidity. (All the same, two of the terrorists tried to kill Lenin, whose car was shot at with revolvers, on 2 January, in the city centre.)

In the factories under their influence, the SRs who came to urge a struggle against the Bolsheviks were rudely received. They were asked if they couldn't 'reach some better understanding with the Bolsheviks, who are devoted to the people's cause'. Through the work of the Bolshevik agitators, the Committees of the Semyonovsky and Preobrazhensky Regiments eventually gave way.

The demonstration of 5 January was both numerous and pathetic.[31] It was attended *en masse* by the petty-bourgeois citizens, who thronged the main thoroughfares of the city. A few rifle-shots fired here and there by the sailors scattered this ineffectual crowd, deserted and disarmed as it was by irresolute leaders. In Sokolov's words, 'it was absurd, ridiculous'. He judges that the Bolsheviks would not have had the forces at their disposal to resist an armed demonstration that was led vigorously. This assessment is doubtless very misguided; all the same, the nervous fatigue among the masses that follows their greatest efforts sometimes makes it difficult for them to renew the pace. The weariness of the Petrograd proletariat might have put the situation in the balance for a day or so.

Meeting in this atmosphere of botched insurrection, the Constituent Assembly felt itself doomed. All that was left of its old illusions was a mixture of fear, stoic resignation and posturing. The delegates had nothing to do except vanish gracefully, posing before history and enunciating memorable words. Such at least, seems to have been the principal concern of the first Parliament of the Russian petty-bourgeoisie, this most piteous of parliamentary assemblies.

A number of us from the Chamber came to ask our leaders, 'If the Bolsheviks use violence, hit us, kill us even, what is to be done?' A very definite answer was made to us, which perfectly fitted the ideology of our fraction: 'Let us remember that we are the people's elected representatives ... and must be ready for the sacrifice of our lives.'

The deputies decided not to separate, so as to be ready to confront tragedy together. And they assembled a stock of ... sandwiches and candles – in case the Bolsheviks cut off electricity and supplies.

To sum up, the SR party, on the day of the Constituent Assembly, lost its nerve at the moment it was due to launch its decisive battle before history. The bloody failures of the resistance to the revolution in Moscow, the Junkers' *coup* and the Stavka's struggle had produced their effect. The politicians of the democratic counter-revolution trembled before the masses.

THE COLLAPSE OF THE ASSEMBLY

Y. M. Sverdlov, the Chairman of the All-Russian Soviet Executive,[32] opened the session of the Constituent Assembly. A tall, broad-shouldered man, his thick hair brushed back from his forehead, his features clear and delicate, his eyes sharp and steely behind pince-nez, his beard pointed: Sverdlov, who was one of the best organizers in the Bolshevik party, had no difficulty in quelling the indescribable din in the first minutes of the gathering. The huge hall of the Tauride Palace, newly decorated for the occasion, had a festive air. Smartly dressed, with red ribbons in their button-holes, the deputies of the majority filled the benches of the right and the centre of the hall. The less numerous left side, on the other hand, had noisy support from the public galleries, which were thronged with soldiers, sailors and workers.

Sverdlov proposed that the Assembly should endorse the 'Declaration of the Rights of the Labouring and Exploited Masses', an authoritative document composed by Lenin and promulgated by the All-Russian Soviet Executive. In it Russia was proclaimed to be a Federative Republic of Soviets, 'a free union of free nations'. According to the text, the Assembly was to associate itself unreservedly with the Socialist revolution; approve the nationalization of the land, 'distributed to the toilers, without payment, on the basis of equal access and use'; approve the Soviet laws on workers' control of production and the establishment of the Supreme Economic Council 'to consolidate the power of the workers over their exploiters and as a first step towards total expropriation' of the means of production and transport; approve the nationalization of the banks; decree the universal obligation to labour, the formation of a Socialist Red Army and the total disarmament of the propertied classes. In the international field, the Decree once again affirmed the principle of a democratic peace, without annexations or indemnities, the repudiation of the colonial politics of bourgeois society, and 'the annulment of the debts owed by the Tsar, the landlords and the bourgeoisie, as a first blow against the international bankers and finance capital'. Finally, the Assembly was to decree that the exploiters could have no place in any of the institutions of authority. It was to limit its own work to 'the general elaboration of the fundamental principles for the Socialist transformation of society'.

The majority did not regard this as their function. Once Sverdlov had finished reading the declaration, they refused any discus-

25. Sverdlov

sion, on the grounds that 'too much time was being wasted', and passed on to the election of a Chairman. The Left (Bolsheviks and Left SRs) proposed the Left SR leader Maria Spiridonova, the former terrorist, whose excellent character and total Socialist dedication were known to all. The majority had previously fixed its choice on V. M. Chernov, the official head of the SR party, its most discredited politician and the least respected by the other parties: a candidate that nobody wanted, in fact. The SRs, in the belief that a Jew could not assume the leading office in their 'popular republic', failed to nominate Abraham Gotz for the chairmanship, though he was their real and respected leader. Chernov was elected by 244 votes, against 153 for Maria Spiridonova. He at once ascended the rostrum to deliver an inordinately long and rambling presidential speech, with the flavour of a ministerial announcement. It was a masterpiece of sweet evasiveness. The speaker invoked the Zimmerwald Conference,[33] advocated 'a general peace of the peoples' as distinct from a separate peace (thereby hiding his loyalty to the Allies beneath the flowery language of Socialist rhetoric), and spoke of the 'Socialist army' which had to be organized. He outlined a complicated constitution which envisaged the collaboration of the Constituent Assembly with the Soviets and the Constituent Assemblies of the different nationalities, proclaimed the definite liberation of the Ukraine and the Russian Moslems, and announced the Popular Federative Republic of Russia. Several times he touched upon the nation's 'will for Socialism', remarking, 'The revolution has merely begun. . . . The people want actions, not words . . . socialism is not equality among poverty. . . . We desire controlled Socialist construction. . . . We shall pass from the control of production to the republic of labour. . . .' Finally, he endorsed the nationalization of the land without compensation.

He was then inept enough to invoke the dead, fallen for the nation in war, at which point he was interrupted by shouts from the galleries and from the benches on the left:

'Murdered by Rudnev,[34] Chernov and Kerensky!'

Chernov's variety of Radical-Socialist eloquence, diplomatic and empty, couched entirely in vague formulas, could now deceive nobody. Bukharin refuted his 'chatter' in a short speech, as brutal as the other had been unctuous. 'How,' he asked, 'can a man talk of the "will to Socialism" and at the same time be the assassin of Socialism?' Was it a matter of a Socialism to be won in two centuries? Of Socialists who were collaborating with the counter-revolution? Which side are you on – with Kaledin and the bourgeoisie, or with the workers, soldiers and peasants? Who is to have the power now? 'Is what you want a miserable little bourgeois parliamentary republic? In the name of the great Soviet republic of labour, we declare war to the death on such a government!' Bukharin concluded: 'Let the ruling classes and their servants tremble before the Communist revolution. The workers have nothing to lose but their chains!'

Tseretelli, the only Menshevik present, presented his party's position with firmness and dignity, and without any attempt to evade: 'He is not a Socialist who incites the proletariat to aim for its final goal without having passed through the stage of democracy which alone can make it strong.' You have taken over production, he challenged the Bolsheviks: have you succeeded in organizing it? The land taken by the peasants has in reality been taken by the kulaks, the rich peasants who possess the farming equipment. Your peace negotiations are risking the destiny of Russian Socialism and democracy on the hazardous throw of a European revolution. You are trampling under foot the bourgeois-democratic freedoms for which we have gone to the gallows. The revolution is in danger of collapsing under the burden it has massed. My party, he said, is not afraid of unpopularity: we shall guard the torch of the working class for the future. He ended his address with an appeal for conciliation among the different parties present. No dictatorship of a minority, or the result will be anarchy, followed by reaction. Let there be instead: a democratic republic, with universal suffrage; expropriation of the land-owners, without compensation; revival, control and regularization of production by the State; an eight-hour day and social insurance for the workers; restoration of democratic liberties; equality for the nationalities, and a struggle for peace.

The debate went on, confused and stormy, but adding nothing to these first basic declarations. Then Raskolnikov,[35] to the applause of the galleries and the jeers of the majority of delegates, read out the declaration of the Bolsheviks which Lenin had drafted:

Not wishing to draw a veil for a single minute over the crimes committed by the enemies of the people, we declare our withdrawal from the Constituent Assembly, relying on the power of the Soviets to decide definitely on the attitude to be adopted towards the counter-revolutionary section of this Assembly. . .

After a moment of surprise, the Assembly proceeded with its agenda. Imperturbably riveted to the presidential chair, V. M. Chernov bent his greying forelock and his Second Empire goatee over the papers in front of him. An endless chain of speeches and declarations unrolled in the void. High in the public galleries, the crowd brooded malevolently over this wan gathering. At about 4 A.M., after the Left SRs had also withdrawn, with a declaration similar to that of the Bolsheviks, the Chairman was just reading out the ten articles of the 'fundamental draft law on the land', when the anarchist sailor Zheleznyakov, who was a member of the guard for the Assembly, came up to the presidential rostrum.

There was silence in the hall. The sailor leaned over slightly and said something which could not be heard. Shocked and anxious, Chernov flopped against the back of his ornamental chair.

'But,' he said, 'the members of the Constituent Assembly are tired too. No amount of tiredness can interrupt the reading of the agrarian law which is awaited by the whole of Russia!'

The sailor spoke again. This time his firm tones, ironic, unthreatening and calm, came out into the hall:

'The guards are tired. Please leave the hall.'[36]

Chernov looked down over the astonished Assembly. 'I have a proposal before me,' he said, 'to close the session without further debate, after adopting the basic draft of the agrarian law.' The phrase 'I have a proposal before me ...' provoked laughter from the galleries. Votes were taken hastily, solemn texts were seen off in a feverish hurry, to the menacing interruptions of the gallery, which chanted with insistent fury: '*That's enough! That's enough!*'

It was boredom, and sheer exasperation with the comedy below, that drummed this sombre fury into the brains of the listeners. Inside the hall, the catches of rifles could be heard clicking back. Comedy was about to turn into drama. But then the goatee of the Chairman could be seen retiring. The session was over.

It was not until the following night that the decree dissolving the Constituent Assembly came out.

> The toiling masses have become convinced by their experience that bourgeois parliamentarianism is outdated; that it is completely incompatible with the construction of Socialism; for only class institutions, not national institutions, can break the resistance of the propertied classes and lay the foundations for the Socialist society.[37]

Lenin spoke in justification of the measure before the All-Russian Soviet Executive. We shall quote a few lines from his speech:

> While no Parliament has ever, anywhere, given the slightest support to the revolutionary movement, the Soviets blow into the fire of revolution and say imperiously to the people: 'Fight: take everything in your own hands: organize yourselves!' It is a mystery to nobody that every revolutionary movement is accompanied by chaos, ruination and temporary troubles. ... But bourgeois society is also war, is also the slaughterhouse.[38]

The dissolution of the Constituent Assembly made a great sensation abroad. In Russia, it passed almost unnoticed.[39]

WORKERS' CONTROL OF PRODUCTION

The economic programme of the Bolsheviks called for workers' control of production and the nationalization of the banks. The decree for workers' control in industry was passed on 14 November. It legalized the intervention of workers in the management of factories; the decisions of the organs of control were binding and

26. Factory workers voting a resolution

all commercial secrets were abolished.[40] The leaders of the revolution had no further plans at this stage. By exercising its control, the working class would learn to direct industry. Through the nationalization of banking and credit institutions, the workers would recover, for the benefit of the State, part of the proceeds levied by capital from their labour, thus diminishing their exploitation. In this way the class would progress towards the complete expropriation of the exploiters (as envisaged in the 'Declaration of the Rights of the Labouring and Exploited People').

This rational form of progress towards Socialism was not at all to the taste of the employers, who were still confident in their own strength and convinced that it was impossible for the proletariat to keep its power. The innumerable economic conflicts that had gone on before October now multiplied, and indeed became more serious as the combativity of the contestants was everywhere greater. The initiatives for acts of expropriation, undertaken as necessities of struggle rather than according to any design for Socialism, came from the masses rather than from the government. It was only eight months later, in June 1918, that the government adopted the great decrees of nationalization, under the pressure of foreign intervention. Even in April 1918 it was envisaging the formation of mixed companies which would have been floated jointly by the State and by Russian and foreign capital.[41]

The liquidation of the political defences of their capitalist exploiters launched a spontaneous movement among the workers to take over the means of production. Since they were perfectly able to take control of the factories and workshops, why should they abstain? If they could, they ought. The employers' sabotage of production entailed expropriation as an act of reprisal. When the boss brought work to a halt, the workers themselves, on their own responsibility, got the establishment going again. Later, there was also the necessity to deprive the counter-revolution of the economic base it had in its wealth.

The Council of People's Commissars had to decree the nationalization of the Russo–Belgian Metal Company's factories, the Putilov Works, the Smirnov spinning-mills, and the power station belonging to the 1886 Electrical Company. Shlyapnikov relates how the management of some of the big factories – notably the Franco–Russian Works in Petrograd – immediately insisted that their works be nationalized: they wanted to get out of the responsibilities of demobilizing industry from war production. Belgian, Swedish and French companies made similar approaches, which were received with a categorical refusal. Some of these managers wanted to avoid answering to their shareholders for the increasingly difficult problems of organization in industry.[42]

The state of war had previously necessitated a system of rationing and requisitions. This path had to be continued, only in a class spirit. The Soviet authorities everywhere undertook the requisitioning of food supplies from merchants, and of warm clothing, footwear and bedding from the rich. Houses were raided for this purpose. Taxation was at a standstill, and so the local authorities imposed levies on the wealthier classes, purely on local initiative and for local use. The following examples will give a picture of the nationalizations that went on. At Ivanovo-Voznesensk, the workers took over two textile mills after sabotage from the employers. In the Nizhni-Novgorod gubernia, various enterprises were nationalized after the management had shown themselves unwilling to resume production. In the Kursk province, sugar refineries, tram undertakings, a tannery and several engineering works passed into the workers' hands for similar reasons. In the Donetz basin, the managers of the coal-mines joined forces with the Whites, and so the miners from seventy-two pits set up an Economic Council which took over their functions. At Romanovo-Borisoglebsk, the flour-mills and oil-works were nationalized following a lock-out.[43]

The Supreme Council for the National Economy was formed on 5 December to co-ordinate the activities of all the local and central organs which managed or controlled production. It included the economic Commissariats: Industry, Food, Agriculture, Finance and Transport. These Commissariats were not, however, subordinated to the Council, which acquired its authority only gradually, after months of work. In the period which we are studying, the local authority is practically the only one which counts. The trade unions, even though apparently fitted to play a capital role in situations of this description, were totally overtaken by events. Too often they were run by Mensheviks, SRs or pure trade-unionists. Their Central Council was paralysed by factional battles. The leaderships of the railwaymen's and post office unions were anti-Bolshevik. Other unions were often more interested in 'getting out of the mess' than in serving the general interests of the working class.

The backward attitude of various sections of workers was all too evident. Sometimes it was a matter of trade unions founding cooperative shops which came all too close, inevitably, to speculating in the midst of famine. Sometimes deplorable conflicts resulted from the pursuit of immediate demands in an irrationally sectional spirit. The revolution is over, let's have double wages! Now is the time for everybody to get easy money! Similarly, in the field of requisitions and expropriations, there were strong anarchistic tendencies, in which workers would exploit a factory they occupied purely for their own benefit, or confiscate the first food train which went through the station nearest to them.

The counter-revolutionaries were well aware of the backward mentality of certain workers and took every advantage of it. Manufacturers working for the State sometimes went to the length of implementing fantastically high wage increases. When factories closed down, the Mensheviks demanded payment of wages in advance. The Mensheviks in the chemical workers' union at Petrograd demanded exceptionally high wage-rates, hinting as a bargain ploy that they controlled large quantities of explosive.[44] At the height of the battle of the barricades, Moscow almost ran out of bread, as the loaders in the flour mills, who cared nothing for the revolution, were out on strike for a wage increase.[45]

The nationalization of the banks was one of the most important measures undertaken before the meeting of the Constituent Assembly. It was made necessary by the resistance of the financial institutions to outside control, their refusal to cooperate with the workers' government, and the part they were playing in the sabotage of economic life. The decree making banking a State monopoly was passed on 14 December. All private banks were amalgamated with the State Bank. The interests of small depositors were completely safeguarded. A second decree ordered an inventory of all individual safe deposits, under penalty of confiscation. Gold coin and bullion was to be requisitioned, and all funds were to be placed in current accounts at the State Bank. The banks were occupied by Red Guards, and any recalcitrant managers were imprisoned. In several areas the staff decided to go on strike against the Bolsheviks' violence.

On the day the decree was passed, there was a lively debate in the All-Russian Soviet Executive between Lenin and a member of the Menshevik-Internationalist fraction, Avilov. The latter, though agreeing 'in principle' with the measure, stressed the great complexity and seriousness of financial matters. 'We must touch nothing,' he said, 'without great caution and then after mature reflection, having assured ourselves the support of the various departments. All that violence will achieve is a fall in the value of the rouble.' Lenin's reply is as typical as the timidity of his adversary:

You talk of the complexity of the matter, and these are first truths known to us all. But anyone who uses this complexity only to interfere with Socialist initiatives is a demagogue, and a mischievous demagogue at that.

You accept the dictatorship of the proletariat in principle, but when we call it by its proper name in Russian, when we speak of *a mailed fist*, you bring in the delicacy and complexity of things.

You refuse to see that this mailed fist creates as it destroys. If we are passing from a principle to its practice, that is very much to our credit. ... We are perfectly aware that the measure under discussion is complicated. But none of us, even those of us with economic training, is going to try to administer it. We shall call in financial experts, but once we have the keys we shall get all the advice the former millionaires used to have. Anybody who wants to work will be welcome, on the condition that he does not try to reduce every revolutionary initiative to a dead letter.[46]

The central machinery of food-supply (cooperatives, etc.) eluded the control of the Soviet government for several months; they were in the hands of various democratic elements. They were too crucial in importance to be touched at the beginning.

THE BOURGEOISIE AND THE PETTY-BOURGEOISIE

The facts examined in this chapter suggest a number of theoretical observations.

(1) In January the proletarian and peasant revolution finished its initial phase, its march of triumph through the whole of this immense country. Everywhere, from the Baltic Sea to the Pacific Ocean, the masses make the revolution, hail it, defend it, impose it irresistibly. Its victory is complete: yet already, in this very period, it comes into collision with the two belligerent coalitions of imperialism, the Central Powers and the Allies. The civil war will continue, or rather be kindled again by foreign intervention. Victorious at home, the revolution finds itself face to face with the capitalist world.

Its victory at home, repeatedly won in the very different circumstances of Petrograd, the Stavka, the Ural, the Don, the

Kuban, the Ukraine, Bessarabia, the Crimea and Siberia, proves to be astonishingly easy despite the ferocious resistance it encountered. It is easy to see why: the revolution is the work of the most active, the most powerful, the best-armed section of the population, i.e. the majority of the proletariat and the majority of the army, which, moreover, has assured itself the sympathy of the great majority of the peasantry. This remarkable conjuncture of circumstances is due to the simultaneous occurrence of the completed bourgeois revolution – which satisfies the rural masses by suppressing the feudal land-owners – and the proletarian revolution in its first beginnings. The proletariat consciously completes the work begun by the bourgeoisie in its struggle for free capitalist development against the old regime. Having completed this work, the proletariat inevitably went beyond it, although with a certain sluggishness. The incompatibility of the exercise of political power with the absence of ownership over the means of production was only revealed gradually, in the course of the struggle, as a result of the struggle against the bourgeoise. The great nationalization decrees will be called forth, in a few months' time, as the result of the civil war rather than through any plan for a speedy Socialist transformation. Reality will bend theory, bend the proletarian consciousness which would have preferred a more rational, less hasty and brutal transition in the conquest of production. In the period we have reviewed, the first hints of this struggle and of its solution may be plainly seen.

(2) Through fear of the proletariat, the bourgeoisie has been unable to achieve its own revolution (that is, to satisfy the peasant masses at the expense of the land-owners): this is one of the deepest causes of its defeat. Through fear of the peasantry, it postponed the summoning of the Constituent Assembly under Kerensky, and formed a bloc with the feudal proprietors, the most reactionary element of the old Russian society. By trailing after the bourgeoisie, the petty-bourgeois Socialist parties condemned themselves to unpopularity. As they had received some revolutionary education under Tsardom, and were subject to a powerful current of influence from the proletariat, these parties remained far enough from the direct influence of the bourgeoisie to be prevented from giving it unconditional support. Victims of their democratic illusions, they tried to maintain an independent form of politics and establish a democratic republic conceived on the French model. The bourgeoisie itself was more perceptive, particularly in its assessment of working-class strength. They wanted a class dictatorship (Kornilov). But at the last moment the middle classes refused to support them: left to its own resources, which numerically were very weak (as always, the disparity between the capitalists' economic power and their numerical strength was enormous) the Russian bourgeoisie was doomed to collapse. From November 1917 to the spring of 1918 it appears to be

crushed, reduced to almost total impotence. It has no leader, no policy of any strength, and not one serious party. Its disarray is total. Alone, and in desperation, a few thousand men at the most, mainly officers led by a handful of generals, took up the defence of its cause. The terrorized bourgeoisie in the capitals was not even intelligent enough to give effective support to the escapades of Kaledin, Alexeyev and Kornilov: these, cold-shouldered by the democratic middle classes, were beaten by the Red Guards in every engagement. The very ease with which they were defeated arose from the refusal of the 'advanced' petty-bourgeoisie to lend them aid.

The division between the bourgeoisie and the petty-bourgeoisie displays the powerlessness of the class of capitalists and land-owners when they are thrown back on themselves. Once beaten, this class is unable to re-establish itself by its own efforts.

(3) This last point holds good to such an extent that a most curious re-grouping of social forces is detectable in these events: the bourgeoisie begins to follow in the wake of the middle classes,

27. 'He who does not work, neither shall he eat': the ex-bourgeois at compulsory labour, 1918

instead of leading them, especially as the latter's conflict with the proletariat worsens.

During the insurrection, the petty-bourgeoisie of the cities, led by Socialists, rallies wholesale to the counter-revolution. Those in the countryside, the rich and middle peasants who are appeased by the decree of land, fail to follow this movement. After its defeat, the urban petty-bourgeoisie, which still believes itself to be revolutionary by virtue of its hatred of Tsarism and its democratic faith, still clings to its governmental illusions without daring to venture on another armed battle; the experiences of the recent period (end of October, beginning of November) have cut too near the bone. The rout of the Constituent Assembly registers the total political incapacity of the middle classes,[47] and confirms us in our conviction that the only classes which are able to decide the destiny of modern societies are the bourgeoisie and the proletariat.

The development of the Russian revolution was closely linked with international politics. The autocracy collapsed at the moment when the Allied representatives, headed by Buchanan, the British ambassador in Petrograd, were cooperating with the big bourgeoisie and leading generals of Russia to engineer a palace revolution against the junta of Nicholas II, which had become a serious obstacle in the prosecution of the war.[1] On their side the Central Powers provided facilities for the return to Russia of Lenin and other internationalist exiles. The Provisional Government rested on Allied support. It promised the Allies that it would implement the treaties Russia had with them, and Kerensky launched the offensive of July 1917 in response to Allied pressure: this became a crucial turn in Russia's own crisis. Immediately following the insurrection in Petrograd, the Second Congress of the Soviets broke decisively with the policy of support for the Allied war. The Military Missions from the Allied Powers intervened in the Stavka episode against Bolshevism. Now, at the hour of the Brest-Litovsk negotiations, the destinies of the Soviet Republic had become an extremely serious international problem for the two imperialist coalitions.

The profound causation behind these international alignments is evident in a number of facts. The revolution was born out of war, but of a war that was in no sense Russian: the international significance of the revolution was determined by these origins, as well as by the characteristics of Russia itself. In the first chapter of this book we gave some statistics in support of the historian M. N. Pokrovsky's dictum that Franco–Russian imperialism can be dated as an entity from the end of the nineteenth century. It is a formula which needs amplifying. The pre-war Russian Empire is one of the five Great Powers of Europe (with Britain, Germany, France and Austro–Hungary), but among these powers, who are characterized by their financial expansionism, Russia is the only one which is not an exporter of capital,[2] being indeed a net importer of capital. By 1914 Britain had one hundred thousand million gold francs' worth of investment in her colonies and overseas; Germany had forty-four thousand million; French foreign investments in 1912 had reached forty-two thousand million, nine-tenths of these in Russia. Of the two-and-a-half thousand million gold francs' worth of annual income accruing to French financiers from their foreign investments, the profits drained from Russia into France are between five and six hundred million francs. Between 1891 and 1900, the development of Russian industry had been extremely intense. From 1910 Russia ranked fourth in the production of metals in the European countries, with a concentration of industry higher than that of Germany. Such are the results of the influx of capital: French, British, German and Belgian. In respect of the extent of its indebtedness to international finance, the situation of Russia can only be compared to that of China: it is virtually a *colonized* nation.

Even before the alliance between France and Russia, the Paris Stock Exchange had begun its conquest of the Russian financial market. The enormous loans raised in France by the Tsarist State sank another gold-mine in Russia, in parallel with the industrial investments. Meanwhile French imperialism pursued its strategic interests as well as its aims of speculation and colonization. French influence was probably crucial in the development of Russian engineering, an industry which devoted itself first to the opening of the Far East to Western trade, through the construction of the Trans-Siberian Railway (the Russo–Chinese Bank, too, was founded in 1895 by Witte with the assistance of the great finance establishments of Paris), and then to the transformation of Russia into a great military power for the coming war. A good part of the loans allowed to the Tsar by France were designated for the construction of strategic roads.

Statistics reveal with impressive eloquence the quasi-colonial character of the dependence of Russia upon foreign, principally French, imperialism. On the eve of the revolution, the Petrograd banks could marshal a capital of some 8,500,000,000 roubles. The share of this belonging to foreign sources was as follows: French banks, fifty-five per cent; British banks, ten per cent; German banks, thirty-five per cent.[3] With the big Russian banks as intermediaries, foreign finance companies controlled Russian engineering sectors in proportions varying from sixty to eighty-eight per cent; locomotive construction in the proportion of 100 per cent; shipbuilding by ninety-six per cent; sixty-eight per cent of machine-manufacture, seventy-five per cent of coal-mining, sixty per cent of oil production. The quasi-colonial character of Russian industry is strikingly displayed in a further fact: the production of the means of production (machinery and equipment) held a distinctly secondary place.[4] The war only intensified Russia's dependence on the Allied imperialisms, from whom a further 7,500,000,000 roubles (over twenty thousand million francs at the current rate) were borrowed in the course of the hostilities.

THE PROBLEM IN JANUARY 1918

An integral part of the imperialist system of the Entente – and its most vulnerable unit – Russia had by January 1918, after forty months of war, reached a desperate economic situation. It was, however, only a little ahead of the other belligerent powers in its positioning on the edge of the abyss. The situation in the rest of Europe at this moment was as follows. Britain, under severe rationing but amply shielded by its navy and its wealth, and well served by its colonies, had now spent some six thousand million pounds on the war, or about a third of its national capital. The expenditures of Austro–Hungary had been at least equal, and its ruin was more complete. Germany's spending was of a similar magnitude: eighty-five thousand million marks out of a total national fortune valued at 300 to 340 thousand millions. The total war expenditure of the belligerents had, according to the Carnegie Endowment, reached $208,000 million. These are colossal figures, and no figure can be given to assess the destruction, the deaths (about ten million at this stage, with twice as many wounded and mutilated), the growth in the mortality rates among the civilian population, the decline in the birth rate, the senseless waste of the labour of entire nations. The total cost of the war has been valued at $320,000,000,000, or 1,600,000,000,000 gold francs.[5] What is certain is that, in the fourth year of the war, European civilization appeared to be stricken to the heart. The Central Powers – Germany, Austro–Hungary, Bulgaria, Turkey – were reduced to living in a 'brilliantly organized famine'. In Germany, the harvest of 1917 had been forty to fifty per cent lower than the average for the years of peace: the soldier's bread ration therefore fell to 200 and even 160 grams per day (about seven and five ounces respectively). The consumption of comestibles had in general fallen by about thirty or forty per cent. The situation for the Allies was better, thanks to American support. The winter of 1917–18 was still a harsh one, with rigorous rationing and a fuel crisis in Britain and France. The area of France under cultivation had dropped by thirty-five per cent in 1917. All the countries suffered from severe scarcities of coal, oil, sugar, grain, chemical products and metals. The various military HQs watched helplessly as their 'human material' decomposed and deteriorated. The last reserves of fighting men in Germany, Austria and France had been called up.

After their shattering defeat at Verdun, with the impossibility of breaking the British blockade demonstrated in the naval battle of Jutland, the famished Central Powers made peace overtures in December 1916: these were repulsed by the Allies. Germany then decided to fall back on a tactic of last resort which had long been advocated by certain of her military chiefs, i.e. ruthless submarine warfare. This was in January 1917. Up till now neutral ships had generally been left alone by German U-boats, and so could supply Allied countries without running much risk. Henceforth they were sunk without warning. The declaration of war against Germany by the United States, whose commercial interests were threatened, now followed. America threw into the balance on the Allied side her immense wealth – she had just siphoned off Europe's gold reserves – her technical prowess, her admirable manpower, which was fresh, well-fed, well-equipped and well-dressed. Between February and May 1917, German U-boats sank 1,374 ships weighing over 2,500,000 tons. The tonnage of ships sunk in the whole year came to six million. But the United States alone was building ships at the rate of a quarter of a million tons a month.

The principal events in December 1917 and January 1918 are: in France, the arrival in power of Clemenceau, who, at the age of seventy-seven, was to govern dictatorially and succour for the war-effort the last energies of a half-dead country; the battles of Cambrai; the end, on 15 December, of the second battle of Verdun, which had gone on since 22 August; the end, a few days later, of the second battle of the Isonzo, which had gone on since 24 October; the battles in Palestine; and, finally, the message to Congress of President Wilson of the United States on 8 January, listing fourteen conditions for peace: end of secret diplomacy, freedom of the seas, liberty and equality in trade, limitation of armaments, settlement of colonial questions by reference to the interests of the peoples concerned, evacuation and reconstruction of occupied territories, return of Alsace and Lorraine to France, establishment of an independent Poland with access to the sea, and the League of Nations. In it could be seen a distant echo of the Russian revolution, a bourgeois liberal's transcription of the slogan of the Soviets: 'peace without annexations or indemnities'.

At this hour, the problem of the war is presented in these terms:

For the Allies: to hold on until the power of the United States is ready; towards this purpose, to prolong the operations on the Russian front at all costs.

For the Central Powers: to impose peace on France and Britain before American power has entered the fighting; to finish operations on the Russian front as quickly as possible, so as to be able to devote all resources to the crushing of the British and French.

For the Russian revolution: to play the game of neither of the rival imperialisms, but to hold on till the maturing of the revolutionary crisis in Europe, now heralded by numerous signs.

THE IMPERIALIST INTERPRETATION OF 'PEACE WITHOUT ANNEXATIONS'

The armistice that had been signed on 2 December at Brest-Litovsk envisaged the speedy opening of peace negotiations. On 9 December, the Russian delegation led by Kamenev and Yoffe and the delegation of the Central Powers headed by the Foreign Ministers of Austro–Hungary and Germany, Count Czernin and Baron von Kühlmann, with General Hoffmann, the commander-in-chief of the eastern front, met at the Brest-Litovsk Fortress. The Russians put their theses first. Count Czernin replied: 'The delegation of the Quadruple Alliance is willing to conclude without delay a general peace without forced annexations and without

28. Brest-Litovsk: coolness at the railway station

indemnities.' In principle, he said, his delegation condemned the continuation of the war for purposes of conquest, the position of the Quadruple Alliance 'having always been thus'. It desired the adherence of all the belligerent powers to these conditions of peace; and it demanded the return of the German colonies now occupied by the Allies.

The Russians then clarified their own position. 'Historical antiquity,' they said, 'does not justify the violence committed by one people against another.'

Was an agreement on its way? 'The Germans are inclined to make many concessions for the sake of achieving a separate peace,' Kamenev had told the All-Russian Soviet Executive on 27 November. But so far only initial probings had taken place. On 15 November (28, New Style) the Central Powers uncovered their guns; Article 2 of their conditions for peace contained the

The Russian government, having recognized, in conformity with its principles, the right of all peoples who form part of the Russian state, without exception, to self-determination, including the right of total secession, takes account of the decisions expressing the will of the peoples of Poland, Lithuania, Courland,[6] part of Estonia and Finland, which have resolved to secede from the Russian state and constitute themselves as completely independent states.

A counter-proposal from the Russians demanded the evacuation of these countries so that they could decide their destinies freely by themselves. The negotiations were suspended, and the two delegations separated for ten days, in order to give the other belligerents time to define their own attitude and examine the situation created by the peace negotiations.

This situation was serious. The Allies had manifested a hostile silence to the pressing appeals of the Soviets, which were addressed to all peoples and to all governments in the war. They were becoming increasingly inclined to behave towards the Russians as enemies. The Austro–Germans, once cheated of the hope (which actually they had never held seriously) of a general peace, showed themselves in their true colours: as imperialists devoid of scruple. Kamenev explained the background of the problem to the All-Russian Soviet Executive on 19 December. The Russians were offering to evacuate 120,000 square kilometres of Austrian and Turkish territory. The Central Powers were offering the evacuation of the Pinsk marshes, and were trying to hold on to 215,000 square kilometres of territory inhabited by nearly twenty million people. The frontier they drew up was purely strategic: it would have kept the road from Petrograd to Warsaw in their hands. 'All we are defending,' declared Kamenev, 'are the limits to which the Russian revolution has extended, not geographical frontiers which are the result of acts of historical violence.' He concluded:

We are faced by a peace imposed by the mailed glove, which would be a denial of the rights of the peoples concerned and an interference with the development of Russia. Such a peace is inadmissible for the Socialist proletariat and for a party governing in the name of international Socialism.

Would the revolution now be forced to wage a mortal struggle for the workers in the countries that imperialism was trying to wrest from it? The All-Russian Soviet Executive addressed a new appeal to the workers of the Allied nations: 'Your governments have still done nothing to make peace: they have not even published the aims for which they are making war. Demand their immediate participation in the Brest-Litovsk talks.' It was a feeble hope.

The great voice of the revolution seemed to be crying in the wilderness.

THE ACCOUNTS OF CZERNIN AND LUDENDORFF

The anxiety of the Austrian and German officials was no less than that of the revolutionaries. They were clearly aware that the fate of the Central Empires, in the outcome of the war, was being determined at Brest-Litovsk. The memoirs both of Count Czernin

and of Ludendorff give many significant details on this point.
Austria, now at the end of its strength, was threatening to conclude a separate peace with Russia or even with the Allies; it was
held back by a fear of German occupation and subsequent dismemberment (so Czernin relates). Germany's exhaustion was so
complete and the discontent at home so great that mutinies swept
the fleet in the summer of 1917, in which the sailors tried to force
a peace through coming out on strike. The disciplinary armour of
German militarism was crumbling. Morale at home was so bad
that the General Staff unsuccessfully demanded control over the
press. In the course of the winter of 1916–17 it had proved necessary in feeding the nation to replace the potato with the turnip, a
vegetable of far less nutritive value. The cruellest ravages of
starvation were avoided, in this land of 'brilliantly organized
famine', only thanks to the grain that came in from conquered
Rumania. In the winter of 1917–18 the problem of food supplies
was even more desperate. Coal and oil were short, and there was
not nearly enough rubber, a serious gap in view of the importance
now assumed by motor vehicles in military operations. The
Chiefs of Staff were alarmed to see their men physically wasting.
Ludendorff and Hindenburg delivered a serious warning to the
Chancellor on 10 September 1917: 'If the army cannot be sent
reinforcements, the outcome of the war will become doubtful.'

There were two contrary tendencies at work among the governments of the Central Empires. The party formed by the Austrians,
the Bulgarians and the Turks (for famine was even worse in Constantinople than in Berlin), along with a section of the German
bourgeoisie, wanted a genuine peace with Russia and the immediate resumption of trading relations. Surrendering before the immediate economic necessities, it realized how impossible it was to
continue the war. Czernin and von Kühlmann represented this
tendency among the negotiators. The other party consisted of the
top General Staff (Hindenburg, Ludendorff, Hoffmann), the
Kaiser Wilhelm II, the engineering and chemical employers and
the farming interests: these wanted the destruction of the Russian
revolution and the dismemberment of Russia, and believed that
in this case a speedy victory over the Allies would follow. Ludendorff's mistake was to believe that America was not in a position
to compensate the Allies for the loss of Russia. His plan was to
impose peace on Russia or deal the Russians a 'short, powerful
knock-out blow', and then to launch an irresistible offensive in
mid-March on the French front, before the arrival of the Americans.[7] He attributed the loss of morale in the army to the demoralizing effects of a lengthy defensive phase. On the matter of peace
with Bolshevism, Ludendorff had no illusions. 'Even in the event
of peace,' he was to write later, 'I know that we shall need large
forces to marshal against Bolshevism.' His keen perception as a
military commander was juxtaposed with an astonishing blind-

29. General
Ludendorff

ness when it came to social factors outside the State and the army.

There was a fearsome ripple across Vienna and Berlin when the Russians, who wanted the negotiations held under international supervision, asked for them to be transferred to Stockholm. The Austro–Germans were afraid that the Russians might break off the talks. Czernin notes that they were awaited with anxiety. There was immense relief when they came back. On their side the Bolshevik delegation had to resist a powerful temptation to break off the talks, in view of the growing internal difficulties of the Central Empires.

THE NEGOTIATIONS

The conference was resumed on 27 December (Old Style). The new Soviet deputation consisted of Trotsky, Yoffe, Kamenev, Karakhan, the historian Pokrovsky and the Left SRs Bitsenko and Karelin. The arrival of Trotsky, 'the man himself', who was already being surrounded with world-wide fame as a chief of the revolution, created a sensation, as Czernin tells us. We will not go over the detail of these utterly fruitless negotiations. The Soviet delegation stuck to its position of absolute respect for the rights of nationalities. When asked point-blank over the table which territories the Germans were willing to evacuate, General Hoffmann ('that gangster in a helmet', in Trotsky's phrase) replied bluntly: 'Not one millimetre.' The delegations parted again, and arranged a further meeting ten days thence.

Let us try to convey some impression of the confrontation made in these talks, virtually unique in history. Has the incompatibility between enemy negotiators ever been so vast? The negotiations were conducted behind the German lines, in the dismal Brest-Litovsk Fortress. The General Staff, ever attentive to small details, arranged hand-grenade exercises a few hundred yards from the Bolshevik delegates' quarters, to tax their nerves with the noise of the explosions.[8] The negotiators were well aware that they represented not so much warring States – the very word 'State', applied to the young Soviet Republic, caused smiles in the diplomatic circles of the world in this era – as incompatible worlds. It was difficult for the two sides even to find any language in common. The ancient fine points of diplomatic convention were lost upon the Russians, and the Bolsheviks' words of revolution left their bargaining partners indignantly uneasy.

30. Von Kühlmann

The discussions on the Quadruple Alliance side were led by von Kühlmann, Germany's Secretary of State for Foreign Affairs, a country gentleman with a senior civil servant's face and an insolent and freezing politeness. Trotsky was quick to note both the quickness and the limitations of his intelligence. He came to Brest-Litovsk as though to a comedy whose script had been prepared beforehand. It was his opinion that the Bolsheviks were desperate, out to buy the favour of the Hohenzollerns at all costs, and would seek only to preserve some appearance. (It was the opinion, too, for a brief while of all Europe's leading statesmen.) Once this hypothesis was no longer tenable, he fell back on another, which was comprehensible to his career diplomat's mentality: that the Bolsheviks were from the outset in league with the Entente, and, once again, were only there to put up a show. 'We had over our opponents,' wrote Trotsky, 'one infinite advantage: we understood them much better than they understood us.'[9]

At von Kühlmann's side the tall and massive hulk of General Hoffmann was often to be seen: a large face, smooth and with pince-nez, all very German. A key figure in the General Staff, Hoffmann aimed for a hardness of character which was intended to be Bismarckian. As for Count Czernin, long and thin, with a 'pacifist' reputation, he was incapable of doing anything but follow his two colleagues, even though he disagreed with them (not that they failed to disagree with each other). 'The Turkish delegates,' Trotsky reports, 'were straightforward enough to ask us, in the middle of a sitting of their commission, to spit on principles and get down to business. As they said these words, they put on the artful look of old and experienced counterfeiters.'[10] Facing these individuals were Trotsky, Yoffe, Karakhan, Kamenev and their friends: veterans of prison, of exile, of riots, 'soldiers of the revolution', in their own description of themselves, men utterly alien from 'a career'. Karl Radek showed up at the end, as the representative of the Polish Social-Democrats.

The tone of the discussions was inevitably somewhat sour. Between Trotsky, particularly, and von Kühlmann and Hoffmann there was a continuous duel in which the dialectical skill of the former stood out in exasperating relief. The quotation of a few exchanges will give some idea of the discussion that went on, and form a useful indication for the reader of the character of the contest.

VON KÜHLMANN: Every peace treaty has to be preceded by some kind of preamble saying that the state of war is at an end and that the two parties henceforth desire to live in peace and concord. .... I suppose that discussion on this point is superfluous.

TROTSKY: I will permit myself to propose the deletion of sentence two of the draft, which by reason of its profoundly conventional and decorative character is out of keeping, I think, with the severely practical purpose of this document [Session of the Political Commission, 29 December (11 January, New Style)].

At the same session Trotsky emphasized the significance of the evacuation of Persia by Russian troops:

VON KÜHLMANN: As Persia is not represented here, and is not, generally speaking, a participant in these negotiations, I think it would be best to leave this question out.

TROTSKY: Most unfortunately for that country, Persia is actually only the object of negotiations.

When von Kühlmann spoke of enlarging the debate on this same point:

TROTSKY: If the question was to be pursued so widely, I should feel forced to mention certain other neutral countries: Belgium, for instance...

General Hoffmann ('I am here as the representative of the German Army!') made regular protests about the Bolshevik propaganda among the troops of the Central Powers. Trotsky made the following disdainful reply to him at the session of 30 December (12 January):

I deeply regret that I have been unable to understand the attitude of General Hoffmann. To my mind, it must spring from our profoundly divergent points of view. I may say that the nature of this difference is amply registered in a verdict pronounced against me during the war. Its precise wording is located in the archives of the tribunal either at Leipzig or at Stuttgart, I am no longer sure which.

Von Kühlmann asks General Hoffmann at this point: 'Would you like to say something?' Hoffmann answers, 'No, that is enough.'

On another day the Central Powers were trying to get Russia to recognize the right of the bourgeois local institutions of Poland and the Baltic States to represent the 'will' of these countries. Von Kühlmann thought he had found one very powerful argument:

VON KÜHLMANN: If, following the orator who has just preceded me, I may touch on the question of India, I should like to ask this gentleman whether he does not consider that, in the event of the evacuation of India by the English troops, the Nizam of Hyderabad would have to be presumed the representative of the Hindu people, if this same people were not able to appeal to the results of a general election?
TROTSKY: I do not have the slightest guarantee that the Nizam will not disappear too, with the end of British rule. In any case, I should like to wait until the stability of his position is attested.

As the determined adversaries of all secret diplomacy, the Bolsheviks had insisted on the publication of the stenographic transcript of the negotiations. Over the helmeted, masked heads of the plenipotentiaries of German imperialism, they would speak to the peoples. Each of their words were heard a long way off, as events were shortly to prove. Von Kühlmann and Hoffmann made numerous protests against the agitational speeches made by Trotsky and Kamenev. They made hasty efforts to have the transcripts edited, but incidents resulted from this which were not to their advantage. Nothing could be more extraordinary than the impromptu theoretical controversies in which General Hoffmann

31. General
Hoffmann

could be seen as the upholder of an ideal bourgeois justice, re-proaching the Bolsheviks for ruling by force. On this point there was a full debate, where the incompetent manglings of the text made the general look even worse.

I must observe [Trotsky said in the Political Commission on 1 January (14 January, New Style)] that General Hoffmann has been quite right to say that our government rests on force. Up to the present moment there have been no other varieties of government in the whole of history. It will always be so, as long as society is composed of hostile classes. But what makes our actions amaze and alarm the governments of other countries is that, instead of arresting strikers, we arrest the employers who organize lock-outs: instead of shooting the peasants who demand land, we arrest and we shoot the landlords and the officers who try to fire upon the peasants...

By 5 January (18, New Style), the talks were at a dead end: the Central Powers were infuriated with the Bolshevik agitation, and the Bolsheviks were faced with the necessity either of continuing an impossible war or of submitting to a disastrous, outrageous and demoralizing peace.

LENIN IN A MINORITY

In this choice, there was no question of principle for the Bolsheviks, who were remote from the illusions of pacifism. As long ago as April 1916, Lenin, in foreseeing the victory of Socialism in one or a few countries, had envisaged the possibility even of offensive wars waged by the Socialist country or countries against the capitalist countries.[11] In April 1917 he wrote that if power belonged to the Soviets 'we would consent to a revolutionary war against any capitalist country because that would in fact be war against the interests of capitalism, not war for the interests of the capitalists of one country'.[12] The principles were not in doubt. But the army was demobilizing itself, the soldiers were going home. The masses no longer wanted to fight. The October insur-rection had been made in the name of peace. The transport system was at its last gasp, production profoundly disorganized, food supplies in an atrocious condition. Famine was more of a danger than ever.

A report of the Tenth Army stated: 'The infantry and the artillery cannons were abandoned in the field.' 'There is no longer a fortified zone,' we were told in a message from the Third Army. The trenches are filled with snow. The material for the defences has been used up for fuel. The roads have vanished under the snow: there are only a few foot-paths leading to dug-outs, kitchens and German brothels. On one sector over ten kilometres long, nobody is left except the Staff HQ and the Regimental Committee.[13]

'Over two thousand cannons were abandoned in the front-line,' notes M. N. Pokrovsky. On the Russian side, the war was simply over.

The German peace terms were, nonetheless, unacceptable. The situation remained confused still, as there were considerable gaps in the reports about the spontaneous demobilization, and large illusions became fed by revolutionary enthusiasm. On 8 January (21), on the eve of the Third Congress of Soviets, an important meeting of leading Bolsheviks was held at Petrograd. There were three different positions in the debate. Lenin's was in favour of peace; Trotsky's position considered that revolutionary war was impossible, but wanted to provoke a breakdown in the negotiations so that any possible surrender would be the obvious result of German aggression; there were also the supporters of revolutionary war. Sixty-five Bolshevik militants attended the conference. Lenin was put in a minority of those present after he had presented his theses on peace. The partisans of revolutionary war got thirty-two votes, Trotsky's intermediate position sixteen, and Lenin's fifteen. It was the same situation at the Central Committee meeting on the following day. Lenin invoked the impossibility of fighting any longer, the lack of horses, the inevitable loss of the artillery in the event of retreat, the ease with which the Austro–Germans could capture Reval and Petrograd. 'The peace that has been offered us is disgraceful,' he said, 'but if we turn it down we shall be swept out of power and peace will be made by another government.' Germany is pregnant with revolution, his argument ran, but the Socialist republic already exists in Russia, and needs a truce in order to gain strength. Trotsky is asking for an international demonstration which will cost us heavily. We are already losing a Socialist Poland, and we are losing Estonia.

The safety of the Socialist Republic is well worth an indemnity of three thousand millions . . . If we really believed that the German revolution was likely to break out after the collapse of the negotiations, we ought to sacrifice ourselves, since the German revolution is superior to our own. But it has not even begun yet. We have to hold on until the general Socialist revolution, and we can only do this by concluding peace.[14]

Zinoviev, Stalin and Sokolnikov supported Lenin; Lomov and Krestinsky voted for war; the case defended by Trotsky, Bukharin and Uritsky – to drag out the negotiations at length – carried the majority. The same solution – 'neither to make war nor to sign the peace' was endorsed once again a few days later, on 14 January, at a joint meeting of the Central Committees of the Bolshevik and Left SR parties. This majority realized that resistance was impossible, but judged that a German offensive, if it came about, would provoke a revolutionary explosion on both sides of the front. The Third All-Russian Congress of Soviets, which met in the meantime, left the Council of People's Commissars with full freedom to act.

Lenin was in a minority then, and not only in the Central Committee. The influential local committees in Petrograd, the Moscow region, the Ural, the Ukraine, etc., declared themselves against his position. The norms of life in this great, disciplined party were so fundamentally democratic that its acknowledged leader yielded before the majority, while continuing ceaselessly to press his own viewpoint. Once more, and this time in his own party, Lenin was battling against the stream.

LENIN'S THESES

In critical situations, Lenin was in the habit of expounding his thought in a condensed format, which was both explicit and concise, that of a set of theses. These theses were never long, and he did not waste words. His theses on peace, consisting of twenty-one articles each of five to fifteen lines, is a model of this kind of writing. We will give a summary of them:

(1) The success of the Socialist revolution is guaranteed in Russia by the support of the worker and peasant masses.

(2) The civil war that has inevitably followed is still far from its maximum peak.

(3) Sabotage, corruption and other indirect methods will keep it going for some months yet.

(4, 5) The revolution needs time. It must have a truce lasting at least several months in order to defeat the bourgeoisie and take up its work of organization.

(6) It is impossible to foresee how long it will take the European revolution, though inevitable and near, to come to fruition.

(7) The first discussions at Brest-Litovsk have shown that the military party has the upper hand in Germany, and is giving us the alternative either of continuing the war or of submitting to an imperialist peace, paying a concealed war reparation of three thousand million roubles.

(8) The utmost has already been done to drag out the negotiations as long as possible.

(9) To make peace by yielding to superior force is not a betrayal of proletarian internationalism:

The workers who in the course of a strike accept conditions for a return to work which are disadvantageous to them and advantageous to the capitalists do not betray Socialism. Only those betray it who trade the assets of a worker's party for the benefit of the capitalists, and it is only transactions like that which are in principle inadmissible.

(10) We are told that, by making peace, we shall be allowing German troops to leave the eastern front, and this will be to play the game of German imperialism. But, from this point of view,

surely revolutionary war would be playing the game of the Anglo–French imperialists.

The British have quite bluntly offered our commander-in-chief Krylenko a hundred roubles per soldier per month if we continue the war. ... The correct conclusion to draw from the situation is that, from the moment of the victory of a Socialist government in one country, questions have to be posed not from the standpoint of which imperialism we prefer to support, but exclusively in terms of the best conditions to develop and strengthen the Socialist revolution which has begun. ... We never advocated defeatism except in relation to the bourgeoisie of one's own country, and we have always repudiated as inadmissible a victory obtained over a foreign imperialism with the aid of a formal or actual alliance with a *friendly* imperialism ...

(12) We are supporters in principle of a revolutionary war, but we have to reckon with real possibilities.

(13) A policy based on fine gestures in no way corresponds to the actual, existing relation of forces.

(14) The army is in no state to make an effective resistance to the Germans, who are quite able to capture Petrograd.

(15) The mass of the peasants and the soldiers are against the war; 'It would be an outright adventure, given the complete democratization of the army, to try to make war against the will of the majority of the soldiers.' The creation of a Socialist army will take months.

(16) Revolutionary war would only be permissible if the German revolution was due to break out within three to four months. Otherwise, defeat would amount to the loss of Socialist power ...

(18) To gamble the fate of the revolution on this chance would be an adventure.

(19) A separate peace will not weaken the German revolution: the example of the Soviets will have an enormous propagandist value.

(20) Peace would liberate us, as far as this is possible, from bondage to imperialism.

(21) A genuine revolutionary war must be an offensive war waged by a Socialist army to overthrow the bourgeoisie of other countries. Such a war is impossible at this moment. We have done all we can for Poland, Lithuania and Courland: the interests of Socialism take precedence over the interests of nationalities.[15]

Lenin's theory was accurately called 'the theory of the breathing space'.

TROTSKY'S THESES

A strong Left tendency in the Bolshevik party was already forming round the extreme-Left militants of the Moscow area (Yaroslavsky, Soltz, Muralov, Sapronov, Ossinsky, Stukov, etc.). Since the end of December the Moscow Regional Committee had demanded the breaking off of the Brest-Litovsk talks, and, indeed, of all diplomatic relations with 'all capitalist countries'. This grouping even thought that economic relations between capitalist and Socialist States were inadmissible. Better, they thought, 'to perish for the cause of Socialism than to bow the head before Wilhelm II'. A democratic peace would come through the rising of the peoples.[16] This doctrine was quite evidently based on a totally abstract revolutionary romanticism.

Trotsky's thesis was essentially different from this. He did not pretend that there was any possibility of a revolutionary war. But he did doubt that Germany, in its profound crisis, with its weary army open to the influence of the Russian revolution, was really capable of taking the offensive. It was necessary, he thought, to put the German working class and army to the test. To which Lenin replied: 'Very tempting – but risky, too risky.'

The press of the Entente made out the Bolsheviks to be paid agents of Germany, and the trying negotiations at Brest-Litovsk as a prearranged comedy to keep up appearances, with the bargaining already agreed.

> Here [said Trotsky] are the Bolsheviks dissolving the 'democratic' Constituent Assembly to make a peace of humiliation and enslavement with the Hohenzollerns, while Belgium and the north of France are occupied by German armies. It is clear that the bourgeoisie of the Entente would be able to steer the mass of the working class into terrible confusion, and even be able to mount an armed intervention against us more easily.[17]

The mass of the people had been in the grip of chauvinism for years. Within the working-class movement, the internationalists formed only tiny groups. If the Bolsheviks did nothing to neutralize the unease that would be created by a separate peace with the Central Powers, would not the attitude of the masses in the Allied countries be disposed towards an intervention in Russia? Whereas if the Bolsheviks only signed a peace when the knife was at their throats, any misgivings would disappear.

To this, Lenin replied obstinately, 'Too risky. Nothing is more precious at the present time than our revolution. It must be put out of danger at all costs.'

Trotsky argued also from the inner-party situation. Immediate peace could bring about a split, in which the departure of the best elements of the Left would inevitably reinforce the Right wing. Lenin answered, 'These fancies will pass. A split is not absolutely inevitable. And if it does happen, those who fall away will come back to the Party. But if the Germans crush us, there will be no coming back for any of us.'

'We remarked,' Trotsky wrote later (in *On Lenin*), 'that if there was only a twenty-five per cent chance that the Hohenzollerns would decide not to make war on us, or simply be unable to, we would have to take the risk.'

Events in Germany began to support this manner of reasoning. In the middle of January, huge strikes broke out in Berlin. On the 18th (31st, New Style), *Pravda* appeared with the headlines: '*It has happened! The head of German imperialism is on the chopping block! The mailed fist of the proletarian revolution is raised!*'

Revolution in Germany! A Soviet in Berlin! The strike movement covered Vienna, Berlin, Kiel, Hamburg, Düsseldorf, Kassel, Leipzig, Halle, etc. Soviets, which were soon to be dissolved, appeared in Vienna and Berlin. The munitions factories closed down.

'NEITHER PEACE NOR WAR'

The negotiations at Brest-Litovsk started again on 18 January. There the Central Powers found themselves fortified by the presence of a delegation from the Ukrainian Republic, whose orators delivered anti-Bolshevik diatribes which were listened to with pleasure by Baron von Kühlmann. The Soviet delegation did not resist the admission of the delegates from the Rada, which still controlled some territory, if only for a few more days. They managed to get a hearing, in return, for a delegation from the Polish Social-Democrats, consisting of Stanislas Bobinski and Karl Radek, who did not mince their words in attacking the regime established in Poland by the German occupation.

The German generals became more and more exasperated. Precious time was being wasted, was it not? Why be made fools of by Bolshevik agitators? 'I felt I was on burning coals,' wrote Ludendorff later. Meanwhile, the press was hostile to the boorish interventions made by General Hoffmann. The Austrians, alarmed by the gravity of their situation at home, threatened to abandon their allies and demanded relief supplies from Berlin. 'We are,' reported Czernin, 'almost at the point of catastrophe in the food supply.'[18] The strikes that broke out in the second half of January bowled them over. 'If supplies are not sent,' cabled the Austro–Hungarian Prime Minister, 'we shall have riots on our hands next week.' He was quite right.

Ludendorff would have liked to break off the negotiations, take the offensive forthwith, and thus provoke the establishment of a new government for Russia that would prove more compliant. 'Look how they are treating us!' he exclaimed. Hoffmann, red-faced, reminded Kamenev, Yoffe and Trotsky that the Central Powers were not the defeated side. The outbreak of the strikes doubtless inclined Wilhelm II to yield to his generals' protestations. A propaganda broadcast from the Bolshevik radio to the German troops, in which the Kaiser fancied that he was marked out by name for the vengeance of his troops, proved the last straw: Wilhelm ordered von Kühlmann to present the Russians with an ultimatum. All that Hoffmann desired was to 'knock them flat with an ultimatum'. In front of the Russian delegation he calmly unfolded his map where the new frontiers were already traced. This time, the Russians had their backs to the wall.

The meeting of 28 January (10 February) found Trotsky unexpectedly aggressive in manner. He made a brief speech which was intended purely for propaganda purposes:

The peoples are demanding an end to this self-destruction of humanity, caused by the spirit of greed and conquest of the ruling classes of all countries. If the war has ever been defensive, it has long ago ceased to be so on both sides. Great Britain is seizing colonies in Africa, Baghdad, Jerusalem. Germany is occupying Serbia, Belgium, Poland, Latvia and Rumania, and is taking over the Moonsund Islands. This is not a defensive war. It is a war for the division of the world.

We are against any further participation in this purely imperialist war in which the ruling classes are paying for their designs in human blood. We are equally hostile to the imperialisms of both camps, and we will no longer consent to shed the blood of our soldiers for the interests of an imperialist party.

Awaiting the hour, which we believe to be close, when the toiling classes of all countries take power, as the working people of Russia have taken it, we withdraw our people and our army from the war. Our peasant-soldier is returning to his labours to till in peace, from this spring onwards, the land which the Russian revolution has taken from the hands of the landlords and given to the toilers. Our worker-soldier must return to his factory, there to produce, not engines of destruction but tools of creation, and to build, side by side with the peasant, the new Socialist economy.

We are demobilizing our army. We refuse to sign a peace based on annexations. We declare that the state of war between the Central Empires and Russia is at an end.

This was what the Austro–Germans least expected. An extraordinary council meeting was called at Homburg Castle to examine this new situation. Those present were Wilhelm II, Chancellor von Hertling, the Vice-Chancellor, Hindenburg, Ludendorff, the head of the Admiralty and von Kühlmann. Their views were divided. The Chancellor, the Vice-Chancellor, von Kühlmann and the Austrians believed that the domestic situation, particularly in Austro–Hungary, did not allow the offensive to be taken against Russia.[19] The possibilities envisaged by Trotsky were thus very real. The generals, on the other hand, demanded an offensive, giving the following reasons: first, without finishing off the Russian front, it would not be possible to take the offensive against the British and French; secondly, the only way by which famine could be avoided in Austria was by occupying the rich grain-lands of the Ukraine; similar economic considerations dictated the occupation of part of Russia; thirdly, it was essential to inflict a serious defeat upon Bolshevism, which could otherwise make a military recovery. The Kaiser shared the opinion of his General Staff.

THE ALLIES AND THE CANCELLATION OF DEBTS

At this same moment, the Soviet government, in annulling Russia's foreign debts, broke definitively with the Allied powers. This was a necessary measure: it may even be said that it was one of the aims of the revolution. We have noted the profound, almost colonial dependence of the Russian Empire on foreign powers. The proletarian and peasant revolution, in lifting the yoke imposed by the propertied classes and by Great-Russian nationalism, could not bow subserviently under the burden of international finance-capital. There was, besides, no other way of avoiding inevitable bankruptcy except by cancelling the State debt, which now reached the stupendous total of 80,000,000,000 gold roubles. (In thousands of millions of roubles, it was made up as follows: foreign loans sixteen; long-term domestic loans, twenty-five; short-term internal loans, nineteen; indirect domestic debts, 4·8; various indirect obligations, about fifteen.) The debt account would have necessitated the payment, on 1 January 1918, of the yearly interest amounting to four thousand million roubles, a sum distinctly higher than the total income of the State in 1913 (which was 3,452 million). The amount of the debt now equalled two thirds of the total national wealth. Revolutionary measures were the only way of avoiding bankruptcy and economic bondage. Any agreements with foreign creditors would simply have intensified Russia's colonial dependence.

The abolition of the national debt was preceded, in a decree of the Council of People's Commissars dated 26 January, by the confiscation of all the share capital of the private banks, which went to the State Bank.[20] The decree of 28 January cancelled all State debts 'contracted abroad by the governments of Russian landlords and capitalists', with retroactive effect beginning in the month of December; dividend coupons for December were invalidated also. Article 3 read: 'All loans raised abroad are cancelled without exceptions and without reservations.' The securities held by savings banks, cooperatives, local democratic organizations and small shareholders (at a maximum of ten thousand roubles' worth of shares) were to be converted into a new stock issued by the Russian Federative Socialist Republic of Soviets. (This scheme was not actually implemented, in the event.) The Soviets were given the responsibility of deciding who were to be the democratic institutions and small shareholders who could benefit from the offer.

This was a sharp blow against international high finance and the Allied imperialisms. Ever since the October Revolution the Allied governments and their representatives in Russia had observed towards the Soviet government – which they still did not recognize – an attitude of sternly hostile expectation. They had refused any reply to the repeated appeals of the Soviet government

Тов. Ленин ОЧИЩАЕТ землю от нечисти.

32. Early Soviet cartoon: 'Comrade Lenin sweeps the world of its rubbish'

for a general peace. On the other hand, we have seen how the Allied Military Missions encouraged the resistance of General Dukhonin; the support given by certain French officers to the Rada in the civil war in the Ukraine had caused a diplomatic incident between M. Noulens, the French ambassador, and the Commissariat for Foreign Affairs; General Berthelot was encouraging Rumania's machinations in Bessarabia. Britain had interned two Russian revolutionary exiles, Chicherin[21] and Petrov, and Trotsky only obtained their release by threatening reprisals against British subjects in Russia. The press of the Entente coun-

tries greeted the Russian revolution with campaigns of slander
and insult, whose violence and prejudice can only be compared
with the insane attacks delivered against the French Revolution
by the English press, William Pitt and the Royalist *émigrés*. In
studying the documents of the period, one is taken aback by a
striking fact: the capitalist world's statesmen, journalists and
most enlightened leaders of public opinion *understood nothing*
about the Russian revolution. The most stupid rumours were
accepted by them as true. Their general opinion was that the Bolsheviks, a set of doctrinaire adventurers brought into power by
the chance results of rioting, would disappear in three to six weeks·
(later it became three to six months) as suddenly as they had
appeared on the scene. Nobody held out any future for them except the gallows. The Allied representatives in Russia shared in
this blindness, except for two men whose voices, flung against the
stream of opinion, had no effect on their governments: the American Raymond Robins and the Frenchman Jacques Sadoul.[22]

On 18 December, Buchanan, the British ambassador, declared
(in what was intended as a conciliatory speech!) that Britain
would await 'the establishment in Russia of a stable government,
recognized by the people'. The semi-official press in Paris and
London put its hopes in Kaledin, Alexeyev and Kornilov. It began
to instigate a scheme for Japanese intervention in Siberia. The
United States reserved its position.

On 31 January, two days after the dramatic scene at Brest-
Litovsk, with the Rumanian army beginning an offensive against
Odessa, tacitly supported by the German Field-Marshal von
Mackensen and with the explicit agreement of the French General
Berthelot, the Diplomatic Corps at Petrograd confronted the
Council of People's Commissars with an insulting and menacing
Note, the key passage of which ran:

The Ambassadors and Plenipotentiary Ministers of the Allied and
neutral governments accredited to Petrograd cause it to be known to the
Commissariat of Foreign Affairs that they consider all the decrees of the
Workers' and Peasants' Government on the cancellation of State debts,
confiscation of property, etc., as non-existent in the degree to which
these decrees touch on the interests of foreign countries.

The united front of the two warring imperialist coalitions
against the workers' and peasants' revolution was now realized.
The hints of possible military cooperation against Germany between the Allies and the Soviets, which came out during the worst
days of the Brest-Litovsk period, had scarcely any consequence.
The politics of the Allied representatives in Russia was dominated,
in reality, by their class-spirit: these were no longer British,
French or American diplomats or officers, they were members of
the bourgeoisie before anything else, and they never forgot it. The
partition of Russia began to be considered more and more seriously

by the statesmen of the world. As General Hoffmann was launching his offensive against the Russia which had 'declared peace' on him, Marshal Foch gave the American press an interview on 26 February, on which the French newspapers thought it best to keep quiet: 'America and Japan,' he said, 'will be able to confront Germany in Siberia.' Active exchanges were pursued in London, Washington, Paris and Tokyo concerning a possible Japanese intervention in Siberia, in other words the conquest of the Russian Far East by Japan. This plan collapsed owing to the resistance of the United States.[23]

For a brief moment the possibility of an alliance between the United States and Soviet Russia was mooted.[24] Trotsky made a formal request for American assistance. Jacques Sadoul took it upon himself to ask, in the name of Trotsky (who had not requested him to do so), for aid from France. On 24 February,[25] he managed to get M. Noulens to telephone Trotsky and say, 'In your resistance to Germany you may count on military and financial support from France.' Despite Sadoul's efforts, this support amounted in practice to precisely nothing.

'THE SOCIALIST FATHERLAND IN DANGER'

The Russian–German front formed practically a straight line from Riga down to Kamenets Podolsk on the Dniester. On 18 February, eight days after the close of the negotiations, General Hoffmann, in violation of the clause of the armistice which required the resumption of hostilities to be notified a week in advance, informed the Soviet government that a state of war had been resumed. The Right-wing press in Germany justified the attack by the necessity to restore order in Russia. Prince Leopold of Bavaria made a speech before his troops in which he told them that they were marching not to fight for conquests but to wipe out the contagion of Bolshevism. 'Germany,' he said, 'is from now on the rampart of European culture against the Oriental pestilence.' Ludendorff's intention, on the other hand, seems not to have been to topple the Soviet power, which (as we know today, but was not known then) would probably have been too much for his forces. He was trying to occupy the Ukraine and deal the Russians a 'short, sharp' blow which would gain control of all their artillery and material, thus making it impossible for them to re-create their army in a short spell.

The German offensive encountered no resistance. German troops advanced without firing a shot, using the railways. In a few days (from 18–24 February) they occupied Reval, Rezhitsa, Dvinsk and Minsk, and they invaded the Ukraine.

These were terrible days. As soon as they had the announcement of the offensive, the Council of People's Commissars cabled the Austro–Germans their consent to a peace. Everyone thought

33. Sverdlov speaks
to Moscow Red
Guards before they
leave for the front

that the Central Powers were not going to reply. An evasive answer came from Berlin: 'Put your proposals in writing.' The most common opinion was that the Germans were not making war now on Russia, but on the Soviets, that they might even have an agreement with the Entente on the restoration of order in Russia and that they would occupy most Soviet territory, probably including Petrograd. The last remaining Russian troops retreated in disorder in front of them, without even bothering to follow the order from the Council of People's Commissars instructing them to destroy arms and munitions if they had to draw back. If the Germans refused the peace offer, there was nothing left for the Soviets except to organize partisan warfare in the occupied territories. On 21 February it was proclaimed that 'The Socialist fatherland is in a state of danger.'

The order was given to mobilize all the country's forces and resources for revolutionary defence; to defend all positions to the last; to destroy all railway lines before the enemy's advance; to destroy all stocks of food, munitions and useful goods rather than leave them for the enemy; to mobilize the population of the towns to dig trenches under the direction of military technicians ('All healthy adults, male and female, belonging to the bourgeois class must join these detachments; those who resist will be shot'); to suspend the publication of all organs hostile to revolutionary defence, sympathetic to the German invasion or to counter-revolution, and conscript the staff of these journals for the work of defence; to 'shoot on the spot all enemy agents, speculators, looters, hooligans and counter-revolutionary agitators'. The seed of the Red terror was in this document. As with the French Revolution, it arose from foreign invasion and the sheer immensity of the danger.

But the peasantry in the countryside did not want to fight. Lenin had founded his entire theory of the breathing space on this fact, and he was right. The Germans advanced onwards without encountering any resistance and took possession of a colossal booty. In one week they progressed two to three hundred kilometres. Sometimes they had resistance from the Red Guards: a desperate resistance, doomed to failure. The passivity of the peasant soldiery contrasted with the enthusiasm of the workers, who by entire factories, along with their wives and older children (just as good for the fighting, they thought) poured along to Smolny to be armed. As for yesteryear's fervent patriots, quite a few of these now welcomed the Germans as liberators.

The Red Guards were now carrying out some of their extraordinary operations in the south under Antonov-Ovseyenko's command (capture of Rostov, defeat of Kaledin), and the Red troops on the Bessarabian front were beating off the Rumanians and keeping Odessa safe. It is worth noting, too, that in fact no terror took place, since the feeling of the masses did not favour terror for a war they did not want to wage.

The capture of Pskov, 257 kilometres from Petrograd (not a very great distance in Russian terms), caused consternation in the capital.

When the new Soviet deputation arrived at Brest-Litovsk on 1 March, they could not improve the situation. The Germans refused to call off their offensive until the peace was actually signed, on the date fixed by them, 4 March. The Soviet delegates informed their government that the Germans intended to penetrate as far as possible into Russian territory, but were using small shock-brigades which were easy to repulse.

In fact, the German offensive had its natural limitations. The partisan warfare, the destruction of highways, the difficulties of the supply line, the state of feeling of the Russian population, the formation of Red bands in the rear of the invader, the strikes, famine and discontent in Germany and Austria, all forced the German command, at the end of the first week of the attack, to face the prospect of large-scale, protracted, difficult and dangerous operations. They were fighting in unknown country against an enemy very different from all those they had encountered previously. All the plans they had for a quick Russian capitulation were now in doubt.

LENIN WINS

As soon as the resumption of hostilities was announced, Lenin proposed the immediate signature of peace terms, at the Central Committee meeting of 17 February. Once again he was put in the minority, though this time by one vote. Bukharin, Trotsky, Yoffe, Krestinsky, Uritsky and Lomov voted against him; Sverdlov, Sokolnikov, Smilga and Stalin with him.

The Central Committee had two sessions on the 18th, the day of the German attack. Two speakers took the floor for each position on those questions where there were clear differences. Each had five minutes – this was no time for long speeches. At the first session Lenin's position was again defeated by seven votes to six (this was on his demand for the immediate resumption of negotiations); it was defended by Zinoviev and opposed by Bukharin and Trotsky. At the second sitting Trotsky informed them of the capture of Dvinsk and the entry of the Germans into the Ukraine.

We are in a revolutionary war [said Lenin] against our own intentions. War is not a matter to be played with. This game has brought us to such a crisis that the revolution will inevitably crash now if you continue any longer with this dithering attitude. Yoffe wrote to us from Brest that there was not even the faintest beginning of a revolution in Germany.

Here we are scribbling away while they are capturing our stores and rolling-stock, while we are collapsing. ... History will note that you surrendered the revolution! We could have signed a peace and got away with it, but we have nothing, we can't even blow up the stuff...

The peasants don't want war, and they will not fight. A permanent peasant war is a Utopia. Revolutionary war isn't just phraseology. If we are not equipped for it, we must sign the peace.

The revolution will not be lost simply because we will be giving the Germans Finland, Latvia and Estonia.[26]

Lenin's potent realism, now terribly confirmed by events, carried the day this time by seven votes to six: it was Trotsky's vote that gave him the majority.[27] Neither Lenin nor the Central Committee dreamed of accusing Trotsky of inconsistency: indeed, he was given the task of drafting, with Lenin, the radiotelegram to the Germans. The demonstration he wanted to make before the proletariat of the West had now been made, the chance he wanted to try for had been tried.

The situation worsened from one hour to the next. The Germans made no haste to reply, but continued their advance aggressively, collecting their enormous loot. And the party became divided, as the Left militants of the Moscow district resigned their posts (on 20 February) 'reserving ourselves the freedom to agitate both within the party and outside it'. (Among those who resigned were Lomov, Bubnov, Uritsky and Pyatakov.) It was clearly a step towards a split. The party press covered up what had happened. Two days later, those who had resigned, along with the remainder of the Left, changed their minds, but declared that they would appeal to the Party Congress.

On 22 February, Trotsky informed the Central Committee of a proposal received from the Allies: France and Britain were willing to aid Russia in its resistance to Germany.

Trotsky believed that this offer should be accepted, inasmuch as the independence of Soviet foreign policy was safeguarded. Bukharin demanded its rejection. Lenin was not at the meeting, but he scribbled a few words hastily on a scrap of paper: 'Please count my vote *in favour* of accepting support and arms from the Anglo–French imperialist bandits – *Lenin.*'[28] By six votes to five, the Central Committee voted to do so. Von Kühlmann's reply to the Soviet note was discussed in the Central Committee on 23 February. It announced the stiffening of the German peace terms, to a considerable degree: Russia must accept the detachment of the whole Baltic area, Poland, Lithuania, Estonia, the Ukraine and Finland. Lenin, firm as ever, declared that 'the politics of revolutionary phrasemongering was finished': he added that if it continued he would resign immediately from the government and the Central Committee. 'If you want revolutionary war we shall give it you,' he said. Trotsky judged that the divisions in the party made revolutionary war impossible, and spoke in favour of peace, but he abstained in the vote: Lenin's thesis was carried by seven votes to four, with four abstentions.[29]

THE TREATY

Sokolnikov, Petrovsky, Chicherin, Karakhan and Yoffe came to Brest-Litovsk to meet von Rosenberg, the German ambassador, and General Hoffmann. This time the Soviet delegates refused any parley. 'We are here,' declared Sokolnikov, 'to sign without the least delay a peace which is being imposed on us by violence.' Again: 'The peace which we are signing,' he said to the session on 3 March, 'has been dictated to us at gunpoint. Revolutionary Russia is compelled to accept it with clenched teeth. . . .' He spent a brief time in frankly denouncing the character and class nature of the plunderer, and concluded: 'Any discussion is useless and we refuse to have any.'

The principal clauses of the treaty, which consisted of thirty articles, were the following. A bilateral undertaking to cease all agitation against the 'governmental or military status' of the countries concerned; the demobilization of the Russian army, including the new Soviet units; the renunciation by Russia of all interference in the affairs of the countries to the west of her new frontiers (all the Baltic States and Poland); the evacuation of Russian troops from the areas of Asia Minor they occupied; Soviet recognition of the People's Republic of the Ukraine and of the treaty it had concluded with the Central Powers; Russian evacuation of Finland and the Aland Isles (which meant the sacrifice of the Finnish revolution); the reciprocal repudiation of war indemnities – though Russia still had to compensate the Central Empires for the upkeep of Russian prisoners-of-war, the damages caused to Austrian and German nationals by the revolution, etc. (a total of three thousand million gold roubles). The exchange of war prisoners was to take place immediately, enabling Germany to recover her fighting manpower. Commercial and consular relations were to be resumed.

Once the peace was concluded, German troops continued their advance into the Ukraine, protected by the treaty; they marched right on to the Don, to the Crimea, to the Caucasus.

PATIENCE, NOT PHRASES

Lenin's policies in this turning-point of the revolution deserve to be thoroughly studied. Lenin put his case with great energy, as was his custom, in his articles for *Pravda* and his interventions at Central Committee meetings. The whole tenor of his argument was directed incessantly against the Left-Communist tendency. In an article of 21 February ('On the Revolutionary Phrase'), he set out to refute its theses. His definitions deserve to be quoted:

The revolutionary phrase is usually a malady which befalls revolutionary parties when these suffer from a mixture of proletarian and petty-bourgeois elements, and the course of events necessitates a sharp turn. Revolutionary phraseology consists of the repetition of revolu-

34. The signing of the Brest-Litovsk peace: Field-Marshal Prince Leopold
of Bavaria appends his signature

tionary slogans without any relation to the objective circumstances of a
given moment or situation. Slogans which are excellent, inspiring, intoxicating, but without any basis: that is the essence of the matter.

He went on to observe that the Moscow and Petrograd organizations of the party, which were advocating revolutionary war,
did nothing to oppose demobilization in time of war. The old
army no longer existed, and the new one had hardly begun to
exist. The phrases with which the Lefts were so lavish expressed
pure sentiment. The reasoning they invoked was simply pitiful.
They appealed to the example of revolutionary France in 1792.
But France only made war *after* her economic revolution; the
French Revolution pitted 'economically and politically backward
peoples against a people who had not been exhausted by a war,
and who had just gained land and liberty'. We have only just
finished a war and have scarcely begun the revolution. Our peasant
'still has not enjoyed one year of work in freedom (freed, that is,
from the landlords and the disasters of war). . . . Feudalism conquered, bourgeois liberty consolidated, a satisfied peasantry

marching against the lands of feudalism: such is the economic basis for the military miracles of 1792–3.'

Germany, we are told, cannot take the offensive because of the imminence of revolution at home. But even when our revolution was in full spate we were not able to stop the Russian bourgeoisie from launching an offensive in June 1917. The German revolution is maturing: to proclaim that it is already mature is no more than phraseology.

We shall be helping Liebknecht by making war, it is being said. Not by making war without effective forces: to start fighting without possessing the necessary effectives is sheer adventurism.

Our forces were no larger in October, we are told. But the masses were with us and we knew it.

Would we be ruined by the economic provisions of the separate peace? German imperialism is growing weaker, whereas our resources are growing month by month. 'The most disadvantageous peace is a hundred times better for us than the lot of a Belgium.'

The peace is disgraceful and dishonourable. Surely we would be betraying Poland, Courland, Lithuania and Latvia, handing them over to Germany? No, for the interests of Socialism take precedence over the rights of nationalities to enjoy self-determination. 'War must be waged on the revolutionary phrase, so that men will not one day have to repeat this bitter truth: the revolutionary phrase on the revolutionary war destroyed the revolution.'[30]

On the following day Lenin published another article on the same subject entitled 'The Itch', under the innocent pseudonym of Karpov. 'Phrasemongering,' he said, 'is a disease as tenacious as the itch.' The article was partly concerned with refuting the Left-wing argument that saw a desertion of principles in the acceptance of aid from the British against the Central Powers: is it possible to fail to comprehend the difference between Kerensky's arms purchases, made from the Allied pirates to continue a war of conquest, and the purchases made by Socialist Russia from these same pirates in order to defend itself against Wilhelm II? The difference is the same as that between a murder committed for theft, and a homicidal act of self-defence.[31]

In his article 'Peace or War?', published on 23 Feburary, Lenin wrote that 'It must be made clear that anybody who opposes immediate peace, even on the cruellest terms, is working for the defeat of Soviet power.'[32]

In a third article on 25 February ('A Painful but Necessary Lesson') he indicated the roots of the ideology of revolutionary warfare. The ease of the revolution's victories at home had been too intoxicating. The lesson provided by the week of the German offensive has been severe but necessary.

What an instructive contrast there is between the two sets of dispatches which the government has been receiving in the last few days. On one side we read a barrage of the most 'determined' revolutionary phrases. ... On the other, the heart-breaking, shameful reports of regiments who have refused to defend their positions, of failures to carry out the order to destroy all stock before retreating: not to mention the stampeding, the chaos, the incompetence, the incapacity, the waste.

It is a crime to accept battle with a powerful enemy when there is no army on one's side: peace is necessary not for capitulation but for a serious preparation for war. We must be able to help the Socialist revolution in the advanced imperialist countries. 'This revolution will only be damaged by delivering the Socialist Republic of the Soviets unarmed to the mortal blows of the enemy. Our great motto "We bank on the victory of Socialism in the entire world" must not be changed into an empty phrase. But every

35. Red Army soldiers reading newspapers

abstract truth, when applied indiscriminately to all concrete situations, becomes reduced to a phrase.'[33]

We should lack a full appreciation of Lenin's thought at this moment if we did not have a detail which Trotsky has recounted.[34] Here is Lenin, the supreme realist, the sworn enemy of all adventures. who weighed all possibilities to the full, never abandoning hope but keeping confidence and a blazing will, determined to hold on, whatever might happen, and win in the end:

And what if the Germans keep marching? [Trotsky asked him.] What if they march on Moscow?

Then we will draw back to the east, the Ural. The Kuznetsk basin is rich in coal. We will set up the Republic of the Ural and Kuznetsk, supported by the industry of the Ural and the mines of Kuznetsk, and aided by the proletariat of the Ural and those workers from Petrograd and Moscow who succeed in joining us. We shall hold on! If it becomes necessary we shall move farther away, even beyond the Ural. We shall go right as far as Kamchatka, but we shall hold on! The international situation will see many changes, and from our Republic of the Ural and Kuznetsk we shall return to Moscow and Petrograd. But if we get ourselves tangled up uselessly in a revolutionary war, and allow the flower of the working class and the party to be slaughtered, it is quite clear that we shall never return anywhere ...

PROBLEMS AND TACTICS

At Brest-Litovsk the October Revolution made its appearance in the international arena, face to face with the whole world of imperialism (for the Allies, though formally absent, still played their part). Lenin immediately discerned the essential objective for this conjuncture: *to save the revolution and gain time.* (Gaining time was synonymous with the salvation of the revolution, which would gain strength while the crisis was maturing within the imperialist coalitions.) Lenin's tactics were unflinchingly dictated by this consideration. His policy was inspired by a ruthless, unclouded realism whose keenness could not be led astray by any burst of enthusiasm. Neither the dazzling victories of the revolution in the interior, nor the great strikes in Germany and Austria, nor even the coming of the first Soviets (forerunners of revolution) in the Central Empires could blur his clear vision of reality: which was that the revolutionary crisis in Germany was still only maturing, that Austro–German imperialism was still very powerful. Hence his conclusion: to bank on the German revolution is to risk the very existence of the Russian revolution. Lenin's realism is all the more impressive in that he displays no *basic* tendency to overestimate the forces of the enemy.

No *basic* tendency: the point about the 'Republic of the Ural and Kuznetsk' confirms us in this view, as does the relatively slight resistance offered by Lenin against Trotsky's thesis, as compared with his intransigent opposition, more in the character of an ultimatum, against the proponents of revolutionary war. His sharp awareness of the fragility of Soviet power seems to move him to the idea that a German offensive could cause it to collapse. Today we know how critical the domestic situation was in the Central Empires, the few advantages and the immense difficulties they encountered in their occupation of the Ukraine, the astonishing vitality displayed by Red Russia. We may be permitted to conclude that even the occupation of the capitals by the invader would not have meant the collapse of the Soviet regime, in short that German imperialism, at that moment, was no longer in a position to destroy the Russian revolution.

This reality must be borne in mind in order to appreciate Trotsky's line at the time. His purpose was twofold, as has been seen: to exhaust all revolutionary possibilities and to convince the proletariat of the West of the intransigence of the Bolsheviks before Austro–German imperialism. The Central Empires hung on for nine months longer after the Brest-Litovsk peace, until November 1918, a proof of the error made in exaggerating the revolutionary chances in these countries during January and February, and a confirmation of Lenin's thesis on this point. But the necessity for convincing Western workers of Bolshevism's intentions before the Austro–Germans still stood. It is worth remembering how fearful were the war manias that still held sway over the masses of Europe and America. In the working classes of all the Allied countries the Socialism of patriotism and office still enjoyed unshakable majorities. The voice of the minorities who sympathized with the Russian revolution could scarcely be heard. In France, old Socialists like Varenne, Renaudel, Sembat and Albert Thomas were becoming increasingly outspoken as advocates of an Allied intervention in Russia. The parliamentary group of the Parti Socialiste Unifié[35] appealed to the Bolsheviks, in a message of mixed reproach, warning and advice, not to conclude a separate peace. The bourgeois press was unanimous in presenting the Bolsheviks as agents of Germany, and the Brest-Litovsk talks as a comedy played out according to rule.[36] In the eyes of the masses in these countries – and I personally remember many conversations to this effect with French soldiers – the Russians, in surrendering before German imperialism, were responsible for prolonging a war already hated by all. If this attitude among the masses had lasted, would it not have enabled the Allied governments to mount a large-scale and direct intervention in Russia? Trotsky's tactic was of great assistance in dissipating this state of mind. After the breaking-off of negotiations, after the disconcerting gesture of the Soviet delegates at Brest-Litovsk, after General Hoffmann's offensive against a disarmed Russia, after the signing of a treaty presented at pistol-point for all the world to see, how could a British or a French worker still believe

BETRAYED.

The Pander. "COME ON; COME AND BE KISSED BY HIM."

in the supposed collaboration between the Bolsheviks and Austro–
German imperialism? As Rakovsky said: 'If the signing of the
Brest-Litovsk treaty in its second draft put an end to the German
offensive, the previous refusal to sign it in its first draft spared us
an offensive from the Entente for a considerable time.'[37]

Through Ludendorff's memoirs and various statements made
by the German representatives at Brest-Litovsk, it is known that
the Austrians and Germans hesitated before launching their offensive against Russia. Chancellor von Hertling and Baron von
Kühlmann had stated their opinion that the situation on the home
front did not allow of an offensive. The generals carried the day,
thanks to the Kaiser's backing. It is still true, though, that the
Central Powers seriously considered a pure and simple acceptance

of the existing state of affairs. The success of the line 'neither peace nor war' therefore seems to have been a *possible* outcome.

By contrast, the line of revolutionary war advocated by the Left Communists and most of the Left SRs was impossible: it simply could not have succeeded. This is already evident through the very ease of the German invasion, and will become more so when we see the difficulties that attend the creation of the Red Army. What were the principal ideas behind this tactic? That of safeguarding the integrity of principles, and that of hastening on the German revolution by an active intervention. The first of these ideas, evidenced in the frequent use of words like 'shameful', 'dishonourable', etc., proceeded from an abstract and dogmatic conception of honour, alien to true proletarian realism: revolutionary honour is not put in question when, without abandoning the struggle, one submits to an unavoidable defeat. The second has its main source in a sentiment which may well be described as romantic. Certainly there can be no condemnation in principle of a revolutionary intervention which tends to quicken the final crisis of the class struggle in a particular country; still, such an intervention must be timely and must use substantial forces, in default of which its consequences can only be disastrous. A healthier tendency may, however, be uncovered in Left Communism during the Brest-Litovsk period, beneath its abstract and undialectical arguments, its emotional exaggerations, its dangerously doctrinaire thought: we may also see, to its credit, the fear of opportunism. It was an unjustified fear, since no real tendency

37. A revolutionary tribunal in session

towards the Right was manifested in the Bolshevik party, but still a useful one.

We have seen the energy which Lenin devoted to attacking the theses of the Left.

It is beyond doubt [Trotsky has written in this connection] that it is because of the vigour with which Lenin posed the question of the need for a temporary surrender – of a 'transition to illegality in relation to German imperialism' as he himself put it at public meetings – that the party and the revolution were spared involvement in a hopeless war which would have ended after two or three months with the total collapse of the Russian revolution.[38]

THE HEALTH OF THE PROLETARIAN PARTY

All the responsibilities of this moment rested on the party, or more precisely on its leading ranks in Petrograd and Moscow. What kind of picture do we see here in the crisis?

This party, so disciplined and so little encumbered by an abstract fetishism for democracy, still in these grave hours respects its norms of internal democracy. It puts its recognized leader in a minority; Lenin's tremendous personal authority does not hinder the militants in the Central Committee from standing up to him and energetically maintaining their point of view; the most important questions are settled by vote, often by small majorities (a margin of one vote, or seven votes out of fifteen present, etc.), to which the minorities are willing to defer without abandoning their ideas. Lenin, when in the minority, submits while waiting for events to prove him right, and continues his propaganda without breaking discipline. Even though impassioned, the discussion remains objective. Neither gossip nor intrigue nor personalities play any important part in what is said. The militants talk politics, without trying to wound or to discredit the comrades on the opposing side. Since the opposition is never bullied, it shows only the minimum of emotion that one would expect in events of this order, and soon recovers from its rash decisions.

Once Lenin gets his majority he does not boast: he has other things to care about. His attitude towards his opponents is both tolerant and firm: tolerant towards persons, immovable towards their ideas. Not that it is his custom to make the typical distinction of liberal-bourgeois parliamentarians between men and their ideas – this although his polemic never stoops to petty personalities. On the other hand, he always does make the distinction between the methods and procedures in struggle that may be used against enemies of the party and those that may be used *within* the party, among comrades; similarly, his tactics at the beginning of 1917 were based on a distinction between struggles against enemies of the working class and struggles waged within the working-class movement. Here his conception of the leader of a proletarian party is vividly displayed. It is a leader whose authority is founded on a recognized superiority, a resolute, self-disciplined but stubborn man, who is not afraid to be in a minority and swim against the current. His mission is not to follow the masses but to enlighten and lead them, since it is precisely the keenest element in their consciousness which speaks through him. This proletarian conception of a party leader may be contrasted with the example of the old opportunist parties influenced by the petty-bourgeoisie, whose leaders can be seen courting popularity by trailing after the masses – anti-militarist and pacifistic when the masses are, patriots when the masses acclaim 'the war to end all war', and 'revolutionary' when they return bloody and beaten from the war.

At this hour, the party really is the courageous 'iron cohort' of Bukharin's later description. It is a living organism, teeming with initiative from the lowest to the highest ranks, disciplined even to its most senior leader, regarding with love and respect the mentors it has formed for itself in long years of struggle, but knowing how to contradict them and put them in a minority. It is equipped with a genuine collective of leadership (Lenin's concern to make leadership a collective responsibility is worth noting), and with healthy political traditions which are able to avoid excesses of authority as well as of democracy. Any differences of tactics were softened by collective habits of thinking, by Marxist education and by the operations of democratic centralization. The centre leads and has to be followed: but this centre is itself the expression of the party and, through the party, of the masses.

If Lenin had been a little more authoritarian, or his comrades had shown a little more excitability, or a little less discipline, or party loyalty, or sense of unity, or if the party's leading core had been a little more rigid, or a little less collective, or intelligent, or firm-willed, or if their Marxist consciousness had been a little less keen – then, either in the Brest-Litovsk days or shortly afterwards, some excellent Left elements in the party would have been broken, or forced out temporarily,[39] or lost forever. A little more, a little less: every living equilibrium rests upon such slight quantities as this. The equilibrium we have discussed may be termed the proletarian party's condition of health.

RESULTS OF THE FIRST IMPERIALIST PEACE

The 'peace of shame' of Brest-Litovsk was the first retreat undertaken by the revolutionary proletariat of Russia, isolated in the face of the imperialist powers through the inaction of the proletariat of Europe. It was also the first collision between the young Soviet State and its imperialist environment. The Russian revolution now found itself alone. To live, it had to gain time: time was everything. At that moment it could have been defeated within three months, and to gain those three months was to keep open all the immensity of the future.

It was also, at least for Europe, the first imperialist peace (the treaty of Bucharest came later, followed by Versailles), dictated to the vanquished party at cannon-point, directed openly towards ends of territorial conquest and economic enslavement.

For the Central Powers this proved to be an irreparable error, though inevitable. The German General Staff had been running the war with its own rigorous logic. The terms of the peace reflected no more than its consistency, the powerful intelligence with which it pursued its designs. Once the blockade around the Central Powers was broken, and their supplies assured through the grain of the Ukraine, the coal of the Donetz and all Russia's raw materials, once their fighting manpower was reinforced through the return of the prisoners-of-war, would not victory now be possible on the western front? That is what the German high command hoped to achieve. It was this hope that impelled Ludendorff, in March, to unleash his great offensive on the Somme, towards Amiens, when he tried to break the Anglo–French lines. But in fact the dialectic of history, following on Brest-Litovsk, made his victory impossible. In the first imperialist peace the peoples of the world thought they saw *the first German peace*. The example of the Russian revolution and of President Wilson's propaganda for the rights of nationalities undermined German imperialism from within. The disgraceful peace imposed upon Russia caused fresh enthusiasm for the war among the Allied and neutral peoples. All thoughts of negotiation now went by the board: the idea of a compromise peace, which had been in the air up till then, simply vanished.

Besides this, the calculations of the Austro–Germans on the consequences of Russia's surrender were falsified by events. Past master in the art of war as it is waged *between imperialists*, skilful in exploiting an occupied Belgium or a Briey basin which French pilots were under orders never to bomb, the German strategists found the tasks of *a class war* beyond them. As they had failed to understand the Bolsheviks (who still managed to understand them) during the peace negotiations, so they neither understood nor prevented the results of their seizure of the Ukraine and southern Russia. The Ukraine supplied them only with a proportion of the food supplies they had anticipated, and then at the cost of innumerable troubles. The occupation of the Russian territories encountered resistance from an armed revolutionary peasant population, whose behaviour was quite different from that of the north of France: more German troops were needed for this difficult work than had been budgeted. The occupation troops, harassed by partisans, often influenced by revolutionary propaganda, and weary of the war against a local populace, lost their morale. The prisoners-of-war repatriated from Russia had become 'Bolshevized'. Conquered Ukraine proved to be the first tomb of German imperialism.[40]

6 · The Truce and the Great Retrenchment

Events in the Ukraine took a very singular turn. In its resistance to the revolution, the Rada asked for aid simultaneously from the Allies and the Central Powers; it obtained support from both quarters. France sent money to the Ukrainian patriots: such patriots, such defenders of order and property – actually they were engaged in selling their country to whichever power bid the higher and proved the stronger. But the press of the Entente, so indefatigible in its rage and denunciation against the 'treason' of Bolsheviks, who were now engaged in a desperate struggle against German imperialism, chose to ignore the very real treason of the Ukrainian nationalist bourgeoisie, a betrayal which was to prolong the World War for several months. The episode forms a striking illustration of the contempt in which statesmen, party leaders and moulders of public opinion hold the truth and the realities of history. The interests of the propertied classes is the only guide they acknowledge; and these interests pressed them to slander the Bolsheviks at all costs as a prelude to slaughtering them later. Let the facts speak for themselves.

On 9 February (27 January, Old Style), the Red Guards entered Kiev. The Ukrainian Rada now controlled only a few towns in the Vinnitsa region. It was then that the Germans offered it their armed backing to impose a recognition of the Rada on the Soviets. This they accomplished through the provisions of the Brest-Litovsk treaty. The adventurer, Petlyura, an artful cut-throat, was already the Rada's real leader. On the very day the Reds entered Kiev, he signed a treaty with the Central Powers in which he undertook, in exchange for their military support, to supply a million tons of grain (later to become 2,160,000 tons), 180,000 tons of meat, 30,000 sheep, 40,000 tons of sugar, etc. He also undertook to see to the needs of the German occupation forces.

From the Rumanian front to the borders of the Caucasus, the workers' Red Guards and the first Soviet troops had just won a series of brilliant victories. The revolution was triumphant everywhere. The 'Soviet Republic of Odessa' and the Soviet Executive on the Rumanian front compelled the Rumanian aggressor to call off hostilities on 8 February; then, supported by Muraviev's little Red Army of less than 4,000 men, which had travelled from Kiev within a single night, they launched an offensive in the direction of Jassy. The Rumanian conquerors of Bessarabia suffered a severe defeat at Rybnitsa, losing twenty cannon. The Diplomatic Corps at Jassy became alarmed, and through its mediation

КРАСНЫЙ ОКТЯБРЬ
В КРЫМУ ГРУППА боевиков 2
ЕВПАТОРИИ КРАСНОГВАРДЕЙЦЕВ б. КР.ПАРТИЕА
О.РЕВОЛ. ПОДПОЛЬНИКОВ ПО ЕПИЕ.ОРУ ВЕЯ.ТИЯ В
бОЛЬШЕВИКАМИ 1947-18я

38. Red Guards during the fighting for the Crimea, January 1918

Rumania signed a treaty on 8 March ending the Russo–Rumanian quarrel. Rumania formally renounced its claim to Bessarabia and agreed to evacuate the country. This is also the period of the White defeats in the Don, the Crimea and the Kuban. The successes of the Reds, achieved despite the numerical weakness of their troops, are to be explained by the spontaneous assistance they gained from the poor peasants and the working-class population.

Such was the situation when the Austrian and German forces entered the Ukraine with twenty-nine divisions of infantry and four and a half divisions of cavalry, a total of between 200,000 and 250,000 men. Against these forces, Antonov-Ovseyenko and his sturdy lieutenants Pyatakov, Evgenia Bosch,[1] Muraviev, Sivers, Sablin and Kikvidze[2] could muster about 15,000 poorly organized fighters, who were dispersed in tiny groups all over this immense territory. The German columns encountered savage resistance here and there from pockets of revolutionaries, but were able to smash these centres without much difficulty. There was in fact no shortage of arms or men on the revolutionary side – the peasants would have eagerly supported any resistance to the invasion. What was missing was organization. There was no State, not even any local institutions possessing any authority, no trained cadres, no cohesion or co-ordination. All the old institutions had collapsed and their successors were still being formed, painfully and against odds, in the midst of chaos. Armed bands sprang up practically everywhere. The cheap white bread of the Ukraine attracted adventurers from all over Russia. Its country districts and its small towns seemed to offer a marvellous stamping ground for all kinds of hare-brained scheme-mongers, from Ukrainian Socialists (all more or less infected with nationalism) through Left SRs to anarchists or semi-anarchists. Little local armies were formed under their own party flag. Often the name and banner of a revolutionary organization served merely to dignify the existence of a feudal armed band. The influence and even the organization of the Bolshevik party left much to be desired: conflicts arose within the party between Ukrainians and Russians, militants in the localities and those at the centre – for in the hearts of the Bolsheviks, the national question was far from being resolved.

The anarchists and the Left SRs, often working in unison, played a most important role. For a short while the anarchist Baron ran a dictatorship in Ekaterinoslav. At Nikolayev the anarchists rose in revolt, but abandoned the town to the Germans, against whom the citizens, left unaided, kept up a battle for four days. The band led by Marusya Nikiforova, which flew the black flag of anarchism, fought a street battle in Elisavetgrad for two weeks against the counter-revolutionary populace. Bands of White officers from the Rumanian front (for example, Drozdovsky's forces) kept crossing the Ukraine in order to get to the Kuban. The Czechoslovak legions were at large in the heart of the country, under orders from the Allies to retreat before the German advance and take up positions on the Volga. The German settlers in the region were in revolt. Petlyura's nationalist commandos, or *haidamaks*, held various points in the countryside. Villages that bristled with machine-guns defended themselves ferociously against all comers. Local republics were inaugurated, such as that of the Donetz workers. Red brigades, totally undisciplined, often drunk, often commanded by adventurers who had later on to be shot, discredited the authority of the Soviets with the local populations. Shooting, looting and assassinations went on everywhere. Sometimes strong formations retreated before the enemy without firing a shot; magnificent resistance came from odd handfuls, like the thirty-five Red fighters who held back two German regiments at Putivle. At the rail-junction of Lozavaya a whole unit, the Lenin Battalion, was wiped out covering the Reds' retreat.

Amid such frightful chaos, the revolutionary struggle demanded an uncommon strength of personality. In this period a woman emerged as one such figure of distinction, the old Bolshevik militant Evgenia Bosch:[3] by a noteworthy injustice of fate, she has become a little-known character. Here G. Chudnovsky, one of the conquerors of the Winter Palace, met his death.

Most of the battles were waged along the railways; armoured trains played a capital role in the whole campaign. The stages of the German advance are worth remarking: at Chernigov, 14 March; Kiev, 16 March; Poltava, 30 March; Kherson, 10 April; Crimea, 20 April; Rostov-on-Don, 6 May. The Germans had come in after grain. They stopped at nothing to compel the farmer to deliver his stocks to them. There are stories of peasants flogged *en masse*, tortured, buried alive. The occupation regime, welcomed so joyously by the bourgeoisie and petty-bourgeoisie, swiftly became a reign of terror. The Ukrainian peasantry met it with a secret, scattered resistance, implacably harassing the invader. Blood flowed in the tiniest hamlets.

THE PROLETARIAT'S DEMOCRATIC REVOLUTION IN FINLAND

The treaty of Brest-Litovsk sealed the sacrifice of the Finnish proletariat, in whom the Russian revolutionaries had rightly placed their greatest hopes.[4] If Russia was, as Lenin emphasized on many occasions, one of the most backward countries in Europe, Finland was one of the most advanced nations in the world. Everything in its situation seemed to promise an easy victory for Socialism: its customs, its political culture, so similar to that of the most progressive democracies of the West, the victories of its labour movement, and even its industrial structure.

The people of Finland had known neither serfdom nor despotism. A part of Sweden since the twelfth century, a country of small owners who had never been conquered by feudalism, Finland passed to Russia in 1809 through the alliance between Napoleon and Alexander I. Constituted as a Grand Duchy, it enjoyed a large degree of autonomy within the Empire which was all the more effective because the Finns defended it cannily against their Grand Dukes – the Tsars of Russia. Finland kept its own Diet, its currency, its postal system, its schools, its militias and its internal administration. It evolved in Western fashion, like the Scandinavian countries. Nicholas II's brutal attempts at Russification only succeeded in alienating the whole of Finnish society. Two years after the 1905 revolution, as a result of which the Tsar was forced to give Finland a constitution, the Finns introduced universal suffrage. At the first elections in 1907, the Social-Democrats won eighty seats out of 200 in the Sejm. The elections of 1916 gave them an absolute majority: 103 out of 200. They voted in the eight-hour day and an intelligent programme of social legislation.

Then, Socialist parliamentarianism found itself in peril of its life. Was it, after all, possible to travel peaceably towards Socialism, ballot-form in hand? The Finnish bourgeoisie made an alliance with Kerensky against the 'Red Diet' with its Social-

Democrat majority: the Provisional Government in Petrograd ordered its dissolution, thus continuing, when it came to the choice, the political line of Tsardom. Russian sentinels stood on guard outside the locked doors of the Parliament in Helsinki. At the subsequent elections, the Social-Democrats gained votes (from 375,000 in the previous year to 444,000) but lost seats (from 103 down to ninety-two). This result was due to the cynical but skilful fraud practised by the bourgeois parties.

But just as the Finnish proletariat could scarcely resign itself before this electoral defeat, so the Finnish bourgeois could as little remain satisfied with such a precarious 'victory'. Matters had to be settled with an extra-parliamentary conclusion. The bourgeois had long foreseen this outcome, and made conscientious preparations for a civil war. It was a showdown which the Finnish Social-Democratic Party, formed over twenty years in the mould of German Social-Democracy, had hoped to avoid. Ever since 1914 the bourgeoisie of Finland had been preparing to use the imperialist war to gain its national independence by force of arms. The 27th Jägers Battalion of the German army was made up of 3,000 young Finns from the wealthy and the well-to-do classes, who were in service against Russia, the ancestral enemy. Clandestine military schools existed in various parts of the country. After the fall of the Tsar, a corps of volunteer riflemen was organized in the north to maintain law and order. This was General Gerich's *Schutzkorps*, the first-ever White Guard unit, which was formed quite openly. Its headquarters was at Vaasa on the Gulf of Bothnia. Meanwhile, the bourgeoisie insistently demanded the withdrawal of Russian troops, who had been sent to Finland at the beginning of the war to guard the country against a German invasion.

The October Revolution was echoed in Finland by the great general strike of mid-November (14 November, Old Style; 27, New Style). This was provoked by a serious famine, which was confined to the poor classes, and by the reactionary politics of the Senate, who wanted to install a dictatorial Directorate headed by the reactionary Svinhufvud. Work stopped everywhere. The railways were at a standstill. The workers' Red Guards, with support here and there from Russian soldiers, occupied the public buildings. There were bloody clashes everywhere between Reds and Whites. The deputies sat and talked. Terrified, the bourgeoisie agreed to the eight-hour day and the new social legislation, as well as to the democratization of executive authority, which passed from the Senate to the Sejm (or Diet). And the general strike, the workers' own victory, was consummated in the introduction of a bourgeois Cabinet, presided over by the same reactionary Svinhufvud! It was a revolution aborted. In the opinion of the Finnish revolutionaries, the seizure of power could have been managed at this moment, and would even have proved very easy – the support

of the Bolsheviks being decisive. But, as Comrade O. W. Kuusinen,[5] formerly one of the principal leaders of Finnish Social-
Democracy, was to write later: 'Wishing not to risk our democratic
conquests, and hoping to manoeuvre round this turning-point
of history by our parliamentary skill, we decided to evade the
revolution. . . . We did not believe in the revolution; we reposed
no hope in it; we had no wish for it.' With leaders animated by a
spirit like this, the cause of the Finnish proletariat was in terrible.
peril.

If the general strike had shown the workers their strength, to
the bourgeoisie it had revealed their danger. The bourgeois classes
of Finland realized that, left to their own resources, they were
doomed. Svinhufvud asked Sweden to intervene. The Whites were
busily arming in the north, where they had set up depots for
their food supplies. The government was astute enough to prolong
the famine in the working-class centres, making sure that food
reserves were not made available for the workers. The proclamation of Finland's independence changed nothing. The proletariat
became increasingly apprehensive of the possibility of a Swedish
or German intervention. On top of it all, the Sejm now, by
ninety-seven votes against eighty-seven, passed a resolution making clear reference to the need for a bourgeois dictatorship. Once
again the problem of power faced the workers, in even starker
terms than during the general strike of November. This time it
was obvious to the Social-Democrats that all chances of settling
matters by parliamentary means had vanished. It was necessary
to fight.

On the night of 14 January (27, New Style), the Red Flag was
hoisted over the Workers' House at Helsinki. The city was rapidly
captured, and the Senate and government fled to Vaasa. In a few
days, almost without resistance, the Reds took over the largest
towns, Åbo, Viipuri and Tammerfors, and the whole of southern
Finland. So peaceful a victory might have been disquieting. The
Social-Democratic leaders (Manner, Sirola, Kuusinen, etc.)
formed a workers' government, the Council of People's Delegates,
under the control of a central Workers' Council of thirty-five
delegates (ten from the unions, ten from the Social-Democratic
party and five from the workers' organizations of Helsinki). Their
notion of activity was 'to march day by day towards the Socialist
revolution', as the People's Delegates put it. They introduced
workers' control over production, which was relatively simple
given the marked concentration of key industries: wood, paper
and textiles. They were successful too in stopping sabotage on the
part of the banks. Public life and production very soon resumed a
practically normal existence.

Was the dictatorship of the proletariat possible? Was it necessary? The leadership of the movement did not think so, although
industry employed about half a million persons out of a total

population of three million. The proletariat and the agricultural day-labourers formed a mass of about half a million altogether. The small and middle peasants, who were in a majority in the countryside, could have been won to the revolution or neutralized by it. Unfortunately, however, 'until they were defeated, most of the leaders of the revolution had no clear idea of the aims of the revolution' (according to Kuusinen). *Their aim was to establish, without the expropriation of the rich or the dictatorship of labour, a parliamentary democracy in which the proletariat would have been the leading class.*

The principal measures passed by the Council of People's Delegates were as follows: the eight-hour day; compulsory payment of wages for the days of the revolutionary strike; the emancipation of domestic servants and farmhands (who were hired by the year by the farmers and subject to very harsh regulations); the abolition of the old system of land distribution, which was based on tribute and compulsory labour as rent; the abolition of rent for small tenants; judicial reform; the abolition of the death penalty (which had very rarely been exercised previously); tax exemption for the poor (the minimum taxable income being set at 2,400 marks in the towns and 1,400 marks in the country, instead of 800 and 400 marks, and a further tax being imposed on incomes over 20,000 marks); a tax on dwellings of more than one room; the liberation of the press from its ancient restrictions; workers' control in the factories.

A little while later, during the civil war, other measures were introduced: requisitioning of grain and potatoes; the closing down of the bourgeois press; the prohibition of the flight of capital abroad; the general obligation to labour for all able-bodied adults between the ages of eighteen and fifty-five years. It was a workers' revolution conducted in the name of an ideal democracy, characterized in the form of a draft constitution at the end of February 1918 which was to be put to a referendum in the spring. This attractive project is worth summarizing.

The supreme authority of the 'People's Republic of Finland' was to be an assembly of representatives of the people elected every three years by direct and secret balloting under universal suffrage with proportional representation; women were to have the vote and the electoral age was twenty years. In addition to the usual liberties, the constitution would have guaranteed the inviolability of the person, the right to strike, the right of strikers to guard factories against the employment of blacklegs, and the neutrality of the armed forces in labour disputes. Any modification in the constitution had to be subjected to a referendum. Minorities in the Assembly, if they amounted to one third of the votes, had the right to veto all measures, except tax laws, until the next session. Any bill introducing indirect taxes or customs dues (which chiefly affect the poor classes) had to have a two-thirds majority. The import of primary commodities was to be exempt from taxation. In the event of war the government was empowered to take special measures against 'the enemies of the constitution'. The right to rise in insurrection was accorded to the people in the event of an attack on the constitution by their representatives. The people even had to have the right of initiating legislation: any proposed law presented by 10,000 citizens had to be discussed forthwith. Functionaries and magistrates were to be elected for a term of five years, and could be re-elected. At any time a deputy could be compelled to stand for re-election on the demand of one fifth of his electors. The Council of People's Delegates, who would exercise executive power, were to be voted in for three years by the Assembly; the Assembly would also appoint the Council's president and vice-president who could not be re-elected for more than one more consecutive term and would enjoy no special powers. The government would be under the supervision of a 'Control Commission on the Administration and Application of the Laws'. The veto of two members of this Commission was the minimum required to freeze any act of new legislation. The other clauses dealt with the election of judges, who were to be subject to control from the government, autonomy of local institutions and the provision of workers' representatives in all administrations.

In contrast with the practice of the bourgeois democracies, this constitution would have unified, in the Assembly of popular representatives, all legislative, executive and (to a certain degree) judiciary powers. The government was reduced virtually to the exercise of executive functions. On this project, one Finnish revolutionary has remarked:

> In theory, the highest conceivable degree in the development of bourgeois democracy was attained – a degree which is in practice unrealizable under the capitalist system. Bourgeois democracy has to either go on and be transformed into the dictatorship of the proletariat, if the proletariat is the winner, or become the dictatorship of the bourgeoisie if the proletariat is defeated.[6]

It was a truly noble scheme, if somewhat Utopian. 'The weakness of the bourgeoisie,' Kuusinen has said, 'led us into being captivated by the spell of democracy, and we decided to advance towards Socialism through parliamentary action and the democratization of the representative system.' Such was the influence of reformist illusions upon the Finnish Socialists. Such was their fatal ignorance of the laws of the class struggle.

THE WHITE TERROR IN FINLAND

The bourgeoisie displayed a much greater realism. It immediately launched a small White army, the bulk of whose forces, to the tune of about 5,000 men, were formed from the *Schutzkorps* (27th Jägers Battalion of the German army, consisting of young Finns, as we have mentioned), a brigade of Swedish volunteers and others recruited from the bourgeois and petty-bourgeois youth. Mannerheim, a former general of the Russian army, of Swedish origin, took the command of these troops and promised 'to restore order within a fortnight'. The arming of the Whites was completed with the proceeds from several lucky raids against the Russian garrisons in the north, which had actually been committed with the complicity of their commanders.

The Red Guards numbered only about 1,500 men at the beginning of hostilities, and these were poorly armed. Initiative rested with the Whites who, since they controlled the cities of the Bothnian Gulf, Uleaborg, Vaasa and Kuopio, as well as agrarian Finland in the north, held a continuous front from the Gulf to Lake Ladoga. There were Russian garrisons at Sveaborg, Viipuri and Tammerfors, a town in the centre of the country, and part of the Baltic fleet happened to be at Helsinki. Antonov-Ovseyenko, Dybenko and Smilga had established Bolshevik organizations among these troops and crews. The Russian garrison at Tammerfors, commanded by Svechnikov, a revolutionary officer, repulsed Mannerheim's first attacks. Under the protection of the Russians the Red Guards of Finland were able to arm and complete their organization. At this point Soviet troops had to retire from Finland under the provisions of the Brest-Litovsk treaty. All that remained of them were about a thousand volunteers incorporated in the Red Guard, and many of these were longing to get back home. Eero Haapalainen, a Finnish Socialist, and Svechnikov directed operations. The Reds opened a general offensive at the beginning of March: this failed, but the setback strengthened the Reds' determination to win. Between 15 January and 1 April, the organizational efforts of the workers' government succeeded in assembling a force of 60,000 men (of whom about 30,000 were stationed in the rear) and in winning numerous partial victories at the front.

Svinhufvud, the head of the White government, obtained the backing of Wilhelm II. Twenty thousand Germans under the command of von der Goltz disembarked at Hanko, Helsinki and Lovisa, taking the Reds from behind. Helsinki was captured after a bitter street battle in which the Germans and Whites made workers' wives and children march in front of them – around a hundred of these were killed. The capture was followed by atrocious reprisals. The Workers' House was bombarded by artillery. A Swedish newspaper published the following item: 'Forty Red women who were said to have had arms were led out on the ice and shot without trial.'[7] Over 300 corpses were picked up in the street.

Within the workers' government the moderate current represented by Tanner was so strong that rigorous measures were only adopted against White agents behind the lines when it was too

late. Often the counter-revolutionaries appearing before the tribunals were sentenced to nothing more than a fine or a mild term
of imprisonment. Any summary executions were entirely due to
the initiative of the Red Guards. The irresolution of the government, the differences in policy among its leaders, their refusal to
push the revolution any further, and the timidity of the agrarian
reforms, as well as the effect of the Brest-Litovsk treaty, all helped
to weaken the Reds. The landing of the German troops had a
most demoralizing impact. The power of Germany had reached
its maximum at that moment.

Mannerheim surrounded Tammerfors, where 10,000 Reds led
by a few Russian officers resisted furiously. The town was captured in house-to-house fighting after street battles lasting several
days. Two hundred Reds were shot there, including two excellent
leaders, Colonel Bulatsel and Lieutenant Mukhanov. Several
thousand of the Reds managed to flee, around 2,000 were killed
in the fighting or massacred later, 5,000 were taken prisoner.[8]

The decisive battle was fought at Tavastehus, between Tammerfors and Helsinki. Between 20,000 and 25,000 Reds converged on
this point, pushed from north to south by Mannerheim and in the
opposite direction by von der Goltz; their retreat to the east was
cut off. Against the orders of their commanders they brought their
families with them and often all their meagre possessions. It was
the migration of a populace rather than the march of an army.
Capable of turning at any moment into a chaos of fugitives, this
mass of people was hardly able to manoeuvre. The Whites raked
them with shrapnel. When surrounded, they fought heroically for
two days before surrendering. A few thousand of them cut a way
out for themselves to the east. The surrender was followed by a
massacre, in which the killing of the wounded was the rule. Ten
thousand prisoners remained; these were interned at Riihimäki.
On 12 May Viipuri fell. A few thousand Red Guards took refuge
in Russia.

The victors massacred the vanquished. It has been known since
antiquity that class wars are the most frightful. There are no more
bloody or atrocious victories than those won by the propertied
classes. Since the bloodbath inflicted on the Paris Commune by
the French bourgeoisie, the world had seen nothing to compare in
horror with what took place in Finland. From the very beginning
of the civil war 'in the zone occupied by the Whites, membership
of a workers' organization meant arrest, and any office in one
meant death by shooting'.[9] The massacre of the Socialists reached
such a scale that people lost all interest in the topic.' At Kummen,
where forty-three Red Guards had fallen in battle, nearly 500
persons were executed afterwards. There were 'hundreds' shot at
Kotka, a town of 13,000 inhabitants: 'They were not even asked
their names, but led out in batches. ·...' At Rauma, according to
bourgeois newspapers, 'five hundred prisoners captured on 15

May received the punishment they deserved on the same day'. 'On 14 April two hundred Red Guards were shot in the district of Töölö in Helsinki. ... The Reds were hunted down from house to house. Many women were among the victims.' At Sveaborg public executions took place on Trinity Sunday. Near Lahti, where thousands of prisoners were taken by the Whites, 'the machine-guns worked for several hours each day. ... In one day some two hundred women were shot with explosive bullets: lumps of flesh were spattered out in all directions. ... ' At Viipuri 600 Red Guards were lined up in three rows along the edge of the fortress moat and machine-gunned in cold blood. Among the intellectuals murdered we may mention an editor of the journal *Social-Democrat*, Jukho Rainio and the writer Irmari Rantamala who, when taken by boat to the place of execution, 'jumped overboard in an attempt to drown. His coat prevented him from sinking and the Whites killed him in the water with rifle-fire.' No statistics exist on the number of those massacred: current estimates vary between ten and twenty thousand.

There is, however, an *official* figure for the number of Red prisoners interned in concentration camps: 70,000. The camps were ravaged by famine, vermin and epidemic. A report signed by a well-known Finnish doctor, Professor R. Tigerstedt, notes that 'between 6 July and 31 July 1918, the number of detainees that were held in the camp at Tammerfors and the adjacent prison varied between 6,027 and 8,597. 2,347 prisoners died in these twenty-six days and the weekly mortality-rate among detainees

39. The Finnish Revolution: soldiers of the White 'Protective Corps' shoot down Red Guards, 1918

was as high as 407 per thousand.' By 25 July there were still 50,818 revolutionaries imprisoned in Finland. In the September of the same year 25,820 cases were still awaiting investigation by the courts. The bourgeoisie became temporarily interested in the possibility of exporting its captives to supply manpower to Germany. A bill was passed authorizing the transportation abroad of men condemned to forced labour. Germany, now depopulated by the war, would have exchanged chemical and mineral products for this penal labour force. The implementation of this project was prevented by the German revolution.

The purge of Finnish society continued for months in all fields. On 16 May warrants of arrest were issued against all former Social-Democratic deputies still living in the country. (The revolutionaries had either perished or escaped by now.) Three of them allegedly 'committed suicide' in prison in the night of 2 July. Ten more were condemned to death. The Supreme Court set aside this verdict in January 1919 and pronounced one death penalty, six sentences of imprisonment for life, four of twelve years, one of eleven years, five of ten years, five of nine years, fifteen of eight years and two of seven years: 'Many of the condemned,' writes Kataya, 'were that type of Social-Democrat who, with all the artfulness of traitors to Socialism, had spent all their lives serving bourgeois society. The bourgeoisie avenged itself blindly.' It is usual for the White terror to strike indifferently at the reformists – for whom the triumphant bourgeoisie no longer has any use – and the revolutionaries. Once order was re-established, the Finnish bourgeoisie toyed with the idea of a monarch drawn from the Hohenzollern family. The increasingly precarious situation in Germany caused it to abandon this plan.

It seems to be no exaggeration to declare that the total number of Finnish workers struck down by the White terror (whether killed or given long prison sentences) was more than 100,000: about a quarter of the entire proletariat.[10] 'All organized workers have been either shot or imprisoned,' wrote a group of Finnish Communists at the beginning of 1919. This fact permits us to draw an important theoretical deduction on the nature of the White terror, which has been confirmed since by the experience of Hungary, Italy, Bulgaria, etc. The White terror is not to be explained by the frenzy of battle, the violence of class hatred or any other psychological factor. *The psychosis of civil war plays a purely secondary role.* The terror is in reality the result of a calculation and a historical necessity. The victorious propertied classes are perfectly aware that they can only ensure their own domination in the aftermath of a social battle by inflicting on the working class a bloodbath savage enough to enfeeble it for tens of years afterwards. And since the class in question is far more numerous than the wealthy classes, the number of victims *must* be very great.

The *total extermination* of all the advanced and conscious elements of the proletariat is, in short, the rational objective of the White terror. In this sense, *a vanquished revolution – regardless of its tendency – will always cost the proletariat far more than a victorious revolution, no matter what sacrifices and rigours the latter may demand.*

One more observation. The butcheries in Finland took place in April 1918. Up to this moment the Russian revolution had virtually everywhere displayed great leniency towards its enemies. It had not used terror. We have noted a few bloody episodes in the civil war in the south, but these were exceptional. The victorious bourgeoisie of a small nation which ranks among the most enlightened societies of Europe[11] was the first to remind the Russian proletariat that *woe to the vanquished!* is the first law of social war.

THE 'INDEPENDENCE' OF THE CAUCASUS

Meanwhile, the Caucasus was detaching itself from proletarian Russia. This old 'Imperial Lieutenancy', a sumptuous mountain territory a little smaller than France, possessing nearly ten million inhabitants and an inexhaustible natural wealth, had been undergoing a national revolution of extreme complexity. The Caucasus had been conquered for the Russian Empire over a century of fierce warfare, from 1760 to 1864. It was divided, on both the European and the Asiatic faces of its peaks, into a number of highly variegated countries, comprising ten or more nationalities. This area was to provide the intrigues of imperialism, as well as the ambitions of its own middle classes, with a field for exercise even more tempting and profitable than the Ukraine had been. Its rich resources were bound to excite economic appetites: the grain of the Kuban, the oil of Azerbaidjan, the manganese and copper of Georgia, the cotton and tobacco of Armenia, the vegetable oils of the north, the wines of Armenia and Georgia: a stupendous spoil. The whole design required the installation of democratic republics in the region, a perspective which appeared all the easier since Russian oppression had inflamed nationalist sentiment among the proud, bellicose small peoples of the Trans-Caucasian countries. Georgians, Armenians, Cherkassians, Ossetians, Abkasians, Adzhars, Turks, Tartars, Persians, Jews and Russians lived in the area between the Caspian Sea and the Black Sea, in a long wait for freedom, whose coming was conceived in numerous different ways. Powerful traditions had been deposited by the revolution of 1905, which was marked in the Caucasus by terrorist acts and great popular victories, with a wake of merciless repression. The principal social forces in play were:

(1) The Russian proletariat of Baku, the oilfield capital.

(2) The petty-bourgeoisie, artisans and intellectuals of Georgia, who for a long time had been under the influence of Menshevik Social-Democracy.

(3) The Revolutionary National-Socialist party of Armenia, the Dashnaktsutiun.

(4) The reactionary Moslem party, the Mussavat.

(5) The army of the Caucasian front where the influence of the SRs, though still powerful, was steadily being overtaken by that of the Bolsheviks.

There were two political centres: Baku, on the Caspian Sea, with its concentrated proletariat and its Bolsheviks; and Tiflis, which was in the power of the Menshevik intellectuals, the administrative centre and Georgian capital, strategically sited at the heart of the region at the crossing of the main roads and railways.

During 1917 the Caucasus, which had achieved *de facto* independence, had not intended to secede from Russia. The nationalities took it for granted that they would exercise a broad autonomy within an All-Russian democracy. The Regional Military Soviet, the Regional Council of Workers' Soviets and the Regional Committees of the large parties formed a democratic government at Tiflis which operated in virtual unison with the Kerensky administration. The Mensheviks of Georgia did affect a more lavish use of the language of class struggle than their Russian counterparts, but this was only a mixture of doctrinaire verbiage and political cunning. Tiflis received the news of the October Revolution with incredulity, and then issued an indignant condemnation of the

40. Stepan Shaumya Georgievich

scandalous Bolshevik usurpation, pronouncing grandly against all dictatorship and in favour of democracy. A regional government was set up there on 11 November (24), headed by Mensheviks (Gegechkori, Chkenkheli) and SRs (Donkoi). Baku and the army remained outside its control.

Inside the Soviet at Baku the news of the Bolshevik victory in Petrograd and Moscow resulted in a shift of power. The Bolshevik fraction, up till now in the minority, became the leading group in it. Such remarkable characters as Stepan Shaumyan and Dzhaparidze were among its leaders. Shaumyan was forty years old. Armenian by birth, and imbued with a solid polytechnical education in Europe, he was a Marxist trained by exile and activity abroad which had given him valuable experience of the working-class movements of Switzerland, Germany and Britain. He had been a Bolshevik since the split of 1903: a close colleague of Lenin, he had been arrested, imprisoned or exiled many times over. He was known as the tireless editor of the party's clandestine journals, as an organizer of memorable strikes in 1914, as an intransigent 'defeatist' during the war and as a sound theoretician. Among the ranks of the great Bolsheviks Shaumyan was a figure of the first importance. Alexei Dzhaparidze was also a Bolshevik from 1903, and one of the founders of the working-class movement in Baku; he was of bourgeois origin, with four experiences of exile, in 1907, 1910, 1913 and 1915, each time returning to his post in illegal work. The experience of these leaders was tested to full stretch in their guidance of the Baku Soviet's work. The results of the elections to the Constituent Assembly, which had been held at the end of November, give a revealing picture of the difficulties in their way. The 107,000 votes had gone as follows: Bolsheviks, 22,000; Moslems (Mussavat, etc.), 29,000; Armenian Dashnaks, 20,000; Kadets, 9,000; Mensheviks, 5,000; SRs, nearly 19,000; Jews, 2,000. The Left SRs and Left wing of the Dashnaks joined their votes with the Bolsheviks, who were now stronger than any one of their rivals. But they had to reckon with the powerful influence of Armenian and Moslem nationalisms, as well as with the resistance of a strong Right-wing minority. These were exceptionally precarious conditions in which they assumed power. These facts should be remembered: they explain what happened later.

The condition of the army of the Caucasus was beyond description. Whole divisions were literally decimated by typhus and scurvy, epidemics which sprang from filth and poverty.[12] This army of desperate men soon became 'infected with Bolshevism'. General Przhevalsky ordered it to be demobilized, while the government at Tiflis was parleying with the Turks, and an attempt was made to form small armies based on the nationalities. A frightful tragedy which has so far gone unchronicled now took place. The Russian peasants who formed the mass of the troops tried to return, still armed, to their homes. But the democratic counter-revolution had no intention of allowing reinforcements of this order to join the Bolsheviks, and wanted to organize its own military establishment. Georgian Mensheviks, Turkish 'federalists' from the Mussavat, Kurd highlanders, Armenian nationalists, all now proceeded to 'disarm', forcibly, the military trains on their way to Russia, stopping them in the mountain gorges. Often the Russian troops resisted. On the pretext of disarmament, they were robbed of their personal belongings; and entire regiments had to march for days, barefoot and in rags, the target of revengeful nationalist populations. In several places there were standing battles, followed by massacres. The Russian military trains were often simply derailed. Often the Armenians, Turks, Tartars, Georgians or Kurds went on to fight among themselves; from one mountain slope to the next, villages blazed in flames.

In mid-February (Old Style) a Parliament, the Trans-Caucasian Sejm, was established at Tiflis. The majority in it was controlled by the Georgian Mensheviks, the Armenian Dashnaks, and the Turkish federalists (Mussavat). It was led by Chkeidze, Tseretelli, Noah Jordania, Ramishvili and Gegechkori, old Menshevik Social-Democrats, who negotiated with every available nationalism or reactionary tendency against the Bolshevik menace. The 'Trans-Caucasian Republic' declared itself independent. 'The crimes of Bolshevism,' declared Tseretelli, the ex-minister of Kerensky, 'have cost it the loss of Trans-Caucasia.' Another Menshevik went so far as to declare, 'We do not know now which is the worst peril for us, the danger from Turkey or the danger of Bolshevism.'[13]

The Sejm legislated an agrarian reform, doomed to remain a paper measure through its inspirers' impotence. It refused to join in the negotiations at Brest-Litovsk, but negotiated with the Turkish commander-in-chief, Vekhib Bey, at Trebizond. One detail: although the independence of the Caucasus was proclaimed in April on the specific demand of the Turks, i.e. of the Central Powers, Vekhib Bey tried to occupy Batum (Georgia's only po t on the Black Sea), as well as Kars and Ardagan in Armenia. The Georgians were inclined to fight for Batum, but the Moslem federalists refused to take arms against Turkey: the Trans-Caucasian Republic was over. The Central Empires now insisted on the formation of separate national republics, Georgian, Armenian, Azerbaidjani, mutilated and rival units: divide and rule. The national-socialistic parties accepted willingly enough. The Mensheviks proclaimed the independence of Georgia at the end of May. In mid June, German troops occupied Tiflis; an official communiqué from Noah Jordania's Socialist government told the population that 'German troops have been called in by the government of Georgia to defend the frontiers of the republic' (13 June). Against whom? one might ask. *Ertoba*, the central organ of the Georgian Social-Democratic party, said it straightforwardly: against the Bolsheviks. Noah Jordania later told the Georgian Constituent Assembly, 'I prefer the imperialists of the West to the fanatics of the East.' These 'Socialist' intellectuals, representing an artisan and rural petty-bourgeoisie, would later call in the Allies as they called in the Germans, backing Denikin as they now backed the Moslem reactionaries against Baku: in short, would not shrink before any weapon that presented itself whenever it was a question of fighting the proletarian revolution.[14]

THE BAKU COMMUNE AND THE MASSACRE OF THE TWENTY-SIX

The Soviet at Baku, led by Shaumyan, was meanwhile making itself the ruler of the area, discreetly but unmistakably. Following the Moslem rising of 18 March, it had to introduce a dictatorship. This rising, instigated by the Mussavat, set the Tartar and Turkish population, led by their reactionary bourgeoisie, against the Soviet, which consisted of Russians with support from the Armenians. The races began to slaughter each other in the street. Most of the Turkish port-workers (the *ambal*) either remained neutral or supported the Reds. The contest was won by the Soviets.

From this point, the first Soviet Republic of Azerbaidjan began to organize itself. Shaumyan became President of its Council of People's Commissars, which in May nationalized first the oil industry and then the Caspian tanker fleet. It was a measure difficult to implement: the running of the oil industry demanded skills which the proletariat did not possess. Moscow's help would have to be called in. The SRs, the Mensheviks and the Dashnaks, for their part, defended the firms which had been expropriated.

Soon hunger struck the town. Baku was blockaded by an army of counter-revolutionary Moslem peasants, with officers sent in by Menshevik Georgia. The Mussavat had by now set up a rival government at Ganja, and an imam in Daghestan was preaching holy war against the Bolshevik city. Grain was in short supply. In May, June and July the inhabitants could be given only minute rations of nuts and sunflower seed; the small quantities of corn that the Soviet managed to bring in by sea were reserved for the troops. Attempts at requisitioning were made by the small Red Army of Baku, a poorly disciplined, poorly officered body composed largely of Armenians who were alien to the revolutionary spirit of the proletariat. These drank in excess and plundered the Moslem peasants, causing disaffection among them.

The Cheka at Baku executed no more than two unfortunates; these were two members of the proletarian government, caught out in dishonesty.[15]

The Mussavat was planning to capture the town with the assistance of Turkish troops. Some Russian troops who had been summoned from Persia (actually on some suspicion of counter-revolutionary tendencies) held them back for a while. In the famished city the Socialist parties were thinking in terms of an appeal to the British forces in the north of Persia. On 25 July the Soviet, despite the uncompromising opposition of the Bolshevik representatives, voted to call in the British. 'The British,' said Shaumyan, 'only want our oil; they have no food supplies to give us.' He was only too terribly right. Meanwhile the suspect Russian troops were disorganizing the front; the threat of a Turkish and Tartar onslaught hung over all. The Dashnaks had actually been negotiating since 21 April with General Dunsterville, the commander of the British troops in Persia. 'Our friends,' wrote the latter in his *Memoirs*, 'seemed to be in a position to overthrow the Bolsheviks shortly and call us in. ...'[16] The People's Commissars resigned and were replaced by a democratic Directorate, under the mysterious title of 'People's Dictatorship', composed of SRs, Dashnaks and Mensheviks. The Bolsheviks, having tried in vain to reach Astrakhan by sea, set up a camp for last-ditch resistance, defended by their artillery, in the centre of the port, on board the ships which also held a number of workers' families. A group of comrades headed by Mikoyan[17] still conducted activity semi-clandestinely in the working-class districts, resisting the so-called 'democracy'. Eventually some hundreds of British troops landed.

On the night of 14 August the Bolsheviks once again weighed anchor. Owing to bad weather, their heavy tanker vessels, loaded with cannon, horses and passengers – for whole families were fleeing – could not reach the open sea. Gunboats caught them up. The Caspian fleet had kept its officers from the Tsarist regime, and the Soviet had made the grave blunder of neglecting political work among the sailors. The local government now demanded the handing over of Shaumyan and the other main proletarian leaders, threatening to open fire if they were refused. The Reds surrendered after undergoing an hour's bombardment in mid-sea, against which they were powerless to retaliate. They tried to get Shaumyan away but failed. About forty Bolshevik militants were arrested. They remained in prison until the British and the Directorate both fled before the advance of the Tartars and Turks in mid-September. Mikoyan freed them from the prison where they had been left to lie and wait for slaughter. Dzhaparidze, Shaumyan and his friends, to the number of twenty-six, now embarked with other fugitives for the Trans-Caspian area, governed to all appearances by a vague sort of SR government but actually by half-a-dozen British officers. They were arrested at Krasnovodsk. Captain Reginald Teague-Jones demanded the execution of the twenty-six commissars, in the name of General Thomson and the British Mission at Ashkabad.[18] The prisoners were to be shot in the course of being 'transported to India' for internment. On 30 September, three whole days after being arrested, the twenty-six Bolsheviks were shot in a deserted spot on the railway-line from Ashkabad.

At around 6 A.M. [relates a witness], the twenty-six commissars were told of the fate awaiting them while they were in the train. They were taken out in groups of eight or nine men. They were obviously shocked, and kept a tense silence. One sailor shouted: 'I'm not afraid, I'm dying for liberty.' One of the executioners replied that 'We too will die for liberty sooner or later, but we mean it in a different way from you.' The first group of commissars, led from the train in the semi-darkness, was dispatched with a single salvo. The second batch tried to run away but was mown down after several volleys. The third resigned itself to its fate . . .[19]

Thus perished Shaumyan, who has been called 'the Lenin of the Caucasus'. Thus perished the heroes of the Baku Commune. 'Captain Teague-Jones told me of his satisfaction that the execution had taken place in conformity with the wishes of the British Mission,' wrote Funtikov later, who was a Socialist-Revolutionary member of the Trans-Caspian government.[20]

The Turks and Tartars had by now invaded Baku. For three days they cut the throats of the Armenians, the Russians, the workers, the Reds. Georgadze, the Georgian Minister of War in the Socialist government of Tiflis, nevertheless remarked shortly afterwards to the Turkish General Nuri Pasha when the latter was the guest of honour at a banquet: 'I congratulate you on chasing the Bolshevik usurpers from Baku and establishing your splendid democracy there.' Socialist Georgia had let the Turkish troops pass over its territory.

LENIN AT THE THIRD CONGRESS OF SOVIETS

The Third Congress of Soviets had taken place at Petrograd from 10 to 18 January (23–31). Its composition can be gauged from that of the All-Russian Executive which it appointed and which consisted of 160 Communists, 125 Left SRs, seven Right SRs, seven Maximalist SRs, three anarchist-Communists, two Mensheviks and two Menshevik-Internationalists. Trotsky and Kamenev reported on the negotiations at Brest-Litovsk. The most important debates were those concerning the organization of the power of the Soviets. We shall give details only of Lenin's contributions, which happen to be of capital importance.

He began his report on the work of the Council of People's Commissars by expressing his pleasure at the fact that Soviet power had so far lasted *five days longer* than the Paris Commune (which had only lasted two months and ten days). He emphasized the importance of the alliance between the proletariat and the poorest peasants, as confirmed in the united front between the Bolshevik and Left SR parties; and he stressed once more that there was no question of imposing Socialism upon the peasantry. He also affirmed the necessity of violence:

Never in history has any question relating to the class struggle been settled other than by violence. We are supporters of violence on the condition that it proceeds from the exploited toiling classes and is directed against the exploiters ...

To those who were urging an end to the civil war he asked their views on the example which had been set by the propertied classes with their pitiless repression. 'We are still very far from exercising real terror, because we are strong.' The confiscation of the capi-- talists' goods would be enough to make them cringe. He told them of a remark made by an old woman, overheard by chance in a railway station: 'The people is no longer afraid of the man with a rifle.' After that, what does it matter to us that we get called 'dictators' and 'usurpers'? And he announced the creation of the Red Army, a nation in arms.

He denounced two social evils: the sabotage of the intellectuals and the egoistic impulses of the backward masses. 'The professors, teachers and engineers are making their knowledge into an instrument for the exploitation of labour: they are saying, "We want our intelligence to serve the bourgeoisie or we shall not work at all."'

But the worst social elements bequeathed to us by the old regime are the scoundrels who are animated by one desire only: to take and then run off. All the badness from the past is concentrated in them, they must be chased out of the factories. It is worth remembering this reference by Lenin to the crude individualism of the backward citizens, which is developed and encouraged by capitalist competition and is particularly powerful among the petty-bourgeoisie. Lenin will continually return to the problem to denounce it, to fight it, to expose the immense dangers in it. Against the revolution's thieves, adventurers and profiteers he will ceaselessly appeal to the initiative of the masses. He tells the peasants, 'Do what you please with the land: undoubtedly you will make mistakes, but it is the only way to learn.' He tells the Congress that 'the proletariat has in a number of places been contacting the managers' associations in order to secure for itself the direction of whole branches of production'. He concludes with some general reflections on the place of the Russian revolution in the world revolutionary process:

Marx and Engels used to say: the Frenchman will begin it, the German will finish it. They said 'The Frenchman will begin it' because he had acquired, in the course of revolutions over many decades, the revolutionary dedication and initiative which have placed him in the vanguard of the Socialist revolution. ... We say, though, that the movement will begin most easily in those countries which are not among the exploiting powers with all the possibilities of plunder (from the colonies) to corrupt the better-off layers of the working class. ... The Russian has begun it, the German, the Frenchman and the Englishman will finish it – and Socialism will triumph.

Lenin made some very clear allusions to the suppression of the State.

Anarchist ideas [he said] now assume living forms in this epoch of the radical demolition of bourgeois society. However, it is still necessary first of all, in order to overthrow bourgeois society, to establish the strong revolutionary power of the toiling classes, the power of the revolutionary State. ... The new tendencies of anarchism are definitely on the side of the Soviets.

Speaking a few days later to the agitators who were going off to one of the provinces, he again expresses one of the ideas which he loved to repeat: 'Each worker, each peasant, each citizen must understand that he alone can bring help, and that he has nothing to rely on except from himself'.[21]

THE PROBLEM

Could the Soviet Republic survive under the burden of Brest-Litovsk? This was the great question. It had lost forty per cent of its industrial proletariat (for the Austro–Germans occupied the Donetz basin with its mines), forty-five per cent of its fuel production, ninety per cent of its sugar production, sixty-four to seventy per cent of its metal industry, fifty-five per cent of its wheat, i.e. the major part of its export grain.[22] Russia, whose external trade had rested for centuries upon the export of grain, was to find herself thrown back on her own resources and doomed to inevitable poverty. 'The peace of Brest-Litovsk,' it was being said, 'means slow death to the revolution' (in Lozovsky's words). This conviction helped to nurture the idea of revolutionary war. The discussions at the first All-Russian Congress of the People's Economic Councils (26 May–4 June) are informative on the ideas current in the majority of the party. Radek, who gave the report on the economic consequences of the treaty, stressed that the revolution would henceforth become severely dependent on foreign powers and the world market. He advocated a policy of concessions and loans from private capital (a line which nowadays looks somewhat Utopian). Only new enterprises were to form the subject of concessions, and these were to be established outside the main industrial regions of the country (the Ural, Donetz, Kuznetsk and Baku); the State would share in the profits and would reserve the right to buy the enterprises back at the end of a certain interval. The Congress had no choice but to content itself with this hypothetical solution. It also decided to develop the industries in the Ural as well as the cotton production of Turkestan. Old Kalinin declared, 'It is in the Ural, in the north and in Siberia that we shall lay the foundations of our future power.'[23] These were the despairing solutions produced by revolutionaries who had been determined never to despair. Was such a Russia viable – mutilated like this, living under the constant menace of an all-powerful imperialism, a prey to the growing conflict between the towns and the countryside? The most optimistic affirmed the possibility only out of sheer necessity. The party was splitting, with the Left

Communists (who were moving nearer the Left SRs) becoming increasingly convinced that the peace was an evil fouler than the worst war, while Lenin and the majority of the party listened to the earth tremors of Europe and waited for Germany's collapse.

The growing antagonism between town and country was evident in the inflation, the famine and the general chaos. The value of the rouble fell dizzily. Since taxes were no longer collected – rightly in the circumstances – the government's only resources were the banknotes it issued. Industrial production had declined terribly, so that the prices of manufactured goods kept rising. The peasant received in exchange for his corn only paper roubles with which he could buy nothing except an ever more restricted supply of manufactured articles, and these with great difficulty; and so he resorted to barter: foodstuffs against goods. A whole host of small speculators operated as middlemen between him and the town. The cities had been in a state of famine even before the revolution; so there were no reserves left. Amid this collapse individualist instincts had free play: it was easy to find a personal way out and impossible to make bread available for all. Nothing less than the discipline and collective consciousness of the proletariat could have managed even a partial success against these forces. The inflation of 1917–18 may be judged from the following figures: the total issue of paper roubles from the Imperial Bank as of 1 January 1917, was a little more than nine thousand million; in the course of 1917 14,721 million roubles were issued and twelve thousand million in the first five months of 1918.[24]

This internal situation in Russia must be kept in mind if the dissensions within the Bolshevik party are to be understood.

LENIN AT THE SEVENTH CONGRESS OF THE RUSSIAN COMMUNIST PARTY

On 24 February the Moscow Region Committee passed a resolution in defiance of the Central Committee, refusing to submit to 'the measures relating to the implementation of the peace treaty'. This motion was accompanied by an explanatory document, which stated:

The Moscow Region Committee, considering that a split within the party is probable in the near future, resolves to rally all serious revolutionaries and all Communist elements in struggle against the supporters of a separate peace and the moderate elements of the Communist movement. It would be in accordance with the interests of the world revolution, we believe, to accept the sacrifice of Soviet power, which is becoming purely formal. As in the past, we see our essential task to be the worldwide extension of the ideas of the Socialist revolution and, in Russia, the vigorous exercise of the dictatorship and the pitiless repression of the bourgeois counter-revolution.

'Strange,' replied Lenin, 'strange and monstrous.' Far from

improving the chances of the German revolution, he pointed out commonsensically, the sacrifice of Soviet power would do it considerable harm. Did not the workers of Britain become cowed by the defeat of the Commune in 1871? Did not France in 1793 and Prussia under the boot of Napoleon's armies show the power that could be held in a tenacious will?

Why cannot events like these be repeated in our history? Why do we have to fall into despair and draw up resolutions which are more dishonourable – yes, truly! – than the most dishonourable peace, referring to a 'Soviet power which is becoming purely formal'? Never has any foreign invasion made a popular political institution 'purely formal' (and the power of the Soviets is not only a popular political institution: it is an institution far superior to all others known in history).

Foreign invasion, on the contrary, would only increase the sympathy of the people for Soviet power . . . as long as the latter does not embark on adventures. . . . Russia is on the road to a new national war, a war for the defence and preservation of Soviet power. It is possible that this epoch, like that of the Napoleonic wars, will be an epoch of wars of liberation (I speak deliberately of wars, not *a* war) forced on Soviet Russia by the invaders. It is quite possible. And that is why despair, dishonourable despair, is more dishonourable than any viciously oppressive peace treaty imposed on us by the absence of an army. The consequences of tens of such oppressive treaties will not lead to our defeat if we know how to consider war and insurrection *seriously*. The invaders will not kill us if we do not permit ourselves to be killed with despair and phrasemongering.[25]

The Left Communists – 'Communists of misfortune' as Lenin called them – at first, from 5–19 March, published a daily newspaper: this was the *Kommunist*, the organ of the Petrograd Committee of the party, edited by Bukharin, Radek and Uritsky. *Kommunist* was moved soon afterwards to Moscow, where it appeared weekly from 20 April until June. Obolensky-Ossinsky and V. M. Smirnov joined the editorial team in this period. Among the collaborators of this organ of the Left may be noted: Bubnov, Bronsky, Antonov (Lukin), Lomov (Oppokov), M. Pokrovsky, E. Preobrazhensky, Y. Pyatakov, Soltz, Unschlicht, Kollontai, V. Kuibishev, E. Yaroslavsky, Sapronov and Safarov. These names give some idea of the strength and quality behind the Left movement.

The two tendencies faced each other at the Seventh Party Congress which was held in Petrograd from 6–8 March, a few days before the capital was transferred to Moscow (on the 10th, under the threat of a German occupation). The only subject discussed was the peace treaty. Lenin (supported by Zinoviev, Smilga, Sverdlov and Sokolnikov) attacked the theses of the Lefts. Trotsky, though a supporter of war, rallied to Lenin's thesis on the grounds that revolutionary war could not be fought with the party divided. The menace of a split, which was feared by all sides, hung over the congress until the end of its work. But the delegates' concern for unity prevailed. The oppositionists were given representation on the Central Committee as well as on the commission for the revision of the programme.

From Lenin's various statements to the Congress we shall select those which offer the greatest historical and theoretical interest. He remarked first that the first months of the Soviet regime had been a triumphal march, but afterwards the inevitable difficulties of a Socialist revolution had made their appearance. For:

one of the essential differences between the bourgeois and the Socialist revolution is that the first, which is always born out of the feudal order, builds up its forms of economic organization bit by bit within the old regime, through the development of commerce which slowly modifies all aspects of feudal society. The bourgeois revolution has one task only: to remove, eliminate and destroy all the foundations of the old order. When it accomplishes this task the bourgeois revolution fulfils its whole mission, as it ends up by creating the system of commodity production and facilitating the growth of capitalism. The situation of the Socialist revolution is quite different. The more backward the country is where the zigzags of history cause it to begin, the more difficult is the transition from the old capitalist relationships to the new relationships of Socialism. As well as the tasks of destruction there are other tasks, infinitely difficult: those of organization.

The Soviet Socialist Republic came to birth so easily because in February 1917 the masses created Soviets before any party had time to issue this slogan.

Thus, the difference between bourgeois and proletarian revolutions is that the former benefits from forms of organization which are already in existence, while the latter has to create everything from scratch. And 'assault tactics' cannot be applied to economic and administrative work. The Socialist revolution 'will be infinitely more difficult to begin in Europe than in Russia. With us, it was infinitely easier to begin, but will be hard to continue with: in Europe on the contrary it will be easier to continue once it has started.' We have had to disarm in the presence of the imperialist beast and

our salvation, I repeat it, lies in the European revolution ... and if you say that the hydra of revolution is hidden in every strike and he is not a Socialist who does not understand that, you are quite right. Yes, the Socialist revolution is hidden in every strike; but if you say that every strike is a step forward towards the Socialist revolution, you are saying the emptiest of stupidities.

It is absolutely true that without the revolution in Germany we shall perish. We may not perish in Petrograd or Moscow: perhaps at Vladivostok.... In any case we shall perish if the German revolution does not come. This in no way diminishes our duty to face the most critical situations without idle boasting. The [German] revolution will not be coming as rapidly as we expected. History has proved that. We must take it as a fact.

We demobilized because the army was our society's diseased limb: the sooner it is dissolved the sooner the organism will recover. 'We must know how to beat a retreat.'

As for the split in the party, we shall cure it (Lenin said) with our historical experience and the aid of the world revolution. He waged a polemic against the fantasies of *Kommunist*, which were completely refuted by the facts, and against the absurd attempt to transpose the insurrectionary methods of October to the international scene. *The truce is a fact*, he said. He re-told the shattering tale of the eleven days of revolutionary war: they thought Petrograd would be lost, and such an emptiness stretched before the Germans that towns like Yamburg[26] were 'recaptured' by telegraph operators who were amazed to find that no Germans were there. 'There it is: the terribly bitter, outrageous, painful and humiliating truth – but a hundred times more use than your *Kommunist*.'

What was to be done now? There must be order. Let the worker learn how to handle arms, be it for only an hour a day. That is going to be more difficult than writing the most beautiful romances. 'Our peace is another peace of Tilsit', so let us profit from it to prepare war. 'History tells us that peace is a truce before war, and war is a means of obtaining a slightly better peace.' The whole speech was couched in these terms of realism and tenacity. 'We will retreat as far as we have to. Perhaps tomorrow we shall abandon Moscow. We shall know how to meet that test. And when the day comes we shall begin the struggle again.' And, having crossed swords with Bukharin, who was blaming the Central Committee for its 'demoralizing tactic', and with Trotsky, who was urging a war against the Ukraine, he said in conclusion: 'I want to lose space in order to gain time.'[27]

THE THESIS OF HEROIC SACRIFICE

The arguments of the Left Communists became the object of a painstaking analysis whose accuracy Bukharin was gracious enough to acknowledge in a preface written later in 1925. The Left Communists' case was founded, both then and before the conclusion of the treaty, upon deeply rooted feelings: indignation, sorrow, anger and a tragic pessimism on the future of the revolution, all the more tragic in that it was mingled with an almost blind enthusiasm which involved a desire for total sacrifice. This feeling was expressed in a number of surprising declarations: 'If the Russian revolution itself does not flinch, no one can master it or break it';[28] 'So long as the revolution ... does not capitulate, it can fear no partial defeat, however grave. The great Republic of the Soviets can lose Petrograd, Kiev or Moscow, *but it cannot perish.*'[29]

Such affirmations are amazing. How was the country to hold on in reality? A 'mobilization of spirits' was needed. Bukharin wrote that 'When the masses see the German offensive at work ... a true holy war will begin.'[30] What if there is no army? Then we will use guerrilla warfare. Guerrilla war was, during the whole duration of the revolution, one of the white hopes of all revolutionary romantics. The strength of the guerrillas would lie above all in their Socialist convictions and 'in the social character of the new army that is being mobilized'. Here a very perceptive idea was mixed up with a very misleading idealism. A new army could and must be born, based upon the class interests which are the source of revolutionary enthusiasm; it was still childish to argue that German technique could be opposed with Socialist convictions.

These theories were justified by a doctrinal affirmation and by a distortion of reality. The statement of doctrine was: No compromise! The revolution must not manoeuvre, nor retreat, nor agree to compromises. The only tactic it must apply was that of maximum intransigence. Better perish than live at the cost of a compromise! This was the basic doctrine of Left Communism, and one must give it the credit of a healthy reaction against opportunist tendencies. (We have seen how the Left Communists opposed all relations with the capitalist powers.) The distortion of reality, which was obviously unconscious, consisted in denying the existence of the respite won from German imperialism and even of disputing its possibility. The prospect of peace, said Bukharin, was 'illusory, non-existent'. Peace, wrote Kollontai, had become 'an impossibility'. 'This is not peace,' wrote Radek after the signing of the treaty, 'it is a new war.'

Reality became blurred in the sight of these passionate revolutionaries owing to their intense feelings; the struggle continued but the truce was a fact, imperfect and uninspiring as it was. With his typical common sense, Lenin asked them: 'How can you deny the existence of the truce when we have already had five clear days to get on with the evacuation of Petrograd?'

The conclusions of the Left Communists summarize, in a single, clear, theoretical statement, both their sense of exaltation and the curious blend of optimism before history and pessimism before immediate reality which was so characteristic of their tendency:

We do not seek to conceal from ourselves the possibility that the rigorous application, on both the home and the international front, of a proletarian policy has many dangers, and might result in our overthrow for the moment; but we believe it to be better that we should, in the interests of the world proletarian movement, succumb to the overwhelming pressure of external forces while we are still in an authentic state of proletarian power, than that we should survive by adapting ourselves to the circumstances.[31]

It has been the general custom in Russia to view this ideology as a petty-bourgeois deviation, to use the hallowed expression. And doubtless most deviations from proletarian ideology, of their various kinds, are in general the work of intellectuals, and reflect more or less faithfully states of consciousness characteristic of the middle classes who occupy a position intermediate between the proletariat and the bourgeoisie. Doubtless, too, the sentiments of wounded pride, outraged patriotism and heroic sacrifice (the 'Death before Dishonour' school) are much more congenial to the mentality of the middle classes, and particularly of the intellectuals, than to the realistic, utilitarian, dialectical and deeply revolutionary spirit of the proletariat. But it is, as I see it, no longer deniable that this Left-wing tendency also represented something else: a reaction against the danger of opportunism. Lenin belonged neither to any Left nor to any Right: he was simply revolutionary, inflexibly yet pragmatically, and without fine phrases. However, up till the time of Lenin, all the points at which men had opted to 'manoeuvre' in the name of revolution had been occasions for them to fall straight into opportunism. We must also remember another essential fact. Never before had there been a successful proletarian revolution. Some of the best revolutionaries now became inclined to continue the tradition of heroic proletarian defeats, by means of a sacrifice whose fruitfulness for the future deeply and understandably impressed them. It was, however, one of Lenin's great merits to have insisted that this tradition must be broken with.

DOCTRINE AND ACTION AT THE SEVENTH PARTY CONGRESS

In these crucial days the Seventh Congress of the party also devoted its attention to problems of theory. Lenin succeeded at last in getting the name of the party changed there: the Social-Democratic Workers' Party of Russia thus became the Communist Party (Bolshevik) of Russia, a change which he had advocated ever since the beginning of 1917. This also provided an occasion for him to stress, once again, how the concept of democracy had been transcended by the State of the Soviets, conceived as it was on the model of the Paris Commune, and to recall to the delegates that Socialism aspires to the suppression of all governmental constraints and the application of the rule 'From each according to his abilities, to each according to his needs'. In refutation of the theory propounded at this juncture by all the Socialist adversaries of the revolution to the effect that 'Poverty cannot be socialized', he quoted some prophetic lines by Friedrich Engels, written in 1887. Engels had even then foreseen the world conflagration, and predicted the overthrow of kingdoms, devastation on an immense scale and, amid all this, 'the victory of the working class or the creation of conditions which will make this victory possible'. Lenin declared too that human culture was indestructible, though he admitted that its renaissance at the present time might well prove an arduous task.

Bukharin, Sokolnikov and Vladimir Smirnov proposed the deletion of the current theoretical section of the party's programme which was devoted to an explanation of the growth of commodity production: they thought that this section was outdated and that it would be enough for the programme to define imperialism and the era of Socialist revolution. This view was erroneous on several points, for even in the epoch of imperialism both commoditv production and the simplest forms of capitalism continue to develop in the backward countries. But in his reply to them Lenin treated the matter more broadly. One page of his speech must be quoted in full.

Commodity production begot capitalism and capitalism led to imperialism. Such is the general historical perspective, and the fundamentals of Socialism should not be forgotten. No matter what the further complications of the struggle may be, no matter what occasional zigzags we may have to contend with (there will be very many of them – we have seen from experience what gigantic turns the history of the revolution has made, and so far it is only in our own country; matters will be much more complicated and proceed much more rapidly, the rate of development will be more furious and the turns will be more intricate when the revolution becomes a European revolution) – in order not to lose our way in these zigzags, these sharp turns in history, in order to retain the general perspective, to be able to see the scarlet thread that joins up the entire development of capitalism and the entire road to Socialism, the road we naturally imagine as straight, and which we must imagine as straight in order to see the beginning, the continuation and the end – in real life it will never be straight, it will be incredibly involved – in order not to lose our way in these twists and turns, in order not to get lost at times when we are taking steps backward, times of retreat and temporary defeat or when history or the enemy throws us back – in order not to get lost, it is, in my opinion, important not to discard our old, basic programme; the only theoretically correct line is to retain it. Today we have reached only the first stage of transition from capitalism to Socialism here in Russia. History has not provided us with that peaceful situation that was theoretically assumed for a certain time, and which is desirable for us, and which would enable us to pass through these stages of transition speedily. We see immediately that the civil war has made many things difficult in Russia, and that the civil war is interwoven with a whole series of wars. Marxists have never forgotten that violence must inevitably accompany the collapse of capitalism in its entirety and the birth of Socialist society. That violence will constitute a period of world history, a whole era of various kinds of wars, imperialist wars, civil wars inside countries, the intermingling of the two, national wars liberating the nationalities oppressed by the imperialists.

We have only just taken the first steps towards shaking off capitalism altogether and beginning the transition to Socialism. We do not know and we cannot know how many stages of transition to Socialism there will be. That depends on when the full-scale European Socialist revolu-

41. Partisans from Irkutsk on the anti-Kolchak front, 1919

tion begins and on whether it will deal with its enemies and enter upon
the smooth path of Socialist development easily and rapidly or whether
it will do so slowly. We do not know this, and the programme of a
Marxist party must be based on facts that have been established with
absolute certainty. The power of our programme is in that alone.

The same militants advocated the deletion of the minimum programme of the party. Before the October Revolution Lenin had
opposed this proposal, but now saw nothing against the deletion.
All the same, he added that 'It would be Utopian to think that we
will not be thrown back once again.'

He dwelt further on the distortion by the Social-Democrats of
the Marxist teaching on the State: as he had done repeatedly in
1917 he defined the nature of the Republic of Soviets:

A new type of State, without a bureaucracy, without a police, without a permanent army, which replaces bourgeois democracy by a new democracy, causes the labouring masses to act as vanguard, and confers upon them legislative, executive and military power, thereby creating the means whereby these same masses will be educated. We are just beginning this work in Russia, and for the time being we are beginning it badly.

Perhaps we are doing badly what we are doing, but we are pushing the masses into doing what they must. And may the workers of Europe say among themselves: 'What the Russians are doing badly, we shall do better.'[32]

I shall give only a brief summary of the draft programme submitted by Lenin to the Seventh Congress. In it the power of the Soviet is defined in ten theses, which provide what is surely the most developed exposition of his ideas.

(1) Unity of all the poor and exploited masses. (2) Unity of the conscious, active minority for the re-education of the whole labouring population. (3) Abolition of parliamentarianism, which separates legislative from executive authority. (4) A unity between the masses and the State which will be closer than in the older democratic forms. (5) Arming of the workers and peasants. (6) More democracy and less formalism, greater facilities for election and recall of delegates. (7) Close links between the political authority and production. (8) The possibility of eliminating bureaucracy. (9) The transition from the formal democracy of rich and poor to the real democracy of the toilers. (10) Participation of all members of the Soviets in the management and administration of the State.

After this comes the listing of a number of measures, both political (those aimed towards the 'gradual total abolition of the State') and economic, such as 'socialized production' administered by the workers' organizations (trade unions, factory committees, etc.); compulsory enrolment of the whole population into consumer cooperatives; the registration of all commercial operations (since money is 'not yet abolished') conducted by the producers' and consumers' communes; general obligation to work ('which we discreetly extend to include those peasants who live off the fruits of their own labour'); the establishment of ticket-books for labour and consumption for all persons either with an income of over 500 roubles per month or employing wage labour or domestic servants; the concentration of all financial operations in the hands of the State Bank; control and accountancy of all production and consumption, first by the workers' organizations and eventually by the whole population; organized competition among producer and consumer cooperatives, with the aim of improving the efficiency of labour while reducing its duration; systematic steps towards collective dining facilities, by groups of families; the abolition of indirect taxes and their replacement by a progressive income tax and a levy on the takings of the State's monopolies.

CREATION OF THE RED ARMY

Finland, the Baltic countries and the Ukraine were now occupied by the Austro–German forces. The Turks were in the Caucasus, which was still supposedly 'independent'. The British were occupying Baku, and the Rumanians had taken over Bessarabia.[33] On 6 April, the Japanese landed at Vladivostok. The revolution was encircled by iron and fire. It needed an army. And this army had to be created from a sheer void.

On 2 (15) January, during the Brest-Litovsk negotiations, a decree on the constitution of a Red Army of volunteers had been promulgated.[34] The Red General Staff – consisting of the remnants of the General Staff of the former regime – called on the local Soviets to show their initiative by recruiting new military formations, with the battalion of 150 men as the basic unit. This appeal was taken up: when the actual Red Army took shape later, it was to be formed on the skeleton provided for it by these first improvised units. A Supreme Council of the Army was established on 1 March. From these very first days Trotsky stood out as the indefatigable inspirer of this creation of an army. 'We have need of a properly organized army, a new army,' he proclaimed on 19 March to the Moscow Soviet. 'We shall work twelve hours a day if necessary ... but we shall march forward on the path of discipline, work and creative action.'

Determined labour, revolutionary discipline: these were the slogans he repeated, inserting and implanting them in the brains of his listeners. On his proposal, the decree on general and compulsory military training was passed on 22 April. It was a preparatory measure only: a large section of the population was still hostile to the regime. The army now being organized had to be made up from volunteers whose social origins and political opinions had to be the prime consideration. But a modern army is a highly complex machine. The machinery cannot be set in motion and its functioning cannot be guaranteed without specialized skills. Where were the technicians of war to be found? There existed only those from the old regime, those belonging to the enemy classes. Trotsky argued, from an early stage, that these specialists must be employed. In order to carry this policy he had to overcome widespread resistance and well-founded anxieties. Even Lenin offered objections at first, but then withdrew them. In Trotsky's *On Lenin* we read:

'Without serious, experienced military men,' I told Vladimir Ilyich, 'we shall never get out of this chaos.'
'That seems fair enough. But what if they start to betray us?'
'We shall put a commissar next to each one of them.'
'We'll put two commissars,' cried Lenin, 'With burly fists. At any rate we are not short of burly Communists!'

The leading organs of the new Red Army were conceived on the following pattern: one specialist (a career officer) and two Bolshevik commissars. The military staff, it seems, accepted this pattern of control without too much difficulty. Accustomed to passive obedience and to the service of the State, they submitted once authority was imposed on them. In their memoirs the White generals complain of the facility with which the Bolsheviks recruited the technical personnel of the Red Army. After all, these latter had to make a living. Patriotic sentiment also had its appeal for them. Nevertheless, there were numerous officers who were to enter the Red Army and remain enemies of the revolution. The army became infiltrated with a permanent conspiracy. Trotsky had to answer the arguments of those who feared that the army, headed as it was by former generals, might become an instrument of counter-revolution. He replied that, manned by workers and poor peasants, and officered by strong forces of Communist commissars, it need fear only individual betrayals. He had to attack the manners and customs which had been instituted by the revolution itself. For many long months the military leaders had been elected, a principle made imperative by the need to democratize the old army.

So long as power belonged to the enemy class and the leading elements of the army were the instrument of that class, we had to break the resistance of the high command through introducing the election of officers. But power today is in the hands of the working class, from whose midst the army is being recruited. In these conditions – I say this in all frankness – the election of officers has no further political utility and is technically inadequate. In fact, it has already been abolished by decree.

However excellent these reasons were, they were not imposed easily. How could it be otherwise, when first-class revolutionaries, proletarians, were being replaced in the high command by the generals who ran yesterday's firing-squads and by officers who remained counter-revolutionaries at heart? It was a high command controlled by commissars, it is true, but how competent were these? But it was necessary. 'The creation of the army,' Trotsky would say, 'is a matter of life or death for us.'

No administrative machinery existed that was capable of mobilizing the forces required for the army. The party had to take over from the State, revealing once against the key importance of its mission in history. The Red Guards, the partisan units (numerous in the south, but anarchical, undisciplined and infinitely resistant to control), and a few regular (but only just regular) units left over from the old army furnished the Republic with her first soldiery, which was of very uneven and unreliable quality. The recruiting campaign produced quite useful results, though still insufficient. On 1 April, Petrograd supplied 25,000 volunteers and Moscow 15,000. One hundred and six thousand volunteers joined up within six weeks.

FAMINE

The months of April and May were marked by an extreme intensification of the food shortage. We may recall that the fall of the
Tsar in February 1917 had been accompanied by cries of 'Bread!
Bread!' shouted in the workers' districts of Petrograd. Ever since
1916 supplies even for the army had been so poor that in 1917 the
troops had received only fifty-three per cent of their meat ration.[1]
The disorganization of transport had reached a climax as the
result of the spontaneous demobilization of the army, followed by
the German advance and the sporadic guerrilla warfare. The best
elements of the proletariat streamed from the factories to fight or
labour for the revolution; production was being sabotaged by the
employers, abetted by the technical staff. The prices of manufactured goods, which were getting harder and harder to find, went
up, while the value of the paper currency, depreciated by constant
re-issues, simultaneously declined. The peasants became tempted
to withold their corn from a State which forbade them to sell it
and offered in exchange what was only a derisory price, whether
in paper money or in goods: grain became the target of speculation and sold at four or five times its normal price. These tragic
facts summed up the problem of supplying food to the large
towns, the working class that was the revolution's vital force, and
the growing army.

A monopoly of the grain traffic had been secured by the Provisional Government immediately after the collapse of Tsarism;
but its running had been entrusted to Committees of Supply made
up of dealers, factory-owners, landlords and rich peasants. The
Soviet government gave the institution a quite different character.
The Mensheviks, SRs and peasantry urged the People's Commissars to abolish the monopoly. But it was actually a vital necessity.
Free trade in grain would have left the State armed with the means
of issuing paper currency but actually powerless in the face of
speculation, which would be master of the market. The rich or
comfortable layers of the peasantry would have been the best fed,
indeed the only ones to be fed. It would have been virtually impossible to organize the regular transport of foodstuffs. The
better-off peasants, enriched at the expense of the towns, would
have in a short while become a formidable force. The State monopoly had to be defended to the death, and that is what was done.

A decree of 2 April authorized the bartering of commodities
with the countryside, a first step towards regularizing the difficult,
chaotic relations between city and peasantry. The fall in the value
of paper money had necessitated the direct barter of goods

against grain; but it had turned out that the goods delivered by the State fell into the hands of the rich peasants or kulaks.[2] The new decree specified that the exchange was henceforth to be conducted via the associations of poor peasants. This was the first invitation to the struggle between rich peasants and poor, destined within a few months to become a bitter civil war. In the end, on 13 May, it became necessary to proclaim 'the dictatorship of food supplies'. The decree establishing it instituted the compulsory delivery to the State of all excess grain held by individuals, deductions being made for the amounts necessary for their own subsistence, for sowing, etc. These deductions were fixed by regular norms. The poor and the workers were urged to unite against the kulaks in the struggle for grain. The Commissariat for Food Supplies was authorized to act with the utmost vigour. It was, in short, a formal declaration of war by the dictatorship of the proletariat against the kulaks. On 20 May the 'Food Army' was created. Its effective troops were to number between 40,000 and 45,000 even up to 1919. It was this force that carried out the requisitioning in the countryside.

The famine was so acute that at Tsarskoye Seloe (now Dietskoye Seloe), not far from Petrograd, the people's bread ration was only 100 grams per day. Rioting resulted. Cries of 'Long live the Constituent Assembly!' and even 'Long live Nicholas II!' were heard (this on 6–7 April). On 19 April there were 'hunger riots' (an expression familiar from long ago) at Smolensk, 'fomented' (or so it was said) by anarchists. At the end of April all movement into the famished and overpopulated province of Samara was prohibited. The bitterness, despair and anger sown by the famine, even in working-class areas, turned the middle classes of the cities, now ruined and totally incapable of understanding the revolution, into a receptive stratum for all varieties of counter-revolutionary propaganda. Discontent among the rich and prospering sections of the peasantry threatened to gather into a formidable rural Vendée.

In this period [writes one worker-militant], hardly any horses were to be seen in Petrograd; they were either dead, or eaten, or requisitioned, or sent off into the countryside. Dogs and cats were no more visible either. ... People lived on tea and potato-cakes made with linseed oil. As a member of the EC of the Vyborg Soviet [in Petrograd] I know that there were *whole weeks* in which no issues of bread or potatoes were made to the workers; all they got was sunflower seeds and some nuts. ... The balance of forces consisted of starving towns face to face with a hundred million hostile peasants. Soviet power seemed to be in a desperate position.[3]

THE DISARMAMENT OF THE ANARCHISTS

These conditions formed the background for the disarmament of the anarchists, which took place on the night of 11–12 April.

The unimportance of the anarchists' influence among the worker-masses is attested by the small number of seats they held in the Soviets and in the Congress of Soviets, where, as a rule, they never added up to more than half a dozen out of the several hundred deputies; a number of libertarian groups, in addition, boycotted the Soviets, as being organs of authority. However, their little groups had become conspicuous, ever since May and June of 1917, in the bloody events at Durnovo's villa in Petrograd,[4] and then by their role in the July days which were the prelude to the October insurrection; these demonstrations were partly their work. At Kronstadt and other places they had battled bravely against Kerenskyism, side by side with the Bolsheviks. In spite of their ideological disarray,[5] most of them had fought well in October. On the morrow of the proletarian victory, their movement had gathered an exceptional vigour. No power stood in their way; they proceeded with the requisitioning of houses at their own behest; the Bolshevik party negotiated with their organizations on equal terms; in Moscow they had a big daily newspaper, *Anarkhiya*. (*Golos Truda*, or *Voice of Labour*, the anarcho-syndicalist journal in Petrograd, which at various moments had rivalled Lenin's *Pravda* in influence, folded up only through the fault of its editors, who were divided among themselves on the problem of revolutionary war; Voline[6] and his friends abandoned propaganda to form themselves into a partisan detachment, and went off to the front where they proved quite useless.)

Anarkhiya, edited by the Gordin brothers,[7] devoted itself to a feverish propaganda, of an entirely idealistic and demagogic quality, which seemed to be in no contact with any reality. Let us go through a few issues of this sheet, from April 1918. It must be remembered that this is the time immediately before the collapse of anarchism in the Russian revolution: after 12 April, it no longer exists. 'We are against the Soviets on principle,' write the brothers Gordin on 7 April, 'since we are against all forms of State.' 'They are saying that we intend to overthrow the Bolsheviks. Nonsense! We were opposed even to overthrowing the Mensheviks!'

The same source, 10 April: 'We considered and still consider the seizure of power to be a fatal error ... but in October we fought in the front ranks.' Again: 'We are threatened, but we are calm. It is impossible that we should perish: what is great cannot perish.' There was one single practical slogan in big black letters across the journal's two pages: a humanitarian slogan directed against the Cheka (which at this moment was fairly mild): '*Don't shoot men arrested without arms.*' This sort of language, however violent it might be from time to time, appears to have been harmless. But that was not the problem.

In Moscow alone, the anarchist forces, divided into a multitude of groups, sub-groups, tendencies and sub-tendencies, from individualism to syndicalism, via Communism and not a few other quite fantastic 'isms', amounted to several thousands of men, armed for the most part. In this environment of famine, the sincere demagogy of the libertarian propagandists was well received by the backward elements of the populace. A 'Black General Staff' directed these forces, who indeed constituted a sort of armed State – irresponsible, uncontrolled and uncontrollable – within the State. The anarchists themselves admitted that suspicious elements, adventurers, common criminals and counter-revolutionaries were thriving among them, but their libertarian principles did not permit them to refuse entrance to their organizations to any man, or to subject anyone to real control. They sensed acutely that their movement needed to be purged, but this was impossible without authority or a disciplined organization. Splits among them and this reverence for principle was slowly leading to the political suicide of the movement, which was becoming more compromised each day.

Anarkhiya often published 'important notices' like this one: 'Council of Anarchist Federation. Regrettable abuses are going on. Unknown persons are conducting arrests and extorting funds in the name of the Federation. The Federation declares that it will not tolerate any confiscations for the purpose of personal enrichment.' (This on 1 April.)

'The Black General Staff announces that it will not assume responsibility for any operations unless effected on an order signed by at least three of its members and in the presence of at least one member.' (The same date.) The General Staff suspected its own members so much that two signatures alone were not enough! These precautions against banditry were in vain.

Did some of the anarchists think of dealing the besieged Bolsheviks a death-stab in the back? Strength has a certain logic, and they were strong. On either 7 or 8 April, Jacques Sadoul met Alexander Gay,[8] one of the anarchist leaders who had rallied to the Soviet cause. 'He thundered against the Bolsheviks,' Sadoul recalls (Gay, be it noted, was on the extreme Right of anarchism, among the 'Soviet anarchists' who were allies of the Communist party).

Several towns in the south were already under anarchist control. Gay believed that at that moment he had several thousand armed men at his disposal in Moscow. But the time for action was not yet ripe. The monarchists had joined the movement, trying to exploit it for their own ends. These impure and dangerous elements first had to be purged. In a month or two, the anarchists would dig the grave of the Bolsheviks – and the reign of the beast would be ended.[9]

I myself know that a little while previously a meeting of the leaders of the Anarchist Federation had been held at which the possibility of a rising against the Bolsheviks had been discussed.

But what then? How could they escape the necessity of taking power? Two influential orators, B— and N—, opposed the idea of an uprising on the grounds that it would be 'senseless to take on the responsibility and the fatal discredit for an economic situation which was beyond repair' and that 'we could not hold on for long'.

Several incidents such as an attack on an American car, the murder of several Cheka agents followed by the summary execu‑ tion of several bandits, and arrests of 'expropriators' who were promptly claimed by the Anarchist Federation, led Dzerzhinsky, the President of the Cheka, to insist on the liquidation of the Black Guard. 5,000 Soviet troops took part in this operation, on the night of 11–12 April. The houses occupied by the anarchists and defended by their machine-guns were surrounded. The occu‑ pants were given twenty minutes to surrender. In several places there was bloodshed; artillery was used against the Anarchy Club; the siege of one libertarian citadel lasted ten hours. In this way, twenty-seven houses were taken, twenty groups disarmed and 500 people arrested. The killed and wounded amounted to a few dozen. No anarchist known as such died in the course of this skirmish, which was followed neither by summary executions (as has been rumoured) nor by other rigorous measures. The daily newspaper *Anarkhiya* re-appeared on the 21st with the headline: '*Down with absolutism!*'[10]

To what extent were counter-revolutionaries taking advantage of the privileged position of the Black Guard? On this point I shall quote only one piece of evidence, that of General Goppers,[11] who took part in the officers' conspiracies of the 'Fatherland and Freedom Defence League'. The leaders of the League did not know of any place in Moscow where they could house their squads.

One can rely on the fighting capacity of an organization [writes Goppers] only if its members are subject to military discipline . . . and under the command of a leader. The anarchist clubs gave us the oppor‑ tunity of organizing ourselves properly. They were tolerated by the Bolsheviks. . . . At the beginning of April, sixty or seventy of our mem‑ bers were installed in these clubs. We no longer had to rack our brains to find somewhere to put up our members arriving from the provinces. All I had to do was provide them with a pass and direct them to the head of our 'anarchist department' who would place them in a large house occupied by the libertarians. At the head of our anarchists we had an artillery captain whose appearance and character exactly matched the literary picture of the anarchist . . .

The counter-revolutionary officers who were arrested during the disarmament of the anarchists only had to play out their role patiently in order to be liberated at the end of several weeks. I know of several other similar reports from counter-revolutionary sources. They establish in particular that the clubs of the 'Third Revolution' were frequented by foreign officers.[12]

THE REVOLUTION AND ITS DISSIDENTS

The disarmament of the anarchists was effected with little difficulty in Petrograd, Vologda and other places. On 15 May there was an anarchist rising at Tsaritsyn (now Stalingrad). On 17 May a rising of Maximalists and libertarians occurred also at Saratov. The Ukraine remained a lively focus for the anarchist movement; here guerrilla warfare was to go on for years.

Thus, a straight police operation terminated the role of anarchism in the Russian revolution. There was no need even to mount a political campaign against it. Neither press nor agitators waged a campaign to prepare the masses for the disarmament of the libertarians or to justify the action. Formidable as their Black Guardsmen were, their political influence was nil. Their whole power lay in a few machine-guns which had fallen into the grasp of a small number of determined men.

The anarchist 'party' was rendered incapable of any practical initiative through its divisions, its Utopian spirit, its contempt for reality, its thunderous phrasemongering and its lack of organization and discipline. Whatever it enjoyed in the way of real capacities and energies were wasted in small and chaotic struggles. It was, for all that, a distinctive and armed party which, as we have seen, tried to organize itself along with its own General Staff. But it was an amorphous party without definite contours or directing organs – that is to say, without a brain or nervous system – a strange sort of party which was at the mercy of the most contradictory aims and was unable to exert any control over itself. It was an irresponsible party in which individual intelligences dominated by cliques, by alien pressures of a highly suspect kind and by group instincts, dissipated themselves to no effect. It was an unworkable party for a time of social war: for any war in modern conditions demands of its combatant units the centralization of information, thinking and will. It demands levers which are smoothly obedient to the decisions of leadership, and a clear view of facts and possibilities, which can come only through a clear-cut theory.

In disarming the anarchists, the Bolsheviks – and the Left SRs who at least gave tacit consent to the operation – obeyed the imperative necessity of securing the rear of the revolution. Could the revolution tolerate the anarchist strongholds behind its back, outside its control? With the formation of the Red Army, a long phase of struggle was now opening between the guerrilla forces and the organizers of regular troops. (We shall return to this theme later.) The defence of the Ukraine had cruelly shown up the weaknesses of guerrilla bands. These detachments, often composed of adventurers, often of excellent revolutionaries, most usually of a mixture of the two, refused to carry out orders 'from above' and tried to make war according to their own fancy. In order to create an army the resistance of these tendencies had to be broken. And in order to break them, it was necessary to do away with the guerrilla regime in the capital itself.

For the first time the Bolsheviks were obliged by the anarchists to suppress by force a dissident minority within the revolution. Sentimental revolutionaries would have hesitated. But what would have been the consequence? Either the Black Guard would have eventually organized a rising, and Moscow would have undergone some days of infinitely perilous disturbance (it is enough to think of the famine and the waiting counter-revolution already powerfully organized): or else the Guard would have gradually been dissolved, after a whole series of incidents with uncertain outcome. Any revolution which could not subdue its dissidents when these were armed to form an embryonic State within the state would be offering itself, divided, to the blows of its enemies.

The party of the proletariat must know, at hours of decision, how to break the resistance of the backward elements among the masses; it must know how to stand firm sometimes against the masses, among whom hunger (for example) may plant a spirit of defeatism; it must know how to go against the current, and cause proletarian consciousness to prevail against lack of consciousness and against alien class influences. Even more must it know how to bring dissent to obey. Such dissidence proceeds from minorities; it would, however, be quite stupid to bully these. One has at this point to make the distinction between counter-revolutionaries and the revolution's own dissenters. The latter are not enemies; they belong to our class; they belong to the revolution. They want to, can and should serve it in one way or another. They are neither fatally nor necessarily nor absolutely in the wrong. To use against them methods of repression which are indispensable against the counter-revolution would quite clearly be criminal and disastrous; all it would achieve would be to replace disagreement by bitter and bloody splits.

The Bolsheviks did not fall into this error. Their press was at pains to declare that no obstacles would be placed in the way of the anarchists' continued existence or their propaganda. Once disarmed, these maintained their press, organizations and clubs. The small groups that represented the three or four libertarian tendencies, whose membership was constantly being pulled in opposite directions – some being attracted towards Bolshevism and eventual assimilation into the Communist party, others gravitating towards the most intransigent anti-Sovietism – were from this point to vegetate on without exercising any noticeable influence.[13]

TWO THESES. BUKHARIN: CONTINUE THE OFFENSIVE

We have already seen the confrontation of the different platforms at the Seventh Congress of the Communist party, where a split was avoided only through the over-riding concern of all for unity and – even more – through Lenin's patience. The Left Communists were declaring that a split was becoming hard to avoid: they had their own leading bodies (Moscow Regional Committee, Ural Committees, etc.), their own journal (*Kommunist*), and their supporters were practically everywhere. They refused to stand for the Central Committee of the party and were elected on to it under protest. Lenin emphasized on that occasion that the Central Committee's obligation to pursue a firm policy 'did not mean that all its members had to have the same opinions'; any other ruling would be 'a step towards a split'; 'every member of the Central Committee has the chance to make his responsibility clear without resigning or making a scene'. As Lenin put it again, 'the comrades are quite capable of defending their point of view without leaving the Central Committee. We must try and get rid of this fashion of resigning from the Committee.' Once elected, the Left Communists declared once again that they refused to sit on the Central Committee. The president of the session answered them quite simply: 'The comrades who have been elected will be asked to come: they have a perfect right not to come.'[14]

Discord again flared up over the precarious truce that had been won at Brest-Litovsk. What was to be made of it? Which way were we to go? Lenin answered these questions with a power and a sharpness characteristic of his genius, in his report to the All-Russian Soviet Executive on 29 April, published as a pamphlet under the title *Immediate Tasks of the Soviet Power*.[15] Trotsky, in full agreement with Lenin, had (as we have seen) provided the motto for a victorious revolution: *work, order, discipline*. But such resolutions could not give any complete satisfaction to a revolutionary party in a revolutionized country. The Left Communists (Bukharin, Preobrazhensky, Pyatakov, Yaroslavsky and Radek) saw all this as symptomatic of a dangerous Right deviation. They argued their position in a set of fifteen theses published on 4 April, which we shall summarize. The first part of the theses explained away the fact that the majority of workers had approved of the peace of Brest-Litovsk: it was the weary de-classed elements that had carried the day. Analysing the situation created by the peace, the authors concluded that the imperialist system would collapse 'during the forthcoming spring or summer', a prospect that could be only slightly retarded in the event of a German victory.

The theses blamed the Central Committee for its long-standing failure to decree the total nationalization of industry and the socialization of production. They also denounced the danger be-

ing risked by the party in 'the reconciliation between the proletariat and the poorest peasants', with all the pitfalls of a petty-
bourgeois politics:

If this tendency prevails, the working class will lose its leading role
and the hegemony it possesses in the socialist revolution, which has won
the poorest peasants to throw off the yoke of finance-capital and the
landed gentry; the working class will be no more than a force surrounded by the petty-bourgeois mass which views its task not as the
proletarian struggle, in alliance with the working class of western
Europe, to overthrow the imperialist system, but as the defence of a
fatherland of small farmers against imperialist incursions, a defence
whose objectives can be attained through a compromise with imperialism. If an active proletarian policy is abandoned, the conquests of the
workers' and peasants' revolution will begin to degenerate into a system
of state capitalism, marked by economic relations typical of the petty-
bourgeoisie.

The party could be led on this path by the temptation to preserve
Soviet power at any cost whatsoever to the international revolution. In foreign policy, agreements with capitalist states and diplomatic manoeuvre would take the place of revolutionary agitation;
in the economic field, there would be covert agreements with the
capitalists, cooperative managers and rich peasants; in place of a
socialized industry there would be set up, in concert with the captains of industry, trusts which would have the outward appearance
of State enterprises. The Soviets would lose their independence,
and from a State of the commune type Russia would pass to a
government of centralized bureaucracy. There would be labour
discipline through piece-work, etc. The Soviet State, now separated
from the world labour movement, would turn into a national
petty-bourgeois state.

'The proletarian Communists want a quite different kind of
politics. We must not try to preserve a Soviet oasis in the north
of Russia, at the price of concessions which will transform it into
a petty-bourgeois State. ...' What were the demands of the Left
Communists? An active international policy, rejection of all agreements that could turn the Republic into an instrument of the
imperialists (an allusion to the Brest-Litovsk treaty and to Trotsky's negotiations with the Allies); no capitulation before the
bourgeoisie. Suppression of the counter-revolutionary press. Obligation to work for all intellectuals and technicians. Confiscation
of property. Establishment of consumer communes. An offensive
waged by poor peasants against the rich. A large scale of autonomy to the local Soviets.

Lenin and his policies, moreover, became the object of attacks
that were sometimes extremely violent. The organizations of the
Ural area demanded a new party congress. The 'State capitalism
created by Lenin' was not spared by these critics. From a criticism of one-man authority in industry and the transport system

they went on to open references to personal dictatorship inside the party. 'The ruling minority, led by Comrade Lenin,' it was said on one occasion, 'has nothing in its head except words.' This 'minority' was dubbed 'opportunist', 'capitalist' and 'myopic'. The passions of this opposition were so heated that the Left SRs became emboldened to sound them out on the possibilities of arresting Lenin. ... This episode was revealed by Bukharin in 1923; he was well qualified to know the truth about it. All the elements of a split were present.[16]

TWO THESES. LENIN: SUSPEND THE OFFENSIVE

Lenin's reply is called *Left Infantalism and the Petty-Bourgeois Mentality*. The Lefts, he said, admit that 'the conclusion of peace has already caused the conflict between the imperialist powers to become more acute', without remarking that this is a perfectly good justification for the peace being signed. They announce the collapse of imperialism during the coming spring and summer. This 'childishly helpless formulation' evades an indisputable truth. No serious political person can commit himself to saying when the collapse of a system has to begin. The Lefts deplore the fact that 'the masses have become firmly imbued with an inactive peace mentality'. This statement is seen by Lenin as something monstrous. What could be more natural than the need to take breath after three years of frightful butchery? Anyone who deplores this fact shows that he himself is imbued with the mentality of the de-classed petty-bourgeois intellectual.

The revolution, we are told, cannot save itself at the cost of making concessions. But it is a matter now of not walking straight into a trap. *At the present time* we are avoiding battle. If you don't want to retreat, say so, and don't use equivocating phrases about 'an energetic international policy'. At this moment we have either to fight or not to fight. Since 25 October we have been supporters of national defence: but of serious defence! 'It is in the interest of capitalism to destroy its enemy (the revolutionary proletariat) bit by bit. It is in our interest to do all that is possible ... to postpone the decisive battle until the moment (or until *after* the moment) when the national revolutionary contingents have fused in a single great international army.' When there are not enough forces available for a standing fight, it is necessary to be able to retreat.

In the economic field, the Lefts are advocating a most determined policy of socialization. 'But even the greatest possible "determination" in the world is not enough to pass *from* confiscation *to* socialization. ... Today, only a blind man could fail to see that we have nationalized, confiscated, beaten down and put down more *than we have had time to count. ...*' We are in peril, are we, of an evolution towards State capitalism? But that would be a great step forward! It would be a stage towards Socialism.

Lenin enumerates the elements that constitute the Russian economy: (1) patriarchal peasant farming; (2) small commodity production (this includes the majority of those peasants who sell their grain); (3) private capitalism; (4) State capitalism; (5) Socialism. Russia is so vast and varied that all these different types of socio-economic organization are intermingled. That is what constitutes the specific feature of the situation. What elements predominate? 'Clearly, in a petty-bourgeois, peasant country the petty-bourgeois element is dominant, for the great majority of those working the land are small commodity producers.' The proof is in the fact that the grain monopoly is being undermined by profiteering. In this struggle, State capitalism is the ally of Socialism. Let us take a lesson from Germany, where State capitalism has been established for the benefit of the Junkers and the militaristic capitalists. It is precisely for that reason that the proletarian revolution will be able to conquer easily in Germany. In these matters we must copy Germany even more energetically than Peter the Great copied from Europe, and not shrink even from dictatorial methods.

Socialism is inconceivable without large-scale capitalist engineering based on the latest discoveries of modern science, and without a rational organization which keeps tens of millions of people to the strictest observation of a unified standard in production and distribution.[17]

Lenin recalled that even in September 1917 he had written: 'Socialism is merely the next step forward from State-capitalist monopoly ...'

Marx, in the 1870s, admitted the possibility, for Britain, of a peaceful victory of Socialism on condition that the capitalists allowed themselves to be 'bought out'. And why not, if the trouble of a civil war could be avoided at this price? Lenin dealt with this case in reply to those who condemned the payment of high salaries to specialists. We must be able, he said, to combine two methods: merciless repression against uncultured capitalists, and methods of compromise towards the others – it is reasonable for the proletariat to give good pay to experienced managers. In their defence of the worker, the Left Communists succeed only in repeating word for word the demagogic pronouncements of certain Mensheviks.

Lenin's reply to the Left is serious, honest and devoid of polemical exaggerations and personal attacks; on the contrary, it juxtaposes, next to its sternest arguments, a number of expressions of esteem addressed to Bukharin. With all its formality, it possesses vehemence, but of a serious sort which keeps to fundamentals. As such it is a model for a pamphlet intended for discussion within the party.

The pamphlet *Immediate Tasks of the Soviet Power* had been written shortly before. It is the most complete and concise exposition of Lenin's politics in this period. In bourgeois revolutions the role of the proletariat is a destructive one; it is the bourgeois minority that takes on the labour of construction, and it is supported in this by the spontaneous growth of the market, the 'chief organizing force of anarchically built capitalist society'. Every Socialist revolution, on the other hand, impels the proletariat into a creative role in planned production and distribution. And it can succeed only if the majority of the toilers exercise their initiative within it. 'Only if the proletariat and the poor peasants display sufficient class consciousness, devotion to principle, self-sacrifice and obstinacy, will the victory of the Socialist revolution be assured.' We have *convinced* and *won* Russia, we have gained a majority among the workers and seized power. The principal task now is to *organize* and *administer* the country. When that problem is solved – and not before – the Soviet society will have become a Socialist society.

Keep regular and honest accounts of money, manage economically, do not steal, observe labour discipline – these are now the conditions of the country's salvation and, with the application of Soviet power, form 'the necessary and sufficient condition for the final victory of Socialism'. The bourgeoisie has been conquered, but not uprooted; it is now a matter of preventing any possibility that a new bourgeoisie can arise, a task which is much more difficult. 'Although we have certainly not finished off capital, and although it is necessary to continue the offensive of the workers against it, the fact is that, in order to go on advancing successfully *in the future*, we must "suspend" our offensive now.' 'If we decide to continue to expropriate capital at the same rate at which we have been doing it up till now, we shall certainly suffer defeat, because our work of organizing proletarian accounting and control has obviously *fallen behind* the work of *directly* "expropriating the expropriators".' It is not that we have made errors in our tactics; every social struggle has its own logic, but a violent attack is not always appropriate. 'We achieved victory by methods of suppression; we shall be able to achieve victory also through methods of administration.'

The high salaries to be paid to experts are indeed 'a step backward' in relation to Socialism, but a necessary step back. We must improve the functioning of the banks, shoot bribe-takers, consolidate the State monopolies (in grain, leather, etc.) and begin introducing compulsory labour service – but this only gradually and carefully, and applying it only to the rich. The meaning of Socialism is accounting and control: anarchism and anarcho-syndicalism, which oppose State control and accounting, only reveal their bourgeois outlook. 'The Socialist State can arise only as a network of producers' and consumers' communes, which conscientiously keep account of their production and consumption, economize on labour, and steadily raise the productivity of labour, thus making it possible to reduce the working day to seven, six and even fewer hours.' The decree passed on cooperation is a compromise with the bourgeois cooperatives, the Soviet government having abandoned the principle of compulsory enrolment in the societies without entrance fees.

The raising of the productivity of labour and the improved organization of labour demands, firstly, the development of heavy industry and, secondly, discipline among the work force. In this respect the situation is bad. 'Without the victory of conscious discipline over petty-bourgeois anarchy, there is no Socialism.' We must apply piece-work and make use of what is progressive in the Taylor system.[18] 'Like all other progress under capitalism, this system is a combination of the refined brutality of capitalist exploitation and a number of remarkable scientific discoveries.' Socialism does not deny the role of competition, whatever its detractors say. On the contrary it opens to the masses limitless possibilities of competition, through social forms of advertising, competition between communes, etc.

Several pages of the article are devoted to justifying the dictatorship of the proletariat. 'An iron hand is necessary.' 'Dictatorship is iron rule, government that is revolutionarily bold and ruthless in repressing both exploiters and hooligans. But our government is still excessively soft. . . .' Compulsion is necessary both against the counter-revolution and against petty-bourgeois individualism. We have had to provide certain individual executives, on the railways, with dictatorial powers. The Left S Rs launched extraordinary agitation against this proposal. However, it is irrefutable that 'in history the dictatorship of certain individuals was often the expression, the vehicle, the channel of the dictatorship of the revolutionary classes. Undoubtedly, it was compatible with bourgeois democracy. . . . There is *no* contradiction in principle between Soviet [i.e. Socialist] democracy and the possession of dictatorial power by certain individuals.' The Socialist dictatorship is distinguished from any other in the fact that it arouses and stimulates the organization of the masses. But the management of large-scale industry demands unity of will, 'the subordination of the will of thousands to the will of one'. We are moving from the phase of public meetings to the phase of 'iron discipline'. Guarantees of democracy and the means of struggle against bureaucracy are to be found in the Soviet system itself (with its absence of formalism, working people as the electors, right of recall freely exercised by the voters, participation of all in the life of the State, control of the government by the masses).

The more resolutely we now have to stand for the dictatorship of individuals in certain definite executive functions, the more varied and numerous must be the forms and methods of control by the masses in order to counteract every shadow of a possibility of deformation in the power of the Soviets, ceaselessly to drag out the weeds of bureaucracy.[19]

The pamphlet concludes, as one might have expected, with a ringing indictment against the petty-bourgeois revolutionary romantic who is suspicious of organization, practical necessities and new manoeuvres. 'Hysterical impulses are of no use to us. What we need is the steady advance of the iron battalions of the proletariat.'[20]

THE DIALECTIC OF EVENTS

Politics become verified through the facts. Lenin was right against the Left Communists on two essential points. The country was at its last gasp: it was indeed necessary to 'suspend the offensive against capital', in order to consolidate the positions already won, assemble new forces and prepare an offensive for later on. And the revolutionary crisis now maturing in Europe guaranteed the Russian revolution its chance of shortly being able to resume its onward march. The Left Communists were following their emotions, their zeal as an enthusiastic minority, rather than any clear-headed dialectic proceeding from social facts. Thus, as with the issue of 'revolutionary war', they became trapped in the revolutionary subjectivism to which intellectuals of middle-class origin are prone, and abandoned the outlook of proletarian realism.

The source of their error is clear. All their fears of the impending degeneration of the proletarian State would have been justified given the stabilization of European capitalism. But they themselves (and rightly) proclaimed the imminency of imperialism's collapse, that is to say of a new source of energy, this time international in scope, for the revolution. On such a perspective, a calm period could hardly any more be seen as a real threat; rather it would have to be viewed as a period for the necessary accumulation of forces.

Another misunderstanding they displayed was their failure to see the contrast between revolutionary duty before and after the seizure of power. Before the take-over, it is necessary to destroy: after it, it is necessary to build. It is not easy for destroyers to turn into builders; that is why goodwill and a Marxist sense of the tasks involved in the revolution's aftermath are all the more essential.

All the same, Lenin displayed great moderation in his handling of the Left Communists, both in his polemic and even more so in practical politics. The moderate tone of the majority on his side contrasted strikingly with the turbulence, violence and intransigence of the Left minority. That no split occurred is due to Lenin, who did not want that sort of outcome. He was all too conscious that the Lefts were genuine Communists of real worth, and that there were healthy features even in their errors. Suppose the party had signed the 'infamous peace' of Brest-Litovsk without reacting painfully, had accepted the suspension of the revolutionary offensive in total unanimity, without any repercussions in its membership, and in a crisis as grave as this, had been quite devoid of ideological struggles, with all that these imply in the way of restless critical thinking, passion and the search for new solutions – would such a party have been alive and healthy, truly capable of confronting its huge responsibilities? As for the majority which accepted the truce and suspended the offensive, did it not include Right-wing elements in whose eyes the pace of revolution had already gone too fast and too far? As we have remarked concerning the debates of Brest-Litovsk: until the Year One of the Russian revolution of workers and peasants, working-class history contained no examples at all of a revolutionary movement which was not in the end swallowed, corrupted and betrayed by opportunism. The notion that the workers' revolution needed to manoeuvre was quite acceptable in principle; but any manoeuvre that was undertaken provoked fears of Right-wing deviation, and these fears were legitimate and proper. The Left Communists who reacted so forcefully had a case to make. They stood out against a danger from the Right which undoubtedly existed, though in the event the civil war stopped it getting any further.

The truce turned out to be much shorter and flimsier than Lenin seems to have anticipated. In *Immediate Tasks of the Soviet Power* he had outlined the plan for a great operation of reconstruction which was to have been started at once, but was immediately frustrated by the civil war. Yes, it was necessary to call off the offensive against capital and proceed by skilful administration instead of compulsion: necessary, but impossible. The civil war, resumed by the Allies through the Czechoslovak intervention, was on the contrary to necessitate an even greater reliance upon methods of compulsion. From June on, the government had to fall back on the measures advocated by the Left Communists, whose practical programme thus became realized – under Lenin's guidance. However, what was in their eyes the normal method of continuing a social revolution actually amounted to a fresh escalation of civil war, and a civil war whose consequences were far more of a hindrance than a help to the progress of Socialism. If the Allied armed intervention had not taken place, the Soviet Republic would have been able by the spring of 1918 to enter on the Socialist organization of production and administration, which in the end it only managed by 1921, after the introduction of the New Economic Policy, with more concessions to the rural petty-bourgeoisie than would have been necessary three years earlier. Here we may consider the remarkable continuity in Lenin's ideas: in 1921, once the war was over, he had only to take up his plan of April 1918 once again, adapting it to new circumstances.

However this may be, from June onwards the imperative measures were rationing, the establishment of consumer com-

42. Hetman Skoropadsky (in white hat) with German advisers in Kiev

munes, confiscations, nationalizations, the introduction of Committees of Poor Peasants and compulsory labour, just as the Left Communists had demanded in April. From June the revolution had to unleash all its energies, as each day demanded more. Nevertheless, it will be in order, discipline and work, along the paths pointed by Lenin and Trotsky, the paths of methodical organization in production, administration and revolutionary defence, that Russia's safety is found. Hesitations dissipate; the Left finds itself with no further justification for existing; the profound unity of the party is forged once more.

COUNTER-REVOLUTION IN THE UKRAINE. THE FAMINE

It was in the Ukraine that the classic cycle of counter-revolution, which was to unroll many times in the course of the civil war, was first displayed completely. Its normal phases are as follows: the middle classes, having at first supported the proletariat, take up arms against it and form an alliance with the very reactionary forces they have just fought against. Just as the middle strata had only joined with the proletariat to exploit it, so reaction only allies

43. Field-Marshal Eichhorn

itself with them for the sake of exploiting them. The alliance wins. A regime of anti-worker 'democracy' is instituted, and the petty-bourgeoisie seems to have triumphed – until the moment, not long delayed, when they are knocked down from behind by a *coup* from the reactionaries.

The People's Republic of the Ukraine, which had 'summoned' the Germans, soon found itself at the mercy of its 'protectors'. These found themselves displeased by a Rada too radical for their taste, and summarily dissolved it (Kiev, 26 April), locked up its ministers and established prior censorship of all publications. Meanwhile, a 'Congress of Farming Folk' awarded the title of sovereign Hetman to the Russian General Skoropadsky, who was in the good graces of the *Kommandatur*. Skoropadsky assumed personal rule to give 'peace, law and fruitful labour' to the country, and announced the convocation of a Sejm, the re-establishment of private property ('the basis of culture and civilization'), agrarian reform and legislation for the working class. In the interim, the Hetman was given the powers of an autocrat by a 'provisional constitution'; it was decreed that all land should be restored to the big owners and the State should requisition the grain; the workers were deprived of any right to strike or assemble. The petty-bourgeois nationalists hid themselves away in the countryside.

The real master of the country was Field-Marshal Eichhorn. His orders were law. Soon Skoropadsky was to ask for the whole country to be occupied by German troops so that order could be guaranteed. These troops, whose sole interest was in the requisitioning of grain, Germany's last hope now, went to the extreme of using poison gas against peasants. All for Order! At the end of May Skoropadsky had to proclaim a state of siege. He lasted while the Germans lasted.

Skoropadsky's *coup d'état* re-stocked the counter-revolution with a vast, rich and fertile territory. Now the feeble neighbour of a Germanized Ukraine, Russia seemed to be doomed. As we have seen, famine was sowing a crop of riots. It seemed that the hour for casting off the Bolshevik usurpation had arrived. As an immediate consequence of the events in the Ukraine, counter-revolutionary activity flared up over the whole of Russia. Until the end of April the petty-bourgeois parties, the Mensheviks and SRs had declared themselves as opposed to civil war. Precisely then, they came out as partisans of the use of armed force against Bolshevism.

White Finland was demanding back Fort Ino, on the Russo–Finnish border (the Bolsheviks, rather than hand it over, blew it up on 14 May); Mannerheim seemed ready for war. The Germans had just occupied the Crimea and were expected to capture Voronezh, in the south-east of Russia. At this moment famine held sway over the whole of Europe; the populace was rigorously rationed in London and Paris, and in Vienna and Berlin lacked every necessity. All the same, inside Russia it was easy to put all the blame on the Soviets. The bourgeois press spread panic. On 9 May it published reports that the Germans were insisting on the right to send their troops into Moscow and Petrograd and that the Bolsheviks were thinking of forming a coalition cabinet. 'Stop playing with fire,' cried the popular orator Volodarsky in the columns of Petrograd's *Krasnaya Gazeta* (*Red Gazette*): 'If we have to, we will crush you forever!' Proceedings were instituted against the press, involving a dozen or so bourgeois dailies (*Vechernya Viesti*, *Zhizn*, *Rodina*, *Narodnoye Slovo*, *Drug Naroda*, *Zemlya* and *Volya*)[21] and some S R journals. Several of these were closed down. It was the end of freedom of the press, through sheer force of circumstances. 'You asked for it, gentlemen!' wrote Volodarsky. But on 15 May he is more specific: 'Freedom to criticize the action of the Soviet government and to agitate in favour of another government are granted by us to all our opponents. We will guarantee freedom of the press for you if you understand it in this sense. But you must give up false newsmongering ... lies and slander.' In the midst of its immense danger, that is how strong the party of the proletariat felt itself to be.

Hunger riots began to multiply, and anti-semitism reared its head again. Even at the Putilov Works an S R speaker shouted out on 8 May, 'Let's throw the Yids into the Neva, get a strike committee going and stop work.'

Agitation conducted by the S Rs and Mensheviks called demonstrations in the streets and prepared for a general strike. The demands were: free trade, wage increases, payment of wages one, two or three months in advance and 'democracy'. The intention was to incite the working class itself against the revolution. To cap it all, the electricians at Putilov were out on strike. The best elements among the workers were away fighting; those in the factories were precisely the less energetic, less revolutionary sections, along with the petty folk, yesterday's small shopkeepers and artisans, who had come there to find refuge. This proletariat of the reserve often allowed itself to fall under the sway of Menshevik propaganda. In April the Communist party had to mobilize its strength in Moscow to defend its positions in the Soviet, now under threat, against the Mensheviks. Big factories in the Ural region were also under Menshevik influence. At the beginning of May there were scattered risings of workers here and there against the Bolsheviks. The S Rs launched a bloody attempt at insurrection at Saratov.

This critical moment was the occasion for publicizing the slogan: *He who does not work, neither shall he eat*. If there is not enough bread for everyone, then, in these days of social war, the toilers will be served first. Perhaps they will be the only ones to be served! Their share will be 100 or 200 grams of bread per day, with herrings, other fish and other rations, if there are any, two or three times a week.[22] Zinoviev, President of the Petrograd Soviet, organizes the first workers' food brigades, whose purpose is to go out to the countryside and requisition the grain of the rich peasants.

The Germans have robbed the revolution of the corn of the Ukraine. The Allies send the Czechoslovak forces, now encamped over the regions of the east, the signal for rebellion. And so the two capitals are cut off from the grain supplies both of the Volga and of Siberia.

PLOTS AND PREPARATIONS FOR ALLIED INTERVENTION

The Allies were still hostile, but disorientated.[23] By a declaration of 19 March, drafted in moderate terms, they had committed themselves not to recognize the Brest-Litovsk peace. Negotiations went on between Trotsky and the Americans (Colonel Robins) and the French (Captain Sadoul) on the possible collaboration of the Allied missions in organizing the Red Army and assisting the transport system. Japan, with talk of the presence in Siberia of 'German war-prisoners armed by the Bolsheviks' and of 'the danger of the Germans controlling the Trans-Siberian Line', was making ready to occupy the railways across Siberia. The British reactionaries encouraged these designs, which were constantly thwarted by President Wilson since any extension of Japanese power in the Far East was utterly unacceptable to the Americans. On 4 April, Admiral Kato organized a landing at Vladivostok, following the murder of a Japanese businessman. The displeasure of the United States nipped these events in the bud, but the incident was a warning to the Soviets. Its sequel will be seen later.

The Soviet authorities in Murmansk were cooperating with Admiral Kemp of Britain in an effort to forestall the occupation of the port by the Finns and Germans.[24] The Allied legations, who felt insecure in the capitals, had withdrawn now to Vologda. M. Noulens, the French ambassador, a diehard bourgeois reactionary, showed a resolute hostility against any agreement with the Bolsheviks, whose fall from power he anticipated (and plotted for). An advocate of military intervention by the Allies in Russia (on the formal pretext of re-establishing an eastern front against the Central Powers), he intended to get his way. In diplomatic circles he was fond of making such smart and terse remarks as: 'We shall not be allowing any further Socialist experiments in Russia . . .'; 'We pay, so we call the tune . . .'; 'You have to know how to talk to these Russians'; and 'Their opinions have not the slightest importance . . .'.[25] French politics at this point was in the hands of the big imperialist bourgeoisie. On 14 April, M. Clemenceau disclosed that France recognized neither the Soviets nor the Brest-Litovsk peace. A fortnight later, Francis, the US ambassador in Russia, took his turn to argue sharply for intervention *against* the Bolsheviks. The secret memorandum he addressed to his government in Washington explained that Count Mirbach, the German representative in Moscow, had become 'the real dictator of Russia' and that, in any case, the Allies could not remain indifferent before the presence of Bolshevism.[26] The false argument was a cover for the real one.

These facts must not be lost sight of. From this moment onward, the pressure from outside, from German bayonets, is linked in its campaign against the revolution with the pressure from within, in the form of extensive conspiracies fomented by the diplomatic and military representatives of the Allied powers.

The leaders of the counter-revolutionary parties (SRs, Mensheviks and Kadets) had recently, in March, set up a common organization, the 'League for Renewal' (*Soyuz Vozrozhdeniya*). 'The League,' one of the SR leaders has written, 'entered into regular relations with the representatives of the Allied missions at Moscow and Vologda, mainly through the agency of M. Noulens.'[27] With the reservations of hypocrisy, no direct cooperation between the Central Committee and the Allies was envisaged, only a cooperation from the activists which would not officially commit the parties. The League for Renewal was the main clandestine organization of the 'Socialist' petty-bourgeoisie and of the liberals who were determined to overthrow the Soviet government by force.[28] In Moscow the Octobrists, representing the big bourgeoisie, joined the organization and linked it with the 'Right Centre', a united front of reactionary tendencies inspired by the generals Alexeyev and Kornilov. The Octobrist party was to the Right of the Constitutional Democrats (Kadets): it based itself on the Imperial edict of 17 October 1905, which granted Russia a sham constitution. There was thus a chain of counter-revolutionary organizations running uninterruptedly from the most 'advanced' Socialists to the blackest reactionaries. The Military Commission of the SR party organized the League's 'combat groups', whose command was entrusted to a general. The League's political platform rested on three points: (1) the impossibility of a purely Socialist government; (2) the Constituent Assembly; (3) (as a provisional measure) a Directory invested with dictatorial authority. The local committee of the League in Petrograd was composed of two Popular-Socialists, one SR (A. R. Gotz, the leader of the party), one Kadet, Pepeliaev (who was to be one of Kolchak's ministers) and two Mensheviks, Potresov and Rozanov. In June, M. Noulens sent the League a semi-official Note from the Allies approving of its political programme and promising it military assistance against the German–Bolshevik enemy.

The former SR terrorist Boris Savinkov[29] had formed another organization, the 'Fatherland and Freedom Defence League', which aimed to group the most advanced and pugnacious elements of the counter-revolution on a platform sufficiently vague

44. Boris Savinkov

to satisfy both monarchist or radical-minded officers and the SR intellectuals. Savinkov's League was organized in clandestine groups of four or five persons at the most, the nuclei of a small secret army that had enough hierarchy and centralization to offer minimum scope for repression, while permitting determined action at the appropriate moment. The League proceeded to install its men in the Soviet institutions concerned with food supply, the militia and the army that was now in formation. With intelligence passed on by a delegation and a good deal of luck, the 'Extraordinary Commission for Struggle Against Sabotage and for Repression' (Vee-Cheka), still consisting of a small staff of about 150 persons, inexperienced and mostly drawn from the working class, managed to uncover this conspiracy. Mass arrests took place in Moscow, and the capital was declared to be in a state of siege (this at the end of May). But the arrested plotters were treated mildly. The Vee-Cheka undertook executions only rarely, in quite exceptional cases. The Left SRs opposed the application of martial law to Savinkov's accomplices, as Dzerzhinsky and his Bolshevik colleagues would have liked. With Savinkov still at large, the League, which had been decimated at Moscow and Kazan, continued its preparations for an uprising. We shall be meeting it again. These organizations were not the only ones. The soil of the young Republic was being thoroughly mined, in more senses than one. All these clandestine associations received indiscriminate encouragement from the Allies.

THE RISING OF THE CZECHOSLOVAKS

The Allied representatives had conceived a large-scale plan of operations, whose success would have ended Soviet rule.[30] A rising by the Czechoslovak forces in the Ural and Volga regions and in Siberia was to coincide with a series of counter-revolutionary *coups* in the towns near Moscow and with the landings of the Japanese at Vladivostok and the British at Archangel. Starved, encircled and demoralized by a swift succession of defeats, the two workers' capitals would fall; 'order' would have been restored.

A former officer from the French Military Mission in Russia, Pierre Pascal, who subsequently became a devoted and serious revolutionary, has explained the plan in these terms:

> The insurrection at Yaroslavl and the Czechoslovak rising were organised with the direct collusion of the agents of the French Mission and of M. Noulens. The Mission was in constant relations with the Czechs, to whom it sent officers and funds.... The counter-revolutionaries were to seize Yaroslavl, Nizhni-Novgorod, Tambov, Murom and Voronezh in order to isolate and starve out Moscow. This plan began to be implemented with the insurrections in Yaroslavl, Murom, Tambov, etc. I can still see General Lavergne sketching a large circle with his finger on the map around Moscow and saying, 'That's what Noulens wants. But I

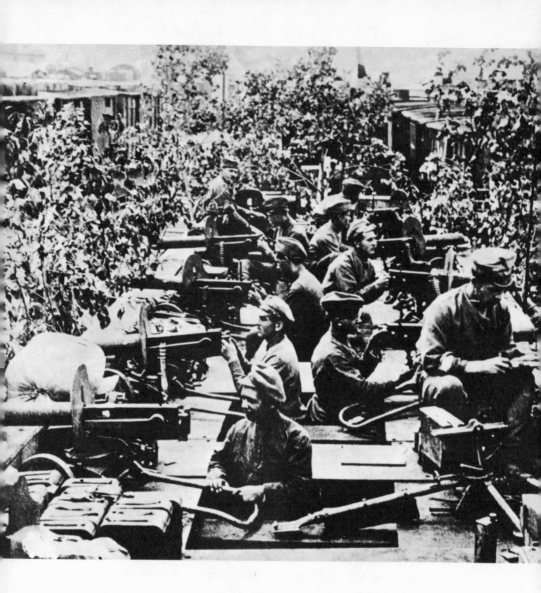

shall feel guilty because, if our plan succeeds, the famine in Russia will be terrible...'[31]

We have various testimonies of a similar description. The final plan of action for the Czechoslovak troops was settled on 14 April in Moscow, at a meeting of counter-revolutionary organizations attended notably by General Lavergne, head of the French Military Mission, Colonel Corbeil, one of his colleagues, and the head of the British Mission, Lockhart.[32]

The Czechoslovak Legion in Russia had been built up gradually during the war. Czech and Slovak prisoners from the Austrian front were organized under the auspices of a National Council whose leaders took their instructions from Masaryk and the heads

45. Czechoslovak troops on an armoured train during the intervention

of the national movement that had been set up in Paris. These troops had witnessed the vicissitudes of the Russian revolution without taking part in them. They were earmarked for the front in France, where they were to travel via Murmansk or Vladivostok. However, once the American intervention in the war had made up the shortage of troops from the Somme to Alsace, it occurred to the statesmen of the Entente that the Czechoslovaks might be used in the service of the Russian counter-revolution. Under the leadership of Allied officers, the Czechoslovak units refused to recognize the treaty of Brest-Litovsk, though they retreated before the Germans out of the Ukraine into the east. The Council of People's Commissars, in an effort to avoid conflict, authorized their evacuation – retaining their arms – via Siberia. The landing of the Japanese at Vladivostok, while the Czechs, to the number of about 30,000, were spread out along the Trans-Siberian Railway, faced the revolution sharply with the danger that the whole of Siberia might be occupied. Trotsky, as People's Commissar of War, forthwith demanded the disarmament of the Czechoslovaks and their movement, for purposes of evacuation, towards Archangel rather than the east of Siberia. The plan for the Czechoslovak offensive had been studied in all its details at a conference in Chelyabinsk attended by British, French and Russian officers as well as by SR members of the Constituent Assembly. On 25 and 26 May, the Czechoslovaks suddenly occupied Chelyabinsk (Ural region), Penza, Syzran (on the Volga) and Novo-Nikolayevsk (in Siberia). In these three regions they disposed of some 20,000 men, in well-equipped units commanded by Gajda, Voitsekhovsky and Čeček. An order by Trotsky dated 25 May decreed that any Czechoslovaks captured bearing arms would be shot on the spot. All facilities were offered, on the other hand, for those who would surrender arms and accept either evacuation via the north or Russian citizenship. The majority preferred to resist.

The rising of the Czechoslovak Legion completed the encirclement of the Soviet Republic, which was now cut off from the industry of the Ural, the fertile lands of the Volga and the granaries of Siberia. The Orenburg Cossacks took up arms again.

These Czechoslovaks, now called upon to deal the death-blow to the Bolsheviks, were in their overwhelming majority radical Republicans, followers of Masaryk, and Social-Democrats. Their devotion to democracy was for them, in the presence of the harsh conditions of the proletarian dictatorship, a factor making for incomprehension, indignation and revulsion. The Russian Socialist parties influenced them with the rumour that the Bolsheviks, as the paid agents of the Germans, were preparing to hand them over to their masters. With the support of the counter-revolutionary

Socialists, the Cossack peasants and the officers' leagues, the Czechoslovaks launched a series of successful operations which gave them Samara (8 June), which became their base, Syzran (19 June) and Ufa (13–23 June), thus offering a whole territory to the counter-revolution. This formed, as we shall see, the signal for a general attack upon the Soviets. Counter-revolutionary movements broke out in various parts of the countryside. The Right SRs assassinated the orator Volodarsky at Petrograd (20 June); the Left SRs, the allies of the Bolsheviks and still in the government, prepared a *coup d'état* to govern alone and tear up the Brest-Litovsk agreement; the Anglo–French expedition landed at Murmansk (2 July).

NATIONALIZATION OF BIG INDUSTRY

It was under the weight of these circumstances that the expropriation of the capitalist class was now undertaken. There is no better statement on this than some lines by the economist Kritsman:

After the proletarian revolution had undergone a preparatory period of eight months, distinguished in the economic sphere by hesitation and indecision, it took the pressure of an increasingly savage civil war and of the pro-capitalist intervention by the Kaiser's Germany, which used the Peace of Brest-Litovsk for its own ends, for the proletarian government to proclaim the expropriation of the expropriators by nationalizing large-scale industry with the decree of 26 June 1918.[33]

The main stages in the expropriation of the possessing classes were as follows:

The expropriation of the capital of the State[34] through the formation of the Council of People's Commissars on 8 November (26 October) 1917; the expropriation of agriculture (decree on the nationalization of land, passed on the same day); the expropriation of finance capital (decree on the nationalization of the banks, 1 December (14) 1917); expropriation of transport capital (decree on the nationalization of water transport, 12 January (25) 1918); expropriation of credit and principally of foreign credit (decree on the cancelling of loans, 14 January (27) 1918); the expropriation of commercial capital (decree instituting the monopoly of foreign commerce, 23 April 1918); the expropriation of the capital of rich peasants (decree establishing the Kombedy, or Committees of Poor Peasants, 11 June 1918); and the expropriation of big industrial capital (decree on the nationalization of large-scale industry, promulgated on 28 June 1918)[35] (Kritsman).

These measures were completed by the decree abolishing the right of inheritance that was promulgated on 1 May. Any inheritance over 10,000 roubles was to revert to the State, and the relatives of the deceased who were incapable of working were entitled to no more than a pension, to be determined by the local authorities.

At this juncture it will be appropriate to stress the reverse which had befallen workers' control in production. From November to

46. V. Volodarsky

May, control was organized through the local initiatives of the workers, with assistance from the Supreme Council of the Economy. But it was more and more obvious that matters could not rest there. The managers, deprived of their political power and under proletarian control, felt themselves to be at the mercy of their employees and threatened in the exercise of their property rights: they struggled, resisted, sabotaged. Control now appeared as a transitional measure, reflecting the hesitations of the revolution; it had either to become meaningless or else to pass on to the stage of expropriation. Sometimes astute managers who had obtained the confidence of their factory committees would profit from the workers' inexperience in the direction of enterprises, in order to get themselves a living at the expense of the Supreme Economic Council. They did good business in this new variety of plunder from the State.[36]

Other capitalists, more numerous, liquidated their enterprises in one way or another, spirited away their stocks, stole or sold their equipment, and vanished with the cash they had realized. From now on the factory committees had to organize these firms as they became abandoned and promptly expropriated. There was also sabotage by the technical staff, which necessitated a regime of straight working-class dictatorship in the factories. 'Nationalization was a reprisal rather than an economic policy.'[37] This conquest of the enterprises by the factory and works committees had its risks. Each committee thought in the first place of the interests of its own enterprise (i.e. of the workers it represented); from this it was an easy step to defending this interest by every means in its power, without any concern for the general economic interests of the country. Every enterprise, even though it might be backward, ill-equipped or dealing with a relatively inessential industry, demanded its own right to life, that is to re-stocking, to credit, to work. The consequence was an extraordinary mess, with the factories operating anarchically, each for its own benefit. As one comrade writes,

We were building, not a Soviet Republic, but a republic of working-class communities based on the capitalist factories and mills. Instead of a strict ordering of production and social distribution, instead of measures towards the Socialist organization of society, the existing state of affairs reminded one of the autonomous communes of producers that the anarchists had dreamed of.[38]

By 15 May 1918, 234 enterprises had been officially nationalized and a further seventy sequestrated. Heavy industry, i.e. manufacturing and engineering, was chiefly affected. It was imperative to make these measures general and systematic: the country was devastated and split into fragments, with the defeated employers striving to lay down impossible terms. Milyutin, who announced the forthcoming nationalization of large industry to the Congress of Economic Councils, told them of the battle between the government and the oil-well proprietors. The big oil men were demanding, as a condition of continuing production, that the same profits should be given them as before the revolution, while at the same time they wanted to restore the conditions of work operating in 1916. Convinced as they were that the workers would be incapable of managing oil-production, they threatened to stop all output in their failing enterprises if any attempt was made to force them to comply with Soviet law.

The decree of 28 June 1918 nationalized all industries engaged in mining, engineering, textiles, electrical goods, wood, tobacco, glass, ceramics, leather, cement, rubber, transport, etc., with a capital of half a million roubles and over. A few details of the implementation of this scheme will show how premature it appeared even in the eyes of its authors. The Supreme Council of the Economy was entrusted with the administration of the nationalized industries, but these were declared to be 'leased gratis to their former owners', who were obliged to carry on managing their affairs, and authorized 'to receive profits' (whose existence was now somewhat problematic). The technical staff and the directors remained in office, appointed by the State and responsible to it. Any case of desertion of duty was to be punished by the revolutionary tribunals.

The Congress of Economic Councils shortly decided on the creation of plant managements in the form of collective bodies, two thirds of whose members were to be nominated either by the Regional Councils or by the Supreme Council: half of these nominees could be selected by the trade unions on behalf of the appointing authority. The other third of the collective was elected on the spot by the workers of the enterprise.

IN THE FACE OF FAMINE

Speaking in Moscow before a popular meeting, Trotsky displayed a sheaf of telegrams: 'Viksi, Nizhni-Novgorod province: the shops are empty, work is going badly, shortage of 30 per cent of the workers through starvation. Men collapsing with hunger at their benches.' From Sergïev-Posada the telegram says: 'Bread, or we are finished!' From Bryansk, 30 May: 'Terrible mortality, especially of children, around the factories of Maltsov and Bryansk; typhus is raging.' From Klin, near Moscow: 'The town has had no bread for two weeks.' From Paslov-Posada: 'The population is hungry, no possibility of finding corn.' From Dorogobuzh: 'Famine, epidemics. ...' All the same, as Trotsky established, the country did have grain. The reserves of the northern Caucasus alone were to be valued at 140 million poods (a pood being thirty-six pounds in weight), while no more than fifteen million poods a month were needed to keep the big towns supplied. The famine was the result of class war. The rich peasants were refusing their corn to cities that could offer no more than worthless paper money in exchange. In White Russia, they were burying their stocks and planting crosses on top of the mounds to deceive the searchers.

The discontented sections of the community demanded the abolition of the grain monopoly and of the maximum-price system. Thus, against all the evidence, they declared their faith in capitalist methods and the self-interest of the wealthy rural petty-bourgeoisie. We have already explained how, with the exhaustion of industrial stocks, the inflation and the run-down of the transport system, a return to free trade in grain would have meant an era of frenzied speculation and of hopeless famine for the poor. Three great revolutionary measures were set in hand, which were to carry the class struggle resolutely into the rural areas: the formation of Committees of Poor Peasants, the requisitioning of excess grain, the dispatch of workers' food brigades. Lenin analysed these in a 'Letter to the Workers of Petrograd' and in a speech on the struggle for grain made before the All-Russian Soviet Executive. The famine was caused by the revolt of the bourgeoisie against the new laws: so he who does not work will not eat! The famine proves 'the abysmal stupidity of the contemptible anarchist windbags who deny the necessity of a State power (and, what is more, a power ruthless against the bourgeoisie and the disorganizers of government) for the transition from capitalism to communism'. Bread would be sufficient for all only if there was rigorous accounting and equal distribution. Either working-class consciousness would triumph by breaking the kulak resistance or reaction would take over. Half-measures were quite useless. 'Attempts to secure bread or fuel "in retail fashion", each man for "his factory", would only increase the disorganization and encourage profiteering.' It was the task of the revolutionary minority to involve the masses 'in a crusade against the profiteers, the kulaks, the parasites, the disorganizers'. Salvation must lie in this activity of the masses.

One of the greatest accomplishments of the October Revolution is that the advanced worker, as the leader of the poor, as the leader of the toilers of the countryside, as the builder of the State of labour, has *gone among the people....* But when he became the leader of the poor peasants he did not become a saint. He led the people forward, but he also became infected with the diseases of a disintegrating petty-bourgeoisie.... Having begun the Communist revolution, the working class cannot instantly discard the weaknesses and vices inherited from the society of capitalists and landlords, of exploiters and parasites, of the filthy gain and self-enrichment of the few based on the poverty of the many. But the working class can vanquish the old world – and in the end certainly and surely will vanquish it – with all its weaknesses and vices, if it hurls ceaselessly against the enemy its fresh forces, ever greater, ever more experienced and tempered in the struggle ...[39]

At the All-Russian Executive Committee of Soviets, on 4 June, and at the Congress of Factory Committees on 27 June, Lenin recalled that Germany was the country of 'brilliantly organized starvation'; that the war was the prime cause of the famine; and that the Russian proletariat owed its role as vanguard of the world revolution not to its own merits, but to the will of history. He used a striking phrase: 'We are now facing the most elementary task of any human society: to defeat famine. ...' Here he rebuts the Menshevik case for a compromise with the capitalists. The difficulties in the struggle against famine come from the fact that it faces us with questions of organization. 'Success in an uprising is infinitely more easy.' In the struggle against reaction, the proletariat could count on support from a section of the middle classes: but against the famine it must stand alone to confront a task of organization that will be authentically Communist. Three master-ideas inform the new decrees: centralization (avoiding the dispersal of scattered efforts, and the pitfalls of 'every man for himself'), union of the toilers (crusade against the kulaks), union of the poor peasants with the workers (class struggle in the countryside). Some phrases are worth noting:

They say that our food brigades are degenerating into gangs of bandits. It is quite possible.

When the old society perishes, its body cannot be nailed up in a coffin and lowered into the grave. The corpse decomposes in our midst: it rots and infects us.

We have no police, we shall not have a special military caste, we have no apparatus: only the conscious unity of the workers.

All over the world the workers are organized. But virtually nowhere has any systematic, painstaking effort been made to unite those who live out in the countryside, in small-scale agricultural production, in forgotten corners, in darkness, stunted by their whole condition of living ...

We have always said: the emancipation of the workers must be performed by the workers themselves. We have always said: they cannot be liberated from outside; they themselves must learn how to solve historical problems ... and the more difficult these problems are, the more we see that millions of men must take a part in solving them.

You must thoroughly understand, delegates from the factory committees, that nobody is going to come and help you, that from other classes you can expect not assistants but enemies, that the Soviet government has no loyal intelligentsia at its service.

Remember that if you in your factory and works committees concern yourselves with the workers' purely technical or financial interests, the revolution will not be able to keep a single one of its gains. ... Your factory committees must become the basic state nuclei of the ruling class ...[40]

As an example, Lenin cited the case of the workers in the small town of Yelets, who took the initiative in making house-to-house searches and requisitions against their bourgeoisie.

WAR AGAINST THE RICH PEASANTS

The famine was not caused simply through the inevitable effects of the war. It also marked the beginning of the long war of the peasants against the workers' cities, which was to end only in 1921 with the coming of the New Economic Policy (the *Nep*), whose cardinal point was the re-introduction of the free trade in grain. At the moment of the October Revolution the peasant movement, now reaching its peak, fused with the workers' movement: it had given the latter the backing of its limitless elemental force, and assured it of support from the army, which was composed in its immense majority of country people. In exchange the proletariat gave it an organization, objectives, slogans and a political direction. However, once the land was seized, the peasants were satisfied: their victory was total and final, while the struggles of the proletariat had scarcely begun. From the high point of the common victory in October and November, the cross-purposes between peasants and workers were to make themselves increasingly felt. There was first the question of the large agricultural estates: the peasants, profoundly attached to individual property and anxious principally for their own enrichment, wanted to divide them up, while the Soviet government sought to turn them into agrarian communes. There was the problem, already discussed in these pages, of the shortage of goods, the inflation and the feeding of the towns. During the war the peasants had accumulated paper roubles by the billion; the Soviet State, quite unavoidably, insisted on a maximum price for grain, which they were forbidden to sell on the market as they pleased. With the banknotes offered to them in exchange for their grain, they could buy practically nothing. And why should they sell on credit to the proletarian revolution? When an agitator explained to them that, if the maximum price was abolished and free trade permitted, all that could result would be a roaring inflation followed by a fantastic increase in the prices of manufactured goods, the cold reply was: 'Well, you won't get grain from us at any price.' (These were the typical words used.) Over the whole country a mass mobilization of kulaks against the Soviets was gathering with terrible force.

We must note Lenin's attitude to this threat. Party comrades came to see him from all corners of the country. One worker from Petrograd, who had managed to extricate himself with some difficulty from the Volga peasants among whom he had been trying to conduct propaganda, came at the beginning of July to confide his anxieties on the subject to 'old Ilyich'.

Lenin listened to him with the mischievous smile that lit up his eyes when the facts were proving him right.

When I assured him that the peasants would give us a thrashing, Vladimir Ilyich burst out laughing: 'But of course, comrade, they'll thrash us, and not for the first time, if you don't knock down the kulaks before they knock you.' And, taking a piece of paper, Lenin addressed to the workers of Petrograd a few urgent words which he asked his visitor to pass on. Here are the main parts of this brief message:

Comrade K— has been in Simbirsk gubernia and has himself observed the attitude of the kulaks to the poor peasants and to our government. He has perfectly realized what no Marxist and no class-conscious worker can doubt, namely, that the kulaks hate the Soviet government, the government of the workers, and *will inevitably overthrow it* if the workers do not *immediately* make every effort to forestall the attack of the kulak on the Soviets and to *smash* the kulaks before they have the chance to unite.

The class-conscious workers *can* do this at present; they can rally around them the poor peasants, defeat the kulaks completely and smash them, *provided that the vanguard* of the workers understand their duty, exert their whole strength and organize *a mass campaign in the country districts.*[41]

The task was, in short, to take the civil war into the countryside, appeal to the poor peasants against the rich, and engage in this battle with relentless energy. And for this purpose to call, once more, on the initiative of the workers.

Organize [said Lenin to K—], and go off. We will give you whatever the country's stores possess. Already the Soviet government has enormous stockpiles of confiscated goods. ... We tried to keep by some reserves but everything is getting stolen and pilfered. You will be using it in the interests of the revolution to rally the poor peasants to your side.

The following two telegrams, addressed around the beginning of August to Evgenia Bosch, the comrade who had been sent to the Penza region to fight the rural counter-revolution, give an idea of the strictness with which Lenin meant this struggle to be waged:

(1) 9 August 1918. Urgent. Penza. Executive, copy to Evgenia Bogdanovna Bosch. Message received, you must organize à picked guard. Exercise pitiless mass terror against the kulaks, the priests and the Whites, imprison suspects in concentration camps outside the towns. Telegraph back implementation. Chairman of Council of People's Com. *Lenin.*[42]

(2) 11 August 1918. In repressing rebellion five districts, take all measures to requisition all excess grain. For this, designate (not seize, designate) hostages from the kulaks, rich, parasites, bound to deliver and transport the grain. ... The hostages to answer with their lives for the speedy and punctual delivery of the demanded quantities.[43]

The workers' 'crusade' now turned to the countryside. All industrial centres now saw the formation of food brigades which went off to seek grain in the remotest corners of the land. The venture entailed bloody struggles. The participants were often massacred, and more than one Bolshevik commissar was found by his comrades in an abandoned barn, his belly slit open and stuffed with grain. .... Still, tens of thousands of proletarians carried the revolution into the country districts: the amount of grain they procured for the cities may have been insufficient, but was by no means negligible.[44]

ANARCHY AND SOVIET DEMOCRACY

Let us consider briefly the state of the country and the regime at this moment. The working class was showing numerous symptoms of exhaustion and demoralization. Its best sons had left its ranks for the front line or for work in Soviet institutions. Its position as the victorious class meant that it attracted a host of doubtful elements: pseudo-workers, ruined shopkeepers, speculators. The famine was forcing it close to the peasants: usually the Russian worker came from peasant parentage. Production was very low, and the factories lived as best they could, idle more than half the time, and riddled with theft. Raw materials and fuel were lacking and discipline practically non-existent. A report by Shlyapnikov, presented at the end of March to the All-Russian Soviet Executive, is full of telling details. The trains are often running without lighting or signals. Practically none of the signals on the line are working! 'People keep saying there is no paraffin nor any candles, but the fact is that it all gets stolen.' On occasions the trains cannot start because of the absence of staff. Everyone is absent sick, orders from the management are not carried out, plunderers are sheltering behind the committees. At Klin, not far from Moscow, on the line to Petrograd, the shed for the rolling stock has been made into a club – and the wagons left lying to clutter the tracks. Everybody is going in for speculation, offering and receiving bribes, supporting the profiteers and thieving from the system. Shlyapnikov can see only one cure for these evils: to interest the railwaymen in efficiency on the job and introduce piece-work in the depots just as in the factories. A report by Nevsky in June tells us that productivity in transport has gone down by fifty or seventy per cent while running costs have increased by 150 per cent. The dilapidation of the stock is frightful, especially in the country areas and the regions close to the front: windows smashed, doors battered in, disgusting filth.

Some of the big factories had become centres of demoralization and formed a favourable soil for counter-revolutionary agitation. At Petrograd the Soviet censured the workers of the Obukhovo factory who spent all their time in meetings and recriminations. The Putilov Works were scarcely any better, with incident after incident. The Mensheviks fomented strikes in the big workshops of Sormovo (which now produced two locomotives a month in place of eighteen) and at Kolomensk, and the arrest of their agitators instantly provoked a strike. At Yaroslavl and Zlatust the SR and Menshevik parties were masters of the streets.

The local Soviets, unprovided with food supplies or money, were at a desperate turn. They imposed extraordinary levies on their wealthier citizens, confiscated goods and seized firms' current accounts, thus drying up the sources of the State's regular revenue. They also taxed commodities in transit over their territories. The Soviets of Tsaritsyn, Samara and Kazan taxed the oil sent from Baku to Moscow (and sometimes even seized it), so that if and when it got to its destination its price had increased fivefold. The Soviets at Yalta, in the Crimea, taxed all exported tobacco with a prohibitive duty, thereby depriving the cigarette factories at Rostov, Moscow and Petrograd of their basic raw material. Without proper control, and for ill-defined purposes, the Nizhni-Novgorod Soviet levied an extraordinary contribution of twenty-seven million roubles from the rich in its area. The Military Revolutionary Committees, which were often headed by partisan fighters, also exacted levies and undertook requisitioning on their own account.[45]

These details will give a fair indication of the financial state of the country. The budget as forecast for the year was between eighty and a hundred thousand million roubles; the most opimistic estimates of the actual revenue put it at fifteen thousand million.[46]

There was the same chaos in food supply. Each Soviet, each factory and each family bent every effort to feed its own without caring for anybody else. All the measures undertaken by the Food Commissariat were cancelled out by a host of highly varied and egocentric local initiatives. Trains carrying grain were requisitioned *en route*, turned from their destination, and seized strictly according to the rule book, with edicts duly drawn up and signed by the 'responsible' local authorities – or else straightforwardly pillaged. The whole Petrograd–Moscow line thus kept itself alive by buccaneering, at starving Petrograd's expense. All the railways were infested with the 'bag-men', small-scale profiteers or other enterprising citizens, who set off at their own risk and peril to look for foodstuffs in the countryside. They travelled in bands, formed crowds, captured trains by assault, corrupted railway workers, and went off each with his fifty or a hundred pounds of corn. In the Kursk gubernia there were estimated to be 20,000 bag-men devoting themselves to speculation; in the Saratov gubernia there were 50,000.[47]

This quickening social decomposition demanded urgent and energetic counter-measures. Moral influence had already done all that it could. In the face of this mounting anarchy, the centralization of authority appeared ever more necessary. The Food Commissariat sought, and obtained, from the Vee-Tsik the right to quash the decisions of local Soviets and to dismiss their officials.

To replace local anarchy by State intervention; to replace committees by responsible leaders; to involve the workers in production; to repress the counter-revolution which had long been vigorous in the countryside, and was now penetrating the proletarian centres: these are the pressing urgencies of the hour.

The debate on these measures takes place in the All-Russian Soviet Executive (Vee-Tsik), for the Republic, despite its lack of a written constitution, has a constitutional structure already crystallized, and a whole system of inner democracy. The dictatorship of the proletariat is not the dictatorship of a party, or of a Central Committee, or of certain individuals. Its mechanism is complex. Each Soviet, each Revolutionary Committee, each committee of the Bolshevik party or the Left S R party holds a portion of it and operates it after its own fashion. Lenin himself is obliged to follow strict rules. He has to convince a majority in the Central Committee of his party, then discuss with the Communist fraction in the Vee-Tsik and then, in the Vee-Tsik itself, brave the fire of the Left S Rs, anarchists and Internationalist Social-Democrats, all doubtful allies, and of the Right S Rs and Mensheviks, irreducible enemies.[48] All the decrees are debated during sessions which are often of tremendous interest. Here the enemies of the regime enjoy free speech with a more than parliamentary latitude. With monotonous enthusiasm they celebrate the praises of the Constituent Assembly. Impotent but courageous – in fairness they must be granted that – they tirelessly develop the prosecution's indictment of the dictators. 'The autocracy of the commissars has within six months produced the total ruin of Russia, laid waste by German imperialism,' cries a Right S R, who demands the Constituent Assembly, the cancellation of the Brest-Litovsk treaty and re-entry into the war on the side of the Allies. The lawyer Kogan-Bernstein (a Right S R) shouts at the Bolsheviks: 'Get out before you are chased out! You are only in power thanks to bayonets!' He denounces 'the October counter-revolution' and 'Lenin the insensible'. Along with Martov he cries: 'Down with the dictatorship, long live the Republic, long live the Constituent Assembly!' 'You are savages, madmen, bandits!' screamed another, at the end of the session of 14 May, at Sverdlov's imperturbable face.

The arguments of the adversaries of Bolshevism amounted to the following: everything that was wrong came from the usurpation of power by Lenin's party and its intention to burden the country with a premature transition to Socialism by dictatorial and bureaucratic methods. The cure lay in a return to democracy (bourgeois democracy), which would be endowed with wise laws by the Constituent Assembly and escorted into Socialism by the proletariat.

The end of these tempestuous debates came at the session of 14 June, when the Bolsheviks put on the agenda: 'Anti-Soviet activity by parties represented in the Soviets.' L. Sosnovsky, who

gave the report, concluded in favour of the expulsion from the
All-Russian Executive of the representatives of those parties which
were instigating civil war against the Soviets and allying themselves with the enemy. A resolution was passed to this effect, and
the local Soviets were asked to follow this example. The Left SRs
voted against. It was an important step towards a monopoly of
politics in the proletarian dictatorship. Up till now this dictatorship had not seemed incompatible with the legal existence of
parties, groups and journals which were hostile, oppositional,
neutral, doubtful or conditionally friendly. The Vee-Tsik had
been acquiring a sort of parliamentary flavour. We have already
seen the circumstances in which the suppression of the bourgeois
press had been begun. Now the open alliance of the Right SRs
with the Czechoslovaks and the strike propaganda of the Mensheviks,[49] chiming in with the intervention, determined the outlawing of the two parties. It is true that this was still not an
irrevocable step: Lenin would later ask his old opponents
Martov, Dan and Abramovich on the Vee-Tsik: he was not afraid
of them and he thought their opposition might be useful.

At the end of June, simultaneously with the victories of the
Czechoslovaks and the troubles in the countryside, the agitation
of the Mensheviks in the cities reached its peak. At Petrograd a
committee of workers' delegates proclaimed a general strike for
2 July; this was a failure, but a number of factories came out. On
20 June, the revolvers of unknown assailants murdered the party
tribune Volodarsky, an orator and journalist of immense fire, as
he was returning from a meeting in a factory. It was the first
successful political assassination committed by the counter-
revolution.

CLASS STATE, CLASS ARMY

There was as much need of arms as of grain. Bread and an army –
or the Republic was doomed. 'Voluntary enlistment,' Trotsky was
soon to write, 'has reached only a third of our expectations.' The
early Red Army attracted too many unstable elements who came
into it only to get fed for a while – and to acquire arms for themselves. The land of Socialism could after all be properly defended
only by the collective of able-bodied citizens: mass mobilization is
demanded by the conditions of modern war, as the revolution's
leaders perfectly well knew. In their view, voluntary enrolment
was no more than 'a provisional compromise arising from
tragically difficult circumstances'. The All-Russian Soviet Executive had, on 22 April, decreed universal and compulsory military
training for all men aged between sixteen and forty (for youngsters
from sixteen to eighteen it was called preparatory training). This
instruction had to be given them for twelve hours a week, at a
minimum, over eight weeks. At the same time as this measure, the
Executive also approved the text of the Red soldier's oath:[50] 'I, a

47. Red Army recruits at rifle training

son of the toiling people, assume the title of soldier in the workers'
and peasants' army; I swear' to learn the bearing of arms, to look
after my weapons, ammunition and equipment with care, to accept
discipline, to safeguard my dignity and that of my comrades, 'to
direct my every thought and action towards the great aim of the
emancipation of the workers', and 'to spare neither my strength
nor my life in battle for the Soviet Republic, for Socialism and for
the fraternity of all peoples ... may I earn contempt and punishment if I violate this oath'.

The victorious offensive of the Czechoslovaks, achieved without striking a blow, revealed the military feebleness of the Republic. Dispersed as they were over vast tracts of territory between
the Volga and Vladivostok, the Czechoslovaks nowhere amounted
to a substantial force; they became formidable only through the
contrast of their cohesion, discipline and resolve against the disarray and disorganization on the other side. On the Trans-
Siberian line and in the Chelyabinsk region no effective resistance
was put up to the intervention by the local Soviets. Some Soviets
tried to avoid the necessary battle, to the cost of neighbouring
areas. They refused to acknowledge the seriousness of what had
happened, believing it was a matter of misunderstandings, fragmentary mutinies or incidents which would eventually be sorted
out; they did not see that it was war, and war to the death. When

the Czechoslovaks occupied Chelyabinsk the Soviet, which had tolerated the enemy's preparations for nine days without doing anything, now spent two days in useless deliberations, refused to arm the Hungarian prisoners who offered to fight, and disregarded the workers' forces that came together spontaneously. Other Soviets, notably in Siberia, negotiated with the Czechs and concluded truces with them, thus facilitating the enemy's work through their own political stupidity. Trotsky's merciless order, to shoot those who refused to surrender their arms, was nowhere carried out. It was a costly clemency.

There were still units of the former army, in a disorganized condition, all over the country, if only anyone had been able to use them. (The best of the Red Guards were fighting in Siberia, on the Manchurian border, against the Ataman Semyonov, and in other parts against the White bands.) The initiative of the revolutionary masses, which had caused the October Revolution to continue its triumphal march through November and December, was now faltering, for a variety of reasons: the best revolutionary cadres had been wrenched from the local Soviets by the first selection; the country was living off the feeling of a victory gained, so that the tension had slackened; privation and danger had instilled a certain weariness among the workers remaining in the rear – and their very presence in the rear was an indication of their backwardness; the peasantry was vacillating. From now on the failing initiative of the masses had to be made up by compulsion and organization, and a regular army substituted for the permanent insurrection of the guerrilla units.

It was Trotsky's unflinching, tireless energy that took on all the organizational tasks of the army that had to be dragged out of chaos. Numerous points of resistance had to be broken within the revolution itself. Left SRs and Left Communists, symbolizing a very common state of mind, stood up for the guerrillas, combated the theory of the revolutionary army, and opposed the employment of former officers. The Left Communists' theses denounced 'the *de facto* re-establishment in the army of the old officers-corps and the command of the reactionary generals'. They defended the principle of election of leaders. Within a few months the cruel disappointments dealt to their cause by reality would totally dissolve these objections.

The proletariat has no military leaders of its own: 'then let it take to its service those who have served other classes,' said Trotsky. But these officers, these generals are surely counter-revolutionaries? Yes, they are: a dual command is instituted. By the side of each offices will be placed a commissar, as adviser and political guarantor. The commissar receives reports jointly with the commander, whose orders he countersigns, 'thus attesting before the workers and peasants that the orders are not counter-revolutionary machinations'. The responsibility for all operations

48. Ataman
Semyonov

rests upon the commander alone. It is not the job of the commissar to assess the military merits of any orders given; all he can do if he disapproves of them from this viewpoint is refer them to the Military Revolutionary Committee (Order of the Commissar of War, 6 April 1918).

Measures were set afoot to *compel* officers to serve in the Red Army. 'We must finish with military parasitism', and so deprive the counter-revolution of its reserves. The officers have had their training at the expense of the people: let them serve the people. (An appeal addressed to those who have enlisted with the Ataman Krasnov and are burning down the Don valley promises them not only the pardon of the proletariat *but also fresh appointments* if they will surrender forthwith; those who fail to do so will be shot.) Furthermore, proper respect must be accorded to the officers and generals, 'even conservative ones, who accept work in the difficult circumstances that we face; they are worth more than the false, intriguing Socialists'. 'We shall discover among them many more first-rate men than we expect. ...'[51]

The Mensheviks cannot resist raising the ghost of Bonapartism before the All-Russian Soviet Executive. 'An army? Generals? Watch out for the Kornilovs, remember Napoleon!' The army's organizer gives them their answer in his imperious, mocking, metallic tones: Kornilov? But it was you people who nourished and made him. Our army will be a class army, just as our State is a class State. 'We affirm and proclaim the proletarian monopoly of the army.' If our generals intended to imitate their predecessors in revolutionary history we shall know how to remind them of our laws. And we must observe that Dan and Martov are ill-advised in their quotations from French history: they might have remembered that in the era of large-scale mechanized industry, of finance-capital and the proletariat, Bonapartism can no longer assume such crude forms as it did at the end of the eighteenth century.

Still, the desire to repeat the role of Pichegru[52] is not wanting among the military leaders. Admiral Shchastny opens the sequence of betrayal. He had distinguished himself in the last days of April by leading the Baltic fleet to safety when, blocked by ice at Helsinki, it was in danger of falling into the Germans' hands. Shchastny then steered it into Kronstadt. The orders he gave stated: Defend the fleet and prepare to blow it up in case it falls into enemy hands. The admiral instigated suspicion among the crews against the government, which was being cunningly accused of planning the destruction of the fleet. Some officers of the mine-laying division gave out the slogan: dictatorship of the fleet. Trotsky had the admiral arrested. 'When gentlemen admirals and generals, in a time of revolution, start playing their own politics, they must expect to take the consequences. Admiral Shchastny has lost the game,' said Trotsky to the Supreme Revolutionary Tribunal on 20 June. The admiral was executed.[53]

8 · The July-August Crisis

1. Western Russia

THE MAP OF RUSSIA

The months of July and August 1918 were the most critical for the
revolution. Even the crisis of July 1919, which was longer, and
more oppressive and painful, did not reach this pitch of paroxysm
in the class war. The Soviet Republic, which had experienced the
full force of German imperialism, now underwent the shock of
Allied intervention in the very heart of the country. The monstrous coalition between the Central Powers and the Allies was
now realized *de facto* against the Soviets, just when Ludendorff
was launching, on the Somme and the Aisne, his last desperate
offensives towards Paris. Ataman Krasnov, now in control of the
Don region, was simultaneously supplied with arms and munitions
by the Germans and encouraged by the Allies.

Look at the map. On the frontier of Finland, the Finnish–
German troops menace the railway to Murmansk. In the north
the Allies (the British) occupy the coast of Murmansk, Kem,
Onega, Archangel and Shenkursk. The northern front extends
over nearly 850 miles. The German front stretches in practically a
straight line from the Gulf of Finland to the Ukraine for over

350 miles. The Germans hold down Pskov and Minsk, and are in occupation of the entire Ukraine. Around Rostov, Ataman Krasnov is turning the domain of the Cossacks into a counter-revolutionary State. The Kuban is almost completely occupied by the Whites under General Alexeyev. Menshevik Georgia is, as we know, 'independent'. Baku is calling in the British. The southern fronts extend over 900 miles. Dutov's Cossacks control the countryside in the Orenburg (southern Ural) region. On the Volga the Czechoslovaks hold Kazan, Simbirsk (today Ulyanovsk) and Samara; Kursk, Voronezh and Tsaritsyn (today Stalingrad) are threatened. The Republic is in effect reduced to the area of the Grand Duchy of Moscow, just as in the fifteenth century. The ambassadors of the Allies are at Vologda. In the interior, the counter-revolution is seizing Yaroslavl and pressing on Rybinsk, Kostroma, Murom and Nizhni-Novgorod, in the immediate vicinity of the capital. In the rural areas the rich peasants are instigating uprisings: the provinces of Tambov, Ryazan, Yaroslavl and Penza are at the mercy of the kulak Vendée. We shall be attentively following the events in Moscow and Petrograd, no less serious in their implications. Peril is everywhere.

The following figures will give an idea of the intensity reached by the famine. For rationing purposes the population of the large cities is divided into four categories: (1) Heavy physical labour. (2) Ordinary physical labour and intense intellectual labour. (3) Intellectual labour. (4) Not occupied. Here, simply as an exam-

2. Siberia

49. British officers interrogating a Bolshevik soldier

ple, are the rations allocated to these categories in Petrograd on 3–4 July and 14–15 August.

Ration for two days

Category	3–4 July	14–15 August
(1)	200 grams of bread, 2 eggs, 400 grams of fish, 5 herrings	200 grams of bread
(2)	100 grams of bread, 2 eggs, 400 grams of fish, 5 herrings	100 grams of bread
(3)	100 grams of bread, 400 grams of fish, 5 herrings	50 grams of dried vegetables, 5 herrings
(4)	50 grams of bread, 5 herrings	5 herrings

On 2 July the Allies occupy Murmansk. According to their official story they mean to protect the stocks of arms, munitions

and provisions in the port against the designs of the German–Finnish forces. The French Military Mission arms Serbian and Italian prisoners-of-war and sends them to the north. The hesitations of the Allied governments in the matter of intervention have not ended, but a state of mind favourable to intervening has been created in western Europe as the result of the Brest-Litovsk peace, now denounced as 'an act of treason to the Allied cause' and to be followed by important German offensives on the French front; this hysteria extends to the mass of the people, who often believe the legend that the Bolsheviks have 'sold out to the Kaiser'. The arrival of American troops in France had remedied the man-power crisis and made it possible for operations in Russia to be seriously envisaged. In addition, Europe's statesmen have now begun to understand the social implications of Bolshevism. The most enlightened of them on this score are, naturally, the Allied diplomats who have taken refuge at Vologda. Messrs Francis, the United States ambassador, and Noulens, his French opposite number, are (as we have already seen) strong supporters of intervention; the British chargé d'affaires, Lockhart, supports them unreservedly. The Allied diplomatic and military missions in Russia have two objectives at present: to prevent Soviet power from consolidating itself and to prove to the governments of London, Paris and Washington, through the success of the internal counter-revolution, that an energetic intervention would both be opportune and have serious chances of victory.

Several counter-revolutionary governments are now taking shape in Siberia, where the Czechoslovaks have colonized the

3. Black Sea and Caspian Sea

length of the Trans-Siberian Railway and the Japanese are occupying Vladivostok.

This map of Russia should be borne well in mind by the reader if he is to follow events.

50. Lenin and
Sverdlov in Mosc◦
for the unveiling o◦
the Marx–Engels
Monument,
November 1918

THE LEADERS

Let us pause briefly to look at the men who dominate these events. Later, they will acquire the semblance of giants: men will search avidly to decipher their human qualities from the deeds, facts and dates of history. But at this moment their greatness appears to us as something homely, and they themselves as simple. The distribution of roles among them is complete: each fulfils his own task.

Vladimir Ilyich Ulyanov ('N. Lenin' is an old pseudonym for illegal writing) is forty-eight. He is a man of average stature, quite broad in the shoulders, rather stout, with a rapid stride and a lively way of gesturing. His cheekbones are powerful, his nose fleshy, his forehead high and made higher by a spread of baldness. A short, almost red beard lengthens the face, whose blue eyes often twinkle with mischief. Such simplicity in a man of genius is astonishing. He laughs freely; he looks gay and easy-tempered. When he listens, with his hand at his forehead, he sometimes has a sharp look about him, and sometimes guards his eyes and keeps his features hardened in a terrible expression of unbending thought: but one of his very common expressions is a broad smile of amusement, either approving (as if to say: 'Yes, that's it!') or sarcastic. As an orator he is devoid of emphasis and averse to rhetoric: zealous to persuade and prove, with a dialectic that is rigorous, bound together by common sense, powered by sheer obstinacy; his hands make short, frank movements that seem to materialize the argument. As speaker and as publicist he is an impressive realist who carries and even forces the conviction of his hearers. Lenin is of bourgeois origins. His life-history: propaganda and agitation since the age of twenty, at the University of St Petersburg. He has memories of a brother, a young terrorist, who was hanged. Then a year in prison, two years of exile in Siberia, emigration to Munich and then London, the founding of the party, ceaseless polemics and struggles, the research and development of a theory, clandestine activity in Russia during the 1905 revolution, international congresses, and daily toil in Geneva, Paris, Cracow, Zürich throughout the war. The same insistent effort over fifteen years: building the party, preparing the revolution. The same existence, with its paradoxical regularity, as a professional revolutionary in Britain, Switzerland, France and Galicia: humble lodgings, libraries, editings of small illegal journals, meetings: comrades, tea-gatherings, long bicycle-trips. The hours of darkness have come: but there have been no falterings, no doubts. He is a trained scholar who has at his finger-tips four languages (Russian, English, German, French), Marxist sociology,

the history of capitalism and the labour movement, and the politics of Russia. In order to confute the idealist tendency in the
party he dedicated himself to philosophy. This revolutionary now
has the experience of three revolutions. A unity which blends
action, thought, word, personal living and political vocation is the
cardinal trait of his character. Lenin is hewn from one single
block: his whole being is tensed perpetually on his task, his mis-

sion, which fuses with the mission of the proletariat. His prestige
as the founder of the party and guide of the revolution is immense;
for all that, people within the party he has created do not fear to
contradict him, and this is just what he wants. His utilitarian outlook may sometimes be brutal, but his hands are absolutely clean.
At this moment he is chief both of party and of government. He
maps out the routes and points to the destination. He is the brain
of the revolution. In Sadoul's words: 'Lenin is a superb thinking-
machine, a willing analytic mechanism of incredible precision and
strength, inserted into the great revolutionary movement whose
motor it has become, marvellously adapted as an integral part of
the whole.'[1]

Leon Davidovich Trotsky (real name Bronstein) often appears
as Lenin's equal, though he himself gladly recognizes the latter's
pre-eminence (not that these considerations have any importance).[2]
At the Seventh Party Congress the two leaders were elected on to
the Central Committee with the same number of votes. Thirty-
nine years old. A man of lank proportions, broad-shouldered,
with a military bearing and a restrained natural elegance. Long
face, lofty forehead, a mass of unruly hair, green eyes that look
out with a metallic glint, piercing, alive, shrewd and searching

51. Trotsky and colleagues at a military parade in Moscow, 1919

from behind the pince-nez lenses; a clean-cut profile, a large mouth whose line accentuates the firmness, and sometimes the hardness, of his other features. A small pointed beard further extends and emphasizes this face of strength and delicacy. It is a closed, distant personality, yet affable. The gestures are authoritarian, like his manner of talking. From the rostrum comes a voice of astonishingly powerful modulation, audible from afar, rapping out its brief, incisive, mordant sentences, which are constructed with the assurance of a consistently clear dialectic: each dictum scientific in precision, impeccable in form. A bitter, haughty, exact irony which neatly pierces the opponent. Trotsky's eloquence, concentrating intelligence and will, sweeps along crowds, because it transmits greatness, force and necessity in a language of epic clarity. The style of the journalist equals that of the orator, with a superb fusion between essence and form. Biography as follows: born in 1879 in the Kherson gubernia, of Jewish and bourgeois origin. A revolutionary since his seventeenth year. At eighteen and nineteen, a member of the Workers' Union of Southern Russia (illegal, naturally), at Nikolayev. Two years in prison (a Marxist education undergone in the jail). Two years of exile in Ust-Kut (Siberia). Escape. Emigration. Vienna, Zürich, Paris, London, first period of collaboration with Lenin in 1903, in editing *Iskra*. After the split in the Social-Democratic party in 1903, separates from Lenin on questions of organization and joins the minority (Menshevik) opposition for a short while; soon, when the Mensheviks turn out to be supporters of collaboration with the liberals, leaves them and remains outside the two factions, somewhat to the Left of the Bolsheviks. Illegal return to Russia during the revolution of 1905. An adversary of all opportunism and a supporter, from this time on, of the proletarian dictatorship and the Socialist revolution, he collaborates with the Bolsheviks. President of the Petrograd Soviet. Arrested with the Soviet on 3 December. Imprisonment, theoretical and historical work, deportation to Obdorsk, on the River Obi in the Arctic, escape and flight abroad. In Vienna, collaboration with the German and Austrian Socialists, publication of *Pravda* together with Yoffe. War correspondent in the Balkans. Expelled from Austria in 1914; an internationalist during the war, condemned in Germany; in Paris, edits *Nashe Slovo* and works with the French syndicalists around *Vie Ouvrière*. Expelled from France in 1916. Expelled from Spain, travels to New York: collaboration with the revolutionary press in America. Leaves for Russia on the beginning of the revolution and is interned in Canada. From this time, has propounded a concept of revolution similar to that of the Bolsheviks. Returns to Petrograd; after the July events, spends a time in Kerensky's jails. In the course of these struggles, and the studies that have gone with them, the theoretician has acquired a European culture; he has four languages. The principal organizer of the October Revolution now has the task of organizing the defence of the Soviet Republic. He goes to war, forges the blade, carries the responsibility on all fronts. He incarnates, in its keenest expression, the revolution's will to survive.

Lenin and Trotsky have in common a method of work based on punctuality, economy of time and resources, discipline, responsibility and initiative among collaborators. They are born organizers; and they train team after team of organizers.

External defence must be complemented by defence in the interior. The man to whom the party has entrusted the difficult mission of unmasking the permanent conspiracy, of serving the proletariat as the epitome of vigilance, severity and terror, is called Felix Edmundovich Dzerzhinsky. He is tall and thin, with angular features and acute eyes. His mortal enemies – and he has

52. Dzerzhinsky

no other sort, since the struggle between him and them is to the death – admire his ascetic honesty, his unbreakable self-possession, his amazing capacity for work. Forty-one years, a Pole of bourgeois origin. A Marxist revolutionary since his eighteenth year. Five times imprisoned, thrice deported, thrice escaping, sentenced in 1912–14 to ten years of forced labour, a political prisoner for five years, liberated on the fall of Tsardom, member of the Petrograd Military Revolutionary Committee which organized the insurrection of 1917, Chairman of the Commission for Repression of Counter-Revolution (Vee-Cheka) since it was first set up. Dzerzhinsky is a man of faith. Since adolescence he has devoted his life, with a poet's ardour, to the transformation of man and of life. His *Prison Journal* is suffused with a profound idealism. 'He had the deepest imaginable love for men,' wrote Karl Radek, 'and it was only the conviction that any weakening would be calamitous for the masses that enabled him to strike so inflexibly with the sword of the revolution.'[3]

From time to time the tall frame and the intellectual's face of Yakov Mikhailovich Sverdlov could be glimpsed behind Lenin. We have already made our acquaintance with Sverdlov.[4] He is organizer extraordinary to the party and to the Republic, whose constitution he has just drafted.

Grigori Yevseyich Zinoviev (Radomyslsky), a collaborator of Lenin's since 1907, theoretician, popularizer and orator, is defending, at Petrograd, one of the most advanced and most threatened outposts of the Republic. As President of the Executive Committee of the Northern Commune, he is the dictator of a great workers' city, starving, cholera-stricken and vulnerable to surprise attack. His colleague Volodarsky, a garment-worker returned from the United States, unsparing as a speaker and a writer, has just been assassinated by unknown men (by Right SRs, it will be discovered later, when the organizer of the murder goes over to Bolshevism). Zinoviev, with his tousled head, smooth, rather flabby face, nonchalant stance, rounded gestures, deep, sometimes strident and always audible voice, Zinoviev with his merciless choice of words often confronts and subdues, in the old capital's factories, the discontent and anger of a proletariat whose best sons are at the front, and which is dying of hunger.[5]

Another man must be named here, who is not visible on the scene: Dr Adolph Abramovich Yoffe, the Republic's ambassador to Berlin, accredited to his Imperial Royal Majesty Wilhelm II. Functions whose delicacy requires a discreet penumbra, whose importance demands quite unusual skills. The foundations of the German Empire are being mined, the edifice can be heard cracking. Its fall will be the salvation of the Russian revolution, and perhaps the signal for the revolutionary explosion in Europe. This first Bolshevik ambassador, who in a time of war flies the Red Flag over his home in Berlin, has a paradoxical mission: to avoid a resumption of hostilities and to prepare the German revolution. No Spartacist's house is more closely watched than his residence: none more assiduous than he in practising the cult of appearances. But the mission is being accomplished. Dr Yoffe is thirty-five: large forehead, pronounced Jewish physiognomy, powerful lips, an Assyrian beard, the grave demeanour of a man of science or of business trained in Berlin. At the age of sixteen, in the town of his birth in the Crimea, he was already a Social-Democrat. He did his medical schooling in Germany, from which indeed he was expelled in 1907 by Chancellor von Bülow. He has seen the inside of prison several times, has organized the transmission of illegal literature in the Caucasus, organized the escape from Sebastopol of a comrade from the *Potemkin*, performed a large number of clandestine missions in Russia during the years of reaction, undergone a sentence of hard labour and four years' deportation to the Tobolsk gubernia, right up to the revolution. The revolution has a worthy representative at the court of the Kaiser. Bolshevism's first ambassador to Germany was to follow a long and brilliant career as a revolutionary diplomat. He led the peace negotiations with Estonia, Lithuania, Latvia and Poland (1920–21), represented the Soviets in China, where he skilfully steered Sun Yat-sen to a pro-Soviet orientation, then in Tokyo, then in Vienna (1925). Having become the victim of an incurable illness, he took his own life in 1927 (in Moscow), having declared his solidarity for the last time with the opposition in the Communist party.

There is another great figure that does not appear, in this work, in the first rank, even though he belongs to that level. We have had to concentrate our attention on the very heart of events, deliberately neglecting the fortunes of the revolution in the Ukraine. Bolshevism, with the aid of peasant uprisings, is engaged in a contest for this abundant granary against Skoropadsky's dictatorship, which rests on the German occupying armies. Bolshevism's man in Kiev is called Christian Rakovsky. At this moment he is negotiating a peace between the Ukraine and the Soviet

Republic; in reality, he observes, waits, struggles and prepares. Later he will be, for some years, head of the Soviet government of the Ukraine, the soul of the proletarian revolution in this land devastated over four years by some fifteen invasions and armed restorations from the counter-revolution. Christian Rakovsky is now, at the prime of his life, a veteran Socialist of Europe, an old hand at international congresses, gallicized by long spells in Paris, Russified by long-standing contacts with the Russians. Bulgarian by birth, Rumanian by nationality, he bears a name which is inscribed in the history of Bulgaria and which has recently entered the annals of Rumania. A revolutionary internationalist before and during the war, associated with the concept of a Balkan Socialist Federation, prosecuted in many trials, feared in Bucharest as the regime's mortal enemy, tracked by assassins, Rakovsky emerged on May Day from the prison at Jassy to the acclamation of the Russian soldiers who had opened its doors for him: he immediately formed the first revolutionary government of the Rumanian republic at Odessa. Lithe and svelte, of Latin appearance and temperament, this gentleman of the handsome, hairless countenance, this tribune of the lashing tongue blends an unshakable revolutionary integrity with a Western intelligence of infinite subtlety.[6]

THE PARTY AND ITS MEN

Behind these great figures of the foremost rank there naturally stands a multitude of others, ready to replace them if they vanish: these too are energetic, powerful, great in their way. The revolution is rich in men, because it awakens to creative activity innumerable masses from social strata which are full of young, unused vigour. The personalities of the second rank are numerous, and deserve study. Numerous also among these are men who await no more than the event which will arouse them to a new stature. Nonetheless, the selection of leaders that has been achieved has nothing arbitrary or unjust about it: the passage of the years enables us now to make this judgement. It is the result of twenty years of revolutionary preparation and of eighteen months of turmoil: not of the caprice of a congress or of an electorate's balloting.

And yet these men have their greatness and strength only through the greatness and strength of the party, which itself derives its power from that of the masses, of the classes in society. We shall not deal here in any depth with the problem of the role of personality in history. The classes, the masses, the party work through the agency of individuals; their choice of individuals demonstrates precisely the fitness of these larger forces for victory. Had Lenin and Trotsky been assassinated in September 1917, would not the revolution's chances of victory have declined immeasurably? Would not their disappearance at this juncture, in July–August 1918, have been like the loss of an experienced sea captain who, in a ship in mid-ocean assailed by tempest, computes within his skull the maximum chances of safety? Lenin had suffered this very uncertainty: 'Tell me,' he said one day to Trotsky, 'if the Whites kill you and me do you think Bukharin and Sverdlov will be able to pull through all right?' That phrase of the English which is so remarkably accurate in business matters, *The right man in the right place*, applies with even more force to the class struggle. And it is a fact of serious significance that neither the Tsarist regime nor the Russian bourgeoisie was able to find or to introduce in their appropriate places the men whom they needed, whereas the proletariat found them at once; just as it is significant that, increasingly over the whole world, the bourgeoisie is forced to borrow its political leaders and statesmen, if not from among the proletariat, at least from the Socialist movement.

We have noted how Lenin, in emphasizing the salutary role of individual authority, has demonstrated the compatibility between personal dictatorship and the dictatorship of the proletariat. The limitless strength of the revolutionary classes now appears to us, in short, as an elemental power that must be canalized, dammed, directed and organized so as to prevail against the forces of the counter-revolutionary classes, which are already organized. An effectively organized and directed social class will in the last resort be able to impose its will upon classes which are stronger but which lack organization and direction. It is like the difference between a multitudinous mob and a small army. The party works as the yeast of organization among the worker and peasant masses. At such moments its function takes many forms: it expresses the most general, most basic aspirations of the crowds, and translates them into conscious actions; it attracts, mobilizes, staffs and disciplines the most active elements of the class it represents: it selects from these the administrators, agitators and leaders; it establishes between the leaders and the masses a network of continual contacts and exchanges, be it through great assemblies, congresses, meetings or the daily work-round; finally it ensures the predominance within the working class of the conscious element over the backward strata, the victory of intelligence and the higher instincts over alien influences, ancient vices and the baser instincts.

THE FIFTH CONGRESS OF THE SOVIETS

The Anglo–French expedition landed at Murmansk on 1 July; the Whites entered Orenburg on the 2nd; the Czechs entered Ufa on the 3rd. The Fifth All-Russian Congress of Soviets met on the 4th.

1,164 delegates were present. Of these 773 were Communists, 353 Left Socialist-Revolutionaries, seventeen Maximalists, ten non-party, four anarchists, four Internationalist Social-Democrats and three representatives of nationalities. The Congress opens with an urgent statement from the Commissar for War, Trotsky. The political battle is now on with a vengeance. In the Kursk region, close to the Ukrainian frontier now held by the Germans, a disquieting agitation is being conducted among the Red troops. They are being incited to war against the Germans. Some units are demanding an offensive. One commissar has been killed and a brigade leader wounded. Guerrilla strikes into Ukrainian territory have taken place. Certain fanatics have threatened the head of the peace delegation in the Ukraine, Rakovsky, with their grenades. All this must stop. 'I have given the order,' states Trotsky, 'to shoot the agents of the enemy who are fomenting these disturbances; I demand the approval of Congress for this action.' The hall echoes with shouts. 'Executioner! Kerensky!' cry the Left SRs. From the rostrum their leader Kamkov openly endorses 'the broad, healthy movement which is leading the revolutionaries of Russia irresistibly to the aid of their brothers in the Ukraine'. This explicit backing for the guerrillas who are seeking to create a state of war as an accomplished deed excites indignant objections. The vehemence of the Left SRs at once breaks into a kind of paroxysm. 'Allow us to speak,' they shout, 'before you shoot us!' Zinoviev defends Trotsky's proposal, which is carried by a two-thirds majority. 'The safety of the Republic,' it is proclaimed, 'is the supreme law. Those who oppose it will be put down.' The SRs demonstratively leave the meeting, then return to it, and the duel is resumed even more violently.

Maria Spiridonova[7] now attacks the Bolsheviks with a passion bordering on hysteria. She speaks of the martyred and betrayed Ukraine; accuses the 'Bolshevik usurpers' of ruining the peasantry, of sending the Germans secret trains loaded with gold, of being in the service of Germany. Lenin shakes his head as he listens. His rebuttals, which are sometimes drowned in interruptions, are notable for their common-sense. 'A party which drives its sincerest representatives to wallow in this mire of lies and errors is a doomed party.'[8] To want to tear up the Brest-Litovsk treaty is to put the peasants' neck into the big landlords' noose. It is essential to gain time: the Republic is getting stronger, the rival imperialisms are at their last gasp. Civil war is necessary to Socialism, but the parties must not base themselves on the standpoint of the starving individual, but on that of Socialism. The Left SRs are setting the peasantry against us: merciless war upon those Socialists who desert us while some are cornering all the grain and others are dying of hunger! We shall not shrink from any struggle whatsoever. We shall subject everything to State audit and nationalize everything, if necessary. Our practical solutions are: monopoly and taxation of grain; fixing of a maximum price; reduction of the prices of manufactured goods by fifty per cent for the poor peasants and twenty-five per cent for the middle peasants.

It is at this point in the debate, with the atmosphere electric with opposing currents, that the news comes, at 4 A.M. on 6 July, that Count Mirbach, the German ambassador in Moscow, has just been assassinated in his Legation by Left S R terrorists belonging to the staff of the Cheka. The Congress, which is meeting in the Bolshoi Theatre, immediately suspends its deliberations, but the Left S R deputies are prevented from leaving. They spend the evening in a state of mortal anxiety, expecting at some moments to be delivered by the insurrection that they have organized, at others to be massacred by these Bolshevik 'agents of Germany'.

ASSASSINATION OF COUNT MIRBACH. THE LEFT SR RISING

On 6 July, at about 3 A.M., two functionaries of the Cheka arrived by car and presented themselves at the German Legation. They brought with them papers concerning an obscure Lieutenant Mirbach, who was a prisoner of war. The ambassador, a secretary and the two visitors sat together in a drawing-room decorated with grey and pink silk hangings. One of the visitors, Blyumkin, opened his briefcase smartly, saying 'Look, here is an item which ...', pulled a Browning automatic out of it and fired point-blank at Count Mirbach. The ambassador, wounded, rushed into the neighbouring reception room, where he fell. The terrorists followed close behind him. One of them threw a grenade on to him, which failed to explode. The other (Blyumkin) picked it up and threw it again, with more force, at the man lying at his feet. The wounded man was blown to bits. The explosion threw the terrorist out of the window; an official fired at him but his companion dragged him to the car. They got away without pursuit.[9]

Dzerzhinsky went to see the Central Committee of the Left S R party: there he learnt that the party assumed the entire responsibility for the assassination, and was taken prisoner. A detachment of special troops from the Cheka under the command of Popov formed the principal nucleus of the Left S R forces, which that evening took the offensive at several points of the city. They took the central post office by surprise, and made haste to send telegrams everywhere decreeing as null and void any decisions of the Council of People's Commissars, 'the Socialist-Revolutionary party being from now on the only governing party'. 'The people want war with Germany!' declared the Left S Rs. Meanwhile the population watched the operations of the troops in the streets with an indifference tinged with hostility. The Left S Rs had at their disposal from 800 to 2,000 men, sixty machine-guns, half a dozen field-guns and three armoured cars. Some squads of anarchists and Black Sea sailors joined their forces. They had, as it appears, concealed from their own partisan forces the project of forcibly seizing power from the Bolsheviks, right up to the last moment, and so the confusion of morale among their troops condemned them to inactivity within a very short spell. Their whole strategy was limited to a few blasts of cannon-fire at the Kremlin.

The Bolsheviks could call on the Lettish riflemen, a serviceable remnant from the old army, commanded by an officer named Vatsetis,[10] non-party but loyal, and on an international brigade composed mainly of Hungarian prisoners-of-war, headed by a Communist by the name of Bela Kun. The local commandant, Muralov, also had available some detachments of the young Red Army. These forces were put under the direction of two of the men who had seized the Winter Palace in 1917, Antonov-Ovseyenko and Podvoisky.

By midday on the following day, the rising was crushed. A few shells on the headquarters of the Left SR Central Committee had put the insurgents to flight. Nearly 300 of them were arrested. Several of them were executed; among them Alexandrovich, an excellent young militant who had participated in all the actions of 1917 and enjoyed a general esteem. An assistant of Dzerzhinsky's at the head of the Cheka, he had deceived his chief and his comrades in accordance with his party's discipline, in order to prepare the insurrection. He died bravely. His death was much more than the penalty paid for a breach of duty: it was the ransom exacted by the peace with Germany.

THE END OF THE SOVIET ALLIANCE

The Left SR party had committed suicide. What had it been aiming after? Its speakers at the Fifth Congress had defined its aims: 'To tear up the Brest-Litovsk treaty (which is fatal to the Russian and the international revolution) in revolutionary style; to appeal to the solidarity of the German workers ...'; and to modify the peasant policy of the Soviet government. This party claimed to represent the interest of the 'toiling peasants'.

This last point is of considerable importance. During the debates in the Vee-Tsik in mid-June on the Committees of Poor Peasants, advocated by Lenin and bitterly attacked by Martov, the Left SRs had stated their position in vigorous terms. We agree, they said, that the civil war must be taken into the countryside against the kulaks; but we think it is nonsensical to try to distinguish between the poor and the middle peasantry (in the attempt to enlist the poor, proletarian or semi-proletarian masses). It is necessary, they said, to count not on the poor peasant but on the middle peasant, who will be 'the most reliable support of the Socialist revolution in the countryside'.[11] Against Lenin's formula 'the poorest peasantry' the Left SRs wished to substitute the expression 'labouring peasantry'. In other words: whereas the Bolsheviks founded their policy in the countryside on the interest and the energy of the rural proletariat, the Left SRs defended the interests of the rural petty-bourgeoisie – the mass of middle peasants – whom they hoped to involve in the struggle against the kulaks. Hence their differences with the Bolsheviks on the problems of food supply. While the latter worked for centralization in order to combat anarchy and the free play of local and personal egoisms, the Left SRs would have liked to leave the maximum initiative, authority and command to the peasant Soviets, which were obviously, for the most part, under the control of middle peasants.[12]

These differences became sharper and clearer during the discussions on the decree concerning the supply of manufactured goods to the Committees of Poor Peasants. This decree, Karelin declared, harmed the interests of the labouring (i.e. middle) peasants; it opposed the populations of infertile districts to those in fertile districts; it was part of the system of bureaucratic dictatorship which was undermining the local Soviets. It was criminal to counterpose Committees of Poor Peasants to the Soviets of labouring peasants.[13]

These facts allow us to characterize the Left SR party as the party of the middle peasantry. Hence we can immediately understand its vacillations,[14] its anarchistic tendencies, its aversion towards the centralized State and the regular army, its penchant for guerrilla warfare, its democratic mentality which was so often opposed to the dictatorial spirit of the Bolsheviks. But were the middle peasants, then, in favour of war? Of course not, since it was they, more or less, who had imposed the peace. The fact that their party committed political suicide for the sake of provoking war was due to its having become the plaything of other forces (which we shall see working out later) through the lack of political independence so characteristic of the petty-bourgeoisie, the feverishness of its emotions and the fuzziness of its politics.

In July 1918 the peasantry, which had from July the previous year up till January and February supported the Bolsheviks as instruments for the expropriation of the landlords, had now as a whole become hostile to them. On the key question of the trade in grain, peasant interests allied the middle peasants with the kulaks. The Left SR party, whose leading circles were made up of sincere Socialist intellectuals, had by now lost its social base. Between the intentions of its leaders and the aspirations of the class which lent it strength, the gap was widening. All that could issue now was some kind of adventure. In such situations all that remains for revolutionary idealists is to try their luck for the last time, to fall and break their necks.

The defeat of the SRs, coming as it did after the disarmament of the anarchists, marked (in Trotsky's words) the end of the Soviet alliance that had been cemented the previous November through the combined efforts of the peasant masses and the proletariat. Once the bourgeois revolution carried out by the rural masses had run its course, the contradiction between these aims and the aims of the Socialist revolution made itself felt with increasing cruelty. The ideologues of the petty-bourgeoisie, torn by contradictory interests and sentiments, split from the party of the proletariat, not without much inner turmoil. It is the moment chosen by influences from abroad to intensify their pressure.

The end of the Soviet alliance produces in its wake a formidable concentration of power. Up till this time, the dictatorship was in a way democratic; constitutional forms were spelt out within its structure. The multiplicity of local activity, the existence of parties and groups, the demands of public opinion, the democratic traditions of revolutionaries trained in the school of Western democracy, and the weakness of the central authority all worked in this direction. The debates within the Bolshevik party, too, have shown us the vitality of its internal democracy. But everything changes at this point. The Allied intervention, striking simultaneously with the rebellion of the kulaks and the collapse of the Soviet alliance, poses an unmistakable threat to the survival of the Republic. The proletarian dictatorship is forced to throw off its democratic paraphernalia forthwith. Famine and local anarchy compel a rigorous concentration of powers in the hands of the appropriate Commissariats. The catastrophe of the transport system compels a recourse to draconic methods of authority on the railways. The war, the total encirclement of the revolution and the inadequacy of spontaneous foci of resistance compel the establishment of a regular army, to supplement and supplant the guerrilla formations. Bankruptcy compels the centralization of financial policy. Conspiracy compels the introduction of a powerful apparatus of interior defence. Assassinations, peasant risings and the mortal danger compel the use of terror. The outlawing of the Socialists of counter-revolution and the split with the anarchists and Left S Rs have as their consequence the political monopoly of the Communist party and the extinction, for practical purposes, of the constitution. With the disappearance of political debates between parties representing different social interests through the various shades of their opinion, Soviet institutions, beginning with the local Soviets and ending with the Vee-Tsik and the Council of People's Commissars, manned solely by Communists, now function in a vacuum: since all the decisions are taken by the party, all they can do is give them the official rubber-stamp.

The defeat of the Left S R party is final. Many of its organizations and members break with it. Up till 1923 it retains the mere ghost of a legal existence, with a small review and a few deputies in a few of the Soviets. After the bloody days of July it splits into three tendencies. Certain of its militants found the 'People's Communist party', shortly to be absorbed by the Bolshevik party. Others, persisting in the anti-Bolshevik struggle, will engage in dreams of a Third Revolution, cooperate with Makhno and the

Ukrainian anarchists, and assist in 1919 in the anarchist attempt
to kill the Moscow CP committee.[15] Spiridonova and Kamkov
will adopt an attitude similar to that of these 'activists', and be
interned. A third group, led by the former People's Commissar
for Justice, Steinberg, will try to keep for the party some legal
existence as a loyal opposition, seeking a liaison with those
Socialists in western Europe who attempt, in vain, to found a
Left Socialist International between the Socialist and the Communist Internationals, which is sometimes called the 'Two-and-a-
Half International'.[16]

YAROSLAVL

During the street fighting in Moscow the counter-revolutionary
forces took over Yaroslavl. This ancient city, situated on the Volga
on the Archangel railway line between Moscow and Vologda, is
an industrial concentration (16,000 workers out of nearly
100,000 inhabitants) and a religious centre, celebrated for its fine
sixteenth- and seventeenth-century churches. Reactionary influences had been so successful in this provincial environment that in
the spring of 1917 officers had been known to murder Jewish
soldiers and non-believers had been lynched by the mob. The
Mensheviks were able to provoke strike movements there and the
Bolsheviks were hated like the plague. It had been necessary to
break the resistance of the post and telegraph offices and the employees engaged in food supply. The populace was rationed; the
Soviet raised forced levies from the bourgeoisie. Public proces-
sions were organized by the clergy, who were held personally
responsible by the Soviet for any disorders. The town was actually
held by two or three hundred determined Communists led by
Nakhimson, a young doctor of philosophy from Berne University
who had fought in the 1905 revolution, and the watchmaker
Zakheim: both being Jews. Meanwhile the Fatherland and Freedom Defence League was concentrating its forces there secretly.
The League, which could count on several thousand reliable supporters, had at first intended to start simultaneous insurrections in
Moscow, Rybinsk, Murom, Kostroma, Yaroslavl and Kazan.
The preventive measures taken by the Cheka in Moscow and
Kazan forced it to abandon this extensive plan of operations. At
the beginning of July Boris Savinkov arrived at Yaroslavl accompanied by his assistants, including Colonel Perkhurov, who had
been appointed to the command of the local forces. This high-
ranking officer had served the Red Army on a number of occasions
and had only recently been an inspector of artillery with a partisan
corps. He now had two or three hundred ex-officers in his
organization.

On the night of 6–7 July, 110 of his men assembled not far from
the town. Their arms amounted to about a dozen revolvers. They

began by seizing the artillery depot and getting themselves armed. The mounted militia surrendered without a struggle and a Red regiment decided to stay neutral and allow itself to be disarmed. The Whites had been promised the support of several hundred workers; in the event they got hardly a few dozen. Arrests of the Communists began. Nakhimson and Zakheim were captured when just out of bed, and shot on the spot. The town awoke to find itself in a state of siege, and under the authority of the 'volunteer army of the north', commanded by the 'old revolutionary' Boris Savinkov and Colonel Perkhurov, acting on behalf of General Alexeyev (then away organizing the volunteer army of the south, with Denikin). Several commissars, including one Bolshevik, went over to the Whites. Intellectuals, high-school pupils, middle-class youngsters flocked to enlist in hundreds under the banner of 'order'. News of sweeping Czechoslovak victories was being given out.

The Whites arrested around 200 Communists and suspects and, not knowing what to do with them, interned them on a barge moored between the two banks of the Volga. These 200 captives, men, women and children, wounded, sick and dying, were crammed on top of each other in their floating prison, in which they spent thirteen days, exposed to the fire of the belligerent forces; they received nothing in the way of food.

The Mensheviks, who had been informed of the reactionary *coup* that was being organized, had decided to observe complete neutrality.

The Communists, although surprised by this attack, delivered at the moment when the political conflict with the local Left S R branch was occupying all their attention, soon recovered and concentrated around the city all the Red units they could call in. They made use of the powerful artillery they had at their disposal to begin immediately with a bombardment that was to last twelve days. A ferocious battle ensued. When the promised descent of the Allies from Archangel failed to materialize, the Whites knew they were lost. They tried in vain to call the surrounding countryside to insurrection, but the peasants demanded arms for the sole purpose of defending their villages against the Bolsheviks and were unwilling to engage in any further operations. Perkhurov managed in the end to escape from the city by boat, under cover of fog, at the head of fifty officers.[17] Most of the Whites refused to risk a break-through; hoping to escape the vengeance of the revolution by a subterfuge, they surrendered on 21 July to a German lieutenant who headed a committee of prisoners-of-war, and declared themselves to be the prisoners of Germany. The town, full of corpses and smoking ruins, had now exhausted its bread supply.

The extraordinary Red General Staff for the Yaroslavl front issued an order to the population decreeing that:

any person who wants to save his life must leave the city within twenty-four hours and surrender on the American Bridge. Those who remain in the town after this interval will be treated as rebels. After twenty-four hours, no quarter will be given to any person. The town will be mercilessly bombarded by heavy artillery, using poison-gas shells. Any who remain in it will perish in the ruins, along with the rebels, the traitors and the enemies of the workers' and poor peasants' revolution [20 July].

The population, terrified at this announcement, came out into the fields in throngs to surrender at the designated point; there they filed in their entirety past the tables of the Cheka, which had been drawn up in the open air. Three hundred and fifty Whites were arrested in the course of this summary tribunal and shot without delay. Fifty-seven officers had already been executed when the Reds entered the town. It was the first serious episode of the terror.

The futile battle of Yaroslavl left 4,000 workers without jobs and 40,000 persons homeless. Fourteen factories had been destroyed, 2,147 houses out of 7,618, nine out of ten schools, twenty public buildings out of forty-seven.[18]

THE POLITICS OF M. NOULENS

The battle of Yaroslavl was, as a matter of fact, no more than one episode in the Allied intervention in Russia. In the previous chapter we have already mentioned the plan for encircling Moscow which had been envisaged by General Lavergne. The testimony of Boris Savinkov before the Moscow Revolutionary Tribunal in 1924, which moreover accords fully with *all* the written sources in this affair (and there are many of them) is absolutely clear.

I thought at first [said Savinkov] of operating in Moscow; but the French [Consul Grenard and General Lavergne, the latter speaking on M. Noulens's behalf] told me that the Allies felt that it was possible to continue operations against the Germans on the Russian front. ... They informed me that a sizeable landing of Anglo–French forces would be taking place at Archangel, with this purpose in mind, and that it was necessary to support this expedition from the interior. The plan was to occupy the north of the Volga basin, when the British and French would support the insurrection. We were to take Yaroslavl, Rybinsk, Kostroma and Murom. The French would concentrate on Vologda. But they deceived us. The Allied landing did not take place and we found ourselves on our own at Yaroslavl. ... The French knew all the resources we could call on ... I saw Grenard and Lavergne several times. ... The French put money at my disposal. Our own funds [those of the Fatherland and Freedom Defence League], which were on a relatively small scale, came from three sources. There were insignificant donations; I had 200,000 roubles (Kerensky issue) via a Czech intermediary named Klepando. The French gave about two and a half million Kerensky roubles.[19] An official brought me the money, in small amounts at first; when the insurrection was in the offing they gave a huge sum all at once, two million I think...[20]

The French advised me to seize Yaroslavl, Rybinsk and Kostroma. I hesitated, as I felt that our forces were insufficient. For a while I was thinking of transferring them all to the Czechs, and even gave the order for a section of them to go off to Kazan, which was still held by the Reds, to start a rising there when the Czechs came near. But I had a message from Vologda via Grenard in which Noulens confirmed categorically that the landing at Archangel would be taking place on 5 and 10 July (or else 3 and 8 July, I cannot remember exactly) and asked me at all costs to begin the action on the upper Volga precisely on that date.

The British did not land at Archangel until a month later, on 3 August. There was never any question of a French landing. All the indications are that M. Noulens wanted popular insurrections against the Bolsheviks as a means of influencing his government to support his own interventionist policies.[21] Savinkov's activities on the upper Volga were to complement those of the Czecho-slovaks and the Right S Rs farther down the river. A kind of S R government had been functioning for a month in Samara, receiving its directives likewise from M. Noulens. One of the leaders of the S R party at this time, who was also a leading figure in the so-called Constituents' movement, wrote:

In June we received an official note from M. Noulens ... giving a categorical confirmation of the Allied governments' decision to supply forces for joint action against the Germano-Bolsheviks; such forces were to be large enough to take the weight of the struggle in the first stage and to enable the anti-Bolshevik contingents to form themselves into a big regular army. The Allies rejected any possibility of co-existence with the Bolsheviks and proposed the formation of a single coalition government, to take the form of a directorate of three persons, armed with dictatorial powers until the existing Constituent Assembly could meet. ... The Allies, in addition, intended to recognize the Assembly only in respect of its right to invest the directorate with its authority and to prepare fresh Constituent elections.[22]

A letter from M. Stephen Pichon, then Foreign Minister in Clemenceau's cabinet, to the Foreign Minister of the Samara government, Vedenyapin (a Right S R), written at the same time or shortly afterwards, contains a note to exactly the same effect.[23] The Right Centre (Prince E. N. Trubetskoy, P. B. Struve, Gurko) and the League for Renewal, dominated by the liberal bour-geoisie, equally collaborated with the French. The Left S Rs, too, though sincere and determined adversaries of all these counter-revolutionary groups, appear to have had relations with the French Military Mission. I have been assured from several quar-ters that the latter supplied the grenades which were used in the murder at the German Legation. Savinkov testified: 'I remember one conversation that I had, I think, with Grenard. He told me that the French had given facilities for the assassination of Count Mirbach by the Left S Rs.'

We can be certain that the Soviet regime's pro-war party was in contact with the Allies. One is therefore led to conclude that the French, being as much informed of the Left S Rs' plans as they were of Savinkov's and the Czechoslovaks' activity, managed to apply a certain division of labour between the various parties, unbeknown to one another. It was they who, after a certain fashion, achieved a unified command over two rival fronts. The betrayal of Muraviev, to be related below, strengthens this conviction of ours.

MENACES AND TREASON

For several days Russia lived under the menace of a renewed war with Germany. In spite of some reassuring statements made to the Reichstag by the Chancellor, Germany presented the Soviet Republic on 14 July with a Note demanding that a battalion of uniformed troops be allowed into Moscow to ensure the security of the Imperial embassy. It would have amounted to an occupation of Moscow. The Russian reply, drafted by Lenin, was an outright refusal.

We would have been obliged [Lenin told the Vee-Tsik] to reply to this action as we have already replied to the Czechoslovaks' mutiny and the British military operations in the north: by an expanded mobilization, calling on all adult workers and peasants to resist and, if a temporary retreat should become necessary, to destroy by fire all stores without exception to prevent them falling into enemy hands. War would then be for us a fateful but absolute and unconditional necessity and this would be a revolutionary war waged by the workers and peasants of Russia, shoulder to shoulder with the Soviet government until their last breath.

But Germany, preoccupied by the failure of its last offensives on the French front, was no longer in a fit condition to invade Russia. All that happened was that the German Legation was transferred to Pskov, in occupied territory.

The attempted insurrection of the Left S Rs had one jarring echo on the eastern front. There the Red troops operating against the Czechs and the counter-revolutionary bands had been placed under the supreme command of Colonel Muraviev, whose role in the defence of Petrograd after the October victory and in the capture of Kiev a little later we have already recorded.

He was a born adventurer. He considered himself to be a Left SR (membership of this party was a convenient solution for a number of people who wanted to be adopted by the Soviet regime without demeaning themselves by submission to Bolshevik discipline). He had, I believe, lectured in tactics at a military academy. A bluffer and a braggart, Muraviev was not lacking in certain military capabilities: quick-wittedness, daring and the art of addressing soldiers and giving them heart [Trotsky].

As an organizer he was a spirited character. Having received the directive of his party, and being still ignorant of the outcome of

the Moscow *coup*, Muraviev suddenly announced that he considered himself to be at war with Germany, ordered his troops to
wheel round towards the east, had the Simbirsk Soviet surrounded
and presented himself there to demand their support.[24] He was
received in the Soviet by angry shouts, insults and threats; completely isolated, he was killed on the spot (12 July). A young
officer named Tukhachevsky[25] continued with the operations
against the Czechoslovaks on his own initiative. The Lett Vatsetis
took over the high command of the front.

THE SOVIET CONSTITUTION

When it resumed its sessions on 10 July, the Fifth Congress of Soviets
adopted the draft constitution for the Russian Federative Soviet
Republic which had been drawn up by Sverdlov. Article I consists
of the 'Declaration of the Rights of the Exploited and Labouring
People'. Article II states the general principles: dictatorship of
the proletariat and the poorest peasants 'in order to abolish the
exploitation of man by man and to build Socialism which will
have neither classes nor a State'; 'the Russian Republic is a free
association of toilers ...'. The supreme authority there is to belong
to the Congress of Soviets, and between Congresses to the All-
Russian Soviet Executive (Vee-Tsik). The Church is separated
from the State and education from the Church 'in order to guarantee freedom of thought to the workers'. 'In order to guarantee
the toilers the real freedom to express their opinions, the Republic
... abolished the subjection of the press to capital and offers to the
working class and the poor peasantry all the technical and
material means for publishing newspapers ... [etc.] and for distri-
buting them freely in the country.' The freedoms of assembly,
association and education are guaranteed by similar measures.
'The Republic ... considers labour to be an obligation for all its
citizens, and adopts the motto: *He who does not work, neither
shall he eat!*' There is to be compulsory military service, with only
the workers having the privilege of bearing arms. Foreign workers
living in the Republic are to enjoy all political rights. The Republic
offers asylum to all those in foreign countries who are wanted for
political or religious crimes. All nationalities are to be equal.
Individuals or groups who make use of their rights against the
Republic may be deprived of them.

Article III concerns the structure of authority. The All-Russian
Congress of Soviets consists of representatives of local Soviets,
the towns being represented by one deputy for every 25,000 inhabitants and the country areas by one deputy for every 125,000. This
article formalizes the dominance of the proletariat over the
peasantry. Congresses will be held at least twice a year. Extraordinary Congresses may be summoned either by Vee-Tsik or on
the demand of Soviets representing one third of the country. The

Congress is to elect its All-Russian Executive of 200 members at the maximum, responsible to itself. This Executive selects the Council of People's Commissars and enjoys legislative power. Its members are to perform specific missions or do other work in the Commissariats. The Executive may annul or suspend any measure taken by the Council of People's Commissars, which is to submit its most essential decisions to it for approval. The People's Commissars are to number seventeen (Foreign Affairs, War, Navy, Interior, Justice, Labour, Social Insurance, Public Education, Posts and Telegraphs, Nationalities, Finance, Communications, Agriculture, Commerce and Industry, State Control, Supreme Council of the Economy, Public Health). At the head of each Commissariat is placed a collegium whose members are nominated with the approval of the Council of Commissars; the members of the collegium can appeal from it to the Council and to the Vee-Tsik Bureau. The Council of People's Commissars is responsible both to the Congress of Soviets and to Vee-Tsik.

The All-Russian Congress of Soviets authorizes, amends and supplements the constitution, directs general policy, declares peace and war, fixes the plan for the nation's economic life, votes the budget, regulates financial and similar agreements, legislates and amnesties. In between Congresses, Vee-Tsik enjoys all these powers with the exception of amending the Constitution and ratifying peace treaties. Matters of emergency importance are thus anticipated as falling within its domain.

The various Soviet Congresses are laid down as follows. Regional Congresses are to have one delegate from town or district Soviets per 25,000 inhabitants, and one per 5,000 electors on town registers, with 500 delegates at a maximum. These norms are to form a limit on the deputies elected to the Regional Congress from the Provincial Congresses. The Provincial Congress is to have one delegate from the ward or district Soviets per 10,000 inhabitants, and one delegate per 1,000 town electors, with 300 delegates as a maximum per province or gubernia. The Ward Congress is to have one representative per 1,000 inhabitants, to a maximum of 300 deputies, and the County Congress (in the rural areas) one deputy for each ten members of local Soviets. These congresses will constitute the supreme local authorities and will elect Executive Committees.

The Soviets, or Councils, are constituted in the towns in the ratio of one deputy per 1,000 inhabitants; they are to number not less than fifty nor more than 1,000 members. In the country areas and in towns of less than 10,000 inhabitants, one deputy is to be elected per 100 inhabitants, with a minimum total of three and a maximum of fifty for each village; the period of election is three months. The Soviets are to elect Executive Committees. Their local powers are very extensive.

The right to vote is enjoyed by all toilers of both sexes, soldiers and sailors. The following may not vote or stand for election: persons who exploit the labour of anyone else; persons living off unearned income or engaged in commerce; priests, monks, former police officers, members of the former ruling dynasty, the insane and those condemned to deprivation of civil rights. Elections are to take place 'according to custom' (which amounts to specifying a vote by show of hands) in the presence of an electoral commission and a representative of the Soviet. The credentials of those elected are to be verified by a mandates commission appointed by the Soviet; electors may at any moment recall their deputy and proceed to fresh elections.

Article V of the constitution deals with the budget. Section 79 makes it clear that the financial policy of the Republic 'works towards the expropriation of the bourgeoisie and prepares the general equality of all citizens', without hesitating to infringe on private property in the pursuit of this end. The Congress is to delimit the income of the State and that of the localities. All expenditures of the Exchequer are to be controlled by the central government. Article VI concerns the emblem of the Russian Socialist Federation of Soviet Republics: sickle and hammer on a red background, within the rays of the rising sun, the whole surrounded by a crown of wheat-ears. Motto: *Proletarians of all lands, unite.* The Red Flag is to bear the initials of the Republic.

This constitution was not debated. Its role was purely that of sanctioning and codifying the organization of a new form of State which had been born, as it were, spontaneously, from the base to the summit. Its distinguishing features were: unification of legislative and executive powers, political monopoly for the labouring classes, dominance of the proletariat over the peasantry, participation of the masses in public life and class dictatorship. The profusion of electors, deputies, Soviets and Congresses, and the rights that these enjoyed, appeared to provide the most substantial guarantees of a labour democracy; the dictatorship was assured by the multi-stage character of elections and the centralization of powers. But, as we have seen, the bloc between the Soviet parties had just collapsed precisely at this moment. Soviet democracy gave place, through the force of irresistible historical necessities, to the dictatorship of the Bolshevik party; the constitution was to become increasingly a project for an ideal proletarian democracy for whose realization neither the time nor the means was available. Any normal functioning of this array of institutions, so simple in their social character, yet of an enormous scope and practical complexity (since they implied a mobilization of the political activity of millions of labouring people), would have presupposed, in default of an actual revolutionary upsurge, at least peace, security and a level of sufficient prosperity to permit a free, rich, variegated and constant political life to be conducted in the nation, reflected in innumerable initiatives. But it was just at this moment that mortal peril converted the Republic into an entrenched camp, defended by a phalanx of staunch and conscious revolutionaries in the front rank, in whose hands the dictatorship was to function as the decisive weapon. We must note that up to this time no one had formulated the theory, later to acquire the force of law, according to which the dictatorship of the proletariat is naturally exercised by the Communist party. This theory will be imposed later, by life.[26]

CONSEQUENCES OF THE CZECHOSLOVAK VICTORIES

The situation on the front was worsening daily. The Czechoslovaks entered Ufa on 5 July, Verkhne-Uralsk on the 7th, Zlatust on the 8th, Syzran on the 10th, Simbirsk on the 22nd and Ekaterinburg on the 25th; they crowned this series of successes on 6 August with the capture of Kazan. (In the meantime counter-revolutionary attempts on the lines of Yaroslavl had taken place at Murom, Rybinsk and Arzamas on 11 July, and Nizhni-Novgorod on the 14th; the British occupied Onega on the 31st and, with support from the Whites, Archangel on 2 August.)

The Czechoslovaks thus occupied the middle stretch of the Volga and the Ural mountains. They held down the country's most important river artery, the granary of European Russia, the mining and industrial region of the Urals and the roads of Siberia. Farther to the south, General Dutov's Cossacks were occupying Uralsk and Buzuluk, so that communications with Turkestan were practically cut off. The strategic aims of the Czechoslovaks were to link up with the Allies who were landing on the White Sea coast, and to support the Japanese intervention which might very easily be extended, it seemed, as far as the Ural region via the Trans-Siberian Railway.

The regular, efficiently commanded Czechoslovak formations, which aroused support everywhere from the counter-revolutionary elements of the population, found themselves faced in battle only by improvised, indisciplined and anarchical units, good at most for a guerrilla war against an adversary exposed to the hatred of the masses. One corps of 1,105 bayonets, for instance, which held the front near Myas, not far from Chelyabinsk, was made up of thirteen local detachments, the smallest of which contained nine men and the largest, from Perm, 570. It had twenty-four horsemen and nine machine-guns. However, the four companies that came from Perm had not a horse among them while the thirty-nine volunteers from Katai had twelve. Each detachment had its own leaders and tried to act as it liked. The basis of their organization was the local factory. Some data concerning a certain Simonov Brigade give some idea of their military preparation. Here there were about 100 experienced soldiers, about 100 who had done some drill five times or less, and about 600 totally ignorant of the handling of weapons. 'Armed to the teeth, after any fashion they could manage, they did not know how to make use of their arms.' These bands sometimes fought very well, and sometimes very badly; they knew almost nothing of the art of reconnaissance, of the main forms of defence, of the most elementary precautions to be taken in a march across country. They might abandon a position simply to carry on a leisurely debate about what to do a little further off; or retreat before the enemy, without bothering to warn other comrades, simply to take a rest ('We're fed up with it!'). We shall quote a passage from a report on some operations on the river Kyshtyma:

At about eleven the firing slackened off. The leader of the detachments from Rozhdestvenskoe telephoned to say that his men had learnt that the enemy had captured some villages close to their own and had decided to leave the line and defend their own village; the workers had taken the same view, so the orders that had been given could not be carried out. ... The Seventh Ural Regiment left its positions to take a breather without telling anybody. When asked about it, its leader answered: 'The men wanted to get themselves dry and have a sleep; they decided to go off only for half an hour but are still sleeping; I can't do any more.' After one very ragged battle it was found that out of 2,200 troops only 900 were left, many of them barefoot and without rifles; out of four cannon three remained, out of fifty machine-guns twelve working and five damaged; two detachments were missing without trace. The T— detachment stationed machine-gunners around its village and decided not to budge.[27]

These partisans were beaten with ease by the Czechoslovaks.

At the same time, a general drive towards mobilization was taking place: battalions, regiments and divisions sprang up almost spontaneously on the initiative of hosts of militants. These mobilized officers in their service, and created general staffs and the machinery for supplies. The Red Army was born as much from these numberless initiatives as from the organizing effort directed by Trotsky. In a speech before the Moscow Soviet on 29 July, Trotsky defined the tasks of the moment: 'Our troops lack cohesion. The servile drill of the old army must be replaced in the Red Army by a sharp, clear consciousness of the absolute necessity to fight.' This was the revolutionary master-idea of the Red Army's creator. All the regular armies of modern times have had a triple backbone to stiffen them: the State, the court-martial (with the death penalty) and the cult of the fatherland to complement the rest (the anti-militarist joins the colours like any other citizen). The Red Army must be, above all, the organized expression of the workers' collective consciousness; its discipline must rest on the soldier's personal convictions.

The force that the old armies acquired through long months of drill, training, and practice with weapons, cementing units mechanically together, must be provided by us in the spiritual plane, by introducing into our army the best elements of the working class: that will ensure us victory, despite the weakness at command level.

In each unit a core of Communist revolutionaries must be placed to be its life and soul: five to ten workers will suffice. Moscow had already given the army two or three hundred agitators, commissars and organizers; it must give twice as many again. The Petrograd Soviet has resolved to send a quarter of its members, 200 men, to the Czechoslovak front. If we pay this price the treacherous officers will be broken down over and over again. We will shut them up in concentration camps at the front, 'we will case them in with commissars whose revolvers are at the ready'. The commissars will be the living incarnation of the army, the force that determines power: 'Let him who feels he is not of this stamp be off and packing! Let him who remains give his life!'

The Communist backbone of the Red Army goes off to organize a vast service of political agitation, propaganda, education and action, such as no army has known before. In place of passive obedience the proletarian revolution substitutes the obedience of a discipline that is based on political consciousness.

In Petrograd, Moscow and other industrial regions, the working-class youth is mobilized. 'Victory or death' is the slogan issued to all. 'Sons of the working class, we have made a pact with death, and therefore with victory' (Trotsky). These are not idle words; for death is everywhere.

THE END OF THE ROMANOVS

The Czechoslovak intervention settled the fate of the Romanovs. Ever since the first days of the revolution, the royal house had been the field of a persistent battle between those who wanted to preserve the dynasty and those who wished to annihilate it. This struggle had begun on 16 March 1917, when the Soviet had demanded that Prince Lvov's Provisional Government should arrest Nicholas II. Shortly afterwards the British ambassador in Petrograd sounded out the government on the possibility of transferring the Imperial family to Britain. These discussions went on while the Romanovs were interned in their usual residence of Tsarskoye-Seloe (now Dietskoye-Seloe) close to the capital. After the serious riots of July 1917 the Kerensky Cabinet, in order to give some satisfaction to the revolutionary masses, and also to whisk the 'august captives' out of their reach, exiled the Imperial family to Tobolsk. Nicholas II, his closest relatives, his retinue of five courtiers and thirty-five servants left Tsarskoye-Seloe on 14 August in a special train that flew the pennant of the Japanese Red Cross. They were lodged in Tobolsk in the mansion that had belonged to the governor-general on 'Liberty Street'. The instructions of the Provisional Government placed them 'under the protection' of their escort: the soldiers performing this duty decided of their own accord to take all possible measures to prevent an escape. In this large Siberian town the former Emperor enjoyed a tolerable existence, like a man of modest property under surveillance. There, while the civil war was ranging across the country, he spent quiet winter evenings, a good bourgeois at his fireside. Nicholas II read through the foreign reviews; Alexandra Feodorovna played bezique with old General Tatishchev; the four Grand Duchesses devoted themselves to the proper occupations of ladies. In the night and the snow, revolutionary soldiers kept guard on the doors. A commissar from the Provisional Government, a Socialist-Revolutionary who had known exile in Siberia, lent every attention to the desires of His deposed Majesty. Archbishop Hermogenes of Tobolsk, an old friend of Rasputin, assisted by his clergy, succoured the 'martyr Emperor' with their active solicitude. Meanwhile monarchist officers were preparing to liberate him. This situation lasted even after the October Revolution.

However, among the guarding party a group of soldiers came together, who swore that they would never allow the Romanovs to escape alive; the soldiers of the escort searched the ex-Emperor's quarters, confiscated his Cherkassian dagger, compelled him to remove his braid of office, and rationed him. The Ural Regional Soviet insistently demanded of Vee-Tsik that the royal captives be transferred to Ekaterinburg, and sent Red Guards to watch over the points through which they would have to pass, in case of an escape. Some Bolsheviks from the Ural arrived at Tobolsk with the object of arranging the execution of the Romanovs there, at their own risk and on their own responsibility. The prisoners were thus enveloped by two opposing conspiracies: one for their rescue, the other for their death.

The officers and the monarchist clergy lacked energy, intelligence and even dedication to their aim. At one point, it seems, they had available a force of several hundred men as well as considerable funds. Quarrels over money and influence between a Lieutenant Soloviev and a priest named Vassiliev caused them to miss the moment to act. The Ural Soviet at last obtained Vee-Tsik's authority for the transport of the Romanovs to Ekaterinburg. Vee-Tsik entrusted an adventurer by the name of Yakovlev to conduct the transfer at the head of a troop of workers on horse. Simultaneously, the Ural Executive Committee dispatched another party, under more reliable command, to bring back Nicholas II 'dead or alive' (this was the end of April). From the start, Yakovlev's behaviour aroused such suspicions that the Ural Executive resolved to take the Romanovs off him, by force if necessary. The soldiers from the Tsar's escort were also afraid that this might be an escape attempt, and made Yakovlev take eight of them with him. Yakovlev took the Tsar, the Tsarina, their daughter Maria and five other persons in sledges over the frozen Irtysh towards Tiumen. The extraordinary caravan passed

53. The Tsarina Alexandra and Tsar Nicholas II

through Pokrovskoe, the village in which Rasputin had been born.
Nicholas II and Alexandra Feodorovna received the last homage
of their last subjects on the threshold of the house of that 'holy
man' who had been so instrumental in bringing about their downfall. Their last chance now came. Yakovlev tried to change the
itinerary given in his instructions, and to take the Romanovs not
to Ekaterinburg but towards Moscow, via Omsk, Chelyabinsk
and Samara. His plan was to offer them asylum in the mountains
during the journey, and await events there. The Omsk Soviet

refused to let the party cross their territory and ordered him to turn back. Faced with the threat of being outlawed, he complied.[28]

In the meantime, the Regional Congress of the Communist party had met at Ekaterinburg and demanded the death of the Tsar. Nicholas II was received in the working-class capital of the ʿUral region by an energetic Bolshevik, Byeloborodov, Chairman of the Regional Soviet Executive, who had directed the conduct of the whole matter. The former Tsar was housed in the sumptuous mansion of the engineer Ipatiev, who had been given twenty-four hours to move out. The other members of the Imperial family arrived at the end of May with an entourage of twenty-three persons. However, they were allowed to keep none of these except Dr Botkin (who was needed for the Tsarevich Alexei, always in bad health), a cook, a scullery-boy, a footman and a maid. From now on their guard was composed of factory workers. Three sentries watched night and day in the corridors next to their rooms. The prisoners were allowed out into the garden only for half an hour each day.

The Ural Soviet was now demanding the Tsar's death. The Left SRs were insisting on it. Certain anarchists and Left SRs, mistrusting the Bolsheviks, prepared an assault upon the Ipatiev house. The Bureau of Vee-Tsik had different ideas; it wanted to conduct a trial of the last Tsar before the proletarians of the Ural. This was to open at the end of July, and Trotsky was to take the role of public prosecutor. Further developments were cut short by the approach of the Czechoslovaks. The Ekaterinburg Cheka had just uncovered an officers' plot and arrested a number of agents sent by the ambassador of Serbia, Spalaiković. On 12 July the Soviet noted that it was impossible to proceed with the trial: the Czechoslovaks were approaching the town from both sides and could capture it before the end of the week. The decision was taken to execute the Romanovs without delay and to destroy their remains completely so that no relics might be left for future use.

A worker from the Verkhne-Isetsk factory, Pyotr Zakharovich Ermakov, was deputed to carry out the execution with a squad of reliable men. On the night of 15–16 July, around midnight, Nicholas II, the Tsarina, the Tsarevich Alexei, the four young Grand Duchesses, Dr Botkin and the former heir's governess and tutor, eleven persons in all, were asked to assemble in a ground-floor room. They expected to be transferred again somewhere else. They stood in a row facing a group of armed men. The sentence of death, in the name of the Regional Soviet, was read out to them, and they had no time to take it in properly. All that Nicholas II said was, in a surprised tone: 'So we're not being transferred to another place?' He was never to recover from his surprise. Moments later, the Romanovs were no more than a heap of corpses hurled against a bullet-pitted wall. Their remains were taken, rolled in bedclothes, by lorry to an abandoned mine eight versts from the city. There their clothing was meticulously searched: the garments of the Grand Duchesses were found to contain a large number of diamonds; the bodies were burned, and the ashes buried in a nearby swamp. This destruction was so effective that the Whites, despite two years of obstinate searching, found almost nothing. The Grand Duke Mikhail Alexandrovich, the Tsar's brother, in whose favour the latter had abdicated, had disappeared for some days. He was living at liberty in Perm; a group of workers, headed by Myasnikov, a determined old Bolshevik, had kidnapped him on the night of 12–13 July, pretending to make an arrest. The local authorities believed that he was in flight; but he had been shot.

A number of other members of the royal house were interned in a disused school in the small factory town of Alapayevsk, 250 miles to the north-east of Ekaterinburg: the Grand Dukes Sergei Mikailovich, Igor, Constantine and Ivan Constantinovich, Prince Palei, Elisabeta Fyodorovna, widow of the Grand Duke Sergei assassinated in 1905, and Princess Helena of Serbia. These were shot on the night of 17–18 July and their remains thrown down a mine shaft.

The Bureau of the All-Russian Soviet Executive learnt of the Romanovs' execution during its session on the 18th. A draft decree on public health was being debated; Semashko was giving the report. Sverdlov entered and sat down at his place, just behind Lenin. When Semaskho had finished, Sverdlov leaned over towards Lenin and murmured a few words to him.

'Comrade Sverdlov requests a moment to make a communication.'

Sverdlov said, with his level voice:

'I have been informed that Nicholas has been shot at Ekaterinburg, on the order of the Regional Soviet. Nicholas wanted to escape. The Czechoslovaks were approaching. The Bureau of Vee-Tsik approves.'

There was silence.

'We will pass,' said Lenin, 'to the detailed examination of the draft.'

A decree confiscating the property of the Romanovs was issued on the 19th of the month.[29]

9 · The Terror and the Will to Victory

A democratic government was being established in the Volga region under the protection of Czechoslovak bayonets. It was born at Samara on 8 June: the Czechoslovaks captured the town at dawn, and a committee of four S R members of the Constituent Assembly (I. Brushvit, B. Fortunatov, V. Volsky and I. Nesterov) assumed power the same evening. In the name of the Constituent Assembly it proclaimed the dissolution of the Soviets and the restoration of democratic liberties. Meanwhile the Bolsheviks were being massacred in the streets. The Committee informed the local court-martial of the names of any person resisting the authorities. A State Security Department with extraordinary powers was set up on 9 August.

The S R Constituent Assembly Committee assumed power in the towns of the Volga following in the train of the Czechoslovaks. Each town became, as it was captured, the scene of a protracted massacre of Communists and suspects. 'At Simbirsk, most of the Red soldiers captured in the town were shot. There was a real epidemic of lynchings,' wrote the *Vestnik* (*Monitor*) *of the Constituent Assembly Committee* on 28 July. In Samara itself the Committee had to order an end to the summary executions 'on pain of having to answer for these acts'. [*sic*]. This democratic government was reduced to begging the Czech commander in the town to protect the workers from the violence of reaction in their own districts. At Kazan, while the Czechoslovaks pursued the retreating Reds, men with weapons and white armbands roved the streets searching houses and arresting suspects; armed with previously prepared lists and led on by informers, they cut every 'Bolshevik' throat on the spot. For several days the streets were strewn with disfigured, undressed corpses. Any Reds found wounded were killed. Some of the bodies had their documents pinned to the chest: the title 'commissar' was displayed to explain why a man had his eyes poked out. After the passing of the first fury the reprisals go on, hardly less summary and not a whit less harsh. Class hatred is let off its leash. Each Red prisoner who walks the street, flanked by guards, is delivered to the rage of a well-dressed mob. 'Young women slapped them and spat in their eyes. The corpses were trampled underfoot; the eyes of the dead were gouged out,' writes one witness. The trial of any Bolshevik amounted to the formality of a brief interrogation before execution.

The old municipal institutions were born again, and the bourgeois newspapers reappeared with their announcements of the flight of Trotsky, the Allies' irresistible intervention, the atrocities of the Chinese, Letts and Germans who made up the Red Army. The Metropolitan Bishop of Kazan summoned the faithful for the defence of the Church. The university placed itself patriotically at the disposal of the government. 'The professors, the generals, the students and the old people of all classes are forming a militia so that the young men can go off to the front' (*Monitor of the Committee*). The organization of a National Army was set going.

Russia's gold reserves, which were deposited at Kazan, had fallen into the hands of the counter-revolution, and were to provide a financial base for its cause over a long period. These reserves came to 657 million gold roubles (6,500 million roubles of the existing currency) and 100 million in banknotes, plus 'an enormous hoard of securities and stocks of gold and platinum'.[1]

The Constituent Assembly Committee passed decrees ratifying the nationalization of the land and the expropriation of the big landlords, but restored to their former owners all industrial enterprises that had been nationalized, municipalized or seized. It took vigorous measures to organize the bourgeois classes, and abolished workers' control over production. Its programme can be summarized in a few words: neither a monarchist reaction nor Socialist experiments; restoration of bourgeois democracy.

The foreign policy of the Constituent Assembly Committee is already sufficiently known to us through a letter from M. Stephen Pichon to Vedenyapin, the Minister of Foreign Affairs at Samara;[2] it also formed the subject of negotiations between Timofeyev, a member of the SR party's Central Committee, and the French agents, Charles Dumas and Ehrlich. Military operations assumed more importance. Commander Alphonse Guinet, of the French Military Mission, was influencing the Czechoslovak National Council; it was he who advised a quickening of the offensive against Simbirsk, Kazan and Saratov in order to give assistance to the Allied effort. Another French officer, Captain Condot,[3] paid a visit to Simbirsk for the purpose of hastening the capture of Kazan. In the eyes of the Allies, the Constituent Assembly Committee was the embryo of Russia's future national government.

What were the social forces on which the Committee relied? The Menshevik Maisky, a former member of this government of democratic counter-revolution, has drawn a precise portrait on this point. The hostility of the working class towards the Committee was so great that the latter's attempt to create a docile 'Soviet' with Menshevik assistance collapsed miserably, with the 'Soviet' promptly passing a Bolshevik resolution. Mobilization was a dismal failure in the countryside. It got together scarcely 15,000 men, who had to be put away in barracks under the guard of White officers, instead of the 50,000 expected to respond to the appeal. These units, formed of young peasants dragged by force from their own villages, were quite unreliable. Sometimes they surrendered to the Reds after tying up their own officers. Only the petty-bourgeoisie gave a rapturous reception to the new government; however, its democratic fancies, its attachment to the Republic and the Red Flag (which the 'Socialist-Revolutionaries' still flew on public buildings) very quickly upset the officers, who were mostly monarchists, the liberal industrialists and the clergy. The bourgeoisie, which hankered for some kind of military dictatorship, began to view democratic illusions more and more as a watered-down variety of Bolshevism. It was waiting for its own moment.[4]

TOWARDS THE TERROR

Little by little, more and more completely, the class war enveloped the whole of the countryside. The kulaks hid the grain, sounded the alarm when the food brigades approached, sometimes engaged in standing battles, but more often stole out at night to murder the workers who had come looking for grain. The poor peasants formed committees which worked as a substitute for the food supply organization, and conducted requisitionings themselves. In the smallest villages, a war to the death flared up around the corn. There were interventions by Red troops. The newspapers were full of reports of this kind:

> Smirnovo district, Orel gubernia. When a detachment of Red soldiers came to take the grain, the kulaks raised loud shouts of 'By what right do you come to take what you have not sown?' It was impossible to persuade them. They fired upon the brigade, killing the commissar and several soldiers. The Provincial Executive sent along a strong detachment accompanied by armoured cars. The kulaks have been taught a good lesson [21 August].

There were incidents of priests refusing burial to those who were assailing the property of the Church. At Livny, not far from Orel, a whole district rose in rebellion, with more than 300 counter-revolutionaries killed in the struggle and the subsequent repression (20–23 August).

In the cities the famine was dreadful. Often the food services had to distribute raw grain instead of bread. When there was bread it came mixed with straw and various assorted grains. Private bakeries were closed, and the prices of all foodstuffs and manufactured goods were fixed by decree. Nevertheless the population was forced to resort to speculation with its high prices (which, though illegal, took place openly in the squares occupied by the huge standing markets, sometimes surrounded by squads of soldiers ready to carry out summary confiscations). Increasingly barter replaced commerce in the stricter sense, and payment in kind eliminated the use of paper money. The *Krasnaya Gazeta* of Petrograd discussed the problem of the fuel which the city needed but could not pay for, and noted: 'We have stocks of copper

which we can give [to foreign buyers] in exchange for coal . . .'
(issue of 1 August). The towns continued to empty. The wealthy
converted their riches into diamonds or foreign banknotes,
acquired on the black market, and crossed the frontier, a journey
not without risks. Anybody who could move into the countryside
did so, lured by the presence of grain there. The population of
Petrograd fell from 2,319,000 on 1 November 1915 to 1,480,000 on
1 July 1918, and continued to decline with great rapidity.[5]

Among the populace, hatred simmered and brooded. The
Council of People's Commissars decreed that anti-semitism was
'outlawed'. Whole groups of counter-revolutionaries (chiefly
officers), corrupt officials and bandits were being shot, five, ten or
fifteen at a time, with increasing frequency. It was not yet the
terror: only its unmistakable prelude. At night the towns slept
under a suffocating darkness of ambush and conspiracies. The
commanders of the Petrograd garrison had to issue a special
order to their troops instructing them to 'be economical with the
ammunition': for the night patrols were firing in utter confusion
in the darkened streets (17 August).

The population of the factories and workshops was enlisted in
the detachments of the food brigades and the Red Army. Often
the Soviets introduced compulsory labour for the bourgeoisie on
public-works projects. On 3 August, Kuzmin, Press Commissar
of the Northern Commune (of Petrograd) suppressed all bourgeois publications, in a departmental minute of three lines: some
were still being published up till then. The Cheka announced that
food saboteurs would be 'ruthlessly annihilated'. On 24 August a
decree was issued abolishing private property in housing in all
cities.

It is difficult to catalogue the various counter-revolutionary
organizations unmasked and promptly destroyed by the Cheka
(which wasted no time in any profound analysis of their nature).
The case of the Polish legionaries, for instance, ended with 600 or
so arrests at Vologda. To this town the French Military Mission
had dispatched, and equipped with French documents, counter-
revolutionaries of Polish origin who were supposed to be members
of a Polish Corps then in formation. Two large organizations,
mainly composed of officers, were uncovered: one devoted to the
disorganization of transport, similar to Savinkov's apparatus,
with which it was doubtless linked; the other consisting of
Constitutional-Democrats, i.e. an agency of the liberal bourgeoisie.
There were 150 arrests in Moscow. The Cheka proceeded noise-
lessly. These cases, which were scarcely mentioned in the press – if
at all – were snuffed out in darkness. Actual executions, however,
were still exceptional.

Eventually Zinoviev, as Chairman of the Council of People's
Commissars of the Northern Commune, published a warning that
enemies of the Republic would from now on be executed.

Counter-revolutionary agitation, incitement of Red soldiers to disobedience, the giving of assistance to the Whites or the foreign powers, espionage, corruption, pogroms, thefts, banditry, sabotage and 'other crimes' would be 'immediately punished by death'. The Cheka would conduct the shootings, and the names of those shot would be communicated to the press (18 August). No preliminary trial was envisaged in these rules; the list of crimes was so long and vague that the redoubtable Commission actually enjoyed unlimited power. The weapon of the terror is now ready; but it will be used by the revolution only after the attempts at assassination that are at the moment being planned.

The return of L. Kamenev to Russia shattered any remaining illusions, if any still lingered, on the attitude of the Great Powers to the revolution. Kamenev had left for western Europe in April, charged by the Communist Party Central Committee with the task of informing Western Socialists and public opinion of the truth about the Soviets, and doubtless too with the opening of official negotiations with the governments. He was surrounded by spies wherever he went, and assailed with slanders in the European press; France had refused him entry and Britain had expelled him. On his return the Whites of Finland had kept him in prison for several months. He came back now, to tell the proletarians of Russia: 'Comrades, we are alone.' (Speech to the Petrograd Soviet, 7 August.)

The Republic, too, now changed its tone towards the foreign powers. An appeal, under the signatures of Lenin, Chicherin and Trotsky, went out to the workers of France, Britain, America, Italy and Japan, exhorting them to stop the intervention:

If the Allies wish to help us in our sacred task of resistance, let them assist us in restoring our railways and our economic life, for a weak Russia is in no position to defend itself. But the Allies have not replied to our appeals. All they think of is to make us pay back the interest on the loans assigned in other times by French capital to Tsarism to lead it into the war, for which the Russian people has already paid in rivers of blood and in heaps of corpses.

Too long we have tolerated the impudent insults of the representatives of imperialism and permitted to remain in Russia those who not long ago licked the boots of Tsarism.... We have taken no reprisals against them, even though their hand in the conspiracies was clearly visible...

The Ukraine, still occupied by the Germans, at this juncture became a blazing furnace. A Left SR terrorist, Boris Donskoi, shot Field-Marshal Eichhorn at Kiev on 30 July. From the middle of July till the middle of August, the railway workers struggled against the invader through strikes and acts of sabotage. German railwaymen had to be imported in order to keep the main lines open. On 7 August the Military Revolutionary Committee of the Ukraine, a clandestine body naturally, declared war upon Hetman

54. Nestor Makhno

Skoropadsky and the occupying forces. Peasant risings burst out simultaneously everywhere. The regions of Poltava, Kiev, Chernigov, Ekaterinoslav were ablaze with war. An anarchist schoolmaster and former political prisoner, named Nestor Makhno, opened up guerrilla warfare at 'Gulai-Polye, with fifteen men at his side; these attacked German sentries to obtain weapons. Later on, Makhno was to form whole armies.[6] The Germans repressed these movements with the utmost vigour, executing prisoners *en masse* and burning down villages; but it was all too much for them.

THE COUNTER-REVOLUTION ATTEMPTS ASSASSINATION

With the Republic surrounded, starving and infested with conspiracies, it remained to deal a decisive blow at its head. The role of the proletariat's true leaders is crucial precisely because they cannot be replaced. Personal merit, authority, influence, all are historical products formed by the working class with the assistance of time and of the events for which nothing can substitute. The dominant classes which have attained a high degree of culture are in a position, during their periods of good fortune, to create in large quantities the leaders that they require. Whereas the working class, given its present state of oppression and lack of culture, can make up for the absence or the death of its leaders only by political organization. This is one of the grave problems confronting it in periods of crisis. The German working-class movement has still, after ten years, failed to find a replacement for Karl Liebknecht and Rosa Luxemburg. It remained, then, to strike down the revolution in the person of its leaders. The terrorist traditions of the Right S R party were awakening persistent initiatives in this direction. The S R Central Committee, it is true, had declared that individual assassinations were impermissible now that Tsardom had fallen; but, following on the dissolution of the Constituent Assembly, the Brest-Litovsk treaty and the pressure of the Allies, the mentality and the politics of the party had undergone a profound change. Meeting from 7 to 14 May, the Eighth National Council of the S R party had solemnly approved the principle of foreign intervention in Russia, in terms that were scarcely modulated even by hypocrisy:

Considering that the policies of the Bolshevik government threaten the very independence of Russia, this Eighth SR Party National Council is of the opinion that this danger can be removed only by the immediate liquidation of the Bolshevik government and the transfer of authority to a legitimate government elected by universal suffrage.... Such a government could permit, for purely strategic purposes, the entry of Allied troops on to Russian territory, on condition that non-interference by the foreign powers in Russian domestic affairs and the territorial integrity of the country were guaranteed...

This amounted to yet one more statement, sufficiently clear in its own terms, that against the Bolsheviks all means are good. The terrorist's Browning automatic is not so different as it may seem from the aeroplane of the Czechoslovaks.

There existed at Petrograd an S R 'Battle Organization', a small compactly organized terrorist group. This group remained somewhat independent of the Central Committee, which reserved the right to disavow it if the necessity arose; it kept a close watch on Uritsky and Zinoviev, ready to put them out of the way; it had already assassinated the tribune Volodarsky. The chief of the group was K. I. Semyonov who later, in 1921, was to cross over to Bolshevism and shed a clear light on the terrorist activities of his old party. The terrorists – there were about ten of them – grouped themselves in Moscow in order to make simultaneous preparations for the assassination of Lenin and Trotsky. They divided Moscow into four sectors; in each of these one observer and one executioner, assiduous in their attendance of the public meetings at which Lenin spoke on Fridays, waited for the opportunity to shoot him. This surveillance lasted about five weeks. The executioners consisted of two women, Konopleva and Kaplan, and two workers, Ussov and Kozlov. This last pair both encountered Lenin and lost their nerve. 'I faltered,' Ussov recounted later, 'I had lost my faith; I had to leave the organization.'

On 30 August, as on the preceding Fridays, terrorists waited for Lenin at all the big workers' meetings. Novikov, an old S R worker, who had been posted outside the Michelson works, saw him arrive; the terrorist Fanny Kaplan, a former anarchist, was in the hall armed with a pistol, whose bullets Semyonov, the group leader, had tried to poison. Lenin arrived alone; no one escorted him and no one formed a reception party. When he came out, workers surrounded him for a moment a few paces from his car. It was at this moment that Fanny Kaplan fired at him, three times, wounding him seriously in the neck and shoulder. Lenin was driven back to the Kremlin by his chauffeur, and just had the strength to walk upstairs in silence to the second floor: then he fell in pain. There was great anxiety for him: the wound in the neck could have proved extremely serious; for a while it was thought that he was dying. The wounded man's own strength carried him through. Lenin was back on his feet in around ten days.

Five days later, the SR party's Central Committee declared that it was 'completely dissociated' from the attempt. (It had made a similar declaration after the murder of Volodarsky.) This disavowal, which was evidently impelled by the fear of terrible reprisals and by the party's awareness of its unpopularity, had a most distressing effect upon the terrorists themselves: the party's tradition was one of claiming and glorifying the attempts committed by its Battle Organization. 'We were going to our death,' one of them said, 'in the name of the Central Committee, and the Central Committee was disowning us!' So shameless was the duplicity of the SR leaders, Gotz and Donskoi, that at the very hour when they were drafting this repudiation their men were preparing to derail Trotsky's train. They believed that the disappearance of the Red Army's leader would cause the total collapse of the front. Watch was kept for Trotsky near the Kremlin, the War Commissariat and the military departments. Five agents, with the task of blowing up his train, went on a technical course prepared for them by an experienced terrorist. Trotsky was to leave for the front on the 6th. Two terrorists, one of them a woman, waited for him at the station: if he escaped their bullets, Helena Ivanova was to make sure that his carriage blew up. All night long she waited in vain on the line to Kazan. Trotsky had gone by the Nizhni–Novgorod line.

Both capitals came into the scheme together. On the very day that Lenin fell in Moscow, the President of the Petrograd Cheka, Moise Salomonovich Uritsky,[7] was killed by Kanegisser, an SR student, who tried to seek refuge in the British Club. Kanegisser was a member of the People's Socialist party, which was even more Right-wing than the SRs proper. Did these actions have any direct links with the forces of foreign intervention? Pierre Pascal, who was in charge of coding at the French Military Mission, reports: 'I personally deciphered a telegram which had to do with the use of terrorism. I declare categorically that the French Military Mission encouraged the acts of assassination that were committed in Russia.'[8] We shall see shortly how, for their part, British agents were making preparations to have Lenin and Trotsky put

out of the way. Finally, Savinkov declares that the agents of the Czechoslovak National Council, who kept him supplied with funds, wanted him to spend the money in organizing terrorist attempts.

THE SEPTEMBER DAYS

Coming at such a moment, these simultaneous outrages could not fail to provoke a terrible wave of fury in the party and the proletariat. The feeling was that the moment of reckoning had now come in which the revolution had no alternative but to destroy or be destroyed. Before the enemy from abroad could be subdued, it was necessary to vanquish the enemy that lay within. The *Krasnaya Gazeta* of Petrograd wrote:

Now it is the time for our turn. ... We used to say that we would answer the death of one with the death of a thousand: now we are obliged to act. Out of the way with the sentimentalists who are afraid to shed innocent blood! What bourgeois does not have on his conscience the ruined lives of working-class women and children? There are no innocents among them. Each drop of Lenin's blood must be paid for by the bourgeoisie and the Whites in hundreds of deaths. ... The interests of the revolution demand the physical extermination of the bourgeoisie. They have no pity: it is time for us to be pitiless [31 August].

The same article emphasized that only those representatives of the bourgeois classes who had shown positive loyalty towards the regime deserved any mercy. Another editorial in this journal, on the same evening, went on:

> *Blood for blood!* But no, we are not going to have a massacre, in which individuals hostile to the bourgeoisie might be killed and real enemies of the people would get away. It will be in an organized manner that we shall seek out the bourgeoisie, the well-fed ones and their hirelings...

To organize the terror means to limit it.

On 2 September, as the Cheka is carrying out its summary executions, the Soviet government, determined to take decisive steps against the foreign intervention, has the British Missions raided and the British chargé d'affaires, Lockhart, arrested. The Anglo–French conspiracy is thus summarily unmasked. A proclamation from Vee-Tsik converts the country into an armed camp whose defence is entrusted to a Revolutionary War Council headed by Trotsky. (We shall use the terms 'Revolutionary Council of the Army' and 'Revolutionary War Council' interchangeably, since both are accurate translations – readers will have to remember that only one organization lies behind these two names.) On the next day, Red terror is instituted in a decree signed by Petrovsky, People's Commissar of the Interior. Up till now (the order runs) the Soviets have taken only minor reprisals against the massacres of proletarians in Finland, the Ukraine and the Czech-occupied areas.

> An end to this clemency and slackness! All Right SRs known to the local Soviets are to be arrested immediately. From among the bourgeoisie and the officers, large numbers of hostages are to be seized. At the least sign of White-Guard resistance or activity mass shootings are to be the rule, without further discussion. Provincial Executive Committees must take the initiative along these lines.... These measures are to be instituted at once: the Commissariat is to be informed immediately of any local authorities who drag their feet in these matters.

On 7 September the Cheka of Petrograd announced that 512 counter-revolutionaries had been shot, including ten Right SRs. Several days later the Petrograd newspapers appeared carrying interminable lists of the names of hostages: Grand Dukes, aristocrats, officers of all ranks, Right-wing journalists, financiers, industrialists, merchants, between five and six hundred in all, had been arrested in this way. At Kronstadt, 500 counter-revolutionaries were shot, according to an oral report delivered in mid-September at the Northern Commune Conference of Extraordinary Commissions. Executions were much fewer in Moscow, where lists of those shot were released to the public. In the first ten days of the terror there were around sixty executions: several Grand Dukes, the former Ministers Khvostov, Protopopov, Shcheglovitov and N. A. Maklakov, some officers and ex-policemen, a blackmailer and a lawyer charged with possession of weapons.

It is difficult to come by even an approximate picture of the scale of Red terror in the provinces. Information of a highly fragmentary, almost random character was available in the newspapers. At Perm, we learn that fifty hostages were shot, followed by another thirty-six; at Tver, nothing happened except the imprisonment of 150 hostages; from Penza, where one nobleman and some officers were shot in the first days, a telegram came on 25 September: 'The murder of the worker Yegorov has been avenged by 152 lives.' From Kostroma they wrote that seven Whites had been executed and that 'the big bourgeoisie is in our power and we are keeping them busy cleaning the barracks'. At Nizhni-Novgorod, forty-one priests, officers, policemen and capitalists were killed; at Orlov (near Viatka) twenty-three; at Shui, eight; at Kursk, nine. The Cheka of a little place called Kirma sent Moscow a list of 'twelve counter-revolutionaries, bandits, thieves and defrauders who have been executed'. At Ivanovo-Voznesensk, a large textile centre, 184 hostages were arrested and a concentration camp was established, but only a small number of executions took place.

After 5 September, the party made visible efforts to moderate the terror. Petrograd's *Krasnaya Gazeta* wrote: 'The bourgeoisie has been taught a cruel lesson. ... Let our enemies leave us in peace to build a new life. If they do so, we shall ignore their simmering hatred and stop hunting them out. The Red terror is over, until the White terror begins again. The destiny of the bourgeoisie is in its own hands.' On the following day it asked: 'Are the White Guards going to risk the heads of their hostages? The front at home has been secured, the bourgeoisie is terrorized, its fighting organizations are destroyed, its plots revealed, its plotters punished. ... From now on, let us deal with the military front.' But in fact, these September days, so reminiscent of their parallel in the French Revolution, mark – like their predecessor, and for similar reasons – the inauguration of the era of the terror.

THE LOCKHART AFFAIR

The Vee-Cheka had known for some while that the threads of all the counter-revolutionary conspiracies could be traced back to the foreign Missions stationed in Russia. On the very day of Uritsky's murder it raided the British Consulate at Petrograd. There were some bloody incidents; Captain Cromie resisted and was killed,[9] one Cheka agent was killed and two were wounded. As a result, several counter-revolutionaries who had taken refuge at the Consulate were arrested, and arms and documents were seized. The British chargé d'affaires in Moscow, Lockhart,[10] was closely watched over a period of some weeks, even in his most secret activities. Like most foreign observers, he was principally interested in the Red Army squadrons whose formation was then under way, and most of all in the Lettish contingents, whose qualities of discipline and organization were exceptional. Lockhart established contact with a Lettish officer, whom he introduced to Grenard, the French Consul, and to Lieutenant Sidney Reilly – all without suspecting that he had landed himself with a Red counter-espionage agent. The Vee-Cheka was thus admirably informed from the beginning. Organizations for espionage and counter-revolution existed in both the capitals. Two officers, the Englishman Reilly and the Frenchman de Vertemont, together with an individual named Kalamatiano,[11] were put in charge of the operations in Russia that were to be set in hand after the Military Missions had left. There were plans for the occupation of Vologda and for a *coup* in Moscow in the middle of September. The People's Commissars were to be arrested in the Kremlin during one of their Council meetings. Reilly, who was well-informed on the Commissars' mode of working, laid special importance on the simultaneous arrest of Lenin and Trotsky, and was confident that he could bribe the Kremlin guard. (Lieutenant Sidney Reilly was to be shot on the territory of the Soviet Union in 1928.) After their arrest, the two leaders of the revolution were to be conveyed immediately to Archangel, 'although [as Reilly added] the safest thing would be to shoot them on the spot'.[12] Mr Lockhart transmitted sums of money to Red officers on various occasions, to a total of 1,200,000 roubles; he also supplied them with false papers with the heading and seal of the British Mission.[13]

Explosives, lists of conspirators and military documents were discovered by the Red authorities, who also learnt that the British and French were planning to destroy two bridges in order to cut off Petrograd's food supply. On the night of 31 August–1 September, the Vee-Cheka raided a clandestine meeting. Among those picked up was an Englishman who at first refused to disclose his name: it was Mr Lockhart. He was released shortly after, but a few days later was interned again in the Kremlin, where he was treated with such consideration that he made a special point of thanking Peters, one of the members of the Extraordinary Commission. General Lavergne and Consul Grenard only escaped arrest by taking refuge in the Norwegian Legation, which was kept under the strictest surveillance by the Reds. At this moment Litvinov and some other Bolsheviks were being detained in Britain and France; the Commissariat of Foreign Affairs successfully proposed an exchange of prisoners.

The press of the whole world ran indignant commentaries on the Bolsheviks' criminal assaults against the sacred diplomatic rights of extra-territoriality and immunity. The Bolsheviks had put themselves 'outside the code of civilization'. The governments of London and Paris threatened to take reprisals against any Bolsheviks who fell into their hands. Nevertheless, on Soviet territory the conspiracy of the Powers was defeated.[14]

SVIAZHSK

The fate of the revolution was being decided at this very time at a small, obscure railway station, about forty miles from Kazan on the route from Moscow. There the victorious advance of the Czechs and the Whites was halted against a line of pathetic, hastily dug trenches, behind which stood nothing but a will of iron. On 8 August, with the eastern front in complete disarray, Trotsky's special train left for Kazan, carrying nearly 200 Communists picked from the most determined cadres. The train journeyed slowly, since it had to smash the resistance of the railway workers in its path. The line was so insecure that the passengers, who were organized on a strict military discipline, were put on the alert several times. The Whites had just captured Kazan; some Red regiments of comparatively recent formation had been betrayed by their officers and disintegrated before the enemy. The chaos among the Reds had almost resulted in the capture by the Whites of Vatsetis, the commander-in-chief of the whole front. With a handful of men to support him, he managed to clear a path for himself among the fugitives and the pursuers. What now remained of the Soviet forces hung on to the little station of Sviazhsk, on the bank of the Volga. It was here that Trotsky's train stopped. Its locomotive drove off, and in the decrepit yard nothing was left but this group of carriages that held the staff headquarters, the revolutionary tribunal and all the departments of an army that did not yet exist. (This train of Trotsky's was to become legendary. It was to be seen over the next four years on all the fronts, with the Revolutionary Army Council holding permanent session there; its carriages were fortified by armour-plate or sacks of earth, and equipped with machine-guns and a cannon. However, the train at Sviazhsk at this time lacked organization and equipment of this kind.) Another train followed, 'manned by three hundred cavalry-men, along with an aeroplane, a garage-truck for five cars, a radio-telegraph office, a print-shop and a tribunal: in short, a small military settlement'.[15]

Sviazhsk barred the Czechoslovaks' access to the river-bed road to Nizhni-Novgorod and the railway line from Kazan to Moscow. Its defenders knew it was the key to central Russia, the final bastion for which they must be prepared to die to the last man.

Those who slept on the station floor, in straw strewn with broken glass, were afraid of nothing, and almost past any hope of victory. Nobody wanted to know when the business would be over. . . . Each hour of life had the fullness and freshness of some miracle. A plane came to drop bombs on the station; the sickening bark of machine-guns came nearer, and then went away again, as did the murmuring voice of the big guns; and the soldier in his ragged cape, with a floppy old hat on his head and worn-out boots – this was the image of the defender of Sviazhsk – would consult his watch with a grin and say to himself :'At 0300 hours, or at 0400 hours, or at 0620 hours, I am still alive, then ... Sviazhsk is holding on. Trotsky's train is over there, with a lamp shining in the window of the Political Department. Another day over.' There were practically no medicines, heaven knows how the doctors managed to dress wounds. The misery of our situation banished shame and fear; as the soldiers went to get their soup, they passed before the dead and the wounded lying in the open on their stretchers. Then came the rainy days of August. Our thin, badly armed lines never yielded at any point, the bridge stayed under our control, and the reinforcements began to arrive from the rear.[16]

Communications were now restored.

Trotsky's organizing genius now became apparent: across railways that were openly sabotaged he could get to Sviazhsk not only fresh artillery but everything that was needed for resistance and for offensive. This, it should be noted, was in 1918, in a period when the excitement of demobilization was still strong, when the sight of a squad of well-dressed soldiers walking in the streets of Moscow would cause a sensation. To do this was to beat back the current, to fight against the weariness of four years of war, and against the stormy waters of the revolution itself, which over the whole country was sweeping aside the old hated discipline like so much flotsam. . . . Against all odds, the rations, the newspapers, the boots and the capes reached us.

What sort of men were the defenders of Sviazhsk?

Suddenly around Rosengoltz, there in his carriage, maps and typewriters seemed to shoot up from God knows where: the offices of the Revolutionary War Council had arrived. Rosengoltz set himself about building a powerful organizing apparatus, along lines of geometrical exactitude, its branches precisely defined. A simple, indefatigable character, Rosengoltz (despite the huge pistol that hung from his belt) had nothing at all martial either in his bearing or in his pale, rather gentle face. The great strength he emanated came from his personal capacity to regenerate, to reorganize, to rouse the circulation of a sluggish bloodstream to a feverish pace. . . .

Ivan Nikitich Smirnov (an old Bolshevik from Siberia and a former worker) was the Communist conscience of Sviazhsk.[17] Even among the non-party soldiers, and among Communists who had not known him before, his absolute honesty and correctness were instantly recognized. It is likely that he never realized how he was feared, how men were afraid to be found cowardly and weak before him of all men, before this man who never raised his voice and was content to be simply himself, calm and courageous. . . . We knew that in the worst moments of danger he would be the bravest, the most fearless. At Trotsky's side we could die in battle with the last cartridge gone, oblivious of our wounds; for Trotsky incarnated the holy demagogy of battle, with words and gestures summoning up the most heroic pages of the French Revolution's history. But with Smirnov beside us we could feel calm and clear-headed when we were right up against the wall, facing interrogation by the Whites in some hell-hole of a prison. That is what we used to whisper among ourselves on those nights of a quick-freezing autumn, lying jumbled in our heaps over the station floor.

These sketches by a woman fighter from Sviazhsk have seemed worth quoting: they sum up a whole spirit. A personal calibre and a moral nobility of this level makes men invincible; and it is the privilege of the greatest causes to raise men precisely to this level.

Little by little, faith in victory, against an enemy who had been enormously superior in numbers, arms and organization, began to crystallize: we could capture Kazan again! Fresh troops were arriving; a small airfield was laid down, though the aircraft at its disposal numbered only a squadron. The enemy began to realize that a force was being assembled at Sviazhsk that might soon prove formidable. The White attacks were regularly beaten back. Then two of the most remarkable leaders of the counter-revolution, Savinkov and a talented young strategist named Kappel, who was later to be killed in Siberia after ferocious battles, conceived an audacious plan of taking Sviazhsk by surprise. The Whites made an extended circling manoeuvre, cutting the line to Moscow, and marched on Sviazhsk from behind. An armoured train mounted with naval guns was sent to intercept them, but being badly commanded it was captured and burnt. The enemy was now less than six miles from Sviazhsk, cutting off any retreat overland.

Panic now seized the Red forces. The army's Political Department thought only of ensuring its own speedy evacuation along the Volga. A regiment which held the front by the river broke and scattered in flight; commanders and commissars headed the rout. These mobs of deserters invaded the ships of the Volga flotilla. The disarray seemed to be total. All that remained at Sviazhsk consisted of the offices of the Fifth Army's headquarters, Trotsky's train and the staff in charge of the stores.

Leon Davidovich mobilized the entire manpower of the train, office-boys, telegraphists, ambulance-men, in short anyone who could hold a rifle. These were about five hundred men; the Whites numbered double this. The offices were emptied, the rearguard no longer existed. Everything was thrown into the battle against the Whites. The whole of the road down to the first houses in Sviazhsk was ripped up by shell-fire. The battle lasted for several hours. The Whites thought they were up against some formation of fresh, highly organized troops that their intelligence services did not know about.

Wearied after a forced march of forty-eight hours, they exaggerated the strength of their opponents, not realizing that what faced them was no more than a handful of improvised troops who had only Trotsky and Slavin (an old officer who commanded the Fifth Army) at the back of them. They drew back. In order to make it quite clear that his troops were there to stay, Trotsky had deliberately omitted to have a locomotive coupled to his train. The bulk of the Fifth Army, numbering some 10,000 men, was gathering in front of Sviazhsk and on the further bank of the Volga for the offensive against Kazan. If Sviazhsk had been lost the result would quite possibly have been the destruction of this army.

The decisive effect of the victory of Sviazhsk was consolidated on the following day by a further exploit. A number of small torpedo-boats had been brought from Kronstadt along the canals, to form the Red Volga flotilla under the command of Raskolnikov, a young Bolshevik naval officer, and Markin, who was to die a hero's death. Trotsky and Raskolnikov had concocted a scheme of extraordinary daring: to burn the enemy's small fleet, which was anchored at Kazan. The Red flotilla sailed down the Volga in the depth of night, with all lights doused. The torpedo-boat carrying Trotsky and Raskolnikov was the only one that succeeded in passing the narrow entrance to Kazan harbour. With her rudder broken, the boat was for a moment in fantastic danger, caught against the side of an enemy vessel. The whole of the White flotilla was set in flames; the Reds retired without losses.

FIRST VICTORY: THE CAPTURE OF KAZAN

On the following day, twenty-seven Communists who had yielded to the panic and taken flight were tried and shot. Several of them were old militants. A measure of this extreme severity was undoubtedly necessary.

> The whole army [writes Larissa Reissner] was saying that the Communists were cowards, that they were exempt from the law, that they could desert and get away with it. ... Without the extraordinary gallantry displayed by Trotsky, the commander-in-chief and the members of the Revolutionary War Council, the prestige of the Communists working in the army would have been finished for a long time.

The Communists were the heart and soul of the army.

This ruthlessness was no novelty. Over the twenty-five days that Trotsky's train had been at Sviazhsk, revolutionary enthusiasm, or more exactly fanaticism, had been waging a merciless struggle against indiscipline and disorder. On 14 August Trotsky published the following order:

> I learn that the detachment of partisans from Petrograd has deserted its positions.
>
> I have ordered Commissar Rosengoltz to investigate the facts of the matter.
>
> The soldiers of the Red Army of Workers and Peasants are neither cowards nor scum. They want to fight for the liberty and happiness of the toiling people. If they retreat or fight badly, it is the fault of their commanders and commissars.
>
> I give a warning: if a unit retreats, first the commissar will be shot, then the commander.
>
> Courageous soldiers will be rewarded according to their merits and will be given commissions.
>
> Cowards, profiteers and traitors will not escape bullets.
>
> I answer for this pledge before the whole Red Army.

The Petrograd partisans, who had perhaps imagined that their status as volunteers from the capital would give them some indulgence, were sternly dealt with by a military tribunal: several dozen of them were sent to their deaths.

No army on active service has ever avoided measures of such rigour: war has always forced men to stand between the bullets of the enemy and the bullets of their comrades if ever through faint-heartedness they become the enemy's allies. The collective's instinct for self-preservation needs this iron law in order to vanquish the individual's identical instinct. And so these actions require no comment. At the very most we are bound to emphasize once again the nature of the conditions in which the discipline of the Red Army was forged. At the beginning of his stay in Sviazhsk, Trotsky had to draft a long document in order to have a few typewriters sent across to his headquarters. On 19 August, he addressed a long reproof to the sailors of the Red flotilla:

When I paid a visit yesterday to the Flotilla headquarters, I was dumbfounded by the spectacle that was presented to my eyes. The boat is full of strangers, but nobody is there to check passes – these indeed do not even exist. Anyone who pleases can go in. It is impossible to tell who is in charge of the vessel, or to know who runs the communications section. Men are sent out to various places and nobody knows who sent them. ... When they go off they leave their dinghies abandoned for someone else to collect. No organization, no sense of responsibility. There are numerous women and children on board. No practical work is possible in these conditions. No military secrets can be kept. I have seen Commissar Markin with a mechanic who did not know how to start an engine. 'It's always the same,' Markin said. 'When we have to retire to the rear the engines work perfectly; when we have to advance to the line of fire the engines go on strike!' Comrade sailors! This state of affairs cannot go on. ... Let us think of the position of the country. If we capture Kazan we will have breached the enemy front, Simbirsk and Samara will simply fall into our hands.... [This persuasive argument ended with these words:] Everything must be set going militarily. Do not yield an inch of ground. Take from the enemy every inch you can manage. Take the offensive boldly and courageously. He who risks nothing always possesses nothing. I shake you fraternally by the hands, comrade sailors!

The leader who used this language and signed orders of the strictest inflexibility *had to* expose himself to fire, with his men, from time to time, in the front rank. This builder of an army worked his way through persuasion, through example and through rigour.

His inward certainty of victory gave him a self-assurance that could be terrible. In towns occupied by the enemy he had Notices of Warning scattered in the following terms:

Citizens of towns which are temporarily captured by the White Czech forces remain subject to the laws of the Soviet Republic.
No person has the right to invoke the duress of the invaders to justify

acts of treason committed against the power of the workers and peasants.

Whoever, during the rule of the White Czechs, lends assistance to the enemy, will be shot.

The personal goods and estates of any participants in bourgeois sedition, as well as of their accomplices, shall be confiscated.

These goods will be used to compensate the families of the workers and peasants who have fallen under the blows of the counter-revolutionaries and, more generally, the toilers who have suffered under the bourgeois rebellion. [15 August 1918].

Workers mobilized by the Whites were ordered, on pain of death for any default, to pass over to the Reds (order of 27 August on mobilization).

The persuasion, the example, the harshness, the assurance, the organizing skill of the Communist chiefs accomplished a miracle within four weeks. At the time when Trotsky's train arrived, all that existed at Sviazhsk (according to the report of one able member of the Revolutionary Council, S. I. Gusev)[18] was a formless mass of ten to fifteen thousand men, divided up into several dozen regiments, some formed long ago, others made up from little partisan groups. Some of these formations were so demoralized that they refused to enter battle, as was the case with the Fourth Latvian Regiment, whose two leaders – both Communists – were sent before the revolutionary tribunal.

The other units, if they fought at all, often gave way before an enemy that was less numerous than they, but active and better organized. ... The political departments, the tribunal and the intelligence services were staffed by inexperienced people. To sum up: little or no self-confidence, lack of initiative, passivity, indiscipline from top to bottom. ... Trotsky's special train imbued the doomed station of Sviazhsk with the determination to win, strong initiative and an active rhythm in all departments of the army's machinery. From the very first days it could be sensed that a sharp change had taken place; it began to be felt first in matters of discipline. The severe methods practised by Trotsky were supremely adequate and necessary in this time of partisan warfare, indiscipline and insufferable conceit.

Out of the straggling horde of beaten soldiers from Kazan there came a powerful, self-assured army which was to enter Kazan once again.

When the news of Fanny Kaplan's attempt arrived, Trotsky returned for a few days to Moscow; there he was able to inform Vee-Tsik that the situation was stable and in hand, and that the Red forces were able to cope with any unpleasant surprises. On 9 September, the sailor Markin knocked out an enemy battery inside Kazan itself. On the following day the Reds recaptured the city.

The workers in the arsenal at Kazan had risen against the Whites a few days previously, and been massacred. All young men in the city had been conscripted by the Constituent Assembly

Committee and marched away by force. The bourgeois population had been in flight during four whole days, in interminable
convoys of fugitives, taking away with them everything that they
could. In the courtyard of the prison, a row of fresh corpses: the
arrival of the Red cavalry commanded by the legendary Azin had
interrupted the executions. Trotsky's voice echoed out in the
Soviet:

   ... Now that the workers are being charged with committing cruel-
ties in the civil war, we must reply, instructed by our experience: the
only unpardonable sin which the Russian working class can commit at
this moment is that of indulgence towards its class enemies. We are
fighting for the sake of the greatest good of mankind, for the sake of
the regeneration of mankind, to drag it out of the darkness, out of
slavery...[19]

THE VOLGA, THE URAL, THE KUBAN

Two days later, on the 12th, the First Army under the command
of Tukhachevsky captured Simbirsk. On the following night it
forced a way across the Volga. To do this it had to gain control of
an iron bridge, one kilometre long, which was straight in the
enemy's line of fire. A driverless locomotive was sent towards it,
full steam ahead, followed by an armoured train, then by an
infantry brigade. Artillery thundered from both banks of the
river; the battle was lit up by barges set aflame by the Whites. The

enemy, unnerved by this frontal attack, retreated in disorder. The army which achieved this exploit was a youthful one. Tukhachevsky, coming to his command at the end of June, had found it living inside trains from which it never ventured out, being content to do its fighting along the railway tracks. 'The general staff was composed of five comrades. ... No administration existed; no one knew how many troops there were; the provision of food was entirely due to the ingenuity and energy of one comrade who intercepted all trains passing through the region ...'[20]

The plan drawn up by the Revolutionary War Council was now being put into operation. From the White Sea to the Black Sea, twelve armies had been successfully formed. Their disposition was as follows: in the north, blocking the advance of the British past Shenkursk, in the Dvina region, was the Sixth Army. Between Perm and Ekaterinburg lay the Fourth; between Perm and Kazan, the Second. At Kazan, the Fifth; farther south, now threatening Samara, was the First, under Tukhachevsky; at Saratov, the Fourth; at Tsaritsyn, the Tenth (under Voroshilov); in the Northern Caucasus, the Eleventh and Twelfth. These armies all number between eight and fifteen thousand men, except for the Tenth (an imposing force of 40,000 men, 240 cannon and thirteen armoured trains facing Ataman Krasnov's Don Cossack army, which was almost equally matched) and the two north Caucasian armies: the latter, over 100,000 Reds, kept a similar number of Whites occupied with a mobile war that was prodigal in exterminations, sackings of towns, atrocious reprisals and deeds of valour.

The Red Army came into being in a class struggle that, owing to the terror, had turned into a primitive, even though organized, version of the struggle for life. We will dwell for a moment on a few brilliant pages of this epoch, which are far too little known. Better than any lengthy exposition, they will provide an understanding of what this war was, and of why the Reds were bound to win.

57. Blyakher

In May, the workers of Ekaterinburg and the miners of Chelyabinsk had assembled their first contingents to do battle against Dutov's Cossacks close to Orenburg. When the Czechoslovaks marched towards the Ural, all the factories rose to arms, creating new brigades which massed around the earlier volunteers. The people of Ekaterinburg, Verkhne-Uralsk and Troitsk thus formed a small army of some 10,000 men (possessing sixty machine-guns and a dozen cannon), but with so few officers that commissions had to be conferred on Communist party members, members of the Soviets and former officers. The command of this force fell upon a Bolshevik worker who had been an NCO, Blyukher. The Czechs captured Verkhne-Uralsk, and Blyukher's small army was swollen by some 2,000 refugees. The proletarians of the captured town came out in carts, bringing their families and all their most treasured possessions: the samovar, the bedding, the household linen. They also brought a gold reserve of 130 kilos. The army was practically surrounded. Where could they go? Should they try and reach Turkestan? Or work back along the lower Volga? They decided to cross over the ridges of the Ural range so that they could link up with the Red Army in the north. It was both a guerrilla war and a people's migration. At every big factory the army was reinforced with fresh partisans and new contingents of fugitives. Just by Verkhne-Uralsk itself, at a point where it was necessary to force their way through, the partisans, short of ammunition, had to make a charge with bayonets and pikes against an eminence defended by Cossacks, officers and high-school pupils. Face to face the combatants stood and recognized one another, inhabitants of the same streets, neighbours, cousins, workers and bosses, sometimes fathers and sons. They wavered for a moment, reluctant to seize each others' throats. Then body tangled with body in frenzied battle. The Reds passed on.

The armament of both sides was appalling. Old rifles were wrenched from museum displays, hunting-rifles were brought along, pikes and clubs were crudely fashioned, like those of the Jacqueries of medieval times; bullets were moulded by any apparatus that came to hand; wooden rattles were used to simulate machine-gun fire. In the rear, children of ten drove the carts, where the women and the wounded lay keeping up a hail of gunfire. Neither the Whites nor the Reds took any prisoners. Perfect discipline and superb organization sprang up in this army, where soldiers and leaders received the same pay (150 roubles a month), where the commanders went into battle like everyone else, where cartridges were in such short supply that they became a precious object of barter. At the end of a month of privations and struggles, with the Urals behind them, they reached the factories of Bogoyavlensk and Arkhangelsk, close to Ufa. There a new act of heroism became necessary, since the breakthrough at this point looked extraordinarily difficult: they had to abandon their families. The immense sacrifice was voted by a mass of raised hands, in a crushed silence. On 2 September at Krasny Yar, Blyukher's army, swept with constant machine-gun fire from the Whites, was trapped by the side of a deep river, the Ufa. A bridge was constructed in a single night, with tree trunks crudely joined together. Again, the Reds passed on. They had imagined that every man among them was doomed to perish. Their command, determined to make a stand till the last cartridges were gone, had made the final arrangements: each soldier was to keep his last bullet for a comrade; the army commander, the last to be left standing, was to be the only one to kill himself. When the other side of the river was reached, 200 prisoners were taken; not one of them was spared. Finally, on 13 September, the Ural partisans effected their link with the Third Red Army, near Kungur to the south of Perm. In fifty days of fighting over the Urals peaks they had covered about 1,000 miles.[21]

Some 1,200 miles from them, during approximately the same dates, another Red Army was performing a similar exploit. 16,000 guerrillas, followed by a population of refugees·(some tens of thousands of souls), who had been separated from the Red forces of the Kuban as the result of a defeat, fought a long retreat over the Taman Peninsula which takes the mountains of the Caucasus towards the Crimea. There they found themselves blockaded in a hopeless position. Only one path was open to them: the dike that extends towards the south alongside the azure waters of the Black Sea. The sea was patrolled by German cruisers; the mountains overhanging the dike were full of enemy soldiers. Along the shore were small towns, ruined and famished: no chance of obtaining food from here. Overhead, a scorching sun. This human flood followed the line of the dike. They had to march without stopping so as not to die of hunger. Their necessity created discipline, order, leaders. A former captain, a peasant's son named Epifany Kovtyukh, laid down the law of common safety for the partisans. His column, breaking through every obstacle in its way like a battering-ram, soon felt irresistible. The army and the refugees kept alive on maize, nuts and wild fruit. Half-naked in their rags, leaving stragglers to die by the roadside, they journeyed on in the burning dust. On 16 August, after a fortnight of marching and fighting without quarter, they found their path barred by the impregnable outpost of Tuapse, which was defended by a Georgian garrison. The enemy, there in his eagle's nest bristling with guns, was sure of victory. But some of the partisans managed to scale the rock-face with the help of bayonets driven into the winding crags. At dawn, the Reds rushed into the fortress, and were merciless. Then the army marched against Maikop, where General Pokrovsky was engaged in an orgy of blood-lust: hangings, sabrings, shootings, to an estimated total of 4,000 dead (the town has 45,000 inhabitants). In the glades on their journey the Reds found crucified women. They smashed Pokrovsky's cavalry, they captured Maikop, they captured Armavir (25 September).

Epifany Kovtyukh's retreat from Taman has been described by the writer Serafimovich in a novel which both sticks fairly closely to the historical truth and effectively reconstructs the atmosphere: *The Iron Torrent*. There is a translation of it in French.[22]

No decisive military importance can be attached to the heroism of the Ural fighters, nor to that displayed by the partisans of the Kuban; but these things should be known if the victory of the Reds is to be understood. Sviazhsk, the Ural, Tuapse – these three simultaneous feats of daring witness the same social imperatives, the same drive to win, or, more simply, to survive.

RISE AND DECLINE OF THE DEMOCRATIC
COUNTER-REVOLUTION. THE UFA DIRECTORATE

Meanwhile, as the Reds were gaining strength, the democratic revolution was correspondingly finding itself in the midst of increasing difficulties. The Constituent Assembly Committee in Samara had received a warm welcome only from the wealthy classes. It now had to suppress revolts inside the factories and disturbances in the country districts, which had become indignant with the mobilization and the requisitionings. Even the bourgeoisie detached itself from the Samara regime and began to look towards Siberia, where reaction appeared predestined to assume a dominant role. The 'Socialist-Revolutionary' government enjoyed, in fact, two sources of support: the bayonets of the Czechoslovaks and the White terror. The most significant episodes of the struggle in this phase were: the massacre of the insurgent workers from the Kazan arsenal, a few days before the Reds entered the city; the massacre of the workers of the munitions factory at Ivashchenko, near Samara, who had also revolted – here 1,500 men, women and children were sabred down;[23] the massacre of the 306 political prisoners who had been evacuated towards Ufa following the fall of Samara.

The White officers who were sent into the countryside to mobilize conscripts treated the peasants according to the old customs of Tsardom. They arrested suspects and sometimes gave estates back to the expropriated landlords. They ordered floggings for the recruits, the local dignitaries, suspects and complainers. Here, as an illustration, is a passage from one of the many reports published in the Constituent Assembly supporters' own newspapers:

District of Klyuchevsk. A Cossack brigade of two hundred men surrounded the town and stopped everyone from going out until the workers had returned from the fields. In the evening eighteen persons were arrested. Those due for recruitment had hidden away; their fathers and mothers were flogged. In the morning, those arrested were taken into the square, where they were forced to undress and lie down on their clothing. All of them were then flogged, and two peasants were taken into a courtyard and shot.

Colonel Galkin, the organizer of the National Army, ordered trials for the relatives of peasants who had deserted, and for any local authorities who displayed insufficient energy in the campaign against desertion. The growing unpopularity of the Constituent Assembly supporters in the countryside materially assisted the activity of the Reds.

At this time, about twenty counter-revolutionary governments existed between the Ural and Vladivostok. The Committee for the Constituent Assembly seemed to be the one with the most authority; it was the only democratic one, with the greatest support from the Czechoslovaks, and the most influential in European Russia. Its principal rival was the Regional Government of Siberia, whose seat was at Omsk and whose territory extended as far as Chelyabinsk. The government of the Ural, headed by a liberal industrialist, L. A. Krol, had cordial relations with the open reactionaries at Omsk (bourgeois Kadets and Cossack generals, these last with real effectives at their command enjoying the use of sabres and horses). The Czechs kept up their end of the front only to give the Russians an opportunity to establish a national army, and were pressing for the creation of a Russian central authority. There thus arose the idea of a Conference of the various anti-Bolshevik governments.

The Ufa Conference, meeting from 8–25 September, assembled the representatives of the Constituent Assembly; the Samara Committee for the Constituent Assembly; the Regional Government of Siberia at Omsk; the Provisional Regional Government of the Ural; the Cossacks of the Ural, Siberia, Eastern Turkestan, Yenisei, Astrakhan and Irkutsk; the Bashkirian government; the Alash-Orda Kirghizian government; the National Council of Turks and Tartars; a provisional Estonian government; the Congress of Towns and Zemstvos of the Volga, Ural and Siberia; and the Central Committees of the following parties: SR, Menshevik Social-Democrats, People's Socialist, *Unity* Social-Democrat (*Edinstvo*, Plekhanov's group), People's Freedom (Kadet party), League for Renewal. The several governments of the Far East were not represented. The SR democrats from Samara (N. Avksentiev, Gendelman, Argunov, Zenzinov, Catherine Breshko-Breshkovskaya, Volsky and Vedenyapin) set the tone from the first in this variegated assembly, which brought together, elbow to elbow, sincere Socialists, former terrorists, monarchist generals, Cossack atamans, businessmen, industrialists, liberal professors, bourgeois leaders of national minorities, foreign agents and adventurers.

The Conference, with a benediction from the Archbishop Andrei, opened with a religious service held in the cathedral square. In it two tendencies were immediately at loggerheads: on one side the SRs, who wanted a democratic, parliamentary, republican counter-revolution led by a government responsible to the Constituent Assembly; on the other, the generals, the bourgeoisie and the most far-sighted men of action, who wanted a military dictatorship at first, followed by a regime based on the reactionary forces. Each of these tendencies leant for support upon a government: it was Omsk versus Samara. The Kadet orator L. A. Krol advocated 'an authority that will be strong, supreme, personal, uncontrolled and responsible to no one'. The capture of Kazan by the Reds weakened the position of the SRs; however, the Czechoslovaks were hostile to the monarchist reactionaries. The Conference adopted a compromise solution by establishing a Directorate of five members, armed with the most extensive powers pending the convening of the Constituent Assembly. These five were: the most Right-wing of the Right SRs, N. Avksentiev, the party's outstanding orator; a Kadet bourgeois, N. I. Astrov; a liberal general, Boldyrev; a liberal representative of the Siberian government, Vologodsky; and the old Populist Socialist Chaikovsky. Chaikovsky was absent from the proceedings, and was to be called on to head the National Government of the North at Archangel, under the British occupation. Among the deputy members were the SRs, Argunov and Zenzinov, and the old monarchist General Alexeyev.

The Directorate set itself the following tasks: the abolition of the Soviet regime; the return of the lost territories to Russia; the cancellation of all treaties concluded by the Bolsheviks; the implementation of the treaties linking Russia with the Allied powers; the resumption of the war against the German coalition; the formation of a powerful national army; the establishment of a democratic regime. This programme received the approval of the representatives of Czechoslovakia and France (in the person of M. Jeannot), and Mr Alston, the British chargé d'affaires in Siberia, sent his government's best wishes to the conference:

> The British people observes with relief that Russia, justifying the trust that the Allies have never ceased to place in her, is returning to the field of battle. They offer her a helping hand, in a spirit of joy. May the Conference of Ufa succeed in founding the new Russia, strong and free...

The counter-revolutionaries' rear was in a state of ferment, stricken by demoralization. Their front line was caving in under the Red Army's battering-ram. The Czechs, tired now of bearing the brunt of resistance to the Reds almost unaided, were giving way. The Japanese were beginning their systematic plan of conquest in the Far East.[24] The forces of outright reaction, encouraged by the Allies, were engaged in establishing military dictatorship in Siberia. But the party of the middle classes, utterly unable to draw any lesson from its own experiences, totally blinded by its democratic illusions, continued to build on sand in the midst of the hurricane.

THE TERROR BECOMES PERMANENT

After the September days, the terror does not die away; it slackens and becomes systematic. The newspapers are already publishing several times a week the communiqués of the Extraordinary Commissions: these, in every corner of the country, are proceeding with summary executions of criminals and counter-revolutionaries. One issue of *Izvestia* (for 24 October 1918), which we cite simply as an example, contains two columns of information of this sort. It is worth going through. The Cheka of Yegorievsk district has had a counter-revolutionary priest interned in a monastery for three years. That in Ivanovo-Voznesensk has sentenced a speculator, who insulted a commissar during a search, to five weeks of imprisonment and a fine of 30,000 roubles. That in Meschovsk district has shot a former police-official, 'a keen Black Hundreds member', and adds, 'The population is calm.' That in Kozel announces simply that it is suppressing agitation among the priests and kulaks. At Mineyevsk, a Right SR has been executed. At Perm, they are mainly using fines; the Commission is publishing a bulletin to keep the population informed of what it is doing. Then comes a new headline: '*War Against Corruption*'. An investigating magistrate from the All-Russian Central Commission, and his office-boy, have been convicted of bribe-taking and been shot. There follows a list of sixteen criminals executed by order of the Central Commission: forgers, bandits, a Cheka soldier who forged a stamp from a cooperative, a Cheka commissar who tried to sell a revolver. The Commission at Kotlas has shot a citizen guilty of conducting counter-revolutionary agitation. The Commission in Shui announces the execution of seven 'thieves, assassins and provocateurs'.

This cutting from *Izvestia* gives quite a good picture of the Red terror, which is not only a necessary and decisive weapon in the class war but also a terrible instrument for the inner purification of the proletarian dictatorship itself. 'The Extraordinary Commission,' writes one of the men who directed the terror,[25] 'is neither an investigating commission nor a tribunal. It is an organ of struggle, acting on the home front of the civil war by the methods of investigation, the tribunal and armed force. It does not judge the enemy, it strikes him.' It is not concerned with establishing and grading the guilt of individuals; it asks itself what social class, what background the adversary belongs to, whether he is dangerous and if so in what measure. The Commissions conducted investigations that were sometimes summary, sometimes long and complex, always in virtually total secrecy, without admitting the right of defence. The investigating judge reached his conclusions on his own responsibility; the Commission pronounced sentence without hearing the accused. When there was any question of the death penalty the verdict had to be agreed unanimously (at the beginning the Commissions were composed of twelve members, with a single vote sufficing to veto a death sentence). Executions usually took place in absolute secrecy, to avoid arousing untoward emotions among the populace. In large cities they were often carried out in cellars, by revolver.

The local Commissions were gradually, though not without friction, made subordinate to the Central Commission.[26] A special section was established to combat espionage and counter-revolution in the army and navy, and another for the surveillance of the transport system.

The Commissions undertook a census of the whole bourgeois population for the purpose of selecting hostages from them. Dzerzhinsky and the other chiefs of the Vee-Cheka repeatedly instructed them to avoid arrest except in cases when it was really necessary. An Order No. 83, some time in November 1918, even ordered the release from confinement of those members of the KD (Constitutional Democrat) party, the organization of the big bourgeoisie, who had not engaged in any noteworthy political activity.

The Commissions held a number of local and regional conferences. One of these, in mid-October in Petrograd, brought together the heads of all the Chekas in the north-west. It transpired there that the Commissions still had only very spasmodic sources of funds, such as fines and levies. Zinoviev, who presented the report, mentioned the Left SRs, who had just incited a disturbance in the city, and stressed that from now on 'only the Communist party could function freely'. In addition, he pointed to the dangerous vices and pretensions of certain Commissions who were tending to substitute themselves for the local authorities. A tendency towards a dictatorship of the Extraordinary Commissions was becoming visible. He emphasized sharply how necessary it was to punish corrupted commissars with the severest rigour.

Peters, one of the heads of the Vee-Cheka, protested in the same month at 'the undesirable forms that the system of terror was assuming in the provinces' (*Izvestia*, 29 October). A dispute arose over the respective spheres of competence of the Commissariat for the Interior and the Chekas. There can be no doubt that a large number of abuses were committed. The running of the prisons, in this epoch of famine, epidemics and an extreme hardening of personal behaviour, was simply detestable (and provoked several interventions in the press from influential Communists); many cases dragged on for ages, others were polished off crudely. Karl Radek was one of the first to propose new forms of terror, more rational than summary executions.

The bourgeoisie [he declared] must be hit in its economic privileges. Before winter begins let us requisition the warm clothing, the comfortable houses, all the surplus that comes from individual affluence; let us give it all to the army, to the workers. Let us pass draconic legislation against conspiracy.... It is impermissible for there to be luxury restaurants in Moscow like the Praga; it is impermissible that the bourgeoisie should muffle itself in costly furs while the Red soldier at the front suffers from the frost...

That was the state of things still (*Izvestia*, 6 October).

What was the scale of the Red terror? All that we have available to answer this question is very incomplete data. No regular statistics were issued in the first months; the official figures published by Latsis[27] are based on information often of a random character. With these reservations in mind, let us examine them. The Extraordinary Commissions were set up, as we know, in December 1917. In the first six months of their activity they executed only twenty-two people. In the last six months of 1918, more than 6,000 executions were proceeded with. The monthly average of executions for 1918 is: counter-revolutionaries, 380; dishonest and criminal officials, fourteen; speculators, three.[28] The Red terror, in four years of revolution, perhaps spilt less blood than what flowed on certain days during the battle of Verdun.

OUTLINE OF A PARALLEL: 1793 AND 1918

Some striking parallels can be traced between the French Revolution and the Russian revolution, even in the details of events and actions. Even the dates provide some impressive coincidences. Thus, the days of 2, 3, 4, 5 and 6 September, in 1792 and 1918, are marked in both cases by the extermination of domestic enemies inside the prisons. The Paris of 1792 rose to arms mercilessly when the news came of the entry of the Prussians into Verdun. The proletarians of Petrograd and Moscow took up the sword once the Czechs had captured all the major towns on the Volga, and when the British were seizing Archangel and Murmansk. In both revolutions, decisive crises appeared in the summer months, July, August and September. This was true of France in 1792 and 1793, in Russia in 1917, 1918 and 1919. Doubtless these months are the most propitious for the waging of war, for reasons climatic, biological (human energy reaching its peak of expression at this time) and social (the closeness of harvest-time).

The crisis of July–August–September 1918, whose direct and necessary result was the Red terror, vividly recalls the situation that beset the French Revolution during the same months in 1793, after the betrayal of Dumouriez and the Vendée rebellion, with Normandy, Bordeaux and Lyon all in revolt. Charlotte Corday had murdered Marat; the coalition powers were invading France; the British were capturing Toulon; conspiracy, treason and famine were undermining the revolution from within; William Pitt was organizing the coalition of Europe for the defence of civilization against the *sans-culottes*; the London press was supplying horrifying details on the 'Jacobin atrocities'. The Commune of Paris and the Committee of Public Safety gave the enemies of the revolution their reply: the mass call to arms, the terror, the Law of the Maximum. The revolutionary tribunals were no less prompt in their operation than the Extraordinary Commissions. In France as in Russia, it was necessary to galvanize the spirit of the army, subdue the generals by demanding their heads in case of defeat, and send members of the Convention into the armies. Carnot fulfilled the same role as Trotsky.

The Jacobin terror seems to us to have been much bloodier than the Bolshevik one. Certainly it was crueller: 'At Angers the condemned were led to the place of execution ... to the sound of music, with the roads lined with members of the revolutionary authorities dressed in festive costume and with soldiers.'[29] At Nantes and Lyon and in the Vendée, the revolution cut off heads by thousands; in Paris, 1,376 fell in nine days after the decree of 22 Prairial.[30] It should be noted that France at this time had between twenty-five and thirty million inhabitants.

But historic necessity needs no justification. There has never been a war, never a revolution without terror. In the class war, terror has from time immemorial been the favourite weapon of the propertied classes. Turn back to the history of the Reformation and the religious wars, of the Jacqueries, of the English revolution in the seventeenth century, of the War of Secession in the United States.[31]

And remember above all the experience of these last ten years. The discipline of all the armies of the Great War, all of them so lavish in heroism, rested in the end on terror: does anyone know the number of those sent to the firing-squad by courts-martial? In central Europe, in Finland, in Spain, in Italy, in the Balkans, capitalism when threatened has resorted to the White terror, which is elevated by fascist dictatorship into a permanent system.

Besides, it is out of White terror that Red terror is born. The workers and peasants, little enough inclined to take to the sword, in view of their inexperience in power and the generous idealism of many revolutionaries, learnt their lesson from the defenders of Tsardom and of capitalism. It is even somewhat disconcerting to see the leniency of the victors towards the vanquished, both after the fall of the autocracy and after the October rising. After the Red October, the ultra-reactionary leader Purishkevich was quietly set at liberty. The Cossack ataman Krasnov, captured with arms in his hands, was released on parole. The Moscow Junkers who massacred the workers in the Kremlin arsenal were simply disarmed. It took ten months of bloodier and bloodier struggles, of plots, sabotage, famine, assassinations; it took foreign intervention, the White terror in Helsinki, Samara, Baku and the Ukraine, it took the blood of Lenin before the revolution decided finally to let the axe fall! This in a country where over a whole century the masses had been brought up by the autocracy in the school of persecutions, flogging, hangings and shootings!

During the same period, in the territories occupied by the counter-revolution, the White terror claimed infinitely more victims. There are no statistics to enlighten us on this point. But the facts reported in great profusion in the memoirs both of White and of Red combatants are truly frightful. We have pointed out a few: General Pokrovsky massacring 4,000 men at Maikop (northern Caucasus); 1,500 workers killed by the Whites and Czechs at the Ivashchenkovo factory near Samara. In the small town of Troitsk (Ural region) the White–Czech forces slaughtered several hundred Reds. Bands of Kornilov's officers passed through the little town of Lezhanka (in the Don region); they had just received casualties of three dead and seventeen wounded; they left behind them, in this one village, 507 corpses.[32] Larissa Reissner's account tells us that in the time of the Czechoslovaks the corpses never stopped drifting along the Volga. But with these numberless victims the 'civilized world' – that is to say, the capitalist world – has scarcely ever concerned itself, except to make sure that the numbers went up. It shut its eyes to the White terror, the work of its own soldiers. It was the Red terror that plunged it into a holy fury.

THE THEORY OF TERROR

The writings of Lenin contain no more than a few references, incidental and formal, to the terror. The stark necessity to break, ruthlessly and decisively, the resistance of the propertied classes was self-evident in the eyes of Lenin and the Bolsheviks, who for this very reason thought it superfluous to prove the matter theoretically. From the first days of the revolutionary government, Lenin had pressed for stern measures and fought against the 'pacifist illusions' and 'impermissible weaknesses' of his immediate circle.

> Stupidities, stupidities [he would repeat]. Do they think they can make a revolution without shooting people? Do you think that you can master your enemies by disarming yourself? What other methods of repression are at your disposal? Imprisonment? Who, during a civil war, will allow himself to be deterred by that when both opponents have the same hope of coming out top?[33]

He added a footnote to one page of his pamphlet *Left Infantilism and the Petty-Bourgeois Mentality*, written in May:

> Let us look squarely at the truth again: the pitiless harshness which is necessary for the victory of Socialism is still lacking in us, and it is not that we lack determination. We are quite determined enough. But we have been unable to *catch* quickly enough a sufficient number of the speculators, marauders and capitalists who break the Soviet laws. ... In the second place our tribunals are lacking in firmness when, instead of shooting defrauders, they give them six months' prison. These two faults have the same social root: the influence of the petty-bourgeois element, its flabbiness.[34]

He was too realistic to avoid the conclusion that 'in a revolution, greater energy is equivalent to greater humanity' (Trotsky). Hesitations and weaknesses have a heavy cost. The more decisively a struggle is waged, the less long and costly it is, the better chance of success it offers. 'The clemency which treats with tyranny is barbarous,' Robespierre declared to the National Convention.

The theory of terror was expounded by Trotsky in 1920, in a book devoted to the refutation of a work by Karl Kautsky with the same title: *Terrorism and Communism.*

The Red terror [Trotsky writes] is not to be distinguished in principle from the armed insurrection, of which it is no more than a continuation. The terror of a revolutionary class in power can be condemned 'from the moral point of view' only by a person who (verbally, to be sure) condemns all violence on principle.

Terror is powerless – and even then, only in the ultimate reckoning – when it is exercised by reaction against a class which has rebelled through the laws of its historical development. Against the reactionary class, on the other hand, which is reluctant to leave the stage, it cannot but be efficacious.

It is for this profound reason that the Red terror is always far less bloody than the White terror. The toiling masses use terror against classes which are a minority in society. It does no more than complete the work of newly arisen economic and political forces. When progressive measures have rallied millions of workers to the cause of revolution, the resistance of the privileged minorities is not difficult to break at this stage. White terror, on the other hand, is carried out by these privileged minorities against the labouring masses, whom it has to slaughter, to decimate. The Versaillais accounted for more victims in a single week in Paris alone than the Cheka killed in three years over the whole of Russia.

The key to victory in civil war is basically the same as that in wars between states. It is a question of annihilating a part – the best part – of the human forces of the enemy and of demoralizing and disarming the others. Modern warfare tends increasingly to nullify any distinction between combatants and non-combatants. The destruction of the railway centres and industrial complexes of the enemy is as important as the task of destroying his armies. The destruction of the proletariat working in the rear to supply the front line with machinery and munitions will be, in all wars of the future, an objective quite as important as the destruction of the soldiers in the first line of battle. On all these points, civil war anticipates the code of war between states. It recognizes no non-belligerents; it searches everywhere, without quarter, for the living strength of the hostile classes. Before a social class can be struck to the heart and admit its own defeat, terrible losses must be inflicted on it. Its sturdiest, bravest, most intelligent sons must be cut down. The best of its life-blood must be drained. (So we have, in the first days of inter-State warfare, the holocaust of the fighting armies, of the flower of the nations' youth, which would otherwise be quite absurd.) That is how it has always been in the past. Must it be always so in the future? Certainly the regimes of White terror now installed in many countries of Europe are doing their utmost to ensure that tomorrow's reckoning for today's ruling classes will be truly frightful. Nonetheless, let us have confidence in the power of the proletariat to spare humanity, in the social wars of the future, from too great a blood-letting. Like the Jacobin terror, the Red terror was directly provoked by foreign intervention.

In 1918, international working-class solidarity was still not strong enough to prevent all foreign intervention from moving in against the revolution. If it had been, revolutionary Russia would easily have been spared four years of civil war. A victorious proletariat which is shielded against foreign invasion by the international solidarity of the workers will need no terror, or else will need it only for a very short time. It will be the responsibility of the possessing classes to gauge the balance of the contending forces with sufficient realism to avoid initiating disastrous battles against a proletariat which is assured of victory. Proletarian organization; class-consciousness; fearless and implacable revolutionary will; active international solidarity: these, we believe, are the factors which, if they are present in a certain degree of strength, may make the Red terror superfluous in the future.

10 · The German Revolution

July and August had been no less decisive in the West than in Russia. The great spring offensives of the Germans, begun at a moment when the American forces were still away from the battle and Russia had opted out of fighting, had failed to break the Allies' will to resist. The German pincer-movement had managed only to get nearer to Paris. At the end of April, Hindenburg's and Ludendorff's troops had moved from their positions at Cambrai, St Quentin and La Fère and advanced as far as Albert, Montdidier and Noyon (battle of the Somme); at some points they penetrated fifty kilometres ahead, and their progress threatened Amiens and the link between the British and French armies, as well as Compiègne and the road to Paris. At the end of May, a further effort had taken them on from L'Ailette on the Marne, another advance of forty kilometres which was marked by the capture of Soissons and Château-Thierry.

However, now that the greatest industrial and financial power in the world, the United States, had entered the war, it had become impossible for the Central Empires to achieve victory, so long as the Allies did not slacken. The ruthless submarine warfare which might have brought Britain to her knees before the American intervention was now no more than a pointless waste of forces and money: the American and British shipyards were every month building *more* vessels than the U-boats sank. The exhaustion of the Allied armies was more than recompensed by the arrival of the excellent human material sent from the USA, since the end of April, at a rate of 300,000 men per month.

Germany and Austria were at the limit of their strength, while the United States had scarcely begun its own effort, marked by a calculated enthusiasm. The occupation of the Ukraine had yielded only a little grain for the benefit of the Central Powers, and the Russian front continued to immobilize considerable German forces: twenty-two divisions, and these all the more vulnerable (as events would soon show) to 'the contagion of Bolshevism' since they were composed of reservists. Around the middle of July, Chancellor von Hinze had asked Ludendorff about the chances of bringing off an unmistakeable victory, and had received the astonishing reply: 'I answer categorically: Yes.' This pronouncement, excessively categorical as it happened, resulted in the offensive of 15 July which was the start of the catastrophe. A sharp attack was launched between Reims and Château-Thierry, towards Épernay. After crossing the Marne, however, the Germans ran up against a new and immovable front: their effort was crushed within twenty-four hours. Two days later, Foch turned to the offensive against the 'Château-Thierry pocket', beginning his action at Villers-Cotterêts with a formidable tank attack. It was the beginning of the end. In the closing days of July, the Germans retreated back over the Vesle.

'The eighth of August was the German army's blackest day in the whole of the World War,' as Ludendorff remarked. On it the third battle of Picardy began, between Albert and Moreuil. There the tank established irrevocably the superiority of the Allies' military technology. The Second German Army broke, and its losses were so great that several divisions had to be re-formed.

The extraordinary new fact, which brought the leaders to a realization of the approaching end, was that *the soldiers were no longer willing to fight.*

Events occurred which would have been thought impossible in the German Army: our soldiers surrendered to enemy horsemen; whole units laid down their arms when a tank approached. A fresh division going bravely up to the firing-line was met by the retreating troops with shouts of: 'Strike-breakers!' and 'They still haven't had enough of the war!' The officers, who had often lost all their influence, tailed behind the movement. ... The war had to be ended [Ludendorff].[1]

From now on the Germans were falling back along the whole front, under the insistent, measured pressure of an enemy that was increasingly coming to dominate them. From one week to the next their resistance seemed about to collapse altogether. The General Staff demanded that the government should seek peace without further delay.[2]

On 15 September, the Allies attacked in Macedonia, between Vardar and Czerna. From the American diplomatic staff who were still, most conveniently, accredited to Sofia, they knew that Bulgaria was at her last gasp. The peasant soldiers were refusing to fight, and the Second and Third Divisions abandoned their positions without any resistance. The Bulgarian army disintegrated in the space of a few days. Tsar Ferdinand, enraged at the state of affairs, sent Stambolisky, the leader of the peasant opposition, who was just out of jail, to the front. A Republican army was marching on Sofia. These events are still obscure. What is certain is that in order to strangle the revolution energetic intervention was necessary, first from the German forces, who kept the rebel army off Sofia, and then from the Allied forces. Tsar Ferdinand abdicated in favour of his brother Boris. The opposition party got control of the government. Under the cannon of the foreigner, the peasant revolution continued to trouble the nation. Bulgaria's official surrender, made to Franchet d'Esperey, was on 27 September.

Austria, on the verge of collapse, was already suing for peace (Note to the USA of 14 September). On 4 October Germany and Austria made a joint proposal for an armistice to President

Wilson. A new government came into power in Berlin, with Prince Max of Baden as Chancellor and Scheidemann, the Social-Democrat, as Deputy Chancellor. Long weeks went past in arduous negotiations with President Wilson. The Central Powers accepted the Fourteen Points he had put out in January (open diplomacy, freedom of the seas, commercial equality, right of self-determination of peoples, independence of Poland, League of Nations). Wilson declared that he would parley only with a democratic Germany. The work of the blockades and the tanks was completed by propaganda for democracy and the rights of nationalities. It was a revelation of the superiority of the structurally most advanced capitalist countries over empires that were burdened down with survivals of an *ancien régime*. Germany, now beset by the spectres of invasion and revolution, agreed to all conditions. Emperor Charles of Austria suddenly discovered a reformer's soul within himself and proclaimed, on 16 October, a 'federative State'. He was too late. The Czechs, tired of waiting on his edicts, organized themselves into an independent state. On 31 October, revolution descended on the streets of Vienna and Budapest.

In Sofia, in Budapest, in Vienna, in Berlin all eyes are now on Russia: it is the example, the hope, the faith. Clandestine or open Soviets are being established everywhere. An illegal conference of the Spartacus League at Berlin, on 7 October, decides that Soviets must be founded; Liebknecht is amnestied and released from prison while the General Staff draws up detailed plans for the repression of disorder. The signal for the outbreak of the revolution is an insane decision by the Admiralty. The fleet is ordered to sail out and engage in a final battle, self-evidently hopeless, with the Allies for the sake of German honour. The Kaiser's admirals want to end with a flourish. The sailors do not have the same reasons for dying; on the contrary, they have found new reasons for living. The crews, now organized around clandestine Soviets, mutiny, and the workers of Kiel support them in a general strike (28 October–4 November). The Social-Democrat Noske makes speeches to the insurgent sailors – in vain. The flame of rebellion is spreading nearer. On 6 November the Social-Democrat statesmen confer under the chairmanship of Prince Max of Baden with General Groener on 'the best means of maintaining the monarchy'. The obstinacy of Wilhelm II, who refuses to abdicate, compromises the dynasty in the eyes even of its last defenders. Max of Baden assumes the Regency on 9 November; Fritz Ebert, a Social-Democrat deputy and former saddler, becomes Imperial Regent;[3] the Kaiser hastily leaves the army headquarters at Spa, by car, and departs for Holland, while Karl Liebknecht, from a balcony of the Imperial Palace in Berlin, proclaims the Republic and the coming of Socialism.

From the Scheldt to the Volga the councils of workers' and

58. Council of People's Commissaries, December 1918. From left to right: Scheidemann, Landsberg, Ebert, Noske and Wissell

soldiers' deputies – the Soviets – are the real masters of the hour. Germany's legal government is a Council of People's Commissaries, made up of six Socialists.

All events in Russia from the end of September to the end of January 1919 take place against this glowing background. This period is marked by a victorious offensive of the Russian revolution on all fronts, simultaneously with the immense victory which the German revolution means to the revolutionary Marxists who have prophesied and anticipated its coming: it is the realization of their deepest hopes, the beginning of the revolution in the West.

EVERYTHING FOR THE GERMAN REVOLUTION

The Vee-Tsik and the Moscow Soviet met in joint session on 3 October, the day on which a new German Cabinet was formed under the auspices of Prince Max of Baden and of Scheidemann. Lenin, who was still recovering, could not attend, but a short letter from him was read out.

The German crisis [he declared] means either that the revolution has begun, or that it is imminent and inevitable. The government is wavering between a military dictatorship, which has existed *de facto* since 2 August 1914 and has ceased to be feasible now that the troops are unreliable, and a coalition with the Socialists. The admission of Scheidemann into the cabinet will only hasten the explosion, because the impotence of the miserable lackeys of the bourgeoisie will soon be exposed. The crisis is only beginning. It will end infallibly in the seizure of power by the proletariat.

The proletariat of Russia must bend its every effort to aid the German workers ... who are called on to wage a most stubborn struggle against their own and British imperialism. The defeat of German imperialism will for a while have the effect of increasing the arrogance, cruelty, reaction and annexatory designs of French imperialism...

The Russian proletariat will understand that soon they will have to make the greatest sacrifices in the name of internationalism. The time is approaching when circumstances may require us to confront British and French imperialism and come to the aid of the German workers, who are struggling against the yoke of their own imperialism.

We must build up grain stocks for the German revolution, and speed up our efforts to create a powerful Red Army.

We had decided to have an army of one million men by the spring; now we need an army of three million. We can have it. And we shall have it.

The sharpest changes in the situation are possible: it is still in the bounds of possibility that German imperialism and Anglo–French imperialism will ally together against the Soviet power.[4]

Trotsky traced a broad outline of events:

It can be said that, as materialists, we have understood the nature of these events and forecast their outcome. History is accomplishing itself, against our will perhaps, but following the curve that we have traced. And even though heavy sacrifices may be necessary, the end will be that which we have predicted: the downfall of the gods of capitalism and imperialism. It seems as though history has wanted to give mankind a final, shattering lesson. The workers were too lazy, apathetic and indecisive. It is quite certain that we should never have been faced with this war if the working class had shown enough determination in 1914 to oppose the designs of the imperialists. But nothing of the sort happened: the working class needed to be given a new, a cruel lesson from history. History permitted the most powerful, the most organized nation to raise herself to an inconceivable height. The 420 cannon dictated the will of Germany to the whole world. Germany seemed to have enslaved Europe forever. ... And now, see how history, having raised German imperialism to this height and hypnotized its masses, plunges her dizzily into an abyss of impotence and humiliation, as if to say: Behold! It is destroyed – go and sweep Europe and the world free of its debris...

Trotsky took pains to establish that the salvation of Germany lay in the seizure of power by the proletariat:

Germany would then attract to itself a powerful current of sympathy from the peoples and oppressed masses of the world, above all from France. ... The French working class, which has shed more blood than that of any other nation, is waiting, deep in its revolutionary heart, only for the first signal from Germany...

He concluded:

If the proletariat of Germany undertakes the offensive, the first duty of Soviet Russia, in the revolutionary struggle, will be to take no account of national frontiers. Russia of the Soviets is no more than the vanguard of the German and the European revolution. ... The German proletariat with its technical expertise, on the one hand; our ill-organized but vastly populated Russia, full of natural resources, on the other – these will form a redoubtable bloc against which all the waves of imperialism will be smashed. ... Liebknecht has no need to conclude a treaty with us. We shall help him without a treaty, to the limit of our strength. We give everything to the world-wide proletarian struggle. Lenin has urged us in his letter to build an army of a million men for the defence of the Republic of Soviets. This programme is too restricted.[5] History tells us: perhaps tomorrow the German working class will call you to its assistance; create an army of two million men...

Such were the sentiments, and such the teachings, not only of the Bolshevik party but of all the revolutionaries of Russia, be they Left SRs, anarchists or Menshevik-Internationalists. Had not Lenin written during the debates on the Brest-Litovsk peace that, in the presence of a German revolution which was threatened in its decisive battle, 'it would not only be expedient but a downright *duty* to risk a defeat and even the loss of Soviet power'.[6] The Socialist Republic of a backward country might be called upon to sacrifice itself for the Socialist revolution (which would be much more important for the international proletariat) in an advanced country, i.e. one with a far stronger industrial base and a more numerous proletariat. From the standpoint of proletarian internationalism, this proposition displays the simple rigour of an axiom. Lenin wrote on 20 August, in his *Letter to American Workers*:

He is not a real socialist who fails to understand that, for the sake of victory over the bourgeoisie, for the seizure of power by the workers, for the sake of beginning the world proletarian revolution, we cannot and must not shrink before any sacrifice, be it the sacrifice of territory, be it a sacrifice which inflicts on us heavy defeats at the hands of imperialism. He is not a real socialist who has failed to prove *by deeds* that he is willing for 'his' country to make the greatest sacrifices so that the cause of the Socialist revolution may take a real step forward.[7]

The resolution adopted by Vee-Tsik pledged to the proletariat of Germany and Austria the unstinted support of the Russian working class; the Revolutionary Military Council was instructed to 'undertake an expanded programme for the formation of the Red Army'; the Commissariat for Food was ordered to set up a food fund without delay for the benefit of the German and Austrian workers.

NEW DANGERS

Lenin, who had by then recovered from his wounds, spoke on 22 October at a joint session of Vee-Tsik, the Moscow Soviet and the Council of Trade Unions. He spoke to the theme that 'never have we been so near the world revolution and never have we been in such a perilous position, because this is the first time that Bolshevism has been regarded as a world-wide danger'. Before the collapse of the Central Empires it could have been thought that the Russian revolution was specific to Russia. But now the opposite was obvious: 'Bolshevism has become the world-wide theory and tactics of the international proletariat.'

The studied prudence of some of the formulations is to be noted:

A popular revolution, and perhaps a proletarian revolution, in Germany has become inevitable.

Let us take care not to interfere with the revolution in the Ukraine. One must understand the variations in growth of every revolution. In each country – and we who have seen and experienced it should know this better than anybody else – the revolution proceeds in its own way ...

Interference by those who do not know the rhythm at which the revolution is growing may hamper those intelligent Communists who are saying: 'Our principal effort must be to make this a conscious process.'

No revolution is worth anything unless it can defend itself; but a revolution does not learn to defend itself at once.[8]

The decomposition of German imperialism was, paradoxically, causing immense dangers for the Russian revolution. The Allies from now on had a free hand in their activities against the Soviet Republic. Bolshevism was now threatening them on the Rhine, not simply on the Vistula. The German and Allied bourgeoisies could perfectly well, in these new circumstances, become reconciled with each other against the Soviets. A tacit bargain had apparently been struck between Germany and the Allies over the occupation of the Ukraine. One must expect an attack by the Allies in the south, either through the Dardanelles and the Black Sea or through Rumania. Lenin's vision was clear. The Allies were indeed thinking of occupying the Ukraine. General Franchet d'Esperey was planning large-scale operations in southern Russia. As we shall see, this campaign began to be implemented, with serious and bloody consequences.

Lenin's speech made no reference whatever to the recent dissension that had arisen around the Brest-Litovsk peace. This is a leader modest in his victories, so modest that they pass him unconcerned. The correctness of the ideas he expounded in February, in his polemic against Left-Communist proponents of revolutionary war, is now unmistakeably revealed. The great spring offensives launched by Hindenburg and Ludendorff on the western front had shown the enduring strength of German imperialism, which was still to hold on for nine more months. We know today that General Hoffmann was trying to persuade the German General Staff to launch a decisive onslaught against the Soviet Republic. The precarious and painful respite that had been won through the Brest-Litovsk treaty had allowed the revolution to gather strength, to master its enemies on the home front and to begin the construction of the Red Army; and during this same interval the troubles that were undermining German imperialism had reached an extreme intensity.

Two closely connected problems were on the agenda for the leaders of the Russian revolution:

(1) To ensure the victory of the proletariat in Germany.

(2) To hold fast against the Allies, now the victors in the world war.

For the Allied powers would be attacking Bolshevism with all the more energy now that the menace of the German proletariat had appeared. The triumph of the working class in Germany would achieve the united front of the workers of Europe against the capitalists of the world. The destiny of humanity was now at stake.

THE FACTS OF THE GERMAN REVOLUTION

As far back as 1908, one of the most famous theoreticians of German Social-Democracy had been at pains to demonstrate that Germany was ripe for the Socialist revolution.[9] No other country at this time formed a better embodiment of all the pre-conditions for social transformation: a high degree of industrial concentration, an extraordinary development of technology, the social predominance of the proletariat, the rapid growth (still under way) of working-class organization. The total population of Germany was 61,700,000, of whom 27,420,000 were working adults. This active population was composed as follows: 6,049,135 property-owners (22·9 per cent), 1,588,168 employees (5·8 per cent) and 19,782,595 proletarians (72·3 per cent). These statistics, from the official census of 1907, are still debatable: in particular, the category of 'property-owners' comprises, in addition to members of the middle and upper classes, a large number of small farmers whose social situation was very akin to that of the proletariat. At all events, the predominance of the industrial proletariat in Germany is not in dispute. One analysis of the class distribution of the working population (dating from 1925) gives the following picture:

Proletarians	16,000,000
Semi-proletarian elements (lower-grade employees and poor peasants)	5,700,000

Petty-bourgeois (artisans, rich peasants, middle and higher-grade employees and officials)	10,100,000
Capitalists and managerial staff for capitalist society	2,000,000

This makes a total of 33,800,000: of these, 20,600,000 are calculated to be wage-earners.[10]

On the basic background of the German revolution, social statistics are fraught with controversy, though the general trends are clear. To the 27·4 million fit adults of the 1907 census must be added a further 4·6 million in extra-occupational categories: the army, naval crews, rentiers, pensioners and so on. The 1923 *Yearbook of the Communist International* (Russian edition) gave the following figures for the period pre-dating the revolutionary mobilization of that year: independents, 4·43 million; semi-proletarians, 3·47 million; employees, 3·22 million; workers, 22·7 million. The noticeably smaller figures that we have reproduced for 1925 are from the same source, but were published in 1925, i.e. after the reverse suffered by the German Communist party,[11] in *The Social-Democratic Parties* (preface by E. Varga). We will

59. Liebknecht

accept them with due reservations, trusting that our statisticians will show more care in the handling of their figures and perhaps less concern for their opportune presentation.

In the general election of 1912, the Social-Democratic party had won 4,250,000 votes: it enjoyed the backing of wealthy cooperatives and the most powerful trade unions in the world, and by 1914 had 1,086,000 members. True enough, during the war (by 1917) this figure had fallen to 243,000, but this was overwhelmingly due to the suspension of public political activity. However, on 2 August 1914, no more than two heroic figures, Karl Liebknecht and Otto Rühle, could be found among 100 party deputies, to vote against the war:[12] all the others, the whole leadership and general staff of the Socialist proletariat, had voted *for*. This was no more than the sudden climax of a long evolution. The great workers' party had been sapped by petty-bourgeois opportunism, whose dominance had been facilitated by the economic expansion of capitalism, a national prosperity based in part on the profits of colonial exploitation and exports, and the existence of a working-class aristocracy that was satisfied, well-paid and linked, in aspirations and way of life, with the pushing middle classes. More and more, the leading circles of the party had become accustomed to identify their destiny with that of the Empire.

Upon this shifting terrain, complex struggles unfolded between the different tendencies of Socialism: in these it was opportunism that always finally carried the day, backed as it was by all the forces of capitalist society. In these battles of ideas that were constantly renewed between small revolutionary minorities and the great realists of the party leadership, the invariable outcome was a further deception of the workers' consciousness, a new vocabulary with which to trick the masses, while continuing to employ a revolutionary language that had lost its basic meanings. Little by little, class collaboration was substituted for the class struggle; the theory of the peaceful conquest of Socialism through parliamentary democracy consigned to oblivion the necessity for the dictatorship of the proletariat, as proclaimed by Marx; a phrase-mongering and lying patriotism draped the party congresses with the national flag, side by side with the red banner of the workers' International. Erudite theorists even proposed to revise the basic principles of Socialism in the light of the progress made by German capitalism. And these men, even as the Empire poured its metal into cannons, devoted their energies to demonstrating that the journey to the city of Socialism was now afoot, along the path of peaceful reforms.

For over a quarter of a century the labour aristocracy, from among whom were recruited Social-Democracy's leading sections, had gradually come to identify its own interests with those of the social system whose prosperity guaranteed their comfort. The vote of 2 August 1914 only revealed, brutally and openly, the crossing which the officer-corps of Socialism had long ago made to the side of the bourgeoisie.

An Independent Social-Democratic party, dissatisfied with the unconditional support given to imperialism by leaders like Scheidemann and Ebert, had split off and constituted itself in 1917: it reflected both the protest of the worker masses against the Sacred Union and the old centrism that loved to use revolutionary phraseology to mask a politics of moderation, compromise, temporizing and the Golden Mean. Its ideologues proved to be the very people who had worked hardest over the last ten years to corrupt Socialist thought: Eduard Bernstein, inventor of revisionism, and the pacifist Kautsky, now ready to become the prophet of Wilsonism.[13] In the absence of a revolutionary organization of the masses, it was with the influential Left of this party (Haase, Daümig, Crispien) that Yoffe had to collaborate on the eve of the German revolution.

The only authentically revolutionary proletarian group that could be compared in class-consciousness with the Russian Bolshevik party was the Spartakusbund (Spartacus League), founded in January 1916 by the outstanding veterans of the struggle against opportunism. It included a tiny band of leaders who were capable of great things: the old Polish conspirator Leo Tyshko, a past-master of clandestine work; the historian Franz Mehring, responsible for some of the most brilliant applications of the historical-materialist method; Rosa Luxemburg, the only brain of Western Socialism in the same class as Lenin and Trotsky; and the intrepid Liebknecht. But these leaders, habituated to a struggle 'against the stream', had no great army of masses behind them, for all their popularity. The Spartakusbund was 'more of an ideological tendency than a party', as Karl Radek put it. And it had had no alternative but to affiliate, in April 1917, to the Independent Social-Democratic party.

Ranged against the German proletariat, so singularly lacking in that essential weapon for the class war – the revolutionary party conscious of its tasks – stood the most educated, the most organized, the most conscious bourgeoisie of all, the bourgeoisie that had known how to train war leaders like Hindenburg, Ludendorff, Mackensen, von der Goltz, von Klück, the bourgeoisie that had produced its Krupps, its Albert Ballins, its Hugo Stinnes, its Walter Rathenaus, its Hugenbergs, its Klöckners, its Thyssens and so many others.[14]

THE COUNTER-REVOLUTIONARY SOCIALISTS WIN POWER

It was a bourgeoisie too wise to try and reverse the situation when the troops, exhausted, demoralized, without hope of winning the war, fled from the front. We have already seen how Ludendorff understood at once that the war was over and that not an hour must be wasted before making peace. Once the dream of a Greater

Germany had exploded, nothing was left for the hard-headed men who had dreamt it but to save the imperialist order. And this could only be saved by coming to suitable terms with the masses. What had never been comprehended by the Savinkovs, Kornilovs, Kerenskys and Chernovs of Russia (or by Buchanan, Paléologue and Albert Thomas)[15] when the tide of Bolshevism ran high was grasped immediately by Imperial Germany's rulers in September to November 1918. Their guiding idea was to be swept along by the revolution in order to avoid being swept away by it. The German expression is here strikingly appropriate: *Sich an der Spitze stellen, um die Spitze abzubrechen* – put yourself at the spearhead of the movement in order to smash it.

Nowhere in Germany did the military leaders resist the troops. When the Soldiers' Councils (Soviets) were formed, the staff chiefs were skilful enough to get their own creatures elected on to them in many places. The Kaiser's field-marshals and the big bankers took it upon themselves to call into the government Ebert and Scheidemann, Socialist leaders of the utmost decorum, but with influence among the masses. Prince Max of Baden's Cabinet smoothed the way for the Council of People's Commissaries[16] of the Socialist Republic which was formed on 12 November. All

60. Armed Spartacists marching in Berlin, 1918

Germany lay in the power of the Soviets. The very names, Council of Commissaries, Workers' Councils (*Arbeiterräte*), were an echo of the Russian revolution. But these Soviets were paralysed by the dominant Social-Democratic majorities. The Council of People's Commissaries was in reality only the demagogic camouflage for a normal coalition Cabinet. In it three Majority Social-Democrats, Fritz Ebert, Landsberg and Scheidemann, notorious for their loyalty to the bourgeoisie, cohabited with three indecisive Independents, Hugo Haase, Dittmann and Barth. It was this government that undertook the foundation of a democratic Socialist republic for Germany. It prescribed order and calm for the citizens until the elections should take place. It was reluctant to accept the harsh Armistice terms dictated by the Allies, and signed them only under the urgent pressure of the General Staff. From its inception, the government had two paths to choose from: social peace and peace with the Allies – in other words, defence of capitalism, repression of the revolutionary movement, united front with the Allies against the Soviet Republic; or civil war, alliance with the Russian Soviets, revolutionary war for the defence of Germany. In such a civil war, the victory of the proletariat was assured; but Wilson and Foch would never have agreed (at least, so it was believed) to sit down and negotiate with Bolshevism.[17] The interest of the nation would therefore have required the development of the struggle on a new plane, that of the proletarian revolution itself; but for this it would have been necessary to dare, and, in order to dare, to desire the victory of the proletariat, to wish it and believe in it. The whole of Social-Democracy's past ran counter to such a prospect. And the bourgeoisie and petty-bourgeoisie preferred a capitalist Germany crushed underfoot by the Allies to a proud and strong proletarian Germany, born out of the ruins of imperialism.

The People's Commissaries refused any appeal to Yoffe. They turned down the Russian grain that had been offered to them by Vee-Tsik. They steered clear of any interference with the old bureaucracies, and kept the reactionary generals in their posts of command.[18]

The Socialists of counter-revolution were in power.

The struggle was now to open between them and that revolutionary minority of the proletariat, grouped around the Spartacus League and the Left of the Independent Social-Democrats, which was demanding a dictatorship of the proletariat.

YOFFE, THE SOVIET AMBASSADOR, IS EXPELLED FROM BERLIN

In Russia, the momentum of events quickens. The Red Army becomes organized, wins battles, captures cities. The Extraordinary Commissions are having enemies shot. The factories, the transport systems, the towns are locked in a desperate struggle against the famine. Daily life is completely dominated by the expectation of revolution in Europe. The eyes of the whole nation are turned towards the West. Famine, typhus, deaths, one town captured, one town lost – what do these matter? In Berlin, Paris, Rome, London, the world's future is being decided. The internationalism of Russia's Soviets runs deep and true: nothing breaks its attention.

The newspapers of the period are astonishing. Each day, in large type with headlines across the page, they carry last-minute dispatches, vague rumours picked up in Stockholm by anxious ears: riots in Paris, riots in Lyon, revolution in Belgium, revolution in Constantinople, victory of the Soviets in Bulgaria, rioting in Copenhagen. In fact, the whole of Europe *is* in movement; clandestine or open Soviets are appearing everywhere, even in the Allied armies; everything is possible, everything. On 15 October, Vorovsky telegraphs Zinoviev from Stockholm: *Revolution builds up in France* (so runs the headline of his dispatch in the newspapers); 'a workers' popular movement began two days ago, and is spreading energetically in Paris. ... The workers are demanding the immediate release of all political prisoners. ... A Soviet of Allied soldiers has made contact at the front with the Soviet of German soldiers ...'

On 5 November, with the red flags already floating over Kiel, Chancellor Max of Baden decided to take a step which had been long demanded by the General Staff. He broke off diplomatic relations with Soviet Russia. Yoffe was asked to leave Berlin within twenty-four hours. Some Russian diplomatic luggage had got opened 'by accident' and was found to contain revolutionary leaflets in German.[19] In addition to these grounds, which might well set Russia in a bad light before the German masses, it was also alleged that there had been a reluctance to punish the assassins of Count Mirbach.

An interesting exchange of telegrams shortly afterwards (on 10 December) sheds some light on Yoffe's activities in Berlin. The Soviet ambassador had in fact freely admitted helping the German revolutionaries with money, arms and ammunition, via Haase and Barth, the Independent Social-Democrats, who acted as intermediaries. Haase and Barth, who were both members of the Reich's Socialist government, felt obliged to deny the truth of this declaration; whereupon Yoffe replied to them with a crushing letter whose principal passages we reproduce:

It goes without saying that I was not so unwise as to deliver personally and directly to Comrade Barth – a newcomer to the working-class movement who inspired in me only a limited confidence – the sums which were destined for the purchase of armaments. ... People's Commissary Barth, however, was perfectly aware that the hundreds of thousands of marks which he had admitted receiving from German comrades derived from my establishment as their ultimate source. He said as much in the conversation we had a fortnight before the revolution, when he reproached me for not having provided the two million marks he had asked for. ... If only I had provided this sum, he said, the German workers would have been armed long ago and ready for a victorious uprising. ... Herr Haase and his friends have on many occasions been supplied by me with material – by no means always of Russian origin – for the speeches they made in the Reichstag. ... The Independent Social-Democratic Party received material assistance from us for the publishing projects on which our writers collaborated with them. ... Does not Herr Haase believe that we were acting together in the common interest of the German and international revolution? I would never have brought up these reminiscences of our work together if Herr Haase had not adopted the viewpoint of the von Kühlmanns ... who actually consider our cooperation with the German USPD a crime and have expelled us from Germany for that reason. If the new German government, which calls itself Socialist and revolutionary, goes to the extent of openly denouncing us for the actions we undertook jointly with its members when they were still revolutionaries, then the political obligations which would constrain me in the case of party comrades or honest opponents lose all their force. I will now take the opportunity of informing the legal adviser to the Russian Consulate in Berlin, Reichstag Deputy Oskar Cohn, that the sum of 500,000 marks and 150,000 roubles which he received from me the night before I left Berlin, in his capacity as a member of the USPD, is not now to be paid into the account of his party. The same applies to the fund of ten million roubles which Dr Cohn was previously authorized to draw upon for the service of the German revolution.[20]

KRASNOV AND THE GRAND ARMY OF THE DON

During these months the new perils that Lenin had warned against are manifested in all the regions where the civil war still rages. The Germans and the Allies take it in turn to join the war.

After the victories of the Red Army on the Volga, the Revolutionary Military Council concentrated its attention on the Don. The Don country had been conquered easily enough by the Reds at the beginning of the year (the suicide of Ataman Kaledin may be recalled here) but rose in the spring with the approach of the German forces. Ataman Krasnov (the same general who had marched upon Petrograd on the eve of October 1917, was taken prisoner and then released on parole) set forth during April and May at the head of this Cossack counter-revolution. By July he had at his disposal 27,000 infantrymen, 30,000 horsemen, 175 cannon, 610 machine-guns, twenty aeroplanes, four armoured trains and eight gunboats. The territory ruled by the 'Grand Army of the Don' is a state enjoying the recognition of the Central Powers and a rather extraordinary constitution: it is bounded on the west by the Ukraine of Hetman Skoropadsky, to the north by Soviet Russia, to the east and the south by the Kuban Cossack territory, where Denikin's National Army is being formed. This new state is no more than the personal fief of a military adventurer, under the Kaiser's suzerainty. The Don constitution voted by the Krug (the Cossack Assembly) decrees the Ataman to be an autocrat. He exercises supreme command of the armed forces, is sole director of foreign policy, appoints all ministers and military leaders, can declare a state of siege, authorizes all laws and exercises both the right of veto against all legislative measures and the right of pardon. Private property is declared inviolable. In the religious sphere the Orthodox rite has official precedence. All the same, the Ataman moves with the times: he even speaks of the 'war of the capitalists'. An agrarian reform is decreed for the benefit of the Cossack poor. The landlords are to be expropriated with compensation, and cultivated lands are declared to be common property. These concessions to the peasant revolution go along with some sham attentions given to the counter-revolutionary Socialists, one of whom is given the Ministry of Public Education in the Novo-cherkassk[21] administration. An organ of the SRs, the *Pryazovski Krai* (*The Land of Azov*), appears in the capital there, side by side with a monarchist organ. As to the treatment of the workers: one military commander sends to the commandant of Yuzovka, a working-class city, two telegrams on the same day: 'It is forbidden to arrest workers. The orders are to hang them or shoot them. 10 November. No. 2428'; 'The orders are to hang all arrested workers in the street. The bodies are to be exhibited for three days. 10 November. No. 2431. Signed *Zhirov*.' The same methods are used at Rostov. At Taganrog, General Denisov warns the population that he will use asphyxiating gas if there are any disturbances. Meanwhile, according to Articles 15 to 23 of its Fundamental Laws, the Don country was endowed with all the democratic freedoms imaginable. With disarming frankness Krasnov declared that 'All the so-called conquests of the revolution were swept away.'

On 5 May the Ataman requested the Kaiser's partnership and protection against Bolshevism. He asked for arms, and for Wilhelm II's arbitration in the dispute that had arisen between the Ukraine and the Don over the possession of Taganrog. General von Arnim arrived in the Don country, which was being supplied with weaponry and ammunition in great abundance by Germany. On 28 June the Ataman sent a fresh letter to the Kaiser, expounding his plan for the creation of a great Cossack State, in vassaldom to Germany, extending from the Sea of Azov to the Caspian. This enemy of 'anti-national Bolshevism', this patriot, calculates the best possible amputations of his own country; he asks the German invader to cede to him Voronezh and Tsaritsyn, Astrakhan, the Kuban, the Terek.[22] He proposes a treaty favourable to German business interests and offers the products of his land: grain, leather, wines, oils, tobacco and livestock. He even stabs his brother-in-arms Denikin in the back: the Kuban is Denikin's base of operations. 'German domination,' he tells the Cossack Assem-

bly, 'will be easier to put up with than domination by the Russian muzhik-bandit.'

However, during November, at the very time when the rupture of diplomatic relations between Berlin and the Soviets sets off speculation about a full-scale German intervention in Russia, German imperialism collapses. Its armies of occupation in the Ukraine are in total disorder: its soldiers now have only one desire, to get back home at all costs. Without losing a moment, the patriot Krasnov appeals to the Allies. In his memoirs he records the promises lavished on him by his new friends. At the conference at Jassy in Rumania, M. Hainaut,[23] a French consul, 'insists on a definite undertaking from the German command that order should be kept in the Ukraine, through their auspices, until the arrival of the Allies'. General Berthelot promises to send several French divisions before the middle of December. It is no longer to the Kaiser that Ataman Krasnov sends his petitions, but to General Franchet d'Esperey.

The Don [he informs the latter] is a democratic republic, at whose head I stand. ... The Don's only war is with Bolshevism. ... Without the aid of the Allies, the liberation of Russia is impossible. ... Three or four army corps, 90,000 to 120,000 men, would liberate Russia within three to four months. ... The occupation of the Ukraine by foreign troops is becoming imperative...

Equally imperative, it would appear, will be the presence of Allied garrisons at Tula, Samara, Saratov, Tsaritsyn, Penza and Moscow. ... At Jassy General Berthelot gives formal assurances to the emissary sent by Krasnov: 'The Ukraine will certainly be occupied, either by an Anglo–French army, or by troops which Germany will be compelled to leave behind there.' Further, if need be, 'the whole army from Salonika' will be sent into Russia.

A British Military Mission, headed by General Poole, pays a visit to Denikin's headquarters at Ekaterinodar. British and French officers (Dupré, Faure, Hochain,[24] Ehrlich) visit the Don country; they are welcomed with *Te Deums*, feted by ancient Cossacks, decorated, cheered by rows of girls dressed in white. Poole is no less categorical than Berthelot: 'I will call in a brigade from Batum immediately!' he declares. However, London recalls him.[25] At the end of January 1919, Captain Fouquet, the representative of General Franchet d'Esperey, finally presents the Ataman with the draconic conditions laid down by the Allies. The Ataman is to subordinate himself to General Denikin, the supreme head of the Russian armed forces; he will 'submit, in matters military, political and administrative, to the authority of General Franchet d'Esperey'. All his orders will be countersigned by Captain Fouquet. The Don government will reimburse all French citizens who have suffered any damages through the revolution: 'the average revenue of all businesses that were lost during the disturbances will be restored to them, plus a five per cent indemnity over all the output of the said enterprises since 1914'.

Krasnov was undertaking a war of extermination against the Reds, using both surprise attacks and large-scale strategic operations. Twice, in October 1918 and January 1919, he managed to encircle Tsaritsyn,[26] the gateway to the Lower Volga, but it was heroically defended by the Tenth Army (Tulyakov, Voroshilov and Stalin). His attempt to mobilize the peasantry for his cause proved a failure. In the first days of November Trotsky arrived on the southern front, visiting Voronezh, Tsaritsyn and Astrakhan: he galvanized morale and lent his decisive impulse to the organization of a regular army. In these parts this was a particularly difficult task. The civil war set village against village and, often, rich against poor in the same village. Everywhere bands of guerrillas were being formed around leaders who became folk-heroes. In order to replace these brave but bizarre squadrons by a proper army, it was necessary to break their resistance, their group cohesion, their personal traditions. Sometimes the villages were in a state of fortification for their own static defence, without regard for the rest of the front. When a particular band had to leave its district, it melted away. The leader-heroes wanted to be independent of everybody else, and the first attempts at centralization provoked some dangerous reactions from them. In the Kuban, Sorokin took prisoner the Revolutionary Council which was being placed over his command, and sent it to the firing-squad. Mironov, Avtonomov, Sakharov, Potapenko and many other local commanders mutined against the central power, in the name of the revolution. Their rebellion was put down. Vigorous centralization was brought to the southern front by regiments recruited in Moscow, by the worker-commissars and by a Revolutionary Council of the Army headed by the metal-worker Shlyapnikov (the army itself was commanded by a former Tsarist officer who had rallied to Bolshevism, P. P. Sytin). From now on, Krasnov's attacks broke against Red lines that were becoming harder and stronger. At the beginning of 1919 the establishment of an efficient Red cavalry, commanded by a dauntless NCO named Budyonny,[27] testified to the rallying to the Red cause of the middle and even the wealthy Cossacks: the cavalry being a relatively wealthy branch of the armed forces.

The task of the Red Armies in the south was well defined by Trotsky:

We have to move up into the space between the departing German imperialism and the approaching Anglo-French militarism. We must take over the Don, the northern Caucasus, the Caspian region, render assistance to the workers and peasants of the Ukraine, and get back to our own Soviet home where there is no room either for the auxiliaries of Britain nor for those of Germany. ... The pulse of our revolution beats on the southern front: there the lot of the Soviet power is being cast.

THE COLLAPSE OF SAMARA

The liberation of the Volga region, achieved in early October with the capture of Samara and Stavropol, amounted to all that Trotsky said. The Red Army followed up its successes by penetrating the Ural province (capture of Bugulma, 16 October).

Ever since the fall of Kazan and Simbirsk the SR Constituents' capital had been living in a state of terror. Sudden panics arose in the city, stopping the traffic. The population was hiding in cellars, the shops were closed, the local bourgeoisie crowded itself into trains and went off. The Constituent Assembly Committee, increasingly aware of its powerlessness, decided to dissolve and hand over its power to the Ufa Directorate, in which it had little confidence. The Czechs, worn out by long months of battle, did not want to see any more fighting. The White volunteers were too few to be of any use. The mobilized peasants deserted *en masse* or went over to the Reds. To cap it all, Ataman Dutov would not let the SRs have any help from the Cossacks at Orenburg. The Directorate was wasting its days hopelessly in a succession of intrigues.

It was not even possible at Samara to find a military leader who was capable of organizing the evacuation of the city. The various liberal societies passed resolutions declaring resistance to the death, the SRs formed combat groups or decreed the conscription of the whole masculine population: but nothing serious was done, and the Reds approached inexorably. The order for evacuation, issued on 4 October, was the signal only for a general rout.

> It was a nightmare. ... General Tregubov, the military governor, took flight on the first train out. The Commission for Evacuation disappeared. ... There was nobody to issue documents and passes. Every man made straight for the station without thinking of anybody else, to secure a place in one of the trains. The chaos was unbelievable. There were no carriages or locomotives. The luggage from State institutions or private persons was piled three floors high on the yard in front of the building. Thousands of State functionaries, members of the various parties, influential personalities and terrified small gentry crushed their way into the station, amid the sobs of women and children. On every face, panic and ruthless egoism. Each one thought: Me first!, and brutally beat his way towards the coveted berth in a goods-wagon.[28]

A few details may be noted. The government's special train, packed with passengers, found itself abandoned at the last minute on a perilous stretch of line. The Czechs cornered all available rolling-stock in order to evacuate their own troops. The delegates from the Constituents' Committee, who visited the Czech Chief of Staff to ask him for a locomotive, found only insults to meet them.

The scene is recorded for us by Maisky, a Menshevik member of the Samara Cabinet. The delegates had just left Volsky, the SR head of the government, drunk and despairing in the remains of an alcoholic orgy, breaking glasses and shouting: 'I drink to dead Samara! Can't you smell the corpse?' The city was gripped by terror and depression. When they arrived at the Czech HQ an officer there greeted them with an outburst of laughter: 'Where's your army? He, he, he, he. Go on, tell me now, where's your army?' The word 'government' sent him into fits of mirth. 'Government?' he spluttered, 'You the government?' He rolled a paper pellet and threw it contemptuously.

We have dwelt on these details of the collapse at Samara because they are typical. The contrast between this degradation and the heroic tenacity of the Reds at Sviazhsk, the Ural, Tuapse, springs from the difference in human quality manifested by the contending social forces. The Reds' superiority in spiritual resources – confidence, energy, intelligence and endurance – is strikingly evident. The same will be observed during the whole course of the revolution. Later on, other bankruptcies, more serious and more bloody, will cause the collapse of Samara to be forgotten; and Sviazhsk will be eclipsed by other exploits. The world will see the proletarians of Orenburg withstand a lengthy siege till their victory; Petrograd holding against all odds under Trotsky's defence; Tsaritsyn twice invested by the Whites and twice victorious; the Red Army taking by assault two impregnable fortresses, Kronstadt and Perekop. On the other hand, the Rumanian and French occupiers will undergo the débâcle of Odessa; the British occupiers, the débâcle of Archangel; Denikin will end his career by the hideous evacuation of Novorossisk; Kolchak by his flight down the Trans-Siberian Railway; Wrangel in the disaster of the Crimea. We have already noted the character of the primacy in social forces to which this moral superiority corresponds. We will add, from the events of the Don and Samara, one further characteristic which will be reproduced again and again in all the episodes of the counter-revolution: the brutally self-interested attitude of the foreigners, British, French and Czechoslovaks. The Allied officers arrogantly dictate their commands to the counter-revolutionary chiefs, desert them as soon as the situation worsens, lash them with their contempt when the moment of reckoning arrives, and clear off to save their own skins on the first trains in any evacuation. Without foreign bayonets the counter-revolution is impotent; yet 'national' Russia is treated by its allies as a conquered territory. Here is one of the most curious apparent paradoxes of the civil war: in it, bourgeois patriotism will be seen constantly enslaving itself to the foreigner, while proletarian internationalism fulfils its mission by excelling in the defence of the nation.

THE ALLIES IN SIBERIA: KOLCHAK

The fall of Samara reveals the decay of the democratic counter-revolution. The reactionary forces are now concentrated in Siberia, around the government at Omsk. The conflict between the SR Constituents and the Siberian counter-revolution (headed by the Kadets, who support a Right-wing dictatorship) sharpens from day to day. The Siberian government keeps the Ufa Directorate under severe constraint. At Omsk, the officer-corps is playing an unusually powerful role: no administration can stay in power without its support. Its very influence demoralizes it, for public life becomes a sequence of military plots and intrigues. Any politicians with a liberal reputation risk arrest, kidnapping or murder at any moment: thus the SR minister Novoseltsov disappears at the end of September. The Siberian capital at this time offers a complex spectacle of military anarchy: the Directorate, allegedly the supreme authority, is respected by nobody; a Council of ministers, purged by assassinations, is at loggerheads with the liberal Duma whose majority consists of Socialist-Revolutionaries; the Czechoslovaks, 'democrats' but dedicated to order as their first priority, reserve their allegiance; juntas of officers legislate in the shadows. Industrialists and generals, who are agreed on the principle of a personal dictatorship, meanwhile come up with the formation of a 'national united front'. The Directorate and the Omsk government reach agreement – as an exception rather than a rule – on the appointment of Admiral Kolchak as Minister of War (4 November).

These internal dissensions are compounded by the schemes of foreign powers. The Japanese, supported by Ataman Semyonov, pursue their operations in the Far East; the Czechs rule the Trans-Siberian line as conquerors; their leader General Gajda humiliates the Russian officers, conducts requisitionings, shoots Bolsheviks and suspects (five people were shot without trial on 25 October at Krasnoyarsk); the Allies send Generals Knox and Janin,[29] who are officially invested by Lloyd George and Clemenceau to take the command of all Allied forces in Siberia.

Point for point, the experience of the Ukraine, where the democratic parties of the middle classes could do nothing except open the path for black reaction, is repeated in Siberia. Such, indeed, is the inevitable function of these parties in civil wars, since the peculiarity of the petty-bourgeoisie is to have no politics of its own. It is always situated between two dictatorships – that of the proletariat, or that of reaction; its destiny is to prepare the latter, up to a certain point, and then to submit to it. The SR Directorate has nothing to offer except the empty eloquence of its leaders. At Omsk, these gentlemen feel just as distressed, just as powerless, under the threat of the military, as they did in Petrograd not so long ago, in the days of the Constituent Assembly under the threat of the proletariat. The very same illusions fortify their spirits. The vocation of the parliamentary martyr rises in their breasts. The Menshevik Maisky, who has fled from Samara, has a conversation with Avksentiev, the great man of the Directorate and the SR party: impressive beard, idealist's forehead, an austere rhetoric.

Avksentiev told me bluntly, 'We are living on top of a volcano, we expect every night to be arrested.'
I asked him, 'Do you think your policy is right?' He replied, 'Yes, it was impossible for us to act otherwise. We are the martyrs of compromise. Do you laugh at that? There are such martyrs, and perhaps Russia needs them more than anything else.'

A few minutes later Maisky asked another member of the Directorate, 'But aren't you going to try to resist?' 'And what could we do?' was the answer, with a gesture of despair.

On the night of 18–19 November, the members of the Directorate and their political associates were at last arrested by the Cossacks. The strategic points of the city were dominated by the machine-guns of the British Colonel Ward. On the same day a decision of the Siberian government bestowed upon Admiral Kolchak the title of Supreme Ruler. The admiral, 'accepting the cross of office', declared that he intended to follow neither the path of reaction nor that of the factions; his sole object would be the formation of a strong army to fight Bolshevism. The Russian people would 'thenceforth organize its own liberty'. The *coup* had been prepared with the agreement of the Allied representatives: Colonel Ward, the French Consul Regnault, the American Harris and the Czech Štefanik.[30] The members of the Directorate left for exile a few days later, escorted by Russian and British soldiers. General Janin arrived at Omsk on 14 December: the Allied order-paper actually made the 'Supreme Ruler' of Omsk a subordinate of this general!

The SR Constituents tried in vain to oppose this turn of events. Their resistance committee, headed by Chernov, allowed itself to be arrested. The SR party decided to abandon the struggle against Bolshevism and to return to its insurrectionary and terrorist methods, this time against the Siberian reaction. It was too late. A few of its militants got shot, and that was all.

A study of the Siberian counter-revolution, which reached its maximum success in 1919, is beyond the scope of this book. The military dictatorship and the Allied intervention achieved these results. By the spring of 1919 Kolchak found himself at the head of an armed force strong enough to appear temporarily superior to the Red Army. But, as with all the White armies, this was a class army, formed principally from officers and youngsters from the well-off classes. The regime instituted by the Supreme Ruler was one of White terror. The peasants deserted, refused to supply food, and resisted the requisitionings, the return of the landlords, and the arbitrary rule of the old authorities who had come back

62. Funeral of miners shot at Yuzonka by Denikin's men, 1919

more arrogant than ever. Soon the whole of Siberia was streaked
with columns of fire. Repression was everywhere the rule: in the
rebellious villages, muzhiks were shot in dozens, the women were
flogged, the girls raped, the cattle stolen. The townships that were
bombarded or incinerated can be numbered in hundreds. Soon,
droves of Red guerrillas began to swarm in the Siberian bushland.
At the end of December, a workers' insurrection organized by the
clandestine section of the Communist party broke out in Omsk;
its repression cost 900 victims. In the general massacre, several
SR and Menshevik members of the Constituent Assembly were
executed. In cases of railway sabotage, the villages suspected of
complicity were burned down; for each 'act of banditry' from the
Reds, between three and twenty hostages were shot.

Kolchak's *coup d'état* answered the wish of the Allies for a united command over the counter-revolutionary forces. At the very moment when events at Omsk were unfolding their course, there was a conference at Jassy (Rumania) whose host was the British ambassador, Barclay: it included the French ambassador, M. de Saint-Aulaire, an American diplomat, an Italian diplomat, the leaders of the liberal (Milyukov) and monarchist wings of the bourgeoisie, and the SR leaders (Fundaminsky).[31] The principal matter was the question of a military dictatorship in Russia. It may be said that it was the Allies who imposed on the Russian counter-revolution its principal leaders, Denikin and Kolchak, whose every least action was supposed to be invigilated by the generals Franchet d'Esperey[32] and Janin.

63. Admiral Kolchak

SIXTH CONGRESS OF SOVIETS. CANCELLATION OF THE BREST-LITOVSK TREATY

The first anniversary of the October Revolution was commemorated by the Sixth (Extraordinary) Congress of Soviets, held from 6–9 November, at the very hour of the German revolution. It was a singularly lifeless Congress: virtually an enlarged session of Vee-Tsik. There was not, and could not have been, any controversy owing to the extremely homogeneous make-up of the assembly, which out of the 950 voting delegates was composed of 933 Communists, eight Revolutionary-Communists, four Left SRs, two Narodnik Communists,[33] one Maximalist, one anarchist and one non-party delegate. The only speakers were Lenin, Trotsky, Sverdlov, Radek, Steklov, Kamenev, Kursky and Avanesov.[34] The only reactions from the hall consisted of prolonged applause and unanimous votes.

The Congress decided once again to propose peace to the United States, Britain, France, Italy and Japan, countries that were at war with Russia even though they had never declared it. A resolution on amnesty was adopted, instructing the Extraordinary Commissions to keep under arrest only avowed and active enemies of the regime: there was a further resolution on revolutionary legality.

During the proceedings the news came of the Red Army's capture of the factories at Izhevsk (Ural region). This was a great advance, since the munitions works at Izhevsk and Votkinsk had gone over to the counter-revolution under Menshevik influence. Trotsky announced that in the Kotlas district a party of fifty-eight British soldiers had gone over to the Reds.

The Congress showed extreme caution in its evaluation of events in Germany. The motion adopted after Lenin's report spoke of the need to instil into the masses a clear awareness of the new dangers that were present and 'the conviction that we shall be able to defend and preserve the Socialist fatherland and the victory of the world proletarian revolution'. Yoffe had just been expelled from Germany, and a two-pronged attack was now expected against Communist Russia from the Central Powers and the Allies.

Lenin took the platform twice, to commemorate the first anniversary of the revolution and to explain the international situation.

We have always realized [he said] that it was not because of any merit of the Russian proletariat that we happened to begin the revolution, which was impelled by the world-wide struggle: it was because of Russia's weakness, its backwardness and the special influence of military strategic circumstances that obliged us to place ourselves at the head of the movement until the other detachments should come up.

He drew the balance-sheet of a year of struggles: from workers' control we had passed to workers' organization of industry; from the general democratic struggle of the peasants for land to the differentiation of classes in the countryside; from military impotence to the creation of the Red Army; from isolation to joint action with the proletariat of western Europe. 'We began with workers' control, we did not decree Socialism at once, because Socialism can only take shape when the working class has learnt how to administer.' He spoke of the peasant question, referring to the July crisis of kulak revolts. 'We confined ourselves to leaving the way open for Socialist transformation in the countryside, though we knew full well that the peasantry was still, at the time, unable to enter on this path.' No democratic republic had done as much for the peasants. It had not been until the famine struck that war broke out between the workers and the kulaks; of which the principal result had been the mass mobilization of the working people of the towns and the countryside. And now 'the alliance of the rural poor with the workers in the cities is laying the foundation for real Socialist construction'. 'No matter what happens to us,' Lenin declared, 'imperialism will perish.'

In his second speech he said that:

international relations have been confronting us as a central question, not merely because the essence of imperialism is now the firm, stable linking of all the states in the world into one single system – or rather into one mass of blood and filth – but also because Socialist victory is inconceivable in one country but demands the most active collaboration of at least several advanced countries, among which we cannot number Russia.

Convinced of this conception from the very first moment, the Russian proletariat has bent its efforts towards enlightening the masses of other countries, without hoping for any immediate results. 'Even if we were to be suddenly wiped out, we would have the right to say, without concealing our mistakes, that we have made full use, for the world-wide Socialist revolution, of the interval that destiny offered to us.' Once again he repeated, as a rider to these general observations, that 'never have we been so near the world revolution, and yet never have we been in such a dangerous situation'. Lenin's last remarks were:

We have no cause whatsoever for despair or pessimism. We know that the danger is great. It may be that fate has even sterner tests in store for us. It is not excluded that they can crush one country: but they will never be able to crush the world proletarian revolution...[35]

Trotsky reported on the situation at the fronts, which gave grounds for considerable hope. The liberation of the south, he said, was now on the order of the day.

The Armistice of 11 November, drawn up between the Allies and Germany, insisted as one of its conditions upon the cancellation of the treaties of Brest-Litovsk and Bucharest. Two days later, Vee-Tsik proclaimed that the treaty of Brest-Litovsk was null and void. The Republic of Soviets offered its fraternal alliance to all the peoples liberated from imperialism.

THE UKRAINE IS RECONQUERED

During the German occupation and under the rule of Hetman Skoropadsky, the Ukraine had never for a moment been free of trouble. The class struggle continued in all its fury. The effect of compulsory requisitionings was to force the peasantry to take up arms. The nationalist-Socialist parties of the petty-bourgeoisie were offended by the condition of national humiliation and transmitted the discontent of the rural masses. In the working-class centres, the illegal organizations of the Bolshevik party kept up the good fight. The Left SRs undertook their terrorist acts. The countryside was full of irregular bands called *haidamaks* (part of the tradition of the Ukraine), of partisan forces under the red (Bolshevik) or black (anarchist) flag. In the middle of September the nationalist groups that had officially declared war on the Hetman began to gather an army of volunteers around Belaya-Tserkov. This insurrectionary movement was directed by two old nationalist-Socialist leaders, the writer Vinnichenko and the schoolteacher Simon Petlyura, who had both been prominent figures in the Rada, of piteous memory.

As soon as the members of the occupying forces heard the news of events in Vienna and Berlin, they only had one thought: to get back home. The only form of organization the Austro–Germans could now boast was that required to evacuate the country in good order, and this was provided by the Soldiers' Councils.

The Germanized Ukraine disintegrated instantly. All over it Red forces sprang into being, while regular units of the Red Army marched upon Gomel, Kharkov and Kiev. The troops of Vinnichenko and Petlyura, who at the first moment of the collapse were stronger than the Reds, launched simultaneous attacks everywhere against the panic-stricken authorities of the Hetman.

The Germans retreated without offering battle. Around 15 November, Petlyura felt strong enough to declare the Hetman an outlaw. In this bloody chaos, two rival powers arose at once: the nationalists' Directorate and the Soviet government. Thus power became contested between the petty-bourgeoisie, urban middle classes and wealthy peasants on the one hand and the workers and poor peasants on the other.

The Directorate offered a programme which at first sight was very close to that of Bolshevism: expropriation of the large estates in favour of the peasants (the land was declared to belong to the tillers); an eight-hour working day; labour legislation; the rights of combination and strike; recognition of factory committees; 'exclusive authority of the labouring classes', i.e. workers, peasants and intellectuals; the speedy summoning of a Congress of Toilers.[36] Soviets were to be tolerated on condition that they limited their activity to the defence of local and corporate interests. This plausible revolutionism did not stand up for long to the shocks imparted by reality. The force of the revolution lay, in the cities, with the proletariat; in the country, after the hasty departure of the landlord, the gendarme, the Hetman and the German *Kommandatur*, it lay with the poor peasant, and the latter was immediately locked in struggle with the rich and middle peasantry who proclaimed that the revolution was over now and that the only remaining task was to consolidate private property against the threat of Bolshevism. Scarcely did Petlyura's soldiers plant the yellow-and-blue national flag in a town or village when the struggle flared out once again between them and the Soviet, the Communist party, the workers and the peasants. On the morrow of its ephemeral victory the democratic counter-revolution once more found itself placed between two dictatorships. And, as usual, it opted at the decisive hour in favour of military reaction. The political suicide of the Ukraine's Directorate is pitiful to behold. Here is the text of the declaration it addressed in January to the French commanders:

The Directorate places itself under the protection of France and requests the French authorities to guide it on all diplomatic, military, political, economic, financial and judicial questions until the conclusion of the struggle against Bolshevism. The Directorate looks to the generosity of France and the Allied powers in the event of any fresh settlement of the frontier and nationality questions.

According to the terms of the treaty signed at the end of January 1919 with France (represented by General d'Anselme), the Directorate declares the Ukraine to be an integral part of a single and indivisible Russia (so much for 'national independence'); it transfers its powers to a coalition cabinet (so much for 'the exclusive authority of the toilers'); it abandons the project of summoning a Labour Congress, promises to tolerate no Soviets on its territory, and entrusts the command of its troops to a

General Staff composed of General d'Anselme, the officer in charge of Allied troops, one representative from General Denikin's volunteer army, one representative of the Polish Legionaries and one representative of the Ukrainian republicans. In return, the Allies pledge themselves to keep the Ukrainians supplied with munitions.

The essence of this curious treaty was contained in two economic clauses, drafted in even harsher terms, which were divulged later in a note from Rakovsky to M. Stephen Pichon. France would acquire over the Ukraine, for five years, extended rights amounting to those over a protectorate; she would receive fifty-year concessions on the Ukrainian railways. The seriousness of these plans for controlling the Ukraine would shortly be revealed by the occupation of Odessa and Kherson by the French, Greeks and Rumanians (December–March), the activities of the French fleet in the Black Sea and the military engagements at Kherson and Sebastopol.

These efforts failed in view of the purely temporary character of the victories won by the nationalists who had sold out the Ukraine. Petlyura captured Kharkov on 23 November and Kiev on 14 December. But, meanwhile, a Congress of Soviets held at Ekaterinoslav had established the Bolsheviks' Government of Workers and Peasants under the presidency of Yuri Pyatakov.[37] The Reds rallied the middle peasants behind them and slowly won back the country districts; the towns were already theirs. The units of partisans were absorbed into the Red Army. The anarchists and their sympathizers, who were going from strength to strength under the powerful leadership of Makhno, lent their support to the Soviet power despite many hesitations; while the Allied forces in the Black Sea ports became subject to the influence of revolutionary contagion. It remains true that the Soviet government (with Rakovsky as the Chairman of the Council of People's Commissars) would beome installed in the big Ukrainian centres only around January and February, and even then not definitively. Nowhere else in Russia would the civil war be so hot and fierce as in the Ukraine, where fourteen governments replaced one another within four years. But, in this country, whatever men try to build against the proletarian revolution will prove to be built on sand: whatever blood they shed will be in vain, for always the sand will shift from beneath their feet.[38]

VICTORY OF THE WORKERS IN RUSSIA

'The shortest path to linking up with the revolution in Austro–Hungary passes through Kiev: just as the roads through Pskov and Vilna lead us to the German revolution.' These words of Trotsky define the character of the great offensives which the Red Army launches at this moment in the Baltic countries and in the Ukraine.

What are the forces in play at this moment? On 15 September the Red Army numbered 452,509 combat troops and 95,000 auxiliary or rearguard troops. By around the spring of 1919 it will reach and surpass the total of a million fighting men. Let us now try to reckon the enemy forces: between 30,000 and 40,000 Allied soldiers (British, American, Italian, Serbian and French) were in occupation of Archangel, Onega, Kem and Murmansk; 40,000 Finns were threatening Petrograd and Karelia; in Estonia, Latvia and Lithuania the White Guard resistance was 30,000 to 40,000 strong, with assistance from the German volunteer corps (30,000 men) under von der Goltz. The Polish army was being mustered, and would be over 50,000 in the spring. 20,000 French and Greek troops occupied Odessa and Kherson. 40,000 Czechoslovaks were spread out along the Trans-Siberian Railway. Three Japanese divisions and 7,000 Americans were operating in the Far East. To these 300,000 foreign bayonets there must be added the forces of Russia's counter-revolution: the Don Cossack army, 50,000 men; Kuban Cossacks, 80,000; Kolchak's 'national army', 100,000 (by the spring); Denikin's volunteer army in the Kuban, 10,000 to 15,000; the troops of the Ukrainian Directorate, 10,000 to 15,000; the counter-revolutionary bands of the Ukraine, over 20,000: all making a total of over 250,000 men.

The two sides were therefore scarcely equal. The forces of counter-revolution are far better armed and provisioned but are dispersed and divided, and often reluctant to fight (this is the case with the foreign troops). The Reds, passionately defending their single stretch of territory, have control over the vast railway network that converges towards Moscow. The Allies are disunited: the Reds enjoy the formidable unity of the dictatorship of the proletariat.

Red offensives are pushed to a victorious conclusion on all fronts. Pskov, the gateway to the Baltic countries, is taken on 20 November. Narva, the key to Estonia, falls on the 28th; Minsk, the capital of White Russia, on 9 December. The collapse of the Germans entails the bankruptcy of the nationalist semi-governments in the Baltic states. In Estonia, Lithuania and Latvia, Soviet governments are constituted and are granted recognition in a decree from Vee-Tsik on 23 December. Ufa is captured on 31 December; Kharkov and Riga, 3 January; Vilna, 8 January; Mittau on the 9th; Shenkursk, on the River Dvina in the Arctic Circle, and Ekaterinoslav, in the heart of the southern Ukraine, on the 26th. Through Uralsk, Orenburg and Iletsk, the way was clear again to link up with Turkestan, itself in the throes of civil war.

The return of the Ukraine and the Baltic states to the Soviet fatherland appears as the first international consequence of the German revolution. But, at the very hour when the Russian proletariat is making ready, through the force of its victories, to join hands with the proletariat of Germany, the latter is going down in defeat on the barricades of Berlin. The murder of Karl Liebknecht and Rosa Luxemburg signals the crushing of the proletarian revolution in central Europe.

DEFEAT OF THE WORKERS OF GERMANY

Here we can mark out only the principal stages of the German revolution. Following on the Armistice, the Socialist government of People's Commissaries showed two main concerns: to appease the demands of the Allies (for fear of a foreign occupation) and to contain Bolshevism, which heralded new crises for them. Social-Democracy consolidated itself in power as the party of social conservatism, of the defence of the capitalist order. In the country at large, the only real authority lay with the Workers' Councils (*Arbeiterräte*); but in these the Social-Democrats held overwhelming majorities. The Congress of Councils of Germany, meeting in Berlin from 16–25 December, rejected by 344 votes against ninety-eight a motion proposed by the Independent Social-Democrat Ernst Daümig, which affirmed the principle of 'power to the Soviets'; instead it transferred all authority to the People's Commissaries who were then instructed to convoke the Constituent Assembly. After this explicit abdication by the leading organizations of the working class, the sole opportunity for the revolutionary proletariat lay in an insurrectional initiative. If it had been organized and led by a Communist party, it would without doubt have been strong enough to win this crucial battle. Future possibilities seemed to offer the chance of a striking recovery. The Spartacus group, pursuing its propaganda for the dictatorship of the proletariat, was gaining in influence. The sailors from Kiel and the proletarians in the workers' quarters of Berlin dreamed only of following the example set by their Russian brothers. So long as these forces did not meet with a sanguinary repression, the social order was not safe. On this point, the Social-Democratic leaders found themselves in accord with the military chiefs. We will turn to the memoirs of Gustav Noske, the former editor of the Chemnitz Social-Democrats' *Volksstimme*, who, in the crisis of January 1919, at the head of the reactionary officer-corps, took on the task of butchering the working class that he represented in the Reichstag. We find the section devoted to the joint session of the government and the Central Executive of Workers' Councils, on 6 January 1919, and read:

> Nobody made any objection when I expressed the view that order would have to be restored by force of arms. The Minister of War, Colonel Reinhardt, drafted an order appointing as commander-in-chief General Hoffmann, who happened to be a short distance from Berlin at the head of several units of troops. It was objected that this general would be too unpopular among the workers.
>
> There we were, standing around in Ebert's office, all very nervous.

64. Pioneers of the party: a Marxist social gathering of 1893, with (left to right) Dr Simon (Bebel's son-in-law), Frau Simon, Klara Zetkin, Friedrich Engels, Frau Bebel, August Bebel, an unidentified youth, Frau Bernstein and Eduard Bernstein

Time was getting short: our people were gathering in the streets, demanding arms. I insisted that a decision must be taken. Somebody said: 'Perhaps you'll do the job yourself?' To this I replied, briefly and resolutely: 'I don't mind, somebody's got to be the bloodhound! I'm not afraid of the responsibility!' It was decided forthwith that the government would grant me extraordinary powers for the purpose of re-establishing order in Berlin. In his draft, Reinhardt struck out the name of Hoffmann and replaced it by mine. That is how I was appointed to the post of commander-in-chief.[39]

On the same day, a bloody provocation lit the tinder for the explosion. Emil Eichhorn, a courageous revolutionary of the USPD, had filled the post of Chief of the Berlin Police since the beginning of the revolution.[40] He had turned the *Polizeipräsidium* into a proletarian stronghold. Permanent conflict existed between this revolutionary headquarter, the government and the Social-Democratic commandant of Berlin, Otto Wels. A workers' demonstration which Eichhorn had authorized was met in the centre of Berlin, on Wels's orders, by volleys of firing from the troops. Noske's appointment was thus countersigned in the streets by the blood of sixteen dead workers. The government announced the dismissal of Eichhorn, who refused to resign a post he held not by grace of the ministers, but from the revolution.[41] These provocations precipitated the entry of the proletariat into the streets at a time when, as Karl Radek wrote to the Central Committee of the

recently formed Communist Party of Germany, the Soviets had
no more than a nominal existence, and had still not experienced
any political struggle which could release the power of the masses:
these, in consequence, remained in bondage to the influence of the
Social-Democrats. In these conditions it was out of the question to
think of the seizure of power by the proletariat.[42] Radek's advice
was to avoid the clash and to undertake an agitational campaign
unmasking the treason of the People's Commissaries and the
Executive of the Workers' Councils; the aim of this campaign
would be to seek fresh elections for the Councils, thus enabling
the revolutionary proletariat, as it prepared the offensive, to conquer the organs of power by legal means. The Central Committee
hesitated. Liebknecht was drawn along by the mass current: without consulting the Central Committee he signed a manifesto,
along with the Independents Schultze and Lebedour, deposing
Ebert and Scheidemann from the government. Not only was this
a grave lapse of discipline; it committed the very error that the
Bolsheviks had been stern enough to avoid during the troubles of
July 1917, when they held back the Petrograd masses who yearned
to engage in a premature battle against Kerensky. The inexperience of the proletariat's best leaders here became one of the prime
causes of its defeat. Liebknecht, without his party, initiated an untimely insurrection which he was unable to guide. The Central
Committee, surprised by the turn of events, issued neither insurrectionary slogans nor strategic directives. 200,000 determined
proletarians, a magnificent army ready for any sacrifice, who
would have been formidable if only they had been backed by a
well-led party, marked time for several long hours along the damp
avenues of the Tiergarten.[43] Nobody gave them any orders. No
Revolutionary Committee knew how to make use of their energy.
'The leaders were in conference, in conference, in conference,'
wrote Rosa Luxemburg on the following day. 'No, these masses
were not ready for the seizure of power, or their initiative would
have discovered others to stand at their head, and their first revolutionary action would have been to compel the leaders to stop
their interminable conferences in the *Polizeipräsidium*.'[44] The
testimony of Noske confirms this judgement: 'If these crowds,
instead of being led by prattlers, had possessed resolute leaders,
conscious of where they were going, they would have been masters
of Berlin before midday ...'[45]

No revolutionary leaders worthy of the name. A Communist
party that was too young, too inexperienced, without cadres,
without a Central Committee capable of daring initiative. Masses
of workers marching to do battle, but themselves too subservient
to the traditions of Social-Democratic discipline to make up with
their own action for the deficiencies of leadership and party. The
understandable impatience and great personal courage of Liebknecht, who is afraid to let the hour of action pass. Rosa, clear-

65. Noske

sighted but powerless. Thus did the immediate causes of defeat congeal together. The insurrection was quelled by Noske's monarchist bands, composed in the main of officers.

Karl Liebknecht and Rosa Luxemburg, denounced by *Vorwärts* as the instigators of civil war, were arrested on 15 January after the street-fighting, and perished the same day. Liebknecht was taken in the evening to the Tiergarten and shot from behind 'while attempting to escape'. Rosa Luxemburg was taken from the hotel where she was being detained, and put into a saloon car; there, her skull was shattered with a revolver-shot by Lieutenant Vogel. Her corpse was thrown into a nearby canal. The murderers of Liebknecht and Luxemburg went scot-free.

PRINKIPO

The defeat of Germany's proletarian revolution was reassuring to the Allies; indeed, they had made their own special contribution to it. The Spartacists of Berlin were actually taking on the whole capitalist world. Wilson, Clemenceau, Lloyd George, Orlando[46] and Foch (whose remark 'Better Hindenburg than Liebknecht' became well-known) gave discreet support to the 'Socialist' Noske, the Stinnes, the Krupps, the Groeners and Hoffmanns. The frontier of Bolshevism had now retreated from the Rhine to beyond the Vistula, where under Daszyński's Socialist government the Polish Republic was being established as another bulwark of the old Europe. However, the bloodbaths of Berlin brought no remedy for the social crisis that gripped the continent. The situation continued to be revolutionary in the defeated countries and tended in

66. German troops move in against the Spartacists, Berlin, 1919

67. Karl Liebknecht (centre) and Rosa Luxemburg at a party congress, Leipzig, 1909

that direction in the victor countries. France, Britain and Italy lived in anxiety over a demobilization which would throw into unemployment millions of embittered and weary workers; these, moreover, were used to handling grenades and were not inclined to take promises for an answer. The year 1919 was to be marked by events of immense importance: the Soviet Republic in Bavaria, the proletarian dictatorship in Hungary, the worsening of the crisis in Italy, demoralization of the French troops in Odessa, mutinies in the French Black Sea fleet. In addition, the difficulties of mounting an effective intervention were fully evident at the meeting of the Allies (Paris Conference) that was called to re-draw the map of the world after the ruin of the

Central Empires. Intervention could not bring all the fruits ex-pected of it – i.e. the restoration of capitalism in Russia – except at the cost of a fresh war which would probably be both long and harsh. But the state of morale in the victor-armies and the attitude of the working class in the belligerent countries on both sides made it clear that hostilities could not be re-opened on a large scale against the revolution of the toilers. Hence the hesitations of the Paris Conference before the Russian problem, which was only an isolated aspect – scarcely isolated, at that – of the international problem. Two tendencies came out clearly in the discussion. Clemenceau advocated a forceful policy, doubtless in the belief that a quick military victory was possible over Bolshevism. Lloyd George and President Wilson were more cautious: they envisaged long-term actions such as diplomatic sabotage, undeclared war, indirect war through bribed satellite states and blockades: it may be that they counted on the effects of famine, physical exhaustion and the degeneration of Bolshevism itself. These differences of opinion were complicated by conflicts of interest: of these last, the most serious was keeping the Americans and the Japanese neu-tralized, from fear of each other, in the Siberian Far East.[47]

Such is the explanation of the contradictory tendencies among the Allies, at the point when the defeat of the German revolution coincided with the victories of the Red Army. A radio message from the Paris Conference on 23 January 1919 invited all govern-ments enjoying a *de facto* existence on the territory of the former Russian Empire to send representatives to a peace conference which was to be summoned on the Island of Prinkipo, near Con-stantinople, in the presence of the Allies. On 4 February, the Soviet government notified the Great Powers of its agreement to the opening of negotiations, and showed itself as willing to offer a heavy price to gain peace. This amounted (or so it was assumed) to a continuation of the politics of Brest-Litovsk in transactions with the Allies, for the same reasons that had led to Brest-Litovsk. Chicherin's note stated, as some of its principal points:

The government of the Soviets declares that ... it is ready to make concessions to the powers of the Entente on the question of debts. It does not refuse to recognize its financial obligations to those of its credi-tors who are citizens of the Entente powers. ... It proposes to guarantee the payment of interest on the loans by a fixed quantity of raw materials. ... It is ready to grant, to citizens of the Entente powers, mining, forestry and other concessions, on condition that the internal running of these concessions does not interfere with the social and economic order of Soviet Russia. ... The fourth point, on which the Soviet government believes that the proposed negotiations might have a bearing, concerns territorial concessions: for the Soviet government does not wish to exclude in principle from the negotiations the question of the annexation by the Entente powers of certain Russian territories ...

This offer of annexations went a stage further even than Brest-

Litovsk politics: its causes doubtless have to be sought in the Berlin defeats. The limits of the retreat were, however, clearly defined; indeed, with the exception of the territorial concessions they still form the policy of the USSR, i.e. recognition of debts on certain conditions, economic guarantees for financial agreements, industrial concessions provided that these do not affect the Soviet regime. The very opening of negotiations at Prinkipo signified the Soviets' recognition of the counter-revolutionary states that were in the course of construction in Siberia, the Don country and the Caucasus. This was an extremely dangerous policy, which fortunately came to nothing owing to the response of the leaders of the counter-revolution, Kolchak and Denikin, doubtless taken on the advice of the Allied generals. Relying on the forthcoming spring offensives, they refused to reply to the offer of the Entente powers and to Chicherin's Note. That was a grave miscalculation on their part.

The objectives of the rulers of the Soviet Republic at this point were very simple: to gain time, to consolidate Soviet power even in a restricted and amputated terrain, maintaining there the focus of the proletarian revolution, and to keep future options open: 'gaining time by ceding some space if necessary', and allowing the European revolution, now increasingly imminent, to mature. Events since then have shown how far the Western proletariat was from matching the demands of the hour. The efforts of the revolutionary proletarians in the West would certainly not have been assisted by the crystallization of a number of counter-revolutionary states around a Soviet Russia mutilated by the terms of an onerous and humiliating peace. Consider the prospect of a Red Russia, deprived of the corn of the Kuban and Siberia, of the Donetz coal, of iron from the Ural, of oil from Baku, thrown back on her own resources by the inactivity of the Western proletariat: would such a Russia have succeeded later in conquering – or even in holding out against – a Siberia, a Caucasus, a White south in which capitalist states, more or less colonies of the Entente, would have become consolidated with the aid of the victorious powers? Through the intransigence of the White side, the dangerous diplomatic manoeuvrings of Lloyd George and Wilson turned out for the benefit of the Soviets. Once again it was demonstrated that the proletarian republic would not shrink from any sacrifice in order to declare peace to the world, even while its enemies were compelling it into a war to the death.

The failure of the Prinkipo proposals cost the Russian revolution three further years of heroic struggle. But it was through these struggles that the historic grandeur of the Republic was durably forged: the territory of the USSR became extended from the Gulf of Finland to the Pacific, from the Arctic Circle to Asia Minor, across one sixth of the globe. For the moment, the Allies continued to prepare their spring offensives, in Poland, Siberia,

Archangel, the Baltic lands, the Don region and the Kuban, and planned the encirclement of the Russian Commune with a ring of counter-revolutionary states. All this while, not one country dared to declare war formally upon the Soviets. This unconfessed war found an official form in the perfidy of the blockades. Beginning with the first months of 1919, not one letter, not one food parcel, not one package of goods, not one foreign newspaper could enter Red Russia, except as contraband across the lines of barbed wire.

11 · War Communism

1918 was the first year of the blockade. Russia's imports in 1914 were 936 million poods[1] and her exports 1,472 million: in 1917 they had fallen to 178 million and fifty-nine million respectively. In the Year One of the revolution imports were no more than 11.5 million poods and exports 1·8 million. For 1919 the figures would fall to zero. The effects of this total blockage of trade between Russia and the outside world were worsened by the dismembering of the country which, with two thirds of the population inside its boundaries, had only forty-five per cent of its grain, ten per cent of its oil production, eight per cent of its sugar output and twenty-three per cent of its cast-iron. Sixty per cent of the railway tracks were in the hands of the Whites. The destruction of transport was catastrophic.[2]

We have seen how the famine depopulated the large cities: Moscow and Petrograd had lost half of their population. Migration into the countryside, where food was easier to come by, was a general trend.

The decline of production was uninterrupted. It should be noted that this decline had already begun before the revolution. In 1916 the output of agricultural machinery, for example, was down by eighty per cent compared with that of 1913. The year 1917 had been marked by a particularly general, rapid and serious downturn. The production figures for the principal industries in 1913 and 1918 were, in millions of poods: coal, from 1,738 to 731 (forty-two per cent); iron ore from 57,887 to 1,686; cast-iron, from 256 to 31·5 (12·3 per cent); steel, from 259 to 24·5; rails, from 39·4 to 1·1. As a percentage of 1913 production, output of linen fell to seventy-five per cent, of sugar to twenty-four per cent, and of tobacco to nineteen per cent.[3]

The large enterprises failed more easily than the smaller ones, since they were much harder to keep supplied and were more closely dependent on the general level of production. The importance of small-scale concerns and of artisan craftsmen therefore grew visibly.

The railways, which were almost completely cut off from supplies of coal and oil, went over to burning wood, to the extent of seventy per cent of the whole system.

Wages doubled or trebled; the price of grain on the free market (which was illegal, but a necessary recourse for the proletariat for at least half of their foodstuffs) went up sevenfold. The part played by incomes other than wages in the workers' budget assumed a growing importance: from 3·5 per cent in 1913 to thirty-eight per cent in 1918. What were the sources of these extras?

Simply theft from factories and warehouses. The purchase of food absorbed seven tenths of the worker's earnings, instead of a half. It was this state of affairs that impelled the workers to return to the countryside. In December 1918, the factories of Kolomensk had no more than 7,203 workers on their books, as compared with 18,000. Even this roll-call was largely one of absentees: on one morning in April 1919, only 1,978 showed up for work out of the 5,779 on the books. The State, the Red Army and the party continued to drain off the best forces from this exhausted proletariat. Strikes provoked by the famine would multiply till they reached the great outbreak of the following spring (1919).

THE FINANCIAL SITUATION

The economy was, not surprisingly, in deficit. The extraordinary levies raised from the bourgeoisie played an appreciable role in the conduct of the civil war by sharpening class alignments, but yielded no substantial revenues to the State. The pace of events was too quick, and the resistance of individuals too entrenched, for that.

The war imposed extraordinary burdens upon the young republic. The army, the proletariat, officialdom, all had to be supported by the State, a total of thirty to forty million persons. Let us look at the national budget for 1918. The principal headings are as follows.

Income: 15,580 million roubles, of which 11,834 million are from taxes, in the proportions 68·9 per cent from direct taxes, 5·1 per cent from indirect and 1·9 per cent from customs dues. Expenditure:46,706 million roubles, subdivided as follows: Central State institutions take eight million (less than 0·1 per cent); Supreme Council of the Economy, Commissariats of Food, Finance and Agriculture 15,770 million (33·8 per cent); transport 8,428 million (eighteen per cent); public education 2,994 million (6·4 per cent); War Commissariat, 15,133 million (32·4 per cent). It will be noticed that the war costs as much as Food, Industry and Agriculture put together. The deficit is colossal: 32,000 million, twice the total income.

These figures reveal the disproportion between the State's needs and its resources. Its requisitions and issues of currency were ineffective in making up the deficit. Inflation reached fantastic proportions, unknown to previous history.[4] In November 1917 there were 18,917 million paper roubles in circulation; on 1 January 1918 there were 27,313 million and on 1 January 1919 61,265 million. In the meantime, the value of the rouble had gone down 230 times. The real value of all these thousands of millions was inescapably shrinking. The 27,313 million in circulation on 1 January 1918 represented a purchasing-power of 1,117 million gold roubles; the 61,265 millions circulating on 1 January 1919 represented no more than 266 million gold roubles.[5] Never had monetary circulation been more feeble; and never, in consequence, were exchanges between the socialized productive sector and the peasant-based free market more difficult.

Issues of notes in the year 1918 amounted to 33,952 million roubles, with a real value calculated at 523 million. The real value of the requisitioning undertaken for 1918–19 has been estimated at 127 million gold roubles.[6]

The inflation and the requisitions bore down particularly heavily upon the countryside, from which basic foodstuffs and raw materials had to be extracted. Conditions of life there, however, were still relatively better than those in the towns. Agricultural production suffered from the ills of the time least of all. Russia's total production was 12,000 million roubles before the war, fifty per cent from agriculture; it was now down to four to five thousand million, eighty per cent of this from agriculture.

The depreciation of the paper currency encouraged the general tendency towards exchanges in kind. Commerce became replaced by barter. Food and articles of prime necessity were distributed among the workers through the State, at nominal prices, as a kind of omen of the total abolition of money. Free public utilities were another first step in this direction.[7]

AGRICULTURE

Even before the revolution, the agricultural sector had suffered from the war. The main effect of the revolution was to ruin the large estates. Around 30,000 large proprietors were expropriated, but the peasants were in no position to resume the cultivation of the lands they had won. The disappearance of large areas of cultivation was a further cause which accentuated the decline of agrarian production.[8]

The results of the rural revolution are expressed in some eloquent statistics. The proportion of land in Russia cultivated by the peasants leaped from fifty-four to ninety-six per cent. The peasants became the real owners of virtually all the estates; but the war, the devastation of transport and the weak condition of industry prevented them from taking advantage of their gains.

A process of levelling among the peasantry was soon completed, with a rapid fall in the numbers both of rich and of poor. The number of farmers owning one horse rose from 43·8 to 79·3 per cent (as of 1920), with a corresponding decline in the proportions of those owning several horses or no horses.

Harvests fell dramatically. The cultivation of raw-material crops for industry was in serious peril, since no payment was being made for them.[9] Agriculture lost its commercial character, as the peasants tended increasingly to produce solely for their own consumption and no longer for the market, the State being in no position to supply any recompense for exchanges of corn. Anything they did sell went by preference on the illegal market, where they could get four times the price.

THE DIALECTIC OF ECONOMIC LIFE

We will try and trace the dialectic of events in the economic field. As we have noted, the decree of 14 May had effectively supplanted exchange by a policy of requisitioning. The few manufactured goods that could be spared for the countryside were given to the poor peasants as an inducement to assist the proletariat in confiscating the grain of the rich. This formed one of the decisive measures for the class war in the villages. Through it, the proletarian revolution at once became established in the countryside. Up till now it had interested only the working-class population: twenty million people. From now on it would interest the whole rural population except the kulaks: 130 million people. The chaotic struggles undertaken by the peasants throughout this period cannot obscure the significance of the fact that at all times, in all places, in battle after battle, they secured the final victory of the Soviets. The economic levelling which proceeded among them parallels this fact of politics and helps to explain it. The victory of the proletariat over the kulaks deprived the counter-revolution of its last economic base.

However, the civil war now sweeping through the townships and hamlets was another new factor assisting in the decline of agricultural output; the economic levelling was accompanied by the atomization of cultivated tracts. The sharpening crisis of agriculture, which struck first at the industrial crops – the least necessary for the peasants themselves, and the most dependent on exchange with the towns – reacted back on the size of the industrial sector by blocking its intake of raw materials.

In industry, measures of nationalization continued. The graph they describe is itself significant. In April there was one such measure, in May seven; from July to October the average rate was 170 a month. In June, 357 enterprises had been nationalized; in September, 860 (including whole industries: mining, transport, electricity, oil, rubber, sugar, etc.). This expropriation of industry, verging ever closer to a total nationalization, placed an increasingly numerous population of workers within the responsibility of the Socialist State, and compelled it hastily to establish a body of functionaries, managers and administrators who could not be recruited straight away from among the working class. The bureaucracy was born, and was rapidly becoming a threat.

The zigzags of party policy may be reviewed at this point. In April, Lenin (aware of the dangers of a rash socialization of the entire productive sector) was saying: 'If we go on expropriating capital at this pace, we shall infallibly be beaten.' He fought against the Left Communists, who advocated the most radical economic measures. But in June, the expropriation of all the main industries was undertaken as a riposte to foreign intervention. A decree instituting the tax in kind was passed in March. As in 1921, it would have pacified the countryside: but it was never implemented. By May, the dictatorship of food supplies was installed through the sheer necessities of scarcity, and carried the social war into the villages. Owing to the destruction of transport, the famine, the economic responsibilities of the State, and the imperative necessity to feed the proletariat (the living force of the revolution) and keep the war industries going, a rigorous rationing system had to be introduced, with all its consequences of bureaucracy and paper-work; the State monopoly of grain could endure no further weakening. From now on, the suppression of the private market was a task of urgency. But it was never carried through successfully. Economic life took on a dual form: the organized, socialized sector comprising large-scale industry, and the anarchic, clandestine sector, much bigger than the former, embracing most of agriculture and the artisan crafts. Every day, in every city, the forbidden markets assembled dense crowds in the public squares. The statification of production and consumption provoked, in retaliation, the creation of a whole illegal economy.

Speculation was answered by repression. Force was invoked to subdue the clandestine economic network. The latter defended itself by corruption. Corruption was met by terror. Nevertheless, the cities' sources of food, to the extent of two thirds, were found in the illegal market. Concessions had to be made to small-scale private initiatives: individuals were authorized to seek provisions for themselves in the countryside, to a limit of twenty-five kilos. This measure of relief for the general misery was costly: it added to the disorganization of work and of transport.

In February 1919, important measures in the progress towards a Socialist agriculture were set in hand (the organization of Soviet farms and of agrarian communes); a few days later, the Communist Party's Seventh Congress concluded that small peasant production was bound to continue yet for a long time, and took several measures which tended to support and restore it. (Ever since the Sixth Congress of Soviets, it had been decided to wind up the Committees of Poor Peasants and return to the normal rural Soviet institutions.) All the same, the problem of the countryside would only be resolved much later, in 1921, and even then provisionally, by the establishment of the tax in kind and the return to a free market.

PROLETARIAN INITIATIVES AND THE BUREAUCRACY

It was in these conditions that the proletariat sought to organize Socialist production and distribution, in other words to take economic power into its own hands. In the factories, workers' management committees ousted the capitalist and his technical–managerial staff. The expropriation of capital – industrial, commercial, real-estate[10] and rural – was so complete that the bourgeoisie became transformed, in the phrase used by one Russian economist, into a kind of ex-bourgeoisie in rags or 'lumpen-ex-bourgeoisie'. By contrast, it needed sustained efforts to flush out the petty-bourgeoisie from each one of their last economic strongholds in the cooperative system. The decree of 7 December nationalized the cooperative Moscow People's Bank: the bourgeoisie was refused the right to vote and be elected in cooperative societies. A final blow to petty commerce was dealt by the decree of 21 November which instructed the Food Commissariat 'to ensure provision for the population in all products and to replace the functions of private trade'. Many were the voices in the party which demanded the outright liquidation of cooperatives, 'the servitors of capitalism', and the total statification of distribution. This path would shortly be begun with the introduction of the compulsory cooperative system.

Industry was now managed by fifty-two centres of production (*glavki*), manned by worker committees in which the trade unions had a predominant influence: these succeeded in getting the war industries going non-stop and with increasing efficiency, despite appalling difficulties. At the end of the Year One, a change of heart took place among many of the intellectuals and technicians: an important minority of these joined the managerial councils of the Socialist State. The difficulties involved in the distribution of raw materials and fuel necessarily led to centralization, which was achieved only at the cost of a bitter struggle against separatist tendencies and local power centres. Centralization as a general line of policy, in the army, in transport, in provisioning, and even in the functioning of the party's machinery, was the outcome of the war. The revolution had begun with the slogan: 'Power, in all its fullness, to the Soviets.' Now, however, the play of local egoisms, the lack of competent personnel and the activity of troublemakers were setting in motion a reverse tendency, that leading towards a dictatorship of the centre, for the sake of the higher interests of the revolution.

Local Soviets could be seen demanding the abolition of the local branches of the centralized industrial administrations and trying to run everything for their own convenience within their own territories (e.g. Tambov). Separatist tendencies were so powerful at the periphery that the Soviet Republics of Estonia and Latvia proposed the opening of negotiations with the Council of People's Commissars in Moscow on commercial exchanges, and the conclusion of formal commercial treaties. One of the leaders of the Latvian Soviet government, Stuchka, demanded that the Russian Socialist Federation of Soviet Republics hand back the industrial equipment which had been evacuated from Riga.

The State was still so weak that, given the incompetence of the normal institutions for their work, it often became necessary to resort to the system of Extraordinary Commissions equipped with dictatorial powers. One Extraordinary Commission of this kind was set up to organize the provisioning of the army. Nothing but harm to the progress of centralization could come from the functioning of such Commissions.

In every administrative organ, the revolutionary proletariat found itself using a substantial corps of employees and functionaries belonging to the old petty-bourgeoisie of the cities. In one year, from the first six months of 1918 to the first six months of 1919, the membership of the only trade union for Soviet officials quadrupled, from 114,539 to 529,841. The general scarcity imposed both a census of consumers and a census of all available products. What techniques could be applied, what personnel could be employed? Everything had to be improvised from scratch, with personnel that were often corrupt and were in any case, by reason of their social origins, totally unfitted to grasp Socialist principles and the implacable necessities of the class struggle.

The mass of folk bent all their ingenuity into getting what they needed out of the stock of products; the party bent all its efforts to the task of allocation, as a first priority, to the army, the workers, the children and the mothers. But it entrusted the execution of its directives to bureaux who twisted them, while dubious elements in the population carried on massive fraud. Documents, minutes, government bonds, ration cards formed a phenomenal mass of paper, serving a variety of purposes: accounting, rationing, the classification of the populace into categories, the means of fraud and the livelihood of the corps of functionaries, who were hostile to the regime in their immense majority. Typical of the indignation against this bureaucracy was a slogan that we find in one journal: '*Up against the wall with the bureaucrats!*' (*Krasnaya Gazeta*, 21 October). The article was a denunciation of the characteristically criminal attitude of the hospital staffs to working-class people.

At the beginning of 1918 the organized forces of the proletariat reached the total of 115,000 Communist party members and 1,946,000 trade-union members; a year later, it was 251,000 Communists and 3,707,000 trade-unionists. The functionaries were thus far more numerous than the party membership; and they infiltrated too into the ranks of the party.

THE FIRST ATTEMPT TO ORGANIZE A SOCIALIST SOCIETY

The present work cannot include a description and analysis of the social system that was later, inaccurately, termed 'War Communism'. This system attained its full development only in 1919–20, i.e. beginning with the Year Two. We must, however, pay some attention to it in the form it presents during the winter of

1918–19. We can at least form a general idea of what it meant. In the years since then, the Russian proletariat has had to retreat on a number of fronts before the peasant masses, with their attachment to private property and freedom of trade;[11] the New Economic Policy or *Nep*, begun in 1921, has profoundly modified people's conceptions of the system which preceded it. The erroneous description 'War Communism' has now stuck: some theoreticians have defined it as a form of Communism in the sphere of consumption.[12] In reality, it was also an ambitious attempt to organize Socialist production. The Russian Communists, with their intense theoretical clarity and their skill in political manoeuvre, never thought simply of using expedients necessitated by war, valid only for a time of war: they thought of building towards the future, of starting a sweeping fulfilment of their Socialist programme. If the civil war, freshly kindled by foreign intervention, compelled them to get on with the job faster than they had anticipated, it was not because it imposed on them measures that were contrary to or grossly different from their intentions: it simply made the total application of the proletarian programme a *sine qua non* of safety. Only the intransigence and the audacity of their policies could ensure the victory of the workers' revolution.

So-called 'War Communism' was *a project for the organization of the Socialist society*, undertaken in the most difficult circumstances. On this point we accept the conclusions of the economist L. Kritsman, who proposed to define it as 'the organization of the natural economy of the proletariat'.[13]

The whole of the social structure was founded on production, at whose base was the industrial enterprise. Relations of work became the essential, primary relationships between men (instead of property relations or the relations between owners and non-owners). The trade unions, whose base cells were now the Factory Committees, were increasingly assuming managerial functions in production: in this process the direct management of production by the producers was beginning to be realized, and the organization of production began to be merged with the organization of the working class. From top to bottom of society's rungs, an exclusive and imperious class sense reigned. 'The bourgeois, outcast and despised, deprived of property and honour, has become a pariah' (Kritsman). On every wall the rule, borrowed from St Paul's epistle, 'He who does not work, neither shall he eat', was blazoned abroad. It was the suppression of parasitism, suppression of individualism in labour, the reign of collective methods in work and management.

This regime did spring out of the war, but out of the war between the classes: it proved that a proletarian revolution must realize itself in order to win. The more complete is its realization the more durable is its victory; nothing will kill it more quickly than moderation. But this social system was exhausted by the war: the project of an uncompromisingly Socialist organization of production was revealed as premature, through the isolation of the revolution within national boundaries, through the losses inflicted on the proletariat and through the immense numerical preponderance of petty producers for the market – the peasantry – over the industrial population. It would be just as irrational to blame the general decline of production upon 'War Communism' as it would be to hold War Capitalism, which enabled Germany to survive for several years, responsible for the famine and economic collapse which caused the final ruin of the Central Powers. The conquest of production by the proletariat was in itself a stupendous victory, one which saved the revolution's life. Undoubtedly, so thorough a re-casting of all the organs of production is impossible without a substantial decline in output; undoubtedly, too, a proletariat cannot labour and fight at the same time; but the very rapidity with which Socialist industry recovered in the USSR once the civil war was over shows that the methods of Socialism were not at fault here. The role of errors and exaggerations has to be assessed: but however important this may turn out to be, our general conclusions should need no modification.

The Russian proletariat managed a number of achievements: the formation of a powerful army, the development of war industries, the building of its own State. These substantial results encourage us to believe that, if international circumstances had proved somewhat more favourable, it would have not missed the opportunity to achieve successes of at least an equal order, in the sphere of Socialist production.

THE MENSHEVIKS CHANGE THEIR ATTITUDE.
THE PROLETARIAT AND THE MIDDLE CLASSES

The lessons of a year of struggle now brought results. Among the urban middle classes, whose antipathy to the proletariat had been long and ingrained, a new evolution could be seen. Many intellectuals at last declared themselves neutral; the bravest and most advanced rallied to the regime. The Central Committee of the Menshevik Social-Democratic party acknowledged, in an explicit resolution during October, that 'the revolution of October 1917 had been historically necessary' and constituted 'a factor in the international proletarian revolution'. In December, a conference of the Menshevik party officially reversed its old policy and condemned as counter-revolutionary the demand for the Constituent Assembly. It was a total retreat from the positions of democracy. The Menshevik Central Committee proclaimed that the forces of the party would mobilize for the defence of the Republic, and offered to come to an agreement with the Communist party. The sole Bolshevik response was a demand, unsuccessful as it turned out, that the Menshevik party should formally condemn those of its groups and members who had gone over to the counter-revolution. Restored to the All-Russian Soviet Executive, the Mensheviks would attempt to work for some time now as a loyal opposition. They were able to get a journal published in Moscow. 'We will legalize you,' Lenin told them, 'but we will keep State power *for ourselves alone.*'[14]

A similar movement was in evidence among the Social-Revolutionaries. Several members of the Samara government broke with their party, to move towards the Bolsheviks. A professor of the University of Petrograd, Pitirim Sorokin, a former S R deputy to the Constituent Assembly, announced in a brief but sensational letter to the press that he was giving up politics, where too many errors had a habit of getting committed. Lenin saw this declaration as 'a symptom of the evolution of a whole class, the petty-bourgeois democrats. One section will come over to our side, one section will remain neutral, while a third will deliberately join forces with the monarchist Kadets.' This evolution should be encouraged: 'A revolutionary proletariat must know whom to repress and with whom – and when and how – to come to an understanding. It would be silly and ridiculous to insist only on tactics of repression and terror against the petty-bourgeois democracy when the course of events is compelling them to turn to us.'[15] Anxious to give every support to this development, Lenin urged that the party should chase out of its ranks those false Communists from bourgeois intellectual circles who had entered it in the hope of sharing the spoils of power, and replace them by men of a different quality who only yesterday had been the conscious foes of the proletariat. This courageous distinction between the nonentity who had jumped in at the first chance and the convinced adversary who lays down his arms is worth remembering. Lenin added a warning that a few reverses against the Bolsheviks would be enough to provoke the petty-bourgeoisie, a class doomed to perpetual hesitations, to start vacillating back again in its old directions.[16]

The same topic occasioned a long exposition from Lenin on the relationships between the proletarian revolution and the petty-bourgeoisie.

We had to exercise the dictatorship of the proletariat in its harshest form. It took us several months to break through a whole epoch of illusions. But if you look at the history of the west European countries, you will see that they did not get through these illusions even in decades. We had to dispel the petty-bourgeois illusion that the people are an integral unity and that the will of the people can be expressed in some way other than through class-struggle. If we had made any concessions to petty-bourgeois illusions, to illusions about the Constituent Assembly, we would have destroyed the proletarian revolution in Russia. We would have sacrificed the interests of the world revolution to narrow national interests.

The terror had been born from the conflict between proletarian internationalism and the patriotism of the middle classes. Now it was necessary to seize the opportunity to pass on to other methods. Otherwise, 'inflexibility will become sheer stupidity'.

The intellectuals lived a bourgeois life. ... When they swung towards the Czechs, our slogan was: terror. Now that there is this change of heart, our slogan must be one of *reconciliation*, the establishment of good neighbourly relations. ... We cannot build our state if we do not utilize such an important heritage of capitalist culture as the intelligentsia. We can now treat the petty-bourgeoisie as a good neighbour under the strict control of the State. ... We tell the petty-bourgeois democracy: we are standing firm. We have always known that you were a weak lot. But we don't deny that we need you, because you are the only educated group in the country.

In regard to the middle peasantry, another petty-bourgeoisie and the most numerous of all, Lenin's doctrine is that these will never become Socialists out of conviction, only when they see that there is no other way. 'No amount of decrees can transform small-scale production into large-scale: we must do it bit by bit, winning credibility, through the actual course of events, for the inevitability of Socialism.'[17]

LITERARY LIFE

The change of heart among the advanced petty-bourgeoisie found striking parallels in literary circles. It may be said that Russia's writers had been unanimously hostile to Bolshevism. We have already seen the attitude of Maxim Gorky, despite his long years of friendship with Lenin. We have seen him attacking the 'cruel Socialist experiment of Lenin and Trotsky' which, it appeared, could lead only 'to anarchy, to the unleashing of the base instincts ...'. Gorky was now one of the first to rally to the Soviet regime, acknowledging the greatness of the revolution and the necessity to defend and serve it. He issued an appeal to all:

The experiment now undertaken by the Russian working class and by those intellectuals who have fused spiritually with it, this tragic experiment which will perhaps drain Russia to the last drop of her blood, is one of greatness, from which the whole world can learn. Almost every people in its time feels a Messianic mission, feels itself called to save the world, to breathe new life into its best forces. Come with us in our journey towards the new life for which we labour: come, without sparing us, without sparing anything or anyone, among all the sufferings and all the errors ...

Leonid Andreyev, Ivan Bunin, D. Merezhkovsky, A. Kuprin, the most influential prose-authors of Russia, who had all cut a revolutionary figure under Tsardom, remained incurably hostile. But the poets (and this is a remarkable fact) reacted to the profound meaning of the revolution, in a rich display of brilliant intuitions.

The greatest Russian poets rallied in the space of a few months, and gave the revolution a body of literature unique in its power. Valeri Bryusov, a man steeped in classical culture, hailed the advent of the righteous barbarians who were destined to renew civilization. Alexander Blok, a disciple of the mystic Soloviev, wrote the most popular and the purest masterpiece of the heroic years, *The Twelve*: twelve Red Guards are journeying through night and snow, weapons in their hands, and ahead of them – unknown to them – there goes the invisible Christ, crowned with roses.[18] This Christian conception of the revolution is found again in the Symbolist Andrei Byely's *Christ Lives Again*, and in the poems, pervaded by Orthodox mysticism, of Nikolai Klyuev and Sergei Essenin. In 1919, with the exception of Gorky, all the great writers of Russian prose are either counter-revolutionary or very hostile; almost all the great poets have rallied to the revolution.

68. Maxim Gorky

These great exceptions apart, literary production was interrupted, and ceased. Any writers who wrote at all devoted their energies to politics.[19]

Among the working class and in the party, the movement of the *Proletkults* (proletarian-culture circles) was becoming extended. The ambition of these circles was to renovate the whole of human culture in conformity with the aspirations of the proletariat. They discussed serious problems and in the larger cities formed lively groups who met to concern themselves with poetry, the theatre and literary criticism. The only outcome of the movement would lie in its encouragement of a certain number of poets, who were often to wind up in the usual grooves of the factory, victorious labour and proletarian heroism.

The theoreticians of Communism were themselves so absorbed by action that in the course of 1918, apart from articles for the press and speeches delivered to large meetings, they produced only a few thin booklets. The most outstanding of these were: N. Lenin, *The Proletarian Revolution and the Renegade Kautsky*; L. Trotsky, *The Revolution of October*, a historical sketch commissioned by the Central Committee; and the pamphlets of K. Radek on *The German Revolution*.

EDUCATION, SCIENCE AND ART

The civil war raged its way through the intellectual order as well. After Alexander Blok had written *The Twelve*, literary men refused to shake his hand. Compromise with the Bolsheviks still spelt infamy to most intellectuals. The Academy of Sciences, almost in its entirety, immured itself in a state of wilful hostility towards the Soviet government. It would take years of obstinate struggle before the passive resistance of the teaching profession in the universities could be overcome. The overwhelming majority of the school-teachers were hostile; their trade union had to be purged and reorganized inch by inch; influence in the schools was fought for, and won, step by step.

Under the direction of Lunacharsky,[20] the Commissariat of Public Education set going a radical transformation of the educational system. The old structure with its inferior schools reserved for the people and its high schools reserved in practice for the bourgeoisie, was replaced by the common labour-school; the old syllabuses, which trained subjects for the Tsar and believers for the Orthodox Church, were replaced by a necessarily improvised scheme which was anti-religious, Socialist and based upon the educational role of work – the aim was to train producers who would be conscious of their role in society. Projects were drawn up to unify the school and the workshop. In order to implement sex equality from childhood onwards, co-education was frequently introduced in the schools. But everything had to be organized from scratch. The old textbooks were good only for burning. A large proportion of the old teaching staff resisted, sabotaged, refused to understand, and waited for the downfall of Bolshevism. The schools were appallingly barren of equipment: paper, exercise books, pencils, pens were all scarce. Hungry children in rags would gather in winter-time around a small stove planted in the middle of the classroom, whose furniture often went for fuel to give some tiny relief from the freezing cold; they had one pencil between four of them; and their schoolmistress was hungry.

69. Alexander Blok

In spite of this grotesque misery, a prodigious impulse was given to public education. Such a thirst for knowledge sprang up all over the country that new schools, adult courses, universities and Workers' Faculties were formed everywhere.[21] Innumerable fresh initiatives laid open the teaching of unheard-of, totally unexplored domains of learning. Institutes for retarded children were founded; a network of institutions for pre-school infants was created; the Workers' Faculties and the special short courses placed secondary education within the grasp of the workers. Soon afterwards the conquest of the universities was to begin. In this period too, the museums were enriched by the confiscation of private collections: extraordinary honesty and care characterized this expropriation of artistic riches. Not one work of any significance was lost. In those troubled days a number of precious collections (notably, some of those at the Hermitage) had to be evacuated: they all reached their destination safely. The life of the scientific laboratories struggled on heroically. Sharing in the privations of the community, severely rationed, without lighting or (in winter) fuel and water, scholars of all political loyalties nearly always carried on as usual with their work.

Every evening the theatres, now nationalized, presented their customary repertoire, but to a new sort of audience. The ballet companies, organized for the delight of an aristocracy long since shot, gave their performances in the midst of the terror; the gold-vaulted theatres were thronged with working men and women, with young Communists, their skulls shaved as a precaution against typhus-carrying fleas, and with Red soldiers on leave from the front. And with the same memorable voice that had thundered *God Save The Tsar* in times gone by, Chaliapin sang *The Song of the Bludgeon* to assembled trade-unionists.

During festivals, the public squares were decorated by Expressionist painters. Monuments to the heroes of the French Revolution and to the Socialist pioneers were erected in wood or plaster. Most of these works have since disappeared: they were in any case mediocre.

The press had now lost the richness and variety of democratic times. Little by little, it became reduced to three sorts of organ obeying a solitary inspiration: the organs of the Soviets (*Izvestia*, or *Monitor*, in the capitals), the organs of the Communist party (the two *Pravdas*, or *Truth*), and those of the trade unions.

LIFE AND MANNERS

The winter of 1918–19 was frightful in the large cities that were ravaged by famine and typhus and deprived of fuel, water and illumination. The water and sewage pipes froze up inside the buildings. Families would crowd together around the little stoves that were nicknamed *boorzuiki*, a term ironically derived from 'bourgeois'. Old books, furniture, doors and floor-boards were used in lieu of firewood. In Petrograd and Moscow, most of the mansions constructed in wood went for fuel. Through the interminable nights of the Russian winter all lights were kept down to a flicker. Water-closets no longer worked: piles of excrement accumulated in the court-yards, shielded by constant snow-falls but storing up epidemics for the spring. Queues hung about aimlessly in front of the cooperatives; huge illegal markets, interrupted by police-raids, assembled in the squares. Here the survivors of the ex-bourgeoisie came to sell off the relics of their fortunes. The inevitable speculation was combated by regular house-searches and seizures of property.

The weakest were slowly being killed off by the blockade. The dictatorship managed the impossible in its efforts to succour its first priorities, the workers, the army, the fleet and the children. The sections most cruelly affected by the famine were the former wealthy and well-off classes. It was not a rare spectacle to see old people collapse in the streets for want of food. Mortality-rates rose sharply, especially among children and the old: the number of suicides, on the other hand, sensibly diminished.

The workers had chased the dispossessed bourgeoisie out from their mansions, and now installed themselves in the modern residences of the once-wealthy quarters. Each building, Bukharin wrote, must be populated by proletarians in arms and become a citadel of the revolution. Unfortunately, even the most comfortable appointments of the bourgeois living-quarters often proved impossible to adapt to the needs of their new occupants. In the cities, depopulated as they were, there was thus a shortage of suitable buildings for children's homes, schools and communal dwellings: the architects of the old social order had had quite different needs in mind.

The Soviets instituted compulsory labour for the bourgeoisie in the form of public-service brigades. This service was, as it turned out, most successfully evaded. In late September no more than 400 fit ex-bourgeois could be found in Petrograd for 'rearguard labour'. Requisitions of warm clothing were made, with each bourgeois compelled to hand in one warm suit.

The legal recognition of free union between the sexes, the easing of divorce, the legalization of abortion, the complete emancipation of women, the ending of the authority of heads of families and of religious sanctions: these did not produce any real weakening of family ties. This destruction of old impediments made private life simpler and healthier, and rarely provoked any crises. In Petrograd and Moscow, criminality (as strictly defined) was down to a peace-time level. Prostitution never disappeared completely, but the disappearance of the rich classes who were its clients reduced it to relative insignificance.

Religious life went on much as usual even though many counter-revolutionary priests had fallen foul of the Cheka. The clergy still divided itself into no more than two factions: the partisans of active resistance, whose leader was the Patriarch Tikhon, and the partisans of passive resistance. The Communist Party and the Council of People's Commissars affirmed repeatedly that the liberty of religious believers would not be interfered with.

Conditions of life varied noticeably from one region to another. All the cities were plunged into darkness once evening drew in. Life was austere and tranquil in Petrograd, the most famished and most imperilled of the towns. The same privations seemed to be experienced more neurotically in Moscow, a capital already bureaucratic and lacking the tonic atmosphere of the front line. The cities were hives of the starving. The towns of the Ukraine lived under a cloud of terror, the prey of warring bands, ceaselessly plundered, fleeced and devastated by new occupying forces: night over Kiev was filled with cries of panic. There were times when the real masters of Odessa appeared to be the bandits.

The famine was, however, less acute in the Ukraine. The rural areas were less troubled by hunger, but had to become quite self-sufficient since they were now thrown back entirely on their own resources.

THE FIRST ATTEMPT TO ORGANIZE A SOCIALIST SOCIETY

An observer who travelled through Russia at this moment would have gathered the impression, at once striking and misleading, of a general hostility manifested by the populations towards the Soviet power. This antagonism was a very real one among the expropriated classes and in most of the middle class. The change of heart we have described, important as it was, still showed itself only among the most advanced and articulate elements in the petty-bourgeoisie. The petty-bourgeois masses in the countryside were too close to the kulak in their general outlook not to feel threatened when he was attacked; in the towns, the same masses had been living off trade and other functions close to the bourgeoisie proper, and faced an apparently hopeless situation. In many areas they were more numerous than the proletariat, which had been eaten away by the civil war. And we have already seen how the social composition of the working-class population was being changed.

This class was still the only element of the population on whose loyalty the revolution could reckon. But it was suffering excessively. The individual worker saw only the narrow horizons of his own life; he was often lacking in the education and information that would have enabled him to see the necessary connections between facts, to entertain broader perspectives and larger consequences; and his instinct for self-preservation resisted the higher demands of the collective when sacrifices were demanded. The workers' sufferings were too great for them to desist from complaining, from recriminating, sometimes from despairing altogether. The agitation of the anti-Soviet parties was skilful in exploiting these feelings. If the Russian working class still held fast, if it knew how to triumph, the honour of this achievement belongs to the Communist party above all.

This party still numbered no more than 250,000 members: but those who came to it in these times were selected by history itself. Adventurers too, it is true, flocked in under its banner, hoping to fasten on the benefits that usually go with power. This minority of false Communists, though statistically negligible, did much harm since they helped to discredit local Soviet administrations by their abuses: in an appreciable measure they facilitated the conquest of the Ukraine by Denikin (for, naturally, they made sure to go where the grain was). Nevertheless, it remains true that the overwhelming majority of workers who joined the party voluntarily mobilized for the fronts of the civil war. And this meant that they accepted every conceivable risk.

The working class often fretted and cursed; sometimes it lent an ear to the Menshevik agitators, as in the great strikes at Petrograd in the spring of 1919. But once the choice was posed as that between the dictatorship of the White generals and the dictatorship of its own party – and there was not and could not be any other choice – every fit man that remained took his rifle and came to stand in the silent line before the windows of the local party offices.

At this moment, the party fulfilled within the working class the functions of a brain and of a nervous system. It saw, it felt, it knew, it thought, it willed for and through the masses; its consciousness, its organization were a makeweight for the weakness of the individual members of the mass. Without it, the mass would have been no more than a heap of human dust, experiencing confused aspirations shot through by flashes of intelligence – these, in the absence of a mechanism capable of leading to large-scale action, doomed to waste themselves – and experiencing more insistently the pangs of suffering. Through its incessant agitation and propaganda, always telling the unvarnished truth, the party raised the workers above their own narrow, individual horizon, and revealed to them the vast perspectives of history. After the winter of 1918–19, the revolution becomes the work of the Communist party. We do not wish to imply that the role of the masses in the revolution was slighter simply because it was very different from what it had been at the year's beginning; but all that the masses now accomplished was accomplished only through the medium of the party, just as a highly differentiated living organism senses the external world and acts upon it only through its nervous system.

The consequence is that the party undergoes, in a certain sense, a transformation: a rigorous adaptation to its new functions and to the necessities of the hour. Discipline in it becomes, increasingly, stricter: a strictness made imperative through action, through the inner purge to neutralize alien influences which would otherwise exert a dominating power. The party is truly the 'cohort of steel' of a later description. All the same, its thinking is still very lively and free. It welcomes the anarchists and Left SRs of yesterday. The prestige of Lenin has grown even further, since the attack that shed his blood and following the confirmation of his predictions in the German revolution; but his simplicity is such that no one is afraid to contradict or criticize him. His personal authority is solely that of an intellectual and moral pre-eminence, universally acknowledged.

Nobody is afraid to contradict Lenin or to criticize him. His authority was so little imposed, the democratic manners of the revolution were still so natural, that it was a matter of course for any revolutionary, no matter how recent a recruit, to express himself frankly in the presence of the man who headed the party and the State. Lenin was more than once criticized unsparingly, in factories or conferences, by totally unknown people. He listened to his contestants coolly and replied to them in a common-sense manner. When sharply attacked in 1920, at a meeting of Executive

Committees of the Moscow Gubernia on 15 October, with a large attendance of peasants, he began his reply by saying:

> I have noticed from the beginning that you have come along with a very strong urge to pull the central government 'down the banks'. That would be a useful thing to do, certainly, and I feel it is my duty to listen to everything that anyone has said against the government and its policies. And I think it would be wrong for anyone to close the debate ...[22]

The party's old democratic customs now give way to a more authoritarian centralization. This is necessitated by the demands of the struggle and by the influx of new members who have neither a Marxist training nor the personal quality of the pre-1917 militants; the 'old guard' of Bolshevism is justly determined to preserve its own political hegemony.

A new moral law is generated within the party and, through the extension of its activity, becomes the law of the society now in travail. A law for workers and fighters, it is based on the concept of the revolutionary mission of the proletariat. Necessity, utility, conformity with the aim pursued, solidarity are its first principles; it knows no better justification than success, than victory; it demands the continual subordination of individual interests to the general interest. Every Communist, every participant in the revolution feels himself to be the humblest servant of an infinite cause. The highest praise that can be bestowed on him is to say that he 'has no private life', that his life has fused totally with history. At the command of the party, he was yesterday an army commissar, an educator of men in the front line; today he is a Chekist, merciless as the directives he receives from his Committee; tomorrow, he can be seen out talking to the peasants in the country districts (at the risk of being murdered by nightfall), or running a factory, or conducting some dangerous secret mission behind the enemy's lines. There is not one militant who does not fulfil two, three, five or six different duties at once, who does not incessantly change them from one day to the next, upon the party's orders.It is the party that does everything. Its orders are not to be discussed. 'Conformity with the aim pursued' governs all actions.

The moral health of the party is proven in its absolute honesty. It does not acknowledge the conventions of deceit, the double-talk, the old confidence trick of the two ideologies (one for 'the *élite*', the other for 'the masses'), the divergence between what is thought and what is said, or between what is said and what is done. We were living off plain, clear ideas, ideas of a transfixing simplicity. Ideas, slogans and actions are one: a formidable unity which is both the cause and the consequence of an unswervingly proletarian line of politics. For the source of the social lie is simply the desire to satisfy, or at any rate to appear to satisfy, social interests which are actually incompatible.

LENIN AGAINST KAUTSKY

The principal work of N. Lenin from this period (*The Proletarian Revolution and the Renegade Kautsky*) is devoted, as its title would indicate, to a polemic against the old theoretician of Social-Democracy who had just published a short book in Vienna on *The Dictatorship of the Proletariat*.

Lenin pays close attention to the new twists which Kautsky gives to the Marxist teachings on the State and the dictatorship of the proletariat. Operating within the field of an obscurely pure theory which opposes the ideal dictatorship of the majority to the dictatorship of parties and persons, Kautsky tried to eliminate any notion of revolutionary violence by recalling that Marx entertained the hypothesis of a peaceful revolution for England. Lenin follows him step by step in the argument, tirelessly recalling the most elementary truths of the class struggle: the role of the State as the instrument of domination by one class, the necessity to break the expropriated capitalists' resistance, the falsity of bourgeois democracy which is only a mask for capital's dictatorship, and the authentically democratic character of the proletarian dictatorship. We have seen these ideas live in a year of revolution. Let us merely note here what judgements Lenin delivers on the revolution now in progress.

Is it a bourgeois revolution, as Kautsky declares, destined ultimately to open the way to a capitalist development in Russia?

Beginning with April 1917 ...[23] we publicly declared to the people that the revolution could no longer stop at this stage [at the objectives of the bourgeois revolution] for the country had marched forward, capitalism had progressed, devastation had reached fantastic proportions which demanded (whether one like it or not) progress towards Socialism. For *there was no other way* of advancing, of saving the war-weary country or of relieving the sufferings of the working and exploited people.[24]

For the first time, a revolutionary Marxist was showing how the misery that was born from the imperialist war impelled the transition to Socialism. Speaking in December before the First Congress of Committees of Poor Peasants, Lenin returned to this topic in order to demonstrate the impossibility of a return to an agriculture run on the old individualist work-techniques: 'The war has left us only want and ruin. It is impossible to live in the old way, and the waste of human strength and labour that goes with small-scale peasant cultivation cannot continue. ... Collective farming will treble the productivity of human labour.'[25] These ideas, inspired by a straightforward proletarian realism, were quite contrary to the traditions of the Second International, which envisaged the Socialist revolution as something to be achieved at the peak of capitalist development, in a society that had reached a high degree of affluence. The traditional viewpoint of scientific

Socialism was revealed now as Utopian, but it took Lenin's audacious sense of reality to think of justifying Socialism in terms of the heritage of misery left by a bankrupt capitalism.[26]

He replied to Kautsky:

Our revolution is Socialist. First we fought with *the whole* of the peasantry against the monarchy, the landlords and medievalism (and that revolution was bourgeois-democratic). Then we fought with the poor peasants, the semi-proletarians and all the exploited against capitalism – including the rich peasants, the kulaks and the speculators – and to that extent the revolution became a Socialist one.[27]

Lenin's assessment of the Brest-Litovsk treaty and the German revolution may be quoted here:

If we had not concluded peace at Brest-Litovsk we would have handed power over to the Russian bourgeoisie and done the greatest possible damage to the world Socialist revolution. At the cost of national sacrifices, we have preserved an international influence of such scope ... that the two imperialisms have become weakened and we have become stronger and begun the creation of a real proletarian army.

... The German workers would have won even greater successes if they had made their revolution *without considering* national sacrifices (it is solely in this that internationalism consists), if they had stated (and proved *by deeds*) that the interests of the world revolution take precedence for them over the integrity, security and tranquillity of their own national State.

The biggest misfortune and the biggest danger for Europe is that it has *no* revolutionary party. It has parties of traitors like the Scheidemanns, the Renaudels, the Hendersons and the Webbs, and servile characters like the Kautskys. But it has no revolutionary party.[28]

70. Karl Kautsky

THE STATE OF THEORY. AT THE THRESHOLD OF THE YEAR TWO

Let us summarize the main ideas of the time.

The era of imperialist wars and of international proletarian revolution was opened by the Great War of 1914–18; a return to capitalist stability had become impossible in the countries which had been led into the abyss through the development of finance capital; the task of rescuing, in a devastated Europe, the heritage of a threatened civilization now fell to the revolutionary proletariat. The struggle between the workers' revolution and the dying capitalist order will be lengthy, and marked by setbacks; the proletariat's victories may well be followed by defeats and by restorations of capitalism; but its reverses will prepare the ground for final victory. Already, in the countries defeated in the war, there are rumblings of revolution. The victorious countries have won some time: but they will be unable either to re-establish their production, now gravely affected, or to guarantee their labouring masses that minimum of prosperity which is necessary to social stability. The old world is doomed. Under the well-aimed blows of the proletariat, the capitalist–imperialist system has snapped at its weakest point, in a backward country only recently industrial-ized. And this was possible because the system here was weakest; because the proletarian party had been moulded here through Marxist intransigence, the struggle against despotism and the ex-perience of 1905; because the Socialist revolution benefited from a bourgeois revolution which, though necessary, was feeble and tardy, unable to complete itself; because on the ruins of the Tsarist regime the Russian proletariat found itself faced only with an inexperienced, disarmed bourgeoisie which had not had the time to constitute its own class-State; because the war did not allow the capitalist states of the West to intervene on the side of the Russian bourgeoisie effectively and in time. To this concurrence of circumstances the victory of the proletariat in Russia is due.

From now on the Republic of Soviets is the principal centre of the proletarian revolution: if it succumbs, the chances for the Western proletariat's victory will worsen, the defeat of capitalism will be delayed; but if, on the other hand, the proletarian revolu-tion is suppressed and beaten in the West, the Soviet Republic will be in danger of perishing. Its fate is inseparable from that of the international proletariat. 'We shall perish,' Lenin told the Moscow Soviet on 23 April 1918, 'unless we can hold out until we receive powerful support from workers who have risen in revolt in other countries.'[29] And again:

You know that it is much harder for them to start the revolution in the Western countries than it was for us because the workers there are in the presence not of a rotten autocracy but of the most unified and most cultured capitalist class; but you know that the revolution there has begun, that it has gone beyond the frontiers of Russia and that our chief assistance, our chief hope, is the proletariat of western Europe, and that the world revolution, our essential support, has begun to move.[30]

'I must tell you,' he added a few days later, 'that given a proper distribution of grain and other goods, the Soviet Republic can hold out for a very, very long time.'[31]

It was a matter of holding out, and at the same time converting Socialism *into a reality*. All the main measures of the regime, which a few years later, after the retreat of the proletariat before the rural petty-bourgeoisie (*Nep*, in 1921), would improperly be called 'War Communism', were considered to form the begin-nings of the Socialist order whose completion the international revolution would render possible. Two years later, in 1920, Bukharin would publish a bulky text on the organization of Socialist production through the paths and methods followed hitherto (*Economics of the Transition Period*); *Nep* was not en-visaged in it. Lenin, in a speech for May Day (in 1920) said, 'We shall work for decades, without respite, to make collective volun-tary labour [the *unpaid* labour of 'Communist Saturdays'] a matter of custom and habit. ... We shall make the rule "From each according to his ability, to each according to his need" enter the consciousness of the masses.'[32]

These ideas, which in the spring of 1919, at the foundation of the Third International, constituted the prevailing opinions, formed an accurate and powerful whole: as, indeed, they still are. For there are no predestined victories in the class struggle. The triumph of the proletariat in the aftermath of the war was just as possible as the victory of the bourgeoisie, and perhaps even more probable. The fact that neither the bourgeoisie nor the international proletariat brought off a decisive victory does not allow us to conclude the inevitability of the outcome. The working class had the worst of the battle in central and south Europe (Germany, Austria, Hungary, Italy, Bulgaria), but nothing supports the conclusion that their defeat in these countries was always a certainty. The non-existence or inexperience of the Communist parties and the fatal role of reformist Socialism (which, at the most crucial moment, came to the aid of the capitalist regime) show on the contrary that the poor development of the class consciousness of the proletariat was one of the principal causes of this defeat. In this epoch of social war, hope for the rapid development of proletarian class consciousness was more than legitimate, it was absolutely right and necessary. The world bourgeoisie got the worst of the battle within the boundaries of the old Russian Empire. But the victory of the Russian proletariat, due in the last resort to the resistance of the workers in the West against the anti-Soviet intervention, was also far from inevitable. In order to put it seriously in jeopardy, all that would have sufficed would have been a few political errors, a few hesitations, the disappearance of a few men. The struggle of the classes throws into combat masses of human beings: all other factors being equal, victory rests with the firmest, the most conscious, the most decisive.

At the end of Year One, the class war is engulfing the whole of Europe; on the Russian sector of the front the workers are winning; the struggle is still indecisive in central Europe and the Balkans; the proletarian offensive is maturing in Italy; on the quiet sectors of France and Britain the bourgeoisie is preparing intervention in Russia and, if necessary, in Germany. *The proletarian revolution is international.* Starting out from Petrograd and Moscow, it is shaking all Europe, is unsettling America and is about to awaken Asia.

The Allied governments, without daring to announce it publicly for fear of their own peoples, are engaged in hole-and-corner preparations for the great offensives of the spring against the Soviet Republic. Two counter-revolutionary states are being organized under their protection in Siberia and south Russia. Kolchak is to march on the Urals, on the Volga, possibly on Moscow; Denikin is to invade the Ukraine and advance on Moscow; Rodzhyanko[33] and Yudenich,[34] based on Estonia and supported by a British naval squadron, will attack Petrograd, while Finland, if the overtures go through successfully, will give the city its *coup de grâce*. The British will come down the Dvina from Archangel, the French, the Rumanians and the Greeks will occupy the Black Sea ports. ... Such are the vast designs now being hatched in the ministries of Paris and London,[35] where the defeat of Bolshevism is taken as assured. And it is there that the statesmen make their biggest mistake, for it has still not dawned on them that a new era has begun.

Vienna, Leningrad, Dietskoye Seloe, 1925–8

Notes

Except for the notes to the Introduction and Postscript, material added to Serge's own notes by the present editor appears in square brackets.

Introduction

1 Victor Serge, *Memoirs of a Revolutionary* (London, 1967), pp. 261, 263.

2 Victor Serge, *De Lénine à Staline* (Paris, 1937), p. 15. The English translation of this work, *From Lenin to Stalin* (New York, 1937), wrongly dates the composition of this passage as 1919.

3 Serge, *Memoirs of a Revolutionary*, pp. 69, 71–2.

4 Quoted in Daniel Guérin, *L'Anarchisme* (Paris, 1965), pp. 113–14, 189. The anarchist confidant, Gaston Leval, promptly published this critical judgement of the regime side by side with Serge's current eulogies of the Soviet state, terming the latter 'conscious lies'.

5 See e.g. Noam Chomsky, 'Objectivity and Liberal Scholarship', in *American Power and the New Mandarins* (London, 1970); Daniel and Gabriel Cohn-Bendit, *Obsolete Communism: The Left-wing Alternative* (London, 1969); Paul Cardan, *From Bolshevism to the Bureaucracy* (London, 1966). A Social-Democratic and liberal case, tracing Stalinist institutions back to Lenin's political theories, has of course been presented many times: see, for example, Leonard Schapiro, *The Origin of the Communist Autocracy* (New York, 1965), pp. 343–4, 360–61. The argument relating Leninist politics to Kautskyan Social-Democracy stems from the critique offered from the late 1920s onward by the Left Communist Karl Korsch, for example, in *Marxism and Philosophy* (New York, 1930); it can occasionally be found in contemporary pamphlets by far-Left groups.

6 H. R. Trevor-Roper, preface to Burnett Bolloten, *The Grand Camouflage: The Spanish Revolution and Civil War, 1936–9*, 2nd edn (London, 1968), pp. 2–3.

7 L. D. Trotsky, *History of the Russian Revolution* (London, 1965), p. 1079.

8 *ibid.*, pp. 1079–80.

9 Lionel Kochan, *Russia in Revolution* (London, 1970), p. 269.

10 Trotsky, *op. cit.*, pp. 933–5.

11 Oliver H. Radkey's analysis, in *The Election to the Russian Constituent Assembly of 1917* (Cambridge, Mass., 1950), pp. 25–7, convincingly correlates the percentages of troops voting for the Bolsheviks with their relative proximity to the metropolitan strongholds of Bolshevism. By December 1917, moreover, even the armies remote from these centres, such as those on the Rumanian, south-western and Caucasian fronts, were swinging sharply from the SRs to the Bolsheviks: see Radkey, *The Sickle under the Hammer* (New York, 1963), pp. 343–4.

12 Radkey (*The Election to the Russian Constituent Assembly*, p. 53) provides the following enlightening figures on the polarization in Moscow, from the June and September municipal elections and the Constituent Assembly ballot (voting figures in thousands; figure in brackets indicates percentage of poll):

Party	June	September	November
SR	374·9 (58)	54·4 (14)	62·3 (8)
Bolshevik	75·4 (12)	198·3 (51)	366·1 (48)
Kadet	108·8 (17)	101·1 (26)	263·9 (35)
Menshevik	76·4 (12)	15·9 (4)	21·6 (3)

13 Radkey, *The Sickle under the Hammer*, pp. 283–92.

14 *ibid.*, pp. 258–77.

15 *ibid.*, p. 493.

16 Quoted in Stalin's 1918 attack on the Mensheviks, 'The Logic of Events', in J. Stalin, *The October Revolution* (Moscow, 1934), pp. 20–21.

17 L. D. Trotsky, *Stalinism and Bolshevism* (Bombay, 1952), pp. 17–18.

18 E. H. Carr concludes, of the amalgamation between factory committees and trade unions, that 'in practice the fusion did not prove difficult to effect' (*The Bolshevik Revolution 1917–1923* (London, 1966), Vol. 2, p. 74).

19 A. M. Pankratova, '*Les Comités d'Usines en Russie à l'Époque de la Révolution*' (partial translation of her 1923 pamphlet cited below by Serge in Chapter 7, note 38), *Autogestion* (Paris), No. 4, December 1967. The Sixth – and last – Conference of Petrograd Factory Committees in January 1918 was not actually 'unanimous' in its support of the new party line: see Paul Avrich, 'The Bolshevik Revolution and Workers' Control in Russian Industry', *Slavic Review* (New York), 1963, Vol. 22, pp. 47–63, for a good history of the politics of the committees. But principled opponents of government policy were few among committee spokesmen.

20 Serge, *Memoirs of a Revolutionary*, *loc. cit.*

21 Sir Paul Dukes, *The Story of 'ST 25'; Adventure and Romance in the Secret Intelligence Service in Red Russia* (London, 1938), pp. 178–9; the instigators of the resolution were immediately seized, with their families, by the Cheka and shot. However, S R and Left Kadet agitation, based on several large factories and extending into units of the Red Army, was continued into March and April (*ibid.*, pp. 360–61).

22 Propaganda on the rift between Bolsheviks and workers was especially esteemed by the interventionist British government which was then nervous of its own labour force: at a War Cabinet meeting on 14 November 1918, Lloyd George stated that 'it was important that the public in England should know what Bolshevism meant in practice.... Here we had a great, inflammable industrial population and it was very desirable that our industrial population should know that industrial workers had suffered equally with the rest of the population at the hands of the Bolsheviks' (Minutes of War Cabinet meeting 507, in Public Record Office File, FO 371/3344).

23 Jean Maitron, '*De Kibaltchiche à Victor Serge*' (a selection, with commentary, of Serge's anarchist journalism and letters from prison, over 1909–19), in *Le Mouvement Social* (Paris), No. 47, 1964. The parallelism between Serge's enthusiasms, for bandits and for Bolsheviks, was suggested to me by Richard Greeman, to whom it was originally propounded by Vlady Kibalchich (Victor Serge's son).

24 Victor Serge, *Destiny of a Revolution* (London, 1937), pp. 138–9.

25 Serge would later slightly amend his anti-ideological bent: the 'seeds of reaction' or 'the germ of all Stalinism' might well be implanted within Leninist or even Socialist doctrine, but would require the soil of specific historical circumstances in which to flourish. Victorious Bolshevism was also prone to 'a natural selection of authoritarian temperaments'. This new theoretical emphasis can be seen in his 1933 'political testament' addressed to friends in France shortly before his arrest (given in his *16 Fusillés à Moscou* (Paris, 1947), p. 46). It aroused the ire of Trotsky when propounded in Serge's 1937 article '*Puissances et Limites du Marxisme*' (see *Memoirs of a Revolutionary*, pp. 348–9, and also pp. 133–4); and is developed again in the last book Serge published in Europe during his lifetime, *Portrait de Staline* (Paris, 1940), pp. 56–8.

26 These quotations, from Trotsky's polemics of 1904 and 1907 respectively, are reported in Jean-Jacques Marie, *Le Trotskysme* (Paris, 1970), pp. 11, 15.

27 The critique offered by Rosa Luxemburg was not, strictly, an attack on 'Leninism', a term which never enters either her 1904 articles (subsequently reprinted after her death under the incorrect title *Leninism or Marxism*) or her analysis of the Soviet regime – closely resembling that of Serge – written in late 1918.

28 Lenin's advice on referenda 'of the opinion of every member without

exception, in the most important cases at any rate' is given in his *Collected Works* (London, 1969), Vol. 11, p. 441, and his insistence on a clear mandating of delegates from their locals (at a St Petersburg district conference in 1907) is *ibid.*, p. 434.

29 On Lenin's proposal, each of the larger local Soviets in Russia was sent a summary of the two sides' positions on the question of war or peace with Germany in February 1918, and asked to indicate which course it favoured. The results were published day by day in *Izvestia* as they came in. (See the notes to Lenin's *Collected Works*, Vol. 27, p. 559.) So little did party discipline operate that almost half the urban Soviets voted in favour of continued war, against the Central Committee and State policy. The consultation with the Soviets was in no sense a referendum (it was undertaken just after the Council of People's Commissars had voted for peace); but it threw Soviet official policy to the mercy of popular opinion, and remains without parallel in any country as an example of democratic opinion-sounding on a crucial question of foreign policy.

30 See, for example, Chomsky, *op. cit.*, p. 116. A recent critique, Maurice Brinton's *The Bolsheviks and Workers' Control, 1917–1921* (London, 1970), attempts documentary justification for the view that the shifts in early Soviet industrial policy over 1917–18 were caused by the 'monstrous aberration' of 'Bolshevism', supposedly 'the last garb donned by bourgeois ideology'. The compilation omits any treatment of (a) the breakdown of Russian industry in this period, (b) the actual politics of the Bolshevik trade-union spokesmen (who are seen as 'Leninists'), or (c) of the demands for centralised planning that were acceptable to the factory committees themselves.

31 A useful analysis of the economic gradualism of Marx, Engels and Lenin is contained in Y. Wagner and M. Strauss, 'The programme of *The Communist Manifesto* and its Theoretical Foundations', *Political Studies* (Oxford), Vol. 17, 1969, pp. 470–84.

32 Didier L. Limon, '*Lénine et le Controle Ouvrier*', in *Autogestion* (Paris), No. 4, December 1967, provides a clear account of the controversy on workers' control in Russia during 1917–18 with many details of the theoretical standpoints of the contenders.

33 For the politics of the liberal tendency in the Russian Communist party at this time, see Schapiro, *op. cit.*, pp. 73, 77–8, 86, 152. Lozovsky was actually expelled from the party in early 1918 for his constitutional deviations. Both he and Ryazanov were political liberals (voting, for example, against the dispersal of the Constituent Assembly) and industrial centralizers; Ryazanov even calling for 'control by the State over the workers' (Limon, *op. cit.*, p. 106).

34 The conjunction, in Left Communist thinking, of demands for nationalization and central planning with demands for shop-floor power in factory management (see their proposals at the May 1918 Congress of National Economic Councils, summarized in Schapiro, *op. cit.*, p. 140) identifies them as the only faction of Russian Socialism, within or outside the Communist party, whose conception of 'workers' control' approximates the one which is current among the Socialist Left today.

35 The extent of SR complicity in terrorist and putschist manoeuvrings is a matter of controversy (though the guilt of the Left SR section, in the light of their behaviour in the July–August crisis, would appear undeniable). Schapiro (*ibid.*, pp. 153–4, 164–5) emphasizes the pacifism and restraint of the Right SRs, aside from the 'freelance activity' of lone individuals like Kaplan and Savinkov. Radkey, on the other hand, while absolving the Right SR Central Committee from responsibility for terrorist acts, points out how the loose nature of the party opened its organization and membership to military plotters and pro-Allied jingoists in receipt of Western interventionist funds (Radkey, *The Sickle under the Hammer*, pp. 330–34, 452–5, 492–3).

Chapter 1: From Serfdom to Proletarian Revolution

1 [1 hectare = 2·47 acres.]

2 Pyotr Lavrov (born 1823; died in Paris, 1900) developed the Populist theory of peasant movements and edited the clandestine journal *Vperyod* (*Forward*) for the Russian underground. Author of *Historical Letters*, of the *Essay on the History of Thought*, and of works dealing with the Paris Commune and the question of the State. [Nikolai Mikhailovsky (1842–1904) developed the political theory of 'critical populism', which looked to the peasant commune to provide a form of small-scale democracy in opposition to the huge impersonal institutions of industrialism. Mikhailovsky opposed both the terrorists and the Marxists; his writings had an influence in the Right wing of the S R party.]

3 [Vera Zasulich later became active in the populist 'Black Repartition' and then in the Russian Marxist movement. In the 1903 split she supported the Mensheviks and during the war joined Plekhanov's patriotic *Edinstvo* group. She died in 1919, an opponent of the Bolsheviks.]

4 Mezentsev was executed by the writer Stepniak (Kravchinsky), the author of *Underground Russia*.

5 A. Rambaud, *A History of Russia from the Earliest Times to 1877* (New York, 1886).

6 M. N. Pokrovsky, *History of Russia* (New York, 1931).

7 The liberal N. V. Chaikovsky was to end his career unfortunately. For a long time he devoted his efforts to the Russian cooperative movement. Then in 1919, during the Allied intervention in Russia, he headed the White government at Archangel. He died in emigration in 1926.

8 Yuri Osipovich Martov (Tsederbaum), a theoretician and polemical writer of great talent, was to become, throughout his life, the adversary of Lenin and the leader of Menshevism. An internationalist during the world war, he attempted for a brief period (1919–20) to maintain an attitude of loyal opposition to the Bolsheviks. He died in emigration in 1923.

9 The evolution of Pyotr Struve deserves some attention; having passed from reformism to liberalism, he later became an admirer of Stolypin. Today, Struve is one of the leaders of the monarchist emigration; he played a prominent role in the circles around Denikin and Wrangel. [Author of numerous books on Russian politics and economics, Struve died in 1944.]

10 Both belong today to the liberal emigration. In October 1917, Prokopovich succeeded Kerensky as head of the clandestine 'government' which directed sabotage against the revolution. [This attempt to reconstitute the 'Provisional Government' was short-lived. Prokopovich and his wife Kusskova went into exile and ran a Russian research institute in Prague. He died in 1955 and she in 1959.]

11 This first organ of Russian Social-Democracy had on its editorial board, along with Lenin, five future Mensheviks: Plekhanov, Martov, Axelrod, Potresov and Vera Zasulich.

12 The French Socialist Millerand joined, in 1899, a Cabinet of 'republican defence' where one of his colleagues was the executioner of the Paris Commune, Galliffet.

13 V. Nevsky, *History of the Russian Communist Party (Bolshevik): A Short Outline (Istoriya R K P (B): Kratki Ocherk)* (Leningrad, 1926), p. 170; Lenin intended the revolutionary organization to 'unify the Socialist science and revolutionary experience, acquired over decades by the revolutionary intelligentsia, with the special skills of the advanced workers: knowledge of the working-class environment, and the gifts of mass agitation and mass leadership'.

14 Jordania, from 1920 to 1922, was President of the Menshevik Republic of Georgia. [After the Bolshevik invasion of Georgia he went into exile and died in 1953.]

15 See A. I. Spiridovich, *The Socialist-Revolutionary Party and its Pre-*

decessors (Partiya Sotsialistov-Revoliutsionerov i ee Predshestvenniki), a work written by a police official from the documents of the Okhrana. [Not available in Russian: the first edition of 1915 was sold only to Tsarist officials, and the second augmented edition of 1917, after the opening of the Okhrana archives, was given to the Political Red Cross to sell, with a few copies for the S R party itself. Spiridovich had another edition printed on the press of the Stavka, but this was seized by the Bolsheviks. There is a French translation, *L'Histoire du Terrorisme Russe, 1886–1917* (Paris, 1930).]

16 Mikhail Gotz died in 1908, and Gershuni died in Paris in 1920, following many years of bitter struggle on which he left some remarkable memoirs (available in a French translation); Breshko-Breshkovskaya, who went over to bourgeois liberalism in 1917, has become one of the 'stars' of the White emigration; V. Chernov, who is now in emigration, was one of Kerensky's ministers and then Chairman of the Constituent Assembly, leading his party from the denial of its programme to political disaster. [Breshkovskaya died an exile in Prague in 1934; Chernov, after emigration in western Europe, died in New York in 1952.]

17 Statistics supplied by the Museum of the Revolution in Leningrad. Terrorist acts of purely local significance (and there were hundreds of these) are not counted in these figures. [A more recent authority gives a figure of over 4,000 lives taken by S R and anarchist terrorists during 1906 and 1907 alone: Paul Avrich, *The Russian Anarchists* (Princeton, 1967), p. 64.]

18 M. N. Pokrovsky, *A Brief History of Russia* (New York, 1933), Pt III; L. D. Trotsky, *1905* (Paris, 1923); N. Rozhkov, *History of Russia (Istoriya Rossii)* (Petrograd, 1926), Volumes 11 and 12.

19 The *desyatina* is about 2½ acres.

20 Gapon managed to escape and lived abroad for some while. He resumed contact with the Imperial police, took part in its schemes and was executed as an agent-provocateur in 1906 by a Socialist-Revolutionary acting under instructions from Azef.

21 [The Zemstvos were organs of rural self-government encouraged in the late nineteenth century by Tsar Alexander II: though strictly limited from above, they organized local welfare services and provided an important focus for liberal-constitutional agitation in the 1900s.]

22 The cruiser sailed under the colours of the Red Flag for eleven days. Other ships shrank from engaging in combat against her and her crew, and took refuge in Rumania once their supplies were exhausted.

23 Antonov-Ovseyenko will appear again in our story when we come to the October Revolution.

24 The initiative in the pogroms was taken by the police and by the 'Black Hundreds' (Union of True Russians), an ultra-reactionary organization under the patronage of the authorities. Nearly 4,000 Jews were killed and 10,000 injured in 110 separate towns and localities; 500 perished in Odessa alone.

25 In 1905 the Bolshevik party had twelve or thirteen thousand members and, though including a large number of intellectuals, exercised its influence over the straightforwardly proletarian elements of society. The Mensheviks numbered about 15,000 members: their influence was chiefly among the petty-bourgeoisie, the artisans, and sometimes (in Georgia particularly) sections of the peasantry. The Russian proletariat amounted to some three million workers at this time. The two fractions of Russian Social-Democracy thus organized only one per cent of this total between them. See Nevsky, *op. cit.*, Chapter 11. [Serge's estimate of the influence of the two fractions of Social-Democracy among the Russian working class is a considerable oversimplification. Both Bolsheviks and Mensheviks had a working-class base in the main cities, even though their proletarian membership was relatively small. For a detailed presentation see J. L. H. Keep, *The Rise of Social Democracy in Russia* (Oxford, 1963), pp. 165–82, 230, 274. A recent careful statistical study does tentatively distinguish between the firmer working-

class base of the Bolsheviks and the greater petty-bourgeois and national-minority composition of Menshevism over 1905–7: David Lane, *The Roots of Russian Communism* (Assen, 1969), pp. 44, 49–51, 209–13.]

26 'On Guerrilla Warfare' (30 September 1906); N. Lenin, *Collected Works* (London, 1969), Vol. 11, pp. 213–14.

27 M. N. Pokrovsky, 'How Did the War of 1914 Begin?', in *Proletarskaya Revoliutsiya*, 7 (30), 1924.

28 The assassination at Sarajevo was committed at the instigation of the Russian General Staff; see Victor Serge, '*La Verité sur l'Attentat de Sarajevo*', in *Clarté*, No. 74, 1 May 1924. [The evidence implicating the Tsarist General Staff is examined in V. Dedijer, *The Road to Sarajevo* (London, 1967); Dedijer rejects the incrimination of the Russians.]

29 [Emile Vandervelde: leader of the Belgian Socialist party and a prominent figure in the Second International; fervent supporter of the Allied cause from the outset of the war, when he joined the Belgian government.]

30 [2 August marked the day when the French Socialist party voted for 'national defence'. 4 August was the day when the German Social-Democratic party voted unanimously for the war-credits in the Reichstag.]

31 Nevsky, *op. cit.*, p. 386. [Probably an attempt by Serge to vindicate Trotsky's war-time position by citing a recent and reputable party history.]

Chapter 2: *The Insurrection of 25 October 1917*

1 'Speech of Comrade Bukharin at the Commemorative Evening in 1921', in *Proletarskaya Revoliutsiya*, No. 10, 1922. After relating this incident, Bukharin concludes, 'We could have seized power in Petrograd even at this time. We decided not to do so, since we had to depend on winning decisive victories in the provinces as well.'

2 I. Flerovsky, 'Kronstadt in the October Revolution', in *Proletarskaya Revoliutsiya, ibid.*

3 L. D. Trotsky, *The Russian Revolution* (London, 1918) [included as *The History of the Russian Revolution to Brest-Litovsk*, in *The Essential Trotsky* (London, 1963)].

4 Victor Serge, *Lénine 1917* (Paris, 1923), p. 55.

5 [V. P. Nogin: People's Commissar in the first Soviet government; supporter of a broad coalition with the Mensheviks. Died in 1924.]

6 Serge, *op. cit.*, p. 45.

7 K. Grasis, 'October in Kazan', *Proletarskaya Revoliutsiya*, No. 10 (33), 1924.

8 [The Maximalist party was a small direct-action group which had split from the Socialist-Revolutionary party to engage in spectacular acts of terrorism against the Tsarist regime.]

9 V. Bonch-Bruyevich, 'From July to October', in *Proletarskaya Revoliutsiya*, No. 10, 1922. The author of this article was one of Lenin's close associates.

10 My sources for these facts are the 'reminiscences of the fighters of October' published by *Proletarskaya Revoliutsiya* in 1922, and a little book *Moscow in October 1917* (*Moskva v Oktyabre 1917*) [N. Ovsyannikov, ed.] (Moscow, 1919). The argument of the comrades who opposed the insurrection is given and magisterially refuted in Lenin's 'Letter to the Comrades' of 16–17 October 1917 (*Collected Works* (London, 1969), Vol. 26, pp. 195–215).

11 [In Italy, during 1920, over two million workers came out on strike in a wave of militant action in the major industrial cities, culminating in the factory occupations of the spring and autumn; throughout the south, and especially in Sicily, peasants seized the estates. No political leadership of the movement came from the Italian Socialist party, and the decline of the revolutionary wave heralded the consolidation of Mussolini's fascist squads. (See Angelo Tasca (A. Rossi), *Naissance du Fascisme* (Paris, 1967), pp. 95–107, 438–40). Serge's invocation of the German 'missed opportunity' of

1923 is much less apt: revolutionary militancy in the German working class was very localized and sporadic even in this critical year, and the failure of the revolution to materialize cannot be laid to the account of the K P D and Comintern tacticians, clumsy as these were. Werner T. Angress's *Still-Born Revolution: The Communist Bid for Power in Germany, 1921–23* (Princeton, 1963), provides a full and fair analysis of this complex battleground. For the variations of Serge's own attitude to the 1923 German events, see below, note 30.]

12 Numerous documents which have been recently included in Volume 21 of Lenin's *Collected Works* (new Russian edition) seem to indicate that a substantial Right-wing trend was taking shape within the party, to which it would have liked to assign the role of a powerful proletarian Opposition inside a parliamentary democracy. Not only did this tendency fail to comprehend that the question of democracy was an irrelevancy (Russia having only the choice between two dictatorships); it was also the victim of the most dangerous illusions conceivable.

13 'The question is not what this or that proletarian, or even the whole of the proletariat at the moment, *considers* as its aim. The question is *what the proletariat is*, and what, consequent on that *being*, it will be compelled to do' (Karl Marx in *The Holy Family*).

14 The personal predictions of Lenin in 1914–15 (in *Against the Stream*) and on the Russian revolution in September 1917 (*Letters from Afar*) should be compared with President Wilson's hopes in 1918–19: the illusions of Wilsonism formed a powerful contribution to the victory of the Allies, in which they served political ends diametrically opposed to those of their propounder. Lenin's clear vision and effective action can be compared also with the blindness and ineffectuality of the statesmen of the modern bourgeoisie: the leaders of German imperialism in relation to the catastrophe of Germany; Clemenceau and the Versailles treaty; Poincaré and Cuno and the Ruhr conflict of 1923.

One must at once distinguish between the intentions of President Wilson who advocated national self-determination, freedom of the seas and the League of Nations, and the social role played by Wilsonism, the final ideology of the Allied war; personally Wilson appears not to have wanted to produce the result that he actually achieved, i.e. that of serving the cause of one imperialist coalition against another.

15 A satisfactory French translation of these works, unfortunately without explanatory notes or a historical introduction, has been published by La Librairie de l'Humanité. I have provided a detailed analysis of these writings of Lenin in *Lénine 1917*.

16 Lenin, *Collected Works*, Vol. 26, pp. 22–3.

17 [From the article 'Insurrection', in the *New York Daily Tribune* of 18 September 1852, signed by Marx but actually written by Engels (and later published in the collection *Germany: Revolution and Counter-Revolution*).]

18 Trotsky was still interned in a concentration camp at Amherst in Canada at the time when Lenin arrived in Russia, and only reached Petrograd in the first days of May. The articles on the Russian revolution that he wrote in America strike a note similar to those by Lenin in the same period. After 5–6 May, he was in close contact for common activities with the editorial board of *Pravda* and the Bolshevik Central Committee. At this time he was a member of the so-called 'Inter-District' organization of Social-Democrats, which also included Volodarsky, Lunacharsky, Manuilsky, Karakhan, Yoffe and Uritsky, and which fused with the Bolshevik party in July 1917.

Trotsky addressed the Petrograd Soviet for the first time on 5 (18) May, the day after his arrival from America. He urged it first, to challenge the bourgeoisie; second, to put its own leaders under control; third, to have confidence in its own revolutionary strength. 'I believe', he concluded, 'that the next action on our agenda will place power in the hands of the Soviets.'

19 An engineering worker from the Bolshevik emigration, Shlyapnikov undertook illegal activity in Petrograd in the last months of Tsarism, on which he has written some interesting memoirs: *The Eve of 1917* (*Kanun Semnadtsatogo Goda*) (Moscow, no date). He became one of the organizers of the Russian Metal Workers' Union and then, in October 1917, Commissar for Labour. In 1921 he was one of the leaders of the 'Workers' Opposition' in the Russian Communist party. [He capitulated to Stalin in 1926, was expelled from the party in 1933, was sent to an 'isolator' in 1935, and died obscurely in 1943.]

20 G. Georgievsky, *Essay on the History of the Red Guard* (*Ocherki po Istorii Krasnoi Gvardii*) (Moscow, 1919).

21 The way the insurrection was carried out reconciled the two theses. It took place on the day of the Soviet Congress, but began in the early morning; the Congress began its deliberations only in the evening, while the shooting could still be heard going on.

Lenin proved mistaken on another point at this time. In the early days of October he wrote to the Central Committee that 'Victory is certain in Moscow: nobody will resist us there. At Petrograd we can afford to wait: it is not necessary to begin with Petrograd.' In fact, of course, the victory was safe in Petrograd, where the insurrection had a painless triumph, while in Moscow it encountered fierce resistance. [Serge's comments at this point relate to the controversies in Russian party history, from 1924 onwards, which enrolled the differences between Lenin and Trotsky (on the timing of the insurrection) into the current polemic against Trotsky. Trotsky (in his book *Sur Lénine* in 1924) had justified his own timing of 1917 as against Lenin's; this in turn was made much of by Stalin (in his speech 'Trotskyism or Leninism?' of November that year). Serge is here content to state the legitimacy both of Trotsky's and Lenin's position on the insurrection.]

22 [Cavaignac and Galliffet: French generals who were the military saviours of the bourgeoisie against the workers, in 1848 and 1871 respectively.]

23 [Actually a mistaken reference by Serge; the witness for the scene was N. N. Sukhanov: *The Russian Revolution* (London, 1955) pp. 584–5.]

24 Flerovsky, *op. cit.*

25 N. Podvoisky, a member of the Bolshevik party for many years, was one of the founders of the party's military organization. Later he became People's Commissar for War of the Russian Socialist Federation of Soviet Republics, then of the Ukrainian Soviet Republic. Subsequently, he devoted himself to the tasks of military training among youth and physical education generally. [Disappeared from public view in the 1930s; died in 1948.]

Antonov-Ovseyenko, a former officer and journalist who had been in political emigration, was active in Paris during the war in producing the internationalist journals, *Golos*, *Nashe Slovo* and *Nachalo*. He joined the Bolsheviks in 1917 and became a Red Army leader in the civil war. He headed the Political Directorate of the Red Army in 1923, and then the Soviet mission to Czechoslovakia. [A lapsed Trotskyist, Antonov-Ovseyenko steered the GPU terror against revolutionary dissidents in the Spanish civil war, was recalled to Moscow and shot without public trial in 1938.]

Lashevich, an old Bolshevik militant, later became a member of the Revolutionary War Council in Petrograd (1919–20) and in Siberia (after the fall of Kolchak). He became Commissar for War in 1926 and died in 1928. [Lashevich had been a supporter of the Zinoviev opposition of 1925–7, and capitulated with it; his death was apparently by suicide.]

26 S. Mstislavsky, *Five Days* (*Pyat Dnei*) (Berlin, 1922).

27 A. Schlichter, 'Memorable Days in Moscow', *Proletarskaya Revoliutsiya*, No. 10, 1922; Boris Voline, 'The Moscow Soviet before October', *ibid.*

28 N. Norov, 'On the Eve', in N. Ovsyannikov (ed.), *Moscow in October 1917* (*Moskva v Oktyabre 1917*) (Moscow, 1919). See also Victor Serge, '*La Révolution d'Octobre à Moscou*', *Bulletin Communiste*, 1 September 1921.

29 Ilya Noskov, 'The Kremlin Massacre', in Ovsyannikov, *op. cit.*

30 [This characterization of the 1923 Hamburg rising misses any consideration of its most important defects: firstly, the isolation of the insurrection itself from any concurrent action in the rest of Germany (since Hamburg was the only town to fail to receive the order calling off a nation-wide rising originally projected by the German Communists); secondly, the isolation of the few hundred Communist shock-troops in the city from the rest of the working class. Victor Serge's maturer reflections in *Memoirs of a Revolutionary* (London, 1967), pp. 171–2, exhibit this double isolation quite clearly, and the eulogy of the 'new type' of revolution here simply seems to be making the best of a job for which Serge himself, as a Comintern emissary in Germany in the early 1920s, may well have shared some responsibility.]

31 Larissa Reissner, *Hamburg auf den Barrikaden* (Berlin, 1925).

Chapter 3: The Urban Middle Classes Against the Proletariat

1 N. Lenin, *Collected Works* (London, 1969), Vol. 26, p. 256.

2 John Reed, *Ten Days that Shook the World* [London, 1967].

3 The war-aims of the Allies were expressed, through the Versailles treaty, in the dismemberment of Austro–Hungary, the annexation of all the German colonies (2,950,000 square kilometres containing 12,400,000 inhabitants), the annexation of 70,000 square kilometres of German territory (with 6,500,000 inhabitants), and the imposition on Germany of a war-damage reparations payment which was at first fixed at 172,000,000,000 gold francs. The principal war-aims of the Central Powers were: the annexation of the French colonies and of the Briey coal-fields, the annexation (open or concealed) of Belgium, Serbia and Salonika, and territorial expansion in the east (against Poland and the Baltic states). The treaties of Brest-Litovsk and Bucharest mirror these aims most precisely.

4 Lenin, *Collected Works*, Vol. 26, pp. 260–61.

5 L. D. Trotsky, *The History of the Russian Revolution to Brest-Litovsk* [(London, 1918) reprinted in *The Essential Trotsky* (London, 1963)].

6 'In the Allied and bourgeois circles of Petrograd, hope for the swift crushing of the revolutionaries has been born again.... All long ardently for the triumphal return of Kerensky and Savinkov. From the latter, merciless repression is anticipated.' Letter from Jacques Sadoul to Albert Thomas, 27 October (9 November) 1917 [*Notes sur la Révolution Bolchévique* (Paris, 1919)].

7 From the report of the trial of the Right S Rs in Moscow in 1922 [given in *Pravda* for June and July of that year].

8 N. Podvoisky, 'The Military Organization of the Russian Social-Democratic Labour Party', in *Krasny Arkhiv*, Nos. 7–8, 1923.

9 S. A.'Piontkovsky, *Documents on the History of the October Revolution* (*Khrestomatiya po Istorii Oktyabrskoi Revoliutsii*) (Moscow, 1925).

10 According to Krasnov's own testimony.

11 Krasnov himself, had he proved victorious, would not have hesitated to shoot or hang his enemies. His call to arms on 28 October 1917 announced merciless measures of repression. We shall see later on the kind of acts he perpetrated in the Don territory. At the outset of a revolution, the greatest humanity lies in the utmost rigour: magnanimity costs too much.

12 A. R. Gotz, one of the leaders and founders of the S R party, had participated in its terrorist activities in 1906–7 and was a wanted man under the Tsarist regime. He suffered exile in Siberia: became a sponsor first of the Kerensky government, then of armed resistance to the Soviets. He was condemned to death in the Moscow trial of S Rs in 1922 [but was reprieved; released in 1927, he worked for many years in the State Bank before being liquidated in 1937 in the Great Purge]. N. D. Avksentiev, another prominent leader of the same party, later became a member of the Siberian 'Directorate' that was deposed by Kolchak. He went into exile [and died in 1943].

13 'I was incensed. It was a rotten disavowal: Gotz had participated in the preparation of the rising and Avksentiev had signed the order . . .': thus the deposition of the S R Rakitin-Brown, read out at the S R trial in Moscow in June 1922. The indictment presented by Krylenko against the defendants, which was widely publicized at the time, is full of overwhelming documentation on all these facts.

14 *Rabochaya Gazeta* (*Workers' Gazette*), official organ of the Russian Social-Democratic Labour party (Menshevik), for 5 (18) November 1917, cited by Ilya Vardin, 'The Mensheviks after the October Revolution', in *Five Years* (*Za Pyat Let*) (Moscow, 1922). Abramovich and Dan, now *émigrés*, still sit as representatives of Russian Social-Democracy in the Executive of the Socialist International.

15 [Jules Guesde (1845–1922) had been an ardent, verbally insurrectionary Socialist and internationalist, and (like Plekhanov) a supporter of a 'hard' opposition to Revisionism and opportunism in the Second International. The outbreak of the world war saw him rally to the patriotic cause, and he joined the 'Cabinet of National Defence'.]

16 Jacques Sadoul, letter of 18 October, in *Notes sur la Révolution Bolchévique*, p. 47. We are aware of the fact that Plekhanov's widow, after years of silence, in 1922 issued a partial denial of the account related by J. Sadoul. But our comrade's notes on the revolution, apart from their other evident general qualities of sincerity and veracity, on this point accord only too fully – unfortunately for Plekhanov's memory – with the facts and the texts.

17 *Novaya Zhizn*, 28 October 1917, cited by A. Anishev in *Sketches of the History of the Civil War* (*Ocherky Istorii Grazhdanskoi Voiny*) (Leningrad, 1925).

18 Aniushkin, 'Last Days of the Municipal Duma', in N. Ovsyannikov (ed.), *Moscow in October 1917* (*Moskva v Oktyabre 1917*) (Moscow, 1920).

19 From Bogdanov's account in the 'Reminiscences of the Fighters of October', *Proletarskaya Revoliutsiya*, No. 10, 1922.

20 From S. Petrovsky's account, *ibid*.

21 A slogan offered by Lenin (in a very precise sense) ever since March 1917.

22 In *Proletarskaya Revoliutsiya*, No. 10, 1922.

23 See L. D. Trotsky, *Sur Lénine* (Paris, 1926), Chapter 5 ('Government Power').

24 Reminiscences of Kozlovsky and Bonch-Bruyevich, in *Proletarskaya Revoliutsiya*, No. 10, 1922.

25 V. Antonov-Ovseyenko, *Reminiscences of the Civil War* (*Zapiski o Grazhdanskoi Voine*), Vol. 1 (Moscow, 1924).

26 I. Dimitriev, 'October at Orsha', *Proletarskaya Revoliutsiya*, No. 10, 1922.

27 This is the Marxist historian, D. Ryazanov, who today directs the Marx-Engels Institute in Moscow. [Ryazanov was arrested after the 'Menshevik Centre' trial of 1931, and died in deportation in 1938.]

28 [Serge was to modify this enthusiasm for Bolshevism's brand of 'patriotism': in *Memoirs of a Revolutionary* (London, 1967, p. 245) he recognizes that this very 'party patriotism' helped in the intellectual crippling of the Communist oppositions.]

29 Jacques Sadoul's *Notes sur la Révolution Bolchévique*, *op. cit.*, give some interesting side-lights on these events (pp. 74–80).

30 The proletarian dictatorship hesitated for a long time before suppressing the enemy press. Immediately after the insurrection, the only bourgeois papers to be suppressed were those openly advocating armed resistance to 'the Bolshevik usurper', 'bloodthirsty anarchy' and 'the *coup d'état* of the Kaiser's agents'. It was only in July 1918 that the last organs of the bourgeoisie and the petty-bourgeoisie were closed down. The legal press of the Mensheviks only disappeared in 1919; the press of the anarchists hostile to

the regime, and the Maximalists, appeared down to 1921; that of the Left Socialist-Revolutionaries, later still. [Serge's chronology of the suppression of the press is only formally correct: it was, for example, only the press of the pro-Soviet fractions of the Left SRs that was allowed to appear. See L. Schapiro, *The Origin of the Communist Autocracy* (London, 1955), pp. 163, 179–82, 192–3, for a detailed account.]

31 *Collected Works*, Vol. 26, pp. 285, 288, 292.

32 *ibid.*, p. 297.

33 This pithy formula is offered by L. Kritsman in his remarkable work analysing the phase of 'War Communism': *The Heroic Period of the Great Russian Revolution* (*Geroicheskii Period Velikoi Russkoi Revoliutsii*) (Moscow, 1925).

34 The French ravaged Kabylia with fire several times during their conquest of Algeria. We may recall, too, the techniques of warfare and control used by the British in India; the sacking of the Winter Palace in Peking by European troops in 1900; the atrocities of the Italians in Tripolitania, of the French in Indochina and Morocco, of the British in the Sudan. And in no war of modern times were the vanquished treated with such ferocity as those defeated in the Paris Commune of 1871.

Chapter 4: The First Flames of the Civil War: The Constituent Assembly

1 Elisée Reclus [the theoretician of anarchism], in his writings on the Russian revolution, remarked in 1905, in an analysis whose penetration might almost be termed prophetic: 'Russia will be shaken from corner to corner, down to the remotest cabin in the land. But inevitably, in addition to the class question, another problem will erupt: that of the peoples with different languages and distinct national cultures. What is termed Russia is in fact an immense tract of conquests within which twenty enslaved nationalities are penned. ...' This is a remarkable page to read over (Reclus, *Correspondance*, Vol. 3 (Paris, 1912)).

2 According to the 1897 census. Obviously the population increased appreciably over the next twenty years, but on the whole its composition will not have varied.

3 G. Lelevich, *October at the Stavka* (*Oktyabr v Stavke*) (Moscow, 1922).

4 N. Lenin, *Collected Works* (London, 1969), Vol. 26, p. 312.

5 *ibid.*, p. 318.

6 V. B. Stankevich, *Memoirs* (*Vospominaniya*), Pt III (Berlin, 1920).

7 'The cavalrymen, exhausted, confused by events and deeply upset, said that they had done their utmost and were still as loyal to the general as in the past. But – "Ah, boyar!" they asked their officers. "What else could we do when all Russia has gone Bolshevik?"' (A. Denikin, *Sketches of the Russian Turmoil* (*Ocherki Russkoi Smuty*) (Paris and Berlin, 1921–5).

8 Alexeyev had been in supreme command of the Russian army during the imperialist war, in his capacity of Chief of Staff of the Tsar-Generalissimo.

9 Denikin, *op. cit.*

10 G. Safarov, *The National Question and the Proletariat* (*Natsionalny Vopros i Proletaryat*) (Petrograd, 1922).

11 [Bessarabia: the territory between the Dniester and the Pruth, formerly a Russian province, annexed by Rumania after the First World War; incorporated into the Soviet Union as the Moldavian SSR in 1940.]

12 The Rumanian boyars formed a sort of landlord nobility: they had suppressed the 1907 peasant rising, killing 15,000 peasants.

13 The following figures will give an idea of what the Sfatul Țării represented. The elections to the Constituent Assembly were held at the same time at which this false 'national parliament' established itself. 600,000 persons, or a quarter of the population, took part in the vote, with the results: Soviet list, 200,000; SRs, 229,000; Jewish minority, 60,000; Kadets, 40,000;

'National Moldavian Party', 14,000. Thus the party which dominated the Sfatul Tării received only 2·3 per cent of the votes; it did not gain a single seat in the Constituent Assembly.

14 On the annexation of Bessarabia, see Chapter 6, p. 208.

15 S. V. Denisov, *Memoirs (Vospominaniya)* (Constantinople, 1921).

16 N. Krichevsky, 'In the Crimea', in *Archives of the Russian Revolution (Arkhiv Russkoi Revoliutsii)*, Vol. III (Berlin, 1924) (an *émigré* publication).

17 Mstislavsky in *Brest-Litovsk: The Armistice Negotiations* [no other reference given].

18 Moonsund or Muhuis is a channel between the Estonian islands of Dagoe [Hiiu Maa] and Oesel [Saare Maa] and the coast of Estonia.

19 The Tsarist hierarchy designated by Peter the Great in 1722 was made up of the civil class, the ecclesiastical class, the military, the naval, that of the Court and that of the sciences. The civil hierarchy, for example, contained fourteen grades, from 'State Chancellor' (corresponding to the rank of General and Field-Marshal in the army) and 'Trusted Secret Counsellor' to 'Collegial Registrar' (a civil rank corresponding to the military grade of Second Lieutenant). Both in conversation and in correspondence, persons had to be addressed according to their rank: Your Nobility, Your High Nobility, Your Most High Nobility, Your Excellency, Your High Excellency, etc.

20 Such was the leniency of the Soviet government that Purishkevich, one of the main instigators of Russian anti-semitism, later regained his liberty and was able to go abroad. He died in exile. His book on *How I Killed Rasputin* is well known.

21 Lenin, *Collected Works*, Vol. 26, p. 354.

22 In a broadsheet of 18 November. See *ibid.*, pp. 323–5.

23 See *ibid.*, pp. 341–6.

24 See L. D. Trotsky, *Sur Lénine* (Paris, 1926), Chapter 4.

25 The seriousness of this error (very characteristic of their politics) committed by the Left S Rs must be emphasized. Separated by an unbridgeable gap from the Right S Rs, but attached to a common tradition, to the party's old name and to old illusions about majority decisions, they presented common electoral lists. Their popularity redounded to the credit of the S Rs of counter-revolution.

26 Lenin, *Collected Works*, Vol. 26, pp. 379–83.

27 Actually more than 600 deputies were returned, but over 150 did not have time to get to Petrograd.

28 N. Sviatitsky, 'The Elections to the Constituent Assembly', in *One Year of Russian Revolution (God Russkoi Revoliutsii)* (Moscow, 1918), cited in Lenin, *Collected Works*, Vol. 30, pp. 253–61. The author's statistics take in Russia and Siberia, with the exception of certain regions (Olonetz, Estonia, Kaluga, Bessarabia, Podolia, Orenburg, Yakutia and the Don). [For a full analysis of the Constituent Assembly election, bearing out the urban-rural split between Bolsheviks and the rest, see Oliver H. Radkey, *The Election to the Russian Constituent Assembly of 1917* (Cambridge, Mass., 1950). Serge's conclusions pay little attention to the great importance of the vote attracted by the highly centrifugal national-minority parties: it is misleading to lump in the vote of the Ukrainian and Moslem S Rs with that of the Russian Right S Rs, since the latter were hostile to the decentralizing national aspirations of the former. Radkey in *The Sickle under the Hammer* (New York, 1963), pp. 456 ff., even calculates that the Right S Rs could not have mustered a majority in the Assembly against the Bolsheviks, Left S Rs, Ukrainian S Rs and smaller S R nationalist groups: '... on the opposite extreme [to the Bolsheviks] a sentence of death was hanging over the ill-fated assembly, as certain as Lenin's if less immediate'.]

29 Trotsky, *op. cit.*

30 Boris Sokolov, 'The Defence of the Constituent Assembly' in *Archives of the Russian Revolution (Arkhiv Russkoi Revoliutsii)* (Berlin, 1924), Vol. 3.

The author of this article remained a believer in the Constituent Assembly.

31 Boris Sokolov admits that most of the demonstrators came from sections of the population (bourgeois or middle-class) who were motivated much more by hatred of Bolshevism than by any sympathy for the authority of the Assembly. These actual *reactionary* elements were already rallying instinctively, as the first important battles of the civil war would soon show, behind the S Rs and the Constituent Assembly. Sokolov's admission is to be noted.

32 The biography of Yakov Mikhailovich Sverdlov is that of a dauntless revolutionary. Born of an artisan family in Nizhni-Novgorod, a pharmacist by profession, Sverdlov was a Bolshevik militant, working in illegality, ever since 1903. Five times arrested, condemned first to $2\frac{1}{2}$ years in fortress confinement (a sentence he served to the full), then to four years' exile in the remote icy region of Narym, he was placed under the most rigorous conditions there after a demonstration of exiled prisoners and nearly died of cold and hunger: he survived only by a miracle of endurance. Five attempts to escape, two successful escapes at the risk of his life. He returned in 1912 to Petrograd to organize the party's clandestine network and was delivered to the authorities by the agent-provocateur Malinovsky. He was again exiled, this time to the Turukhansk region inside the Arctic Circle, where he stayed three years until the fall of Tsarism. On the news of the revolution he made a journey of 5,000 miles by sledge over the Yenisei, at the risk of being caught by the thawing of the ice, and influenced the Krasnoyarsk Soviet in a Bolshevik direction; he then returned to Petrograd, where he became one of the most valued organizers of the party. After the government crisis at the beginning of November he replaced Kamenev as Chairman of the All-Russian Soviet Executive Committee. He died in 1919, of tuberculosis, at the age of thirty-four.

33 [Zimmerwald was the venue, in Switzerland, of the international conference of anti-war Socialists in September 1915, which repudiated all the trends of Socialism who supported the war and looked to the foundation of a new International. A follow-up conference was held at Kienthal in April 1916.]

34 [V. V. Rudnev, a Right S R and Mayor of Moscow between the fall of Tsardom and the Bolshevik revolution.]

35 F. F. Raskolnikov, a Bolshevik militant from the days of illegality, member of the party's military organization, a naval officer in the Baltic fleet during the war, a leader of the Kronstadt Soviet in 1917, jailed under Kerensky following the July days, and a fighter in October. Later represented the USSR in Afghanistan and elsewhere. [Author of a notable 'open letter' denouncing Stalin as a traitor to the revolution, published in 1939; died in exile in 1943.]

36 Quoted from S. Mstislavsky, *Five Days* (*Pyat Dnei*) (Berlin, 1922).

37 Decree of the Assembly's dissolution, drafted by Lenin.

38 On the Constituent Assembly, see further: the stenographic transcript of the first day of the Assembly's proceedings (Petrograd, 1918); Mstislavsky, *op. cit.*; Trotsky, *op. cit.*; Lenin, *Collected Works*, Vol. 26.

39 [cf. Radkey (*The Election to the Russian Constituent Assembly*, p. 2): 'while the democratic parties heaped opprobium upon him [Lenin] for this act of despotism, their following showed little inclination to defend an institution which the Russian people had ceased to regard as necessary to the fulfilment of its cherished desires. For the Constituent Assembly ... no longer commanded the interest and allegiance of the general population which alone could have secured it against a violent death.' W. H. Chamberlin also remarks that 'the dissolution of Russia's first and sole freely elected parliament evoked scarcely a ripple of interest and protest, so far as the masses were concerned' (*The Russian Revolution, 1917–1921* (London, 1935), Vol. 1, p. 370).]

40 'Article 2: Workers' control is exercised by all the workers of a given enterprise through their elected bodies (factory committees, etc.) ... repre-

sentatives of the employees and of the technical staff are included in these bodies. ... Article 7: The organs of workers' control have the right to control all business correspondence. Commercial secrecy is abolished. The owners are obliged to submit to the organs of control all books and accounts, both for the current year and for past years. Article 8: Decisions of the control organs are obligatory for owners of enterprises and may be cancelled only by the decision of the higher organs of workers' control. ... Article 10: Owners and the representatives of workers and employees, elected to carry out workers' control, are responsible before the State ...'

The employers were granted three days' grace in which to appeal against the decisions of the lower organs of control to the higher organs. Local Councils of Workers' Control were instituted, with the task of summoning an All-Russian Congress: their activity was centralized by an All-Russian Council of Workers' Control.

41 See L. Kritsman, *The Heroic Period of the Great Russian Revolution* (*Geroicheskii Period Velikoi Russkoi Revoliutsii*) (Moscow, 1925) and G. Tsyperovich, *Trade Unions and Trusts in Russia* (*Sindikaty i Tresty v Rossii*) (Moscow, 1920).

42 A. G. Shlyapnikov, 'Reminiscences', in *Proletarskaya Revoliutsiya*, No. 10, 1922.

43 A. Anishev, *Sketches of the History of the Civil War* (*Ocherky Istorii Grazhdanskoi Voiny*) (Leningrad, 1925).

44 Shlyapnikov, *op. cit.*

45 A. Schlichter, 'Memorable Days in Moscow', *Proletarskaya Revoliutsiya*, No. 10, 1922.

46 Lenin, *Collected Works*, Vol. 26, pp. 388–90.

47 On this point it is worth quoting some reflections by L. Trotsky in a short book written in 1918 [*The History of the Russian Revolution to Brest-Litovsk*, reprinted in *The Essential Trotsky* (London, 1963)]: 'On what support could a ministry formed by such a majority of the Constituent Assembly depend? It would have had behind it the rich of the villages, the intellectuals and the old officialdom, and perhaps would have found support, for the time being, among the middle class. But such a government would have been completely deprived of the material apparatus of power. In the centres of political life, like Petrograd, it would have met at once with an uncompromising resistance. If the Soviets had, in accordance with the formal logic of democratic institutions, handed over their power to the party of Kerensky and Chernov, the new government, discredited and impotent, would have only succeeded in temporarily confusing the political life of the country, and would have been overthrown by a new rising within a few weeks.'

Chapter 5: Brest-Litovsk

1 [On this point Serge is too crude; Sir George Buchanan was in contact with Duma circles opposed to the Tsar during January 1917, but the extent of his conspiratorial activity was exaggerated by ultra-Right commentators. Trotsky's *History of the Russian Revolution* (London, 1966), p. 91, discounts the story of a 'palace revolution' scheme involving the British Ambassador. Buchanan, indeed, seems personally to have been devoted to the Tsar. See M. Paléologue, *An Ambassador's Memoirs* (London, 1925), Vol. 3, pp. 129–30, and Bernard Pares, *The Fall of the Russian Monarchy* (New York, 1961), pp. 422–4.]

2 There was, for instance, only a very small volume of capital exports to China.

3 V. Nevsky, *History of the Russian Communist Party* (*Bolshevik*): *A Short Outline* (*Istoriya RKP (B): Kratki Ocherk*) (Leningrad, 1926). See on this topic the interesting little book by N. Vanag, *Finance-Capital in Russia* (*Finanzovy Kapital v Rossii*) (Moscow, 1925). At the outset of the March

1917 revolution, Lenin observed that 'Russian capitalism is no more than a branch office of the world-wide firm which manipulates hundreds of billions of roubles, and whose name is Britain and France'.

4 In spite of her rapid economic growth between 1890 and 1901 Russia remained a distinctly *backward* country through a variety of factors: the falling-off of growth after this burst, the backward state of her agriculture, the preponderance of agriculture over industry, the expansion of her population (which outstripped the growth of production), and the small scale of industry relative to population (Russia had 10·2 per cent of the world's population before the outbreak of war, and only 6·2 per cent of the world's iron output).

5 See M. L. Pavlovich, *Balance-Sheet of the World War* (*Itogi Mirovoi Voiny*) (Moscow, 1924).

6 [Courland was the name of a Baltic province of the old Russian Empire; its territory is now divided between Latvia and Lithuania.]

7 'The Germans believe that they can capture Calais and Paris if peace is concluded with Russia. If Germany refrains from any annexations, the Entente will accept an honourable peace': thus Czernin in his memoirs, in a note dated 17 November. In the same book by the same author, the following observation can be culled for the sake of light relief: 'I have been sent some trustworthy information about the Bolsheviks. Their leaders are nearly all Jews, with ideas of the purest whimsy' (O. Czernin, *In the World War* (London, 1919)).

8 This fact is reported by M. N. Pokrovsky, in *Russia's Foreign Policy in the Twentieth Century* (*Veshnaya Politika Rossii v 20 Veke*).

9 L. D. Trotsky, preface to A. Yoffe (ed.), *Peace Negotiations at Brest-Litovsk* (*Mirnye Perogovory v Brest-Litovskve*) (Moscow, 1920). Both these pages and the whole of this little book are of great interest.

10 Trotsky, *ibid.*

11 'The victorious proletariat ... having expropriated the capitalists and organized Socialist production in its own country, would stand forth against the rest of the capitalist world, calling to its side the oppressed classes of the other countries, encouraging them to rise against the capitalists, and intervening where necessary by force of arms against the exploiting classes and their States' (from 'The United States of Europe Slogan', in the Zürich *Sotsial-Demokrat* of 23 August 1916: see the collection of N. Lenin and G. Zinoviev, *Against the Stream* (*Protiv Techeniya*) (Leningrad, 1925).)

12 N. Lenin, *Collected Works* (London, 1969), Vol. 24, p. 175.

13 Quoted from material in the Military Academy by A. Anishev, *Sketches of the History of the Civil War* (*Ocherki Istorii Grazhdanskoi Voiny*) (Leningrad, 1925).

14 See the Appendix by N. Ovsyannikov, 'The CC of the RCP and the Brest-Litovsk Peace', to Vol. 15 of the first Russian edition of Lenin's *Collected Works*.

15 Lenin, *Collected Works*, Vol. 26, pp. 442–50.

16 V. Sorin, *The Party and the Opposition. 1: The Fraction of Left Communists* (*Partiya i Oppozitsiya. I. Fraktsiya Levykh Kommunistov*) (Moscow, 1925).

17 Trotsky, *Sur Lénine* (Paris, 1926), Chapter 3.

18 A scrap of dialogue between Count Czernin and Baron von Kühlmann may be noted here. KÜHLMANN: 'The only choice the Russians have is what sauce they'll be eaten with.' CZERNIN: 'That's just the choice we've got' (Czernin, *op. cit.*).

19 E. Ludendorff, *My War Memories, 1914–1918* (London, 1919), Vol. 2. Emperor Charles of Austria, several weeks after the Homburg decision, still resisted implementing the offensive into the Ukraine, and authorized the collaboration of Austrian troops only under the pressure of famine.

20 Article 5 of the decree reads: 'Shareholders of banks who fail to hand in their securities, or to provide a list of their certificates, within fifteen days

of the publication of this decree, shall be punished by the confiscation of all their property.'

21 George Vassilevich Chicherin came from aristocratic origins and began a career in the diplomatic service, which he abandoned in 1905 in order to go into emigration as a professional revolutionary. He belonged to Menshevik organizations until the war broke out. An internationalist during the war, he was jailed by the British government until the end of 1917. Since the Brest-Litovsk treaty he has been in charge of Soviet Russia's foreign policy. [He was succeeded by Litvinov in 1930 and died in 1936.]

22 [Serge here omits any reference to the only one of the Allied negotiating agents in Russia who had any official standing or any direct access to his government: Britain's R. H. Bruce Lockhart, who at this point was a warm advocate of Soviet–Allied cooperation for the war effort. Lockhart's subsequent involvement in anti-Soviet conspiracy and intervention plans (see notes 10, Chapter 9, and 33, Chapter 10) may well have caused Bolshevik writers, including Serge, to doubt (wrongly) the genuineness of his earlier efforts to secure military cooperation with the Soviets.]

23 [Details of these approaches to Japan, with extracts from the British and United States government archives, are given in R. H. Ullman, *Intervention and the War* (Princeton, 1961), pp. 93–103, 129–30.]

24 [Recent historians of this episode have tended to doubt whether the Bolsheviks could ever have committed themselves seriously to seeking aid from the Allies against Germany; e.g. G. F. Kennan, *Russia Leaves the War* (Princeton, 1956), pp. 471, 497–8; Ullman, *op. cit.*, pp. 119–27; A. B. Ulam, *Lenin and the Bolsheviks* (London, 1969), p. 540. However, Lenin seems to have undergone genuine moods of vacillation before agreeing finally to ratify the peace with Germany; and Trotsky's measures for Allied cooperation, e.g. in the Murmansk landings (see p. 229 and note 24 to Chapter 7, p. 396) and in his plan for having US officers sent to the fro t to remove military stocks, were constructive and specific. See the account in I. Deutscher, *The Prophet Armed* (London, 1954), pp. 385–6, 397–8.]

25 Until 31 January 1917, Russia used the Julian calendar, which was thirteen days behind the Gregorian calendar that had been adopted from the end of the sixteenth century by all other European countries. Up till now we have given dates in Old (Julian) Style, sometimes with dates in Gregorian style following on in brackets. Thus, the Bolshevik insurrection took place in Russia on 25 October, and (for Europe) on 7 November. A decree of the People's Commissars made the use of the Gregorian calendar compulsory from 31 January; but thirteen days had to be telescoped to achieve this, so that February actually began on the 14th. This shifting of the calendar must be kept in mind, or the naïve reader may receive the illusory impression that the march of events has slowed down.

26 Lenin, *Collected Works*, Vol. 26, pp. 522, 523.

27 The voting was: for Lenin's proposal (of immediate peace), Lenin, Smilga, Sverdlov, Sokolnikov, Stalin, Trotsky, Zinoviev. Against: Uritsky, Yoffe, Lomov, Bukharin, Krestinsky, Dzerzhinsky. One abstention: Helena Stasova. The Central Committee of the Left SRs, when informed of the position, refused to accept the treaty. See N. Ovsyannikov's appendix to Volume 15 of Lenin's *Collected Works* (first Russian edition).

28 Lenin, *Collected Works*, Vol. 27, p. 557n.

29 The voting was as follows. For: Lenin, Stasova, Zinoviev, Sverdlov, Sokolnikov, Smilga, Stalin. Against: Bukharin, Bubnov, Uritsky, Lomov. Abstentions: Trotsky, Dzerzhinsky, Yoffe, Krestinsky.

30 Lenin, *Collected Works*, Vol. 27, pp. 19, 22, 27, 29.

31 *ibid.*, p. 38.

32 *ibid.*, p. 41.

33 *ibid.*, pp. 63, 65.

34 Trotsky, *Sur Lénine*, Chapter 3. See also Victor Serge, ' *Un Portrait de Lénine par Trotski*', *Clarté*, No. 75, June 1925.

35 [i.e. the French Socialist party (SFIO) formed in 1905 from the unification of the rival currents of the 1890s.]

36 It may be useful to add some points concerning the attitude of Socialists abroad at this juncture. At the end of January 1918, a number of members of the parliamentary group of the Parti Socialiste Unifié were still occupying ministerial posts in the Clemenceau government, with the approval of their fellow-deputies! See P. Louis, *Histoire du Socialisme en France* (Paris, 1925), Chapter 11. The Russian revolution was still defended within the working-class movement by a feeble, if growing, minority. As for the German Social-Democrats, we know from their declarations at the Magdeburg trial in January 1925 that they entered the strike-committee movement of 1918 only as antagonists to this 'weakening of national defence' and in order to speed its termination, i.e. to sabotage it. At this time their influence was still powerful.

37 Quoted by Trotsky in his preface to [A. Yoffe (ed.),] *Peace Negotiations at Brest-Litovsk* (*Mirnye Peregovory v Brest-Litovske*).

38 *ibid.*

39 But will we ever know how temporary it might have been? Once he has left the party or been rejected by it, even the best proletarian militant is more likely to lose his way than to return to it. It requires an exceptionally developed theoretical consciousness, as well as a rather uncommon control over the emotions, to continue to serve the party side by side with the party.

40 Ludendorff was only broken when his soldiers followed the example of the Russians and refused to fight. His realization that it was the beginning of the end came when the troops going up into action were met by those withdrawing into the trenches with cries of 'Black-legs! *Streikbrecher!*' (Ludendorff, *op. cit.*, Vol. 2).

Chapter 6: The Truce and the Great Retrenchment

1 Evgenia Bosch's book *A Year of Struggle: The Struggle for the Regime in the Ukraine* (*God Borby: Borba Za Vlast Na Ukraine*) (Moscow, 1925), forms a remarkable contribution to the history of this epoch. Antonov-Ovseyenko's *Reminiscences of the Civil War* (*Zapiski o Grazhdanskoi Voine*) (Moscow, 1924–9), are also of interest.

2 Kikvidze, a Maximalist Socialist-Revolutionary released from jail by the February revolution, was at the age of twenty-three one of the architects of the October Revolution on its western front. A partisan leader, then head of a division of the Red Army, he became one of the revolution's most talented generals. He fought against Krasnov, and was wounded thirteen times. He was killed at the age of twenty-five, in the Don district, on 11 January 1919.

3 An indefatigable militant, a Bolshevik founding member, who experienced both Siberian exile and emigration abroad, Evgenia Bosch performed a role of the first importance in the Ukrainian revolution, where she directed the work of Soviet organization and the resistance to the German invasion. Exhausted, ill and condemned to inactivity, she took her own life at the beginning of 1924. She was one of the great figures of the Russian revolution, now practically unknown. [As Serge's discussion of Bosch's suicide in his *Memoirs of a Revolutionary* (London, 1967) makes clear, her memory was deliberately suppressed because of her sympathy with the opposition.]

4 'Let us not forget', wrote Lenin from Zürich on 11 (24) March 1917, 'that we have, adjoining Petrograd, one of the most advanced countries, a real republican country, Finland, which from 1905 to 1917, under the shelter of the revolutionary battles in Russia, has developed its democracy in conditions of relative peace, and won the *majority* of its people for Socialism. ... The Finnish workers are better organizers than us and will help us in this field; *in their own fashion* they will form a vanguard pressing towards the

foundation of the Socialist Republic' (*Third Letter from Afar*, before Lenin's return to Russia).

5 The author of these lines, O. W. Kuusinen, rallied to Communism during the Finnish revolution. The quotation above is from his remarkable pamphlet *The Finnish Revolution: A Self Criticism* (*Revoliutsiya v Finlandii: Samokritika*) (Petrograd, 1919). [A slightly abridged version of the English translation published in London, 1919, is given in *Labour Monthly*, February and March 1940.] O. W. Kuusinen belongs today (1929) to the Executive Committee of the Communist International. [He died in 1967, having played an obsequious role in all the turns of Moscow's international policy, including a spell as 'Prime Minister' of the 'Finnish Democratic Republic' set up briefly as a cover for Stalin's invasion of Finland in 1939–40.]

6 Edvard Torniainen, *The Workers' Revolution in Finland* [no other title available] (Moscow, 1919).

7 C. D. Kataya, *La Terreur Bourgeoise en Finlande* (Petrograd, 1919). [Published in French by the section of the Communist International's administration which Serge was put in charge of on his return to Russia in 1919.]

8 M. S. Svechnikov, *Revolution and Civil War in Finland, 1917–18* (*Revoliutsiya i Grazhdanskaya Voina v Finlandii 1917–18*) (Moscow and Petrograd, 1923).

9 We are continuing to quote from C. D. Kataya. Most of these facts have become notorious from other sources, and the description of them given by our comrade is certainly an under-statement.

10 The bourgeois press in all countries kept silence about these facts but spoke at length on 'the crimes of the Reds'. It seems instructive here to cite the figure for the Reds' victims given by *a pro-White author*, Lars Henning Söderhjelm, in a book translated from Swedish into English and intended for propaganda consumption abroad: *The Red Insurrection in Finland in 1918* (London, 1919). Söderhjelm calculates that 'over a thousand' persons perished behind the lines of fighting under the blows of the Reds; however, the statistics he gives indicate only 624 persons.

11 Finland has practically no illiterates.

12 S. Shaumyan, 'The Baku Commune of 1918', *Proletarskaya Revoliutsiya*, No. 12 (59), 1926.

13 D. Oniashvili, speech to the Sejm of Tiflis, 22 April 1918, in the collection of official documents produced by the Menshevik government of Georgia: *Documents and Materials on the Foreign Policy of Trans-Caucasia and Georgia* (*Dokumenty i Materialy po Vneshnei Politike Zakavkazya i Gruzii*) (Tiflis, 1919).

14 See M. Amya, *The Paths of the Georgian Gironde* [no Russian reference available] (Tiflis, 1926); Y. Shafir, *The Georgian Gironde* (*Ocherki Gruzinskoi Zhirondi*) (Moscow, 1925); L. Trotsky, *Russia Between Red and White* (London, 1924). [The Georgian Mensheviks' support for Denikin was in fact soon clouded by the latter's determination to enrol the Caucasian states by force into a united 'Greater Russia', and the British government (which regarded the prospect of a strong Russia, even under the Whites, with some suspicion) intervened to prevent the outbreak of war between Denikin and his Menshevik allies. See R. H. Ullman, *Britain and the Russian Civil War* (Princeton, 1968), pp. 219–20.]

15 In order to avoid interrupting the story of the Baku events, we shall be anticipating, in these pages, material from the later chapters.

16 [A slight paraphrase from Major-General L. Dunsterville's *The Adventures of Dunsterforce* (London, 1920), p. 192: 'I was in touch with Baku by almost daily messengers, and our friends the Socialist-Revolutionaries seemed likely to be able to bring off shortly the *coup d'état* which was to throw out the Bolsheviks, establish a new form of government, and invite British assistance.' Dunsterville's book was printed by the Bolsheviks in a

Russian translation (retitled *Britanskii Imperializm v Baku i Persii*) in 1920, and Serge has probably quoted from this edition.]

17 Today (summer of 1927) People's Commissar of Trade in the USSR. [Mikoyan became a member of Stalin's inner circle: a full Politburo member from 1935, he was active in the Great Purge. He sided with Khrushchev in the de-Stalinization measures of 1956 and 1961 against the Molotov 'anti-party group'; played a leading role in the Russian intervention against the 1956 Hungarian revolution; has now retired from politics.]

18 [The case of the executed commissars of the Baku Commune was to become a *cause célèbre* in Anglo–Soviet relations: Stalin issued a denunciation of 'the shooting of the twenty-six comrades by the agents of English imperialism' in April 1919, and the atrocity was frequently recounted (often with added detail, as in I. Brodsky's famous painting showing British officers directing the actual firing-squad) in popular Soviet histories of the civil war. (Shaumyan was one of those few Bolshevik leaders whose early demise during the revolution rendered them suitable for hagiographical treatment during the Stalinist re-writing of party history, a fact which may partly explain the distortion in the later treatments.) Serge's account is free from these subsequent accretions; but the early Bolshevik version is contested, not only in the British official reply to Soviet accusations of complicity, but in the work of recent historians of British intervention in the Trans-Caspian region. Correspondence on the incident between the British and Soviet governments during 1922 is printed in *HM Government White Paper on Russia, No. 1*, Cmd 1846 (London, 1923); the affair is analysed, with conclusions favouring the British case, in C. H. Ellis, *The Trans-Caspian Episode* (London, 1963), pp. 57–61, and in R. H. Ullman, *Intervention and the War* (Princeton, 1961), pp. 320–24. (Ellis, a member of the British Mission to Trans-Caspia at the time of the shootings, discusses the question also in his contribution to St Antony's Papers, No. 6: *Soviet Affairs* (D. Footman, ed.) (London, 1959).)

The precise measure of British involvement in the executions turns on the evidence of two witnesses, both of whom have an evident interest in their particular version of the story: Funtikov, the head of the Ashkhabad 'Directorate' immediately responsible for the shootings, whose statement, turning the main responsibility on the British Mission, was gathered by a journalist (and fellow SR), V. Chaikin, apparently during Funtikov's spell in Ashkhabad jail during early 1919; and Captain Teague-Jones himself, whose personal history of the incident was collected by the British government during the 1922 correspondence with the Soviet Foreign Office, and accepted by them as the correct version. (Teague-Jones's statement on the affair, dated 22 November 1922, is given in Cmd 1846, pp. 7–11; it demands repudiation by the Soviet government of Chaikin's allegations, and adds 'that I reserve to myself the right to institute proceedings for libel against Vadim Chaikin, and against any or all of the newspapers who have published any of the charges against me, at such time as there shall be a civilized and responsible government in Russia'.)

Certain features of the episode are not in doubt:

(1) The commander of the British forces, Major-General W. Malleson, who throughout the affair was in Meshed, Persia (100 miles from Ashkhabad and 600 from Krasnovodsk, where the prisoners were) was notified of the capture of the commissars on 17 September (two days after their arrest on landing in the port). On the following day he asked the Ashkhabad government 'to give me Bolshevik leaders' names for dispatch to India' (i.e. in order that the leaders themselves should be dispatched, under British auspices, to India); Malleson's reason for this measure was that the commissars' 'presence in Trans-Caspia is most dangerous, as at least half the Russians are ready to turn their coat once more at the slightest sign of enemy success'. See Malleson's telegram to commander-in-chief, India, MD 00538, dated

18 September 1918, repeated in Foreign Office memo of 26 September, Public Record Office, File FO 371/3336; Malleson's own statement of his motivation differs from that given by Ellis (*The Trans-Caspian Episode*, p. 59) who says only that the commissars were to be kept in India as hostages for the British citizens held under arrest in Moscow and Petrograd.

(2) Teague-Jones, who had been informed of Malleson's request to Ashkhabad, was present at the meeting of four members of the Trans-Caspian government which had the task of discussing the fate of the commissars (evening of 18 September).

(3) On the following day, Teague-Jones wired Malleson with the news that it had been decided to shoot the prisoners.

(4) On 23 September, Malleson wired to commander-in-chief, India, with the news of the executions, of whose actual occurrence he had been informed by the Meshed representative of Funtikov's government (*ibid.*, p. 61). The telegram (MD 581, Meshed, 23 September 1918; repeated by commander-in-chief, India, telegram 76707, 25 September: Milner MSS, Box 115, File H–3) comments: 'Apart from question of justice as to which I can express no opinion, politically this alleged execution … means that Ashkhabad government have burnt their boats as regards Bolsheviks.' (This appears to be a declaration, favourable rather than hostile in tone, of the anti-Bolshevik credentials of Funtikov and his colleagues; that is, as Malleson went on to say, they could no longer use the lives of the commissars as a bargaining-counter to save their own skins.) The message ended: 'Ashkhabad Committee are anxious it should be kept secret.'

(5) The British government acceded to this request of the Ashkhabad regime. The world discovered the fate of Shaumyan and his colleagues only in March 1919, when Chaikin published his report on the affair in a Baku newspaper (Ullman, *Intervention and the War*, p. 323). Even when the unsuspecting Chicherin asked for the safe return of the Baku commissars from captivity, as a condition of the release of British hostages held by the Soviets, the Foreign Office, in cabling its ambassador in Holland (the intermediary for the negotiations on hostages) with a draft reply to Chicherin, added the news of the shooting solely 'for your [i.e. the ambassador's] private information', in a postscript headed *Secret*. (Chicherin's message, sent on 19 September, is summarized in Ullman, *ibid.*, pp. 293–4; the Foreign Office instruction, dated on 27 September, is in the Public Record Office, File FO 371/3336.)

The testimonies of Ellis (based in part on interviews with other members of the British Military Mission) and of Teague-Jones contain much that goes beyond this. In particular, Teague-Jones relates that he left the fateful meeting of the Ashkhabad ministers before a decision on the shooting was finally reached. The possibility had been debated in his presence; Funtikov had told the meeting that General Malleson had proved reluctant to take the prisoners and had said to the Ashkhabad representative in Meshed that the Trans-Caspian government 'must make its own arrangements'. (Malleson's telegrams of course establish that, on the contrary, he had been keen to have the commissars sent as prisoners to India; yet Teague-Jones, who knew this at the time, does not indicate that he tried to contradict Funtikov.) Ellis (*The Trans-Caspian Episode*, p. 61) reports that Malleson, when informed of the executions, was 'horrified at the action taken'. (The telegram to his chief in India, quoted above, contains no word of regret, still less of horror.) The British complicity may well, therefore, have been minimal; even though, as Ullman suggests (*Intervention and the War*, p. 324), if Teague-Jones 'had chosen to make an issue of the fate of the twenty-six commissars, Funtikov and his colleagues would have found it difficult to refuse the British request', since they were so dependent on British military support. However, it may well have been more than minimal: Teague-Jones's statement (the only evidence we have from him, since according to Ullman he refused to discuss his experiences in Trans-Caspia – and even changed his surname in order to avoid any publicity) was after all drawn up more than four years after the events it recounts. And any reservations about the executions that were felt by Britain's local representatives, or by their superiors elsewhere, were not serious enough to prevent the continuation of British military and financial support for Funtikov's government, at least until it was replaced (in November) by a new committee headed by the local police chief and enjoying the approval of the British Military Mission (*ibid.*, pp. 325–7).]

19 V. Chaikin, *On the History of the Russian Revolution* (*K Istorii Rossiskoi Revoliutsii*) (Moscow, 1922).

20 Funtikov was tried and shot in Baku in 1926.

21 N. Lenin, *Collected Works* (London, 1969), Vol. 26, pp. 455, 459, 461, 463, 466, 468, 470, 471–2, 514.

22 These figures, given by Karl Radek to the First All-Russian Congress of Economic Councils, were taken up by Milyutin, who stressed that, since part of the Ukraine's coal and manufacturing output was consumed in the Ukraine itself, the loss of actually available resources was appreciably less than stated. This specious reasoning, however, only underlined the gravity of the economic amputations undergone by the Republic.

23 From the stenographic report of the discussion at the First All-Russian Congress of Economic Councils (26 May–4 June 1918) (Moscow, 1918).

24 From Sokolnikov's report, *ibid.*

25 Lenin, *Collected Works*, Vol. 27, pp. 74, 75.

26 Today Kingisepp, on the Estonian frontier.

27 *ibid.*, pp. 89, 90, 91, 95, 98, 101, 104, 105, 106, 110.

28 V. Sorin, *The Party and the Opposition. 1: The Fraction of Left Communists* (*Partiya i Oppozitsiya. I. Fraktsiya Levykh Kommunistov*), preface by N. Bukharin (Moscow, 1925).

29 K. Radek in *Soc. Dem. Brest-Litovsk* [no fuller reference available].

30 Editorial in *Kommunist*, No. 1.

31 *Kommunist*, No. 4.

32 Lenin, *Collected Works*, Vol. 27, 129–30, 131, 133, 135, 136, 137.

33 On events in Bessarabia, see Chapter 4 ('The Tragedy of the Rumanian Front'), pp. 117–19. On 26 (13) January the Rumanians, who had several times been checked by the revolutionary forces, at last captured Kishinev. The Russian General Shcherbachev announced that the city had now been purged of Bolsheviks. A few days later the Sfatul Tării, the national representative body subservient to the Rumanian invader, proclaimed the independence of the Moldavian Republic while all dissidents were being hunted down and shot. It was the first step towards a disguised annexation. The People's Commissars replied by ordering the arrest of the Rumanian ambassador to Petrograd, M. Diamandi: following protests by the diplomatic corps, he was promptly released. On the other hand, the Soviet government seized the gold reserves of Rumania which had been deposited at the Russian State Bank. The reserves were declared 'inaccessible to the Rumanian oligarchy' and 'to be handed over only to the Rumanian people'. On 21 (8) February, France, Italy and Britain proposed an amicable settlement of the Russo–Rumanian conflict. Negotiations began at Odessa between Rakovsky and General Averescu, and peace was concluded on 5 March. Rumania undertook to evacuate Bessarabia within two months. However, the Germans invaded the Ukraine, and the Sfatul Ţării (on 27 March) proclaimed the union of autonomous Moldavia with Rumania. The treaty just signed proved to be no more than a scrap of paper in the hands of the Rumanians, who were listening to French advice. In April a Rumanian politician declared: 'Bessarabia was occupied by our troops... in accordance with an agreement between M. Bratianu and the French General Berthelot. The French General Vuillemin headed the occupation troops in Kishinev...' (Statement of M. Antonescu to *La Victoire* (Paris), 14 April 1918). The Soviet Republic has never recognized this seizure of a country.

34 '*Preamble:* The old army was a weapon in the hands of the bourgeoisie

for oppressing the toiling masses. The transfer of power to the toiling and exploited classes necessitates the creation of a new army, which will be the bulwark of the power of the Soviets, will prepare in the near future for the replacement of a permanent army by the nation in arms, and will serve to assist the impending Socialist revolution in Europe. *Article 1:* Clause 1: The Red Army of Workers and Peasants is formed from the most conscious and organized elements of the toiling masses. Clause 2: Admission to the army is open to whoever is ready to die for the conquests of the October Revolution, the Soviets and Socialism. References for each entrant are required from military committees, democratic organizations constituted on a Soviet basis, parties or trade unions: or at least from two members of such organizations. Collective enrolment will be taken on the basis of a roll-call in which each reply for all, as all for each.'

The establishment of local Military Commissariats through a decree of 8 April marked the beginning of a systematic manpower policy. Up till then the organization of the Republic's forces had been undertaken by M. D. Bonch-Bruyevich, whose plan for successive levies of men, on the western front, then in central Russia, then in the Volga region, had proved a complete failure.

Chapter 7: *The Famine and the Czechoslovak Intervention*

1 The meat requirements of the army's quartermastering department rose in 1917 to 50,281,000 poods; only 26,700,000 poods were available, a deficit of forty-seven per cent.

2 The Russian word *kulak* forms an expressive image, for its literal meaning is 'fist'.

3 V. Kayurov, 'My Encounters and Work with V. I. Lenin in the Year of the Revolution', *Proletarskaya Revoliutsiya*, No. 3 (36), 1924.

4 The anarchists were in occupation of the villa of the ex-minister Durnovo [which they converted into a workers' rest centre]: the Provisional Government tried in vain to dislodge them.

5 Just before the October Revolution, *Golos Truda*, the anarcho-syndicalist weekly edited by Voline, A. Shapiro, Y. Grossman-Roshchin and others, had expressed its disapproval of an uprising which could terminate only in establishing a new authority: adding, however, that it would . . . follow the masses. [Declaration printed in V. Voline, *La Révolution Inconnue* (Paris, 1947), p. 193.] In the same period Kropotkin's disciple Atabekian, stationed in Moscow, was deploring 'the horrors of the civil war'. Old Kropotkin himself, loyal to the Allies and his own illusions of 1914, viewed the Bolsheviks as 'agents of Germany', a position he firmly maintained right down to his death.

6 Vsevolod Volin (Voline) or Eichenbaum, the anarcho-syndicalist militant, had lived for some years in America: he was later to become one of the leaders of the libertarian movement in the Ukraine known as Nabat (Tocsin) which supported Makhno and tried to provide him with an ideology (1919–20). He was banished from the Soviet Republic in 1921. [Voline engaged in relief-work abroad for the persecuted Russian anarchists and published important work on anarchist history; he died in Paris in 1945.]

7 Of the Gordin brothers, one has since become the proponent of an international language of monosyllables, written in signs, the *Ao* language: the other, having in 1920–21 founded the original doctrines of Anarcho-Universalism (which seemed to be about to lead him rapidly towards Communism), has now, I think, retired from political life. [Actually both of the Gordin brothers were arrested for brief periods in the early 1920s: both then emigrated to the United States, one becoming a Protestant missionary and the other a settler in Israel.]

8 Alexander Gay, an Anarchist-Communist, had lived in Switzerland for many years as a revolutionary exile. He was a member of the All-Russian

Soviet Executive Committee. During an illness, he had to go for his health to the Caucasus, where he participated very vigorously in the civil war. He defended Pyatigorsk and Kislovodsk and was one of the organizers of the Red terror in the Terek region. The Whites caught him in January 1919 at Kislovodsk, where he was confined by typhus, and sabred him to death in his bed. A few days later, they hanged his wife, Xenia Gay.

9 Jacques Sadoul, *Notes sur la Révolution Bolchévique* (Paris, 1919), letter to Albert Thomas dated 8 April 1918.

10 [Victor Serge's treatment of this whole incident is somewhat evasive. Despite his insistence that no 'well-known' or 'known' anarchist (*aucun anarchiste connu*) was killed in the actual fighting, a leading anarchist worker named Khodunov, who had been elected to a Moscow Soviet from his factory and had fought in the October Revolution, was shot by the Cheka while in their custody following the raid (G. P. Maximov, *The Guillotine at Work* (Chicago, 1940), pp. 388–9); of the other anarchists killed (on the number of which our sources are vague), it is an arbitrary judgement to declare that none was 'known'. And while *Anarkhiya* did re-appear on or about 21 April, its appearance was subject to harassment from the government drive against anarchist publications. See Paul Avrich, *The Russian Anarchists* (Princeton, 1967), pp. 184–5, and Maximov, *op. cit.*, p. 410. Anarchist groupings were in fact broken up severely in this period.]

11 Karlis Goppers, *Four Defeats* (*Četri Sabrakumi*) (Riga, 1920).

12 See A. Vetliugin, *Adventurers of the Civil War* (*Avantiuristy Grazhdanskoi Voiny*) (Paris, 1921).

13 [For a full description of the various trends of Russian anarchism, several of which were neither pro-Bolshevik nor 'anti-Soviet', and which found, contrary to Serge, great difficulty in keeping open 'their press, their organization and their clubs', see Avrich, *op. cit.*, Chapters 7, 8 and Epilogue.]

14 V. Sorin, *The Party and the Opposition* (*Partiya i Oppozitsiya*) (Moscow, 1925).

15 Lenin, *Collected Works* (London, 1969), Vol. 27, pp. 235–77.

16 Sorin, *op. cit.*

17 Lenin, *Collected Works*, Vol. 27, pp. 333, 334, 336, 339. [It should be noted that 'State capitalism' here, in both Lenin's and the Left Communists' usage, refers to the State-controlled private sector ('grain monopoly, state-controlled entrepreneurs and traders, bourgeois co-operators' in the listing given by Lenin on *ibid.*, p. 336); it does not reflect the more common usage of later years, when 'State capitalism' was applied to a Russia now devoid of a private sector (i.e. in Stalin's day and subsequently), with the State itself being conceptualized as the capitalist.]

18 [F. W. Taylor, the American industrial expert (author of *Principles of Scientific Management*, 1911), pioneered the use of the stop-watch in industry, both as a tool for managerial efficiency and as a means of extracting intensified labour from workers.]

19 Lenin, *Collected Works*, Vol. 27, pp. 238, 241, 244, 245, 246, 247, 259, 265, 267–8, 268–9, 275.

20 Lenin had to defend his theses at the All-Russian Soviet Executive both against Bukharin and against the anarchist Alexander Gay, who even declared that the proletariat of the West was too deeply corrupted for the revolution. . . . Lenin also spent time justifying the slogan 'Steal back the stolen', which had been attributed to him and was still occupying the mind of the whole press. 'But it's a very good slogan', he remarked.

21 *Evening News, Life, The Fatherland, People's Word, People's Friend, Land and Liberty.*

22 The bread-ration laid down by the Petrograd Soviet was, as of 29 May:

(1) For workers performing heavy physical labour, 200 grams;

(2) For workers engaged in persistent physical labour, 100 grams;

(3) For clerical workers, 50 grams;

(4) For capitalists and rentiers, 25 grams.

The unemployed are classified according to their previous employment, within the above categories.

23 See Chapter 5, pp. 160–63, on 'The Allies and the Cancellation of Debts'.

24 [The cooperation between the local Soviet authorities at Murmansk and the British forces under Kemp and Poole was encouraged or permitted by Moscow from 1 March to the end of June. Trotsky notified the Murmansk Soviet that they must 'accept any and all assistance from the Allied missions' – an order which, in the light of the Murmansk Soviet's subsequent break with Moscow and crossing over to the Allied forces (in early July), provided ample scope for Stalinist historians who wished to accuse Trotsky of folly or treason. Serge may here be discreetly repudiating the early stages of this anti-Trotsky campaign on the Murmansk epidsode. See R. H. Ullman, *Intervention and the War* (Princeton, 1961), pp. 116–17, 181–5.]

25 From the testimony of René Marchand, in *Pourquoi Je Me Suis Rallié à la Formule de la Révolution Sociale* (Paris, 1919). On the attitude of the Allies in this period, Sadoul's *Notes sur la Révolution Bolchévique* form a document of the first importance.

26 David R. Francis, *Russia from the American Embassy, April 1916–November 1918* (New York, 1921).

27 A. Argunov, *Between Two Bolshevisms* (*Mezhdu Dvumia Bolshevizmami*) (Paris, 1919).

28 The duplicity of the S R party is blatantly evident in the motion concerning Allied intervention adopted by a National Council meeting of 7–14 May 1918. 'Democracy can in no case rely, for the restoration of the power of the people, upon a foreign armed force, even one in alliance . . .'; however, the independence of Russia can be retrieved only through 'the immediate liquidation of Bolshevik power and the installation of a government legitimized by universal suffrage. . . . This government could permit the entry of Allied troops on to Russian territory, for purely strategic purposes and on condition of the non-intervention of these governments in the internal affairs of Russia' (!!).

29 Boris Savinkov was one of the most forceful characters of the S R party. Born in 1879, a militant since his youth, he became a member of St Petersburg's first Marxist groups, along with Lenin and Martov. He went into exile, and became a member of the Socialist-Revolutionary party, whose terrorist organization he directed from 1903 onwards along with the agent-provocateur Azef. Savinkov organized or took part in almost all the S R terrorist acts between 1904 and 1906 (notably the execution of the minister von Plehve and the Grand Duke Sergei), was condemned to death, and managed to escape. A talented novelist and occasional poet, the author of a set of remarkable memoirs, Boris Savinkov was a dilettante, complex spirit: audacious and practical, but tormented by mystical doubts, and with no belief in anything but personal strength and individual heroism. A patriot during the war, he became during the Kerensky period one of the most passionate advocates of a strong, dictatorial authority, which indeed he felt a vocation to exercise. He took part in Kornilov's abortive *coup*, and subsequently became one of the most active adventurers of the counter-revolution. In 1924 he was arrested on Soviet soil, where he had returned illegally, and confessed, before the Revolutionary Tribunal in Moscow, his error and crime in having misunderstood and opposed the revolution. After being sentenced to ten years' imprisonment, he committed suicide in 1925.

30 [See Editorial Postscript: 'The Allied Part in the Czechoslovak Intervention.']

31 Evidence of ex-Lieutenant P. Pascal at the trial of the Right S Rs in Moscow in 1922. His testimony is in complete accord with what is admitted by S R writers like Lebedev and Savinkov.

32 P. S. Parfenov, *Lessons of the Past: The Civil War in Siberia, 1918, 1919, 1920* (*Uroky Proshlogo: Grazhadanskaya Voina v Sibiri, 1918, 1919,*

1920) (Harbin, 1921). [W. H. Chamberlin points out (*The Russian Revolution, 1917–1921* (London, 1935), Vol. 2, p. 23) that Parfenov cites no source for his statement incriminating the British and French Missions in planning the Czechoslovak rising together with Moscow counter-revolutionaries; he also argues that Lavergne in particular could not have been involved in such a move, in view of the general's undeniable efforts, at this time, to work out methods of cooperation with the Soviet government. 14 April does seem, on the evidence of Lockhart's dispatches, a date several weeks too early for any definite anti-Soviet moves, involving the Czechs, to be concerted. On the other hand, it is precisely in this period that Lockhart's contacts with the White organizations in Moscow become intensified (Ullman, *op. cit.*, pp. 163–4); some meeting of the kind mentioned by Parfenov may well have taken place, even if the Czechoslovak action (especially in the form it actually took, later in May) can hardly have been on the agenda in any detail.]

33 L. Kritsman, *The Heroic Period of the Great Russian Revolution* (*Geroicheskii Period Velikoi Russkoi Revoliutsii*), 2nd edn (Moscow, 1926). It is a matter for regret that this remarkable economic analysis of the Russian revolution has not been translated in the West.

34 The Russian State had been the owner of the railways, etc.

35 On 21 November 1918 came the expropriation of commercial capital (with the decree on the nationalization of domestic commerce); then the expropriation of small-scale industry (nationalized on 29 November 1918); then of the cooperatives (nationalized in November–December).

36 ['Workers' control' in the Russian context thus has an entirely different significance from the slogan of workers' control in Western labour and Socialist movements. In the latter, the concept of the control of an industry by its workers is not applicable to a temporary phase before the actual expropriation of the employers: it relates to forms of industrial democracy which are to be practised within nationalized or socialized economic structure. The weakness of the Bolshevik category of 'workers' control' has its roots in the relative absence of a syndicalist tradition in the Russian labour movement: *Golos Truda*, the anarcho-syndicalist organ, was only set up in Russia during 1917 itself, when most of its editorial team arrived from exile in the United States. (See Avrich, *op. cit.*, pp. 137–9, 142, 148.)]

37 A. Rykov's speech to the First Congress of Economic Councils (26 May–4 June 1918).

38 Quoted by A. Pankratova in *The Factory Committees of Russia in the Struggle for the Socialist Factory* (*Fabzavkomy Rossii v Borbe Za Sotsialisticheskuiu Fabriku*) (Moscow, 1923).

39 Lenin, *Collected Works*, Vol. 27, pp. 392–3, 395, 396, 397–8.

40 *ibid.*, pp. 425, 430, 434, 435, 436, 469, 475, 476–7.

41 *ibid.*, p. 536.

42 Lenin, *Collected Works*, Vol. 36, p. 489.

43 Lenin's style, as the guide of the revolution, may be seen here in these few details. He warned the recipients of his telegram: 'You are personally responsible for the prompt and rigorous application of these measures. . . . Make an appeal to the population explaining them. . . . Keep me informed on the progress of the operations, by telegrams sent to me at least, I repeat at least, every two days.' See *Proletarskaya Revoliutsiya*, No. 3 (26), 1924.

44 A few figures may be useful. The textile centre of Ivanovo-Voznesensk assembled twenty-three detachments (2,243 men in all) who, from September to 1 December 1918, secured almost 2,500,000 poods of grain. In the same period, Moscow received from its own detachments 322 wagon-loads of foodstuffs; previously, only a small number of wagons had got through to the city in some weeks. In three months, 30,000 workers moved from the non-agrarian to the grain-producing provinces. (From the Food Commissariat's report on its activity during 1918–19.)

45 Gukovsky's report to the All-Russian Soviet Executive, 11 April 1918.

46 *ibid.*

47 Tsuriupa's report to the All-Russian Soviet Executive, 9 May 1918.

48 The chair at Vee-Tsik's debates was usually taken by Sverdlov, and the Communist fraction there was headed by Sosnovsky, its usual spokesman. The most frequent speakers, apart from Lenin and Trotsky, who tended to present official reports, were Bukharin (for the Left Communists), Karelin, Trutovsky and Kamkov (Left S Rs), Alexander Gay and Apollon Karelin (anarchists), Lozovsky (Internationalist Social-Democrat), Kogan-Bernstein (Right S R) and Martov and Dan (Mensheviks).

49 In these circumstances, the position of the Menshevik Social-Democrats was utterly false. The right S Rs took up arms for the same practical programme (Constituent Assembly, restoration of democracy) that the Mensheviks wanted: but the latter refrained from resorting to arms, limiting themselves (as they said) to agitation and action among the working class, in the hope of becoming the party of the labour opposition within the democracy still to come. They were accused – and with reason – of being the accomplices of the Whites and the Czechoslovaks. These 'slanderous accusations' they denied, and 'insisted on the truth' – which was, for instance, that the Menshevik workers were declaring themselves neutral as the Red Guards were battling against the Czechoslovaks or Savinkov's squads.

50 The texts of these different decrees were written by Trotsky and voted on his proposal. The decree on military training begins with these words: 'To liberate mankind from militarism and from the barbarism of bloody struggles between the peoples: such is one of the cardinal aims of Socialism.'

51 L. D. Trotsky, *How the Revolution Armed Itself* (*Kak Vooruzhalas Revoliutsiya*) (Moscow, 1923), Vol. 1, 'Documents of April–June 1918'.

52 [Pichegru was a general in the French revolution who joined a plot against the Consulate and was executed in 1804.]

53 [Trotsky's judgement on Shchastny was not shared by the Soviet government's naval commissar, Dybenko, who went so far as to publish a protest against the verdict, and the circumstantiality of the evidence, in Moscow's anarchist newspaper (Maximov, *op. cit.*, pp. 73–4). The sentence and trial actually evoked widespread protests in Russia, more so than the hundreds of summary executions conducted by the Cheka; it even moved Martov to write his pamphlet, *Down with the Death Penalty*. See E. H. Carr, *A History of Soviet Russia: The Bolshevik Revolution, 1917–1923* (London, 1950), Vol. 1, pp. 163–4.]

Chapter 8: The July–August Crisis

1 Jacques Sadoul, *Notes sur la Révolution Bolchévique* (Paris, 1919). This book contains a number of fine portrayals of the men of the Russian revolution: they are strikingly faithful portraits, though a little hasty.

2 'Trotsky proclaims aloud with superb style and, more importantly, with complete sincerity, that Lenin is the uncontested head of the Russian revolution.' 'Lenin and Trotsky form, for all who see them at close quarters, an example of the most confidential unity and of the most fertile collaboration': Sadoul, *ibid.*, letter of 11 May 1918. So close a collaboration, in a complete community of thought and action, is bound to recall that of Marx and Engels. [Sadoul, by the time Serge wrote these lines, had become an unflinching Stalinist: he was to repay this embarrassing reminder of his early enthusiasm for Trotsky by denouncing Serge (whom he had known well in the French Communist colony in Petrograd) as a terrorist during the latter's campaign in 1936 against the Moscow trials.]

3 [Dzerzhinsky died suddenly in 1926, having collapsed in a Central Committee session in which, apparently, he had been fulminating against the Left opposition. In his *Memoirs of a Revolutionary* (London, 1967), Serge quotes another assessment by Radek: 'Felix died just in time. He was a dogmatist. He would not have shrunk from reddening his hands in our blood.']

4 See the biographical note in Chapter 4 (note 32, p. 385) giving a biography of Y. M. Sverdlov.

5 [Zinoviev, at the time that this reference to him was published, was in disgrace both with the Stalin wing of the Russian Communist party (he had been expelled in 1927 for leading the united opposition along with Trotsky) and with the residual Left opposition itself (for he had recanted his dissident views). Hence, perhaps, a certain circumspection in Serge's language about him. Expelled again in 1932 and 1934 from the party, he recanted ever more abjectly down to his 'confession' in the Moscow trial of 1936, where he was sentenced to death.]

6 [Rakovsky was still, at the time of publication, an intransigent Left oppositionist evolving, in his exile and disgrace, one of the first 'new class' theories of the Stalinist bureaucracy. He capitulated to Stalin in 1934, confessed in the 1938 Moscow trial to having been a British spy since 1924, and was sentenced to imprisonment for twenty years, three of which he managed to survive.]

7 In 1906 while still a young student, a member of the S R party even then, Maria Spiridonova executed the governor of Tambov province, who had put down peasant disturbances with signal cruelty. She was arrested, and brutalized by the police: she then spent eleven years in the Siberian convict-prison of Akatui, where the regime was so harsh that suicide became the political inmates' final form of protest. Liberated by the 1917 revolution, Maria Spiridonova became the Left S R party's leader. An irreconcilable foe of the Bolsheviks, she was later detained for many years. [Spiridonova was named in the 1938 Moscow trial in connection with the tale of a conspiracy, between Left Communists and Left S Rs, to kill Lenin in 1918: she did not appear as a witness in the trial, perhaps because she had already been executed.]

8 N. Lenin, *Collected Works* (London, 1969), Vol. 27, p. 527.

9 I have elsewhere published in *Vie Ouvrière*, around the end of 1921, the detailed story of this assassination as it was related to me by one of the terrorists concerned, Y. G. Blyumkin, who had become a Communist after having twice miraculously escaped death in attempts committed against his person in the Ukraine by his 'activist' Left S R comrades who objected to his closer ties with the Bolsheviks. [Blyumkin had joined the Trotskyist opposition and been executed by the G P U just before Serge published this book.] His companion in the assassination, Andreyev, later fought alongside Makhno and was killed.

10 [Vatsetis resigned from his post as the Red Army's commander-in-chief in early 1919, following disagreements on strategy in which his unsuccessful advocacy of a switch to the southern front was supported also by Trotsky. He retained high responsibility in the Red Army in Stalin's era until 1937–8, when he perished in the massacre of army commanders.]

11 On the Left S R rising, see the following: Y. Peters, 'Reminiscences of a Cheka Worker in the First Year of the Revolution', *Proletarskaya Revoliutsiya*, No. 10 (33), 1924; L. D. Trotsky, *Collected Works* (Moscow and Leningrad, 1926), Vol. 17, Pt i; and Dzerzhinsky's report on the incident.

12 See Trutovsky's speech to Vee-Tsik, 20 May 1918.

13 Karelin's speech, same session.

14 In 1917, the Left S Rs opposed Kerensky and Chernov, without going to the length of splitting the party they shared with them. In October, when the insurrection was being prepared, they refused formally to give it any support; once the revolution had taken place, they applauded it. Even then, they refused to participate in the first Soviet government and advocated instead a broad Socialist coalition. In the end, they joined the government; they soon left it in order to criticize it more freely, while practising a policy of support towards it; they finished up with an attempt to govern alone.

15 With a dozen deaths as the result. The Left S R, Cherepanov, who until

then had led an excellent revolutionary career, was one of the authors of this killing. He was shot by the Cheka.

16 [The 'Two-and-a-Half International', or Vienna Union, uniting thirteen moderate internationalist parties (including the British I L P, the German USPD, most of the French SFIO and the Swiss Social-Democratic party) was founded in 1921, and dissolved into the more Right-wing Labour and Socialist International ('Second International') in 1923.]

17 Perkhurov resumed fighting on the Czechoslovak front. Taken prisoner later by the Reds, he re-entered the service of the Red Army and was arrested only in 1921, at Ekaterinburg, at the moment when he was preparing a new *coup*. He appeared before the Revolutionary Tribunal, and was shot in 1922.

18 See *Sixteen Days: Materials on the History of the White Revolt at Yaroslavl* (*Shestnadtsat Dnei: Materialy po Istorii Yaroslavskogo Belogvardeiskogo Myatezha*) (Yaroslavl, 1924).

19 [Lockhart's report to the War Cabinet on his return home ('Memorandum on the Internal Situation in Russia', 1 November 1918, copy in Public Record Office, File FO 371/3337, the relevant section of which is summarized in R. H. Ullman, *Intervention and War* (Princeton, 1961), p. 231) confirms this part of Savinkov's testimony in great detail, down to the sum of two and a half million roubles donated by the French and to Noulens's false information about the Allied landing.]

20 *Průkopnik Svobody*, the organ of the Czech Communists in Russia, revealed in its issue of 28 June 1918 that the National Council which stood over the Czechoslovak troops in Russia had, between 7 March and the beginning of their campaign against the Bolsheviks, received 11,188,000 roubles from a French consul and £70,000 from a British consul. *Průkopnik Svobody* provided in its report all the further details one could desire. [Lockhart, in his report to the British government ('Memorandum on the Internal Situation in Russia', *op. cit.*), lists the Czech National Council as one of the 'various counter-revolutionary organizations in Moscow' with whom 'I began to strengthen my relations' after the failure of his hopes for joint Allied–Soviet cooperation. He adds: 'The French commenced to finance and support these organizations before I did.']

21 'It was precisely because the intervention, which M. Noulens constantly presented as the *firm policy* of the Entente powers, had in fact run up against the most serious objections, that our ambassador was led – in order to overcome the resistance he had encountered (which hurt his pride) and in order to give some force to his arguments – to prove through events themselves that he had fully prepared the ground, so that it needed only a minimum effort to overthrow the Bolshevik government and secure the installation of a national Russian government' (René Marchand, *Pourquoi Je Me Suis Rallié à la Formule de la Révolution Sociale* (Petrograd, 1919).) Sadoul's letters for July 1918 several times use expressions like 'M. Noulens, who has inspired the insurrection now going on in Yaroslavl' (Sadoul, *op. cit.*, p. 99).

22 A. Argunov, *Between Two Bolshevisms* (*Mezhdu Dvumia Bolshevizmami*) (Paris, 1919).

23 Cited by I. Maisky, *The Democratic Counter-Revolution* (*Demokraticheskaya Kontr-Revoliutsiya*) (Moscow, 1923).

24 A message, 'To All, To All, To All', published on 11 July under the signatures of the Chairman of the Council of People's Commissars, N. Lenin, and the War Commissar, L. Trotsky, had stated: 'The former commander-in-chief on the Czechoslovak front, the Left S R Muraviev, is declared a traitor and an enemy of the people. Any honest citizen who crosses his path is instructed to kill him on the spot.'

25 [Tukhachevsky was to play a prominent part in Soviet military history. In his twenties he commanded armies on several civil war fronts, including the attack on Poland in 1920 where failures of coordination between him and Stalin led to the Red Army's defeat and some subsequent enmity between the two men. At first an advocate of 'the military opposition' which

emphasized militias and guerrillas as against Trotsky's centralizing plans for the Red Army, Tukhachevsky later led the modernizing team that re-organized the USSR's armed forces. One of the first Marshals of the Soviet Union to be appointed (in 1935), he was executed after a secret trial in 1937 following the Gestapo's planting of forged documents incriminating him as a German agent.]

26 The present constitution of the USSR follows that of 1918 in its main outlines, with additions on the rights of the federated republics and the Union's central institutions. [The later constitution of 1936, with its guarantees of civil rights and its replacement of indirect by direct election, was of course even more solely 'the plan for an ideal proletarian democracy'.]

27 Cited in A. Anishev, *Sketches of the History of the Civil War* (*Ocherki Istorii Grazhdanskoi Voiny*) (Leningrad, 1925).

28 Yakovlev was to go over to Kolchak in October 1918.

29 V. Milyutin, 'Pages from a Journal', *Prozhektor*, No. 4, 1924. See also P. M. Bykov, *The Last Days of the Romanovs* (*Poslednie Dni Romanovykh*) (Sverdlovsk, 1926); and local publications in the Ural area.

Chapter 9: The Terror and the Will to Victory

1 Admiral Kolchak subsequently drew on this gold reserve, stolen from the Russian nation, as follows: to the French, 876 poods (one pood = approximately thirty-six pounds avoirdupois); to the British, 516; to the Anglo–French jointly, 698; to the Japanese, 1,142 (total: 3,232 poods). Deposited with Japan as security for a loan, 1,500 poods; as security with an Anglo–American finance trust, 3,397; purchases of American rifles, 100; purchase of Remington rifles, fifty; purchase of Colt machine-guns, fifty; total out-goings 5,637 poods. Deposited at Shanghai, 375. Grand total: 9,244 poods (S. Piontkovsky, 'Material on the History of the Counter-revolution', *Proletarskaya Revoliutsiya*, No. 1, 1921).

2 See the reference on p. 268.

3 Or Condeau. We have transliterated the name from the Russian.

4 See I. Maisky, *The Democratic Counter-Revolution* (*Demokraticheskaya Kontr-Revoliutsiya*) (Moscow, 1923).

5 It would fall to less than 750,000 inhabitants in 1919–20.

6 [Makhno's armies liberated large tracts of the Ukraine in the battles of 1919 against Denikin and of 1920 against Wrangel. In the latter offensive the Red Army cooperated with the anarchist forces, despite the harrying of anarchism that was official Bolshevik policy. However, once Wrangel was defeated, the Reds turned against Makhno, surrounding his troops and executing his lieutenants who had gone in to parley with them. Makhno fought his way to the Rumanian frontier with a handful of men; he died in exile in Paris, a demoralized, alcoholic factory-worker, in 1934.]

7 M. S. Uritsky, the son of a Jewish small-trading family in Kiev, and former law student, had undergone three sentences of exile in Yakutia and northern Russia, and several terms of imprisonment. This professional revolutionary, riddled with tuberculosis, knew no private life. He had joined the Bolshevik party at the same time as Trotsky, and was on its Central Committee.

Fanny Kaplan and Kanegisser were shot. The background to these killings was revealed later, at the trial of the Central Committee of the SR party in June and July 1922, held in Moscow, when the main terrorists of the organization had gone over to Bolshevism. The Central Committee members persisted in their denial of any responsibility for these acts, but it was established that they had knowledge of their preparation; that one of them (Donskoi) had met and talked with Fanny Kaplan; and that the terrorist organization was providing them with money from the proceeds of 'expropriations' and had been instructed by them to blow up a gold train on its way to Germany. The SR party wanted to gain the benefit of the assassinations, but not to take too heavy a responsibility for them, the outcome being so uncertain. Donskoi suggested to the terrorist Semyonov that a squad of 'Black Mask' activists be formed, in the style of the anarchists. . . . Fanny Kaplan had been an anarchist terrorist: she had been arrested in Kiev in 1906 and given life imprisonment. In the Akatui convict prison, where she spent ten years, she became an S R. 'I fired at Lenin', she declared, 'because I consider him a traitor to Socialism, because his very existence discredits Socialism. I am unconditionally on the side of the Samara government and the struggle against Germany, side by side with the Allies.'

8 Testimony at the Moscow trial of S Rs, hearing of 28 June 1922.

9 [Cromie, the Naval Attaché of the British Embassy, had been left in Petrograd as the senior embassy official after the Allied diplomats' departure for Vologda: he was entrusted specifically with the task of blowing up what remained of the Russian Baltic fleet in the harbour of the city. Already in early May, the War Cabinet in London had authorized his preparations, and allocated a sum of £300,000 as the sum required by Cromie for 'payment to be made for services rendered' (War Cabinet 'A' Minutes, Minutes 408A and 409A of meetings dated 10 and 11 May 1918; Public Record Office. File Cab. 23/14). At this stage Cromie's destruction of the fleet was to be conditional upon a sudden German descent on Petrograd, and the somewhat chimerical proviso was added: 'Care should be taken not to antagonize unnecessarily the Soviet government.' However, later in the month Lockhart cabled London urging the synchronization of Cromie's explosions with a massive anti-Soviet intervention in the north and at Vladivostok (on Lockhart's intervention plan see Postscript, p. 373, and R. H. Ullman, *Intervention and the War* (Princeton, 1961), pp. 186–8; his message linking Cromie's scheme with the intervention against the Soviet government was sent as telegram 219, dispatched 25 May 1918; in Milner MSS, Box 110, File C–1). In the press after Cromie's death, and in subsequent British accounts, the captain was presented as something of an ordinary diplomat going about his innocent business and foully slain by an intemperate Cheka. Even Ullman remarks: 'At the time of his death his plans for this destruction were far advanced, but there was nothing specifically counter-revolutionary about them. They were wholly connected with Britain's war against Germany.' But, even if the Bolsheviks could be expected to appreciate this distinction, it is invalidated by Lockhart's 25 May telegram, which states: 'If however we are to intervene without Bolsheviks as now seems probable, it will be absolutely necessary for us to destroy Baltic fleet. I have had several conversations with Captain Cromie to this effect.'

Cromie, according to the memoirs of Paul Dukes (a British Secret Service agent active in Petrograd later in 1918), had also been working with a reactionary cabal of Russian monarchist ex-officers in the city (Sir Paul Dukes, *The Story of 'ST 25': Adventure and Romance in the Secret Intelligence Service in Red Russia* (London, 1938), pp. 41, 79). Since one of these, on Dukes's account, was a Cheka double-agent, neither the raid on the British Embassy nor Cromie's death, in the exchange of fire that followed, can be considered as an ill-considered or bloodthirsty action by the Cheka, especially in the siege conditions of the time.]

10 [Accounts of the 'Lockhart affair' are given in: N. Reilly, *Sidney Reilly, Britain's Master Spy: A Narrative Written by Himself, Edited and Completed by his Wife* (London, 1931); G. A. Hill, *Go Spy the Land: Being the Adventures of I K 8 of the British Secret Service* (London, 1932); R. H. Bruce Lockhart, *Memoirs of a British Agent* (London, 1932); Robin Bruce Lockhart, *Ace of Spies* (another biography of Reilly) (London, 1967). All deny that Lockhart had any part in the Kremlin conspiracy. The memoirs of Hill, an agent involved with Reilly in the 'Lettish plot', are of particular interest: Hill, who had been working as a liaison officer with the Reds' own military intelligence service, was deputed officially for anti-Bolshevik work in Moscow, with Reilly and de Vertemont, after the departure of the Allied

missions (Hill, *op. cit.*, p. 212; Reilly, *op. cit.*, p. 30). The Soviet version implicating Lockhart as the main instigator of the assassination plot was repeated with testimony from a Cheka agent-provocateur among the Lettish participants, in the Moscow paper *Nedelya* in March 1966; an English translation is given as an appendix in Lockhart, *Ace of Spies*.]

11 [De Vertemont and Kalamatiano were the heads respectively of French and United States Intelligence in Moscow (Hill, *op. cit.*, pp. 236, 246). Kalamatiano was shot after being found guilty by the Revolutionary Tribunal in the 'Lockhart conspiracy'.]

12 [The Western accounts are at pains to deny this. 'Rather than execute them, Reilly intended to de-bag the Bolshevik hierarchy and, with Lenin and Trotsky in front, to march them through the streets of Moscow bereft of trousers and underpants, shirt-tails flying in the breeze. They would then be imprisoned.' (Lockhart, *Ace of Spies*, p. 76; see also, Reilly, *op. cit.*, pp. 25–8; Hill, *op. cit.*, p. 238, who adds that Reilly's aim was solely 'to kill them by ridicule'.)]

13 [According to Lockhart (*Memoirs of a British Agent*, p. 316), he provided the Letts only with a letter on official British paper, signed by himself, to enable them to pass through the lines of the northern front and defect to General Poole's forces. All the Western published sources deny any personal participation by Lockhart in Reilly's plot to seize the Bolshevik leadership in the Kremlin. Lockhart's own memoirs state that he, Grenard and Lavergue were told by Reilly of his projected *coup*, and warned him not to proceed with it (*loc. cit.*). Serge's account of Lockhart's role in the whole intrigue is relatively restrained: and Lockhart's very lenient treatment at the hands of the Cheka (he was interned in the Kremlin, allowed visits from his Russian woman-friend, and visited several times by Karakhan for chats about diplomatic matters) raise the question of how seriously the Bolsheviks took his guilt, despite the death-sentence passed on him *in absentia* following his repatriation to England.

On the other hand, the possibility cannot be excluded that there was a conscious division of labour in the conspiracy between him and Reilly. The account of Lockhart's son (*Ace of Spies*, pp. 70, 73–5, 90, 98) reveals an extremely close and confidential relationship between the two, both in anti-Bolshevik intrigue in Moscow (Lockhart's subsidization of the White underground was channelled through Reilly) and in the pro-interventionist social circle, including Secret Service agents and senior Intelligence and diplomatic officials, who frequented Reilly's rooms in the Albany from 1918 on (see note 35, Chapter 11). Lockhart Jr reproduces a photograph (*op cit.*, opposite p. 96) of an inscribed cigar-box presented by Reilly to Lockhart. The inscription reads: '*To R.H. Bruce Lockhart, HBM's Representative in Russia in 1918 (during the Bolchevik Regime), in remembrance of events in Moscow during August and September of that year, from his faithful Lieutenant*, Sidney Reilly.' And two very friendly personal letters to Lockhart from his 'lieutenant', dated 23 and 25 November 1918, and discussing the struggle against Bolshevism, are preserved in Milner MSS (Box 110, File C–2). In the first Reilly writes advocating the formation of an 'LDC (League of the Defence of Civilization)' to withstand 'the great cataclysm relentlessly approaching'. ('Next year we will have civil war all over the world. You will find me on the side of the "White Guards" who are bound to lose.') Reilly asks his old colleague to 'do something' to support the approaches he was making through the Secret Service and Foreign Office to find 'a half-way decent job' in order to 'continue to serve . . . in the question of Russia and Bolshevism'. 'I should like nothing better', Reilly concludes his plea, 'than to serve under you.']

14 Only very few details have been published about the Lockhart affair. We have drawn on the communiqués of the Vee-Cheka that appeared in the newspapers of the time, and on the reminiscences of Peters in No. 10 (33) of *Proletarskaya Revoliutsiya*, 1924.

15 A. Morizet, *Chez Lénine et Trotski* (Paris, 1921). This book includes a very interesting interview with the head of the Red Army.

16 Larissa Reissner, *The Front* (*Front*) (Moscow, 1918). The author, the daughter of a Socialist professor, fought at Sviazhsk and in the Volga flotilla. Her little book, of which a German translation has been published, is a psychological document and historical testimony of the first importance. [An English translation of Larissa Reissner's narrative, 'Sviazhsk', was published in *Fourth International* (New York), June 1943; reproduced in *Leon Trotsky: The Man and His Work* (J. Hansen and others) (New York, 1969).]

17 [Arkadi Rosengoltz subsequently joined Trotsky's opposition to Stalin. He soon capitulated, and was appointed first ambassador to London and then Commissar for Foreign Trade. He was arrested in late 1937 and appeared as a major defendant in the Bukharin–Rykov Moscow trial the following year; executed March 1938. Ivan Nikitich Smirnov was known as 'the Lenin of Siberia' through his part in establishing Bolshevik rule there after the revolution. He lost his post in the Soviet government after his membership of the Trotskyist opposition, was exiled in 1927, but capitulated after Stalin's 'Left turn'. Arrested in 1933 and given a ten-year sentence, he was put on trial again with the 'Trotskyite–Zinovievite Centre' in August 1936 and shot with all the other defendants.]

18 S. I. Gusev, 'The Days of Sviazhsk', in *Proletarskaya Revoliutsiya*, No. 2 (25), 1924. [This is a very barbed reference by Serge, since Gusev, an old military rival of Trotsky's from the eastern front dispute of 1919, had become a prominent writer, or rather re-writer, of military history from a Stalinist viewpoint: his brochure, *Our Military Disagreements*, had condemned the 'severe methods' of Trotsky which he had endorsed in the passage cited by Serge.]

19 Speech at the Kazan Theatre, 11 September.

20 M. Tukhachevsky, 'The First Army in 1918', in *Revoliutsiya i Voina*, No. 4–5, 1921.

21 The worker Blyukher became one of the Red Army's best strategists; see M. Golubykh, *The Partisans of the Ural* [no Russian title available] (Ekaterinburg, 1924). [Blyukher, after a mission to the Kuomintang as their chief military adviser, became Red Army Marshal to the Far Eastern army; in this command he inflicted a decisive defeat on the Japanese at Lake Hassan in the summer of 1938. He died in November that year, having been arrested and severely tortured in the N K V D purge of the army.]

22 [Kovtyukh continued his military career: he reached the rank of Army Corps Commander and was shot, probably in July 1938, in Stalin's massacre of army leaders.]

23 The 6,000 workers of Ivashchenko rose as the Red Army approached the city, but prematurely; the Reds did not reach Samara until a week later.

24 In the present work we will be unable to follow the events taking place in the Far East. Ever since the beginning of the year, a 'Russian government' had been in residence at Harbin in Manchuria, under the presidency of 'General' Horvat, the manager of the Chinese-Eastern Railway. Mr Putilov [former owner of the famous Works] played a prominent role in it. It was this government that first proposed the formation of the National Army to Admiral Kolchak; the Admiral had to visit Tokyo to seek the agreement of the Japanese government. The real master of the Far East was the Japanese General Nakashima. Ataman Semyonov was battling against the Reds, at the head of powerful bands of some 1,800 Chinese, Mongols, Buryats, Japanese, Serbs and Trans-Baikal Cossacks. His *de facto* chief of staff was one Captain Kuroki, the son of the Japanese marshal who distinguished himself in the Russo–Japanese war. A Siberian government, headed by the S R Derber, was trying to function at Vladivostok. This town was being disputed between the Bolshevik workers on the one side and the Czechs and White Russians on the other. The Americans landed there in September; a Japanese marshal, Otani, took the supreme command of all the Allied forces in Siberia; and

the Allies formed a council of High Commissioners, on which Britain was represented by Sir Charles Eliot, a former diplomat in Petrograd, and France by M. Regnault, their ambassador to Tokyo. This Council brutally disarmed the Russian officers who were suspected of revolutionary tendencies. In the meantime, the Czech General Gajda was capturing Chita; along the length of the Trans-Siberian Railway he was arranging mass shootings and floggings of the peasants, and proclaiming himself as Generalissimo of the Russian and Czechoslovak armies (September). General Stepanov wrote to General Alexeyev: 'It appears that Japan, which lacks iron resources, will take: 1. Our Siberian coast, which is rich in iron ore; 2. Our part of the Chinese-Eastern Railway; 3. The port of Vladivostok and the Usuri territory.' Japan's designs still encountered the resistance of the USA. A. Denikin, *Sketches of the Russian Turmoil* (*Ocherki Russkoi Smuty*) (Paris, 1921–5), Vol. 3.

25 M. Y. Latsis, *The Extraordinary Commissions for Struggle Against Counter-Revolution* (*Chrezvichainye Komissii po Borbe s Kontr-Revoliutsiei*) (Moscow, 1921).

26 A decree of 2 November regularized the structure of the Extraordinary Commissions. The All-Russian Central Commission (Vee-Cheka) was charged with the task of unifying and controlling all the local commissions, whose decisions it was empowered to quash. Its members were appointed by the Council of People's Commissars; its chairman was a member of the Collegium of the Interior; and representatives to it were delegated directly from the Commissariats of the Interior and of Justice. Its principal members, apart from Dzerzhinsky, its chairman, were Latsis, Peters and Ksenofontov.

The local Chekas were constituted by the Executives of the local Soviets and remained subordinate to them, though the appointment of their chiefs had to be sent for approval.

27 Latsis, *op. cit.*

28 In all, 12,733 persons were executed in 1918, 1919 and 1920, over the whole of Russia. These official Cheka figures, which are admitted to be an under-estimate, can serve only as an indication of the true picture. Evidently they summarize only the organized, controlled and systematized activity of the Commissions. It must also be realized that the civil Revolutionary Tribunals also applied the death-penalty. [W. H. Chamberlin (*The Russian Revolution, 1917–1921* (London, 1935), Vol. 2, pp. 74–5) discusses the figure of 12,733, which must be a gross under-estimate even of 'organized' Cheka activity; he concludes that a total of 50,000 killed would be more probable for the Red terror in the civil war period of 1918–20.]

29 A. Mathiez, *La Révolution Française* (Paris, 1922), Vol. 3, p. 88, on the terror.

30 A figure given by M. Aulard. A reactionary historian, M. Jacques Bainville, concludes, despite his bias, that 'Regardless of its atrocious follies and its ignoble executants, the terror was an expression of the nation. It enlarged the energy of France in the time of one of the greatest dangers she has ever known' (*Histoire de la France* (Paris, 1924)).

31 In reality, the terror has been going on for centuries. From the Middle Ages till the coming of the bourgeois revolution it was the normal regime imposed by the possessing classes on the poor. According to Thomas More, 70,000 thieves, big and petty, were executed in England under Henry VIII. Under Queen Elizabeth vagabonds were being hung at the rate of 300 to 400 a year. In France 'under Louis XVI (ordinance of 13 July 1777) any fit man aged between 16 and 60 who lacked means of support and had no profession could be sent to the galleys'. (See Marx's Chapter 24, 'On Primitive Accumulation', in *Capital.*) The French law currently in force considers vagabondage (defined as the state of being without lodging, work or the means of support) as an offence punishable, if repeated, by 'relegation' to a penal colony, i.e. by a life-long penalty scarcely distinguishable from forced

labour. See Victor Serge, 'The Problem of Revolutionary Repression', in *Les Coulisses d'une Sûreté Générale* (Paris, 1923).

32 See the memoirs of Roman Gul, *Icy Marches* (*Ledyanoi Pokhod*) (Berlin, 1922).

33 L. Trotsky, *Sur Lénine* (Paris, 1926), Chapter 5.

34 N. Lenin, *Collected Works* (London, 1969), Vol. 27, p. 344.

Chapter 10: The German Revolution

1 E. Ludendorff, *My War Memories, 1914–1918* (London, 1919), Vol. 2.

2 Extracts from telegrams sent by GHQ to the government: 1 October 1918, 1300 hours: '... Urgently requested to propose peace forthwith. The troops are still holding but impossible to foresee what may happen to-morrow. Signed: Lersner.' 1 October, 1330 hours: 'If Prince Max of Baden is charged with forming a government at 7 or 8 this evening, I am willing to wait until the morning. Otherwise, I shall feel it necessary to issue a statement to the governments of the world this very night. Signed: Hindenburg.' 1 October (dispatched 2 October, at 0010 hours): 'General Ludendorff has told me that our peace proposals must be transmitted immediately from Berne to Washington. The army cannot wait another 48 hours. Signed: Grunau.' Such was the terror inspired by the army in the breasts of the General Staff! Paul Fröhlich, *The German Revolution* [a version of Fröhlich's *Zehn Jahre Krieg und Bürgerkrieg*, Berlin, 1924] (1926), Chapter 13.

3 [Ebert actually became Reich Chancellor, but a legal fiction of continuity between him and his predecessor as Chancellor and Regent, Prince Max, was maintained so that the officials of the Imperial authorities could recognize the legitimacy of the new government without violating their oaths to the Emperor (E. Waldman, *The Spartacist Uprising of 1919* (Milwaukee, 1958), p. 89).]

4 N. Lenin, *Collected Works* (London, 1969), Vol. 28, pp. 101–3.

5 Long years afterwards, in 1924 [i.e when Stalin, Zinoviev and Kamenev were accumulating every scrap of fact hinting at a divergency between Lenin and Trotsky], these words have been interpreted as the sign of a disagreement between the two leaders. It is enough to refer to the text of Lenin's remarks to see that both leaders were expressing the same idea. In any case, Trotsky was speaking in the name of the party's Central Committee. All we have here is a loose formulation let drop by the speaker, if not a stenographic error of the kind that is so abundant in the transcribed reports of the time. At this point there is only one line of thought, that of the party; on this common basis one can find only a slight nuance of difference, in that the emphasis in Lenin's speech is upon the danger of war with the imperialist Entente, whereas Trotsky is concluding (in his speech of 30 October, at Vee-Tsik) that the Republic enjoys a new respite up to the coming spring, since it is too late for large-scale operations to be commenced this year (a view which would be soon confirmed by events); his whole thought turns now on the offensive to be waged by the revolution in the West. We may discern here, perhaps, either the natural effects of the division of labour between the Chairman of the Council of People's Commissars and the Chairman of the Revolutionary Military Council; or the display of two different temperaments, one inclined to prudence and the other more towards the offensive.

6 From 'Strange and Monstrous', Lenin's reply to the Left Communists, 28 February 1918 (*Collected Works*, Vol. 27, p. 72).

7 Lenin, *Collected Works*, Vol. 28, pp. 65–6. A year later the Soviet Republic was to show itself to be inspired by these same principles when Lenin and Trotsky, in a joint telegram of 18 April 1919, urged the Soviet government of the Ukraine to take the offensive in the direction of Czernovitz (Bukovina) in order to establish a link with Soviet Hungary.

8 *ibid.*, pp. 116, 117, 123, 124. These observations were self-evidently addressed to those Communists who would have liked to force the pace of events in the Ukraine by means of an armed intervention.

9 K. Kautsky, *The Road to Power* (Chicago, 1909).

10 See *Les Partis Social-Démocrates* (a set of monographs put out by the Bureau d'Édition et de Diffusion) (Paris, 1925); also G. Y. Yakovin, *The Political Development of Contemporary Germany* [no Russian title available] (Leningrad, 1927).

11 [i.e. after its failure to mobilize a large working-class base in the events of 1923.]

12 [Liebknecht actually voted with the rest of the SPD parliamentarians in August 1914; and when he did break discipline he was not joined by Rühle till March 1915.]

13 [Wilsonism: i.e. the principles of post-war settlement propounded by the US President.]

14 [Albert Ballin was a Hamburg shipping magnate, Klöckner, Krupp, Thyssen and Hugenberg were Ruhr industrial houses, Hugo Stinnes was an empire-building entrepreneur controlling many newspapers, and Walter Rathenau was the brilliant Jewish capitalist and politician assassinated by Right-wing thugs in 1922.]

15 [Sir George Buchanan and Maurice Paléologue were respectively British and French ambassadors to the Tsarist Imperial Court and Provisional Government; Albert Thomas was the French Socialist leader and Minister of Armaments in the Clemenceau cabinet who visited Russia in the days of Kerensky in an attempt to keep her in the war.]

16 [The German designation of the government, *Rat der Volksbeauftragten*, is a virtual translation of Lenin's 'Council of People's Commissars'; 'Commissaries' is given as the translation of Serge's term *Mandataires*, which he uses here rather than *Commissaires*.]

17 It is true that any consent to negotiate on their part would have been reluctant. But the experience of the Allied troops sent into Russia has shown that the Entente was in no position to wage a victorious war against revolutionary countries. On their first contact with the proletarian revolution, the troops became rapidly disaffected. The revolution would not have stopped at the Rhine. Foch and Wilson would have had to be much more accommodating before a combined Russian and German revolution than von Kühlmann and Hoffmann were at Brest-Litovsk before an isolated Russian revolution.

18 General Groener, Ludendorff's successor at the Supreme General Command, declared at the Munich trial of 1925: 'We [i.e. the High Command and the Social-Democrats] concluded an alliance against Bolshevism. ... I was in touch with Ebert every day. My aim was to take the power away from the Workers' and Soldiers' Councils. We were planning for ten divisions to enter Berlin. Ebert was in agreement with us. ... The Independents and the Soviets demanded that the troops should go in unarmed; Ebert agreed with us that they should go in well-armed. We drew up a detailed plan of action for Berlin: the capital was to be disarmed and purged of the Spartacists. Everything was worked out jointly with Ebert. ... After this, a strong government was to be established. The troops did arrive in December, but as they were set on getting back to their homes, the plan was never implemented...'

19 [It appears that, although Yoffe was indeed conducting revolutionary propaganda in Germany, these particular leaflets were 'planted' in the diplomatic luggage by the Prussian police (Waldman, *op. cit.*, pp. 66–7).]

20 From the Moscow *Izvestia*, 18 or 19 December 1918.

21 [Novo-cherkassk was the capital of the Don territory.]

22 [The Terek region in the Caucasus borders on the river of the same name, which runs into the Caspian Sea.]

23 The name of the consul Hainaut has been transcribed from the Russian, and the spelling may be wrong.

24 The same applies to the name Hochain.

25 [Poole's reports back to the War Office, extracted from the Cabinet

papers, are summarized in R. H. Ullman, *Britain and the Russian Civil War* (Princeton, 1968), p. 49: they recommended large-scale assistance to Denikin (including tanks, aircraft and British troops) to stop the Bolshevik terror from 'depopulating large tracts' and 'destroying civilization'.]

26 Today Stalingrad. [Since 1961, Volgograd.]

27 [Budyonny became a loyal military supporter of Stalin; he was made Marshal of the Soviet Union in 1935 and survived the army purge; he played no serious role in the Second World War.]

28 I. Maisky, *The Democratic Counter-Revolution* (*Demokraticheskaya Kontr-Revoliutsiya*) (Moscow, 1923).

29 [Brigadier-General Alfred Knox, during his spell as Military Attaché to the British Embassy in Petrograd, had in 1917 backed Kornilov's *coup* against Kerensky; in the following year he tried to have Lockhart recalled (during the latter's pro-Soviet phase) and campaigned ardently for the unleashing of Japan upon Siberia (R. H. Ullman, *Intervention and the War* (Princeton, 1961), pp. 11–12, 131, 197–8). General Maurice Janin, the titular commander-in-chief of the Allied force in Siberia, was in practice Knox's subordinate (Ullman, *Britain and the Russian Civil War*, p. 35); his presence at Vladivostok was the expression both of the French stake in Allied intervention (he had long experience in pre-revolutionary Russia and had headed the French Military Mission to St Petersburg in 1916) and of the Czechoslovaks' bargaining for political recognition. The Czech connection had been established when he commanded the Czechoslovak forces fighting in France prior to his arrival in Siberia.]

30 [There is considerable controversy over the precise measure of the support given by the various Allied representatives to the Kolchak *coup*. General Janin claimed later that the British had 'installed' Kolchak to secure 'a government of their own' which would yield them economic concessions in Turkestan. Ambassador Noulens and two of Janin's staff officers made similar charges; General Knox was alleged to have made the necessary arrangements for the *coup* at the end of October 1918. The Czechoslovak Legion publicly protested against the overthrow of the Directorate; even before it had taken place, they were on bad terms with Kolchak. The British government itself was highly embarrassed by the *coup*, since it had just given *de facto* recognition to the Directorate as the government of Russia. The activities of Colonel J. F. Nielson, a member of Knox's Military Mission in Omsk, were investigated by Whitehall as tending to suggest British complicity in the Kolchak take-over; he was cleared, although he and his colleagues in the Mission admittedly had prior knowledge that the *coup* might take place at any moment. Captain Steveni, the other of Knox's adjutants implicated in the charges, was a reactionary pro-Tsarist whose participation in the actual plot is, according to Ullman, 'not inconceivable'. The assistance rendered to the plotters by the machine-guns of Colonel Ward's 25th Middlesex Battalion is not in doubt. See Ullman, *Intervention and the War*, pp. 279–84 and *Britain and the Russian Civil War*, pp. 33–4, and P. Fleming, *The Fate of Admiral Kolchak* (London, 1963), pp. 112–16.]

31 On the Jassy conference, see M. Margulies, *A Year of Intervention* (*God Interventsii*) (Berlin, 1923). [Margulies was a participant in the conference.]

32 Since General Franchet d'Esperey did not come to Russia, the intervention plan involving him was abandoned soon afterwards. [Serge is, of course, wrong in thinking of Janin as a possible effective 'controller' of Kolchak: see note 30 above.]

33 [The Revolutionary Communists and Narodnik Communists were two small splinter parties which separated from the Left S Rs after the attempted Left S R rising in July 1918. The Narodnik Communists dissolved their party and entered the Russian Communist party in November that year, and the 'Party of Revolutionary Communism' (which published its own press with an interesting theoretical position supporting the Soviets but

denying the need for a 'dictatorship of the proletariat') dissolved itself into the Bolshevik ranks in late 1920.]

34 [These were all Bolshevik speakers: Y. M. Steklov was the editor of *Izvestia*, D. I. Kursky was People's Commissar of Justice and V. Avanesov was the secretary of Vee-Tsik.]

35 Lenin, *Collected Works*, Vol. 28, pp. 138, 139, 142, 143, 150, 151, 154, 160, 163–4.

36 The Directorate's first proclamation stated that the propertied classes (the capitalists and big landlords) had dishonoured themselves through their greed, their anti-national egoism and their subservience to the foreigner.

37 [G. L. Pyatakov became one of the ablest of Soviet administrators (he was one of the tiny circle of top Bolsheviks singled out for cautious praise in Lenin's 'Testament' of December 1922). After being a leading member of the Trotskyist Left opposition, he capitulated in 1928 and worked as Commissar for Russian heavy industry, being re-instated into the party's Central Committee in 1934. He was arrested in late 1936, confessed to a variety of conspiracies for assassination and sabotage in the 'Trial of the Anti-Soviet Trotskyite Centre' in January 1937, was sentenced to death and shot.]

38 In 1919 the Ukraine, now entirely occupied by Denikin's White army, was lost to the Soviet Republic. Denikin's offensive against Tula and Moscow was broken by the Red Army and by peasant uprisings in his rear. The revolution finally managed to reconquer the country in 1920. Throughout this succession of struggles Rakovsky continued to head the Soviet government of the Ukraine.

39 G. Noske, *Von Kiel bis Kapp* (Berlin, 1920).

40 [Emil Eichhorn (1863–1925) had headed the German SPD's press office from 1908 to 1917; he then ran the USPD's press service. In his capacity as *Polizeipräsident* of the city during the revolution, he had reported regularly to the Berlin Executive of the Workers' and Soldiers' Councils, encouraged the armament of the workers and established a revolutionary militia, the *Sicherheitswehr*. He joined the KPD in 1920 (G. Badia, *Le Spartakisme* (Paris, 1967), pp. 247, 251, 420).]

41 [He had been appointed by the USPD and the Berlin Executive of the Councils; the latter body was swayed by the government after the ebb of the revolutionary wave in the city, and actually endorsed his dismissal (6 January); Waldman, *op. cit.*, pp. 165–6, 180.]

42 These lines are taken from a letter by Karl Radek to the Central Committee of the KPD dated from Berlin on 9 January. Working clandestinely in the capital, Radek saw accurately and clearly. He warned the party against the danger of submitting to provocation. This letter is a model of political foresight and revolutionary firmness. If Radek's advice had been heeded, the German proletariat would probably have escaped the irreparable defeat of January, preserved its leaders, Karl and Rosa, frustrated the designs of Ebert, Wels and Noske and kept the future open. See K. Radek, *In the Service of the German Revolution (Na Sluzhbe Germanskoi Revoliutsii)* (Moscow, 1921); German translation, 1921. It is to be regretted that this remarkable book, which condenses the experience of a year of decisive struggles in central Europe, has not been translated into French.

43 The Tiergarten is a vast park situated at the centre of Berlin.

44 From an article which appeared in *Rote Fahne* [actually by another hand, during January 1920, though it closely followed Rosa's own thinking in her article, '*Was Machen Die Führer?*' in the issue of 7 January 1919: see Waldman, *op. cit.*, pp. 177–8, 188–9].

45 Noske, *op. cit.*

46 [V. E. Orlando was the Prime Minister of Italy.]

47 [Serge's analysis of the varying policies of the Allied ministers, and of their motivation, is broadly correct. Ullman's account, drawn from the minutes of the British Empire Delegation and of the leading 'Council of Ten' at the Paris Peace Conference, relates the lengths to which Lloyd George

went to ask each participating government how many troops it could provide to crush Bolshevism; the answer, in each case, was 'none' (as the British Prime Minister had doubtless guessed before he asked). Lloyd George was formally opposed to a *cordon sanitaire* against Bolshevism; but both he and President Wilson continued the policy of blockade against the Soviet Republic, jointly with the other Allies, until late 1919. Wilson was the first to disengage from the naval encirclement of Russia's foreign trade, and then on the purely legalistic grounds that (though he was in sympathy with the aims of the blockade) he could not order the US Navy to take action unless Congress had declared war against the blockaded nation. The British Cabinet rose to the occasion by deciding, on 4 July, that 'In fact, a state of war did exist between Great Britain and the Bolshevist government of Russia', so that 'our naval forces in Russian waters should be authorized to engage enemy forces by land and sea, when necessary'. But the formal conclusion of the Versailles treaty some days later, and the prospect of the opening of large-scale trading relations between Russia and Germany (and the neutrals), raised a further question-mark over the usefulness and legitimacy of the blockade. In practice, however, it was continued: Russia's external trade was almost non-existent in 1919 as well as in 1918 (Ullman, *Britain and the Russian Civil War*, pp. 104–8, 287–91.)]

Chapter 11: War Communism

1 1 pood = 36 pounds avoirdupois.

2 During the civil war (1918-21), the following were destroyed, according to official figures: 3,672 railway bridges, 3,597 ordinary bridges, 1,750 kilometres of railway-line, 381 railway depots and workshops and almost 180,000 kilometres of telegraph and telephone lines.

3 Production will continue to fall until the end of the civil war and the institution of the New Economic Policy. For 1920, the following indices are given as a percentage of output in 1913: coal, twenty-seven per cent; cast-iron, 2·4 per cent; linen textiles, thirty-eight per cent. The production of the Donetz basin fell to zero in 1921.

4 Though they were conspicuously outstripped in the Germany of 1923.

5 The corresponding figures of 1921 were: currency in circulation, 1,638,600,000,000 roubles; decline in the value of the rouble, by a factor of 26,533; real value of the money in circulation, 44 million roubles.

6 And, for 1919–20, at 253 million roubles. See E. Preobrazhensky, 'Finance and Monetary Circulation', in *Five Years* (*Za Pyat Let*) (Moscow, 1922).

7 1920 was the year which brought Russia closest to the total abolition of money. All public services were free; rent was abolished; theatre tickets were distributed free among the workers by the unions and factory committees; the post and (in some towns) the tram service were also free. Free meals for children were introduced in 1919.

8 State agricultural production was not begun until the beginning of 1919. The large farming estates had vanished by two thirds; they had lost nine tenths of their horses and were very short of implements. By 1927, large-scale working had been restored only to a slight degree through the operations of State farming and the agricultural communes.

9 At the end of 1920 they had fallen by forty per cent.

10 In European Russia, sixty-four per cent of all urban premises were expropriated. In Moscow the proportion was ninety-five per cent, in Petrograd 98·3 per cent.

11 This followed from the fact that they grew corn for sale on the market: consequently they formed part of the system of commodity production.

12 See the debates of the Fifth Congress of the Communist International (1924) on the question of the programme: contributions of Bukharin, Thalheimer and others.

13 L. Kritsman, *The Heroic Period of the Great Russian Revolution*

(*Geroicheskii Period Velikoi Russkoi Revoliutsii*) (Moscow, 1926). This remarkable work is the only book which undertakes a serious analysis of War Communism.

14 N. Lenin, *Collected Works* (London, 1969), Vol. 28, pp. 212–13.

15 *ibid.*, pp. 190, 191.

16 'It is a truth long known to every Marxist that in any capitalist society the only decisive forces are the proletariat and the bourgeoisie, and that all the social elements which occupy a position between these classes, within the economic category of "the petty-bourgeoisie" inevitably oscillate between these two forces' ('Valuable Admissions of Pitirim Sorokin', *ibid.*, p. 186). But, beginning with the spring of 1919, the Republic found itself faced with difficulties, which grew in September and October; the loss of its power appeared imminent. Once again the middle classes suffered a change of heart, resting their hopes on the return of the bourgeoisie (except, that is, in the regions where the peasants had had first-hand experience of bourgeois rule).

17 *ibid.*, pp. 207, 211, 215, 214, 212 (Speech to the Moscow party workers' meeting of 27 November, section 1: 'Report on the Attitude of the Proletariat to the Petty-Bourgeois Democrats').

18 Alexander Blok was also responsible for the idea of the regeneration of the world by the barbarians of Asia – the 'Scythians' – who would bear with them a new culture, more profound and truly human than that founded in the West on the basis of technological progress. Like Byely, he belonged to the literary circles that were close to the Left S R party.

19 The work of Russia's great writers, yesterday's 'revolutionaries' now turned counter-revolutionary after the seizure of power by the proletariat, are filled with such execration, such horror at 'Sovdepia' [a nickname abbreviation meaning 'land of the Soviet deputies'] that they belong to the realm of social pathology. Andreyev, from exile in Finland, issues his pamphlet *S.O.S.*, an appeal to all the interventions against 'the assassins of the fatherland'. Zinaida Hippius, a talented poet whose literary salon has been the most influential in Petrograd, with a 'mystical anarchism' as its chief trend, looks forward in her verses to the day when 'we shall hang *them* in silence'.

20 [A. V. Lunacharsky, a Bolshevik from 1903 who had broken with Lenin to join Gorky's 'God-followers', rejoined the party in 1917 and held the Commissariat of Education until 1929. He died in 1933 shortly after being appointed Ambassador to Spain.]

21 We cannot give any figures, since the available statistics begin only in 1919. With the arrival of the New Economic Policy over 1921–3, a number of these hastily founded educational establishments disappeared.

22 Lenin, *Collected Works*, Vol. 31, p. 336.

23 Lenin makes a special point of saying 'April', doubtless in order to recall, with the hint of an illusion, the fact that before his memorable April theses the Bolshevik party was still taking its position of 1905, which considered the Russian revolution to be a bourgeois one.

24 Lenin, *Collected Works*, Vol. 28, p. 299.

25 *ibid.*, p. 343.

26 'Misery cannot be socialized!' wrote Charles Rappoport at the end of 1917, in the *Journal du Peuple*, putting the view of the whole Socialist-petty-bourgeoisie of the West in the French labour press. Since the Socialism of misery was impossible, all that could be done was to allow the bourgeoisie to organize the workers' misery for its own profit, upon the pile of ruins left by the war. Such was the feeble logic of reformism. Rappoport, dreaming of a parliamentary democracy for Russia, appealed to the Bolsheviks to 'save the revolution by convoking the Constituent Assembly'. [Another deliberately unkind reference by Serge, since Rappoport had subsequently joined the French Communist party as an orthodox supporter of the Moscow line.]

27 Lenin, *Collected Works*, Vol. 28, p. 300.

28 *ibid.*, pp. 112, 113.

29 Lenin, *Collected Works*, Vol. 27. p. 232.

30 Lenin, *Collected Works*, Vol. 28, p. 348 (Speech of 11 December to the First Congress of the Committees of the Poor Peasants).

31 *ibid.*, p. 381 (Speech of 19 December to the Second Congress of Economic Councils).

32 Lenin, *Collected Works*, Vol. 31, pp. 124, 125.

33 [General Alexander P. Rodzyanko headed the field command of the White army which advanced upon Petrograd in May 1919, backed by Estonia, Britain, the United States and the counter-revolutionary emigration in Finland. (See, for Rodzyanko and Yudenich, John Silverlight, *The Victors' Dilemma: Allied Intervention in the Russian Civil War*, London, 1970, pp. 305-8.) He was the nephew of M. V. Rodzyanko, the 1917 Duma leader and anti-Bolshevik politician.]

34 [N. N. Yudenich, who had been the Tsar's Chief of Staff from 1913, commanded the White army in the Baltic region after the October revolution. In October 1919 he led a final abortive offensive against Petrograd. He died an exile in France in 1933.]

35 [British government files for 1918 provide many examples of the 'vast designs' for intervention on whose precise nature Victor Serge could only speculate. Even before the world war ended, a new anti-Bolshevist geopolitics becomes visible in the official memoranda. Thus, a submission of 22 September 1918 from the Director of Military Intelligence, Major-General Thwaites, endorsed the analysis of the Military Attaché in Stockholm, Brigadier-General H. Yarde Buller: 'I am informed – I do not know if correctly – that Bolshevism was originated by a small nucleus of men in the United States, consisting of not more than six, of whom some were of the Jewish persuasion. Be this as it may, there can be no doubt that it is a fever that is spreading, the germs of which are latent among many people of all nations, and it is of the utmost importance for the future tranquillity of the world that every endeavour be made to stem it.' A prompt anti-Soviet intervention was advocated, with the agreement of Britain's enemies in the war: 'an agreement might be come to with the Central Powers (who are strongly opposed to the Bolshevist movement) by which we could have free use of the Baltic' (Public Record Office, File FO 371/3344).

In the same file R. A. Leeper, head of the Political Intelligence Department of the Foreign Office, submitted a report on 'The Growing Danger of Bolshevism in Russia', dated 14 October 1918: 'As the military power of Germany is being gradually crushed, Germany ceases to be the greatest danger to European civilization, while a new danger – no less deadly – looms up in the near future. That danger is Bolshevism.' 'In the event of the continuation of the war and the intensification of the unrest in Germany, Bolshevism may spread, first to the Russian border provinces and then to the Central Powers, thus becoming a force that would seriously threaten Europe.' Leeper wanted the menace 'dealt with now': a comparatively small army coming from the Urals might advance on Moscow and put it down by force. Meanwhile Leeper's opposite number at the Home Office, Sir Basil Thomson of the Directorate of Intelligence, was already circulating, in 1918 as in 1919, a 'Monthly Review of Revolutionary Movements Abroad' (in Public Record Office; PID File 371/4382) which indicates the official anxiety, if little else. (Thus, Report No. 10, for August 1919, contained a summary of developments in some thirty-five countries in its few pages: 'The unrest in Portugal continues', etc.)

With the ending of the war, the various *ad hoc* justifications for intervention (in the cause of the military front against Germany or of this or that pro-Allied Russian element) had to be dropped, and the ideological note becomes more sustained. Lockhart's 'Memorandum on the Internal Situation in Russia', delivered to the Foreign Office on the first anniversary of the Bolshevik revolution (Public Record Office, File FO 371/3337) notes that

'Our victories over Germany have removed our original pretext for intervention.' He advanced various justifications to replace the 'pretext': the risk of revolution in other countries, loyalty to the committed counter-revolutionary forces, 'humanitarian grounds' and others more material. 'A successful intervention will give the Allies a predominant economic position in Russia. It will be more than paid for by economic concessions. . . . By restoring order in Russia at once, not only are we preventing the spread of Bolshevism as a political danger but we are also saving for the rest of Europe the rich and fertile grain districts of the Ukraine.' Massive intervention, requiring at least 100,000 Allied soldiers, mostly from the United States but with British and French participation, was to be mounted on a 'proper scale', strengthening the existing Allied fronts in Siberia and north Russia, and joining Denikin's forces in the south, in a concerted movement to take Moscow. (R. H. Ullman, *Intervention and the War* (Princeton, 1961), pp. 296–300, provides a summary of the report.) A similar memorandum was tabled, in less lurid strategic detail, by J. D. Gregory, the head of the Foreign Office Russian Department (in Public Record Office, File FO 371/3344).

By 1919, the most ardent Bolshevik-eater in British government circles would be a member of the Cabinet: Winston Churchill, the incoming War Secretary, who would advocate massive intervention in Russia to 'break up' Bolshevik power. In Churchill's early statement of his position, the Allies must engage themselves in Russia 'thoroughly, with large forces abundantly supplied with mechanical appliances'. (These proposals, and the opposition they encountered from Lloyd George, are recorded in R. H. Ullman, *Britain and the Russian Civil War* (Princeton, 1968), pp. 90–98; the pre-Churchillian Cabinet debate on intervention is *ibid.*, pp. 10–14.) In February 1919 Churchill would enter into his close relationship with Sidney Reilly, now working in a freelance capacity for MI1C, the espionage department of Churchill's new ministry. Meanwhile, at the end of the 'Year One', following his return to England in November 1918, Reilly had set up a confidential social circle of anti-Bolshevists in the Intelligence and political departments, some of whom were Secret Service agents in the field, others senior Whitehall officials. Piquant details of this social round are given in the biography of Reilly by Robin Bruce Lockhart (himself a former Intelligence officer with access to much information in this area): *Ace of Spies* (London, 1967), pp. 84, 90–91, 98. Almost without exception, all of the authors of the memoranda for anti-Soviet action quoted earlier were intimates of Reilly in these months and subsequently. On 12 November, Reilly gave a party at the Savoy for Lockhart, Leeper and their wives; on the following day Lockhart organized a theatre and supper outing for Reilly, Gregory and Captain Hill, Reilly's Secret Service aide in Russia. Among the callers at Reilly's expensively furnished flat in the Albany was Sir Basil Thomson of the Home Office Intelligence department. And Reilly was also active in a select club uniting leading members of Britain's espionage and diplomatic services in an annual 'Bolo Liquidation Dinner' where those attending would drink a toast each year to 'the liquidation of the Bolos' – the latter being a nickname for the Bolsheviks. (A menu for one of these functions is given as an illustration in Lockhart's biography of Reilly; it is signed by Leeper, Gregory, Reilly, Hill, Paul Dukes and other agents who had been working in Russia.)

These were only the most articulate and explicit supporters of an anti-Bolshevik crusade (and it may be noted that Dukes, Leeper and Lockhart were to be knighted in the course of their careers, with Leeper going on to be British Ambassador to Greece during the civil war of 1944 and Lockhart returning to the Foreign Office as an Intelligence and psychological warfare director). Less militantly, Sir George Buchanan (the former Ambassador to the Tsar), presented a memorandum on 20 October 1918 arguing for a very drastic intervention but insisting that 'I do not for a moment advocate a crusade against Bolshevism.' The comment on this paper by Lord Robert Cecil (on 31 October) is revealing of the nature both of the proposal and of the standard British attitude on intervention: 'I am afraid that Sir George Buchanan's policy of occupying Moscow and taking in hand the reconstruction of Russia is impracticable' (Public Record Office, File FO 371/3344).

Another interesting exchange occurs in the same file between the young E. H. Carr, then a fairly junior official in the Foreign Office, and Cecil. Carr advocates 'some sort of understanding with the Bolsheviks', on the basis of recognizing Soviet power in the vastly truncated area of European Russia controlled by the Reds: 'we should remain at Archangel and Murmansk where the inhabitants have renounced Bolshevism and in Siberia where the majority also appear to be opposed to it'. The Soviet government would also have to give up any hopes of recovering the Ukraine, Poland, Estonia and possibly White Russia. This mild proposal for controlled co-existence on the basis of the territorial spoils of intervention was turned down by Carr's chief; Cecil insisted that there must be no recognition of the Soviet government on the ground that 'Now that our enemies are defeated the chief danger to the country is Bolshevism.'

Thus, even before the arrival of Winston Churchill in his role of intervener-in-chief, the terms of anti-Soviet military activity by Britain were set. Despite the heated argument at Cabinet level over the extent and purpose of the interventionist action there was an ideologically motivated commitment to war against the Bolsheviks (even though a 'crusade' might be abjured), limited by sundry considerations of what was 'impracticable'. The vast geopolitical designs were curbed by inter-Allied rivalry, tactical subtlety, the post-war demobilization, plain incompetence and often the sheer difficulties of geographical access. For, as Peter Fleming points out (*The Fate of Admiral Kolchak* (London, 1963), p. 30), the common characteristic of all the theatres of Allied intervention against Bolshevism is 'accessibility; the Allies intervened in Russia wherever it was physically possible for them to do so'.]

Editorial Postscript: The Allied Part in the Czechoslovak Intervention

The danger of Russia falling entirely under the power of Germany was imminent, and it became clear that the Allies could no longer hold aloof. ... In June, however, hope appeared from another quarter. Siberia, the land of the peasant proprietor, had never been Bolshevik at heart, and it was here that the reaction started against Bolshevism. It was assisted by the presence of the Czechoslovak army, which had maintained its organization after the Russian collapse, and was encamped at different points along the Siberian railway. When the anti-Bolshevik movement in Siberia began, the Czechoslovaks became masters of many points on the railway, as well as the port of Vladivostok ...

The serious situation of the Czechs, who were now liable to attack by the Bolsheviks from the west, while being cut off from all communication with the Allies by a considerable Germano-Bolshevik force astride the Siberian railway, brought the question of Allied intervention to a head. ... The Czechs were greatly exhausted, the Bolshevik forces opposed to them were constantly increasing in numbers and efficiency under German instructors ...

Attempts to disorganize the rearward communications of the Czechs along the Trans-Siberian Railway by fomenting strikes among the railway employees failed, thanks largely to the vigorous action of a battalion of the Middlesex Regiment under Lieut.-Col. John Ward, M.P.[1] ...

from The War Cabinet, *Report for the Year 1918* (London, 1919)

ALLIED POLICY TOWARDS THE CZECHS

The actual relationship between the behaviour of the Czechoslovak Corps and the various intervention plans of the Allies was quite complex. Considerable differences existed between British and French policy on the proper use of the Czechoslovak troops, and the actual incident that led in May to the Czechs' seizure of the trans-Siberian line (the often-recounted scuffle between Czech and Hungarian soldiers at Chelyabinsk station on 14 May) was of a spontaneous, fortuitous character. The tendency of recent chroniclers[2] has been to emphasize the unplanned sequence of misunderstandings and mishaps that sparked the Czechoslovak rising. Trotsky's provocative action in ordering the Czechoslovaks to be disarmed or else shot down (25 May) is often quoted as the salient incident in the affair; even in the summer of 1918, Karakhan, the Soviet Deputy Commissar for Foreign Affairs, told Lockhart that 'in attacking the Czechs Trotsky had made a political mistake, though he had been fully justified by the bad faith of the French in this connection'.[3] (Later Stalinist historiography even suggested that Trotsky had deliberately provoked the Czechs in order consciously to further Allied interests.)[4] In his autobiography, Lockhart (somewhat disingenuously, as will be evident from the next paragraphs) places all the blame on the French.[5] 'I succeeded in securing Trotsky's good will and, but for the folly of the French, I am convinced that the Czechs would have been safely evacuated without incident.' Yet, as Ullman makes abundantly clear, the main trend of French policy, from December 1917 through to May 1918, was to insist that the whole of the Czechoslovak forces in Russia be *evacuated* with all speed to France, via Archangel, Murmansk or Vladivostok, to relieve the critical manpower shortage on the western front.[6] It was the British who repeatedly pressed for the deployment of the Czechs within Russia itself, in a twofold project that encompassed, first, the use of the westernmost section of the Czechoslovaks 'in resisting German aggression and intrigues at Archangel and Murmansk and along the railways leading to these ports',[7] and, second, the launching of the easterly Czech contingents near Vladivostok 'to start operations in Siberia', following which there could be 'little doubt that the Japanese would move and the Americans would find it impossible to hold back'.[8] Both these early attempts by Britain to involve the Czechs were predicated on Bolshevik co-operation or at least acquiescence; but they were very soon replaced by a similar two-part plan, this time no longer anti-German but anti-Bolshevik (more plausibly, perhaps, since the nearest German troops were hundreds of miles from Archangel and thousands from Vladivostok), in which the Czechs would both second a White officers' rising in the north and head a sweep westwards from Vladivostok, with (if possible) French officers in their command, to link up with the northern counter-revolution in the vicinity of Vologda.[9]

Previous accounts have, however, failed to reflect fully the part played in these schemes by British and French intrigues, both in Moscow and in the two Foreign Offices. From 19 April onwards, Lockhart had been sending back telegram after telegram urging an immediate Allied intervention in Russia, regardless of Bolshevik consent; from 23 May he was pressing for a massive Allied invasion which would not even be preceded by an ultimatum designed to force the Soviet government's acquiescence. Lockhart's shift from his previous attitude of pro-Bolshevik conciliation was associated in large measure with the extensive contacts he had formed, in the fortnight preceding his 19 April telegram, with all the main counter-revolutionary groups in Moscow.[10] In Lockhart's own catalogue of 'the various counter-revolutionary organizations in Moscow' with whom he had relations after the Bolshevik refusal of Allied intervention he includes 'the Czech Council, which was not then openly anti-Bolshevik'.[11]

In collusion with Lockhart, moreover, the agents of the British and French Military Missions in Moscow played a major part in instigating the northern element of the two-part intervention plan against Bolshevism. Before the outbreak of any violence between the Czechoslovaks and the Soviet authorities, Lockhart forwarded to London[12] a dispatch from his aide Captain Denis Garstin: 'I have been approached secretly by two large organizations of old army who say if Allies will help them they will mobilize in Nizhni area. ... If Allies will land at Archangel, hold Vologda and join with loyal Russians in that area they would be increasing enormously chances of Japanese arrival. ... Chief cause of present inactivity is lack of any rallying-point for those elements who are patriotic yet anti-Bolshevik.' In this, the first version of the intervention project that can be traced, Garstin proposed an Allied drive down to the area 'east of Vologda and Volga controlling railheads of Archangel and Siberian railways'. Two Allied divisions would be needed: this figure, and the plan as a whole, had (he stated) received the assent of General Lavergne of the French Mission, as well as of Italy's military representative in Russia. Garstin's plan did not specifically mention the Czechs (though the further development of the idea in Colonel Steel's General Staff paper of 24 May did, as we have seen, include the Czechs as a major element). But one is tempted to speculate that Lavergne's ciphers back to Paris may have done so: at any rate, a dispatch from the British ambassador in Paris, Lord Derby, sent shortly afterwards (on 17 May), conveyed an abrupt turn in the views of the French government, which now – so far from insisting on the immediate evacuation of the Czechs – offered a scheme for anti-Bolshevik intervention in the north very similar to that of Garstin except that it included the Czechs as a constituent.[13] 'Allied policy in Russia' (according to this expression of the current French official view) 'can now rely only on itself, and requires ... occupation with least possible delay of White Sea bases in order to keep in touch, i.e. ports of Murmansk and Archangel at head of line to Petrograd and Vologda, defence of principal stations on these lines which can be undertaken by small naval contingents already on the spot or to be sent there and Serb and Czech contingents now moving in that direction. ... The healthy elements who are now dispersed by anarchy in Russia can only rally round nucleus of foreign forces.'

The wheels of the cumbersome machinery that governed a combined Allied military operation now began to turn. Even as the Czech Corps was taking over the trans-Siberian line, the Permanent Military Representatives attached to the Supreme War Council at Versailles were being asked to consider 'whether some force ought not to be sent to northern Russia as a nucleus round which the Czechs, Serbs and loyal Russians could rally'. The Representatives' recommendation for 'the dispatch of a small contingent of four to six American, British, French or Italian battalions, under a British commander-in-chief' was submitted to the Council's meeting in early June and ratified there.[14] It was in anticipation of the landing of this force that Ambassador Noulens encouraged Savinkov to launch the Yaroslavl rising of 6 July. However, the Allied forces did not get to Archangel until 2 August when Poole's 1,200, mostly French troops, disembarked; substantial contingents (4,800 Americans, 2,400 British and 900 French) were not assembled there till early September. By this time, of course, it was much too late for any link-up with the Czechs. Ironside's northern force of 16,000, which was in position at the end of 1918, was never able to get even half-way to Vologda, the main objective of the original plan.[15]

Two features of the turn of actual events require some explanation, since they run counter to the whole intention of the Allied plan involving the Czechoslovaks. We have Clemenceau's indignant reply, of 22 May, to the British Foreign Secretary's soundings on the possible use of the Czechoslovaks to begin intervention in Siberia.[16] Clemenceau was at pains to reinstate the traditional policy of his government, which insisted that the Czechs be evacuated forthwith to fight on the western front. This fresh insistence may well, however, have proceeded from a French reluctance to follow British plans specifically in the Siberian theatre: Siberia was later in 1918 to prove a rich source of French suspicions as to Britain's alleged possible expansionism.[17]

Against the intervention project we also have to set the fact that the Czechoslovak rising that took place in the very midst of the May discussions did not include any movement towards the north. On the contrary, the Congress of delegates from all the Czech contingents which met at Chelyabinsk on 23 May decided unanimously, against the wishes of their National Council's spokesmen and of the French military representatives who were present, to disregard the order that half of the Corps should make northwards for Archangel. (This refusal stemmed from a determination to avoid splitting up the threatened forces of the Corps.) The local quarrel between Czechs and Bolsheviks therefore deprived the planners of the Archangel–Vologda operation that they had contrived for the Czechs; but the actual intervention that took place, involving 70,000 Czechoslovaks from Penza to Irkutsk and thence (from the end of June) to Vladisvostok, gave them all that they could have wished for – including Britain's aim of drawing in the Japanese and the Americans. A revealing map drawn up by the British General Staff[18] is headed '*Proposals for Allied Enterprise in Russia (assuming French concurrence)*'; it shows the Czechs in occupation of Vladivostok and the Trans-Siberian Railway, and moving to link up with Ataman Semyonov at Chita and with General Poole in the Archangel–Vologda region. All the elements in this grand design were in fact fulfilled – with the exception of the Czech participation in the northern 'enterprise'. In successful counter-revolution, no less than in successful revolution, 'spontaneity' appears to coalesce fruitfully with conscious direction.

CZECHOSLOVAK POLICY IN THE INTERVENTION

The policies of Thomas Masaryk and Eduard Beneš, the main spokesmen for the Czechoslovak national movement in the West, took some time to develop into a line of unambiguous support for Allied intervention to overthrow Bolshevism. In a discussion in the middle of May 1918, with Lieutenant-Colonel L. S. Amery of the War Office, Beneš had declared only a conditional willingness for half of the Czechoslovaks (those gathering at Archangel) to be used 'in connection with an Allied intervention in Russia'.[19] Beneš's conditions were: (1) that the Allied powers should declare publicly their support for Czechoslovak independence; (2) that 'intervention should be a real one, i.e., to be carried right through up to the western frontiers and involve actual operations against the Germans or Austrians'. Beneš was opposed to dragging the Czech Corps back into Russia 'merely to be made to participate in Russian internal disturbances'.

Beneš thus appears to have tried to placate both the British demand for a Siberian intervention with the Czechs, and the French insistence on their return to France to fight on the western front; the question of Czechoslovak participation in the Archangel–Vologda invasion, which was then being considered by the British and the French authorities, did not enter into this discussion. In his memoirs, Beneš says that the Czechoslovak National Council abroad opposed intervention in Russia until July 1918;[20] the Amery conversation of May reveals, however, that this opposition was less than absolute. Up to a point, Beneš' two conditions were met. On 6 June the British government informed him that they now recognized his Council as the supreme organ of the Czechoslovak national movement in the Allied countries, and on 29 June the Council received fuller recognition from France; this went at least part of the way to meet the first pre-condition for Czech intervention. On the second point, while the action involving the Czech Legion was not carried 'up to the western frontiers of Russia', it did incorporate 'actual operations' against the Austrian and Hungarian prisoners of war, who, in the extraordinary Allied mythology of the time, were counted as among the active reserves of the Central Powers, working in secret collusion with the Bolsheviks. Apart from the change in French policy that followed the lessening of pressure on the western front, these factors may have weighed in the National Council's decision during the summer of 1918 openly to support the intervention across Siberia.

This support was not, however, to be given as an actual order, from the Council's central officials to the Czechoslovak contingents in Siberia, until early August. It was then that General

Dietrichs, the Legion's commander at Vladivostok, 'announced that the Czechs have received definite orders from Masaryk to fight Germans in Siberia [*sic*] instead of being transported to Europe and that these orders will be obeyed'.[21] This was already well after the Czechoslovak troops had seized Vladivostok from the Soviets (on 29 June), an action which was to be quickly endorsed by the Allied representatives on the spot (including the French). Earlier, and certainly in the crucial month of May, National Council policy opposed the Czech move eastwards: as we have seen, the Czechoslovak Legion's delegate conference at Chelyabinsk (23 May) actually over-ruled the advice of the Council representatives from Moscow, who wanted them to proceed towards the northern ports.

This advice of the Moscow Czech officials may have reflected some involvement on their part in the abortive northern intervention scheme; or it may simply have expressed their accordance with the main line of policy (i.e. evacuation) advocated by the French who were their main financial backers.

Central French policy, indeed, remained in opposition to the Czech involvement in Siberia, even after it was well under way. As we have seen in the previous section, Clemenceau refused on 22 May to countenance the British plan for Siberia; he quoted Beneš specifically as having refused to condone the use of the Czechoslovaks as the 'point of departure' for Allied intervention.[22] Even on 28 May, with the Legion's action across Siberia now in full spate, Pichon, the French Foreign Minister, was reaching an agreement with Lloyd George for the regular transportation of 4,500 Czechs per month from Vladivostok to Vancouver (and thence to France).[23] This decision alone illustrates how misleading it is to suppose that the Allied governments had sufficient intelligence of Czechoslovak movements in Russia to enable them to plan positively for an all-Russian intervention involving the Czechs. The Bolshevik accounts (including that of Victor Serge) are inclined to assume perfect intelligence on the part of the Allies.

The Legion's role in Allied intervention plans for Russia was intimately linked with the successive stages of diplomatic recognition accorded to the Czechoslovak National Council by the British government. When, during the middle weeks of May, Beneš was pressing London for recognition, the Foreign Office was at first inclined to withhold any such commitment until the United States had been consulted; but by 20 May Cecil was convinced that 'all political encouragement possible' should be given to the Czechoslovaks, without waiting for American agreement, since Britain was counting on 'the Czechoslovak forces in Russia to form the nucleus of intervention at Archangel and Vladivostok'. Britain's Washington ambassador, in a cipher dated 6 June, was asked to inform the US government that Britain's limited recognition of the National Council (granted in the previous week) had been necessary in view not only of the Czechs' cooperation on the fronts in western Europe, 'but also of the fact that there are some 50,000 Czechs in Russia ... whom we have every hope of organizing into an effective force to combat the enemy either in the eastern or the western theatres of war'.[24] The Czechoslovak National Council itself soon became eager to utilize the Legion's actions in Siberia as a bargaining-counter with which to secure full recognition as a government by the Allies. On 16 July Beneš wrote to the journalist Wickham Steed asking for support in the proclamation of a Czechoslovak Provisional Government from the Czech forces in France and Italy: 'I should like this to coincide with the Allied intervention in Siberia so that the proclamation of Czechoslovak independence may form part of the process of intervention in Siberia.'[25] In further memoranda, over the period later in the summer when Beneš was in London pressing his case with the Foreign Office and War Office, the Siberian connection was further exploited.[26] The National Council's ultimate policy was still the evacuation of the Legion to the west but in the meantime 'these troops may render considerable service to Great Britain and her allies by facilitating an intervention in Russia'. The Legion was to be left *provisionally* in Russia to carry out military operations, to hold the Trans-Siberian Railway for the Allies, to enlist the Russian population and to prepare the necessary basis for the Japanese and American intervention'. But the subjection of the Legion to Allied orders should cease, with Janin, Stefanik and the National Council being 'given *real sovereignty as a government*'[27] over the Czech contingents.

Beneš was at pains to establish the reliably anti-Bolshevik character of his countrymen, stressing that 'The Czechoslovak army on principle shoot every Czech found fighting with the Red Guards and captured by them, for instance at Penza, Samara, Omsk, etc. (200 at Samara).'[28] The interventionist refrain was repeated as a justification for recognition in both memoranda: 'The recognition of *the Czechoslovak National Council as a Government* would render enormous assistance to the idea of an intervention in Russia. ... It would serve as the basis for American and Japanese intervention.'

Beneš's diligent lobbying met with a favourable response: on 9 August Balfour issued a declaration according 'Allied nation' status to the Czechoslovaks on behalf of Britain and recognizing the National Council, in accordance with the formula requested by Beneš, as 'the present trustee of the future Czechoslovak government'. There is no evidence that the specific considerations put by Beneš (i.e. recognition as the cover for intervention) influenced the Foreign Office; humanitarian grounds, in removing any pretext for Czechoslovak prisoners to be shot by the Austrians as rebels, seem to have been important.[29] But the situation of the

Legion in Siberia cannot have been far from the British government's judgement of its obligations; on 4 August a special meeting of the War Cabinet had been called with the critical plight of the Czechoslovak Legion (hemmed in at Lake Baikal and Khabarovsk) as the sole item on its agenda.[30]

The house of the Czechs and the Slovaks was thus constructed, by the founders of the new state, on an Anglo–French mortgage sought on the security of the Legion's exploits in the international war against Bolshevism. And on the battlefields of the intervention, Czechoslovak nationalists shot their Czechoslovak Red prisoners, as the first act in the new nation's own civil war.

1 John Ward (1866–1934) was a liberal M P who had in the 1880s been an ardent Socialist (member of the S D F) and a founder of the Navvies' Union (he had worked as a navvy from the age of twelve). Breaking with Socialism on the foundation of the Labour party, during the First World War he recruited five labour battalions for the Middlesex Regiment, where he served as commanding officer, and was knighted for his services in 1918.

2 Such as: G. F. Kennan, *The Decision to Intervene* (Princeton, 1956); R. H. Ullman, *Intervention and the War* (Princeton, 1961), Chapter 6; Peter Fleming, *The Fate of Admiral Kolchak* (London, 1963), Chapter 1 *et seq.*

3 Lockhart's report to Balfour, 1 November 1918, in Public Record Office, File FO 371/3337.

4 Fleming, *op. cit.*, p. 25n.

5 R. H. Bruce Lockhart, *Memoirs of a British Agent* (London, 1932), pp. 272, 284–5.

6 Ullman, *op. cit.*, pp. 151–5, 171.

7 Foreign Office telegram 93 to Lockhart, 20 April 1918; in Milner MSS, Box 109.

8 Lord Robert Cecil (Foreign Under-Secretary, acting in Balfour's absence in the United States) to Clemenceau, 18 May 1918; given in Ullman, *op. cit.*, pp. 169–70.

9 Memorandum (headed 'Very Secret' in red pencil) from Colonel R. Steel, for Director of Military Intelligence, War Office, 'The Direction of Allied Operations in the north east of Russia'; in Milner MSS, Box 110, File C–1; summarized partly in Ullman, *op. cit.*, p. 194.

10 Ullman, *op. cit.*, p. 163–4.

11 Lockhart, 'Memorandum on the Internal Situation in Russia', 1 November 1918, Section 2, 'The Counter-Revolutionary Forces', in Public Record Office, File FO 371/3337. Just how far Lockhart's own contacts with the Czechs' Moscow representatives were on an anti-Bolshevik basis is open to conjecture. According to his son's account, it was the French Intelligence official de Vertemont who 'was trying to persuade the Czechs to take up arms under French officers against the Russians' while Lockhart himself was trying to negotiate with Trotsky to secure their evacuation (Robin Bruce Lockhart, *Ace of Spies* (London, 1967), p. 71). This would imply that the local French policy in Moscow was one of implementing the programme for the Czechs which had been advocated by the British (i.e. anti-Soviet embroilment), while Britain's man in Moscow was pressing, on the contrary, for the policy of evacuation which had been the traditional line of the French government. This conjunction is not impossible, but a conscious division of labour in a double game cannot be ruled out.

12 Lockhart's telegram 175, 10 May 1918; in Milner MSS, Box 110, File C–1; summarized without actual quotation in Ullman, *op. cit.*, pp. 193–4.

13 Lord Derby (Paris) to Foreign Office, telegram 648, 17 May 1918; in Milner MSS, Box 110, File C–1.

14 As summarized in the account given by the then Secretary to the British War Cabinet: Lord Hankey, *The Supreme Command* (London, 1961), Vol. 2, p. 874.

15 Ullman, *op. cit.*, pp. 195–6, 225, 243; R. H. Ullman, *Britain and the Russian Civil War* (Princeton, 1968), pp. 18–21.

16 Ullman, *Intervention and the Civil War*, pp. 170–71.

17 See Chapter 10, note 30.

18 Undated, but located among the documents of early June; sheet 67 in Milner MSS, Box 110, File C–1.

19 Memorandum by Amery, 'Notes of a Conversation with Dr Beneš', 14 May 1918; in Milner MSS, Box 118, 'Czechoslovaks' file.

20 E. Beneš, *My War Memories* (London, 1928), p. 392.

21 Telegram from Sir J. Jordan (Peking) to London, 6 August 1918; in Milner MSS, Box 112.

22 Ullman, *Intervention and the Civil War*, p. 171.

23 'Record of War Cabinet Conversations', 29 May 1918; in Public Record Office, File Cab. 23/17.

24 Beneš letter of 14 May, the discussion of recognition by Foreign Office officials (on 20 May) and the telegram to Washington are in Public Record Office, File FO 371/3135 (folders 85869 and 89425).

25 *ibid.*, folder 127473.

26 Two separate communications by Beneš are extant, both with the title 'Memorandum concerning the Recognition of Czechoslovak National Sovereignty'; these overlap to some extent in content. The earlier, dated 26 July, is in Public Record Office, File FO 371/3135 (folder 130680) and formed the subject of Foreign Office deliberations. The other was presented in the first place to L. S. Amery at the War Office and was forwarded by the latter to Milner on 1 August; in Milner MSS, Box 118, 'Czechoslovaks' file. Reference will be given to each memo separately where an extract departs from their common text.

27 FO memorandum by Beneš.

28 Milner memorandum by Beneš.

29 Balfour's and Cecil's sympathetic consideration of the case, on the grounds of saving prisoners' lives, is in Public Record Office, File FO 371/3135, folder 127473; the discussion of the text of the declaration is *ibid.*, folder 135903. Beneš himself noted in his memoirs that he regarded 'the negotiations which resulted in this declaration as the most important political activity of the National Council during the war'; Beneš, *My War Memories*, p. 407.

30 War Cabinet meeting No. 454, 4 August 1918: minutes in Public Record Office, File Cab. 23/7.

Index

Notes referred to in the index are to be found listed under chapter titles on pages 373–414.

DATE DUE

4-14-76			
OC 6 '95			
GAYLORD			PRINTED IN U.S.A.